A History of Ancient Israel and Judah

A History of Ancient Israel and Judah

SECOND EDITION

J. Maxwell Miller • John H. Hayes

WESTMINSTER
JOHN KNOX PRESS
LOUISVILLE • KENTUCKY

Scripture quotations, unless otherwise indicated, are from the New Revised Standard Version of the Bible, copyright © 1989 by the Division of Christian Education of the National Council of the Churches of Christ in the U.S.A., and used by permission.

Grateful acknowledgment is made to the following for the use of copyrighted material:

Alliance Bible Seminary for selections from *Neo-Assyrian Inscriptions and Syria Palestine* by Kah-jin Kuan, © 1995 Alliance Bible Seminary. Reprinted by permission.

The British Museum for selections from *Chronicles of Chaldaean Kings (626–556 B.C.) in the British Museum* by D. J. Wiseman, © 1961 by The British Museum. Reprinted by permission.

Eisenbrauns for passages from *Assyrian and Babylonian Chronicles* by A. K. Grayson, © 2000. Used by permission.

The Johns Hopkins University Press for a selection from *The Amarna Letters*, ed., William L. Moran, © 2002. Reprinted with permission of the Johns Hopkins University Press.

Princeton University Press for selections from *Ancient Near Eastern Texts Relating to the Old Testament*, ed., James B. Pritchard; 3rd ed., © 1969. Used by permission of Princeton University Press.

University of Chicago Press for selections from *Ancient Records of Assyria and Babylonia*, vols. I and II, by Daniel David Luckenbill, © 1926, 1927, The University of Chicago Press. Reprinted by permission.

University of Toronto Press for selections from *Royal Inscriptions of Mesopotamia: Assyrian Periods*, vols. 2 and 3, by A. K. Grayson, © 1991, 1996. Used by permission.

Society of Biblical Literature for excerpts from *Handbook of Ancient Hebrew Letters: A Study Edition*, © 1982. Reprinted by permission.

Book design by Drew Stevens
Cover design by Mark Abrams

Second edition
Published by Westminster John Knox Press
Louisville, Kentucky

♾ The paper used in this publication meets the minimum requirements of the American National Standard for Information Sciences–Permanence of Paper for Printed Library Materials, ANSI Z39.48-1992.

12 13 14 15 — 10 9 8 7 6 5 4

Library of Congress Cataloging-in-Publication Data is on file at the Library of Congress, Washington, D.C.

ISBN-13: 978-0-664-22358-8
ISBN-10: 0-664-22358-3

Contents

List of Charts, Photographs, Maps, and Texts

Texts

Preface

Two decades after its original publication in 1986—decades rife with controversy and spirited debate about virtually every aspect of the history of ancient Israel—our *History of Ancient Israel and Judah* continues to serve classrooms and to attract readers from the general public. Naturally we are gratified that the volume remains useful, but are aware that it needs to be updated. This would be true if for no other reason than that research has continued to forge ahead in disciplines upon which historians of biblical times are heavily dependent—especially Biblical Studies, Epigraphy, and Palestinian Archaeology. Also there have been some critical new discoveries. One thinks immediately of the Tell Dan Inscription, for example, discovered seven years after our history appeared in print.

Along with the continued research with its new discoveries and insights, there is also the spirited academic debate to take into account. As mentioned above, this has involved virtually every aspect of ancient Israelite history—from basic assumptions about history in general, and views regarding the relative strengths and weaknesses of our sources of information, to the specifics of what may or may not have happened from one year to the next in ancient Israel. This debate was beginning to heat up already twenty years ago, and we anticipated in the preface to the original edition of our history that it was likely to be critiqued from opposite directions—from those on the one side who would see it as overly skeptical of the historical reliability of the biblical materials, and from those on the other who would regard it as overly gullible. This turned out to be the case. Perhaps the most notable trend in the debate as it has continued to unfold has been increasing polarization between scholars who argue for restored confidence in the historicity of the biblical story of ancient Israel and their counterparts who call for even more caution on the matter.

Our history clearly belongs to the cautious side of the divide, where in the meantime, however, the center of gravity of the discussion has shifted further to the left. As some very articulate scholars have pushed caution regarding the historical reliability of the biblical materials to the outer limits of skepticism, notions about the history of ancient Israel that seemed radical in the mid-1980s have come to be regarded today as moderate, or even conservative. The same may be said of our history as a whole. When it first appeared twenty years ago, *A History of Ancient Israel and Judah* was recognized as a radical departure from the biblical narrative and traditional treatments of Israelite history. There was no "Patriarchal (and Matriarchal) Age" and no exodus from Egypt, for example, no early twelve-tribe league, and we argued that Solomon was a ruler of local rather than international consequence. Such views are widely accepted at the present, and our history has come to be seen as less radical, as more moderately cautious.

Radical, moderately cautious, or whatever, readers will find in this new edition few changes in the overall contours of how we envision the history of ancient Israel. Although largely rewritten, the updating has more to do with fine tuning and nuances, documentation, and the way we make our case for our approach and conclusions. During the 1980s, for example, with the legacy of Biblical Archaeology still deeply engrained, it was necessary to devote considerable space to explaining why the biblical presentations of Israel's origins could not be taken even essentially at face value. Today it is equally necessary to make a case for utilizing the biblical materials at all in historical research, and to explain and justify how they are to be used in relation to other ancient written sources and archaeology. Consequently, we have expanded and divided the chapter originally titled "The Quest for Israel's Origins" into two chapters—one that explores in much more detail the nature, strengths, and limitations of epigraphical and archaeological evidence for understanding the origins and early history of Israel, and the other that focuses on the biblical evidence. Another additional chapter examines the strengths and limitations of our sources of information pertaining specifically to the time of the separate kingdoms.

As in the case of the first edition, we divided our responsibilities; and the division is slightly different this time. For this updated edition, Miller takes responsibility for the content and wording of chapters 1–8, while Hayes is responsible for the content and wording of chapters 9–16. Miller prepared the maps and, unless indicated otherwise, provided the photographs. Hayes provided footnote and bibliography data, selected the translations used for the ancient texts, and in some cases prepared new translations. We are grateful to Julie Mavity, Robert Williamson Jr., and Bo Adams for helping us prepare the manuscript.

The documentation of this revised edition is far more extensive than the original edition. We have assumed that our audience primarily reads English, however, and especially for the selected bibliographies at the end of the chapters we have limited the entries to English titles. There are a few exceptions in the footnotes where crucial materials and treatments are unavailable in English. For translations of biblical passages we have used the NRSV. Biblical quotations that differ from the NRSV and for which no source is given are our translations.

J. M. M.

J. H. H.

Abbreviations

AASOR	Annual of the American Schools of Oriental Research
AB	Anchor Bible
ABC	*Assyrian and Babylonian Chronicles*, by A. K. Grayson. Locust Valley, NY: Augustin, 1975; repr. Winona Lake, IN: Eisenbrauns, 2000
ABR	*Australian Biblical Review*
ABRL	Anchor Bible Reference Library
AEL	*Ancient Egyptian Literature*, by Miriam Lichtheim. 3 vols. Berkeley: University of California Press, 1973–1980
AfO	Archiv für Orientforschung
AGJU	Arbeiten zur Geschichte des antiken Judentums und des Urchristentums
AIHH	*Ancient Israel's History and Historiography: Collected Essays Volume 3*, by Nadav Na'aman. Winona Lake IN: Eisenbrauns, 2006
AIIN	*Ancient Israel and Its Neighbors: Interaction and Counteraction, Collected Essays, Volume 1*, by Nadav Na'aman. Winona Lake, IN: Eisenbrauns, 2005
AJ	*Die Annalen des Jahres 711 v. Chr. nach Prismenfragmenten aus Ninivie und Assur*, by Andreas Fuchs. Helsinki: Neo-Assyrian Text Corpus Project, 1998
AJBA	*Australian Journal of Biblical Archaeology*
AnBib	Analecta biblica
ANET	*Ancient Near Eastern Texts Relating to the Old Testament*, ed. by J. B. Pritchard. 3d ed. Princeton, NJ: Princeton University Press, 1969
AnOr	Analecta orientalia
AnSt	*Anatolian Studies*
Ant.	*Jewish Antiquities*, by Josephus
AOAT	Alter Orient und Altes Testament
AOS	American Oriental Studies
ARAB	*Ancient Records of Assyria and Babylonia*, by D. D. Luckenbill. 2 vols. Chicago: University of Chicago Press, 1926–1927
ARE	*Ancient Records of Egypt*, by J. H. Breasted. 5 vols. Chicago: University of Chicago Press, 1905–1907
ASOR	American Schools of Oriental Research
ASORAR	American Schools of Oriental Research: Archaeological Reports

AUSS	*Andrews University Seminary Studies*
BA	*Biblical Archaeologist*
BAR	*Biblical Archaeology Review*
BASOR	*Bulletin of the American Schools of Oriental Research*
BETL	Bibliotheca ephemeridum theologicarum lovaniensium
Bib	*Biblica*
BibOr	Biblica et orientalia
BJRL	*Bulletin of the John Rylands University Library of Manchester*
BN	*Biblische Notizen*
BO	*Bibliotheca orientalis*
BR	*Biblical Research*
BRev	*Bible Review*
BSac	*Bibliotheca Sacra*
BT	*The Bible Translator*
BWANT	Beiträge zur Wissenschaft vom Alten und Neuen Testament
BZ	*Biblische Zeitschrift*
BZAW	Beihefte zur Zeitschrift für die alttestamentliche Wissenschaft
CAH	*The Cambridge Ancient History*, ed. by John Boardman. 2d ed. London: Cambridge University Press, 1982–
CANE	*Civilizations of the Ancient Near East*, ed. J. M. Sasson. 4 vols. New York: Scribner: 1995; reprint in 2 vols., Peabody, MA: Hendrickson, 2000
CBQ	*Catholic Biblical Quarterly*
CCK	*Chronicles of the Chaldaean Kings (626–556 B.C.) in the British Museum*, by D. J. Wiseman. London: British Museum, 1961
CHANE	Culture and History of the Ancient Near East
COS	*The Context of Scripture*, ed. W. W. Hallo. 3 vols. Leiden: Brill, 1997–2002
CurBS	*Currents in Research: Biblical Studies*
DJD	Discoveries in the Judaean Desert
ErIsr	*Eretz-Israel*
ESHM	European Seminar in Historical Methodology
ESI	*Einleitung in die Sanherib-Inschriften*, by Eckart Frahm. Vienna: Ferdinand Berger & Söhne, 1997
ETL	*Ephemerides theologicae lovanienses*
FAT	Forschungen zum Alten Testament
FRLANT	Forschungen zur Religion und Literatur des Alten and Neuen Testaments
GBSOT	Guides to Biblical Scholarship: Old Testament
HAHL	*Handbook of Ancient Hebrew Letters: A Study Edition*, by Dennis Pardee. SBLSBS 15. Chico, CA: Scholars Press, 1982
HAR	*Hebrew Annual Review*
Hen	*Henoch*
HSM	Harvard Semitic Monographs
HSS	Harvard Semitic Studies
HUCA	*Hebrew Union College Annual*
HUCM	Monographs of the Hebrew Union College

IAKA	*Die Inschriften Asarhaddons, Königs von Assyrien,* by Riekele Borger. AfO 9. Graz: Weidner, 1956
IEJ	*Israel Exploration Journal*
IOS	*Israel Oriental Studies*
ISK	*Die Inschriften Sargons II aus Khorsabad,* by Andreas Fuchs. Göttingen: Cuvillier, 1994
ITP	*The Inscriptions of Tiglath-pileser III King of Assyria,* by Hayim Tadmor. Jerusalem: Israel Academy of Sciences and Humanities, 1994
JAAR	*Journal of the American Academy of Religion*
JANESCU	*Journal of the Ancient Near Eastern Society of Columbia University*
JAOS	*Journal of the American Oriental Society*
JARCE	*Journal of the American Research Center in Egypt*
JBL	*Journal of Biblical Literature*
JCS	*Journal of Cuneiform Studies*
JESHO	*Journal of the Economic and Social History of the Orient*
JNES	*Journal of Near Eastern Studies*
JSJS	Journal for the Study of Judaism Supplements
JSOT	*Journal for the Study of the Old Testament*
JSOTSup	Journal for the Study of the Old Testament: Supplement Series
JTS	*Journal of Theological Studies*
LAI	Library of Ancient Israel
LCL	Loeb Classical Library
NAHI	*Neo-Assyrian Historical Inscriptions and Syria-Palestine,* by J. K. Kuan. Hong Kong: Alliance Bible Seminary, 1995
NATLO	*Neo-Assyrian Treaties and Loyalty Oaths,* ed. by Simo Parpola and Kazuko Watanabe. Helsinki: Helsinki University Press, 1988
NEA	*Near Eastern Archaeology*
NIB	*The New Interpreter's Bible*
NJPSV	New Jewish Publication Society Version
NRSV	New Revised Standard Version
OBO	Orbis biblicus et orientalis
OBT	Overtures to Biblical Theology
OIP	Oriental Institute Publications
OLA	Orientalia lovaniensia analecta
OLP	*Orientalia lovaniensia periodica*
OP	*Old Persian: Grammar, Texts, Lexicon,* by R. G. Kent. AOS 33. New Haven, CT: American Oriental Society, 1950
Or	*Orientalia*
OTG	Old Testament Guides
OTL	Old Testament Library
OtSt	Oudtestamentische Studiën
PEQ	*Palestinian Exploration Quarterly*
RA	*Revue d'assyriologie et d'archéologie orientale*
RB	*Revue biblique*
RIMA	Royal Inscriptions of Mesopotamia, Assyrian Periods

R*l*A	*Reallexikon der Assyriologie*
SAA	State Archives of Assyria
SAAB	*State Archives of Assyria Bulletin*
SAAS	State Archives of Assyria Studies
SAOC	Studies in Ancient Oriental Civilizations
SBLABS	Society of Biblical Literature Archaeology and Biblical Studies
SBLDS	Society of Biblical Literature Dissertation Series
SBLMS	Society of Biblical Literature Monograph Series
SBLSBS	Society of Biblical Literature Sources for Biblical Study
SBLStBL	Society of Biblical Literature Studies in Biblical Literature
SBLSymS	Society of Biblical Literature Symposium Series
SBLWAW	Society of Biblical Literature Writings from the Ancient World
SBT	Studies in Biblical Theology
SBTS	Sources for Biblical and Theological Study
ScrHier	Scripta Hierosolymitana
SHANE	Studies in the History of the Ancient Near East
SHCANE	Studies in the History and Culture of the Ancient Near East
SJOT	*Scandinavian Journal of the Old Testament*
SPPHH	*Studies in Persian Period History and Historiography*, by H. G. M. Williamson. FAT 38. Tübingen: Mohr Siebeck, 2004
ST	*Studia theologica*
Streck	*Assurbanipal und die letzten assyrischen Könige bis zum Untergange Ninivehs*, by Maximilian Streck. 3 vols. Vorderasiatisches Bibliothek 7. Leipzig: Hinrichs, 1916.
SWBA	Social World of Biblical Antiquity
TA	*Tel Aviv*
TAD	*Textbook of Aramaic Documents from Ancient Egypt*, by Bezalel Porten and Ada Yardeni. 4 vols. Jerusalem: Hebrew University Press, 1986–1999
Transeu	*Transeuphratène*
TynBul	*Tyndale Bulletin*
TZ	*Theologische Zeitschrift*
UF	*Ugarit-Forschungen*
VT	*Vetus Testamentum*
VTSup	Supplements to Vetus Testamentum
War	*The Jewish War*, by Josephus
WBC	Word Biblical Commentary
WO	*Die Welt des Orients*
WTJ	*Westminster Theological Journal*
ZA	*Zeitschrift für Assyriologie*
ZAW	*Zeitschrift für die alttestamentliche Wissenschaft*
ZDPV	*Zeitschrift des deutschen Palästina-Vereins*

1. The Setting

The immediate setting of the history of ancient Israel and Judah was the central hill country of ancient Palestine, between approximately the twelfth and fourth centuries B.C.E. Yet this history, as the history of any people, must be understood in its broader geographical and chronological context. Palestine represents only a tiny portion of Middle Eastern territory, and the period of ancient Israelite and Judean history is only a small segment of the long sweep of Middle Eastern history.

The Chronological Context

Middle Eastern history is not well known to most Westerners and rather difficult to follow for several reasons. This history spans an enormous length of time. Geographical terms and place names change in kaleidoscopic fashion. Peoples and rulers with strange-sounding names surface, survive for a time, and then melt back into the landscape. In order for one to gain a broad overview, and thus to be able to understand ancient Israelite and Judean history in its broad chronological context, it is useful to divide the Middle Eastern past into four major phases: Prehistoric Times, Ancient Times, Classical Times, and Arab-Medieval and Modern Times (see Chart 1).

Prehistoric Times. There are no written records prior to about 3200 B.C.E., but archaeological findings indicate human occupation in the Middle East extending back a million years. The long period of time prior to written records is often designated "prehistoric," and archaeologists working in Palestine recognize four prehistoric "ages": Paleolithic, Epipaleolithic (or Mesolithic), Neolithic, and Chalcolithic.

Ancient Times. This first three thousand years of recorded history began late in the fourth millennium B.C.E. with the appearance of urban centers and the earliest written records. Archaeologists working in Palestine subdivide it into the Bronze Age (approximately the first two thousand years, ca. 3200–1200 B.C.E.) and the Iron Age (approximately the next thousand years, ca. 1200–330 B.C.E.).[1] Alexander the Great's defeat of the Persian Empire in 334–330 B.C.E. marks the end of Ancient Times.

---

1. Israeli archaeologists sometimes use the rubrics Canaanite Period and Israelite Period for the Bronze Age and Iron Age, respectively. Archaeologists working in Syria generally prefer the rubrics Old Syrian Period, Middle Syrian Period, and New Syrian Period for archaeological phases that correspond roughly to the Middle Bronze, Late Bronze, and Iron Ages, respectively.

CHART 1. Chronological Outline of Middle Eastern History*

Prehistoric Times From the earliest evidences of human occupation in the Middle East, approximately one million years ago, to the earliest cities and the beginning of writing.

Paleolithic Period	before ca. 14,000 B.C.E.
Mesolithic Period	14,000 to 8000 B.C.E.
Neolithic Period	8000 to 4000 B.C.E.
Chalcolithic Period	4000 to 3200 B.C.E.

Ancient Times From the emergence of cities and the beginning of writing to Alexander the Great—i.e., the first three thousand years of recorded history. This was the era of the ancient empires of Egypt, Mesopotamia, and Anatolia. The kingdoms of Israel and Judah appeared toward the end of Ancient Times, during the Iron Age.

Early Bronze Age	3200 to 2000 B.C.E.
Middle Bronze Age	2000 to 1550 B.C.E.
Late Bronze Age	1550 to 1200 B.C.E.
Iron Age	1200 to 330 B.C.E.

Classical Times For approximately a millennium, beginning with Alexander's conquests, the Middle East was dominated by Greek- and Latin-speaking peoples.

Hellenistic Period	330 to 63 B.C.E.
Roman Period	63 B.C.E. to 324 C.E.
Byzantine Period	324 to 640 C.E.

Islamic-Medieval Times The Middle East, including Palestine, fell under Arab rule during the seventh century C.E. Since that time, the Arabic language and Islamic religion have been dominant cultural features of the region.

Early Islamic Period	640 to 1099
Umayyad Caliphate	661–750
Abbasid Caliphate	750–969
Fatimid Caliphate	969–1171
Crusader Period	1099 to 1260
Mamluk Period	1260 to 1517
Ottoman Period	1517 to 1918

Modern Times World War I and the fall of the Ottoman Empire set the stage for the current scene of Middle Eastern politics. Key features have been the emergence of national Arab states and the establishment of the state of Israel.

*The dates provided here must be regarded as very approximate, especially for Prehistoric and Ancient Times. Where precise dates are given for Classical Times and later, they apply primarily to Palestine.

Classical Times. Following Alexander's conquests, a Macedonian version of Greek culture and politics began to dominate the Middle East. For roughly the next thousand years (subdivided by historians and archaeologists into the Hellenistic, Roman, and Byzantine periods), the Mediterranean region was a basin of common culture and the Middle East was dominated by Greek- and Latin-speaking peoples.

Arab-Medieval and Modern Times. With the rise of Islam in the early seventh century C.E., the Middle East fell under Arab rule and the domination of Arab culture. It is still predominantly an Arab realm in spite of various invasions by Turks, Crusaders, and Mongols as well as the emergence of the modern state of Israel.

The Israelites and Judeans as "Latecomers"

The Israelites appeared on the scene at the close of the Bronze Age, and their history unfolded during the Iron Age. They were relative latecomers, therefore, preceded by roughly two thousand years of recorded history and impressive cultural achievements. The peaks of ancient Egyptian civilization—the Old Kingdom, Middle Kingdom, and New Kingdom—had already come and gone. The Sumerian city-states, Hammurabi's Babylonian kingdom, the Hittite Empire, Minoan and Mycenaean civilization—all of this was past history. The Bronze Age had witnessed major literary, technological, and scientific developments, particularly in Mesopotamia and Egypt. Known written materials from these civilizations include business documents, royal inscriptions, biographical and autobiographical narratives, epic poems, correspondence, love songs, wisdom collections, theological and mythological treatises, hymns and prayers, and even recipes, both pharmaceutical and culinary. Technological and scientific achievements can be seen not only in the development of fortified cities, monumental and domestic architecture, tools, weapons, household utensils, and jewelry but also in the development of mathematics and astrology. While most of our knowledge of these Bronze Age developments comes from Egypt, Mesopotamia, and Syria (particularly Ebla, Mari, and Ugarit), archaeological remains unearthed at ancient sites in Palestine—such as Megiddo, Gezer, and Hazor—illustrate that in Palestine also the Israelites and the Judeans were heirs to a long and sophisticated civilization.

Their Origins Shrouded in a Dark Age

During the Late Bronze Age (ca. 1550–1200 B.C.E.), while Mycenaean civilization flourished to the west, Egyptian and Hittite empires dominated the Middle East. These two empires fought to a draw during the second quarter of the thirteenth century, established zones of influence, and enjoyed amicable relations for a time (see *ANET* 199–203). This was Egypt's New Kingdom Period, and Palestine was within the zone of Egyptian power. At the end of the thirteenth century, however, the whole ancient world, the Mycenaean realm as well as the Middle East, entered a period of turmoil and urban decline that marked the end of the Bronze Age and the beginning of the Iron Age. The Egyptian and Hittite empires collapsed. Population groups were on the move.

1. *The Great Pyramids and the Sphinx.* The Great Pyramids at Giza and the Sphinx had been standing for a millennium and a half when Israel appeared on the scene of recorded history.

Major cities were destroyed (although not all at once), and cities that survived dwindled in size. The new settlements that emerged over the next three or four centuries also tended to be small and unimpressive. Few written records have survived from these centuries, probably because there was little literary activity. In short, much of the ancient world entered a "dark age" around 1200 B.C.E., bringing to an end the advanced culture of the Bronze Age and lasting through the opening centuries of the Iron Age.

The earliest reference to Israel in surviving written sources from Ancient Times occurs in an Egyptian inscription from the reign of Pharaoh Merneptah (ca. 1213–1203 B.C.E.). It dates from the very end of the Late Bronze Age, in other words, and on the eve of the turbulent times that followed. This inscription, which will be discussed more fully in the next chapter, contains only a passing reference to Israel and reveals little other than that it locates Israel somewhere in the vicinity of Palestine. After Merneptah's Inscription there is a gap of three and a half centuries, the dark age centuries, before Israel is mentioned again in nonbiblical texts. At that point it begins to occur in Assyrian, Moabite, and Aramaean inscriptions. Still there are only occasional and passing references, but it is clear that the Israel involved at that stage was a small kingdom nestled in the north-central hill country of Palestine. Neighboring this Israelite kingdom on the south was another small kingdom, Judah.

How did these two kingdoms come to be? And how are they related to the Israel mentioned in Merneptah's Inscription? It is tempting to answer these questions with the Bible story. The Hebrew Bible recounts in great detail how the Israelites escaped from servitude in Egypt, wandered for forty years in the desert, conquered and settled Palestine, established a monarchy under Saul and David, enjoyed a golden age under Solomon, and then separated into two neighboring kingdoms, Israel and Judah. We must recognize, however, that the Hebrew Bible was compiled long after the people it describes would have lived and the events it reports would have occurred. For this and other reasons (to be discussed in more detail below) many historians and archaeologists have serious doubts that the Bible is to be trusted on matters of history. Neither is archaeology very helpful for answering the kinds of questions posed above. Archaeology can tell us a great deal about the location of settlements in Palestine during the intervening centuries, what sort of houses and communities the people lived in, and about the lifestyle of the times. But archaeologists are unable, at least at this stage of research, to distinguish an Israelite village, house, tool, or weapon from those of other peoples settled in the area. In short, Israel's origins and early history are shrouded in the opening dark age centuries of the Iron Age.

Israel and Judah among the Peoples
and Empires of the Iron Age

Cities, city-states, and small territorial kingdoms began gradually to reemerge. Written records became more abundant. The darkness lifted. This change was under way and reasonably well established by about 850 B.C.E., and written records attest to various city-states and local kingdoms existing alongside one another, sometimes in peace, often at war. The peoples whom we encounter at this point are those known from the Hebrew Bible (Aramaeans, Philistines, Israelites, Judahites, Ammonites, Moabites, and Edomites) as well as others beyond the horizon of the biblical writers (Etruscans, Phrygians, Lydians, and others). Egypt was emerging from its Third Intermediate Period and about to enjoy a revival under a Cushite dynasty.

Having emerged from the dark age centuries, the kingdoms of Israel and Judah experienced essentially the same fate as the other peoples of Syria-Palestine—that is, they enjoyed a brief time of political autonomy and then fell under the shadow of a series of eastern empires. Already during the ninth century, the ancient city of Ashur, situated on the banks of the Tigris River, reemerged as a powerful empire, consolidated its control over Mesopotamia, and began to expand westward. By the end of the eighth century Assyria was in firm control of the entire Fertile Crescent. Some of the local cities and kingdoms were annexed to the Assyrian Empire; others were reduced to vassal or satellite status. By the mid-seventh century, even Egypt was under Assyria's shadow.

When the Assyrian Empire collapsed toward the end of the seventh century, Ashur's rival city Babylon, situated in southern Mesopotamia, stepped into the breach. Babylon, or the Neo-Babylonian Empire, then dominated the scene for approximately a half century, until eclipsed by Cyrus the Great, founder of the Persian Empire. During an amazingly short period of time (550–539 B.C.E.) Cyrus defeated the Babylonians and conquered more territory than had ever been under a single crown. For the next two centuries, until Alexander marched east, the peoples of the ancient world from Anatolia to Egypt and even to present-day Afghanistan and Pakistan were subject to Persia.

The northern Israelite kingdom did not survive the Assyrians; Samaria its capital was destroyed in the 720s B.C.E. and its territory annexed to the Assyrian Empire. The southern Judahite kingdom lingered on, first as an Assyrian satellite and then as a Babylonian satellite, but ended even as a satellite monarchy when the Babylonians destroyed Jerusalem in 586 B.C.E.

The Impact of Alexander's Conquest

Alexander's conquest of the Persian Empire in the fourth century B.C.E. marked a significant turning point in Middle Eastern affairs—the end of Ancient Times and the beginning of Classical Times according to the chronological rubrics proposed above. Pre-classical Israelite and Judean history can be understood as unfolding primarily in the context of the Fertile Crescent. After Alexander, subsequent Judean and Jewish life is best understood as unfolding within the context of the Mediterranean world. The transition involved a wrenching culture shock.

The invading Macedonians brought with them an impressive cultural heritage that differed radically from that of the east. Even later on in the Hellenistic period, when closer contacts with other civilizations had modified their sense of elitism, the Greeks still felt themselves greatly superior to the barbarians—non-Greek-speaking peoples. And the Greeks had good reason for regarding as unrivaled their highly self-conscious culture. It treasured the freedom of the individual, the values of education, realism in art, the worth of dialogue, discussion, and independence of thought, not to mention its superiority in battlefield tactics and military organization. Yet Judaism too, even in the fourth century, was highly self-conscious. Clash ("your sons, O Zion, against your sons, O Greece"; Zech. 9:13) and synthesis ("there was such an extreme of Hellenization and increase in the adoption of foreign ways"; 2 Macc. 4:13) between the two cultures were inevitable.

The Geographical Context

In modern times we have come to think of all of Palestine (present-day Israel, the West Bank, and western Jordan) as the "Holy Land." It is true that certain biblical texts claimed the whole of Palestine for the Israelite tribes. However, the Israelites shared Palestine with various other peoples—principally the Philistines, Ammonites, Moabites, and Edomites. The Israelites and Judeans themselves were settled primarily in the central hill country of western Palestine (approximately the present-day West Bank), and only during certain periods of strength were the Israelite and Judean kings able to exercise authority beyond this hill country. While the central hill country of western Palestine was center stage, however, Israelite and Judean history must be understood also in relation to three broader geographical contexts: (1) the Fertile Crescent and surrounding lands; (2) the eastern Mediterranean seaboard, which we will refer to also as Syria-Palestine; and (3) Palestine as a whole.

The Fertile Crescent

The name "Fertile Crescent," of modern coinage, refers to a region that has also been called the "Cradle of Civilization." Specifically, it denotes the crescent-shaped band of cultivable land that begins near the head of the Persian Gulf, where the Tigris and Euphrates rivers empty their waters. From there the crescent extends toward the northwest, following the plains and valleys of these two rivers and their tributaries to the borders of the Anatolian plateau. The band bends then to the southwest, to include the eastern Mediterranean seaboard, and ends finally in the wastelands of Sinai (see Map 1). In terms of present-day political boundaries, this Fertile Crescent overlaps Iraq, Syria, Lebanon, Israel, and Jordan.

As the name implies, the Fertile Crescent stands out from surrounding regions that, except for Egypt, are less inviting or even hostile to human settlement. To the northeast (present-day Iran) are the Zagros Mountains and the Iranian plateau. To the north and northwest (Anatolia, present-day Turkey) are the Taurus Mountains. The Mediterranean Sea on the west completes, with these mountains, the borders of the convex edge of the crescent. The concave edge is limited by the northern and western reaches of the Sinai, Syrian, and Arabian deserts, which are lands only seasonally usable and which were, until the widespread use of the camel, a nearly impassable barrier to travel.

Fed by spring rains, the Tigris and Euphrates rivers are subject to periodic violent flooding, threatening life and harvest. Their windswept river plain, Mesopotamia (which means the land "between the rivers"), is fertile, however, and through the use of irrigation canals was highly productive in Ancient Times. Ancient Mesopotamian affairs tended to be dominated by two rival city-states: Ashur in the north (Upper Mesopotamia) and Babylon in the south (Lower Mesopotamia). Both Ashur and Babylon had flourished off and on during the Bronze Age before they reemerged as empires during the Iron Age—thus the terms "Neo-Assyrian" and "Neo-Babylonian" for the Iron Age phases. The Neo-Assyrian Empire flourished first and eventually dominated the whole of the Fertile Crescent. Toward the end, another city, Nineveh, emerged as the capital of the Assyrian Empire. The collapse of the Assyrian Empire was followed by a period of Neo-Babylonian imperialism during the sixth century, after which Persia emerged as the dominating power of the whole Middle East for approximately the next two centuries. The Assyrians and Babylonians spoke dialects of Akkadian, a Semitic language; but the Persians, whose home territory was the Iranian plateau east of the Fertile Crescent, were Indo-Europeans and thus belonged to a different linguistic family.

Southwest of the eastern Mediterranean seaboard, which we will consider more closely below, was Egypt. Although part of Africa and separated from the Fertile Crescent by the Sinai Desert, Egypt might be considered as an extension of the Fertile Crescent because of its proximity and the equally important role it played in ancient history. Herodotus, the sixth-century B.C.E. Greek historian, described Egypt as "the gift of the Nile" (11.5), which was a very perceptive observation. The land drew its sustenance from the river that slithers like a snake through the desert sands, adorning its immediate surroundings with luxuriant growth. The valley of the Nile is bordered to the west by the Libyan wastelands and to the east by an arid plateau, which, interrupted by the Red Sea, continues beyond as the Arabian Desert. Fed by equatorial rainfall in the heartlands of Africa, the Nile had an annual rise and fall that was more predictable than the flow of the Tigris or Euphrates. Its rise always began in July, and by late October all of the agriculturally rich land along the riverbanks was

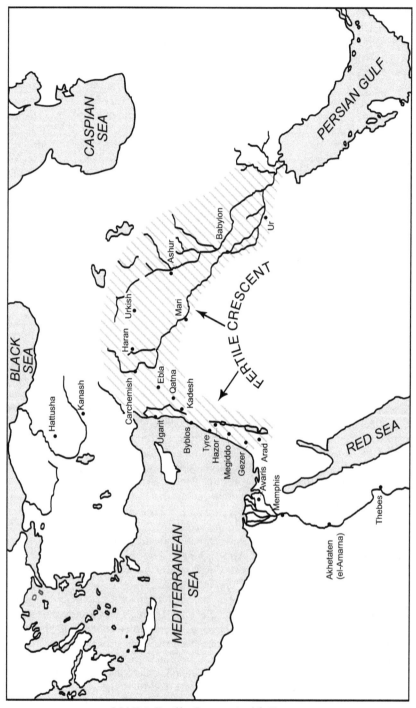

MAP 1. Fertile Crescent with Egypt

inundated. By January the river had returned to its banks, leaving behind richly productive silt. The Nile was also more easily navigable than were the Tigris and the Euphrates, so that in addition to feeding Egypt it served as a means of communication and transportation.

The ancients sometimes spoke of Egypt as two lands: the long and narrow Nile Valley itself (Upper Egypt), and the Nile Delta that creates a broad, flat, and largely marshland as it spreads out to the Mediterranean Sea (Lower Egypt). Located at the juncture of Upper and Lower Egypt was Memphis, the capital of Egypt during its Old Kingdom period. Some 450 miles further south (as the crow flies) and upstream was Thebes, Egypt's capital during the New Kingdom Period. The New Kingdom (1550–1070 B.C.E.) was Egypt's empire age, its heyday as an international power. All of this had passed before the emergence of the Israelite and Judean monarchies. As a result of the geographical proximity, however, Egypt continued as a constant influence and meddler in Syro-Palestinian affairs. During Egypt's better days, it had a long history of control over Palestine, a control that Egypt was never willing to concede even when no longer able to exercise it.

The Eastern Mediterranean Seaboard

It is appropriate now to focus more closely on the eastern Mediterranean seaboard, or Syria-Palestine, which is the southwestern horn of the Fertile Crescent. This is a strip of cultivable land along the eastern coast of the Mediterranean Sea, watered by precipitation from Mediterranean winds. It extends about four hundred miles from the Taurus Mountains in the north to the Sinai Desert in the south, and extends on an average between seventy to one hundred miles into the interior, where it gives way to the Arabian Desert (see Map 2).

Throughout history this strip of land between the sea and the desert has served as a land bridge between Asia and Africa. It narrows toward the southern end, in the region of Palestine, so that one might think of the land bridge as being shaped like an hourglass, with key routes passing north-south through Palestine and forking off in essentially four directions. The northwestern fork led via the Phoenician ports and Anatolia toward Europe. The northeastern fork led around the desert to Mesopotamia. The southwestern fork led along the Mediterranean coast to Egypt and Africa. The southeastern fork led to the Gulf of Aqabah, itself an arm of the Red Sea, and around the gulf to Arabia.

The topography of the eastern Mediterranean seaboard is greatly diversified, broken by mountain ranges and valleys. Common to the entire course of the area are four north-south physiographic features. These are, from west to east: (1) the coastal zone; (2) a mountainous ridge paralleling the coast; (3) a deep depression, actually part of the so-called Great Rift that extends from Syria to east Africa; and (4) another mountainous zone that gradually gives way to the Syrian-Arabian desert. These features are most clearly delineated in present-day Lebanon where they are represented by the Lebanese coast, the Lebanon Mountains, the Bekaa Valley, and the Anti-Lebanon Mountains. At various points this north-south orientation is interrupted by east-west formations that contribute in turn to the variety and brokenness of the terrain. Examples here are the Jezreel

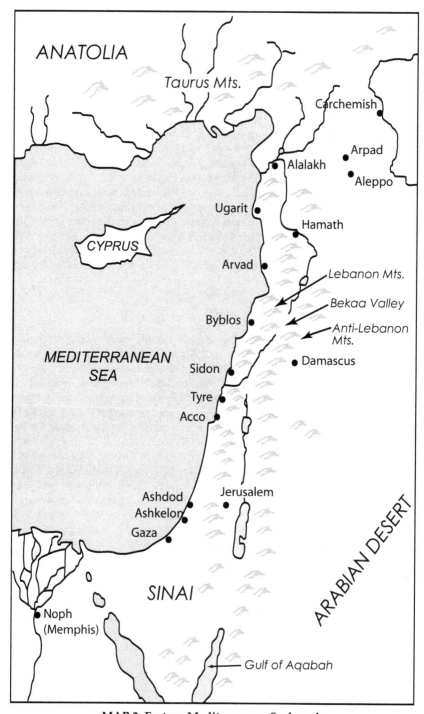

MAP 2. Eastern Mediterranean Seaboard

Valley and the pass between the mountains west of present-day Homs (in Syria). There are no unifying major river valleys comparable to those found in Mesopotamia and Egypt. The only rivers of size are the Orontes River (present-day Wadi al-Assi) that rises in the northern Bekaa and flows first north and then west into the Mediterranean Sea, and the Jordan River that rises at the southern end of the Bekaa and flows southward to the Dead Sea. Agricultural possibilities are reasonably limited and tend toward small-plot farming. The combination of these physical characteristics predisposed the area to particularistic regionalism. Specifically, the situation favored modest city-states and small, localized kingdoms rather than large empires.

The character of the region as lying between continents meant that the population was somewhat heterogeneous and cosmopolitan in Ancient Times, although the vast majority of the people spoke more or less closely related languages that belong to the Semitic family. One would expect this, since the Mediterranean seaboard is the northwestern part of the Arabian Peninsula. This peninsula, shaped roughly like the blade of a hatchet, juts into the Indian Ocean, separating the Red Sea from the Persian Gulf. If one completes the figure, with Mesopotamia forming the socket and the Mediterranean seaboard the back of the head, the resultant area on the map is what may be called the Semitic Quadrant, the homeland of the Semitic peoples.

Being a land bridge between continents, the eastern Mediterranean seaboard, or Syria-Palestine, was an active zone of commerce. While its inhabitants benefited significantly from the commerce, these benefits came with a heavy price. Syria-Palestine was sucked into virtually all the major conflicts between the ancient imperial powers. The cost and futility of military preparedness, the schizophrenia induced by the perpetual need to choose sides, the agonies of defeat, and the lessons of loss are etched in the literature of the region, especially in the Hebrew Scriptures. The architectural, monumental, and inscriptional remains in the region in many instances are not the work of natives, but reflect the hands and languages of the conquerors—Egyptians, Hittites, Assyrians, Babylonians, Persians, Greeks, and Romans. In terms of basic cultural patterns—language, literature, mythological motifs, theological perspectives, and the like—there seems to have been a closer kinship between the peoples of Syria-Palestine and those of Mesopotamia. The close geographical proximity of Palestine to Egypt, on the other hand, meant that Egyptian influence, both political and cultural, was also a fairly constant feature throughout Israelite and Judean history.

Ancient documents apply various names to the eastern Mediterranean seaboard or to subdivisions of it. Early Egyptian scribes used the names "Retenu" and "Hurru" for the seaboard region, for example, while early Mesopotamian (Akkadian) texts refer to the region west of the Euphrates as "Amurru" ("the west"). The Hittites of Anatolia, who spoke an Indo-European language, established a powerful empire during the Late Bronze Age that extended southward into the Mediterranean seaboard. Consequently some ancient texts, both Egyptian and Mesopotamian, refer to the seaboard region as "Hatti." The name "Canaan" also appears in Egyptian and Mesopotamian texts. Generally it seems to refer to the coastal zone and the peoples settled there, but this is not always clear. In certain Egyptian texts from the New Kingdom Period, for example,

"Canaan" seems to refer to Egypt's Asiatic province. Aramaeans begin to be mentioned in the ancient sources early in the eleventh century B.C.E., at which time they appear to have been a largely nomadic people who grazed their flocks between the Euphrates and the Mediterranean. Over the next few centuries, however, the Aramaeans tended to settle down, prominent Aramaean cities emerged (such as Arpad, Hamath, and Damascus), and the region came to be known as Aram.

Like many of the traditional geographical terms we use in English for the various regions of the Middle East, the name "Syria" was coined by Greek geographers. Other geographical terms of Greek origin include "Mesopotamia" (the land "between the rivers"), "Anatolia" (the land to "the east" from the perspective of the ancient Greeks), and "Egypt" (from *Aigyptos*, possibly the Greek pronunciation of one of the early names for Memphis). Greek geographers probably derived the name "Syria" from "Assyria" and used it initially to refer to the Assyrian Empire. Later the term was applied to the region west of the Euphrates, then to the coastal region, and finally to the interior of roughly the northern two-thirds of the coastal zone.

Reference to "the land of Philistia" first appears in nonbiblical texts in the so-called Calah Orthostat Slab of the Assyrian king Adad-nirari III (810–783 B.C.E.; see *COS* 2:276). Herodotus, writing in the fifth century B.C.E. and wishing to refer specifically to the southern part of Syria, called this southern part *syria hē palaistinē* ("Philistine Syria"). Gradually *palaistinē* (Palestine) came to be used as a proper name for the southern part of the coastal zone, and eventually found its way into English.[2] It is in this historical sense that we use the name as the appropriate English term for the geographical region to be described below. Obviously the name is anachronistic for the Bronze Age, and to some extent for the Iron Age as well. The Philistines, from whom the name derives, did not settle in the region until the twelfth century B.C.E.

Palestine

Palestine, a still narrower geographical context for the history of ancient Israel and Judah, has reasonably well-defined boundaries—in the north the foothills of the Lebanon and Anti-Lebanon mountains, in the west the Mediterranean Sea, in the south the Sinai Desert, and in the east the Arabian Desert. Lying between 310 and 330 30′ north latitude and comprising about 9,500 square miles, Palestine is comparable in size to the country of Belgium or the state of Vermont. Its topography may be divided into four north-south zones, which are continuations of the four zones delineated above. These are (1) the coastal plain, continuous with the Phoenician coast; (2) Galilee and the central hill country of western Palestine, continuous with the Lebanon Mountains; (3) the Jordan Valley, continuous with the Bekaa Valley; and (4) the Transjordanian highlands, continuous with the Anti-Lebanon Mountains (compare Maps 2 and 3). The

---

2. For example, a British archaeological society established in 1865 was named the Palestine Exploration Fund, and one of the first major projects funded by this society, a systematic mapping and archaeological survey of the area between the Mediterranean Sea and the Jordan River, was published under the title *Survey of Western Palestine: Memoirs of the Topography, Orography, Hydrography, and Archaeology* (3 vols., London: The Committee of the Palestine Exploration Fund, 1881–83).

general north-south orientation of the region is interrupted by the Jezreel (or Esdraelon) Valley and the Mount Carmel range, which parallel each other in a northwest to southeast direction. The Jezreel Valley, which is a reasonably broad and fertile plain, divides the mountainous backbone of western Palestine, separating the Galilean hill country to the north from the central hill country to the south. The Carmel range is a spur of the central hill country that juts northwestward into the Mediterranean. Thus it creates a natural barrier across the coastal plain, forcing traffic along the coastal road either to detour inward through mountain passes, particularly the one at Megiddo, or to squeeze through the few hundred feet that separate the precipitous Mount Carmel promontory from the sea.

The Coastal Plain. A characteristic feature of the Palestinian coast is its smooth unaccented line, interrupted only by Mount Carmel where it juts into the sea and by the Bay of Acco immediately north of Mount Carmel. The ancient harbor city of Acco was located at the northern end of the bay (in contrast to Haifa, which dominates the bay today from the southern end), and the bay itself represents the northwestern end of the Jezreel Valley. From the Bay of Acco northward, the Phoenician coast, the mountains rise almost straight out of the sea. This leaves little true plain, but provided good harbors for the small and fragile ships of ancient times, harbors that the Phoenicians put to good use. The coastline south of Carmel, where the Philistines were settled, is much smoother, with shallow waters unprotected from the winds—not overly amicable to ancient seafaring. Moreover, much of the southern coast was rendered less accessible by sand dune barriers and low limestone ridges paralleling the shoreline. None of the port cities farther south along the Palestinian coast than Acco—the main ones were Dor, Joppa, Ashkelon, and Gaza—had nearly as good a natural harbor as Acco itself or the other Phoenician port cities farther to the north. During the Roman period, Herod the Great turned the old site of Strato's Tower, just south of Dor, into the successful seaport of Caesarea by constructing an artificial harbor with moles and walls.

The coastal plain is of variable width south of Mount Carmel, from a few hundred feet at the foot of the mountain to about thirty miles in the vicinity of Gaza. Between Carmel and Joppa, where it was known as Sharon, the plain is fertile but was poorly drained in Ancient Times, thus marshy and forested. From approximately Joppa to Gaza, the area of the five main Philistine cities (Gath, Ekron, Ashdod, Ashkelon, and Gaza), the plain was better suited for agriculture, but with an increasing degree of aridity toward the south, where it eventually merges into the desert.

Galilee and the Central Hill Country. The mountainous district between the coastal plain and the Jordan Valley consists of a range of limestone hills of moderate height and rugged contours, along with their associated features. There are essentially two divisions: (1) Galilee, the highlands north of the Jezreel Valley, and (2) the central hill country south of Jezreel. The latter may be divided into (a) the north-central, or Ephraimite, hill country, also called Samaria, which extends from the Jezreel Valley to approximately Jerusalem; and (b) the south-central, or Judean, hill country, which extends from approximately Jerusalem to the Negeb. Ephraim, Samaria, and Judah are of course biblical names used here rather loosely. "Ephraim," for example, refers to the

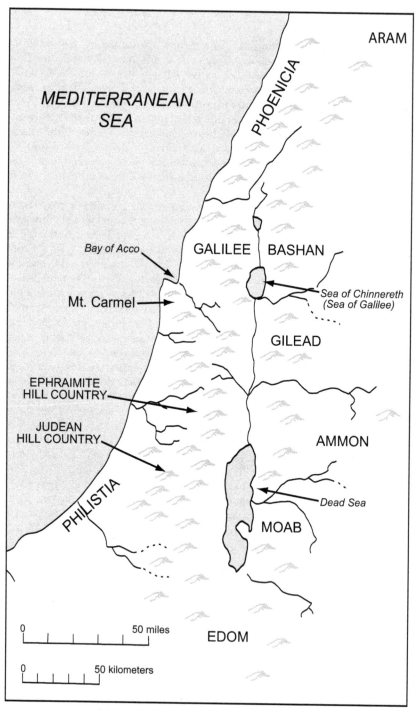

MAP 3. Palestine during Ancient Times

dominant Israelite tribe that inhabited the mountains north of Jerusalem during Old Testament times. Other tribes, particularly Manasseh and Benjamin, also inhabited certain parts of the north-central hill country. The name "Samaria," on the other hand, derives from the city Samaria, capital from the ninth century on of the northern Israelite kingdom, which in turn had as its core the north-central hill country. The term "city" also is used rather loosely in these paragraphs. All of the settlements in ancient Palestine were much smaller than modern cities, and even smaller than the Philistine cities in the coastal plain, to say nothing of their counterparts in Egypt and Mesopotamia.

Upper, or northern, Galilee is rugged country that reaches an altitude of almost four thousand feet. Lower Galilee's hills are somewhat less rugged and interspersed with fertile valleys. Galilee lay outside the main center of Israelite and Judean territory and at the same time in close proximity to Phoenicia and Syria. Accordingly, the Phoenician and Syrian cities exerted considerable influence on the area and at times dominated it militarily and politically. Josephus, a first-century C.E. historian, reports that there were 204 villages and towns in Galilee in his day (*Life* 245). Elsewhere he writes, with some exaggeration, of this area:

> Although surrounded by such powerful foreign nations, the two Galilees have always resisted any hostile invasion, for the inhabitants are from infancy inured to war, and have at all times been numerous; never did the men lack courage nor the country men. For the land is everywhere so rich in soil and pasturage and produces such variety of trees, that even the most indolent are tempted by these facilities to devote themselves to agriculture. In fact, every inch of the soil has been cultivated by the inhabitants; there is not a parcel of waste land. The towns, too, are thickly distributed, and even the villages, thanks to the fertility of the soil, are all so densely populated that the smallest of them contains above fifteen thousand [!] inhabitants. (*War* 3.41–43)

The Jezreel (or Esdraelon) Valley is a broad, flat, and fertile depression that makes a radical break between Galilee and the central hill country. Throughout history this valley has served as a natural route of overland communication between the Mediterranean and the interior. Add to that the fertility of its soil and it is easy to understand why the Jezreel was the most fought-over ground, the natural battlefield, of ancient Palestine. In addition to the port city of Acco situated at the northwestern end of the valley, other prominent ancient cities associated with the Jezreel Valley were Megiddo, Taanach, and Beth-shean. The name "Jezreel" derives from a small city of that name located in the east-central part of the valley, which played an especially prominent role during the period of the Israelite monarchy.

South of the Jezreel Valley, the central mountain range picks up again as the Ephraimite hill country, or Samaria. A key city in this region during Ancient Times was Shechem, situated in a pass between the twin peaks of Mount Ebal (3,083 feet) and Mount Gerizim (2,889 feet). Generally north of Shechem was the old tribal area of Manasseh, characterized by calcareous hills and valleys of fertile farmland. The valleys lead directly into the heart of the region, thus providing easy accessibility. Three other important cities in this area north of Shechem were Samaria, Dothan, and Tirzah.

2. *Jezreel Valley.* View of the Jezreel Valley from Mount Carmel.

Ephraim proper, south of Shechem, is a broad, domed region with heights over 3,000 feet. Jebel Asur, the Baal-hazor of the Bible, reaches 3,332 feet. This was not a region of cities, but many of the towns that figure in the biblical narratives were here, including Shiloh, Mizpah, Ramah, Gibeon, and Bethel. In the southern part of Ephraim, in the area occupied by the tribe of Benjamin, two east-west fault lines cut deep into the hill country, thus providing ancient routes into the interior from the coast to the west and the Jordan Valley to the east. From the west, the Valley of Aijalon (also called "the ascent of Beth-horon" in the Bible) enters the hill country just northwest of Jerusalem. From the east, a double fault line provided two ancient routes from the region of Jericho, one leading to the vicinity of Gibeah and Michmash, the other leading more directly to Jerusalem.

The Judean hill country, from around Jerusalem to the region of Beer-sheba in the Negeb, presents a less fertile, more arid and monotonous countenance than the Ephraimite portion of the central highlands. However, this is not to say that Judah was barren. Forests probably covered much of it during biblical times. Also then, as well as today, careful husbandry of the somewhat meager resources of soil and moisture produced a relatively successful agricultural economic base for village life. This was particularly true of the better-watered western slopes of the hill country, where, through the utilization of painstakingly constructed terraces, olives, grain, grapes, and other typical Mediterranean crops were grown. The chief cities of the Judean highlands, during biblical times as well as today, are Jerusalem and Hebron. Other less prominent settlements during biblical times were Bethlehem, Tekoa, Beth-zur, and Debir.

Running parallel to the western Judean hill country approximately from Beth-horon to Beer-sheba, and separating the Judean highlands from Philistia proper, is an area of low foothills known as the Shephelah (meaning "lowland" or "piedmont"). Because of its double importance as Judah's first line of defense and as a fertile, easily farmed strip, the Shephelah was often a source of conflict between the people of Judah and the Philistines.

The eastern edge of the Judean hill country, between the highlands and the Dead Sea Valley, provided a spectacular and even more efficient line of defense. This is the "Wilderness of Judah," a region of arid steppes, of dizzying naked

3. *Bedouin at well.* Bedouin women drawing water from a well in the Negeb.

stone cliffs overlooking the inhospitable waters of the Dead Sea, of caves and hollows where bandits and outcasts have found refuge through the ages, and of dry streambeds down which the waters of occasional heavy rains rush with destructive fury. Some seasonal pasturage of flocks was possible in this wilderness area; otherwise it was essentially uninhabited in Ancient Times.

On the south, the Judean highlands slope quickly to merge into the Negeb (literally, "the dry land"). Specifically, the Negeb begins with the east-west depression of Beer-sheba and ends in the vicinity of Kadesh-barnea, an oasis that marks the southernmost limit of Palestine. The Negeb is basically a high plateau with very little rainfall—enough to sustain scrub and grassland vegetation—but with soils that, when irrigated, can produce quite abundantly. In biblical times the Negeb was primarily used by shepherds as pastureland, even though some permanent settlements and military outposts were established in places where natural springs provided a supply of water or military defense was required. In effect, therefore, the Negeb represents an extension of the eastern desert across the southern end of Palestine to the Mediterranean Sea and Sinai.

The Jordan Rift Valley. The Jordan Rift Valley, with the Jordan River, the Sea of Galilee, and the Dead Sea in its embrace, represents the Palestinian portion of one of the world's most distinctive geological formations. This is the so-called Great Rift, a furrow on the surface of the globe that extends from Iskandarun in southern Turkey to Lake Malawi in Africa, forming the Bekaa Valley, the Jordan Valley, the Gulf of Aqabah, and the Red Sea along the way. It is this deep rift, exacerbating the distinction between the central hill country on the west and the Transjordanian highlands on the east, that gives Palestine its dramatic topographical configurations. The biblical name for the Jordan Rift Valley is Arabah (Ghor in modern Arabic), although some biblical passages seem to use this term "Arabah" specifically for the southernmost end of the valley, south of the Dead Sea.

4. *Gennesaret.* Plain of Gennesaret and the Sea of Galilee viewed from the southwest.

The sources of the Jordan rise at the foot of Mount Hermon (itself over 9,000 feet in elevation), in the vicinity of the ancient city of Dan. The river is still above sea level where it parallels Galilee. Here also was located until relatively recently Lake Huleh, a lagoon produced by basalt blockage of the river flow and surrounded by marshlands (Lake Huleh has been drained in modern times). On the western bank of the valley along the stretch of the river from Lake Huleh to the Sea of Galilee stood the important city of Hazor. The importance of this city lay in the fact that it was situated at the juncture of main roads to Hamath and Damascus and at the place where the road to Damascus crossed the Jordan. Below Hazor the river plunges rapidly, so that the Sea of Galilee ten miles farther downstream is almost seven hundred feet below sea level. Bearer of a multiplicity of names (Sea of Chinnereth, Sea of Gennesaret, Sea of Tiberias), the Sea of Galilee is a freshwater lake approximately five miles wide by twelve miles long that supported a fishing industry during Ancient Times.

The main portion of the Jordan Valley lies between the Sea of Galilee and the Dead Sea. Moreover, while the direct distance between the two bodies of water is about sixty-five miles, the meandering course of the river between the two is actually three times that long. Of variable width (averaging about ten miles), this main stretch of the river valley is fertile and cultivable where there are natural springs or where other water is available for small-scale irrigation. This is the case primarily in the north, in the vicinity of the Sea of Galilee. Farther south, as the river approaches the Dead Sea, the valley becomes a virtual wasteland, with the springs at Jericho taking on the character of a desert oasis. Close to the river itself and also becoming more pronounced as it approaches the Dead Sea, the valley drops abruptly, sometimes as much as 150 feet, to form lunar-like eroded gray marly flats of fantastic appearance. These frame the *zor,* the biblical "pride of the Jordan," an impenetrable strip of thorny, tangled

5. *Jordan River.* Jordan River near its exit from the Sea of Galilee.

growth along the immediate riverbanks, where wild animals, including lions, prowled in biblical times. Its flow through this depressed canyon within the valley rendered the river difficult to cross and relatively useless for any large-scale irrigation purposes. Its rapid flow, on the other hand, and its excessively winding course rendered the Jordan impractical for navigation. In short, the Jordan River was more of a geographical barrier to communication than a link.

Several tributaries join the Jordan in this stretch between the Sea of Galilee and the Dead Sea, the most important of these being the Yarmuk from the east, which drains the area of ancient Bashan and whose waters merge with the Jordan just south of the Sea of Galilee; Wadi Far'ah from the west, which provides entrance from the valley to the Ephraimite hill country; and Wadi Zerqa from the east, the Jabbok River of biblical traditions, which drains the region of the ancient land of Gilead. Important cities along this stretch of the valley were Beth-shean, at the southeastern end of the Jezreel Valley; Pella, Succoth, and Adam on the east bank; and Jericho with its abundant springs on the west bank.

The Jordan River ends in the bitter waters of the Dead Sea, the biblical "Sea of the Arabah" or "Salt Sea," also later known as Lake Asphaltitis. This sea is actually a landlocked lake filled with mineral soup (about 25 percent mineral content) produced by evaporation. Throughout antiquity its salt, asphalt, and general features were subjects of fascination and the objects of trade. Josephus gives the following description of the sea.

> Its waters are, as I said, bitter and unproductive, but owing to their buoyancy send up to the surface the very heaviest of objects cast into them, and it is difficult, even of set purpose, to sink to the bottom. Thus, when [the Roman emperor] Vespasian came to explore the lake, he ordered certain persons who were unable to swim to be flung into the deep water with their hands tied behind them; with the result that all rose to the surface and floated, as if

impelled upward by a current of air. Another remarkable feature is its change
of colour: three times a day it alters its appearance and throws off a different
reflection of the solar rays. Again, in many parts it casts up black masses of
bitumen, which float on the surface, in their shape and size resembling
decapitated bulls. The labourers on the lake row up to these and catching
hold of the lumps haul them into their boats; but when they have filled them
it is no easy task to detach their cargo, which owing to its tenacious and gluti-
nous character clings to the boat until it is loosened by the monthly secretions
of women, to which alone it yields. It is useful not only for caulking ships, but
also for the healing of the body, forming an ingredient in many medicines.
(*War* 4.476–81)

The Dead Sea is the lowest point on the surface of the earth, with its altitude
and the extent of its shoreline varying from time to time, depending on the
water level. Typically the water level has been about 1,300 feet below sea level,
thus creating a reasonably large lake about 48 miles long, 8 miles wide, and
with a depth of about 1,300 feet in its northern end. The southern end of the
sea, below the peculiarly shaped peninsula called "the Lisan" ("the Tongue")
that protrudes from its eastern shore, is very shallow on the other hand, seldom
deeper than three or four feet. Several tributaries drain into the Dead Sea from
the east, the most imposing being the Wadi el-Mujib, the river Arnon of the biblical traditions, and the Wadi el-Hesa, possibly the biblical river Zered. Located
along the western shores of the Dead Sea were En-gedi, an oasis created by a
warm freshwater spring, and Masada, a massive freestanding mountain developed by Herod the Great as a fortified resort and used by the rebels of the First
Jewish Revolt as their last refuge. Here also is Wadi Qumran, in whose vicinity
were discovered the famous Dead Sea Scrolls.

South of the Dead Sea, the Great Rift continues. The land rises rapidly in the
direction of the Gulf of Aqabah, reaching its highest point, 650 feet above sea
level, some 40 miles north of the gulf. On the gulf itself, actually the eastern
arm of the Red Sea, stood Elath, important as a doorway to South Arabia and
the East African coast.

The Transjordanian Highlands. Almost in a straight line, running from Mount
Hermon in the north to the shores of the Red Sea in the south, the edge of the
Arabian Plateau rises wall-like alongside the Jordan Valley. North of the
Yarmuk River, the plateau was called Bashan in biblical times. Bashan is a relatively well-watered area with rich soils, famous in biblical times for its fat
cattle and fierce bulls. South of the Yarmuk, and roughly paralleling the
Ephraimite hill country, lay Gilead, a strip of land from 25 to 30 miles in
breadth lying along the edge of the plateau and sitting astride the River Jabbok.
This is pleasant, bountiful country, with relatively abundant rainfall, which
permits the growth of forests and the cultivation of olives and grapes. Gilead
being of similar terrain to the central hill country west of the Jordan, it is not
surprising that it was inhabited in biblical times by tribal groups related to
those in the Ephraimite area and that Israelite kings attempted to control
Gilead. This brought them into conflict with the Ammonites and the Moabites,
who also made territorial claims in that area.

Rabbath-ammon (present-day Amman), the chief city of the Ammonites,
was situated at the desert edge on a southeastern branch of the Jabbok. The

Moabites, on the other hand, inhabited the rolling plateau east of the Dead Sea. This plateau provides a north-south strip of cultivable land, approximately 20 miles wide, sandwiched between the rugged slopes of the Dead Sea basin and the desert fringe, and bisected by the steep Wadi el-Mujib canyon (the river Arnon). The area is good for grain cultivation and pasturage of goats and sheep. Chief Moabite cities were Heshbon, Medeba, Dibon, and Kir-hareseth (often identified with present-day Kerak, but this is uncertain).

South of the Wadi el-Hesa (biblical Zered?) was the land of the Edomites, with Bosrah as their chief city. This region becomes increasingly arid as one moves southward; it is similar in this regard to the Negeb and the southern limits of western Palestine. Some biblical texts seem to presuppose that Edom was not limited to the territory east of the Jordan Rift but also extended into the latter region, west of the Arabah. In any case, some of the peoples who inhabited the Negeb and southward during Ancient Times were clearly regarded as being of Edomite stock. Later, during the Hellenistic and Roman periods, Nabateans established a commercial empire in southern Transjordan with its capital at Petra. The Edomites, in the meantime, or Idumeans as they were called during the Roman period, came to be associated primarily with the southern Palestinian region west of the Arabah.

Palestine, a Land of Contrasts. Perhaps no comparably sized area on the surface of the earth is characterized by such diversity of topographical and climatic features as Palestine. In few places other than in ancient Palestine, for example, could one kill a lion "on a day when snow had fallen" (2 Sam. 23:20). As further illustration of the land's topographical and climatic diversity, consider the following hypothetical journey of an ancient traveler from the coastal plain to the eastern desert, crossing approximately at Jerusalem. Our hypothetical traveler would begin the journey, a total distance of less than 80 air miles, by crossing the coastal plain with its tropical climate and growth, including palm trees. From there he or she would ascend the rough, low hills of the Shephelah, passing small fields of barley and wheat, vineyards, olive groves, sycamore and other trees, and scrub growth, similar in many respects to the scenery of southern Europe. Climbing then the Judean hills with elevations over 3,000 feet, our traveler would enter terrain where heavy snowfalls were not unknown and where the land became somewhat more barren, although spotted here and there with growths of forest. After passing Jerusalem and beginning the descent down the eastern slopes of the central hill country, the traveler would encounter a radically different environment: the vineyards, olive groves, and cultivated fields would give way to barren ("wilderness") terrain frequented by tent nomads and their flocks of sheep and goats. A few miles farther along, our traveler would reach the valley of the Jordan, where the summer heat was torrid and the atmosphere heavy. Virtually the whole landscape would be desolate except for the green oasis of Jericho with its springs and tropical appearance. Within the next 20 miles after passing Jericho, our traveler would descend to the Jordan River approximately at the level of the Dead Sea, itself the lowest spot on the face of the earth, and begin an ascent to the Transjordanian highlands. Climbing then to an elevation over 3,000 feet, our traveler would encounter again a landscape of forests and cultivated fields, where wheat and barley grew in a plateau setting.

This diversity of east-west topography and climate is matched by a corresponding diversity from north to south. Only 125 miles separate Mount Hermon with its alpine atmosphere over 9,000 feet above sea level from the Dead Sea with its tropical atmosphere some 1,300 feet below sea level.

Main Roads through Palestine. Two main international highways passed through Palestine. Crossing the Sinai from Egypt and following the coastal plain to the Mount Carmel ridge was "the Way of the Sea" (*Via Maris* in Latin). This route turned inward at the Carmel ridge and slipped through the Megiddo pass into the Jezreel Valley. At that point roads branched eastward to Transjordan, northward toward the Aramaean cities of Damascus and Hamath, and northwestward to follow the Phoenician coast in the direction of Anatolia. The second international route passed through Transjordan, connecting the Gulf of Aqabah and western Arabia with Damascus via Edom, Moab, Gilead, and Bashan. Trajan, after annexing Nabatea to the Roman Empire in 106 C.E., paved this Transjordanian route and named it *Via Nova Trajiana* ("Trajan's New Road"). In recent years this route has come to be known also as "the King's Highway," with reference to Numbers 20:17 and 21:22. However, this may be misleading. First, it is questionable whether the phrase *derek hammelek* in these two passages should be translated "King's Highway." And if so, there remains the question of whether the passages refer to this particular Transjordanian route.

While these two international highways bypassed the central hill country, another road of some secondary importance followed approximately the north-south watershed of the hill country from Shechem via Jerusalem and Bethlehem to Hebron. Crossroads were provided where valleys cut into the hill country from the coastal plain to the west and the Jordan Rift Valley to the east—for example, at Shechem, Jerusalem, and Hebron.

Climate. Palestine has two main seasons: a warm summer that is dry and rainless and a cool winter with rains rolling in from the Mediterranean. Sometime in October the first of the "early rains" moistens the ground enough for plowing and planting. The growing season follows, with most of the necessary moisture coming in the form of sudden downpours rather than the gentler but prolonged periods of precipitation common in more northerly climates. (Jerusalem, for example, gets its 20 or so inches of yearly rainfall, equal to that of London or Paris, in about fifty rainy days, most of them in December, January, and February.) The "late rains" of April and early May are needed to help the crops reach full maturity, and they are normally the last of the rains, although Proverbs 26:1 refers to the occasional havoc caused by "rain in harvest"—an anomalous rainfall in early summer. With the onset of spring, vegetation begins to wither and die, especially the winter growth in marginal rainfall areas, and by midsummer drought conditions prevail. The only climatic relief to the summer drought comes in the form of characteristically heavy dews, particularly in the coastal plain and the higher elevations. The hot, dry blast of the sirocco, or *khamsin*, a southeast wind driving up from the parched desert areas, makes its presence felt from April to early June and from September to November.

Generally speaking, therefore, while some portions of the land receive rain only during the period from December through February, late October through April constitutes the rainy season in Palestine. The "early" and "late" rains

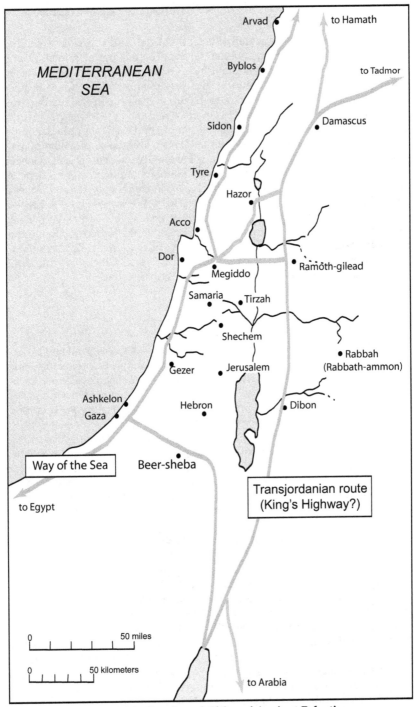

MAP 4. **Main Roads and Cities of Ancient Palestine**

mentioned in the Bible are actually the moderate fall and spring showers that precede and follow the heavy winter storms. The amount of rainfall in any given place in Palestine is controlled by a combination of factors, primarily geographical position and altitude: the precipitation tends to be heavier toward the north and west and lighter toward the south and east, while at the same time higher elevations tend to get more rain than the lower. As it works out, the western slopes of the central hill country and the Transjordanian highlands usually receive the heaviest rainfall, and within these areas the rainfall tends to be heavier in the north. Thus Upper Galilee averages about 40 inches of rain a year, the Ephraimite hill country (Samaria) around 30, Jerusalem 24, and Hebron 22, while Beer-sheba in the Negeb averages only about 9 inches a year. The coastal plain repeats the pattern, with Acco averaging 26 inches a year and Gaza, in the south, 15, but with the highlands of Carmel receiving as much as 35 inches. In the Jordan Valley, where with the rapid drop in altitude below the Sea of Galilee goes a corresponding increase in aridity, Beth-shean has a mean annual rainfall of 12.5 inches, Jericho 6, and the area around the Dead Sea is true desert, with less than 2 inches of rain a year.

Everyday Life in Ancient Palestine

It is difficult for us in modern times to imagine how life was lived and experienced by the inhabitants of Palestine in preindustrial times. Yet we must make an effort to do so, lest we fall into the mentality of medieval artists who depicted biblical characters anachronistically in their own medieval dress and in the physical setting of medieval Europe. Archaeological research is especially useful in this regard. Archaeological surveys help us understand settlement patterns, while excavations of the material remains from ancient times (houses, tools, weapons, pottery vessels, and so on) all contribute to a better understanding of everyday life. Moreover, archaeological research is (or can be) more "democratic" than written sources. The latter tend to reflect the life and thought of the wealthy and educated classes. The archaeologist, on the other hand, can excavate in the poorer sections of town as well as in royal palaces and temples.

Perhaps the most important point to be made is that, because of the topography and climate of Palestine, its inhabitants were predisposed to an agrarian-pastoral village economy and lifestyle. There were no major river valleys, and irrigation never played any significant role in Palestinian agriculture. It is "a land of hills and valleys, watered by rain from the sky" (Deut. 11:11). Also, the two main international routes through Palestine, the coastal road ("Way of the Sea") and the Transjordanian road ("King's Highway"?) essentially bypassed the central hill country. Thus especially the central hill country, which was center stage of Israelite and Judean history, was strewn with small villages whose inhabitants engaged in small-scale agriculture and pastoralism. Even the larger hill country cities—Samaria, Shechem, Jerusalem, and Hebron—must be regarded as nothing more than modest-size towns.

The rhythm and routine of life in preindustrial Palestine was thoroughly immersed in the climatic and agricultural patterns of the land. Fall plowing

6. *Sifting grain.* Husband and wife sifting grain after winnowing.

and sowing, winter pruning, spring harvesting, early summer threshing, and late summer gathering set the dominant agricultural chores. Pastoral pursuits were carried out in the context of this same larger rhythm of life. During the rainy months, when crops were growing, the "wilderness" areas provided pasture; in the summer, the freshly harvested lands could be grazed and the crop residue after threshing used as fodder.

Both the Bible and other ancient Middle Eastern literature provide us with descriptions of the crops produced in Palestine: "a land with flowing streams, with springs and underground waters welling up in valleys and hills, a land of wheat and barley, of vines and fig trees and pomegranates, a land of olive trees and honey, a land where you may eat bread without scarcity, where you will lack nothing" (Deut. 8:7–9). Centuries before this Deuteronomy passage was penned, Sinuhe, an Egyptian traveler, gave the following description of the land: "It was a good land. . . . Figs were in it, and grapes. It had more wine than water. Plentiful was its honey, abundant its olives. Every kind of fruit was on its trees. Barley was there, and emmer wheat. There was no limit to any kind of cattle" (*ANET* 19).

Allowing for theological enthusiasm and touristic exaggeration, these two passages provide an accurate glimpse of Palestinian agriculture in biblical times: cereal crops (wheat, barley) harvested between April and June, various fruits ripening in the summer months, and grapes and olives gathered in late summer and early fall. From these crops came the basic dietary staples: bread, wine, and oil.

Pastoralism, the raising of sheep and goats, was the second basic element in the Palestinian economy, especially in the south and the Tranjordanian highlands. Sheep and goats were well adapted to the Palestinian environment. Both were valued for their secondary products—their wool and hair, and their milk in the case of goats—as well as for the meat they provided. Agrarian and pastoral interests were pursued more in harmony than in competition, although one notices occasional allusions in ancient Middle Eastern literature to differences between the lifestyles of the city-village farmer and the lifestyle of the tent-dwelling shepherd.

Since there was no means of refrigeration, the diet of fresh food was seasonal. As fruits and vegetables ripened, they were consumed before they spoiled. Some could be cured and preserved in various forms: grapes became raisins, jelly, and wine; figs were dried; olives were pickled or made into oil; beans and lentils survived dry; and cereal grains needed merely to be preserved from dampness. The diet was essentially vegetarian, with meat consumed only on special occasions.

Living in a marginal rainfall area where cycles of wet and dry years often oscillate, the people were not unfamiliar with famine and hunger. Simply sustaining life required hard and timely labor, and the products of that labor were often unpredictable, being dependent upon uncertain climatic conditions. Even in years of adequate rainfall, locusts and other pests might pose major threats. Thus one can understand why the biblical proverbs warn that people can plan and work but God controls the outcome, and why many of the biblical ideals of life are associated with agricultural and pastoral images of blessedness and plenty.

The routine and the monotony of the agricultural pattern were broken by festival and ceremonial celebrations that themselves reflected and supported the pattern. Based on the two seasons of the year, the religious calendar contained two main periods of worship and festivity (Exod. 23:14–17). Falling near the spring equinox and the beginning of the grain (barley) harvest was the Festival of Unleavened Bread. This was followed a few weeks later by the Feast of Harvest, which celebrated the conclusion of the harvest. The main festival of the year, on the other hand, was the Feast of Ingathering, which fell near the autumnal equinox. This fall festival was especially a time of feasting, drinking, and dancing (Judg. 9:27; 21:19–23; 1 Sam. 1).

The dominant unit of society was the clan, situated around the village or town. Farming families lived in small towns or open villages, not in houses on their farming plots. During the harvest seasons, members of the family might stay in the fields in temporary lean-tos. Otherwise they walked to the fields in the early morning and returned in the evening. Inside the walled towns, living quarters were tightly jammed together, with space at a minimum. In such towns of a few hundred, close living quarters allowed and demanded familiarity. This could foster egalitarian and communal concerns but could also exacerbate social and economic feelings. The courtyard of the main city gate provided opportunity for gathering and socializing. Here court could be held, hawkers could sell their wares, speeches could be made, the elders could philosophize and gossip, and one could find company and watch the neighbors come and go.

Crafts and special skills tended to be handed down from parents to children. The lack of major technological innovations meant that the skills of one generation rarely differed from those of its predecessor. Even membership in the priesthood tended to be a family and genealogical matter.

7. *Olive trees.* Olive trees on Mount Carmel.

8. *Olive press.* Olive press (reconstructed at Hazor).

9. *Shepherd with sheep.* Minding the sheep was a task often assigned to teenagers in ancient times, as it is today.

Large families were considered a blessing, since they provided labor, social security for a person's future, and continuation of the family name. Because primitive medical knowledge was minimal, disease was a constant companion. It has been estimated that the infant mortality rate may have been as high as 40 percent and that as many as 30 percent of women died in childbirth. The elderly and the sick were the responsibility of the family, which was the primary guardian of human status and privilege. To be an orphan or widow without a family was to be in a state of destitution. Although women had few legal rights in the society, they had numerous responsibilities and a multitude of chores. This is apparent from Proverbs 31:10–31, for example, which describes the traits of the good wife, obviously in this case from a wealthy family.

Travel and contact with other cultures, at least in pre-Hellenistic times, were rare. Even Solomon probably never ventured more than a hundred miles from Jerusalem. Communication was slow, and even the military, the most mobile component of society, traveled primarily on foot. This general lack of outside contacts meant that society tended toward conservatism and was generally suspicious of external influences.

General Bibliography

As a general reference for topics pertaining to the history and archaeology of the ancient Middle East, see J. M. Sasson, ed., *Civilizations of the Ancient Near East* (4 vols.; New York: Scribner, 1995; repr. 2 vols., Peabody, MA: Hendrickson, 2000), and E. M. Meyers, ed., *The Oxford Encyclopedia of Archaeology in the Near East* (5 vols.; New York: Oxford University Press, 1997).

For the historical geography of Palestine, G. A. Smith's classic, *Atlas of the Historical Geography of the Holy Land* (London: Houghton & Stoughton, 1915; with numerous reprints and editions), and Yohanan Aharoni, *The Land of the Bible: A Historical Geography* (rev. ed.; Philadelphia: Westminster, 1979), are still good places to begin. These may be augmented with more recent Bible atlases such as: J. W. Rogerson, *Atlas of the Bible* (New York: Facts on File, 1985); Barry Beitzel, *The Moody Atlas of Bible Lands* (Chicago: Moody, 1985); J. B. Pritchard, ed., *The Harper/Times Atlas of the Bible* (New York: Harper & Row/Time Books, 1987); C. G. Rasmussen, *Zondervan NIV Atlas of the Bible* (Grand Rapids: Regency Reference Library, 1989); and H. G. May, ed., *Oxford Bible Atlas*, revised by John Day (London: Oxford University Press, 1990). The most recent and thorough is A. F. Rainey and R. S. Notley, *The Sacred Bridge: Carta's Atlas of the Biblical World* (Jerusalem: Carta, 2005). Bible atlases necessarily involve interpretation and some take a more thoroughgoing historical-critical approach than others. In this regard see J. M. Miller, "Biblical Maps: How Reliable Are They?" *BRev* 24 (1987) 33–41; and V. H. Matthews and J. C. Moyer, "Bible Atlases: Which Ones Are Best?" *BA* 53 (1990) 220–31.

Authoritative treatments of the archaeology of Palestine are: Amihai Mazar, *Archaeology of the Land of the Bible, 10,000–586 B.C.E.* (ABRL; New York: Doubleday, 1990), and Amnon Ben-Tor, ed., *The Archaeology of Ancient Israel* (New Haven, CT: Yale University Press, 1991). Note also should be made of Edward Lipiński, ed., *The Land of Israel: Cross-Roads of Civilizations* (OLA 19; Leuven: Peeters, 1985), and D. A. Dorsey, *The Roads and Highways of Ancient Israel* (Baltimore: Johns Hopkins University Press, 1991).

For everyday life in ancient Palestine, see David Hopkins, "Life in Ancient Palestine," *NIB* 1:213–27; P. J. King and L. E. Stager, *Life in Biblical Israel* (LAI; Louisville, KY: Westminster John Knox, 2001); and Oded Borowski, *Daily Life in Biblical Times* (SBLABS 5; Atlanta: Society of Biblical Literature, 2003).

Articles on persons, places, and peoples mentioned in the Bible can be found in standard biblical dictionaries. Among the most recent are D. N. Freedman, ed., *Anchor Bible Dictionary* (6 vols.; New York: Doubleday, 1992); P. E. Achtemeier, ed., *HarperCollins Bible Dictionary* (San Francisco: Harper San Francisco, 1996); and D. N. Freedman, ed., *Eerdmans Bible Dictionary* (Grand Rapids: Eerdmans, 2000). Reports on archaeological excavations at various Palestinian sites can be found in Ephraim Stern, ed., *The New Encyclopedia of Archaeological Excavations in the Holy Land* (4 vols.; Jerusalem: Israel Exploration Society & Carta, 1993). A work with articles focusing on historical issues is B. T. Arnold and H. G. M. Williamson, eds., *Dictionary of the Old Testament: Historical Books* (Downers Grove, IL: InterVarsity Press, 2005). Also of much value are N. P. Lemche, *Historical Dictionary of Ancient Israel* (Historical Dictionaries of Ancient Civilizations and Historical Eras 13; Lanham, MD: Scarecrow, 2003) and K. L. Noll, *Canaan and Israel in Antiquity: An Introduction* (Biblical Seminar 83; London: Sheffield Academic, 2001).

2. Epigraphy and Archaeology

Israel emerged on the scene of recorded history at the end of the Late Bronze Age, and its early history is shrouded in the dark ages of the opening centuries of the Iron Age. Whatever else one says about Israel's origins and early history depends on how one interprets the evidence from three sources: epigraphy, archaeology, and the Hebrew Bible. The term "archaeology" often is used rather loosely for anything having to do with antiquities, whether architectural remains, artifacts, inscriptions, or whatever. It will be useful for our purposes to distinguish between archaeology and epigraphy, defining the former as non-written remains (city and village ruins, architectural remains, remnants of tools, potsherds, etc.) and the latter as written materials surviving or recovered from ancient times (memorial inscriptions, royal archives, ostraca, etc.). True, building ruins and other artifacts often bear inscriptions, and most of the archives of ancient texts discovered in modern times have been discovered by archaeologists. Yet written and nonwritten evidence are different, and the archaeologist's work has to do largely with nonwritten evidence.

Epigraphical Evidence

The discovery of written texts and even extensive archives from ancient times, and the decipherment of ancient languages and writing systems, are among the truly exciting accomplishments of modern scholarship.[1] Such ancient writings are doubly advantageous to historians. First, many provide firsthand evidence; that is, they date from the period of time about which they tell. Second, they are verbal, which means that they often communicate very detailed information about specific people and events. Yet epigraphical evidence has limitations. A text may come from the period of time to which it pertains—from the scene of the action, so to speak—but this does not necessarily mean that it is entirely trustworthy. Ancient royal inscriptions, for example, are notoriously propagandistic and given to exaggeration. Perhaps the most serious problem from the historian's perspective is that the written materials discovered thus far are uneven in coverage. Some regions, periods, and peoples from ancient times are represented relatively well in these materials; others receive only

---

1. See G. R. Driver, *Semitic Writing from Pictograph to Alphabet* (rev. ed.; Oxford: Oxford University Press, 1976); and Joseph Naveh, *Early History of the Alphabet: An Introduction to West Semitic Epigraphy and Palaeology* (2d ed.; Leiden: Brill, 1987).

occasional mention. Palestine in general and ancient Israel in particular belong to the latter category.

Epigraphical evidence is relevant to the search for Israel's origins in two regards. First, written materials of various sorts from the end of the Late Bronze Age and the early centuries of the Iron Age—the time frame during which ancient Israel emerged on the historical scene—provide background information about the general circumstances of the times. Second, in addition to the Merneptah Inscription, which actually refers to Israel by name, certain other documents may be particularly relevant for understanding Israel's origins and early history.

Late Bronze and Early Iron Age Palestine as Known from Egyptian Sources

Palestine's Late Bronze Age corresponds to Egypt's New Kingdom Period. This was Egypt's empire age, during which the powerful pharaohs of Dynasties 18–20 extended Egyptian control over Nubia, Libya, and Palestine (for texts see *COS* 2:3–40). Egyptian armies also campaigned into Syria as far as the Euphrates River. In Syria, however, they met with resistance first from the Hurrians and then from the Hittites. Toward the end of the Late Bronze Age/New Kingdom Period, following a crucial battle fought at Kadesh on the Orontes River, a treaty was concluded between the Egyptians and Hittites that reaffirmed their respective zones of influence in Syria-Palestine (see *ANET*, 199–203). This occurred during the reign of Ramesses II (ca. 1279–1213 B.C.E.), and the Egyptian zone of control extended beyond Palestine to approximately Kadesh.[2]

Egypt's New Kingdom officials left relatively abundant written records, and because the empire included Palestine these records provide occasional bits of information about local Palestinian circumstances. For example, accounts of Egyptian military campaigns into Syria-Palestine provide the names of many Palestinian cities and towns. Also, as we shall see below, Egyptian inscriptions, scarabs, and other Egyptian-related artifacts found in Palestine enable archaeologists to correlate Palestinian archaeological data fairly closely chronologically with Egyptian archaeology and history.

Especially useful for understanding local circumstances in Palestine during the Late Bronze Age are the so-called Amarna Letters.[3] These letters were written in the Akkadian language, date from the reigns of the Egyptian pharaohs Amenhotep III and Amenhotep IV, and were discovered at the site of Amenhotep IV's capital, Akhetaten, in the Amarna district of Egypt. Most of the letters derive from the reign of Amenhotep IV (ca. 1353–1336 B.C.E.), whose religious reform destabilized the empire for a time. It was in connection with this religious reform that he changed his name to Akhenaten and transferred Egypt's capital from Thebes to Akhetaten. The Hittites were expanding into Syria-Palestine about that time also, adding to the political uncertainties.

---

2. See K. A. Kitchen, *Pharaoh Triumphant: The Life and Time of Ramesses II* (Warminster: Aris & Phillips, 1982).

3. Available in an English translation in W. L. Moran, *The Amarna Letters* (Baltimore: Johns Hopkins University Press, 1992). See also Israel Finkelstein, "The Territorial-Political System of Canaan in the Late Bronze Age," *UF* 28 (1996) 224–55.

TEXT 1. Amarna Letter from Abdi-Heba of Jerusalem

Say [t]o the king, my lord: Message of 'Abdi-Ḥeba, your servant. I fall at the two feet of my lord, the king, 7 times and 7 times. What have I done to the king, my lord? They denounce me: (I am slandered) before the king, my lord: "'Abdi-Ḥeba has rebelled against the king, his lord." Seeing that, as far as I am concerned, neither my father nor my mother put me in this place, but the strong arm of the king brought me into my father's house, why should I of all people commit a crime against the king, my lord? As truly as the king, my lord, lives, I say to the commissioner of the king, [my] lord, "Why do you love the 'Apiru but hate the mayors?" Accordingly, I am slandered before the king, my lord. Because I say, "Lost are the lands of the king, my lord," accordingly I am slandered before the king, my lord. But may the king, my lord, know that (though) the king, my lord, stationed a garrison (here), Enhamu has taken i[t al]l away, [. . .] . . . [Now], O king, my lord, [there is n]o garrison, [and so] may the king provide for his land. May the king [pro]vide for his land! All the [la]nds of the king, my lord, have deserted. Ili-Milku has caused the loss of all the land of the king, and so may the king, my lord, provide for his land. For my part, I say, "I would go in to the king, my lord, and visit the king, my lord," but the war against me is severe, and so I am not able to go in to the king, my lord. And may it seem good in the sight of the king, [and] may he send a garrison so I may go in and visit the king, my lord. *In truth*, the king, my lord, lives: whenever the commissioners have come out, I would say, "Lost are the lands of the king," but they did not listen to me. Lost are all the mayors; there is not a mayor remaining to the king, my lord. May the king turn his attention to the archers, so that archers of the king, my lord, come forth. The king has no lands. (That) 'Apiru [Ili-Milku] has plundered all the lands of the king. If there are archers this year, the lands of the king, my lord, will remain. But if there are no archers, lost are the lands of the king, my lord. [T]o the scribe of the king, my lord: Thus 'Abdi-Ḥeba, your [ser]vant. Present eloquent words to the king, my lord. Lost are the lands of the king, my lord. (W. L. Moran, The *Amarna Letters* [Baltimore: Johns Hopkins University Press, 1992] 326–27)

10. *Amarna Letter.* One of over 350 cuneiform letters discovered in the el-Amarna district of Egypt and dating from the late fifteenth and early fourteenth centuries B.C.E. This particular letter, measuring about 14 × 8.9 cm. was sent to the Egyptian pharaoh by Abdi-Heba, king of Jerusalem (see Text 1). (*Vorderasiatische Museum, Berlin*)

These letters, directed to the Egyptian court, are correspondence from the rulers of various surrounding lands, including Egypt's Syro-Palestinian vassals. The letters from Palestine reflect a scene of declining cities ruled by petty Egyptian vassals, squabbling with one another, and unable to police disruptive elements in the countryside. Among the petty vassals were Abdi-Heba of Jerusalem and Shuwardata of another city south of Jerusalem, possibly Gath or Hebron. Two letters from Shuwardata accuse Abdi-Heba of disloyalty to Egypt. Five letters from Abdi-Heba insist that it is not he but others who are disloyal and urge Akhenaten to send him military support. We learn further from the Amarna Letters that Shechem, under the rule of Labayu and his sons, had managed to achieve a degree of independence and was exerting some regional influence in central Palestine. Also, apparently taking advantage of the Hittite advance, a region on Egypt's Syrian frontier called Amurru (corresponding to the biblical term "Amorite") had emerged as a semi-independent state.

The Egyptian and Hittite empires collapsed in approximately 1200 B.C.E. in connection with the widespread disturbances and population upheavals that affected the whole ancient world and marked the end of the Late Bronze Age.[4] Among the peoples on the move who probably contributed to the collapse of the Egyptian and Hittite empires were the so-called Sea Peoples. Ramesses III (ca. 1187–1156 B.C.E.) defended Egypt's frontiers against the Sea Peoples and mounted a last-ditch effort to reassert Egyptian authority in Palestine. This effort was ultimately unsuccessful, and Egypt itself slipped into another period of decentralization—the Third Intermediate Period.[5] The rulers of Egypt's Third Intermediate Period were relatively weak and the dynasties involved (Dynasties 21–24) overlapped, ruling different parts of Egypt at the same time. With one exception, the pharaohs of this period seem to have withdrawn almost entirely from involvement in Palestinian affairs. The exception was Pharaoh Sheshonq (biblical Shishak), who founded Dynasty 22 toward the end of the tenth century B.C.E. Sheshonq conducted a military campaign into Palestine and recorded on the walls of the great temple of Amun at Karnak the names of the cities and towns that he supposedly conquered.

Early Iron Age Palestine's Heterogeneous Population

Evidence gleaned from various Bronze Age documents reveals that Syria-Palestine had a heterogeneous population already before the collapse of the Egyptian and Hittite empires, and the situation probably became all the more complex during the dark age that followed. Listed below are some of the groups that would have been present. But first, a word of caution is necessary. Many of the terms and labels that we use even today for contemporary peoples are difficult to define. We mix freely and sometimes use very loosely labels of various sorts—ethnic-cultural labels (Irish, Arab, WASP), geographical labels (European, American, Yankee), national labels (German, Russian, Syrian), and

---

4. See J. M. Weinstein, "The Egyptian Empire in Palestine: A Reassessment," *BASOR* 241 (1981) 1–28; and Robert Drews, *The End of the Bronze Age: Changes in Warfare and the Catastrophe ca. 1200* (Princeton: Princeton University Press, 1993).

5. See K. A. Kitchen, *The Third Intermediate Period in Egypt, 1100–650 B.C.* (2d ed.; Warminster: Aris & Phillips, 1986).

so on. No doubt the ancients did the same thing. Also, ethnic labels can take all sorts of twists and turns over time. The term "Saxon," for example, referred to quite a different group of people in fifth-century England than it does today in the phrase "white Anglo-Saxon Protestant." The terms "Gypsy" and "Egyptian" are related linguistically, but also refer to quite different groups of peoples.

Keep in mind, therefore, that the following is an attempt, some three thousand years after the fact, to identify population groups that were probably not clearly defined even back then. Our evidence consists largely of passing references in documents that date from different times in the Bronze Age. Keep in mind also that names and connotations change over time and that, for the Early Iron Age, we are dealing with scattered remnants of Bronze Age society.

Amorites.[6] The Akkadian equivalent of "Amorite," *Amurru*, appears in Early Bronze Age texts from Mesopotamia with reference to nomadic peoples of the Upper Euphrates region. During the Middle Bronze Age, rulers with Amorite names turn up increasingly in Mesopotamian king lists. For example, Amorite dynasties ruled at Ashur, Mari, and Babylon. By the Late Bronze Age, the name *Amurru*/"Amorite" probably had come to refer generally to the indigenous population of the Upper Euphrates and Syrian interior. Note in this regard that the Amarna Letters speak of a semi-independent state known as *Amurru* on Egypt's Syrian frontier, apparently centered in the Lebanese Bekaa Valley. Although no Amorite writings have been discovered, it is clear from the names of Amorites mentioned in texts of other languages, especially Akkadian, that the Amorites were a Semitic people. The Hebrew Bible often mentions Amorites along with the Canaanites, Hittites, and other indigenous peoples being in the land.

Aramaeans.[7] There must have been some connection between the Amorites and the Aramaeans, who begin to be mentioned in Akkadian texts during the eleventh century B.C.E. Both spoke Semitic languages; both seem to have been largely nomadic peoples when they first appear in written sources; and both seem to have had the Syrian interior as their homeland. But the Amorites are to be associated primarily with the Bronze Age, while the Aramaeans are to be associated primarily with the Iron Age. No doubt some Aramaeans would have migrated as far south as Palestine, and several biblical passages presuppose a close connection between the Aramaeans and the Israelites. Perhaps the best example is Deuteronomy 26:5: "A wandering Aramaean was my ancestor; he went down into Egypt and lived there as an alien, few in number, and there he became a great nation, mighty and populous." Yet the Israelites and Judeans spoke a language more akin to that of the Canaanites than that of the Aramaeans. In fact, modern linguists classify Hebrew as a dialect of Canaanite.[8]

---

6. See R. M. Whiting, "Amorite Tribes and Nations of Second-Millennium Western Asia," *CANE* 2:1231–42.

7. See Edward Lipiński, *The Aramaeans: Their Ancient History, Culture, Religion* (OLA 100: Leuven: Peeters, 2000).

8. Scholars use the name "Canaanite" for the grouping of Semitic languages that includes Ugaritic, Phoenician, Hebrew, Moabite, and Edomite. Ugaritic was written alphabetically with a script derived from Sumerian and Akkadian cuneiform. Another, non-cuneiform, Canaanite alphabetic script was developed and used for Phoenician, Hebrew, Moabite, and Edomite inscriptions. This Canaanite alphabetic script, which reached the western Mediterranean via the Phoenicians, was later modified for writing Greek, Etruscan, and Latin.

Canaanites.[9] Bronze Age documents, both Akkadian and Egyptian, refer to parts of Syria-Palestine as "Canaan." The Amarna Letters associate the cities of Tyre and Byblos with Canaan, for example, and the Phoenicians may be regarded as direct Iron Age descendants of the Canaanites. Archives of texts discovered at the site of ancient Ugarit, a city further north on the Syrian coast, provide our best information about what Canaanite civilization must have been like during the Late Bronze Age. Ugarit managed to survive under the shadow of the Hittite and Egyptian empires without succumbing completely to the imperial agenda of either. As a port city, moreover, it was a meeting place between Mycenaean and Syro-Palestinian civilization. Hundreds of literary documents have been discovered at Ugarit, most of them dating around 1400 B.C.E. These documents witness to the pluralistic character of the city by the very fact that they include texts in so many different languages—Sumerian, Akkadian, Hurrian, Hittite, Egyptian, and Minoan. Most of the documents, however, are in a local Canaanite dialect that scholars call Ugaritic. In addition to providing a wide range of information about Canaanite society, these texts speak of the gods of Canaan, reflect basic religious themes, and inform us about Canaanite cultic practices.

In the Bible, "Canaan" often refers to the whole of Palestine west of the River Jordan; but sometimes it refers to more restricted areas, especially the coastland. Similarly, the biblical writers occasionally refer to the indigenous population of Palestine as "Canaanites" (thus interchangeably with "Amorites"). On other occasions, they seem to distinguish the Canaanites from the Amorites and other indigenous peoples of the land (compare, e.g., Gen. 12:5–6 with 15:18–21).

Hurrians.[10] The Hurrians were another prominent population element during the Bronze Age. One associates them especially with the kingdom of Mitanni, which was centered in the Upper Euphrates region and flourished during the early part of the Late Bronze Age. At that time, before being eclipsed by the Hittites, Mitanni enjoyed far-reaching political influence, and the Hurrians seem to have established a strong presence in Syria-Palestine. Abdi-Heba, for example, the name of the early king of Jerusalem known from the Amarna Letters, is a Hurrian name. There is some possibility that the biblical Hivites were Hurrians, since "Hivite" is translated "Horite" in the early Greek (Septuagint) translation of the Hebrew Bible, and the term "Horite" corresponds linguistically to "Hurrian."

Hittites.[11] We have mentioned several times above the powerful Hittite Empire that flourished in Anatolia and expanded into Syria during the Late Bronze Age. This empire emerged already during the Middle Bronze Age, and

---

9. See A. F. Rainey, "Who Is a Canaanite? A Review of the Textual Evidence," *BASOR* 204 (1996) 1–15; M. S. Smith, "Myth and Mythmaking in Canaan and Ancient Israel," *CANE* 3:2031–41; and Gregorio del Olmo Lete, *Canaanite Religion: According to the Liturgical Texts of Ugarit* (Winona Lake, IN: Eisenbrauns, 2004). For an English translation of the main texts, see M. D. Coogan, *Stories from Ancient Canaan* (Philadelphia: Westminster, 1978); and M. S. Smith, *Ugaritic Narrative Poetry* (SBLWAW 9; Atlanta: Scholars Press, 1997).

10. Gernot Wilhelm, *The Hurrians* (Warminster: Aris & Phillips, 1989); Nadav Na'aman, "The Hurrians and the End of the Middle Bronze Age in Palestine," *Levant* 26 (1994) 175–87; and Gernot Wilhelm, "The Kingdom of Mitanni in Second-Millennium Upper Mesopotamia," *CANE* 2:1243–54.

11. See O. R. Gurney, *The Hittites* (2d ed.; New York: Penguin, 1954); Trevor Bryce, *Life and Society in the Hittite World* (New York: Oxford University Press, 2002); idem, *The Kingdom of the Hittites* (New York: Oxford University Press, 2005). Many of the texts dealing with Hittite international relations can be found in English translation in G. M. Beckman, *Hittite Diplomatic Texts* (2d ed.; SBLWAW 7; Atlanta: Scholars Press, 1999).

11. *Ugarit.* Entrance to the Late Bronze Age palace at Ras Shamra, ancient Ugarit.

12. *Boghazköy.* City gate, guarded by lions, of the ancient Hittite city Hattusas, present-day Boghazköy.

Hittites apparently continued as an elite class in northern Syria well into the Iron Age. Continuation of the Hittites as an elite class during at least the early centuries of the Iron Age is indicated by the fact that Hittite cultural traditions, including hieroglyphic Hittite inscriptions, lingered on in the so-called Neo-Hittite cities of southern Anatolia and northern Syria. A Hittite inscription has been discovered as far south as Hamath, and the biblical traditions indicate Hittite presence as far south as Jerusalem (Ezek. 16:1–5). Abraham is said to have purchased the cave at Machpelah from Hittites (Gen. 23). Recall also that Uriah, Bathsheba's husband whose death David is reported to have arranged, was a Hittite (2 Sam. 11:2–27).

Shashu.[12] Egyptian texts refer to several largely nomadic peoples of the interior of Syria-Palestine, beyond the control of the Egyptian vassals rulers associated with the cities, as *Shashu*. *Shashu* elements would have ranged the Palestinian highlands, which were largely devoid of cities and towns during the Late Bronze Age, and their descendants will have been part of the complex population during the early Iron Age.

Apiru.[13] This is an Akkadian term that appears in texts from various times and places during the Bronze Age. It takes on different shades of meaning depending on local circumstances, but generally refers to people who for one reason or another were marginal to established society. In other words, *Apiru* seems to refer to a social class rather than to an ethnic group. English words like "transients" or "minorities" and in some cases "rebels" or "outlaws" come to mind. The Amarna Letters depict the *Apiru* as unsettled elements in Palestine who were challenging Egyptian authority. They, like the *Shashu*, are probably to be associated primarily with the Palestinian interior, beyond the reach of Egypt's vassal rulers. The biblical term "Hebrew" is related linguistically to *Apiru* and, as we shall see below, probably had a similar range of meanings and connotations.

If the Canaanites, Amorites, and Hittites mentioned in the biblical traditions represented remnants of the old established but now fragmented Bronze Age society, the *Apiru*/Hebrews would have been people marginal to the old establishment. We will need to consider below also how the *Apiru*/Hebrew may have been related to the Israelites and Judahites. For the moment it is sufficient to emphasize that *Apiru*/"Hebrew," "Israelite," and "Jew" were not synonymous terms.

Sea Peoples.[14] Among the disruptive elements contributing to the turbulent times at the end of the Late Bronze Age were several groups of peoples active

---

12. See Raphael Giveon, *Les bédouins Shosou des documents égyptiens* (Documenta et momumenta orientis antiqui 18; Leiden: Brill, 1971); and W. A. Ward, "The Shasu 'Bedouin.' Notes on a Recent Publication," *JESHO* 15 (1972) 35–60.

13. The texts are collected in Moshe Greenberg, *The Ḫab/piru* (AOS 39; New Haven: American Oriental Society, 1955). For an interpretation see A. F. Rainey "Unruly Elements in Late Bronze Age Canaanite Society," in D. P. Wright et al., eds., *Pomegranates and Golden Bells: Studies in Biblical, Jewish, and Near Eastern Ritual, Law, and Literature in Honor of Jacob Milgrom* (Winona Lake, IN: Eisenbrauns, 1995) 481–96. See also Nadav Na'aman, "Habiru-like Bands in the Assyrian Empire and Bands in Biblical Historiography," *JAOS* 120 (2000) 621–24; repr. in *AIIN* 298–304.

14. See N. K. Sanders, *The Sea Peoples: Warriors of the Ancient Mediterranean, 1250–1150 B.C.* (rev. ed.; London: Thames & Hudson, 1985); L. E. Stager, "The Impact of the Sea Peoples (1195–1050 B.C.E.)," in T. E. Levy, ed., *The Archaeology of Society in the Holy Land* (New York: Facts on File, 1995) 332–48; and E. D. Oren, ed., *The Sea Peoples and Their World: A Reassessment* (University Museum Monograph 108; University Symposium Series 11; Philadelphia: University Museum, University of Pennsylvania, 2000).

TEXT 2. Ramesses III's War against the Sea Peoples

Year 8 under the majesty of (Ramesses III). . . . The foreign countries made a *conspiracy* in their islands. All at once the lands were removed and scattered in the fray. No land could stand before their arms, from Hatti, Kode, Carchemish, Arzawa, and Alashiya on, being cut off *at [one time]*. A camp [was set up] in one place in Amor. They desolated its people, and its land was like that which has never come into being. They were coming forward toward Egypt, while the flame was prepared before them. Their confederation was the Philistines, Tjeker, Shekelesh, Denye(n), and Weshesh, lands united. They laid their hands upon the lands as far as the circuit of the earth, their hearts confident and trusting: "Our plans will succeed!"

Now the heart of this god, the Lord of the Gods, was prepared and ready to ensnare them like birds. . . . I organized my frontier in Djahi, prepared before them:—princes, commanders of garrisons, and *maryanu*. I have the river-mouths prepared like a strong wall, with warships, galleys and coasters, *(fully) equipped,* for they were manned completely from bow to stern with valiant warriors carrying their weapons. The troops consisted of every picked man of Egypt. They were like lions roaring upon the mountain tops. The chariotry consisted of runners, of *picked men,* of every good and capable chariot-warrior. The horses were quivering in every part of their bodies, prepared to crush the foreign countries under their hoofs. I was the valiant Montu, standing fast at their head, so that they might gaze upon the capturing of my hands. . . .

Those who reached my frontier, their seed is not, their heart and their soul are finished forever and ever. Those who came forward together on the sea, the full flame was in front of them *at* the river-mouths, while a stockade of lances surrounded them on the shore. They were dragged in, enclosed, and prostrated on the beach, killed, and made into heaps from tail to head. Their ships and their goods were as if fallen into the water.

I have made the lands turn back from (even) mentioning Egypt; for when they pronounce my name in their land, then they are burned up. Since I sat upon the throne of Har-akhti and the Great-of-Magic was fixed upon my head like Re, I have not let foreign countries behold the frontier of Egypt, to boast thereof to the Nine Bows. I have taken away their land, their frontiers being added to mine. Their princes and their tribespeople are mine with praise, for I am on the ways of the plans of the All-Lord, my august, divine father, the Lord of the Gods. (*ANET* 262–63)

along the shores of Anatolia, Cyprus, Egypt, and the eastern Mediterranean seaboard. Their cultural traditions were closely related to Mycenaean civilization, and they appear in written sources as pirates, seaborne raiders, and occasionally as mercenaries. Ramesses III claims to have defeated invading Sea Peoples in a battle somewhere in the vicinity of Amurru, and it appears that some of these Sea Peoples settled along the Palestinian coast. "Sea Peoples" is a collective term coined by modern scholars; Egyptian sources recognize nine

13. *Sea Peoples.* Sea Peoples as depicted on the temple of Ramesses III at Medinet Habu.

different groups, including the *plšt* or Philistines. The Hebrew Bible, on the other hand, may use the name "Philistines" collectively to refer to more than one group of Sea Peoples.

Texts That Relate Specifically to Israel

To this point we have reviewed some of the important background information that epigraphical sources provide relevant to ancient Israel and Judah. Let us focus our attention now on certain texts that relate specifically to the Israelites and Judahites.

Merneptah's Inscription.[15] As observed above, the earliest reference to Israel in any ancient document appears in an inscription from the reign of Pharaoh Merneptah (or Merenptah), who ruled Egypt during the last decade of the thirteenth century B.C.E.—that is, at the very end of the Late Bronze Age when the ancient world was about to enter a dark age. Merneptah was already advanced in age when, following the death of his father, Ramesses II (ca. 1213 B.C.E.), he became the fourth pharaoh of the Nineteenth Egyptian Dynasty. Apparently the most serious threat Egypt faced during Merneptah's short reign was an attempted invasion by Libyan tribes who had combined forces with several groups of the Sea Peoples. Merneptah managed to repel the invaders, and he erected a stela commemorating this event in his mortuary temple at Thebes. The stela bears an inscription, most of which is a poetic eulogy praising Merneptah for the Libyan victory. Near the close of the inscription, however,

15. Much has been written on this stela. See most recently, with bibliography, A. F. Rainey, "Israel in Merneptah's Inscription and Reliefs," *IEJ* 51 (2001) 57–75; and M. G. Hasel, "The Structure of the Final Hymnic-Poetic Unit on the Merneptah Stela," *ZAW* 116 (2004) 75–81.

several lines allude to an earlier campaign Merneptah had conducted into Syria-Palestine.

> The Great Ones are prostrate, saying "Peace";
> Not one raises his head among the Nine Bows;
> Plundered is Thehenu, Khatti is at Peace;
> Canaan is plundered with every evil;
> Ashkelon is conquered;
> Gezer is seized;
> Yano'am is made non-existent;
> Israel is laid waste, his seed is no more;
> Kharu has become a widow because of Egypt;
> All lands together are at peace;
> Any who roamed have been subdued.[16]

Precise and undisputed dates are unavailable for the pharaohs of Dynasty 19, and therefore unavailable also for Merneptah's campaigns into Syria-Palestine and against the Libyans. Unquestionably, however, both operations occurred during the last decade of the thirteenth century B.C.E. Also, while the inscription does not locate Israel geographically, it clearly associates Israel with the general area of Palestine. In Egyptian texts, "Canaan" and "Kharu" (or Hurru) normally refer to the eastern Mediterranean seaboard, either as essentially synonymous terms for that region or with Hurru referring to the northern (Syrian) part and Canaan referring to the southern (Palestinian) part. Ashkelon and Gezer were cities in southwestern Palestine, and presumably Yano'am was a Palestinian city as well. By association, therefore, one can conclude that the Israel mentioned in the inscription also was located in Palestine.

The inscription may provide another clue regarding the entity it calls Israel. In this text, as in most other Egyptian texts, the scribes writing the hieroglyphics attached determinatives (unpronounced hieroglyphic signs) to certain words in order to specify for the reader the category to which the word belonged. It is noteworthy that Merneptah's scribes attached to the name "Israel" a determinative specifying that it referred to a foreign people. Other determinatives in the inscription specify that Canaan, Kharu, Gezer, Ashkelon, and Yano'am were foreign lands or cities, so it is worth noting that the scribes identified Israel not as a land or as a city but as a people.

Hoping to extract still more information from Merneptah's Inscription, scholars have labored over it since Flinders Petrie first published it in 1897. One approach is to analyze the poetical structure of the hymn in order to determine how Israel relates to the other entities mentioned. Some have proposed, for example, that the following two lines should be read as a parallel poetic construction, so that "Israel" stands in parallel to "Hurru":

> Israel is laid waste, his seed is no more;
> Kharu has become a widow because of Egypt.[17]

By this logic, if Kharu was intended to refer to Syria-Palestine as a whole, or to a large portion of that region, then it would follow that Israel also was

---

16. Translation from Rainey, *IEJ* 51 (2001) 63.
17. See L. E. Stager, "Merneptah, Israel and Sea Peoples: New Light on an Old Relief," *ErIsr* 18 (1985) 56*–64*.

14. *Merneptah Inscription.* The Merneptah Inscription, from the reign of Pharaoh Merneptah who lived at the end of the thirteenth century B.C.E., provides the earliest known reference to Israel.

an entity of significant proportions, certainly larger than the city-states of Ashkelon, Gezer, and Yano'am.

Other scholars have suggested a "ring structure" underlying the hymn. One analysis from this perspective parallels "Canaan" with "Kharu," the two of them forming a "ring" that encloses three Palestinian city-states (Ashkelon, Gezer, and Yano'am) and a nonurban agricultural people also presumably located in Palestine (i.e., Israel).[18]

> Canaan is plundered with every evil;
>> Ashkelon is conquered;
>> Gezer is seized;
>> Yano'am is made non-existent;
>> Israel is laid waste, his seed is no more;
> Kharu has become a widow because of Egypt.

Another study focuses on the way the scribes depicted the disaster Merneptah claims to have brought upon Israel: "his seed is not."[19] When this phrase turns up in other hieroglyphic inscriptions, it is argued, the term translated "seed" usually refers to grain—that is, to a people's food supply rather than to their descendants. Associating Israel with grain would suggest that Israel was at least a partially agricultural people.[20]

18. See G. W. Ahlström, *Who Were the Israelites?* (Winona Lake, IN: Eisenbrauns, 1986) 40.

19. See M. G. Hasel, "'Israel' in the Merneptah Stela," *BASOR* 296 (1994) 45–61.

20. It is possible that Merneptah's Syro-Palestinian campaign is depicted in a relief on the outer western wall of the great temple of Amun at Karnak. Unfortunately, the original cartouches that identify the pharaoh responsible for the campaign are no longer clearly legible. Earlier Egyptologists associated the scene with Ramesses II, but Frank Yurco has argued that it should be ascribed to Merneptah. The scene depicts Egyptians attacking several cities, one of which is identified in the accompanying inscription as Ashkelon. Yurco would equate the Israelites with another group under attack in the scene, apparently not identical with the defenders of the cities but dressed similarly in long skirts. A. F. Rainey has challenged Yurco on this latter point, observing that the Israelites might just as well be equated with other "Shashu" warriors in the scene dressed in short skirts. See Frank J. Yurco, "Merneptah's Campaign," *JARCE* 23 (1986) 189–215; and A. F. Rainey, "Anson F. Rainey's Challenge," *BAR* 17/6 (1991) 56–60, 93.

While each of the interpretations summarized above is plausible, none of them is compelling. One suspects that they seek to extract more information about ancient Israel from Merneptah's Inscription than the Egyptian scribe who wrote it intended to give, or would have been able to give. It is possible that the scribe himself knew the name "Israel" only from military informants, had but a vague notion of who the Israelites were (other than that they lived beyond the reach of cities such as Ashkelon, Gezer, and Yano'am), and that he mentioned them as representative of the various peoples of the Palestinian interior. We should probably not make too much either of the determinative that identifies Israel as a foreign people rather than a foreign land. As in the case of the name "Moab," which also makes its first appearance in Egyptian texts about the same time,[21] "Israel" may have referred loosely to both a subregion of Palestine and to the people who lived there. Still, it is noteworthy that an Egyptian scribe would have mentioned Israel alongside Ashkelon, Gezer, and Yano'am as representative of Merneptah's conquests in Palestine.

Throughout the foregoing discussion of Merneptah's Inscription, we have ignored an explanation that some might regard as obvious. Was not the Israel encountered by Merneptah the twelve Israelite tribes described in the Bible— twelve tribes descended from the twelve sons of Jacob who fled from Egypt, wandered in the desert, and presumably would have conquered and settled the land of Canaan prior to Merneptah's Palestinian campaign? This is a possible explanation. Yet we need to be clear that the proposed scenario derives from the Bible and not from the inscription. From Merneptah's Inscription itself, we learn nothing more than that an entity known as Israel was on the scene somewhere in Palestine toward the end of the thirteenth century B.C.E. Moreover, unless one is prepared to fill in the gaps with the Bible story, the connection between Merneptah's Israel and the later kingdom of Israel that begins to turn up in ninth-century inscriptions could be as distant and indirect as that between "Saxon" and "WASP" or between "Egypt" and "Gypsy."

Sheshonq's Inscription and Later Texts. After Merneptah's Inscription, there is a gap of some three and a half centuries, until the ninth century B.C.E., before the name "Israel" begins to turn up again in the epigraphical sources. These were the dark age centuries, of course, from which relatively few written texts of any sort have survived. Yet there are exceptions; and one of these, Sheshonq's tenth-century monumental inscription on a south wall of the temple at Karnak, should be mentioned here. This inscription commemorates a military campaign that Sheshonq conducted into Palestine toward the end of the tenth century B.C.E. The date often given, about 925, is probably reasonably close, but depends heavily on biblical chronology, which will require further comment below. Sheshonq almost certainly is to be equated with the Shishak mentioned in 1 Kings 14:25–27, reported there to have marched on Jerusalem during the reign of Rehoboam soon after Solomon's death. It is rather surprising, therefore, and a matter that also will require further attention below in chapter 9, that Sheshonq's inscription makes no mention at all of Jerusalem, Solomon, Rehoboam, Israelites, or Judeans.

---

21. See J. J. Simons, *Handbook for the Study of Egyptian Topographical Lists Relating to Western Asia* (Leiden: Brill, 1937) 155–56.

The relevant texts from the ninth century are certain Assyrian inscriptions from the reign of Shalmaneser III (858–824 B.C.E.), the Mesha Inscription from Moab, and an Aramaic inscription discovered at Tell Dan in northern (present-day) Israel. These ninth-century inscriptions date from approximately the time that the Omride dynasty was ruling in the northern kingdom of Israel. Accordingly, the first two kings of that dynasty (Omri and Ahab) are the first individual Israelites to find mention in the ancient sources outside the Hebrew Bible. It is interesting that the Assyrian scribes frequently referred to the kingdom of Israel not as "Israel" but as "the land (dynasty) of Omri." Correspondingly, the mention of "the house (dynasty) of David" in the Dan Inscription apparently refers to the kingdom of Judah.

Beginning with these ninth-century references, "Israel" and "Judah" continue to turn up from time to time in epigraphical sources until these two kingdoms met their end. Most of the instances are passing references in Assyrian and Babylonian reports of military campaigns into Syria-Palestine, or in their records of tribute collected from the various peoples whom they encountered there. Since the Assyrian and Babylonian rulers of this period can be dated fairly securely, the occasional points of contact between their inscriptions and the biblical materials serve as valuable benchmarks for working out the chronology of Israelite and Judean history. We will examine all of these ninth-century and other later inscriptions in due course.

Archaeological Evidence

Stratified city ruins, or tells, are perhaps the most typical of the archaeological features surviving in Syria-Palestine from Ancient Times. When people live in one place over an extended period of time (e.g., concentrated in a city or village) they produce occupational debris (abandoned buildings, broken pieces of pottery, remnants of tools and weapons, seeds, bones, and garbage in general). Ancient cities and villages were often abandoned for one reason or another or destroyed in military conflicts; sites that were especially favorable for settlement would often be resettled at a later time; and this cycle could occur again and again. Over the years, therefore, multiple layers or strata of debris would build up. The more prominent cities that flourished through several phases of history usually left conspicuous mounds of debris that archaeologists working in Syria-Palestine refer to as "tells." "Tell" is an Arabic word that means "hill" or "mound," and the corresponding word in Hebrew is *tel*.[22] Archaeologists excavate tells systematically, separating the layers of debris, and attempt to reconstruct from one occupational phase to the next the material culture of the ancient cities that produced the tells.

Hundreds of these ancient city ruins have been excavated in the Middle East since Heinrich Schliemann dug at Hisarlik (ancient Troy) during the 1870s and Flinders Petrie conducted the first such excavation in Palestine at Tell el-Hesi in 1890. Among the prominent Palestinian tells that have been excavated

---

22. We are told in Josh. 8:28, for example, that "Joshua burned Ai, and made it forever a heap of ruins [literally; *tel 'olam*], as it is to this day."

15. *Tell Zeror.* A tell in present-day Israel with excavations in progress.

during the present century are: Tell es-Sultan (ancient Jericho), et-Tell (ancient Ai), Tell el-Mutesellim (ancient Megiddo), Tell el-Qedah (ancient Hazor), Tell Arad (ancient Arad), Tell Hisban (ancient Heshbon), and Tell Nimrin (probably ancient Beth-nimrah). Note that many of the modern Arabic names begin with "Tell" and that there is often a similarity or connection between the second part of the modern Arabic name and the ancient name of the city that the tell represents. The connection between the modern Arabic name Tell es-Sultan and the ancient name Jericho is not so obvious. However, the present-day village surrounding Tell es-Sultan is called Ariha, the Arabic equivalent of Jericho.

While much of our archaeological information about Ancient Times derives from the excavation of tells, two other kinds of archaeological research are important as well. First, we should not overlook the basic mapping of Palestine and other regions of the Middle East, much of which was accomplished by nineteenth-century explorers. Second, in addition to excavating tells, archaeologists also conduct regional surveys to discover and examine thousands of small settlement sites from various periods—small villages, farmsteads, temporary encampments, and so on. These are less conspicuous and impressive than the major tells; some, in fact, are represented by nothing more than a scattering of potsherds. Yet they are equally important for constructing a full picture of ancient society. This is especially true for ancient Israel since the central hill country of western Palestine, the center stage of ancient Israel's history, was occupied for the most part by small village farmers and pastoralists.

The real strength of archaeology is that it produces firsthand, tangible evidence from ancient times. By systematically exploring the settlement remains in a given region, excavating selected tells, and analyzing the material remains recovered during surface surveys and excavations, archaeologists can learn a great deal about the settlement patterns and lifestyles of the people who have

CHART 2. Ancient Names–Modern Names

Ancient Name	*Classical Name*	*Arabic*	*Modern Hebrew*
Jerusalem	Aelia Capitolina	el-Quds	Jersualem
Beth-shean	Scythopolis	Beisan	Beit She'an
Shechem	Neapolis	Nablus	Shkhem
Rabbath-ammon	Philadelphia	Amman	
Acco	Ptolemais	Akka	Akko
Shomron/Samaria	Sebastos	Sebastiyeh	Shomron

lived in the region.[23] Moreover, archaeological data constantly increases; archaeologists conduct new excavations and surveys every year.

Since in Palestine the remains are typically nonepigraphical, however, archaeologists can rarely say that they clearly belong to one ethnic group or to another. Nothing about a broken pottery vessel, or the foundation walls of an ancient house, or a whole village ruin can, in and of themselves, tell an archaeologist that the vessel, house, or village was "Israelite." If the people who lived in the cities and villages, used the tools, and produced the pottery are to be identified in terms of their ethnic identities, or if any details are to be known about specific individuals and events of their history, the artifactual record must be coordinated with and interpreted in the light of written sources. The same is true of dating archaeological remains. Carbon 14 dating is applicable only to organic matter and provides ballpark dates at best. For more exact dating, therefore, archaeologists seek to coordinate their findings with historical events as known from written records. Ceramic typology (pottery dating) plays an important role in this process, but the dates assigned to ceramic forms also depend ultimately on written records.

In the final analysis, therefore, archaeology is most useful for understanding the physical environment of a region and recognizing broad trends in its material culture. Archaeology is less helpful, unless coordinated with written records, for determining the ethnic identity of the people who lived in the region or for dealing with the specifics of their history. Fortunately, for Palestine's Late Bronze Age, there is relatively abundant epigraphical evidence from Egypt to provide context for interpreting the archaeological data. For the early dark age centuries of the Iron Age, on the other hand, there is very little epigraphical evidence.

23. On the interpretation of archaeological data, see Ian Hodder, *Reading the Past: Current Approaches to Interpretation in Archaeology* (Cambridge: Cambridge University Press, 1986); idem, *Theory and Practice in Archaeology* (London: Routledge, 1992); Colin Renfrew and Paul Bahn, *Archaeology: Theories, Methods, and Practice* (3d ed.; London: Thames and Hudson, 2000); Shlomo Bunimovitz, "How Mute Stones Speak: Interpreting What We Dig Up," *BAR* 21/2 (1995) 58–67, 96; and W. G. Dever, *What Did the Biblical Writers Know & When Did They Know It? What Archaeology Can Tell Us about the Reality of Ancient Israel* (Grand Rapids: Eerdmans, 2001), esp. 53–95. The use and relevance of Carbon 14 dating to Palestine's archaeology are discussed in T. E. Levy and Thomas Higham, eds., *The Bible and Radiocarbon Dating: Archaeology, Text and Science* (London: Equinox, 2005).

16. *Archaeological survey.* Archaeological research involves regional surveys as well as excavations. In this photograph, a survey team examines a small site with particular attention to the hundreds of potsherds scattered among its surface remains.

Late Bronze Age Palestine (ca. 1550–1200 B.C.E.)[24]

At the end of the Middle Bronze Age, the Egyptians expelled the foreign Hyksos rulers who had dominated their land for approximately a century (i.e., during Egypt's Second Intermediate Period, 1640–1550 B.C.E.) and chased them as far as Palestine. Numerous cities were destroyed in southern Palestine at that time, almost certainly the results of Egyptian attacks on cities that had been allied with the Hyksos. By the end of the sixteenth century, most of the cities in northern Palestine had been destroyed as well, although it is less clear that this was the work of Egyptian armies. The northern cities could have been victims of the general disorder and violence that would have accompanied the collapse of Middle Bronze Age political structures.

Some of the destroyed cities were rebuilt relatively soon, especially in the north, but Palestine's urban society never fully recovered. Many more cities remained abandoned, and those that continued occupation during the Late Bronze Age were much more modest than their Middle Bronze predecessors. Most of them were unfortified, moreover, or continued to depend on surviving Middle Bronze Age fortifications. It has been estimated that the number of settlements in western Palestine dropped by 30–40 percent during the Late Bronze Age and that the total settled area was reduced by a third.[25] Most of the surviv-

24. See Alfred Leonard Jr., "The Late Bronze Age," *BA* 52 (1989) 4–39; Rivka Gonen, "The Late Bronze Age," in Amnon Ben-Tor, ed., *The Archaeology of Ancient Israel* (New Haven: Yale University Press, 1992) 211–57; Shlomo Bunimovitz, "On the Edge of Empires—Late Bronze Age 1500–1200 BCE," in Levy, ed., *Archaeology of Society*, 320–31; Finkelstein, *UF* 28 (1996) 224–55; and Nadav Na'aman, *Canaan in the Second Millennium B.C.E.: Collected Essays, Volume 2* (Winona Lake, IN: Eisenbrauns, 2005).
25. See Gonen, "Late Bronze Age," 63–69.

CHART 3. Late Bronze Age in Palestine

There were no sudden changes in Palestine's material culture during the course of the Late Bronze Age. Relying especially on Egyptian-related objects discovered at Palestinian sites, however, archaeologists distinguish and assign approximate dates to the following sub-phases.

LBI (ca. 1550–1400 B.C.E.) From the expulsion of the Hyksos from Egypt by the early pharaohs of Dynasty 18 to the so-called Amarna Age.

LB IIa (ca. 1400–1300 B.C.E.) The Amarna Age, during which Amenhotep IV (Akhenaton) initiated a religious reform. This period is illuminated by the Amarna Letters.

LB IIb (ca. 1300–1200 B.C.E.) The time of the early pharaohs of Dynasty 20— Sethos, Ramesses II, and Merneptah—who reasserted Egyptian imperial interests in Palestine.

Note that some archaeological manuals may vary from the above. LB I may be subdivided into LB Ia and LB Ib, with Thutmose III's victory at Megiddo (ca. 1470 B.C.E.) as the transition from LB Ia to LB Ib. LB IIa and LB IIb may be designated LB II and LB III, respectively. Also, some archaeologists are inclined to extend LB IIb (= LB III) to 1150 B.C.E.—that is, through approximately the reign of Ramesses III.

---

ing Late Bronze Age cities were situated in the lowlands. There were exceptions, such as Shechem, Jerusalem, and Hebron, but these exceptions were scattered far apart, leaving most of the hill country sparsely settled. The same pattern of decline is reflected in the local ceramic traditions. Middle Bronze Age styles continued into the Late Bronze Age, but were generally of poorer quality.

While the Palestinian cities and local ceramic traditions deteriorated, however, the material remains of Late Bronze Age Palestine reflect an international character.[26] Along with local wares that continued Middle Bronze traditions, for example, Palestine's Late Bronze Age pottery repertoire included a broad representation of Mycenaean and Cypriot styles. These Mycenaean and Cypriot forms are very useful, along with Egypt-related artifacts, for dating the local wares. Arts and crafts, such as ivory carving, were highly developed in Syria-Palestine during the Late Bronze Age, and some of this will have been produced in Palestine.

All of the above is understandable in the light of Egyptian imperial rule. The Egyptians would not have encouraged the cities to refortify, and may not have permitted it. Instead, they seem to have supported petty vassal rulers who used the declining cities as a base to exploit the land in Egypt's behalf. Economic decline exacerbated by Egyptian taxation would have encouraged people to withdraw from the cities and beyond the reach of Egyptian administration. The

---

26. See B. G. Wood, *The Sociology of Pottery in Ancient Palestine: The Ceramic Industry and the Diffusion of Ceramic Style in the Bronze and Iron Ages* (Sheffield: Sheffield Academic Press, 1990).

Egyptian connection also explains the overall international character of Late Bronze Age Palestine. Egypt was concerned not only to exploit its territories, but also to reap the benefits of international trade. Some of this international trade would have moved through Palestine.

Hazor, the largest of Palestine's Bronze Age cities, was somewhat of an exception to the pattern of urban decline described above.[27] After recovering from a catastrophic destruction at the end of the Middle Bronze Age, Hazor continued to flourish through the Late Bronze Age at about the same size and presumably with about the same level of population. The Late Bronze Age city was well fortified with a defensive system that partially reused the massive Middle Bronze Age system. Two of Hazor's Late Bronze Age temples are particularly noteworthy. One of these featured several small stelae and a small statue of a seated figure, all placed in a niche in its western wall. Depicted on one of the stelae were two hands raised as if in worship before a crescent and full moon. The seated man had a moon crescent on his chest and was holding a cup in his right hand. The other temple consisted of three parts in approximately south-north alignment: a porch, a main hall, and a broad room along the north side of the hall. This broad room was presumably the inner shrine or "holy of holies." The plan is similar to a roughly contemporary temple at Alalakh (in southern Turkey) and an Iron Age temple at nearby 'Ain Dara (in northern Syria). It also calls to mind the description of Solomon's temple in 1 Kings 6–8.

The Early Iron Age[28]

The transition from the Late Bronze Age to the Iron Age is marked by three archaeological developments: (1) Palestine was caught up in the widespread disturbances that affected the whole ancient world approximately 1200–1150 B.C.E. and brought both the Hittite Empire and Egypt's New Kingdom to a close. The local result was the final demise of the already dwindling and declining Late Bronze Age cities. Among the cities that had continued through the Late Bronze Age and were destroyed at the end of that period were Hazor, Megiddo, Beth-shean, Aphek, Beth-shemesh, Gezer, Lachish, and Tell Beit Mirsim. (2) Peoples with Mycenaean-related material culture settled along the Palestinian coast. No doubt these were Sea Peoples, including the Philistines, known from Late Bronze Age Egyptian texts. (3) Small agricultural settlements began to appear in the Palestinian highlands, which up until then had been only sparsely populated. These highland villages, some of which may have appeared even before the end of the Late Bronze Age, have figured prominently in recent discussions about Israel's origins.

It has been estimated, on the basis of recent surveys, that about 250 of these settlements had emerged in the central hill country of western Palestine by the end of the eleventh century, and that the total hill country population at that

---

27. On Hazor see Yigael Yadin, *Hazor: Rediscovery of a Great Citadel of the Bible* (London: Weidenfeld & Nicholson, 1975).

28. See Elizabeth Bloch-Smith and B. A. Nakhai, "A Landscape Comes to Life: The Iron Age I," *NEA* 62 (1999) 63–92, 101–27; L. G. Herr, "The Iron Age II Period: Emerging Nations," *NEA* 60 (1997) 114–83; and K. W. Whitelam, "Palestine During the Iron Age," in John Barton, ed., *The Biblical World* (2 vols.; New York: Routledge, 2002) 391–415.

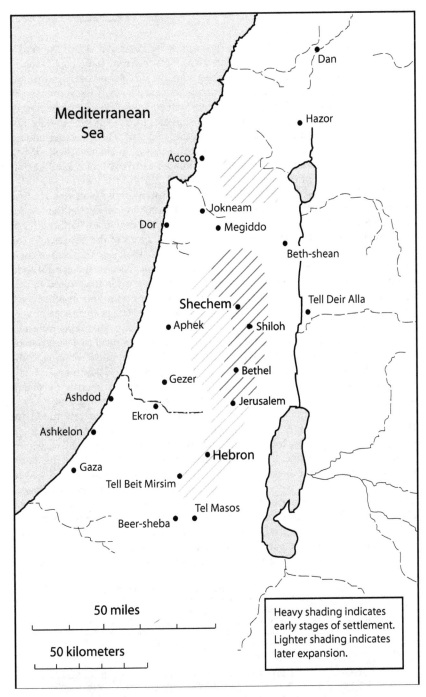

**MAP 5. Geographical Spread of Early Iron Age
Hill Country Settlements**

Based on Finkelstein, *Archaeology of the Israelite Settlement*, 325, 329

time was 60,000–70,000.[29] The latter figure may be excessive. All of the settle-ments were very small and unfortified villages. A few may have had as many as 250 inhabitants, but most probably had considerably fewer, perhaps around 75–100 people. Some of the settlements were located on new plots; others were built over sites that had been abandoned for centuries. Two or more homes were sometimes clustered together, which suggests that extended families, not nuclear families, constituted the primary household unit. These villages had no recognizable public architecture or uniform planning in their earliest stages, except that in some cases the houses were situated in an oval- or circle-like pat-tern with the doors of the houses facing inward.

Individual houses often consisted of a broad room whose wall was abutted by three perpendicular long rooms, and there is some evidence that they had a second story.[30] These have come to be called "four-room houses," although not all of the houses had exactly four rooms. Both the layout of the houses and the artifacts found within them suggest that households took care of much of their own basic needs. Cooking and food processing took place in the central long room; hearths, mortars, pestles, and animal bones are often uncovered in this area. Mangers sometimes found between the center room and another long room indicate that animals could be kept in the house. The pottery assemblage of an Early Iron Age highland household consisted mainly of cooking pots and large, "collared-rim" storage jars, which could have been used to keep grain or liquids such as water, oil, and wine.[31] Zoological and botanical remains, com-bined with house layout and pottery finds, suggest that early highland vil-lagers practiced a combination of agriculture and pastoralism, with sheep, goats, grain, olives, and grapes being particularly important products.[32]

On the whole, the material culture of these highland villages continued Late Bronze Age traditions, which suggests that most of their inhabitants were indigenous to the region. If any of these Early Iron Age villagers were newcom-ers from outside Palestine, this did not make any noticeable impact in the mate-rial culture (as did, for example, the Sea Peoples along the coast). Neither are there sharp differences between the material culture of the highland villagers and that of the remainder of Early Iron Age Palestine. In other words, if one allows for practical differences determined by local conditions, the inhabitants of the highland villages lived in similar houses, used similar pottery, and pos-sessed similar religious paraphernalia as their neighbors in other parts of Palestine.[33] Finally, allowing for natural development and change, there was

29. On the surveys see W. G. Dever, *Who Were the Early Israelites and Where Did They Come From?* (Grand Rapids: Eerdmans, 2003) 91–128; and R. D. Miller II, *Chieftains of the Highland Clans: A History of Israel in the Twelfth and Eleventh Centuries B.C.* (Grand Rapids: Eerdmans, 2005).

30. See Ehud Netzer, "Domestic Architecture in the Iron Age," in Aharon Kempinski and Ronny Reich, eds., *The Architecture of Ancient Israel* (Jerusalem: Israel Exploration Society, 1992) 193–201; C. H. C. J., "A Note on the Iron Age Four-Room House in Palestine," *Or* 66 (1997) 387–413; and Avrahm Faust and Shlomo Bunimowitz, "The Four Room House: Embodying Iron Age Israelite Soci-ety," *NEA* 66 (2003) 22–31.

31. See M. M. Ibrahim, "The Collared-Rim Jar of the Early Iron Age," in P. R. S. Moorey and Peter Parr, eds., *Archaeology in the Levant: Essays for Kathleen Kenyon* (Warminster: Aris & Phillips, 1978) 116–26.

32. See Oded Borowski, *Agriculture in Iron Age Israel* (Winona Lake, IN: Eisenbrauns, 1987); idem, *Daily Life in Biblical Times* (SBLABS 5; Atlanta: Society of Biblical Literature, 2003).

33. Some would make rather more of the differences, such as R. D. Miller II, "Identifying Earliest Israel," *BASOR* 133 (2004) 55–68; idem, *Chieftains of the Highland Clans*.

17. *Iron Age house.* Artistic reconstruction of an Iron Age I house. (Courtesy Madaba Plains Project-Umeri; Rhonda Root)

essential continuity in the material culture of the Palestinian highlands from the Early Iron Age to later phases of the Iron Age.

Questionable Correlations between Archaeology and the Bible

During the early years of archaeological research and throughout most of the twentieth century, many archaeologists and biblical scholars attempted to correlate the constantly increasing archaeological evidence with an essentially uncritical reading of the biblical account of Israel's origins. This approach has been largely abandoned in recent years, for two reasons. First, both the biblical story and the archaeological evidence had to be used selectively, and often given strained interpretations as well, in order to achieve even a loose correlation. Second, an increasing number of biblical scholars and archaeologists have come to view the biblical account of Israel's origins as idealistic and not historically trustworthy. It will be instructive to review some of the proposed correlations between the biblical account and archaeology that linger on in the public media but do not represent the current thinking in most scholarly circles.

The Amorite Hypothesis.[34] Archaeological evidence shows that powerful city-states flourished throughout the Fertile Crescent during the Early Bronze Age

34. This view was widely developed by W. F. Albright and his students. See John Bright, *A History of Israel* (Philadelphia: Westminster, 1959; 4th ed. with introduction and appendix by W. P. Brown [Louisville: Westminster John Knox Press, 2000]).

(roughly the third millennium B.C.E.). Then there was a breakdown of this urban phase toward the end of the millennium, followed by a period of largely nomadic and seminomadic society, and after that a gradual reemergence of urban centers that were to flourish during the Middle Bronze Age. Amurru (Amorites) begin to be mentioned in Mesopotamian texts toward the end of the Early Bronze Age, before the disruption of urban society, and then figure prominently as rulers in major Mesopotamian cities during the subsequent Middle Bronze Age. Building upon this archaeological and epigraphical evidence, scholars formulated during the 1930s what came to be called "the Amorite hypothesis." According to this hypothesis, both the breakdown of urban society at the end of the Early Bronze Age and the following nomadic and seminomadic phase were the results of widespread Amorite movements. As an extension of this hypothesis, it was contended that the biblical patriarchs immigrated to Palestine in connection with the Amorite movements and that the patriarchal narratives in Genesis 12–50 are to be seen against the background of early Amorite society.

Basically, three arguments were advanced in support of this hypothesis: (1) An early-second-millennium date for Abraham, Isaac, and Jacob squares essentially with the Genesis–1 Kings chronology. Specifically, 1 Kings 6:1 dates the exodus 480 years prior to the building of Solomon's temple, while Exodus 12:40 records the Israelite stay in Egypt as having lasted 430 years (however, compare Gen. 15:13; Gal. 3:17). This would mean that Jacob and his sons descended into Egypt approximately during the nineteenth century. Also it would place the Hebrews in Egypt during the so-called Hyksos period (late-eighteenth to mid-sixteenth century) when foreigners with strong Syro-Palestinian connections dominated Egypt. (2) The stories of Abraham's migration from Mesopotamia to Canaan and of the later migration of Jacob and his sons into Egypt make sense, it was argued, when viewed against the backdrop of the largely nomadic phase between the Early Bronze and Middle Bronze ages. For example, there would have been no strong city-states to deter or regulate travel between Mesopotamia and Egypt. (3) The names of the patriarchs and some of the customs reflected in the patriarchal narratives were similar to those known from second-millennium Mesopotamian texts, especially those from Mari (eighteenth century) and Nuzi (fifteenth century).

There are serious problems, however, with this Amorite hypothesis.[35] (1) The idea that the disruption of urban life in Syria-Palestine at the end of the Early Bronze Age and the beginning of Middle Bronze was the result of widespread Amorite movements is itself only a hypothesis and is by no means universally accepted by archaeologists and historians. (2) While the Amorite hypothesis squares fairly well with the schematic chronology of Genesis–2 Kings, it creates problems for the associated genealogical data. Genesis 15:16 assumes a four-generation stay in Egypt, for example, and Moses is identified as a fourth-generation descendant of Jacob (Jacob-Levi-Amram-Moses: Gen. 46:8–11; Exod. 6:18–20). These genealogical data can be made to fit the chronological require-

---

35. A frontal assault on this view was carried out by T. L. Thompson, *The Historicity of the Patriarchal Narratives* (BZAW 133; Berlin: de Gruyter, 1974); and John Van Seters, *Abraham in History and Tradition* (New Haven: Yale University Press, 1975).

ments of the Amorite hypothesis, therefore, only if each generation is allowed an average of a hundred years. Note also that the hypothesis places Israel's ancestors on the scene more than six centuries before we hear anything of Israelites in the Merneptah inscription. (3) The parallels between biblical names and customs, on the one hand, and those known from Middle and Late Bronze Mesopotamian texts, on the other, become less impressive when one takes into account that the sorts of names and customs involved were not confined to the second millennium B.C.E. but were apparently characteristic of the first millennium as well. This renders the parallels relatively useless for pinpointing any particular period as "the patriarchal age." (4) Finally, the biblical traditions never associate the patriarchs with the Bronze Age Amorites but rather with the Iron Age Arameans ("a wandering Aramean was my father," Deut. 26:5) and less directly with other essentially Iron Age groups (Moabites, Edomites, and Philistines).

The Exodus and Natural Catastrophes. Various hypotheses have been advanced that seek to understand the plagues and other miraculous events associated with the exodus in terms of cosmic and natural catastrophes. Some have argued, for example, that the plagues and the parting of the sea resulted from the close passage of a comet or comets during the Bronze Age.[36] A similar suggestion is that the exodus events were related to Late Bronze Age volcanic activity in the Aegean area, possibly the volcanic eruption that occurred on the Island of Thera about 1450 B.C.E.[37] Supposedly the volcanic ash released in the atmosphere would have produced the phenomena associated with the plagues—darkness, unusual precipitation, and so forth—while the sinking of part of the Island of Thera would have produced massive tidal waves. One of these tidal waves, in turn, would have destroyed the Egyptian forces in its backwash against the southeastern Mediterranean shoreline. Another theory has it that the walls of Jericho fell as the result of an earthquake, apparently in perfect timing for the seventh day of the Israelite march around the walls.[38] Theories of this sort attempt to give naturalistic and scientifically acceptable explanations for the more fantastic and miraculous biblical claims. In our opinion, however, these theories presuppose such hypothetical scenarios, such a catastrophic view of history, and such marvelous correlations of coincidental factors that they create more credibility problems of their own than the ones they are intended to solve.

The Ramesside Period as the Setting of the Exodus. The name Ramesses was popular for the Egyptian pharaohs of the Nineteenth and Twentieth dynasties (ca. 1215–1069 B.C.E.), and certain of the pharaohs of this period are known to have undertaken major construction projects in the Nile Delta. Thus the period of these two dynasties has been seen as a convincing setting for the notice in Exodus 1:11 that the Israelites labored on the construction of two Egyptian store-cities called Pithom and Rameses. Ramesses II (ca. 1304–1237 B.C.E.) is often mentioned as the most likely candidate for the pharaoh of the exodus,

36. Immanuel Velikovsky, *Worlds in Collision* (New York: Macmillan, 1950), represents this "catastrophic" approach to history.

37. Hans Goedicke, "The Chronology of the Thera/Santorini Explosion," *Ägypten und Levante* 3 (1992) 60–61.

38. B. G. Wood, "Did the Israelites Conquer Jericho? A New Look at the Archaeological Evidence," *BAR* 16/2 (1990) 44–58.

18. *Statue of Ramesses II*. Although without firm evidence, some identify Ramesses II as the pharaoh of the exodus.

which would allow for the Israelites to reach Palestine in time for their appearance in Merneptah's inscription.[39] Admittedly, the notation in Exodus 1:11 has what some would regard as a ring of authenticity. But this falls short of establishing a firm fixed point between biblical and Egyptian history. For one thing, we would expect Israelite storytellers to be familiar with and to use Mesopotamian and Egyptian names and customs in their narratives. Another problem with this proposed correlation between Egyptian history and the biblical narrative is that it does not square very well with biblical chronology. The Nineteenth and Twentieth dynasties ruled from the end of the fourteenth century until after the beginning of the eleventh century. Yet biblical chronology seems to place the exodus already in the fifteenth century.

Transjordanian Occupational Gap. The results of archaeological explorations in southern Transjordan during the 1930s indicated an occupational gap in the territories of ancient Edom and Moab that began about 2000 B.C.E. and ended with a resurgence of village life during the thirteenth century B.C.E. It seemed reasonable, therefore, to associate this thirteenth-century rise of village life with the rise of the kingdoms of Edom and Moab. The biblical account of the Israelite exodus from Egypt and conquest of Canaan reports, on the other hand, that the Israelites had to deal with Edomite and Moabite kings during the last stages of their wilderness wanderings (Num. 20:14–21; 22:1ff.). An obvious conclusion was that the exodus, the wilderness wanderings, and the conquest must have occurred at least as late as the thirteenth century. If the

---

39. This has been the date advocated by the Albright school. See J. J. Bimson, *Redating the Exodus and Conquest* (JSOTSup 5; Sheffield: JSOT Press, 1978), for a discussion of the issues and an advocacy of a fifteenth-century dating.

Hebrews under Moses had passed through Transjordan at an earlier date, they would not have encountered the kingdoms of Edom and Moab.[40] This line of argumentation was combined with, if not inspired by, the identification of Pharaoh Ramesses II as the pharaoh of the exodus (see above).

More recent archaeological exploration in the Moabite and Edomite regions of southern Transjordan has discredited the idea of a sharp occupational gap prior to the thirteenth century.[41] While there is a noticeable reduction in the amount of surface pottery representing the period in question, especially the Middle Bronze Age, there appears now to have been neither a discrete occupational gap nor a sudden resurgence of settlements. One should think more in terms of a gradual decline in the number of settlements during the Middle Bronze Age, and then a gradual reemergence that began toward the end of the Late Bronze Age and peaked during the latter part of the Iron Age.

Thirteenth-Century Destructions. Archaeological excavations have shown that the end of the Late Bronze Age was a time of widespread city destructions west of the Jordan. Many scholars have been tempted to attribute these city destructions to the invading Israelites and to see this as confirmation of the historicity of the conquest narratives in the early chapters of Joshua (see Map 6).[42] There are, however, three major problems with this use of the archaeological evidence.

1. The Late Bronze Age city destructions in Palestine were part of a general pattern that pertained throughout the ancient world, and it is not clear from the artifactual record that these cities were destroyed simultaneously or as the result of a common enemy. Indeed, it cannot be established archaeologically in most cases that they were destroyed by military action.

2. The sites where artifactual remains indicate city destructions at the end of the Late Bronze Age, with a few exceptions (Lachish, Hazor), are not the ones that the biblical account associates with the conquest under Joshua.

3. Most of the sites that are identified with cities that the biblical account does associate with the conquest, on the other hand, have produced little or no archaeological indication even of having been occupied during the Late Bronze Age, much less of having been destroyed at the end of the period. Prominent among such "conquest cities" are Arad (present-day Tell Arad), Heshbon (Tell Hisban), Jericho (Tell es-Sultan), Ai (et-Tell), and Gibeon (el-Jib).

The Search for a Distinctively Israelite Material Culture.[43] Claims have been made that certain features of Iron I material culture of western Palestine were specifically "Israelite" in origin. If specifically Israelite artifacts could be isolated, this would allow archaeologists, by noting the sites where such artifacts occur, to trace the course and range of early Israelite settlement in Palestine.

---

40. This was argued by Nelson Glueck in a number of publications; see his "Transjordan," in D. W. Thomas, ed., *Archaeology and Old Testament Study* (London: Oxford University Press, 1967) 429–53.

41. See, e.g., J. M. Miller, ed., *Archaeological Survey of the Kerak Plateau* (ASORAR I; Atlanta: Scholars Press, 1991); and J. S. Sauer, "Transjordan in the Bronze and Iron Ages: A Critique of Nelson Glueck's Synthesis," *BASOR* 263 (1986) 1–26.

42. The view of a thirteenth-century conquest has been advocated by members of the Albright school as well as many Israeli scholars: see, e.g., Abraham Malamat, "How Inferior Israelite Forces Conquered Fortified Canaanite Cities," *BAR* 8/2 (1982) 24–35.

43. See W. G. Dever, "How to Tell an Israelite from a Canaanite," in Hershel Shanks, ed., *The Rise of Ancient Israel* (Washington, DC: Biblical Archaeology Society, 1992) 27–56.

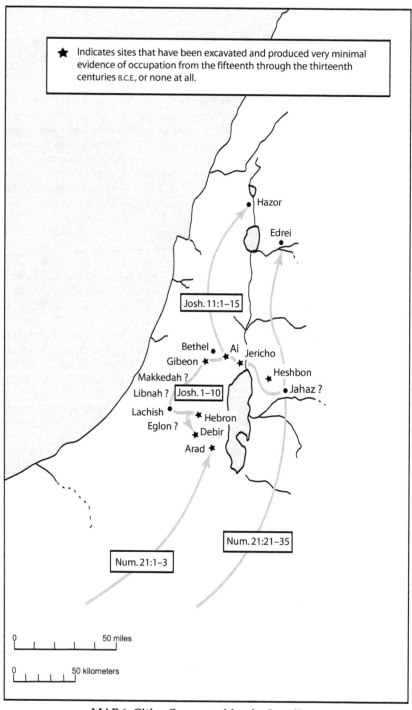

Indicates sites that have been excavated and produced very minimal evidence of occupation from the fifteenth through the thirteenth centuries B.C.E., or none at all.

Hazor

Edrei

Josh. 11:1–15

Bethel   Ai   Jericho
Gibeon ★
Makkedah ?   Heshbon
Libnah ?   Josh. 1–10   Jahaz ?
Lachish ●
Eglon ?   ★ Hebron
            ★ Debir
Arad ★

Num. 21:21–35

Num. 21:1–3

0   50 miles

0   50 kilometers

**MAP 6. Cities Conquered by the Israelites
according to the Biblical Account**

19. *Tell Hisban.* Excavations at Tell Hisban (ancient Heshbon) indicate that the site was not occupied during the Late Bronze Age when, according to a theory widely accepted until recently, the exodus from Egypt and conquest of Canaan would have occurred.

The two items that have been given most serious consideration as being distinctively Israelite are the so-called collared-rim jars and four-room houses. Yet there is nothing intrinsically "Israelite" about either of these features, and in fact they show up in the regions of ancient Ammon and Moab, east of the Jordan River, as well as in the areas generally associated with Israelite settlement. Apparently these items belonged to a commonly shared culture throughout Iron I Palestine and therefore cannot be used to isolate particular sites, geographical areas, or historical periods as "Israelite." The same must be said regarding the fact that pig bones turn up less often among the ruins of the Early Iron Age settlements than at Philistine sites.[44] This may signal a cultural difference between the Philistines and the indigenous peoples of Palestine, possibly even between the Philistines and the peoples of the hill country. But it is hardly useful for distinguishing between ethnic groups within the hill country (e.g., distinguishing between Israelite villages and those of the Hittite, Canaanites, or Jebusites) any more than the absence of pig bones would be useful for distinguishing between Israeli and Palestinian settlements in the West Bank today.

Early Israel and the Early Iron Age
Highland Settlements

The Case for a Connection between Early Israel and the Early Highland Settlements. In all of the proposals reviewed above, it was the Bible story, generally reinterpreted,

---

44. Eating pork is prohibited in the Hebrew Bible (see Lev. 11:7; Deut. 14:8). See Brian Hesse and Paula Wapnish, "Can Pig Remains Be Used for Ethnic Diagnosis in the Ancient Near East?" in N. A. Silberman and D. B. Small, eds., *The Archaeology of Israel: Constructing the Past, Interpreting the Present* (JSOTSup 237; Sheffield: Sheffield Academic Press, 1997) 238–70.

that guided the interpretation of the archaeological evidence rather than the other way around. During recent years, archaeologists and biblical scholars alike have expressed increasing doubts about the historical accuracy of the Bible story, especially the early parts about the patriarchs and matriarchs, the stay in Egypt, the desert wanderings, and the conquest of Canaan. Consequently, more recent efforts in the search for Israel's origins have tended (a) to begin with the Merneptah Inscription, which verifies the presence of an entity known as Israel on the scene in Palestine by the beginning of the Iron Age, and (b) to focus on the small agricultural settlements that were beginning to appear in the Palestinian highlands at that time. The argument for a connection between these highland settlements and early Israel may be summarized as follows.

1. While Merneptah's Inscription does not locate Israel specifically in the Palestinian highlands, the context of the reference does place Israel somewhere in the general Palestinian area.
2. Deeply seated in the Hebrew Bible is the assumption of an early time, before the Israelite and Judean monarchies had come into being, when Israelite tribes occupied the Palestinian highlands, especially the central hill country of western Palestine.
3. Epigraphical sources from later on in the Iron Age verify the existence of two neighboring kingdoms, Israel and Judah, nestled in this same hill country region.
4. The archaeological evidence indicates continuity in the material culture from the Early Iron Age highland settlements to the later villages and towns that would have composed the kingdoms of Israel and Judah.

Clearly these arguments add up to only a circumstantial case for connecting the early Israelite tribes with the Early Iron Age highland settlements. Moreover, the case is not based on epigraphical and archaeological evidence alone. It depends also to some degree, although in a very cautious and circumspect fashion, on the biblical traditions. In our opinion, the main weakness of the case is that it invites oversimplification—more than one scholar has been tempted simply to equate the early highland settlements with early Israel and to call them all "early Israelite settlements."[45]

Danger of Oversimplification. In the first place, the Early Iron Age highland settlements are represented by very meager archaeological remains, and calling them "Israelite settlements" implies that there is something about the archaeological remains that suggests or invites the label "Israelite." The archaeological evidence itself, however, offers no clues as to what the settlers might have called themselves, or been called by others, or what ethnic-like distinctions these settlers might have made among themselves.[46] Neither is the Merneptah Inscription helpful at this point. While it witnesses to the presence of an entity known as Israel in Palestine about the time that these highland settlements were emerg-

45. For example, R. D. Miller II, *BASOR* 133 (2004) 55–68.
46. On the difficulty of defining and ascribing ethnicity, see Elizabeth Bloch-Smith, "Israelite Ethnicity in Iron I: Archaeology Preserves What Is Remembered and What Is Forgotten in Israel's History," *JBL* 122 (2003) 401–25; and R. D. Miller II, *BASOR* 133 (2004) 55–68.

ing, it does not locate Israel specifically in the highlands, and the Egyptian scribe may have been using the term rather loosely as well. Ultimately, therefore, the "Israelite" label for the highland settlements rests on the Hebrew Bible and, in accordance with the biblical perspective, gives precedence to the Israelites over against other peoples that the Bible itself also places in the hill country along with the Israelites—Canaanites, Hittites, Hivites, Jebusites, and so on.

Recognizing the ethnic heterogeneity in Early Iron Age Palestine, and conceding that the archaeological evidence does not enable us to distinguish an Israelite settlement or an Israelite household from non-Israelite ones, some have proposed that we call all the highland settlements "proto-Israelite" settlements.[47] This is justified, so the argument goes, because the area of the highland settlements was later to become part of an Israelite kingdom. Thus regardless of what they might have called themselves at the time—Canaanites, Hittites, Jebusites, or whatever—they were all proto-Israelites because their descendants eventually would be united under Israelite rule. This, of course, is history interpreted from the outcome of events, terminology that privileges the winners. It is comparable to lumping together as "proto-Americans" all of those who in the seventeenth and eighteenth centuries were present in what was later to become the United States—Native Americans, immigrants from various parts of Europe, slaves being shipped in from Africa, anti-British elements, as well as loyal Tories who would return to England or move to Canada after the Revolutionary War. This is not a satisfying approach. One wants to sort out the various elements a bit; and if that is not possible, at least to find terminology that recognizes the heterogeneity of the population.

The proto-Israelite label also raises another question. Which later period of Israel's history is to serve as the reference point for the label? The proponents of the proto-Israelite concept seem to presuppose the time of David and Solomon, and to assume that all those who were united under Davidic-Solomonic rule would have been Israelites. But this only postpones the ethnicity issue, and again depends upon a selective reading of the biblical materials. For the time of David and Solomon also, as we shall see, the biblical narratives presuppose that Israelites represented a self-conscious element within a rather pluralistic population. Moreover, determining the geographical limits of the Davidic-Solomonic realm is a problem in itself. How then are we to determine the geographical limits of the proto-Israelite settlements? Do we identify as "proto-Israelite" all the Early Iron Age highland settlements on both sides of the Jordan River, for example, or only those west of the Jordan? And why, for that matter, should we consider only the highland settlements? Solomon is said to have "ruled over all the kingdoms from the Euphrates to the land of the Philistines and to the border of Egypt" (1 Kgs. 4:21).

We will return below to the question of how earliest Israel may have been related to the Early Iron Age highland settlements. First it is necessary to examine the third source of information about early Israel, the Hebrew Bible.

---

47. See W. G. Dever, "The Late Bronze–Early Iron I Horizon in Syria-Palestine: Egyptians, Canaanites, 'Sea Peoples,' and 'Proto-Israelites,'" in W. A. Ward and M. S. Joukowsky, eds., *The Crisis Years: The 12th Century B.C.: From Beyond the Danube to the Tigris* (Dubuque, IA: Kendall/Hunt, 1992) 99–110; and his subsequent publications.

General Bibliography

Most of the essays in the following three volumes are relevant to the topics of this chapter: W. A. Ward et al., eds., *The Crisis Years: The 12th Century B.C.: From Beyond the Danube to the Tigris* (Dubuque, IA: Kendall/Hunt, 1992); Israel Finkelstein and Nadav Na'aman, eds., *From Nomadism to Monarchy: Archaeological and Historical Aspects of Early Israel* (Washington, DC: Biblical Archaeology Society, 1994); and Seymour Gitin et al., eds., *Mediterranean Peoples in Transition: Thirteenth to Early Tenth Centuries BCE* (Jerusalem: Israel Exploration Society, 1998). Also valuable are Nadav Na'aman, *Canaan in the Second Millennium B.C.E.: Collected Essays, Volume 2* (Winona Lake, IN: Eisenbrauns, 2005); and A. E. Killebrew, *Biblical Peoples and Ethnicity: An Archaeological Study of Egyptians, Canaanites, Philistines, and Early Israel* (SBLABS 9; Atlanta: Society of Biblical Literature, 2005).

Suzanne Richard, ed., *Near Eastern Archaeology: A Reader* (Winona Lake, IN: Eisenbrauns, 2003), contains a number of valuable essays on diverse archaeological topics, as does N. A. Silberman and D. B. Small, eds., *The Archaeology of Israel: Constructing the Past, Interpreting the Present* (JSOTSup 239; Sheffield: Sheffield Academic Press, 1999). The peoples of the ancient Near East are discussed in A. J. Hoerth et al., eds., *Peoples of the Old Testament World* (Grand Rapids: Baker, 1994); and W. D. Dever and Seymour Gitin, eds., *Symbiosis, Symbolism, and the Power of the Past: Canaan, Ancient Israel, and Their Neighbors, from the Late Bronze Age through Roman Palaestina* (Winona Lake, IN: Eisenbrauns, 2003). The issues associated with "biblical archaeology" are discussed in J. K. Hoffmeier and Alan Millard, eds., *The Future of Biblical Archaeology: Reassessing Methodologies and Assumptions* (Grand Rapids: Eerdmans, 2004); and T. W. Davis, *Shifting Sands: The Rise and Fall of Biblical Archaeology* (Oxford: Oxford University Press, 2004). See also D. R. Clark and V. H. Matthews, eds., *One Hundred Years of Archaeology in the Middle East* (Boston: American Schools of Oriental Research, 2004).

Elizabeth Bloch-Smith and B. A. Nakhai, "A Landscape Comes to Life: The Iron Age I," *NEA* 62 (1999) 62–92, 101–27, summarize, with bibliography, the archaeological data. W. G. Dever, *Who Were the Early Israelites and Where Did They Come From?* (Grand Rapids: Eerdmans, 2003), provides a discussion and evaluation of the various theories on Israel's origins.

The history of Palestinian archaeology is discussed in N. A. Silberman, *Digging for God and Country: Exploration, Archaeology, and the Secret Struggles for the Holy Land 1799–1917* (New York: Knopf, 1982); P. R. S. Moorey, *A Century of Biblical Archaeology* (Louisville: Westminster/John Knox Press, 1991); and T. W. Davis, *The Rise and Fall of Biblical Archaeology* (New York: Oxford University Press, 2004).

A full treatment of the complete inscription of Merneptah is provided by Colleen Manassa, *The Great Karnah Inscription of Merneptah: Grand Strategy in the 13th Century B.C.* (Yale Egyptological Studies 5; New Haven: Yale Egyptological Seminar, 2003).

3. The Biblical Evidence

All of the Hebrew Bible is relevant to some degree for researching the history of ancient Israel and Judah, if for no other reason than that it reflects the way that Jews and Christians of classical times understood their religious heritage. Among the biblical writings, however, the so-called historical books are the most directly relevant for any attempt to reconstruct a picture of the past. When read in sequence, these books present two extended and overlapping accounts of Israel's past. The first of the two accounts is narrated in the books of Genesis through 2 Kings (excluding Ruth, which has been repositioned between Judges and 1 Samuel in Christian translations). This long narrative begins with creation and human origins (Gen. 1–11), provides genealogies and narratives about the ancestors of Israel and related peoples (Gen. 12–50), and then tells Israel's story from Moses and the exodus to the Babylonian destruction of Jerusalem (Exodus–2 Kings). Many biblical scholars believe that the latter part of this long narrative account, the part represented by the books of Deuteronomy through 2 Kings, was compiled independently of the Genesis–Numbers part. For that reason, scholars often refer to the Deuteronomy–2 Kings segment as the Deuteronomistic History.[1] Whatever the truth of that theory, the text as we have received it presents a continuous narrative from Genesis through 2 Kings—creation through the fall of Jerusalem. For our purposes, therefore, it seems preferable to refer to the composition as a whole and to use the rubric "Genesis–2 Kings History."

The second biblical account of Israel's past is presented in the books of 1–2 Chronicles, which often is referred to as the Chronicler's History. The Chronicler's History hurries quickly over the time before King David (1 Chr. 1–9), closely parallels and seems to be dependent upon the Genesis–2 Kings History for the period from David to the fall of Jerusalem (1 Chr. 10–2 Chr. 36:21), but then adds a brief notice that Cyrus of Persia, in his first year, proclaimed that the Jerusalem temple should be rebuilt (2 Chr. 36:22–23). The books of Ezra and Nehemiah pick up at that point and continue the story through the careers of Ezra and Nehemiah.

---

1. For discussion of this theory and the issues involved, see Thomas Römer and Albert de Pury, "Deuteronomistic Historiography (DH): History of Research and Debated Issues," in de Pury et al., eds., *Israel Constructs Its History: Deuteronomistic Historiography in Recent Research* (JSOTSup 306: Sheffield: Sheffield Academic Press, 2000) 24–141; G. N. Knoppers and J. G. McConville, eds., *Reconsidering Israel and Judah: Recent Studies on the Deuteronomistic History* (SBTS 8; Winona Lake, IN: Eisenbrauns, 2000); and Thomas Römer, *The So-Called Deuteronomistic History: A Sociological, Historical and Literary Introduction* (London: T. & T. Clark, 2006).

Although many of the stories in the Genesis–2 Kings History and the Chronicler's History are deeply engrained in our Western tradition, most of us know them as individual stories, or segments of stories, or we know them only by passing references and allusions in other literature. For our purposes, however, it is necessary to give attention to the overall story line of the two extended biblical histories, and to consider how the individual characters and episodes fit into the larger picture. Here and at relevant places in later chapters, therefore, we will summarize extended segments of the two biblical histories. Readers who are already well familiar with these materials are invited to skip ahead. Because the Chronicler's History begins essentially with David, we will focus our attention at this point on the Genesis–2 Kings History, and more specifically on Genesis–Judges. Genesis begins with creation, and by the end of the book of Joshua the twelve Israelite tribes have conquered and found rest in the "land of promise." As the narrative continues into the book of Judges, we find them settled alongside various other peoples in the Palestinian highlands.

Summary of the Genesis–Judges Narrative

Origins of the Universe and Human Civilizations (Gen. 1–11). God created the world in seven days, including all the various land, sea, and celestial formations as well as all vegetation and human life (Gen. 1–2). Adam and Eve, the first human couple, were placed in a garden of paradise. Later, God expelled them from the garden because of their disobedience and initiated a family line that was carried forward by a series of patriarchs. These ancient figures enjoyed unusually long life spans, ranging from Enoch, who lived 365 years, to Methuselah, who lived 969 years. Also, there were giants and "mighty men" in the world in those days, some of these being offspring of the gods (Gen. 2–6). Because of human sin and disobedience, God destroyed all humanity in a universal flood. Only Noah and his immediate family escaped (Gen. 6–9).

The descendants of Noah's three sons (Shem, Ham, and Japheth) began to multiply and migrated to the land of Shinar (Lower Mesopotamia), where they started to construct a great tower with its top to reach the heavens. In order to stop the project, God ordained diversity in human language. No longer able to understand one another, the descendants of Noah's three sons scattered to different parts of the world. Among the distant descendants of Shem, in the tenth generation from Noah, was a tent dweller named Abraham. Abraham's father had left Ur of the Chaldees to migrate to the land of Canaan but had settled in the vicinity of Haran (Harran) in Upper Mesopotamia (Gen. 10–11).

The Ancestors of Israel and Related Peoples (Gen. 12–50). After his father's death, Abraham himself migrated from Haran to Canaan. There he lived as a "sojourner" in the land; that is, he maintained his lifestyle as a tent dweller and resisted integration into the indigenous village-agricultural society of the land. God promised Abraham that someday the whole land would belong to his descendants and that his descendants would be great in number. Eventually Abraham made permanent camp near Hebron and became the father of two sons. The older son, Ishmael, Abraham's son born to Hagar, an Egyptian ser-

CHART 4. Holy Shrines at Biblical Places

For reasons explained in this chapter, much of the account of Israel's origins presented in the biblical books of Genesis through Judges must be regarded as legendary. Yet the stories that make up this account have their setting in the real world as it was known to the ancient Israelites, and over the later centuries Jews, Christians, and Muslims have erected shrines at places mentioned in these stories. The photographs in this chapter show the shrines at the following places. Also, see Map 7.

Urfa Current Bible atlases favor Tell el-Muqayyar in southern Iraq as the site of Abraham's home, "Ur of the Chaldeans." Except for the reference to the Chaldeans, however, other geographical details in the stories pertaining to Abraham seem to point to the Upper Euphrates. Also Muslim tradition places Abraham's birth in that region, specifically at Urfa in southern Turkey.

Haran According to Gen. 11:31, Abraham's family emigrated from Ur to Haran. Haran is approximately forty miles south of Urfa, also in Turkey. Haran was a booming city during ancient, classical, and medieval times. Today it is a large tell dominated by the ruins of a medieval mosque.

Hebron Later, as the biblical narrative continues in Genesis, Abraham immigrated to the land of Canaan and settled in the Negeb. When Sarah died, he purchased the cave of Machpelah "east of Mamre (that is, Hebron)" for her burial (Gen. 23). Later Abraham himself and other patriarchs and matriarchs were buried there.

Jebel Musa This mountain is located near the southern tip of the Sinai Peninsula, and the Arabic name means "Moses' Mountain." According to tradition, it was on this mountain that Moses received the Torah, including the Ten Commandments, from Yahweh.

Jebel Haroun During the exodus wandering, Aaron died when the Israelites reached the border of the land of Edom and was buried on top of Mount Hor (Num. 20:22–29). Mount Hor, according to Muslim tradition, is Jebel Haroun ("Aaron's Mountain"), which overlooks Petra in southern Jordan.

Mount Nebo Moses viewed the promised land from Mount Nebo. Then he died and Yahweh buried him there (Deut. 34:1–8). The traditional site of Mount Nebo is in present-day Jordan, at the northeastern end of the Dead Sea.

---

vant in the family, became the father of the desert folk. But the favorite, and the only son of his wife Sarah, was Isaac, born when Abraham was a hundred years old and Sarah was ninety. Meanwhile, Lot, Abraham's nephew who had traveled to Canaan with him, settled in one of the cities of the plain (apparently in the vicinity of the Dead Sea) and barely escaped with his two daughters when God destroyed several cities in that area with fire and brimstone. Lot's wife was turned into a pillar of salt during the escape. His two daughters, in order to continue the family line, seduced their intoxicated father and gave

20. *Urfa Mosque.* Many scholars identify Ur of the Chaldees, Abraham's home, with Tell el-Muqayyar in southern Iraq. But Muslim tradition identifies Ur with Urfa in southern Turkey, and the Grand Mosque at Urfa (Makam Ibrahim Camii) commemorates Abraham's birth. The first arch to the left of the center of this photograph provides access to the cave where, it is believed, he was born.

21. *Haran Mosque.* According to the biblical account, Abraham journeyed with his family from Ur to Haran. The location of ancient Haran is firmly established—approximately 45 miles south of Urfa in southern Turkey. This photograph shows the remains of the medieval mosque at Haran.

birth to two sons from these incestuous unions. The two sons became the ancestors of the Ammonites and the Moabites (Gen. 12–22).

After Sarah's death at the age of 127, Abraham remarried and had further offspring by his second wife and by several concubines (Gen. 25:1–11). These became the ancestors of various Arabic tribes. Before Abraham's death at the age of 175, he obtained a wife for his son Isaac from their kinsmen living in the city of Nahor near Haran (Gen. 23–24). Isaac married Rebekah and settled near Beer-sheba. She gave birth to twins: Esau and Jacob. Esau became the ancestor of the Edomites (Gen. 36), and Jacob, whom God renamed Israel, fathered twelve sons by his Aramaean wives and concubines. These twelve sons became the ancestors of twelve tribes (25:19–35:29).

One of Jacob's sons, Joseph, was sold as a slave by his brothers and was carried into Egypt. Later Joseph was thrown into an Egyptian prison, where he displayed an ability to interpret dreams. With this power he gained his freedom and eventually became the chief administrative official over all Egypt, second only to the pharaoh. Meanwhile a famine in Palestine forced Jacob and his family to migrate to Egypt in search of food. Joseph arranged for them to settle in a place called Goshen. In Egypt the families of the twelve brothers multiplied into twelve tribes (Gen. 37–50).

The Era of Moses (Exodus through Deuteronomy). Eventually a pharaoh came to power "who did not know Joseph" and reduced the Israelites to slavery. God commanded Moses—who, although an Israelite himself from the tribe of Levi, had grown up in Pharaoh's court after being rescued as a babe from the Nile— to lead the people out of Egypt and back to the land God had promised Abraham. The escape from Egypt was surrounded by spectacular miracles, including ten plagues that God sent upon Egypt. After each plague, the pharaoh agreed to allow the Israelites to leave. Then God "hardened Pharaoh's heart" (or the pharaoh hardened his own heart) so that he changed his mind, refused to let the people leave, and thus invited another plague upon his land. When the Israelites finally did manage to leave, the pharaoh, his heart having been hardened once again, assembled his army and chased the people as far as the Red Sea. God parted the waters of the sea, allowing the people of Israel to cross on dry land. When the pharaoh and his army followed, God caused the waters to return and destroy them (Exod. 1–15).

The people made their journey to Canaan in stages. God sent a pillar of cloud by day and a pillar of fire by night to indicate when they should move their camp and where they should pitch their tents. Also he fed them with quail and manna in the wilderness. After three months the people reached a mountain in the wilderness of Sinai. They remained encamped at the foot of the mountain while Moses ascended to the top several times, spoke to God directly, and received from the Deity extensive legal and cultic instructions and regulations. These were put into practice with the understanding that they were to be followed by the people from that time on. The people were still encamped at the mountain when they celebrated the first Passover—the anniversary of the escape from Egypt (Exod. 16–Num. 10:10).

On the twentieth day of the second month of the second year of their journey the cloud was taken up, signaling that it was time for the people to move on. They set out again and eventually came to Kadesh in the southwestern

22. *Hebron Mosque.* This mosque is built over the cave where, according to tradition, Abraham and Sarah are buried.

23. *Saint Catherine's Monastery.* According to tradition, Mount Sinai where Moses received the Torah is identical with Jebel Musa (Mount Moses) in the Sinai Peninsula. Situated at the foot of Jebel Musa is Saint Catherine's Monastery, and over the centuries thousands of pilgrims have climbed the steep rock steps from the monastery to the top of the mountain. This photograph views the monastery from the steps.

Negeb. From there they sent twelve spies, one from each tribe, to explore "the promised land." The spies returned with glowing reports about the land's fertility and produce, but they warned that the cities were too strong to be conquered and that the land was inhabited by giants. Caleb, one of the spies, urged the people to attack anyway, with confidence that God would deliver the land as he had promised. However, the people had lost heart; they began to murmur against Moses and prepared to return to Egypt. Then "the glory of God" appeared at the tent of the meeting and the deity chastised the congregation for their lack of faith, decreeing that the people would wander in the wilderness for forty years—that is, until those who were twenty and older at the time of the incident had been replaced by a new generation. Only Caleb and Joshua (one of the spies who had supported Caleb's urging) were to survive to enter the land. After God's edict, an attempt to enter the land from the south met with defeat (Num. 10:11–14:45).

From Kadesh, Moses sent messengers to the kings of Edom and Moab, apparently as the forty years drew to an end, and requested permission to pass through Edomite and Moabite territory as they approached "the promised land" through Transjordan. This permission was denied. They proceeded anyhow and conquered two Amorite kingdoms ruled by Sihon and Og, respectively. Thus the Israelites gained possession of the whole of Transjordan exclusive of the Ammonite kingdom on the desert fringe and the Moabite and Edomite territories south of the river Arnon. The newly acquired land was assigned to the tribes of Reuben, Gad, and half the tribe of Manasseh as their possessions (Num. 15–36). While still in Transjordan, Moses gave his farewell address admonishing the people to observe the law after they had entered the land and threatening them with exile from the land if they did not (Deut. 1–34).

Conquest of Canaan and Division of the Land (Book of Joshua). After Moses' death in Transjordan, Joshua assumed leadership of the people and began preparations for an invasion of western Palestine. Although some military strategy was involved (for example, sending spies in advance), the crossing of the Jordan and the conquest of Jericho were essentially ritual operations surrounded by miracles. The Jordan River rolled back for the people to cross, as had the Red Sea during their escape from Egypt. When the people marched around the walls of Jericho a specific number of times in a procession led by the priests and the ark, according to God's instructions, the walls collapsed and the city fell into their hands. With subsequent victories at Ai, Gibeon (where God caused the sun to stand still), Libnah, Lachish, Eglon, Hebron, Debir, and Hazor, virtually the whole land fell into their hands. Joshua then assigned the territory west of the Jordan to the remaining tribes. Only the Levites did not receive a territorial allotment. They, being a priestly tribe, were assigned cities scattered throughout the other tribal territories (Josh. 1–24).

The Time of the Judges "before Any King Ruled in Israel" (Book of Judges). Settled in the hill country, but apparently not in control of the lowlands or any cities of significant size, the Israelites were attracted time and again to false gods. Each time this occurred, Yahweh would allow them to fall into enemy hands—Moabites, Canaanites, Midianites, Philistines, and so on. Then the Israelites would repent, cry out to Yahweh for deliverance, and he would send a savior. Perhaps the most memorable of the early heroes who saved Israel and then, for

24. *Mount Nebo.* According to tradition, the mountain ridge at the left of the photograph, marked by a church as early as the fourth century C.E., is Mount Nebo from which Moses viewed the promised land.

the remainder of their lifetime, "judged" Israel were Deborah, Gideon, and Samson (Book of Judges).

The Danites, unable to secure a footing in the territory alloted to them by Joshua, set out in search for another place to live. Finding the city of Laish north of the Sea of Galilee isolated and unsuspecting, they conquered it, destroyed it, and then rebuilt it as their own chief city, henceforth to be called Dan. As they passed through the hill country of Ephraim during their migration to Laish/Dan, the Danites convinced a young Levite priest to leave his post and become their priest. On another occasion, when a Levite, his concubine, and a servant were journeying from Bethlehem to his home in the Ephraimite hill country, they stopped for the night at the Benjaminite town of Gibeah. During the night, the men of Gibeah gang-raped the concubine and left her for dead. Thereupon the Israelites attacked Gibeah and vowed that no one would ever again give a daughter in marriage to a Benjaminite. After defeating Gibeah, they became concerned that, without brides, the tribe of Benjamin would disappear. Thus they massacred the inhabitants of Jabesh-gilead on the grounds that no one from Jabesh-gilead had supported the attack on Gibeah, and presented to the Benjaminites virgins saved from the massacre. Later the Benjaminites were instructed to go to Shiloh at the time of an annual feast of Yahweh and seize more brides when the women of the town came into the vineyards to dance.

Chronological notations scattered throughout the Genesis–2 Kings History combine to provide an overarching chronological framework. Beginning with Adam, created during creation week and 130 years old at Seth's birth (Gen. 1:26; 5:3), and counting forward in unilinear fashion through Seth, Enosh, Kenan, and so on (Gen. 5:6ff.), one reaches the date AM 1946 (AM is the abbre-

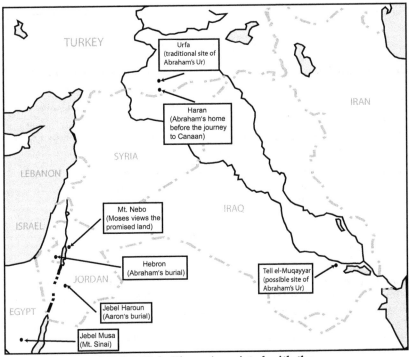

**MAP 7. Holy Places Associated with the
Biblical Account of Israel's Origins**

viation for *anno mundi*, which means "in the year of the world") for the birth of
Abraham (Gen. 11:26). In other words, Abraham would have been born 1946
years after creation. Other notations place the exodus from Egypt in AM 2666
(Exod. 12:40), the founding of Solomon's temple in AM 3146 (1 Kgs. 6:1), and
so on.

Difficulties with Using the Genesis–Judges Narrative
for Historical Research

The biblical account summarized above reports and interprets past people and
events, and the reader is led to understand that these were real people and that
the events actually happened. Yet it is clearly not the sort of history a professional historian would write today, and many modern scholars dismiss it as a
totally unreliable source of historical information. While one may not agree
with such an extreme position, there are ample grounds for skepticism regarding the usefulness of the Hebrew Bible for historical research, and compelling
reasons that the Genesis–Judges narrative summarized above cannot be taken
at face value. Some of these reasons emerge from even a casual reading of
the narrative. Others become noticeable when the text is subjected to literary-
critical analysis.

CHART 5. Judges over Early Israel

Ehud delivered Israel from Moabite oppression by murdering King Eglon of Moab (Judg. 3:12–30)

Deborah the only female judge, urged Barak to fight a powerful Canaanite king, Jabin, who ruled at Hazor (Judg. 4–5)

Gideon tore down shrines to Baal and Asherah and delivered Israel from Midian. He ruled thereafter for forty years (Judg. 6–8)

Abimelech killed his seventy brothers, hired a private army with funds contributed by the people of Shechem and Beth-millo, was made king in Shechem, and "ruled over all Israel for three years" (Judg. 9)

Jephthah led a band of "worthless fellows" to victory against the Ammonites. Before the battle he made a vow that resulted in the sacrifice of his virgin daughter. After the victory, he was installed as permanent "head and leader" of the Gileadites (Judg. 10:6–12:7)

Samson possessed incredible strength, which he used to mock and kill many of the Philistines who were oppressing Israel. Though he was eventually captured and blinded, his final act was killing three thousand Philistines (Judg. 13–16)

Ancient Notions about the Past

The Concept of a "Golden Age." The material in Genesis–Joshua reflects certain historical perspectives that were popular in ancient times but are no longer in vogue. It was a widespread practice in antiquity, for example, to postulate an ideal period in the remote past during which human beings supposedly lived under unique conditions, enjoyed special relationships with the deities, sometimes cohabited with the gods, and had fantastically long life spans. One sees such a view reflected in the early chapters of Genesis, where the earliest ancestors of humanity begin life in a paradise state, are tempted to disobedience by a serpent, intermarry with divine beings, live fantastically long lives, and suffer a universal calamity. Modern understandings of human history informed by geology, archaeology, and paleontology assume a radically different perspective on the origin and early days of human life on earth.

Schematic Chronology. In a manner also typical of historical speculations during ancient times, the Genesis–Joshua narrative sets forth a schematic view of historical chronology.[2] Various manuscript traditions of the Bible—Samaritan, Greek, and Masoretic Hebrew—divide this chronology differently. In the Masoretic or standard Hebrew text, for example, one finds the following schematizations. (1) The unusually long life spans of the earliest ancestors of humanity are understood to have been reduced in four stages. Prior to the

---

2. See Jeremy Hughes, *Secrets of the Times: Myth and History in Biblical Chronology* (JSOTSup 66; Sheffield: JSOT Press, 1990).

flood, people are said to have lived between 900 and 1,000 years. Mahalalel's 895 years, Enoch's 365 years, and Lamech's 777 years are the exceptions. After the flood, there is a gradual reduction from Shem's 600 years to Nahor's 148 years. From Abraham to Moses, the typical age limit is between 100 and 200 years. After Moses, the recorded life spans correspond to present-day norms. (2) The exodus from Egypt occurs 2,666 years after creation. This corresponds to the genealogical data, which places the exodus during the twenty-seventh generation after creation (26 2/3 generations with an average of 100 years per generation equals 2,666 years). Moreover, 2,666 is 2/3 of 4,000 years. By counting forward with the biblical figures and taking into account chronological data that would have been available to later Jews, one arrives at the conclusion that the year 4000 after creation was approximately the date of the rededication of the temple in 164 B.C.E. following the Maccabean rebellion. (3) Forty and multiples of forty are in evidence throughout Genesis–2 Kings. There were forty years of wandering in the wilderness following the exodus. The interval from the exodus to Solomon's building of the temple is recorded as 480 (12 x 40) years (1 Kgs. 6:1). From that point to the return of the exiles from Babylon turns out to be another 480 years. In all of these features, ancient speculative ideas about historical times and chronological periods are in evidence. The modern historian cannot avoid viewing such schematizations with skepticism.

Divine Direction of Human Affairs. Another characteristic of the biblical account of Israel's origins that it shares with ancient literature in general is its emphasis on divine involvement in human affairs.[3] Indeed, in the Genesis–Joshua narrative, divine activity and purpose are considered the primary forces determining the shape and course of the historical process. Yahweh speaks directly with selected persons from time to time. God's participation in human affairs involved public displays of supernatural power: a great flood removes all of wicked humanity from the earth; the confusion in language scatters humanity abroad; a series of plagues climaxed with the drowning of the pharaoh's army and enabled the Israelites to escape Egypt; miraculously provided manna and quail made it possible for them to subsist in the desert for forty years; abnormal occurrences, such as the sudden collapse of Jericho's walls and the sun standing still at Gibeon, gave Joshua and his army an edge over the Canaanites; and on and on. While modern historians do not necessarily reject the idea of divine involvement in history, it is a presupposition of modern historiography that the general cause-and-effect aspects of history are explainable without reference to unique disruptions in natural conditions (such as the waters of the Red Sea rolling back or the sun standing still) or any kind of overt divine involvement in human affairs. In short, modern historians have trouble with miracles.[4]

Lineal Genealogical Descent. A fourth historical perspective that the biblical writers shared with most ancients is the assumption that the origins of the

---

3. For a defense of the view that divine involvement in history should be assigned a place in historiography, see V. P. Long, *The Art of Biblical History* (Foundations of Contemporary Interpretation 5; Grand Rapids: Zondervan, 1994) 99–116.

4. For a discussion of the issues involved in the contrast between critical history and faith-based history, see V. A. Harvey, *The Historian and the Believer: A Confrontation between the Modern Historian's Principles of Judgment and the Christian's Will-to-Believe* (New York: Macmillan, 1966).

various peoples of the world are to be understood in terms of simple lineal descent from different ancestors. In such a view, ethnic groups and their relationships are viewed in genealogical categories. Thus the Genesis–Joshua narrative introduces Israel, Judah, and their neighbors in and around Palestine in terms of extensive family trees. The tribal groups within Israel and Judah are given similar treatment; they are considered to be twelve tribes descended from the twelve sons of Jacob. Modern historians, informed by anthropological studies, recognize that the emergence of population groups is normally a very complex process that cannot be explained or understood in the simplistic categories of lineal genealogical succession.

Common Storytellers' Motifs. Many of the biblical narratives, especially those in Genesis–Judges, are built on motif patterns that had widespread currency in the ancient world. Consider, for example, the favorite storyteller's motif of "the success of the unpromising" (the Cinderella theme). Stories based on this motif tell how one who seemingly had no chance of success or triumph eventually enjoyed a reversal of fate. Abraham, a man without a country; Joseph, an imprisoned slave in an Egyptian jail; Moses, a babe afloat on the crocodile-infested Nile; the Israelites, toiling in servitude to a harsh pharaoh—all of these are presented as the unpromising who, with divine help, ultimately succeeded and were blessed. The Sodom and Gomorrah story reflects yet another motif pattern known from extrabiblical literature, that of divine beings who visit a city to test the hospitality of its people and eventually destroy the inhospitable city. One can compare in this regard the Greek myth of Baucis and Philemon. The presence of such traditional motifs in the biblical narratives raises the possibility that at least some of these narratives are purely products of the storyteller's art, which of course raises serious questions about their usefulness for historical reconstruction.

General Improbabilities

In addition to the schematic chronology and miraculous events that present the historian with credibility problems of a special sort, other aspects challenge credulity. Some of these relate to chronological matters in addition to the encompassing chronological schema noted above. For example, Jacob presumably would have been at least seventy years old when he went to Upper Mesopotamia to secure himself a wife. Simeon and Levi, sons of Jacob, would have been teenagers when they destroyed the city of Shechem (Gen. 34). Other matters unrelated to chronology raise similar credibility issues. Exodus 12:37–39 reports that 600,000 Israelites of fighting age left Egypt. This number plus their wives and children along with the mixed multitude said to accompany them would have totaled some two and a half million. Marching ten abreast, the numbers would have formed a line over 150 miles long and would have required eight or nine days to march by any fixed point. The mere logistics of organizing such a group and sustaining it for forty years of wandering in the wilderness, not to mention the problems two midwives would have had caring for the womenfolk (Exod. 1:15), raise enormous questions for any historian who would seek to use this information.

Internal Contradictions

A close reading of the Genesis–2 Kings History reveals internal contradictions, some of which have troubled interpreters since ancient times. For example, from where did Cain's wife come (Gen. 4:17)? Do not the genealogies in Genesis 4:17–26 and Genesis 5 present irreconcilable contradictions? Did Abraham present his wife Sarah as his sister on two different occasions (12:10–20; 20:1–18) and with essentially the same results in both cases, and did Isaac do the same with Rebekah (26:1–11)? Or have we here variants of the same event, or merely the literary employment of a common plot motif? Did the Israelites flee Egypt without the pharaoh's knowledge, in great haste and without preparation (Exod. 12:39; 14:5a)? Or was the departure very deliberate, with the Israelites organized as an armed military force and only after they had relieved the Egyptians of much of their wealth (11:1–2; 12:35–36; 13:18b–19)? What were the laws given to Moses on Mount Sinai: the Ten Commandments (34:28), the book of the covenant (24:7), or the whole of the pentateuchal legislation? Was Hebron conquered by Joshua during the initial invasion of western Palestine (Josh. 10:36), or by Caleb (Josh. 15:13–14), or by Judah (Judg. 1:9–10)? If Joshua conquered the whole land of Canaan, destroying its inhabitants (Josh. 10:40–42) and settling the tribes in their allotments (Josh. 13–22), how then can one explain the scene in Judges 1 where Judahites, Simeonites, and other tribal groups are struggling for places to settle in the land among the Canaanites after the death of Joshua? Casual readers may not notice such problems in the text or may choose to ignore apparent contradictions of this sort. An historian, however, cannot avoid such problems.

It is possible in most cases to construct scenarios whereby the apparent contradictions turn out not to be contradictions after all. Regarding the conquest of Hebron, for example, one may hypothesize that the city was conquered more than once. Joshua conquered it; then the indigenous people of the land took it back; then Caleb conquered it; after that it was lost again; then finally the tribe of Judah conquered it. But contemporary biblical scholars are more inclined to explain contradictions such as those above in terms of the composite literary character of the Genesis–2 Kings History.

Composite Character of the Genesis–2 Kings History

Most present-day biblical scholars approach the Hebrew Bible from a historical-critical perspective, which means that they analyze the biblical materials with the same assumptions and methods with which they analyze any other ancient sources. These include various techniques of literary analysis such as source criticism and form criticism. Literary analysis of the Genesis–2 Kings History, the Chronicler's History, and Ezra–Nehemiah reveals that all three are compiled works that incorporate many originally independent items (genealogies, stories, songs, collections of laws, and so on). The process by which they were compiled is not entirely clear and may have involved several stages. However, the Genesis–2 Kings History probably did not reach its present form until after the Babylonian destruction of Jerusalem in 586 B.C.E., which is the last major event it reports. For corresponding reasons, the Chronicler's History and Ezra–Nehemiah must be seen as products of the Persian period or later. In short, both the Genesis–2 Kings History and the Chronicler's History were produced long after the people they describe would have lived and the events they report would have occurred. The Genesis–2 Kings History, for example, would have been compiled at least a half millennium after David and Solomon.

The compilers of the Genesis–2 Kings History combined and edited various materials that they incorporated into their account, so that the resulting composite narrative has a degree of unity and coherence. Yet many ragged edges remain. Moreover, the compilers had their own rather idealized views of Israel's past, which they expressed in editorial passages and, to some degree, by editing the incorporated materials. The incorporated materials do not always support their views; and sometimes the incorporated materials, having originated independently, seem to contradict one another. It is this dynamic, from an historical-critical perspective, that explains the many internal contradictions in the Genesis–2 Kings History such as those mentioned above. For example, an historical-critical explanation for the apparent contradiction regarding the conquest of Hebron might be as follows: the compilers of Genesis–2 Kings, wishing to convey the notion that the whole land of Canaan was conquered all at once by Joshua, attributed the deed to him. Also, since they envisioned earliest Israel as consisting of only twelve tribes, they subsumed the Calebites under the tribe of Judah. Yet they incorporated an old tradition in Joshua 15:13–14 that recognizes the Calebites as a distinct tribal group and credits them with the conquest of Hebron.

Folk Materials Embedded in the Hebrew Bible

Early Israel, according to the idealized notions of the compilers of the Genesis–2 Kings History, consisted of twelve clearly defined tribes, each descended from one of the twelve sons of Jacob/Israel. These early tribes were worshipers of a single god, Yahweh, who had revealed himself to the patriarchs and Moses. Standard Israelite lifestyle was governed by a code of laws and religious instructions that Yahweh had given to Moses on Mount Sinai or on the plains of Moab just before the conquest of Canaan. The compilers presumed that Israel was already secure in the land of Canaan by the end of Joshua's career; that ideal boundaries for eleven of the twelve tribes had been established; and that the twelfth tribe, the Levites, had been installed in key cities throughout the land to serve as priests for all the nation. In short, the compilers of Genesis–2 Kings, active during the later centuries of Babylonian and/or Persian rule, conceived of an ideal Israel that had already emerged, taken its rightful place in Palestine, and settled down to normal life by the time of Joshua's death. Correspondingly, they presented the "pre-judges" period as normative for later Israelite and Judean history and sought to convey to their exilic/postexilic community that the only hope for a good future lay in a return to the ancient socioreligious norms.

Embedded in the Genesis–2 Kings History, however, and accounting for much of its content, is a large repertoire of folk materials.[5] These embedded folk materials are not necessarily any nearer to authentic historical memory than the compilers' idealized notions about Israel's past. Yet through these folk materials we hear other voices. They provide us with glimpses of how generations of storytellers and their audiences would have spoken about earlier times.

Genealogies. Genealogies figure prominently in both the Genesis–2 Kings History and the Chronicler's History, especially in the book of Genesis, where a sequence of genealogies trace Israelite ancestry from Adam to the twelve tribes. The overall genealogical system in Genesis seems contrived, because details of the individual genealogies do not always square exactly with the twelve-tribe scheme. But this in itself suggests that the compilers of the Genesis–2 Kings History were working with traditional genealogies rather than constructing an entirely artificial system without any such precedents. Genealogies often function in preliterate societies to express perceived interrelationships between families, clans, tribes, and even larger population groups. Examined from this perspective, the biblical genealogies reveal a great deal about how the ancient Israelites understood their relationships to other peoples of their day, as well as the relationships among the Israelite tribes. Consider, for example, the so-called table of nations (Gen. 10), which identifies, from an ancient perspective, the major peoples of the world and explains their interrelationships. Later genealogies, such as those of Lot and Isaac, signal that the Israelites regarded themselves to be more closely related to the peoples of Transjordan (the Edomites, Moabites, and Ammonites) than to peoples of the coastal zone (Phoenicians and Philistines).

Ancestor Stories. The genealogies of Genesis are filled out with stories about the ancestors of the various peoples of Iron Age Palestine. It is not always clear, however, whether these stories are about individuals or about groups of peoples personified as individuals. The ancient storytellers and their audiences would probably not have bothered with the difference. These were entertaining stories about the ancestors of the Israelites and their Palestinian neighbors, and at the same time characterizations of the Israelites and their neighbors and explanations for long-standing circumstances. According to the stories in Genesis, for example, Jacob (Israel) favored Joseph and Benjamin, his two sons by his favorite wife, Rachel, and when he blessed Joseph's sons he insisted on giving precedence to the younger one, Ephraim, rather than the older one, Manasseh (Gen. 48:8–22). These stories signal that, at least in the narrator's mind, the Benjaminites, Ephraimites, and Manassehites were closely aligned and that Ephraimites tended to have prominence.

Tribal Sayings and Descriptions of Tribal Boundaries. There are two groups of tribal sayings that, although attributed by the compilers of Genesis–2 Kings History to Jacob and Moses, respectively, and presented as blessings (Gen. 49 and Deut. 33), are probably traditional sayings. They are more like caricatures

---

5. On folklore in the Bible see D. G. Kirkpatrick, *The Old Testament and Folklore Study* (JSOTSup 62; Sheffield: JSOT Press, 1988); and Susan Niditch, *Folklore and the Hebrew Bible* (GBSOT; Minneapolis: Fortress, 1993).

of the individual tribes than blessings. It is interesting to compare these sayings with other materials that refer to the tribes on an individual basis, such as the Song of Deborah in Judges 5 and the detailed descriptions of tribal boundaries presented in the book of Joshua. Certain tribes figure prominently in all of these materials, but not always the same tribes, and they are not always located in the same places geographically. Gilead is usually not listed among the Israelite tribes, for example, although it is given individual tribal status in the Song of Deborah. The tribal sayings in Genesis 49:13 and Deuteronomy 33:18–19 associate Zebulun and Issachar with the sea, but this does not seem to square with the tribal boundaries described for them in Joshua 19:10–23. In short, these materials suggest that neither the Israelite tribes nor their geographical locations were as sharply defined as the compilers of the Genesis– 2 Kings history would have us believe.

Stories about Israel's Early Heroes. The artificiality of the compilers' twelve-tribe structure becomes especially obvious when one examines the details of the stories about Israel's "judges" embedded in the book of Judges. This was a time, according to the scenario advanced in the editorial framework, before any king ruled in Israel and "all the people did what was right in their own eyes" (Judg. 21:25). Consequently, the people kept going after false gods. Each time they did, Yahweh allowed them to fall into the hands of enemies. Then they would cry out in repentance to Yahweh, who would identify a champion to lead Israel to victory over the enemy. The victorious hero would then "judge" Israel until he (or she, in the case of Deborah) died. This scenario is filled out with accounts of the exploits of the various judges, the details of which, however, rarely support the scenario. Some of the characters featured in the stories do not fit the profile of divinely ordained deliverers (Jephthah and Samson, for example), while most of the stories have to do with local military actions that involved only two or three tribes. Clearly the compilers of the Genesis–2 Kings History have filled out their scenario with an assortment of traditional folk stories that feature a wide variety of local legendary figures. It is noteworthy, moreover, that these stories tend to focus on legendary figures of the "Rachel tribes"—Ephraim, Manasseh, and Benjamin—or on matters that involved these tribes.

Stories about Early Tribal Conflicts. The book of Judges closes with two long stories about intertribal conflicts. The first of these, in Judges 17–18, recounts how the tribe of Dan migrated from its earlier settlement area in the Shephelah to a new place near the sources of the Jordan River. As the Danites passed through the hill country of Ephraim, they convinced the young priest of an Ephraimite shrine to join them and bring along the cultic paraphernalia from the shrine. This consisted of an ephod, teraphim, a graven image, and a molten image (Judg. 18:14–20). When the Danites reached their destination, an isolated city named Laish, they destroyed the city and rebuilt it for themselves under the new name Dan. The story concludes, "So they maintained as their own Micah's idol that he made, as long as the house of God was at Shiloh" (Judg. 18:31).

The last story in the book of Judges also begins with an incident involving Ephraim and ends with reference to Shiloh. A Levite and his concubine were traveling from Bethlehem to "the remote parts of the hill country of Ephraim"

(Judg. 19:1). They intentionally stopped for the night at the Benjaminite village of Gibeah because it was an Israelite village (unlike nearby non-Israelite Jebus). The concubine was gang-raped in Gibeah. The incident sparked an intertribal war during which the Israelites (who appear to consist mainly or entirely of Ephraimites) vowed not to give any of their daughters in marriage to the Benjaminites. Later on, however, after the Benjaminites had been subdued, the other Israelites (or Ephraimites?) became concerned about Benjamin's future as a tribe. Thus they devised plans to secure wives for the Benjaminites. First, a war party went to Jabesh in Gilead to attack the city and bring back virgins for the Benjaminites. When there were still not enough women after this, the Benjaminites were instructed to go to Shiloh at the time of the annual feast of Yahweh, hide in the vineyards, and each seize a wife when the young women came out in the vineyards to dance.

In connection with these last two stories in the book of Judges, mention should be made of the stories about Eli, Samuel, and Saul (1 Sam. 1–15), to be discussed in chapter 5 below. The Ephraimite hill country, including the Benjaminite territory, is center stage for these Eli, Samuel, and Saul stories also, and we hear more in them about Shiloh, Gibeah, and Jabesh-gilead as well. Eli was the old priest at Shiloh under whom Samuel is said to have trained (1 Sam. 1–3). Samuel was from Ramah, a neighboring village of Gibeah, and is reported to have "judged Israel" on a yearly circuit at three other villages in the immediate vicinity: Bethel, Gilgal, and Mizpah (1 Sam. 7:16). According to the narrative, Samuel anointed the young Saul for kingship, and Saul, a Benjaminite, gained fame by saving Jabesh-gilead from an Ammonite attack. He was then reanointed king over Israel at Gilgal, and chose Gibeah as his chief city.

Again, neither these stories at the end of the book of Judges, nor the Eli, Samuel, and Saul stories that they anticipate, seem aware of a unified twelve-tribe Israel ruled by divinely authorized judges and guided by Levitical priests. These are basically stories about the Ephraimites—conflicts among the families and clans that made up Ephriam, and incidents that involved Ephraim with neighboring tribes.

Folk Materials and Historical Evidence

The stories about tribal conflict at the end of the book of Judges and the stories about Eli, Samuel, and Saul that they anticipate bring us back to the historicity question. The narrators of these stories seem so naively honest about events that are not flattering to anyone involved, and they show such detailed familiarity with the towns, villages, and local topography of the Ephraimite hill country and adjacent regions, that it is difficult to think of their stories as fictional. Upon closer examination, however, one notices themes and motifs that turn up in more than one of the stories. Compare, for example, the scene at Gibeah when the Levite and his concubine stopped for the night (Judg. 19:14–30) with the scene at Sodom when two angels stopped for the night (Gen. 19:1–11). In both cases the travelers were given hospitality by individuals who were not themselves part of the established citizenry of the city—"an old man from the hill country of Ephraim who was sojourning in Gibeah," and Lot, who had recently moved to Sodom—and in both cases the men of the city surrounded the house demanding that the travelers be handed over to them. Compare further the description of the Israelite attack on Gibeah subsequent to the gang rape (Judg. 20:19–36) with the description of the Israelite attack on Ai (Josh. 7:2–8:29). Both narratives follow the same pattern: initial defeat, appeal to Yahweh, ambush tactic, victory. Are we perhaps dealing here with floating motifs or scripts that found their way into different stories?

When we examine the stories about Eli, Samuel, and Saul more closely below, we will see that the characterizations of these three figures are blended. Both Eli and Samuel are reported to have witnessed battles with the Philistines at Ebenezer (1 Sam. 4:1; 5:1) and both are depicted as faithful elderly priests whose office was compromised by two wayward sons. The beautiful story of Samuel's birth following his parents' visit to Shiloh states that Hannah "named him Samuel, for she said, 'I have asked him of the LORD'" (1 Sam. 1:20). But her explanation fits the name Saul (*sha'ul*, which sounds like the verb *sha'al* that means "to ask") rather than Samuel (*shemu'el*, which suggests the verb *shama'*, "to hear"). Both Eli and Saul are reported to have witnessed a disastrous Philistine defeat of Israel's army at a place named Aphek (1 Sam. 4 and 29–31). Were there two separate battles at Aphek that left a strong imprint on Israel's folk memory? Or was there only one battle that came to be, over the centuries of storytelling, associated with both Eli and Saul? For that matter, was there a battle at Aphek at all, or is the "defeat at Aphek" theme entirely folk fiction?

Unfortunately there are no scientifically precise research techniques for distinguishing between fictional elements and authentic historical memory in folk stories, just as archaeologists cannot distinguish Israelite households and villages from non-Israelite ones. We can sharpen up the historical inquiry, however, by separating out three different kinds of questions that historians need to ask of each of the folk stories embedded in Genesis–2 Kings. First, is the event that the story describes likely to have happened, even if only approximately as described? Second, if we conclude that it probably did not and that the story probably reflects more the ancient storytellers' craft than historical memory, might the story nevertheless hark back to actual individuals and events? Even if the story about the incident at Gibeah has the historical information all wrong, for example, did some incident perhaps occur at Gibeah that became deeply etched in Israel's folk memory? Similarly, even if the Gideon, Deborah, Jephthah, and Samson that we encounter in the Hebrew Bible are legendary characters far removed from historical reality, were the legends about them nevertheless based on historical figures? In other words, are we dealing with legendary characters of the King Arthur, Robin Hood, and Davy Crockett sort, or of the Jack and the Beanstalk and Cinderella sort? Third, what about the setting of the story, the general conditions that it presupposes, the societal structures that it assumes, and so on? Can we at least trust this apparently unintentional and indirect evidence, or are the setting and other assumptions about the circumstances under which the story unfolds to be regarded also as a product of creative fiction? In other words, are we dealing with the ancient equivalent to historical novels, or something more akin to *Alice in Wonderland* or to science fiction?

Present-day historians recognize that total objectivity is an unattainable goal in historical reconstruction.[6] Unattainable though it may be, however, objectivity is still a practical goal of modern historiography. What is the modern critical historian to do, then, with the idealistic views of Israel's early history advanced in the Genesis–2 Kings History, or with folkloric materials embedded in this history? Moreover, it is not just a matter of deciding what to do with some of the questionable things that are reported—folk explanations, incredible historical claims, and the like. Equally problematic is that the compilers of the Genesis–2 Kings History, because it was not central to their interests and concerns, often failed to report precisely the sort of information that modern historians consider crucial. Assuming that we could trust the historical accuracy of their record, who exactly was the pharaoh "who did not know Joseph," and what was happening on the international political scene at the time of the exodus? What were the sociopolitical circumstances among the Canaanites at the time of Joshua? These sorts of data are basic to the modern historian's interests but were incidental to ancient storytellers' techniques and of little relevance to the theological message that the compilers of Genesis–2 Kings wished to convey.

Contemporary Approaches to the History of Ancient Israel

When historians disagree on matters pertaining to Israelite history, as they often do, it is usually not because one has more information than another. Rather, they interpret differently the information provided by archaeology, epigraphy, and the Hebrew Bible, and sometimes they place more emphasis on one of these sources than another. Moreover, since archaeological evidence is typically "silent" about its ethnic background unless interpreted in conjunction with written evidence, and since there is so little epigraphical evidence that pertains specifically to early Israel, disagreements regarding early Israelite history usually boil down to disagreements about how much confidence should be placed in the biblical presentation of Israel's past, and how to interpret this presentation. Of course, there is a wide range of views on this matter—all the way from the sentiment expressed on a popular bumper sticker: "The Bible says it; I believe it; and that settles it!" to a postmodern outlook that rejects positivistic historical conclusions based on written documents of any sort, biblical or otherwise.

The Traditional Approach. In the past, treatments of Israelite history generally have followed fairly closely the overall story line of the Genesis–2 Kings History. Conservative treatments, sometimes referred to as "biblical history," would follow it in almost literal detail (at least from the time of Abraham forward), harmonize the Chronicler's History, and interpret archaeological and epigraphical evidence to fit. The presumption here is that biblical accounts should be taken as historically factual unless there are overwhelming reasons

---

6. For a survey of various approaches to writing a history of Israel, though somewhat out of date, see G. W. Ramsey, *The Quest for the Historical Israel: Reconstructing Israel's Early History* (Atlanta: John Knox, 1981; repr. Eugene, OR: Wipf and Stock, 2001).

not to do so.[7] More critical treatments also used the Genesis–2 Kings story line as the point of departure, and followed it fairly closely from the time of David and Solomon forward, but often proposed quite different scenarios for Israel's origins and pre-Davidic times.[8] What all of the treatments had in common was a considerable degree of confidence in the usefulness of the Hebrew Bible as a source of historical information.

The *"Revisionist-Minimalist" Approach.* This confidence characteristic of the traditional approach has been seriously challenged over the past two decades, with a number of very vocal scholars contending that the biblical materials have no relevance for the study of ancient Israelite history other than that the Hebrew Bible is itself a literary artifact from the Persian and Hellenistic periods.[9] Sometimes referred to as "revisionists" or "minimalists," these scholars argue that the Israel one encounters in the biblical narratives is largely a figment of late Jewish imagination, and that whatever authentic historical memory may have contributed to this artificially constructed "biblical Israel" is so thoroughly entangled with and camouflaged by late Judean revisionist notions about their past that it can never be retrieved. Any attempt to derive historical information from the Bible is bound to be more misleading than helpful, and mixing archaeology with the Bible story only compounds the problem. According to the minimalist perspective, therefore, it makes no sense even to speak of Israelite history before the mid-ninth century, when the two separate kingdoms of Israel and Judah begin to show up in inscriptions, and even at that point the only thing to be said for certain about them is that they are mentioned occasionally in inscriptions.[10]

Searching for Ancient Israel without Relying on the Hebrew Bible. A few scholars, while holding similarly negative views regarding the historical value of the Hebrew Bible, are more confident than the minimalists that archaeology, sociology, and other "scientific" disciplines enable us to trace Israel's origins and early history. Their methodological approach therefore, supposedly, is to set

7. For treatments that follow this approach, see Iain Provan et al., *A Biblical History of Israel* (Louisville: Westminster John Knox, 2003); and K. A. Kitchen, *On the Reliability of the Old Testament* (Grand Rapids: Eerdmans, 2003).

8. For examples of histories written along this approach, see J. A. Soggin, *An Introduction to the History of Israel and Judah* (3d ed.; London: SCM, 1999); and M. D. Coogan, ed., *The Oxford History of the Biblical World* (Oxford: Oxford University Press, 1998).

9. Basic works reflecting this point of view are P. R. Davies, *In Search of 'Ancient Israel'* (JSOTSup 148; Sheffield: JSOT Press, 1992); N. P. Lemche, *The Israelites in History and Tradition* (LAI; Louisville: Westminster John Knox, 1998); idem, *Prelude to Israel's Past: Background and Beginnings of Israelite History and Identity* (Peabody, MA: Hendrickson, 1998); T. L. Thompson, *Early History of the Israelite People from the Written and Archaeological Sources* (SHANE 4; Leiden: Brill, 1992); idem, *The Mythic Past: Biblical Archaeology and the Myth of Israel* (New York: Basic Books, 1999) = *The Bible in History: How Writers Create a Past* (London: Jonathan Cape, 1998); and Giovanni Garbini, *Myth and History in the Bible* (JSOTSup 362; Sheffield: Sheffield Academic Press, 2003). On the history of the rise of this radically critical approach to the historicity of OT narratives, see N. P. Lemche, "Is It Still Possible to Write a History of Ancient Israel?" *SJOT* 8 (1994) 165–90; idem, "The Origin of the Israelite State: A Copenhagen Perspective on the Emergence of Critical Historical Studies of Ancient Israel in Recent Times," *SJOT* 12 (1998) 44–64; idem, "Ideology and the History of Ancient Israel," *SJOT* 14 (2000) 165–93; and L. L. Grabbe, "Writing Israel's History at the End of the Twentieth Century," in André Lemaire and Magne Sæbø, eds., *Congress Volume, Oslo 1998* (VTSup 80; Leiden: Brill, 2000) 203–18.

10. True, there is a reference to an Israel in Merneptah's Inscription from the late thirteenth century, but scholars of the revisionist-minimalist perspective point out that this is only a passing reference that tells us little of consequence. One need not assume that Merneptah's Israel was historically continuous in any significant way with the Israel that shows up in inscriptions two and a half centuries later, and certainly it is inappropriate to fill in the intervening gap with the Bible story.

the Hebrew Bible aside and learn what they can by working only with these other disciplines.[11] But while such an approach may be methodologically sound, it is virtually impossible to follow in practice. The biblical story is so deeply engrained in our Western heritage that we cannot simply set it aside, and the studies that purport to do so only illustrate that fact. Almost invariably, at any rate, lurking behind the interpretations of archaeological data that these studies offer, and deeply embedded in their socioscientific explanations, are assumptions about ancient Israel that do not derive entirely from the scientific evidence, but are influenced at least to some degree by the biblical traditions.[12] To the extent that one is successful in bracketing out the biblical traditions and working with archaeology, sociology, and other scientific disciplines alone, the results are necessarily very general. It is possible to draw conclusions from archaeology about settlement patterns in Iron Age Palestine, for example, and to explore what sort of sociopolitical structures might have existed among the Palestinian villagers. For reasons explained above, however, archaeology and sociology alone do not enable us to identify specifically the Israelites among the villagers or to draw any historical conclusions about them in particular.

History of Israel or Sociology of Palestine? This is as it should be, some would argue. Their point is that traditional histories of Israel place too much emphasis on the legendary heroes, kings, and priests who happen to appear in the Bible. More important for understanding our human heritage is the overall and long-range picture of life in ancient Palestine.[13] How did the endless generations of people subsist in that environment, for example, and what changes occurred in their circumstances and lifestyles from one era to the next? Here again, this is a valid point, and studies of the sort envisioned should be encouraged. But while studies that focus on the broad subsistence patterns and sociological trends may be more important in the larger scheme of things, it is still legitimate for those of us interested in exploring what can be known historically about ancient Israel and Judah to do so.

Our Approach

Ancient Israel and Judah are the main focus of this volume. We have attempted to make appropriate use of epigraphy, archaeology, and the Hebrew Bible. We consider it methodologically crucial to examine each of these three sources of information on its own terms and with the procedures appropriate to it, and to determine what can be learned from it alone before attempting to relate its

11. See R. B. Coote and K. W. Whitelam, *The Emergence of Early Israel in Historical Perspective* (SWBA 5; Sheffield: Almond, 1987); and F. R. Brandfon, "Kingship, Culture and 'Longue Durée,'" *JSOT* 39 (1987) 30–38.

12. On the impossibility of dispensing with the Bible in writing a history of Israel, see J. M. Miller, "Is It Possible to Write a History of Israel without Relying on the Hebrew Bible?" in D. V. Edelman, ed., *The Fabric of History: Text, Artifact and Israel's Past* (JSOTSup 127; Sheffield: Sheffield Academic Press, 1991) 93–102; and H. G. M. Williamson, "The Origins of Israel: Can We Safely Ignore the Bible?" in Shmuel Ahituv and E. D. Oren, eds., *The Origin of Early Israel—Current Debate: Biblical, Historical and Archaeological Perspectives* (Beer-Sheva 12; Beer-sheva: Ben-Gurion University of the Negev Press, 1998) 141–51.

13. See K. W. Whitelam, *The Invention of Ancient Israel: The Silencing of Palestinian History* (London: Routledge, 1996).

evidence to that derived from the other two sources. We are especially mindful of the dangers and difficulties involved in attempting to extract historical information from the Hebrew Bible. Even the first edition of this history was characterized by its extremely cautious use of the biblical materials and by its radical departure from previous treatments of Israelite history. If we have learned anything in the meantime, it is that we need to be even more cautious.

Yet we do not share the revisionist-minimalist's extreme skepticism, and point to the mention of Shishak's invasion of Palestine in 1 Kings 14:25–26 as one of the clearest signals that historians need to examine the Hebrew Bible for potentially useful historical information rather than dismiss it out of hand. "In the fifth year of King Rehoboam, King Shishak of Egypt came up against Jerusalem; he took away the treasures of the house of Yahweh and the treasures of the king's house; he took away everything."

Shishak is almost certainly to be equated with Pharaoh Sheshonq, whose campaign into Syria-Palestine is commemorated by an inscription on the walls of the temple of Amun at Karnak. In spite of the fact that both Egyptian chronology and biblical chronology are problematic, both place Shishak/Sheshonq's campaign at approximately the same time, somewhere toward the last quarter of the tenth century B.C.E. Apparently the compilers of the Genesis–2 Kings History were not totally in the dark about Israel's earlier history. Also, as we have seen, the folk materials embedded in the Genesis–2 Kings History, when analyzed critically and individually, allow us to hear other ancient voices than those of the compilers. We think that historians should listen to these voices, rather than dismiss them because they fail to meet all the modern standards of objectivity. In short, we think that, when examined carefully and critically, there is much of historical value to be learned from the Hebrew Bible.

Finally, we are aware that the very concept of history is itself difficult to pin down; and that however one defines the term, history rarely consists of a narrative based on indisputable facts. More often, certainly when it comes to ancient history, it is a matter of best-guess scenarios that emerge from the most convincing interpretations of whatever meager evidence is available. We make no stronger claims than that for the views expressed in the remaining chapters of this volume. They represent our evaluations of the meager and often problematic evidence relevant to ancient Israel and Judah, and our best-guess scenario for the history of these two closely related peoples.

General Bibliography

For discussion of the issues noted in this chapter, see J. M. Sasson, "On Choosing Models for Recreating Israelite Pre-Monarchical History," *JSOT* 21 (1981) 3–24; John Van Seters, *In Search of History: Historiography in the Ancient World and the Origins of Biblical History* (New Haven: Yale University Press, 1983); Giovanni Garbini, *History and Ideology in Ancient Israel* (London: SCM, 1986); Baruch Halpern, *The First Historians: The Hebrew Bible and History* (San Francisco: Harper & Row, 1988); J. M. Miller, "Reading the Bible Historically: The Historian's Approach," in S. R. Haynes and S. L. McKenzie, eds., *To Each Its Own Meaning: An Introduction to Biblical Criticisms and Their Application* (Louisville: Westminster John Knox, 1993) 11–28;

L. L. Grabbe, ed., *Can a 'History of Israel' Be Written?* (JSOTSup 245; Sheffield: Sheffield Academic Press, 1997); N. P. Lemche, *The Israelites in History and Tradition* (LAI; Louisville: Westminster John Knox, 1998); James Barr, *History and Ideology in the Old Testament* (Oxford: Oxford University Press, 2000); N. K. Gottwald, *The Politics of Ancient Israel* (LAI; Louisville: Westminster John Knox, 2001); V. P. Long et al., eds., *Windows into Old Testament History: Evidence, Argument, and the Crisis of "Biblical History"* (Grand Rapids: Eerdmans, 2002); Iain Provan et al., *A Biblical History of Israel* (Louisville: Westminster John Knox, 2003) 3–104; D. M. Howard Jr. and M. A. Grisanti, eds., *Giving the Sense: Understanding and Using Old Testament Historical Texts* (Grand Rapids: Kregel, 2003); K. A. Kitchen, *The Reliability of the Old Testament* (Grand Rapids: Eerdmans, 2004); John Day, ed., *In Search of Pre-Exilic Israel* (JSOTSup 406; New York: T. & T. Clark International, 2004); Jens Kofoed, *Text and History: Historiography and the Study of the Biblical Text* (Winona Lake, IN: Eisenbrauns, 2005); Mario Liverani, *Israel's History and the History of Israel* (London: Equinox, 2005); and M. B. Moore, *Philosophy and Practice in Writing a History of Ancient Israel* (New York: T. & T. Clark, 2006).

4. Earliest Israel

Folk materials embedded in the Hebrew Bible provide a wealth of indirect or "unintentional" evidence about ancient Israelite society. Much of this is background information, information that the storytellers mentioned or alluded to in passing, assuming that their audiences would be familiar with it already—kinship patterns, tribal alliances, cultic practices, and so on. Based on the biblical folk materials, this chapter will attempt to provide a composite picture of early Israelite society. Obviously, given the nature of the evidence, this picture cannot claim scientific accuracy. Yet we think that it is probably not far from reality. Toward the end of the chapter we must address the basic question: What was early Israel? What sort of entity was it; and what would have distinguished an Israelite from a non-Israelite before there was a kingdom of Israel? We begin with two assumptions, neither of which can be proved or disproved. They are judgment calls that we as historians who have labored with the biblical texts (see chap. 3) are prepared to make.

1. The compilers of Genesis–2 Kings presupposed an early time when "there was no king in Israel; all the people did what was right in their own eyes" (Judg. 17:6, 21:25), that is, when Israelite clans and tribes were settled in the Palestinian highlands and lived without any central political authority. Memory of such a time is deep-seated also in the folk materials that they incorporated into their composite work, especially the narratives in the book of Judges. We believe that this is authentic folk memory, rather than a fictitious setting created and crafted by storytellers. There was such a time.

2. The biblical folk materials examined in this chapter are available to us in late, edited versions. Accordingly, the tribal society that they reflect must be understood as a composite of authentic folk memory about earlier times, assumptions based on later circumstances, and adjustments made by the compilers of Genesis–2 Kings in accordance with their idealistic notions about early Israel. We are confident, on the other hand, that Israelite and Judean society was conservative, that most of the societal patterns reflected in the biblical folk materials had their roots in the early centuries of the Iron Age, and that the emergence of monarchy in Israel would not have brought radical societal changes at the local level. Royal rule would have been superimposed upon traditional tribal society rather than displacing it. Consequently, even though we have access to the folk materials only in late edited versions, the picture of Israelite society reflected in these materials, particularly in the Judges narratives, is probably not so far removed from that of premonarchical Israel. It is worth noting in this regard that the societal patterns reflected in these narra-

tives fit well against the backdrop of Early Iron Age Palestine as known from archaeological evidence.[1]

Families, Clans, and Tribes

The biblical materials seem to presuppose three basic social units: the family, the clan, and the tribe (see Josh. 7:16–18; 1 Sam. 10:20–21). Close examination of these materials, in the light of comparative anthropological research, suggests that the family and the clan tended to be more basic to the structure of the society than the tribe.[2]

The family, or in Hebrew the *beth 'ab* ("the house of the father"), was what today would be called "the extended family." Typically, this would have consisted of several generations (the patriarch, his wife or wives, his married sons and their wives, their married sons and wives, all unmarried children, grandchildren, etc.) and various related figures (uncles, aunts, cousins) as well as occasional slaves and strangers. Authority in the family resided with the patriarch. The extended family was probably exogamous; that is, persons generally married outside the extended family, although marriage to one's maternal first cousin may have been considered ideal (see Gen. 25:20; 29:9–30). Various texts even speak of marriage to one's half sister (Gen. 20:8–12; 2 Sam. 13:7–14). The extended family would generally have dwelt close together, a populous specimen perhaps having its own settlement or village. The family was also the basic unit in the ownership of property, cultivation of land, and care of pastoral animals.

The clan consisted of several extended families living in close proximity to one another, interlocked by marriage, and employing communal use of land. Since villages and small towns were characteristic of the Palestinian hill country during the Iron Age, there was no doubt a high degree of correspondence between villages and clans. In typical cases we may suspect that the families of a village functioned as a clan with a shared past and shared ancestry. The families would have exchanged their daughters in marriage and made common use of surrounding farm- and pastureland. Several clans may have been localized in larger towns and their surrounding villages. Government and the administration of justice in the villages/clans were normally in the hands of elders (see Judg. 8:16; Ruth 4:2; 1 Sam. 11:3), who themselves were the heads of families. The village/clan was also an important unit in cultic and religious life (see 1 Sam. 20:6, 29).

The tribe would have served as a larger and more strictly endogamous unit than the clan, that is, persons generally married within the clan. Tribal divisions probably tended to be rather more vague and fluid, and also to be more territorial than genealogical in nature. The essentially territorial character of the tribes is suggested by the fact that several of the tribal names probably originated as territorial designations. Thus the name "Ephraim" probably originated with

---

1. See L. E. Stager, "The Archaeology of the Family in Early Israel," *BASOR* 260 (1985) 1–35.

2. Roland de Vaux, *Ancient Israel: Its Life and Institutions* (New York: McGraw-Hill, 1961) 19–67; F. I. Andersen, "Israelite Kinship Terminology and Social Structure," *BT* 20 (1969) 29–39; Shunya Bendor, *The Social Structure of Ancient Israel: The Institution of the Family (Beit 'Ab) from the Settlement to the End of the Monarchy* (Jerusalem Biblical Studies 7; Jerusalem: Simor, 1996); and J. D. Schloen, *The House of the Father as Fact and Symbol* (Winona Lake, IN: Eisenbrauns, 2001).

reference to the people living in the vicinity of Mount Ephraim. "Gilead" would have been the name applied to people living in the region called Gilead. The same situation was probably the case with "Judah" and Mount Judah. The name "Benjamin," which means "son of the south," is clearly a geographical name derived from the perspective of Ephraim to the north. References to "the land of Benjamin," "the land of Judah," "the land of Naphtali," and so forth also point to geographical entities.

This is not to claim that the tribal divisions were purely territorial and had nothing to do with kinship relations, but to recognize that tribalization probably occurred over time among the families and clans settled in a given area. Living in close proximity, sharing a common lifestyle, facing similar difficulties and common enemies, and exchanging sons and daughters in marriage, the families and clans living in a given area would have developed a sense of kinship over time and expressed this in their genealogies. This gradually emerging sense of kinship would not necessarily have included everyone living in the tribal area. Also on occasion clans and even whole tribes may have moved from one territory to another. In most tribal territories, therefore, there will have existed cities, towns, and enclaves of people who, for one reason or another, were not considered part of the tribe in question. This phenomenon is reflected in the lists of unconquered cities in Judges 1, for example, and in designations such as "the hill country of the Amalekites" (Judg. 12:15), "the territory of the Archites," and "the territory of the Japhletites" (Josh. 16:2–3) for localities within the territory associated with Ephraim and Benjamin.

Tribal Alignments and Territories

As observed in the previous chapter, the twelve-tribe scheme presupposed by the compilers of the Genesis–2 Kings History is artificial and finds no support in the folk materials embedded in their work.[3] The compilers' notion that the twelve tribes were assigned territories that covered the whole of Palestine also is idealistic. The tribal folk whom we encounter in the biblical Judges narratives seem to have been confined largely to the Palestinian highlands, and with territories only vaguely defined. Also they seem to have been associated with small villages and grazing lands, rather than with the modest cities of the Palestinian hill country. There seems to be some sense of kinship among the tribes, but no organized or sustaining unity.

Ephraim and Satellite Tribes

Ephraim proper was that portion of the central hill country between approximately Shechem and Bethel. The Benjaminites ("sons of the south" or "south-

---

3. See A. D. H. Mayes, *Israel in the Period of the Judges* (SBT 2/29; London: SCM, 1974); Barnabas Lindars, "The Israelite Tribes in Judges," in J. A. Emerton, ed., *Studies in the Historical Books of the Old Testament* (VTSup 30; Leiden: Brill, 1979) 95–112; Zecharia Kallai, *Historical Geography of the Bible: The Tribal Territories of Israel* (Jerusalem: Magnes, 1986); idem, "The Twelve-Tribe System of Israel," *VT* 47 (1997) 53–90; and Nurit Lissovsky and Nadav Na'aman, "A New Outlook at the Boundary System of the Twelve Tribes," *UF* 35 (2003) 291–332.

25. *Hill country trail in Benjamin.* In the upper left of the photograph is Nebi Samwil, where, according to tradition, the prophet Samuel is buried.

erners"), associated with Gibeah and surrounding villages, are presumed in some passages to represent an independent tribe, but mentioned in others as if they were simply "southern Ephraimites."[4] For example, while Joshua 18:11–20 presumes that the area between Ramah and Bethel belonged to an independent tribe of Benjamin, Judges 4:5 refers to "the palm of Deborah between Ramah and Bethel in the hill country of Ephraim." The matter of Benjamin's relationship to Ephraim probably was a point of contention at times.

Manasseh was associated with the northern part of the central hill country (from about Shechem northward to the Jezreel Valley).[5] One gets the impression that the Manassites lived in villages surrounding modest cities. One of these was Shechem, a city that had existed during the Late Bronze Age and continued into the Iron Age. Other cities in the Manassite area (according to Judg. 1:27–28) were Beth-shean, Taanach, Dor, Ibleam, and Megiddo. Mention of Beth-shean and Dor (the Dor in the Jezreel Valley) implies that Manassite clans spilled over into the Jezreel Valley, where they intermingled with the Galilee-Jezreel tribal

4. On Ephraim and hill country settlements in the region, see Israel Finkelstein, *The Archaeology of the Israelite Settlements* (Jerusalem: Israel Exploration Society, 1988) 140–77, 187–91; idem, "The Great Transformation: The 'Conquest' of the Highlands Frontiers and the Rise of the Territorial States," in T. E. Levy, ed., *The Archaeology of Society in the Holy Land* (New York: Facts on File, 1995) 349–65; Finkelstein et al., eds., *Highlands of Many Cultures: The Southern Samaria Survey, the Sites* (2 vols.; Monographs of the Sonia and Maaio Nadler Institute of Archaeology 14; Tel Aviv: Institute of Archaeology, Tel Aviv University, 1997). On Benjamin see Burton MacDonald, *The Biblical Tribe of Benjamin: Its Origins and Its History During the Period of the Judges of Israel* (Ann Arbor: University Microfilms, 1975); and Israel Finkelstein and Izchak Magen, eds., *Archaeological Survey of the Hill Country of Benjamin* (Jerusalem: Israel Antiquities Authority, 1993).

5. Adam Zertal, "'To the Lands of the Perizzites and the Giants': On the Israelite Settlement in the Hill Country of Manasseh," in Israel Finkelstein and Nadav Na'aman, eds., *From Nomadism to Monarchy: Archaeological and Historical Aspects of Early Israel* (Jerusalem: Israel Exploration Society, 1994) 47–69; idem, *The Manasseh Hill Country Survey*, vol. 1: *The Shechem Syncline* (CHANE 21/1; Leiden: Brill, 2004).

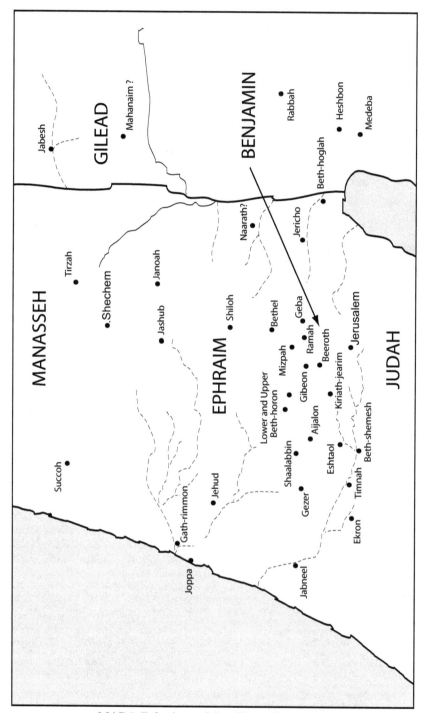

MAP 8. Ephraim and Satellite Tribal Areas

groups (see Josh. 17:11–13). There may have been some Manassite spillover into Transjordan as well. For example, the clan of Machir may have been a branch of Manasseh that crossed over into Bashan and Upper Gilead (see Josh. 12:1–6; 13:29–31; 17:1). The same may have been true of Jair and Nobah, although the references to them are more obscure (see Num. 32:39–42; Judg. 10:3).

Gideon, of the Abiezrite clan from the village of Ophrah, would have been a Manassite hero. According to his story, Gideon mustered a volunteer army and expelled Midianite raiders from the Jezreel Valley. In addition to his own tribe, he was reportedly supported in this venture by Asher, Zebulun, and Naphtali, that is, from three other tribes settled in the area where the Midianites were raiding (Judg. 6:35; 7:23). Note that the Ephraimites, who were called to arms only after the battle was under way, upbraided Gideon for undertaking the venture without calling them (7:24–8:3). Apparently the Ephraimites felt they had some claim on the actions of the Manassites.

Another of the narratives in Judges presupposes a similar dynamic in the relationship of Ephraim to Gilead. When the elders of Gilead, led by Jephthah, attacked and defeated the Ammonites, the Ephraimites mustered for war, crossed the Jordan, and threatened to burn the houses of Jephthah's people. They were offended because, according to the narrative, Jephthah and the Gileadites had not summoned them before the battle (Judg. 12:1–6). Here again the Ephraimites seem to have presumed some special claim over the Gileadites. In fact, the Gileadites involved in this episode are described as "fugitives of Ephraim" (Judg. 12:4), which suggests that they may have been Ephraimite settlers in Transjordan. The presence of Ephraimite settlers in Transjordan would also explain the mention of "the forest of Ephraim" in 2 Samuel 18:6. This forest, according to the context of the passage (see 2 Sam. 18:24–26), must have been in Transjordan roughly opposite Mount Ephraim.

Other Tribes Occasionally Involved in Ephraimite Affairs

The Galilee-Jezreel Tribes. The biblical materials associate several tribes with the Jezreel Valley and Galilee.[6] These tribes receive little focused attention, but enter the picture when their interests overlap with those of Ephraim. Joshua 19:10–39 places the tribes of Asher, Naphtali, Zebulun, and Issachar in the western, eastern, south-central, and southeastern regions of Galilee, respectively, with some spillover into the Jezreel Valley. The tribal sayings in Genesis 49:13 and Deuteronomy 33:18–19 seem to associate Zebulun and Issachar with the sea in some fashion, and the Song of Deborah (Judg. 5:17b) does the same for Asher. Perhaps these three were originally coastal clans that moved into the Galilean mountains, possibly under pressure from (or even including) elements of the Sea Peoples.[7]

---

6. Raphael Frankel, "Upper Galilee in the Late Bronze–Iron I Transition," in Finkelstein and Na'aman, eds., *From Nomadism to Monarchy*, 18–34; and Zvi Gal, *Lower Galilee During the Iron Age* (Winona Lake, IN: Eisenbrauns, 1992); idem, "Iron I in Lower Galilee and the Margins of the Jezreel Valley," in Finkelstein and Na'aman, eds., *From Nomadism to Monarchy*, 35–46.

7. See Adam Zertal, "The 'Corridor-Builders' of Central Israel: Evidence for the Settlements of the 'Northern Sea Peoples,'" in Vasso Karageorghis and C. E. Morris, eds., *Defensive Settlements of the Aegean and the Eastern Mediterranean after c. 1200 B.C.* (Nicosia: Anastasios G. Leventis Foundation, 2001) 215–32.

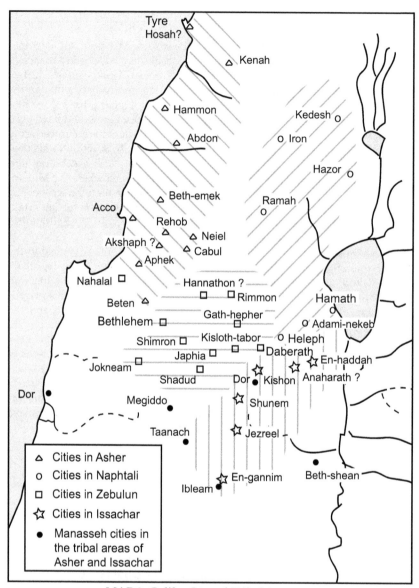

MAP 9. Galilee-Jezreel Tribal Areas as
Suggested by Joshua 17:11–13 and 19:10–39

As with the Manassites, these Galilee-Jezreel tribes are described as settled around cities they did not occupy (Judg. 1:30–33).[8] The Asherites were settled among primarily Phoenician coastal towns—Acco, Sidon, Ahlab, Achzib, Helbah, Aphek, and Rehob. Nahalol, one of Zebulun's two "unconquered cities," was on the river Kishon near modern Haifa. The other, Kitron, has not been located. Naphtali's two unconquered cities, Beth-shemesh and Beth-anath, are also unidentified. Issachar's name, if from *skr*, would mean something like "hired one." This, along with the saying in Genesis 49:14–15, has been taken to suggest that the Issachar clans not only lived among non-Israelites in the fertile Jezreel Valley but also served them as laborers.

The Galilee-Jezreel tribes figure in two of the Judges narratives, both having to do with battles initiated by persons of the Ephraim group but fought in the Jezreel Valley where the Galilee-Jezreel tribes had interests. (1) Gideon of Ophrah's attack against the Midianite raiders in the Jezreel Valley was supported by Asher, Zebulun, and Naphtali (Judg. 6:35). (2) Deborah of southern Ephraim/Benjamin encouraged Barak from Kadesh in Naphtali to engage Sisera of Harosheth-ha-goiim. The prose account of this latter episode (Judg. 4) mentions only Naphtali and Zebulun in connection with the battle, although Deborah's leading role in the affair presupposes that the Ephraim group was involved to some degree. The poetic version (Judg. 5) depicts the Ephraim group as having taken the lead in the struggle.[9]

Dan. The tribe of Dan appears in two geographical contexts: (1) in the coastal plain between the Ephraimite/Benjaminite section of the hill country and the Mediterranean Sea (see the tribal allotments in Josh. 19, the reference in Judg. 1:34, and the Samson stories in Judg. 13–16) and (2) in the city of Dan (Laish) at the foot of Mount Hermon in the extreme north of Palestine.[10] The narrative in Judges 17–18 explains the connection of the tribe with the two areas. We are told that the Danites were unable to maintain their position in the coastal region, whereupon a group of them, in search of Lebensraum, conquered and inhabited Laish, which they renamed Dan. Among the Sea Peoples mentioned in the texts of Ramesses III are, in addition to the Philistines, another related group called the Danuna. There may have been some connection between these Danuna (or Denyen) and the Danites.

Danite affairs impinged on those of the Ephraim group in two ways. (1) The Danite clans, while settled along the Mediterranean Sea, would have been immediate neighbors of Ephraim/Benjamin. Indeed, according to the tribal distributions presupposed in the book of Joshua, Dan's allotment would have fallen essentially within Ephraim's allotment. This apparent overlap probably

8. On urban-rural relations see Avraham Faust, "Abandonment, Urbanization, Resettlement and the Formation of the Israelite State," *NEA* 66 (2003) 147–61.

9. See L. E. Stager, "Archaeology, Ecology, and Social History: Background Themes to the Song of Deborah," in J. A. Emerton, ed., *Congress Volume, Jerusalem 1986* (VTSup 40; Leiden: Brill, 1988) 221–34; idem, "The Song of Deborah: Why Some Tribes Answered the Call and Others Did Not," *BAR* 15/1 (1989) 51–64; Mieke Bal, *Murder and Difference: Gender, Genre, and Scholarship on Sisera's Death* (Bloomington: Indiana University Press, 1988); and J. D. Schloen, "Caravans, Kenites, and *Casus Belli*: Enmity and Alliance in the Song of Deborah," *CBQ* 55 (1993) 18–38.

10. On the city of Dan see Avraham Biran, *Biblical Dan* (Jerusalem: Israel Exploration Society/Hebrew Union College–Jewish Institute of Religion, 1994). There is difficulty in knowing what is Israelite and what is Syrian in the archaeological remains from Dan since Syria controlled the region as much as or more than Israel.

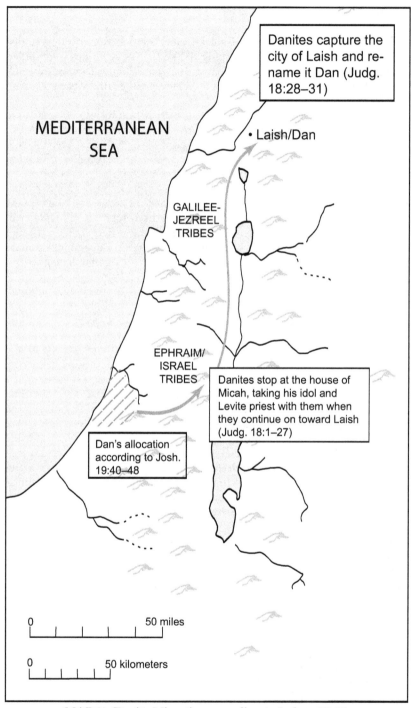

MAP 10. Danite Migration according to Judges 17–18

Danites capture the city of Laish and re-name it Dan (Judg. 18:28–31)

MEDITERRANEAN SEA

• Laish/Dan

GALILEE-JEZREEL TRIBES

EPHRAIM/ISRAEL TRIBES

Danites stop at the house of Micah, taking his idol and Levite priest with them when they continue on toward Laish (Judg. 18:1–27)

Dan's allocation according to Josh. 19:40–48

0   50 miles

0   50 kilometers

arises from the fact that the boundaries defined in Joshua 16 presuppose a "Greater Ephraim" that extended all the way to the Mediterranean Sea, whereas the Danite section in Joshua 19:40–48 does not. This would explain Judges 1:29 also, which places Gezer within Ephraim. (2) The Danites, Ephraimites, and Judeans shared a common enemy—the Philistines. Moreover, in the struggles with the Philistines, the Danites would have been the first and most directly affected. In the stories about Samuel and Saul, the Philistines enjoy superiority over the whole of the southern coastal plain and are penetrating into the central hill country. This means that they would have controlled all the territory allotted to Dan in Joshua 19.

Most of the narrative material in Judges 13–18 pertains in one way or another to the Danites. The first block of this material (Judg. 13–16) consists of the Samson stories, which focus on this legendary strong man of Dan.[11] The second block of material tells of the Danite migration to Laish (Judg. 17–18), although this latter material focuses less on the Danite migration than on an incident that happened as the Danites passed through the hill country of Ephraim: the Danites appropriated the cultic paraphernalia and a priest from one of the Ephraimite sanctuaries. This priest is said to have founded a priestly line, which remained in office in Laish/Dan "until the time the land went into captivity" (Judg. 18:30).[12]

Reuben and Gad. The territorial domains of the tribes of Reuben and Gad are difficult to establish, possibly because elements of these tribes ranged far and wide with their flocks.[13] Both tribes figure in the patriarchal narratives and genealogies, with Reuben identified as the firstborn of Jacob (Gen. 29:31–32; 49:3–4). However, neither tribe is mentioned in the Judges narratives and practically nothing concrete is said about them otherwise. The clues regarding their tribal territory are particularly vague and contradictory. Numbers 32 and Joshua 13 indicate that they were allotted territory in the Transjordanian highlands, from approximately the southern end of the Sea of Galilee to the Arnon River. But while Numbers 32 locates Gad farther south than Reuben, Joshua 13 seems to reverse their positions. Moreover, whatever their relative positions, it is clear from other sources that Reuben and Gad were not alone in this "allotted" territory. Judges 5:17 and 11:1–12:6 place the tribe of Gilead in the area directly east of the Jordan River, for example, while certain prophetical passages seem to presuppose that the entire area east of the Dead Sea (including from the cities of Elealeh and Heshbon southward to the Arnon) was Moabite

---

11. See J. L. Crenshaw, *Samson: A Secret Betrayed, a Vow Ignored* (Atlanta: John Knox, 1978); and Susan Niditch, "Samson as Culture Hero, Trickster, and Bandit: The Empowerment of the Weak," *CBQ* 52 (1990) 608–24.

12. Yigael Yadin, "And Dan, Why Did He Remain in Ships, Judges, v, 17," *AJBA* (1968–71) 9–23; Abraham Malamat, "The Danite Migration and the Pan-Israelite Exodus-Conquest," *Bib* 51 (1970) 1–16; repr. in his *History of Biblical Israel: Major Problems and Minor Issues* (CHANE 7; Leiden: Brill, 2001) 171–85; and Mark Bartusch, *Understanding Dan: An Exegetical Study of a Biblical City, Tribe and Ancestor* (JSOTSup 379; Sheffield: Sheffield Academic Press, 2003).

13. Little is known of these tribes; see F. M. Cross, "Reuben, First Born of Jacob," *ZAW* 100, Supplement (1988) 45–65; repr. in his *From Epic to Canon: Essays in the History and Literature of Ancient Israel* (Baltimore: Johns Hopkins University, 1998) 53–70; L. G. Herr, "Tell Al-'Umayri and the Reubenite Hypothesis," *ErIsr* 26 (1999) 64*–77*; Burton MacDonald, *East of the Jordan: Territories and Sites of the Hebrew Scriptures* (ASOR Books 6; Boston: American Schools of Oriental Research, 2000); and L. G. Herr and D. R. Clark, "Excavating the Tribe of Reuben," *BAR* 27/2 (2001) 36–47, 64–66.

domain (see Isa. 15; Jer. 48). An inscription left by the ninth-century king Mesha of Moab reaffirms the Moabite claim to this latter area, while at the same time noting the presence there of "men of Gad" (see Text 4). Specifically, the Mesha Inscription associates the Gadites with "the land of Ataroth," which is to be identified in turn with the vicinity of present-day Atarus, about eight miles north-northwest of Dhiban.

Finally, certain biblical texts speak of Reubenite and Gadite activity west of the Jordan. Thus Joshua 15:6 (= 18:17) mentions "the stone of Bohan the son of Reuben" near Jericho, while Joshua 22 tells of an ancient tribal conflict that supposedly occurred in the immediate aftermath of Joshua's conquest of Canaan and involved the building of an altar on the west bank of the Jordan by the Reubenites, Gadites, and Manassites. One is tempted to speculate that the actual historical basis of the story, if there is any, was some ancient conflict between the Ephraimite group and the Reubenites (see also Gen. 49:3–4). Perhaps too there was some connection between the "altar" mentioned in this story and "the stone of Bohan the son of Reuben."

In any case, the vague and contradictory information regarding the settlement area of Reuben and Gad is probably best explained by supposing that these two tribes were never confined to a specific territory but ranged rather widely with their flocks. The same may have been true also of other tribes, such as the Kenites discussed below. Accordingly, the grazing range of Reuben and Gad would have partially overlapped territory of the Ephraim-related tribes. There would have been occasional conflicts in the context of symbiotic relations.

Judah

The twelve-tribe scheme espoused by the compilers of Genesis–2 Kings, the supporting genealogies (see also 1 Chr. 2–5), the tribal allotments in the book of Joshua, and the brief "conquest reports" in Judges 1:1–21 all presuppose a "Greater Judah" with ideal boundaries encompassing the entire southern Palestine west of the Arabah.[14] Accordingly, all of the various population elements situated within these boundaries, except for the Philistines, Levites, and Simeonites, are treated as belonging to Judah. Even Simeon, while attributed independent status in the twelve-tribe scheme, is subsumed under Judah for all practical purposes in the tribal allotments. Most of the villages assigned to Simeon are also assigned to Judah, and all of them are situated within the boundaries designated for Judah (compare Josh. 15:2–5, 26–32 with Josh. 19:1–9).[15]

But this "Greater Judah" probably represents the idealized boundaries of the kingdom of Judah. The original tribe of Judah, from which the kingdom got its name, would have covered much less territory. Specifically, it is to be associated

14. See Avi Ofer, "'All the Hill Country of Judah': From a Settlement Fringe to a Prosperous Monarchy," in Finkelstein and Na'aman, eds., *From Nomadism to Monarchy*, 92–121; Volkmar Fritz, "Conquest or Settlement? The Settlement of Nomadic Tribes in the Negeb Highlands in the 11th Century B.C.," in Michael Heltzer and Eduard Lipiński, eds., *Society and Economy in the Eastern Mediterranean c. 1500–1000 BC* (OLA 23; Leuven: Peeters, 1988) 313–40; Gerson Galil, "The Jerahmeelites and Negeb of Judah," *JANESCU* 28 (2001) 33–42; and Ze'ev Herzog and Lily Singer Avitz, "Redefining the Centre: The Emergence of State in Judah," *TA* 31 (2004) 209–44.

15. Nadav Na'aman, "The Inheritance of the Sons of Simeon," *ZDPV* 96 (1980) 136–52.

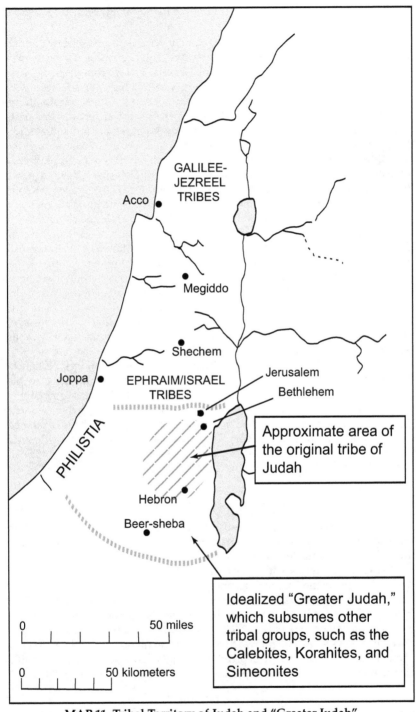

GALILEE-
JEZREEL
TRIBES

Acco

Megiddo

Shechem

Joppa   EPHRAIM/ISRAEL   Jerusalem
         TRIBES   Bethlehem

PHILISTIA

Approximate area of
the original tribe of
Judah

Hebron

Beer-sheba

Idealized "Greater Judah,"
which subsumes other
tribal groups, such as the
Calebites, Korahites, and
Simeonites

0   50 miles

0   50 kilometers

MAP 11. Tribal Territory of Judah and "Greater Judah"

with the hill country between approximately Jerusalem and Hebron. Judah plays a very minor role in the Judges narratives, and even those references may have been "written into the script" by the Genesis–2 Kings compilers.

The opening chapter of the book of Judges credits Judah and Simeon with taking the lead in fighting the Canaanites following Joshua's death (Judg. 1:1–21).[16] Upon close examination, however, the record of Judah's conquests provided in the chapter turns out to be a motley assortment of individual traditions, most of which appear in variant versions elsewhere. For example, the Adoni-bezek affair reported in vv. 5–7 finds its parallel in the Adoni-zedek story of Josh. 10:1–5. The Hebron-Debir episode (vv. 10–15; cf. Josh. 15:16–19) is, as we will see below, probably a Calebite/Othnielite tradition. The reference to Kenite settlement in the Arad region and the explanation of the name of Hormah (vv. 16–17) parallel material found in Numbers 14:45 and 21:1–3; and so on.

The mention of Judah in two other passages is suspect on similar grounds. Judges 10:9 states that "the Ammonites crossed the Jordan to fight also against Judah and against Benjamin and against the house of Ephraim; so that Israel was sorely distressed." This statement occurs in a section of the editorial framework of Judges (Judg. 10:6–16) that develops the theological pattern of apostasy-affliction-repentance-restoration. Moreover, the Jephthah story that this passage introduces has to do with a local Gileadite affair that occurred east of the Jordan. Likewise Judges 20:18 seems to include Judah unnecessarily in the account about an internal Ephraimite conflict.

The two remaining references to Judah in the book of Judges pertain to Judean clans settled on the western slopes of the hill country close to the Philistines and the Danites. In Judges 15:9–11 we hear the Judeans complaining to Samson that his harassment of the Philistines was only making things worse. Then, when the Danites made their trek to Laish, they are said to have encamped at "Kiriath-jearim in Judah" (18:11). These two passages suggest something of the northern extent or expansion of Judahite settlement (see also Josh. 15:5–11, where Kiriath-jearim falls within the ideal boundaries of "Greater Judah").

Other Southern Tribal Groups

Several other southern tribal groups, in addition to Judah and Simeon, find occasional mention in biblical narratives. These include the Calebites, Korahites, Kenizzites, Jerahmeelites, Kenites, and Simeonites.

Associated primarily with the city of Hebron and its agriculturally productive vicinity were the Calebites, as presupposed by Numbers 13–14.[17] This narrative, which reports how Moses sent out an expedition of spies from Kadesh to reconnoiter the land of Canaan, has been edited to conform to the schematic views of the editors of Genesis–2 Kings. That is, it presupposes that the action involved twelve spies, one from each of the twelve tribes, and that they explored the whole land of Canaan. In its preedited version, however, the story probably had to do with a spying expedition specifically directed to Hebron and its vicin-

---

16. See G. A. Auld, "Judges I and History: A Reconsideration," *VT* 25 (1975) 261–85.
17. Walter Beltz, *Die Kaleb-Traditionen im Alten Testament* (BWANT 5/18; Stuttgart: Kohlhammer, 1974).

ity (see Num. 14:22–24), and its main point would have been to confirm the Calebites' right to that area: "But my servant Caleb, because he has a different spirit and has followed me wholeheartedly, I will bring into the land into which he went [that is, Hebron and vicinity], and his descendants shall possess it" (Num. 14:24). This theme reappears in Joshua 14:6–15 and 15:13–19. Note that Judges 1:10–15, a parallel version of Joshua 15:13–19, has the tribe of Judah— "Greater Judah," that is, which would include the Calebites—taking Hebron.

These last two texts mentioned in connection with the Calebites, Joshua 15:13–19 and the parallel version in Judges 1:10–15, describe how Othniel the son of Kenaz the younger brother of Caleb secured the city of Debir south of Hebron. About all that can be deduced from this tale is that Othnielites were settled in the hill country immediately south of Hebron, specifically in the Debir region. However, Othniel is featured again in Judges 3:7–11, the only one of the Judges narratives that actually focuses on a southern hero. The narrative relates how Othniel fought against Cushan-rishathaim, king of Aram-naharaim (Upper Mesopotamia). Several factors suggest that this story is artificial. (1) The name of the Mesopotamian oppressor, Cushan-rishathaim ("Cushan of Double Evil"), sounds like a scribal caricature. (2) What we know of international affairs from epigraphical sources renders it very unlikely that Mesopotamian rulers even campaigned into Palestine during the Late Bronze or Early Iron ages, much less exercised dominion over that area. (3) The text provides no details about the incident, and does not even identify the place where the supposed battle occurred. In short, one has to suspect that this is a fictitious account designed to give "Greater Judah" (under which all of the other southern tribes were subsumed) a share of the action in "the period of the judges."

Elements in the biblical genealogies associate the Calebites and Othnielites with the Korahites, Kenizzites, and Jerahmeelites. Thus Numbers 32:12 and Joshua 14:6, 14 refer to Caleb as "the son of Jephunneh the Kenizzite," while Judges 1:13 (see also Judg. 3:9) identifies Othniel as "the son of Kenaz, Caleb's younger brother," and 1 Chronicles 2:42 describes Caleb as the brother of Jerahmeel. Genesis 36:11 and 15–16, on the other hand, present Kenaz and Korah as brothers among the sons of Esau (= Edom), while 1 Chronicles 2:42–43 presents Caleb as the grandfather of Hebron and great-grandfather of Korah. One hardly knows what to do with these passages, and very little is known otherwise about the Korahites, Kenizzites, and Jerahmeelites. All three of these tribal groups appear to have ranged in the foothills of the southern hill country and in the Negeb, where they intermingled with and were related to the Edomites. First Samuel 27:10 speaks of "the Negeb of Judah" and "the Negeb of the Jerahmeelites," while 1 Sam. 30:29 mentions "the cities of the Jerahmeelites." Korah and Kenaz are listed among the descendants of Esau, who in turn is equated with Edom in Genesis 36.

First Samuel 27:10 speaks also of "the Negeb of the Kenites," and 30:29 mentions "the cities of the Kenites" (some Hebrew and Greek manuscripts, however, read "Kenizzites" instead of "Kenites"), while Judges 1:16 identifies the region around Arad as their place of residence.[18] Judges 4:11–22 and 5:24–30,

---

18. For a classical statement of the view that Yahwism originated among the Kenites, see H. H. Rowley, *From Joseph to Joshua* (London: Oxford University Press, 1950) 148–63.

however, place Jael, a tent-dwelling Kenite, as far north as the Jezreel Valley. The father-in-law of Moses, sometimes called Jethro (Exod. 4:18; 18) but at other times Reuel (Exod. 2:18; Num. 10:29) or Hobab (Judg. 4:11), is identified as both a Kenite (Judg. 1:16) and a Midianite (Exod. 3:1). A widely accepted, and probably correct, hypothesis regarding the Kenites is that they (or at least some segment of the tribe) were itinerant metalworkers who enjoyed a special relationship with and protection among the other Palestinian tribal groups (see Gen. 4:1–16, where the characterization of Cain may relate in some fashion to the Kenites).

Leadership among the Clans and Tribes

As observed above, local government and the administration of justice seem to have found their center in the villages/clans rather than in the tribe, and frequent references suggest that the villages/clans were ruled by a body of elders who themselves were heads of families.[19] Their prominence and position were dependent not upon any elective process but upon social status, wealth, and prestige. Normally disputes were settled and decisions reached in a village public space—at the village gates, if there were gates. When the narratives refer to the elders of a region or a tribe, as in Judges 11, these were probably representatives of the villages/clans in a given locale who came together for unified action in the face of a particular situation or need. Several titles are used in the Judges narratives for persons who exercised leadership roles over and above that of elder. Among these titles are "ruler" or "official" (sar; Judg. 8:14; 9:30; 10:18), "leader" (qatsin; Judg. 11:6; see Josh. 10:24, "chiefs"), "head" (ro'sh; Judg. 11:8), and "judge" (shofet; Judg. 2:16 and frequently). Note, however, that the title "judge" appears primarily in the editorial passages of the book of Judges rather than in the component narratives.[20] We also find a diversity of leadership types reflected in the Judges narratives. Consider the following:

1. Deborah (Judg. 4–5), a prophetess, active in the Ephraimite/Benjaminite region, is said to have sat under a palm, where people came to her for judgment (Judg. 4:4–5).[21] This suggests that she was involved in the settlement of disputes and the arbitration of justice. One could compare the statement that Samuel installed his sons, Joel and Abijah, as judges at Beer-sheba, where they took bribes and perverted justice (1 Sam. 8:1–3). Deborah is also pictured as rallying Barak and the troops to battle against a Canaanite army.

2. Tola, Jair, Ibzan, Elon, and Abdon were wealthy dignitaries with numerous offspring, which seems to explain their leadership status (Judg. 10:1–5; 12:8–15).

19. See Hanoch Reviv, The Elders in Ancient Israel: A Study of a Biblical Institution (Jerusalem: Magnes, 1989).

20. See Tomoo Ishida, "The Leaders of the Tribal League 'Israel' in the Premonarchic Period," RB 80 (1975) 514–30.

21. The figure of Deborah has provided a window to explore the role of women in Israelite society. See J. A. Hackett, "In the Days of Jael: Reclaiming the History of Women in Ancient Israel," in C. W. Atkinson et al., eds., Immaculate and Powerful: The Female in Sacred Image and Social Reality (Boston: Beacon, 1985) 15–38; D. N. Fewell and D. M. Gunn, "Controlling Perspectives: Women, Men, and the Authority of Violence in Judges 4 & 5," JAAR 58 (1990) 389–411; and Susan Ackerman, "Digging up Deborah: Recent Hebrew Bible Scholarship on Gender and the Contribution of Archaeology," NEA 66 (2003) 172–84.

CHART 6. Outline of the Judges

Othniel delivered Israel from the hand of the Cushan-rishathiam king of Aram-naharaim (Upper Mesopotamia) and "the land had rest for forty years" (Judg. 3:7–11)

Ehud Delivered Israel from Moabite oppression and "the land had rest for eighty years" (Judg. 3:12–30).

Shamgar Killed six hundred Philistines with an oxgoad and also delivered Israel (Judg. 3:31).

Deborah Urged on Barak, who defeated Jabin king of Canaan. Deborah is described as a prophetess who was "judging Israel at that time," and Jabin is said to have oppressed the people of Israel cruelly for twenty years from this capital at Hazor (Judg. 4–5).

Gideon Delivered Israel from Midian, who had oppressed the Israelites for seven years (Judg. 6–8). "And the land had rest forty years in the days of Gideon" (Judg. 8:28).

Abimelech One of Gideon's sons. He killed his seventy brothers, hired a private army with funds contributed by the people of Shechem, was made king by all the citizens of Shechem and Beth-millo, and "ruled over Israel three years" (Judg. 9).

Tolah Judged Israel twenty-three years (Judg. 10:1–2).

Jair Judged Israel twenty-two years and "had thirty sons who rode on thirty asses; and they had thirty cities" (Judg. 10:3–5).

Jephthah Commander of a band of "worthless fellows," accepted an invitation to lead Israel in a struggle against Ammonite oppression. It was agreed that he would remain "head and leader" over the people after the Ammonites were defeated. He judged Israel six years (Judg. 10:6–12:7).

Ibzan Judged Israel seven years and "had thirty sons; and thirty daughters he gave in marriage outside his clan, and thirty daughters he brought in from outside for his sons" (Judg. 12:8–10).

Elon Judged Israel ten years (Judg. 12:11–12).

Abdon Judged Israel eight years and "had forty sons and thirty grandsons, who rode on seventy asses" (Judg. 12:13–15).

Samson A man of amazing strength, made sport of the Philistines and killed many of them at a time when they dominated Israel. Eventually captured and blinded, he killed more than three thousand Philistines at the expense of his own life. He judged Israel in the days of the Philistines "twenty years" (Judg. 13–16).

3. Jephthah[22] (Judg. 11:1–12:7) and Abimelech[23] (Judg. 9) appear to have been local warlords with private armies (9:4; 11:3) that they maintained with spoils from raids and "contributions" from those whom they "protected." With judicious use of his army, Jephthah was able to achieve official status ("leader," *qatsin*, and "head," *ro'sh*) over the clans of Gilead. Abimelech achieved a similar status over Shechem and the clans in that vicinity—indeed, the biblical account indicates that the Shechemites proclaimed him "king" (Judg. 9:6).

4. Ehud[24] (Judg. 3:15–30) and Gideon[25] (Judg. 6–8) seem to have represented another type of leader, daring men who took the initiative to muster voluntary armies from their countrymen and challenge foreign oppression. After the success of his venture, Gideon is said to have been offered the crown and to have accepted some form of permanent leadership (Judg. 8:22–28).

Religion and Cult

According to the idealistic views of the compilers of Genesis–2 Kings, the eleven secular tribes of Israel were led in worship by a twelfth tribe of priests, the Levites.[26] These Levites championed a faith in Yahweh, the national god, that contrasted sharply with the religious beliefs and practices of the indigenous peoples of the land of Canaan. It was presumed further by these compilers that Shechem and Shiloh served as central cultic shrines for all twelve of the tribes. Joshua is said to have assembled the tribes at Shechem on two occasions, for example, where he led them in ceremonies pertaining to the Mosaic law and covenant (Josh. 8:30–35; 24). The tent of meeting was brought to rest at Shiloh, according to Joshua 18:1, and Shiloh is presumed to have served as a political center for the tribes thereafter (see, for example, Josh. 21:1–2 and 22:12).

The individual stories in the book of Judges, however, as well as certain other biblical traditions and the material culture of Iron Age Palestine, suggest quite a different situation.[27] Two narratives call for special attention in this regard: the Gideon, Jerubbaal, and Abimelech narrative complex in Judges 6–9, and the story of Micah the Ephraimite in Judges 17–18. Judges 6–9 is a tangle of tradi-

---

22. See David Marcus, *Jephthah and His Vow* (Lubbock: Texas Tech Press, 1986); and Mikael Sjoberg, *Wrestling with Textual Violence: The Jephthah Narrative in Antiquity and Modernity* (Sheffield: Sheffield Phoenix, 2005).

23. See Hanoch Reviv, "The Government of Shechem in the el-Amarna Period and in the Days of Abimelech," *IEJ* 16 (1966) 252–57; Baruch Halpern, "The Rise of Abimelech Ben-Jerubbaal," *HAR* 2 (1978) 79–100; and Wolfgang Bluedorn, *Yahweh Versus Baalism: A Theological Reading of the Gideon-Abimelech Narrative* (JSOTSup 329; Sheffield: Sheffield Academic Press, 2001).

24. On the Ehud story see Robert Alter, *The Art of Biblical Narrative* (New York: Basic Books, 1981) 37–41; Baruch Halpern, *The First Historians: The Hebrew Bible and History* (San Francisco: Harper & Row, 1988) 45–58; and M. Z. Brettler, "The Ehud Story as Satire," in *The Creation of History in Ancient Israel* (London: Routledge, 1995) 79–90.

25. See J. A. Emerton, "Gideon and Jerubbaal," *JTS* 37 (1976) 289–312, and Bluedorn, *Yahweh versus Baalism*.

26. On the Levites see Benjamin Mazar, "The Cities of the Priests and the Levites," in *Congress Volume, Oxford 1959* (VTSup 7; Leiden: Brill, 1960) 193–205; Aelred Cody, *A History of Old Testament Priesthood* (AnBib 35; Rome: Pontifical Biblical Institute, 1969); Chris Hauer, "David and the Levites," *JSOT* 23 (1982) 33–54; and Risto Nurmela, *The Levites: Their Emergence as a Second-Class Priesthood* (South Florida Studies in the History of Judaism 193; Atlanta: Scholars Press, 1998).

27. On family, clan, village, and tribal religion, see E. S. Gerstenberger, *Theologies of the Old Testament* (Minneapolis: Fortress, 2002) 25–160.

tions pertaining to Gideon, Jerubbaal (equated with Gideon in these narratives), and Abimelech. The scene opens at "the oak at Ophrah," which was owned by Gideon's father, Joash the Abiezrite (6:11). The name "Joash" presupposes Yahweh worship, and Gideon is said to have encountered an angel of Yahweh (or Yahweh himself; compare 6:11 with 6:14) at the oak, to whom he offered a sacrifice of meat, bread, and broth. Then, to further commemorate the appearance, Gideon is said to have built an altar to Yahweh and named it "Yahweh is Shalom" (6:24). In a second scene (6:25–32) Gideon proceeds to pull down an altar of Baal and remove an Asherah (sacred tree? or pole? representing the female deity) also belonging to his father, and to build an altar to Yahweh on top of the "stronghold" (6:26). This nocturnally executed destruction of Baal's altar met with opposition from the men of the town, which suggests that it had served as a village shrine (see 6:24). After defeating the Midianites, Gideon made an ephod (a statue of the Deity? some special cultic object?), which he set up in his city, Ophrah.

In the Abimelech episode that follows, we read that seventy pieces of silver were taken from a temple of Baal-berith ("Baal of the Covenant"; 9:4) in Shechem and given to Abimelech for the hire of a private army. Abimelech was subsequently made king by "the oak of the pillar at Shechem" (9:6), no doubt a sacred spot like the oak at Ophrah. Later, when Abimelech attacked Shechem, he approached from the direction of "the Diviners' Oak" (9:37). The people of the city fled to "the stronghold of the temple of El-berith" ("El of the covenant"; 9:46).

According to the story of Micah the Ephraimite (Judg. 17–18), Micah took silver consecrated to Yahweh and had it fashioned into a graven/molten image (a statue of Yahweh?). Along with this image, Micah made an ephod and teraphim (statues? vestments? sacred masks?) and placed all three of these items as cultic furniture in what appears to have been essentially a family shrine. Initially he installed one of his sons as priest. Later he replaced the son with a Levite from Bethlehem in Judah. A Levite priest was apparently regarded as particularly desirable, although it should be noted that "Levite" in this episode does not seem to refer to a genealogical line, since this particular Levite is said specifically to have been from the tribe of Judah. Later on in the narrative, the Levite is recognized by his voice (18:3).

When the Danites passed through Ephraim, they seized the cultic furniture and convinced the Levite to come along with them as their priest, reminding him that it was better to be the priest for a whole tribe than for a single family (18:19). The Levite, subsequently installed in the sanctuary at Dan, is identified in 18:30 as Jonathan the son of Gershom and grandson of Moses; and his priestly line is said to have survived in Dan until the day of the captivity of the land. Micah's image, we are told finally, remained in the Danite shrine "as long as the house of God was at Shiloh" (18:31).

Admittedly these two narratives are beset with problems of interpretation. One cannot deny, however, that they reflect a general religious and cultic situation that is quite different from that presupposed by the compilers of Genesis–2 Kings. We would maintain, moreover, that these two narratives present a more accurate picture of the religious and cultic circumstances that pertained among the early Israelite tribes. Four main generalizations may be made in this regard. (1) Religion and cult as reflected in the Judges narratives had much in common with the age-old practices and symbolism of Syria-Palestine. There was certainly more continuity than contrast. (2) There were probably numerous shrines, high places, altars, and so forth scattered among the clans. Some of these sanctuaries would have been more renowned than others and, correspondingly, would have had a broader constituency. However, a close reading of the Judges narratives does not suggest a single Israelite cultic center during premonarchical times. (3) Nor do the narratives suggest that a single priestly tribe had a monopoly on cultic leadership. Indeed, there appears to have been active competition between certain priestly families or guilds. (4) Finally, although Yahwistic religion seems to have played a significant role among the people, there appears to have been nothing like a uniform religious faith that demanded allegiance to the exclusion of other forms of faith and worship.

El, Baal, and Yahweh

Some degree of continuity between the religion and cult of the "Israelite" tribes and that of the general Syro-Palestinian population should be expected. Indeed, as even the biblical narratives themselves intimate, many of the shrines that had been active during the Bronze Age continued in use among the tribes, in many cases no doubt still with their hereditary priestly families in charge. Several of the patriarchal narratives were probably intended to address this matter. That is, they condone worship at these old Bronze Age shrines by claiming that the Israelite ancestors worshiped at these places long ago and in some instances actually founded the shrines. Thus Abraham is associated with the holy places at Shechem (Gen. 12:6–7), Bethel (12:8), Beer-sheba (21:33), and Mamre near Hebron (13:18); Isaac with Beer-sheba (26:23–25); and Jacob with Shechem (33:18–20) and Bethel (28:10–22).

The Genesis narratives, particularly those that associate the patriarchs with the old Bronze Age sanctuaries, and indeed the name "Israel" itself, imply that Israel's earliest ancestors were worshipers of the deity El (Gen. 16:13; 17:1; 21:33; 31:13; 35:7,11; 43:14; 48:3).[28] Jacob, for example, is said to have built an altar at Bethel and called it "El-bethel" (35:7; see 31:13). Similarly, on property purchased near the city of Shechem, he is said to have erected an altar which he called "El-Elohe-Israel," which would mean "El the God of Israel" (33:20). In Ugaritic texts dating from the fourteenth and thirteenth centuries B.C.E. (see chapter 2), El is the high god, the chief deity in the Syro-Palestinian pantheon. He is presented as the father of years, humankind, and the other gods; and generally depicted as a peace-loving divinity whose will lies behind the operations of the divine and human worlds, although he is at times harassed by the lesser gods and goddesses. In this latter regard, it is interesting to note that the patriarchal worship of El is always placed within a nonmilitary context, unlike the militant Yahwism reflected in the book of Judges.

Some among the Israelite clans and tribes apparently worshiped other Syro-Palestinian gods as well, particularly Baal, known in Ugaritic literature as a

---

28. M. H. Pope, *El in the Ugaritic Texts* (VTSup 2; Leiden: Brill, 1955); F. M. Cross, *Canaanite Myth and Hebrew Epic* (Cambridge: Harvard University Press, 1973) 3–75; and C. E. L'Heureux, *Rank Among the Canaanite Gods* (HSM 21; Missoula, MT; Scholars Press, 1979).

26. *Baal*. Unearthed in the excavations at Ras Shamra (ancient Ugarit), this stela represents a Canaanite deity, probably to be identified with Baal. As the god of storm and rain, Baal was known throughout Syria-Palestine. He holds in his left hand a lance, the shaft of which is a stylized representation of a tree or lightning bolt. (145 cm. high; *The Louvre*)

dying and rising but virile and active god of vegetation and the seasonal cycle.[29] Often mentioned in connection with Baal altars is Asherah, probably a symbol of the female consort of Baal. But it was Yahweh who emerged as the national god of Israel and Judah, although he was probably never worshiped exclusively. Also we must presume, for the reasons given below, that Yahweh would have been perceived and worshiped in much the same fashion as the other gods of the Syro-Palestinian pantheon.

That Yahwism and Baalism existed alongside each other with essentially the same cultic procedures and paraphernalia is apparent, for example, from the Gideon stories summarized above. Yahweh appears first to Gideon at a sacred oak on the family property. Also Gideon's father's name implies Yahweh worship ("Joash," meaning "Yahweh gives" or "Yahweh has given"). Yet we find that the family had a Baal altar as well and an associated Asherah. It is possible, of course, that the scene in which Gideon destroys the Baal altar and Asherah was introduced by later editors in an attempt to render him a more "orthodox" Yahwist. Even taking into account the possibility of extensive secondary editing of the Gideon stories, however, one still has the impression that the lines of distinction between Yahwism and Baalism were vague. The Micah

29. See P. J. van Zijl, *Baal: A Study of Texts in Connexion with Baal in the Ugaritic Epics* (AOAT 206; Neukirchen-Vluyn: Neukirchener Verlag, 1972).

story has a graven/molten image—quite possibly an idol of Yahweh himself—in a Yahwistic shrine. Texts from the late ninth or early eighth century B.C.E. discovered at Kuntillet Ajrud, a caravan or military way station in the southern Negeb, refers to Yahweh and "his Asherah."[30]

Archaeological evidence indicates an essentially continuous religious and cultic scene throughout Palestine during the early centuries of the Iron Age. Nothing has been discovered, in other words, that suggests any notable distinctiveness in temple layout or cultic furniture for the tribal territories described above. Continuity between early Israelite religion and that of the other inhabitants of Syria-Palestine is confirmed further by parallels between the religious and cultic terminology of the biblical materials and the corresponding terminology of extrabiblical documents. Elements of Syro-Palestinian mythology, such as a divine struggle with the cosmic dragon of chaos, also appear here and there in biblical poetry. Indeed, occasional biblical passages suggest that Yahweh was once viewed as a member of the large pantheon ruled over by El. For example, Deuteronomy speaks of the primordial time

> When the Most High [Elyon] apportioned the nations,
>   when he divided humankind,
> he fixed the boundaries of the peoples
>   according to the number of the gods;
> Yahweh's own portion was his people,
>   Jacob his allotted share.
>
> (Deut. 32:8–9)

The origins of Yahwism are hidden in mystery. Even the final edited form of Genesis–2 Kings presents diverse views on the matter. Thus Genesis 4:16, attributed by literary critics to the so-called Yahwistic source, traces the worship of Yahweh back to the earliest days of the human race, while other passages trace the revelation and worship of Yahweh back to Moses (Exod. 6:3).

Several factors may indicate a southern provenance for early Yahwism.[31] It was in Midian, south of Palestine, according to Exodus 3, that Moses first encountered Yahweh. Moses is said to have married a Midianite wife whose father was a priest of Yahweh (Exod. 18). The Midianites seem to have been closely related to the Kenites, moreover, who in turn also were associated with southern Palestine and were afforded a special protective status by the Israelites (see, e.g., 1 Sam. 15:6). Israelite poets sang of Jael, a Kenite heroine in

---

30. For a translation of the inscriptions see *COS* 2:171–73 (with bibliography); for the excavations and presentation of the finds, see Ze'ev Meshel, "Did Yahweh Have a Consort? The New Religious Inscriptions from the Sinai," *BAR* 5/2 (1979) 24–35. For Asherah see John Day, "Asherah in the Hebrew Bible and Northwest Semitic Literature," *JBL* 105 (1986) 385–408; Baruch Margalit, "The Meaning and Significance of Asherah," *VT* (1990) 264–97; S. A. Wiggins, *A Reassessment of 'Asherah'* (AOAT 235; Neukirchen-Vluyn: Neukirchener Verlag, 1993); Tilde Binger, *Asherah: Goddesses in Ugarit, Israel and the Old Testament* (JSOTSup 212; Sheffield: Sheffield Academic Press, 1994); and W. G. Dever, *Did God Have a Wife? Archeology and Folk Religion in Ancient Israel* (Grand Rapids: Eerdmans, 2005). Normally Hebrew does not add a pronominal suffix to a personal name; thus many scholars understand Asherah as an object; see J. H. Tigay, "A Second Temple Parallel to the Blessings from Kuntillet 'Ajrud," *IEJ* 40 (1990) 218.

31. The name "Yahweh" makes its first appearance in nonbiblical texts as a place name in southern Transjordan in an Egyptian text; see M. C. Astour, "Yahweh in Egyptian Topographical Lists," in Manfred Görg and Edgar Pusch, eds., *Ägypten und Altes Testament. Festschrift Elmar Edel* (Bamberg: Biblische Notizen, 1979) 17–34. See also Rowley, *From Joseph to Joshua.*

Yahweh's wars (Judg. 5:24–30). Finally, certain poetical texts associate Yahweh in a special way with the south, and speak of Yahweh coming from that area to aid Israel in warfare.

> Yahweh, when you went out from Seir,
>> when you marched from the region of Edom,
> the earth trembled,
>> and the heavens poured,
>> the clouds indeed poured water.
> The mountains quaked before Yahweh, the One of Sinai,
>> before Yahweh, the God of Israel.
>> (Judg. 5:4–5)

> Yahweh came from Sinai,
>> and dawned from Seir upon us;
>> he shone forth from Mount Paran.
> With him were myriads of holy ones,
>> at his right, a host of his own.
>> (Deut. 33:2)

Although the location of Mount Sinai remains uncertain, biblical texts consistently locate the sacred mountain to the south or southeast of Palestine proper.

The spread of Yahwism and its acceptance among the tribal groups were probably gradual phenomena that would have resulted in local forms of Yahwism varying from place to place. Such local varieties are suggested by passages that refer to Yahweh followed by a place name. Thus 1 Samuel 1:3 refers to "Yahweh Sebaoth in Shiloh" and 2 Samuel 15:7 speaks of "Yahweh in Hebron." Depending on a not entirely certain reading, the texts from Kuntillet Ajrud mentioned above may refer to "Yahweh of Samaria" and "Yahweh of Teman." Micah, like perhaps many other prominent heads of extended families, possessed a family shrine dedicated to Yahweh and in which his son served for a time as priest (Judg. 17). The story of Gideon reveals the practice of Yahwism at the clan/village level (6:11–32). Tribal Yahwism can be seen in the case of the shrine at Dan and the service of the Levite at the tribal center there (Judg. 18). Trans-tribal Yahwism may be suggested in the gathering of Naphtali and Zebulun on Mount Tabor under the direction of the prophetess Deborah (4:10–13).

Perhaps the most noticeable characteristic of Yahweh in Israel's early poetry and narrative literature is his militancy. The so-called Song of the Sea in Exodus 15:1–18 and the Song of Deborah in Judges 5 are typical in their praise of Yahweh, the Divine Warrior, who could be counted on to intervene on behalf of his followers. At Shiloh he was called "Yahweh Sebaoth," that is, "Yahweh of the armies" (1 Sam. 1:3); and the story about David and Goliath has David challenging the giant in the name of "Yahweh Sebaoth, the God of the armies of Israel" (1 Sam. 17:45). Most of the Judges narratives point to a strong connection between Yahweh and warfare. Similarly they suggest that it was during military undertakings that the tribes joined together in a common cause that transcended local interest. Thus it may have been primarily in connection with wars that Yahweh gained status as Israel's national god. During times of peace the tribes would have depended heavily on Baal in his various local forms to ensure fertility. But when they came together to wage war against their common enemies, they would have turned to Yahweh, the Divine Warrior who could provide victory.[32]

Priestly Lines and Houses

Just as the compilers of Genesis–2 Kings tended to subsume numerous and diverse tribal groups under an artificial twelve-tribe scheme, so also they sought to subsume diverse priestly groups under the rubric of the tribe of Levi.[33] The resulting "Levitical genealogy" that emerges is shown in Chart 7. That this is an artificial genealogy is indicated both by its internal discrepancies (see the notes to Chart 7) and the several narratives in the books of Exodus and Numbers that witness to competition and conflict between different priestly lines (Exod. 32; Lev. 10:1–7; Num. 11–12; 16). The Levites themselves may have been a local priestly group from the Judahite city of Bethlehem, David's home, that rose to prominence with the Davidic dynasty. Note that both Levites who appear in the narratives of Judges 17–21 had some connection with Bethlehem (17:7–8; 19:1). Also, as we shall see below, David may have made extensive use of the Levites in his administration.

The genealogical fragment embedded in Numbers 26:58 recognizes five priestly groups, also from the southern hill country, that may or may not have been regarded originally as Levites: Libnites, Hebronites, Mahlites (missing from Greek texts), Mushites (i.e., "Mosesites"), and Korahites. The first two of these five correspond to southern towns (Libnah and Hebron). The last two represent priestly lines that appear elsewhere in the biblical traditions. Numbers 16, for example, reports an uprising by the Korahites that supposedly resulted in their annihilation by divine intervention. Yet the Korahites will appear again. In fact, several of the psalms are attributed to them (Pss. 42; 44–49; 84–85; 87–88), and their presence in southern Judah during the late monarchical period is witnessed by an ostracon discovered near the entrance of the Iron Age sanctuary at Arad.[34] The narratives in which Moses functions as a priest or is concerned with priestly matters may reflect, in some indirect fashion, the priestly role of the Mushite (or Moses) line. If so, we may speculate further that the Mushites had connections (as does Moses in the narratives) with an ancient sanctuary at Kadesh(-barnea). Noticeable especially in this regard is Exodus 15:22–26, which assumes that Marah in the vicinity of Kadesh was the place where Moses received the law. Note also that the Levite who figures in the narrative of Judges 17–18 is identified as a direct descendant of Gershom son of Moses and is said to have initiated a priestly line that served at Dan "until the day of the captivity of the land" (Judg. 17:7; 18:30).

32. On Israelite war see Gerhard von Rad, *Holy War in Ancient Israel*, trans. and ed. M. J. Dawn (Grand Rapids: Eerdmans, 1991); and Susan Niditch, *War in the Hebrew Bible: A Study in the Ethics of Violence* (New York: Oxford University Press, 1993). For the classical statement of the close association of early Yahwism and warfare, see Julius Wellhausen, *Prolegomena to the History of Israel* (Edinburgh: Adam & Charles Black, 1885). On Yahweh as a warrior deity, see P. D. Miller, *The Divine Warrior in Early Israel* (HSM 5; Cambridge: Harvard University Press, 1973).
33. See the works in n. 26 above and F. M. Cross, *Canaanite Myth and Hebrew Epic* (Cambridge: Harvard University Press, 1973) 195–215.
34. J. M. Miller, "The Korahites of Southern Judah," *CBQ* 32 (1970) 58–68.

CHART 7. Levite Genealogy according to Genesis–2 Kings

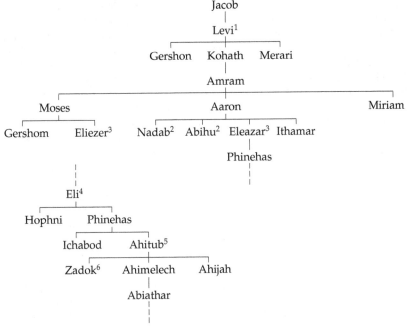

The Levite genealogy is a composite derived from several texts in Genesis–2 Kings and must be qualified at several points:

1. The lineage from Levi through Phinehas is provided in Exod. 6:16–25; 18:3–4; Josh. 21:1; 22:13; 24:33. Miriam is not mentioned in these passages, but is included in this chart on the basis of Exod. 15:20. Note also the genealogical fragments in Num. 26:58, which recognizes five main Levitical families (Libnites, Hebronites, Mahlites, Mushites, and Korahites).

2. It is perhaps not by accident that the first two sons of Aaron (Nadab and Abihu) have names almost identical to those of Jeroboam I (Nadab and Abijah). Both Aaron and Jeroboam are also associated with apostate worship of golden calves.

3. Several priestly figures bear variations of the names Eliezer, including Moses' son Eliezer (Exod. 18:4), Aaron's son Eleazar (Exod. 6:23), and Eleazar the son of Abinadab who took charge of the ark after it had been removed from the Philistine (1 Sam. 7:1). This was apparently a popular priestly name (see also Ezra 10:18 and 1 Esd. 9:19). But we must consider also the possibility that an early Eleazar remembered to have been associated with the ark has been introduced into the Genesis–2 Kings account at more than one place.

4. The priests in charge of the ark at Shiloh in the books of Joshua and Judges are Eleazar and Phinehas, the son and grandson of Aaron (Josh. 21:1; 22:13; 24:33; Judg. 20:28). As the narration continues in 1 Samuel we find the ark still at Shiloh, but in the hands of Eli and his two sons, Phinehas and Hophni. Presumably we are to conclude that Eli was a descendant of Phinehas son of Eleazar son of Aaron. Yet this is never actually stated. Moreover, we must consider whether the name Eli is also a variation of the name Eleazar, in spite of the fact that it begins with a different consonant (*'ayin* rather than *'aleph*). In the latter case, we may be dealing with parallel traditions—that is, the Eleazar and Phinehas supposedly associated with the ark in the days of Moses, Joshua, and the judges may be none other than Eli and Phinehas of Shiloh whom the compilers of Genesis–2 Kings projected back into the earlier period.

5. The Eli>Phinehas>Ahitub>Ahimelech>Abiathar lineage depicted in the genealogy chart is derived from 1 Sam. 14:3; 22:9; 1 Kgs. 2:26–27. Yet 1 Sam. 14:3, which connects Ahitub with the house of Eli, appears to have undergone secondary editing. The original text probably read something like "and Ahijah son of Phinehas son of Eli."

6. 2 Sam. 8:17 identifies Zadok as the son of Ahitub and thus also a descendant of Eli, assuming of course the Ahitub/Elide connection called into question above. However, this verse is also problematic on several grounds: (a) It identifies Ahimelech as the son of Abiathar rather than the other way around (cf. 1 Sam. 22:9). (b) 1 Chr. 6:1–8 traces Zadok's ancestry back to Aaron by a different line that bypasses the Elides. (c) Other lines of evidence discussed in this chapter suggest that the Zadokites represented a separate priestly line altogether from either the Levites or the Elides.

The Aaronites were apparently another quite separate priestly line.[35] Moreover, Aaron is presented in a negative fashion in certain stories that themselves seem to anticipate and serve as polemic against the sanctuary of Jeroboam I at Bethel. Specifically, Exodus 32 depicts Aaron as an apostate priest who builds a golden calf for worship while Moses is away from the camp. The Levites stand over against Aaron in the narrative, siding with Moses and executing vengeance on the people who had participated in the calf worship. Leviticus 10:1–7, on the other hand, relates how Aaron's two sons, Nadab and Abihu, were killed because of improper ritual activities. Note that Jeroboam I, in addition to being accused of introducing golden calves at Bethel and Dan, had two sons who also met untimely deaths. Moreover, their names correspond to the names of Aaron's wayward sons (compare Nadab and Abihu in Lev. 10:1 with Nadab and Abijah in 1 Kgs. 14:1–18; 15:25–32). All of this seems to suggest a connection of some sort between the Aaronites and the Bethel sanctuary. These two narratives that depict Aaron in a negative light contrast with the one in Numbers 17–18, however, which affirms the prominence of Aaron and the Aaronites in Israelite worship. Also, at least one bit of evidence raises the possibility that the Aaronite priests were of southern origin. Specifically, the Aaronite Jehoiada who, according to 1 Chronicles 12:27, was with the Levites who joined David at Hebron may be the same Jehoiada who is identified in 2 Samuel 23:20 as the father of one of David's officers. This latter Jehoiada, father of Benaiah, was from the southern town of Kabzeel.

Other priestly lines, such as the Elides of Shiloh, the priests of Nob, and the Zadokites, will receive attention in later chapters. As we shall see, the editors of Genesis–2 Kings attempted, not very convincingly, to connect these also with the Levitical line.

Shechem and Shiloh

The Judges narratives suggest that the typical sanctuary of the Israelite tribes was a local operation serving one or several clans/villages or perhaps one or two tribes at the most. We learn from the Gideon and Micah stories, moreover, how a single family could set up its own shrine, altar, and sanctuary. The Judges narratives do not support, by contrast, the idea that Shechem and Shiloh were key cultic centers for the Israelite tribes during premonarchical times.

Shechem.[36] Shechem was one of the Bronze Age cities that continued into the Iron Age, and archaeology has revealed that this city possessed a major temple that apparently remained in use into the Iron Age. Also the Abimelech narrative speaks of one or two temples in the city dedicated to Baal/El-berith (Judg. 9). Nearby, but outside the city, was a sacred oak, variously called "the oak of Moreh" and "the Diviners' Oak" (Gen. 12:6; 35:4; Judg. 9:37). This latter sacred spot, along with Mount Ebal and Mount Gerizim, may have been the place that

---

35. R. H. Kennett, "Origin of the Aaronite Priesthood," *JTS* 6 (1905) 161–86; F. S. North, "Aaron's Rise in Prestige," *ZAW* 66 (1954) 191–99; and Moses Aberbach and Leivy Smolar, "Aaron, Jeroboam, and the Golden Calves," *JBL* 86 (1967) 129–40.

36. On Shechem see Eduard Nielsen, *Shechem: A Traditio-Historical Investigation* (Copenhagen: Gad, 1959); G. E. Wright, *Shechem: The Biography of a Biblical City* (New York: McGraw-Hill, 1965); and G. R. H. Wright, "Temples at Shechem," *ZAW* 80 (1968) 1–35.

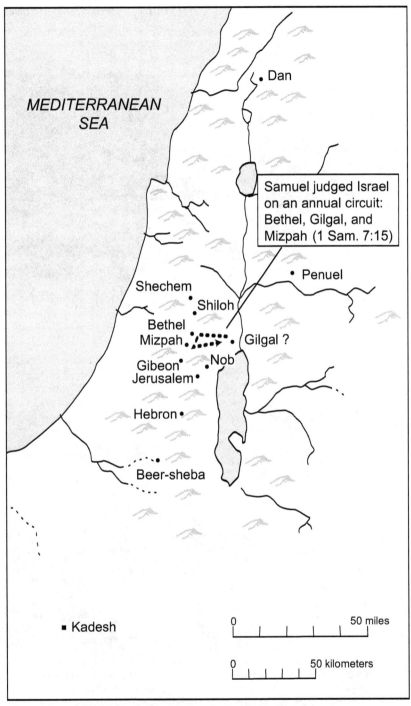

MAP 12. Cultic Centers in the Narratives about
the Early Tribal Period

27. *Shechem.* Ruins of Tell Balatah, ancient Shechem, situated on the slopes of Mount Gerizim. These ruins are surrounded today by the modern city of Nablus.

28. *Shechem temple.* Remains of a Middle–Late Bronze Age temple at Tell Balatah (ancient Shechem) that probably continued in use into the Iron Age. The people in the foreground are standing around a huge limestone slab that was erected in front of the temple. Others behind them are standing in ruins of the temple itself. The whole complex is surrounded by a modern retaining wall intended to protect the ancient ruins from erosion. Still further in the background is Mount Gerizim.

the narrator of Genesis 22 had in mind when speaking of the land of Moriah with its mountains (Gen. 22:2; cf. Gen. 12:6; Judg. 7:1; but see 2 Chr. 3:1).

Two passages in Joshua (Josh. 8 and 24) identify Shechem as a place of worship for the tribes, but literary critics have long since recognized that much, if not all, of the material in these passages derives from the compilers of Genesis–2 Kings. Indeed, the Abimelech story seems to treat Shechem as an essentially non-Israelite city. The editorial stress on Shechem in Joshua 8 and 24 may be less reflective of Shechem's actual role during premonarchical times than it is indicative of the importance of the city in the later kingdom of Israel.

Shiloh.[37] The compilers of Genesis–2 Kings present Shiloh as the major religious and political center for all the tribes during the post-conquest period (Josh. 18:1; 19:51; 21:1–2; etc.). If that were the case, however, it is surprising that Shiloh appears in only one of the Judges narratives, Judges 19–21. Even more surprising is the role that Shiloh plays in this particular narrative.

Judges 19–21 describes a conflict between the Benjaminites and the remainder of Israel. At some point during the hostilities, according to the narrative, the other tribes mustered for battle vowed never again to give any of their daughters to Benjaminites in marriage. Once the Benjaminites were defeated, however, they had second thoughts about the matter. Thus the narrative concludes with raids on Jabesh-gilead and Shiloh in order to secure wives for the Benjaminites. Jabesh-gilead was regarded as an appropriate source for wives, since, as it is explained in Judges 21:12, representatives of this city were not present when the vow was taken. Why Shiloh was considered appropriate is less clear.

> So the elders of the congregation said, "What shall we do for wives for those who are left, since there are no women left in Benjamin?" And they said, "There must be heirs for the survivors of Benjamin, in order that a tribe may not be blotted out from Israel. Yet we cannot give any of our daughters to them as wives." For the Isralites had sworn, "Cursed by anyone who gives a wife to Benjamin." So they said, "Look, the yearly festival of Yahweh is taking place at Shiloh, which is north of Bethel, on the east of the highway that goes up from Bethel to Shechem, and south of Lebonah." And they instructed the Benjaminites, saying, "Go and lie in wait in the vineyards, and watch; when the young women of Shiloh come out to dance in the dances, then come out of the vineyards and each of you carry off a wife for himself from the young women of Shiloh, and go to the land of Benjamin. Then if their fathers or their brothers come to complain to us, we will say to them, 'Be generous and allow us to have them; because we did not capture in battle a wife for each man. But neither did you incur guilt by giving your daughters to them." (Judg. 21:16–22)

The narrative has been edited to bring it into line with the idealistic views of the late compilers of Genesis–2 Kings—thus the references to Phinehas's presence with the ark at Bethel (Judg. 20:27–28), the note about returning to the "camp" at Shiloh after the raid on Jabesh-gilead (21:12), and the rather legalistic observation that the Shilohites could not be accused of breaking the vow

---

37. On Shiloh see D. G. Schley, *Shiloh: A Biblical City in Tradition and History* (JSOTSup 63; Sheffield: JSOT Press, 1989); and Israel Finkelstein et al., eds., *Shiloh: The Archaeology of a Biblical Site* (Tel Aviv: Institute of Archaeology, 1993).

29. *Shiloh buildings*. Isometric reconstruction of Iron I buildings excavated at Khirbet Seilun, ancient Shiloh. The assemblage of pottery vessels shown in photograph 30 came from the room to the left. (Courtesy of Israel Finkelstein)

because their daughters had been taken by force. Scholars have long suspected that the story recalls an ancient conflict of much more limited scope—possibly a struggle between Benjamin and Ephraim, or between the Ephraimites and the individual town of Gibeah. One gets the impression also that in the pre-edited version of the story Shiloh was regarded as foreign territory. Obviously the note in 21:12, which has the Israelites returning to the camp at Shiloh after the raid at Jabesh-gilead, makes no sense in a story that a few verses later will have the "elders of the congregation" explaining to the Benjaminites where Shiloh is located, almost as if they had never heard of the place, and then encouraging the Benjaminites to steal women from there. Moreover, we are still left with the question as to why Shiloh was regarded as an appropriate source for captive women. A likely explanation, in our opinion, is that the preedited version of this story did not presume Shiloh to be an important administrative or cultic center for the Israelites (or whoever took the vow). Indeed the Shiloh-ites, in spite of the fact that they were apparently worshipers of Yahweh, seem to be regarded as non-Israelites.

Shiloh clearly is later viewed as both Yahwistic and Israelite in the stories about Samuel at Shiloh (1 Sam. 1–3), to which we will turn our attention in the next chapter. Yet these stories further complicate matters by indicating that there was a "temple" at Shiloh in addition to a tent of meeting (cf. 1 Sam. 1:7,

30. *Restored pottery from Shiloh.* Restored pottery from the Iron Age I building excavated at ancient Shiloh. See photograph 29. (Courtesy of Israel Finkelstein)

24; 2:22; 3:15) and that the temple, housing the ark (3:3; 4:4), was under the care of the priestly family of Eli.

Defining Early Israel

We need to address now a question that has loomed in the background of our discussion from the beginning: What was Israel? If Israel did not consist of twelve tribes descended from the twelve sons of Jacob, then what sort of entity was it? How might one have defined an "Israelite" or an "Israelite tribe" during the early centuries of the Iron Age before there was a kingdom of Israel? This question cannot be answered entirely satisfactorily or conclusively. But we can sharpen up the question a bit and perhaps make some progress toward a provisional answer. We begin by reviewing some of our earlier observations.

1. A reasonable case can be made that early Israel was connected in some way with the small agricultural settlements that began to appear in the Palestinian highlands at the close of the Late Bronze Age and the beginning of the Iron Age. The name "Israel" finds its first mention in epigraphical sources at that time (Merneptah Inscription), and many of the biblical traditions have as their setting an early time, "before any king lived at Israel," when "Israelite" tribes were settled in the highland regions. However, we cannot simply equate the early Israelites with the Early Iron Age highland settlers, because the same biblical materials assume the presence of non-Israelites in the same regions. Archaeologists are unable to determine from the archaeological evidence which settlements were Israelite and which were not.

2. "Hebrew" and "Israelite" were not synonymous terms. "Hebrew," perhaps related to the Akkadian term *Apiru/Habiru*, would have referred to a social class rather than to any particular ethnic group. A Hebrew was someone who, for one reason or another, was considered marginal to established society—transients, minorities, rebels, outlaws. Abraham, the eponymous ancestor of the Hebrews (Gen. 14:13), is depicted as an immigrant from Ur of the Chaldeans who pitched his tent near the oaks of Mamre and kept a respectable distance from the cities of the plain. Note that the biblical genealogies identify him as ancestor not only of the Israelites, but also of the Ishmaelites and various other peoples as well. The Israelite villagers may have been especially aware of their Hebrew roots and status, but so would some of the other peoples in the pluralistic mix of Palestinian society during the Early Iron Age.

3. Also we need to distinguish between the terms "Israel/Israelite" and "Judah/Judahite." The Hebrew Bible (note that this is modern terminology) is a product of Judah, the southern kingdom; or more accurately a product of Jewish religious leaders who were active after the Babylonian destruction of the Jewish state. These Jewish theologians, active a century or more after the northern kingdom of Israel had ceased to exist, saw Judah as the legitimate heir of ancient Israel, and it is with them that the names "Israel" and "Judah" began to converge. That convergence is now complete with the modern state of Israel— whose "Jewish" founders chose the name "Israel" and revived and adjusted for modern times the language of the Bible called now "Modern Hebrew." However, even the compilers of Genesis–2 Kings did not totally equate Israel and Judah, which for them was but one of twelve Israelite tribes; and our examination of the materials embedded in their account of Israel's origins has revealed that Judah was essentially absent from the "Israelite" scene before the time of David. This matter will require more attention in a later chapter. For the moment, it is sufficient to say that the Israelites and Judahites were neighboring peoples, with much in common, whose histories became entangled.

4. In attempting to define early Israel, we must be mindful that ethnicity is a slippery concept, and that even today we use loose and ill-defined terminology when referring to various groups of peoples. Often it is unclear, or it depends on the context, whether a name is to be understood as primarily a geographical designation, a political designation, or a cultural-ethnic designation. Ethnicity-related names also take on different connotations over time, and may be used as a very general designation in one context or as a rather specific reference in another. Accordingly, it is doubtful that even the ancient Israelites themselves, or their neighbors, would have been able to agree on a crisp definition for "Israel" or "Israelite," and they quite likely would have used these terms differently in different contexts. Thus analyzing how the name "Israel" is used in the Merneptah Inscription will take us only so far toward determining how the name might have been used locally in Palestine. We have observed, for example, that Merneptah's scribe may have had little specific information about Israel and seems to have used the name in a generalized fashion to encompass all the peoples of the Palestinian interior.[38] Compare that to the way the name is used in a local folk story that reflects close familiarity with the central hill country. A Levite, his concubine, and a servant were on their way from Bethlehem to their home in Ephraimite territory. "When they were near Jebus, the day was far spent, and the servant said to the master, 'Come now, let us turn aside to this city of the Jebusites, and spend the night in it.' But his master said to him, 'We will not turn aside into the city of foreigners, who do not belong to the people of Israel; but we will pass on to Gibeah'" (Judg. 19:11–12).

5. We introduced earlier in this chapter the concept of gradual tribalization—the idea that tribal identity developed over time among families and

---

38. This same phenomenon may be illustrated with the name "Moab," which likewise makes its first appearance in epigraphical (Egyptian) sources at the close of the New Kingdom/Late Bronze Age. For the Egyptian scribes, "Moab" seems to have referred generally and inclusively to both the region east of the Dead Sea and the people who lived there. In the Mesha Inscription, however, a local Moabite inscription, the "men of Gad" were apparently not regarded as Moabites even though they had lived in the area from of old.

clans living in close proximity to one another—and recognized that this sense of tribal identity would not have been totally inclusive of everyone living in the tribal area. The same was probably true of Israelite identity; that is, the sense of "Israelite" kinship and solidarity probably emerged gradually, remained somewhat vague, and did not apply to everyone settled in "Israelite" areas. In addition to the fact that they were neighbors with similar lifestyles, three other factors would have contributed to the sense of mutual identity among the Israelite tribes: ancestry and social status; common enemies and occasions of joint warfare; and identification with Yahweh.

Ancestry and Social Status. The early Israelites seem to have recognized that they were largely of *Apiru*/Hebrew ancestry. Many of their non-Israelite neighbors, on the other hand, to the extent that they are remembered in the biblical materials, were remnants of Bronze Age urban society (Canaanites, Amorites, Hittites, etc.). No doubt these neighbors regarded themselves to be of "superior stock." Especially the Philistines, secure in their cities along the coast, must have considered the villagers of the interior as backward people, ripe for raiding or more systematic exploitation. In 1 Samuel 13–14, for example, the Philistines fighting Saul are heard to say, "Look, Hebrews are coming out of the holes where they have hid themselves" (14:11). In a later account, when David and his mercenaries showed up prepared to fight with the Philistines against Saul and the Israelites, the Philistines ask, "What are these Hebrews doing here?" (29:3). They might have said, "Look, hillbillies are coming out of the holes," or "What are these outlaws doing here?"

Common Enemies. Common enemies (such as the Philistines) would have required the emerging "Israelite" tribes to join together in warfare from time to time, and this in turn would have encouraged a sense of solidarity. Note that most of the stories in the book of Judges and 1–2 Samuel have to do with warfare. Observe also that these stories suggest only an emerging sense of solidarity, rather than any sort of formal tribal alliance with firm commitments. Even the so-called Song of Deborah, which is often cited as an early poetic celebration of a unified Israelite victory, mentions only ten tribes; and only five of the tribes mentioned seem to have shown up for the battle (Judg. 5:12–18).

Identification with Yahweh.[39] It was probably in connection with warfare that Yahweh emerged as the chief deity of the Israelites, and this reinforced in turn their sense of mutual solidarity. As we have seen, Yahweh's militancy seems to have been his most noticeable characteristic, and especially in the Judges narratives there is a strong connection between Yahweh and warfare. During times of peace the tribes may have turned to Baal in his various forms to ensure fertility. But when they came together for warfare, joining together in common cause that transcended local interests, they turned to Yahweh the Divine Warrior who could provide victory.

All three of these factors seem to have converged under the leadership of Saul, a Benjaminite, who managed to expel the Philistines from the hill country, lift an Ammonite siege against one of the Gileadite cities, and eventually

---

39. On the problems associated with understanding early Yahwism, see the essays in D. V. Edelman, ed., *The Triumph of Elohim: From Yahwisms to Judaisms* (Grand Rapids: Eerdmans, 1996). For a conservative approach to the issues, see J. C. de Moor, *The Rise of Yahwism: The Roots of Israelite Monotheism* (BETL 91; Leuven: Leuven University Press/Peeters, 1990).

extend the net of Israelite "protection" even into Judahite territory. Saul, as we shall see, may have been closely aligned with the Elide priests of Shiloh.

6. The biblical traditions pertaining to premonarchical times, especially the narratives in the book of Judges, seem to focus on the tribe of Ephraim along with certain neighboring clans and tribes that were closely aligned with Ephraim. Ephraim and its satellite clans and tribes probably represented the earliest identifiable Israel.

Note that the Genesis stories about Jacob, also named "Israel" (Gen. 32:27–28; 35:10), have their setting primarily in the territory of these Ephraimite-related tribes. Joseph and Benjamin are depicted as favorite sons of Jacob/Israel, with Benjamin as the younger. Manasseh and Ephraim are identified as Joseph's sons, in turn, with Manasseh as the older and Ephraim the one destined to dominate (Gen. 48). The occasional references to "the house of Joseph" in the book of Joshua clearly pertain to these three related tribes—Ephraim/Benjamin and Manasseh (see Josh. 17:14–18).

The conquest stories in Joshua 1–9 are primarily local etiologies pertaining to southern Ephraim/Benjamin. Thus the accounts of the conquest of Jericho (Josh. 6) and Ai (Josh. 7–8) explain the existence of two prominent tells in that area (Tell es-Sultan and et-Tell) by attributing their destruction to Joshua.[40] Joshua himself, a hazy and legendary figure, was apparently an Ephraimite hero: he received his inheritance in Ephraim and was buried there (Josh. 19:49–50; 24:29–30). Key figures in the Judges narratives include Ehud (Judg. 3:15–30) and Deborah (Judg. 4–5) from southern Ephraim/Benjamin; Gideon from Ophrah in Manasseh and his son Abimelech (Judg. 6:11, 15; 9); and Jephthah, who led the Gileadites to victory over the Ammonites (10:6–12:7). Most of the so-called minor judges listed in 10:1–5 and 12:8–15 were from one or another of the Ephraim-related tribes. Tola was a man of Issachar but lived and was buried at Shamir in the hill country of Ephraim (10:1–2). Jair, like Jephthah, was a Gileadite (10:3–5), and Abdon was from "Pirathon in the land of Ephraim, in the hill country of the Amalekites" (12:13–15). Only Ibzan and Elon appear to have been from outside the Ephraim-related group, but even they may have been associated with the group in one way or another. For example, Elon is said to have been buried at Aijalon in the land of Zebulun (12:11–12), but the only Aijalon known in the Bible was in the southwestern Benjaminite area.

Not only are Ephraim/Benjamin and Manasseh at the center of the action in the Judges narratives, but also we have noted hints that the Ephraimites were the dominant tribe of this cluster. The story of Jacob/Israel's blessing in Genesis 48 implies Ephraimite dominance over Manasseh. Ephraim and Benjamin are praised in the Song of Deborah for taking the lead in the battle (Judg. 5). In two of the Judges narratives—the stories about Gideon and Jephthah—the Ephraimites seem to feel that they have some authority over the actions of the Manassites and Gileadites. When Gideon mustered a volunteer army and expelled Midianite raiders from the Jezreel Valley, the Ephraimites upbraided him for undertaking the venture without calling them (7:24–8:3). When Jephthah

---

40. This does not square with the results of archaeological excavations at the two sites, however, which demonstrate that the ruins actually date primarily from the Early and Middle Bronze ages.

led the Gileadites into battle against the Ammonites, the Ephraimites threatened to burn Gileadite houses because they had attacked without notifying them.

To summarize, the designation "Israel" probably referred rather loosely at first to certain clans and tribes settled in the north-central hill country. These earliest Israelites would have been conscious of their largely *Apiru*/Hebrew ancestry, which tended to set them apart from other peoples also living in the hill country as well as in other parts of Palestine, and occasionally they joined together under the banner of Yahweh in warfare against common enemies. But there does not appear to have any sort of formal tribal alliance, or supertribal "Israelite" leadership, and even the designation "Israel" may have been more narrowly or broadly intended, depending on the context and circumstances.

At the core of this emerging sense of Israelite identity were the clans of Ephraim settled in the north-central hill country. In its narrowest sense, "Israel" may have been essentially synonymous with "Ephraim." But used more broadly, it would have included the tribes clustered around Ephraim— Benjamin (sometimes and probably originally considered part of Ephraim), Gilead (probably including Ephraimite clans that had migrated eastward across the Jordan), Manasseh, Machir, Jair, and Nobah (the last three closely related to Manasseh in the same fashion as Benjamin was related to Ephraim). Merneptah's scribe, from the distant Egyptian vantage point, used the name "Israel" even more broadly to refer to all of the peoples of the Palestinian hinterland.

We shall see in due course that, in addition to commanding center stage in the patriarchal, conquest, and judges narratives, Ephraim and its satellite tribes were center stage as well for the stories about Eli, Samuel, and Saul, that they represented the core of Saul's Israel, that they remained a contentious element in the Davidic-Solomonic monarchy, and that after Solomon's death they became the core of the northern kingdom of Israel.

General Bibliography

On tribal society in the Near East and early Israel, see P. S. Khoury and Joseph Kostiner, eds., *Tribes and State Formation in the Middle East* (Berkeley: University of California Press, 1990); and N. K. Gottwald, *The Tribes of Israel: A Sociology of Liberated Israel, 1250–1050 B.C.E.* (Maryknoll, NY: Orbis, 1979; repr. with expanded introduction; Sheffield: Sheffield Academic Press, 1999).

On the book of Judges see A. D. H. Mayes, *Judges* (OTG; Sheffield: Sheffield Academic Press, 1985); G. B. Webb, *The Book of Judges: An Integrated Reading* (JSOTSup 46; Sheffield: JSOT Press, 1987); Mieke Bal, *Death & Disymmetry: The Politics of Coherence in the Book of Judges* (Chicago: University of Chicago Press, 1988); G. A. Yee, ed., *Judges and Method: New Approaches to Biblical Studies* (Minneapolis: Fortress, 1995); and M. Z. Brettler, *The Book of Judges* (London: Routledge, 2002).

On early Israelite religion consult M. S. Smith, *The Early History of God: Yahweh and the Other Deities in Ancient Israel* (San Francisco: Harper & Row, 1990; 2d ed.; Grand Rapids: Eerdmans, 2002); idem, *The Origins of Biblical Monotheism: Israel's Polytheistic Background and the Ugaritic Texts* (London: Oxford University Press, 2001); and Ziony Zevit, *The Religions of Ancient Israel: A Synthesis of Parallactic Approaches* (New York: Continuum, 2001). For arguments for an early Israelite monotheism, see Yehezkel Kaufmann, *The Religion of Israel* (trans. and abridged by Moshe Greenberg; Chicago: University of Chicago Press, 1960).

On the general cultural, technological, and agricultural life in the Iron I highlands, see D. C. Hopkins, *The Highlands of Canaan: Agricultural Life in the Early Iron Age* (SWBA 3; Sheffield: Almond, 1985); idem, "Life on the Land: The Subsistence Struggles of Early Israel," *BA* 50 (1987) 178–91; J. W. Rogerson, "Was Early Israel a Segmentary Society?" *JSOT* 36 (1986) 17–26; P. M. McNutt, *The Forging of Israel: Iron Technology, Symbolism, and Tradition in Ancient Society* (SWBA 7; JSOTSup 108; Sheffield: Almond, 1990); N. K. Gottwald, "Recent Studies of the Social World of Premonarchic Israel," *CurBS* 1 (1993) 163–89; Carol Meyers, "'Tribes' and Tribulations: Retheorizing Earliest 'Israel,'" in Roland Boer, ed., *Tracking "The Tribes of Yahweh": On the Trail of a Classic* (JSOTSup 351; Sheffield: Sheffield Academic Press, 2002) 35–45; Shimon Gibson, "Agricultural Terraces and Settlement Expansion in the Highlands of Early Iron Age Palestine: Is There Any Correlation Between the Two?" in Amihai Mazar, ed., *Studies in the Archaeology of the Iron Age in Israel and Jordan* (JSOTSup 331; Sheffield: Sheffield Academic Press, 2001) 113–46.

R. D. Miller II, *Chieftains of the Highland Clans: A History of Israel in the Twelfth and Eleventh Centuries B.C.* (Grand Rapids: Eerdmans, 2005), offers an attempt at writing a history of early tribal Israel.

Valuable essays on the issues and problems associated with the historical books of the Hebrew Bible can be found in B. T. Arnold and H. G. M. Williamson, eds., *Dictionary of the Old Testament: Historical Books* (Downers Grover, IL: InterVarsity Press, 2005).

5. Eli, Samuel, and Saul

As the Genesis–2 Kings narrative continues through the first fifteen chapters of 1 Samuel, it relates how an early Israelite monarchy emerged and existed for a short time under King Saul. Actually these chapters consist of a tangle of legendary stories about Eli, Samuel, and Saul that have been arranged and edited by the compilers of Genesis–2 Kings. The people of the northern kingdom of Israel probably looked back to Saul as the founder of their state, and some of these stories seem to have been told from a northern "Israelite" (as opposed to southern "Judean") perspective. If they hark back to an historical moment in Israel's past and to historical characters—as we think they do, at least for the most part—that time would have been approximately 1000 B.C.E. This was deep in the dark age centuries of the Early Iron Age; there are no epigraphical documents to support the biblical stories; and neither is the archaeological evidence particularly helpful other than to suggest that little change had occurred in general conditions since the beginning of the Iron Age. In this chapter we will (1) summarize the biblical account of Saul's kingship as it stands in 1 Samuel 1–15, (2) attempt to disentangle the individual stories and cycles of stories that the compilers combined and edited to produce this account, and (3) offer some of our tentative guesses regarding the historical circumstances that may have given rise to these stories.

To anticipate the gist of our conclusions, we see Saul as an historical figure—a Benjaminite who gained notoriety by challenging the Philistine hold on the hill country and by managing to keep them at bay for a time. In the process, he emerged as a local warlord of sorts, who ruled Ephraim and the north-central hill country tribes closely associated with Ephraim. It may have been first under Saul that the name "Israel" came to be associated with this cluster of tribes, rather than with Ephraim alone. It was possibly under Saul's leadership also that Yahweh emerged as Israel's chief god. Saul's administration remained rather simple and family connected, better described as a chiefdom than as a kingdom. He seems to have found support in the Elide priests of Shiloh, which may have been the cause of conflict between Saul and Samuel. There are two different stories about a disastrous battle at Aphek in which the Philistines defeated the Israelites. One story associates the battle with Eli and reports the death of Eli and his two sons. The other associates the battle with Saul and reports the death of Saul and his three sons. We suspect that both stories hark back to a single historical battle that involved Saul and his sons and left his chiefdom in shambles.

Eli, Samuel, and Saul according to 1 Samuel

Summary of 1 Samuel 1–15

Samuel, son of an Ephraimite from Ramathaim-zophim (or Ramah? compare 1 Sam. 1:1 with 1:19 and 7:17), was dedicated by his parents for service to the temple of Yahweh at Shiloh. The old priest Eli was in charge of the Shiloh temple at the time. Because of the scandalous practices of Eli's two sons, Phinehas and Hophni, Yahweh rejected the Elide priestly line in deference to another, not yet identified, priestly line that was to emerge in the future. This divine intention was revealed first to Eli by an anonymous "man of God" and then to the boy Samuel in a dream. As Samuel grew to manhood, Yahweh was with him and he became established as a prophet whose reputation spread throughout the land, from Dan to Beer-sheba (1 Sam. 1–3).

In the meantime a battle was fought at Ebenezer between the Israelites and the Philistines. Eli's two sons were killed in the battle; the Philistines were victorious; and the ark of Yahweh fell into Philistine hands (1 Sam. 4). As long as the Philistines held the ark, however, and in whichever of their cities they placed it, their people were smitten with a plague (apparently tumors of some sort). Finally, under the guidance of their priests and diviners, the Philistines took the ark with a "guilt offering" of "five golden tumors and five golden mice," one for each of their cities, and placed it on a new cart led by two cows and sent them away. The cows pulled the cart to Beth-shemesh, where the ark came into the custody of Levites, and a monument ("great stone") was erected to commemorate the event. Yet disaster still followed the ark—Yahweh slew seventy men of Beth-shemesh because they looked into it—so the Ark was transferred from there to Gibeah ("the hill") near Kiriath-jearim, where it was placed in the charge of one Eleazar, whom the Levites consecrated for that purpose (5:1–7:2).

Samuel then gathered the Israelites at Mizpah and led them in rededication to Yahweh. When the Philistines heard that the Israelites had assembled, they came out for battle, whereupon Yahweh "thundered with a mighty voice that day against the Philistines and threw them into confusion; and they were routed before Israel" (7:10). Samuel erected a monument to the event that he named "Ebenezer," the cities that the Philistines had taken were restored to Israel, and the Philistines no longer threatened Israel as long as Samuel lived.

In the remainder of his life Samuel administered justice to Israel from Ramah, where he built an altar to Yahweh. Also he went on a circuit each year to Bethel, Gilgal, and Mizpah, and judged in these places (1 Sam. 7:3–17). When he became old, Samuel installed his two sons as judges over Israel at Beer-sheba. Unfortunately they used the office for personal gain, taking bribes and preventing justice (8:1–3). Eventually the elders of Israel came to Samuel at Ramah and begged him to appoint a king to rule over them. Samuel opposed the idea, but was directed by Yahweh to give them a king anyway, along with a warning of all the evils they could expect from future kings (8:4–9). In the words of Yahweh, Samuel warned them:

> He will take your sons and appoint them to his chariots and to be his horsemen, and to run before his chariots; and he will appoint for himself com-

manders of thousands and commanders of fifties, and some to plow his ground and to reap his harvest, and to make his implements of war and the equipment of his chariots. He will take your daughters to be perfumers and cooks and bakers. He will take the best of your fields and vineyards and olive orchards and give them to his courtiers. He will take one-tenth of your grain and of your vineyards and give it to his officers and to his courtiers. He will take your male and female slaves, and the best of your cattle [or "young men"] and donkeys, and put them to his work. He will take one-tenth of your flocks, and you shall be his slaves. (8:11–17)

In spite of this warning, the Israelites insisted on having a king, a desire to which Yahweh again acquiesced and gave his permission (8:19–22).

Saul, the son of a wealthy Benjaminite named Kish, was taller than any of his countrymen and very handsome. On one occasion, while searching for some asses that had strayed, Saul came to a village in the land of Zuph. It so happened that Samuel was conducting sacrifices at the village on that same day—and in fact Yahweh had revealed to Samuel that Saul would be coming and that he should anoint Saul as prince (*nagid*) over Israel. This Samuel did, and sent Saul on his way with the following predictions and instructions: (1) When Saul returned to the land of Benjamin, he was to meet two men who would inform him that the asses had been found. (2) Then Saul was to proceed to the oak of Tabor, where he would meet three men going up to worship God at Bethel. They were to give him two loaves of bread. (3) From there he was to go to Gibeath-elohim ("the hill of God") where there was a Philistine garrison (or a Philistine governor, or some kind of Philistine monument; the precise meaning of *natsib* in 10:5 is uncertain) and where Saul would meet a band of prophets coming down from the high place. The prophets would be prophesying to musical instruments, whereupon the spirit of Yahweh would come upon Saul and he would prophesy also. (4) When these three events had transpired as signs that God was with him, Saul was to take some unspecified action: "Do whatever you see fit to do, for God is with you." (5) Thereafter Saul was to proceed to Gilgal and wait seven days, until Samuel arrived to offer sacrifices (9:1–10:8).

The first three items in Samuel's prediction went as anticipated. Saul arrived at Gibeah ("the hill") and prophesied to the extent that people began to ask, "What has come over the son of Kish? Is Saul also among the prophets?" After prophesying, Saul ascended to the high place ("Gibeah," according to the Greek text). Next we find him in conversation with an uncle (10:9–16).

At this point, Samuel assembled the people again at Mizpah and proceeded to select a king for them by lot. Saul, even though he had hidden himself among the baggage and was not actually present, was selected. When he was found and stood among the people, he was taller than any, from his shoulders upward. All the people shouted, "Long live the king!" Samuel explained the rights and duties of kingship, wrote them in a book, and laid the book up before Yahweh (10:17–25). Saul returned to Gibeah, where he was joined by men of valor (fighting men) and received "gifts" from the people. Not all of the people supported him, however. There were those who expressed lack of confidence in his abilities—"How can this man save us?" they said—and brought him no present (10:26–27).

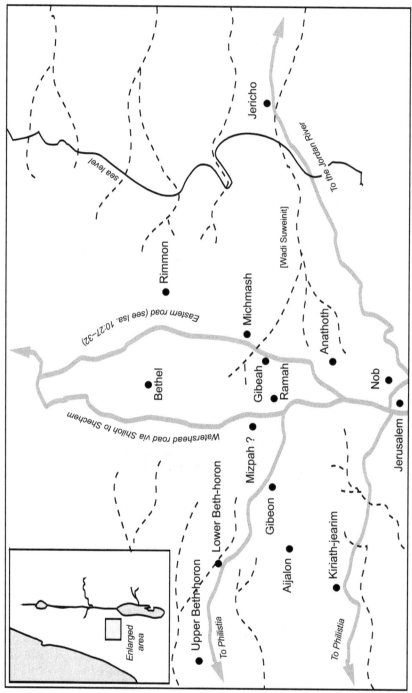

MAP 13. Villages of Benjamin

Soon an occasion arose for Saul to demonstrate his strength. The people of Jabesh in Gilead, their city under siege by the Ammonites, sent messengers to Saul at Gibeah begging for help. Saul called for a general muster of troops, with the warning that he would butcher the cattle of any who failed to respond. Three hundred thousand men of Israel and thirty thousand men of Judah did respond and, under Saul's command, defeated the Ammonites with a great slaughter. The victorious army returned to Gilgal, where they reconfirmed Saul's kingship and offered sacrifices to Yahweh. There were some who urged Saul to take vengeance now on those who had refused to support him initially, but Saul declined to do so (1 Sam. 11).

Samuel addressed the people once again, emphasizing the integrity with which he had served as their leader and the folly of their determination to have a king. Yahweh's affirmation of this farewell address was demonstrated by thunder and rain—which frightened the people, because it was the time of the wheat harvest (late spring/early summer), when rain is unexpected in Palestine (1 Sam. 12).

There followed a major battle with the Philistines, touched off when Jonathan or Saul (compare 13:3 with 13:4) defeated the Philistine garrison (depending still on the proper translation of *natsib*) at Geba. In response, the Philistines mustered 30,000 chariots, 6,000 horsemen, and innumerable troops at Michmash. Many of the Israelites hid. Those who dared to stand with Saul at Gilgal did so trembling, while he waited seven days for Samuel to come and offer sacrifices. When Samuel did not appear at the appointed time, and fearing that his own warriors would desert if he continued to delay action, Saul offered the sacrifices himself. Samuel arrived then, just as the ceremony was completed, and denounced Saul, proclaiming that Saul's kingdom would not continue.

> You have done foolishly; you have not kept the commandment of Yahweh your God, which he commanded you. Yahweh would have established your kingdom over Israel forever, but now your kingdom shall not continue; Yahweh has sought out a man after his own heart; and Yahweh has appointed him to be ruler over his people, because you have not kept what Yahweh commanded you. (13:13–14)

Meanwhile the Philistines had begun to raid in three companies throughout the central hill country and continued doing so until Jonathan conducted a surprise raid on the Philistine garrison (*matstsab*) at Michmash. The Philistines were routed, and the main Israelite army seized the occasion to chase them from the hill country entirely (13:3–14:46). Thereafter Saul was victorious over all of his enemies on every side—including the Moabites, the Ammonites, the Edomites, the Zobahites, and the Amalekites. Also there was more hard fighting against the Philistines throughout Saul's reign (14:47–52).

A battle with the Amalekites occasioned a second angry condemnation of Saul by Samuel. It was on Samuel's command that Saul attacked the Amalekites, and Samuel had specified that everyone and every animal of the Amalekites should be killed: "both man and woman, infant and suckling, ox and sheep, camel and ass" (15:3). Saul did kill all of the people as instructed but spared the Amalekite king, Agag, and some of the best animals. Samuel was

extremely angry and proclaimed again that Yahweh had withdrawn his blessing from Saul's kingship: "Because you have rejected the word of Yahweh, he
has also rejected you from being king" (15:23b).

Yahweh instructed Samuel to go to Bethlehem on the pretense of offering a
sacrifice and to anoint for kingship one of the sons of Jesse, a Bethlehemite.
David was selected, anointed, "and the spirit of Yahweh came mightily upon
David from that day forward." Simultaneously Yahweh withdrew his spirit
from Saul and sent an evil spirit to torment him. A search was made for someone skillful in playing the lyre in the hope that the music would ease Saul's torment. David was chosen for this purpose and thus was brought to the court to
serve as Saul's musician and armor-bearer (1 Sam. 16).

From this point on, the 1 Samuel narrative focuses on David. Occasionally
Samuel, Saul, and members of Saul's family enter into the story, but only as secondary characters. Conflict soon developed between Saul and David, we are
told, and Samuel among others aided David in his escape from Saul's court
(19:18–24). Saul followed close on David's trail while continuing to fight the
Philistines (24:1), until finally David himself joined the Philistine camp
(27:1–4). According to the narrative as it continues in 1 Samuel 28–31, David
was still associated with the Philistines when Saul met them in his last battle.
This battle, which was fought in the vicinity of Mount Gilboa at the southeastern end of the Jezreel Valley (28:4; 29:1, 11; 31:1), was a disaster for Israel. The
Israelites were routed, both Saul and Jonathan were killed, and Saul's kingdom
was left in disarray.

General Characteristics of the 1 Samuel Account

A number of different stories and cycles of stories have been combined, intertwined, and edited to produce the 1 Samuel 1–15 narrative summarized above.
Even though there is general continuity in the overall narrative, a careful
reader will notice disjunctive elements. For example, whereas Samuel is closely
associated with the Elides and plays a central role in the opening chapters of
1 Samuel, he abruptly drops out of the narrative between 4:1b and 7:2, which
describes how the Elides lost possession of the ark, and then he reemerges as
the central figure in the next two chapters. The implication of 4:1b–7:2 is that
the Elides lost possession of the ark before Saul appeared on the scene, while
7:3–14 reports an Israelite defeat of the Philistines under Samuel's leadership
with the result that "the Philistines were subdued and did not again enter the
territory of Israel" (v. 13a). Only a few chapters later, however, we find the
Israelites in desperate battle with the Philistines in the very heart of Israelite
territory. Samuel is still on the scene, and an Elide priest is there with the ark
as well (13:10; 14:3, 18).

The story about Saul's search for the asses in 1 Samuel 9–10 is particularly
confusing because it presents what amounts to multiple endings following
10:5: (1) Saul proceeds to Gibeath-elohim, where he prophesies with a band
of prophets. Compare the variant version of this tradition in 19:18–24 and
note that this latter passage locates the incident of Saul's prophecy at Ramah.
(2) Saul is instructed to go to Gilgal and wait. Compare 13:8–9, where this
thread of tradition reemerges. (3) Saul goes to Gibeah, where there was a Philis-

tine garrison (?), and does "what his hand finds to do"—presumably he challenges the Philistines in some fashion (cf. 13:2–4). (4) Saul returns home (?), where we hear him in conversation with an uncle, and then goes with his family to Mizpah, where he is crowned king.

The stories that compose 1–2 Samuel are folk legends for the most part. They tend to glorify or condemn the personalities involved, emphasize the dramatic, include novelistic features such as conversations between private individuals, lack any clear chronological framework, and so forth. In some cases we are presented with what appears to be variations of the same folk tradition attached to two different figures. Note, for example, the parallel stories about the righteous priest with two unworthy sons. First it is Eli, and then it is Samuel (compare 1 Sam. 2 and 8). Similarly, there are two stories about a Philistine battle at Ebenezer, one that features Eli and his sons, the other featuring Samuel (compare 1 Sam. 4 and 7). Less obvious is the confusion in 1 Samuel 13–14 as to who initiated the battle with the Philistines described there. Was it Saul who attacked the Philistine garrison (*natsib*) at Gibeah, or his son Jonathan who attacked the Philistine camp (*matstsab*) at Michmash across the valley from Gibeah? Probably two different versions of a daring attack in the vicinity of Gibeah/Michmash survived in Israel's folk memory—one attributing it to the young Saul, the other attributing it to the young Jonathan—and both versions are entangled in 1 Samuel 13–14. Finally, there is at least one occasion where a tradition that may have pertained originally to Saul has been transferred to Samuel—the story in 1 Samuel 1 of Samuel's birth and dedication at Shiloh. Two things suggest that this story, in an earlier form, featured Saul rather than Samuel: (1) The explanation of the child's name in v. 20 corresponds to the name "Saul" rather than "Samuel." (2) Saul is said to have been supported by the Elide priests of Shiloh in his later career (14:3, 18). Samuel, on the other hand, while he is connected with Shiloh in this story and its continuation in 1 Samuel 2–3, is never associated with Shiloh in other narratives.

The stories that compose 1 Samuel 1–15 focus on northern, Israelite, characters—principally Eli, Samuel, and Saul—but come to us as reshaped and edited by the late Judean compilers of the Genesis–2 Kings History. In the Genesis–Judges segment of their history, these compilers tended to idealize the distant past and to project later circumstances (or ideal circumstances) back to the time of Moses and Joshua. In this 1–2 Samuel segment they are more concerned to emphasize the legitimacy of the Davidic dynasty (as opposed to Saul's descendants whom David displaced), stress Yahweh's sanction of the Jerusalem cult (over against Shiloh and the Elide priests), and, as will become more apparent in 2 Samuel, to justify Solomon's succession to the throne after David (instead of one of David's older sons). Correspondingly, three tendencies are noticeable in the stories as we now find them. (1) Saul is disparaged, presented as an emotionally unstable character rejected by both Samuel and Yahweh. (2) David tends to be glorified, presented as Yahweh's man who rarely did any wrong, and who repented properly when he did. (3) Samuel is presented as Yahweh's spokesman, presiding over the demise of the Elide priests at Shiloh and the transfer of God's favor from Saul to David.

In order to present Samuel in this role, the compilers seem to have inserted him editorially into several stories that originally did not involve him. We have already noted that Samuel may have displaced Saul in the birth story of 1 Samuel 1, and suggested that his connection with Shiloh in the next two chapters is also editorial. Likewise, as commentators often observe, Samuel seems to have been introduced into the account of Saul's anointment as *nagid* in 9:1–10:16 (originally the story featured an anonymous prophet in "the land of Zuph"), and then introduced secondarily to reconfirm Saul's kingship in 11:7, 12–14 and to reject it in 13:8–15.

Finally, one should observe that the arrangement of the stories in 1 Samuel 1–15 (the sequence in which they are presented) is determined to some extent by the schematic structure of the Genesis–2 Kings History. The compilers would have us see Samuel as the last of the great judges and Saul as Israel's first king. Accordingly, Samuel's farewell address in 1 Samuel 12 concludes the era of the judges in the same fashion that Moses' farewell address (essentially the book of Deuteronomy) concludes the era of the desert wandering, and that Joshua's farewell address (Josh. 23–24) concludes the era of conquest and settlement. The materials pertaining to Saul, on the other hand, have been arranged to fit the literary pattern that the compilers used for the later kings of Israel and Judah. They typically introduce each king's reign with a formulaic introduction that provides pertinent chronological information, and then conclude each king's reign with summary notes about his deeds (compare 1 Kgs. 14:21 and 31; 15:1 and 7–8; 15:9 and 23–24; etc.). In accordance with this pattern, the puzzling chronological notation in 1 Samuel 13:1 introduces Saul's reign, while the summary of his conquests in 14:47–52 concludes it. Also in accordance with the pattern, the story of Saul's victory over the Ammonites at Jabesh-gilead, which explained how he overcame the early opposition of some of his countrymen, is introduced before the notation that introduces his reign, while the account of his victory over the Philistines is placed farther on, in the context of his reign (13:2–14:46). The point to be made here is that the sequential arrangement of the narratives in 1 Samuel has more to do with the schematic literary structure of the Genesis–2 Kings History than with any actual historical sequence of events. More likely, Saul would have expelled the Philistines from his own Benjaminite neighborhood before venturing as far away as Jabesh-gilead.

Separating the Traditions in 1 Samuel

Obviously, any attempt even to speculate on the historical circumstances that may have given rise to the stories combined and intertwined in 1 Samuel 1–15 must begin with an attempt to disentangle these stories and examine them individually.[1]

---

1. A general survey of the issues related to the traditions in 1 Samuel are provided by R. P. Gordon, *1 & 2 Samuel* (OTG; Sheffield: JSOT Press, 1984); see also Bruce Birch, *The Rise of the Israelite Monarchy: The Growth and Development of I Samuel 7–15* (SBLDS 27; Missoula, MT: Scholars Press, 1976); A. D. H. Mayes, "The Rise of the Israelite Monarchy," *ZAW* 90 (1978) 1–19; Baruch Halpern, *The Constitution of the Monarchy in Israel* (HSM 25; Chico, CA: Scholars Press, 1981); W. L. Humphreys, "From Tragic Hero to Villain: A Study of the Figure of Saul and the Development of I Samuel," *JSOT* 22 (1982) 95–117; N. E. Evans, "An Historical Reconstruction of the Emergence of Israelite Kingship and the Reign of Saul," in W. W. Hallo et al., eds., *Scripture in Context II: More Essays on the Comparative Method* (Winona Lake, IN: Eisenbrauns, 1983) 61–77; and Walter Dietrich and Thomas Naumann, "The David-Saul Narratives," in G. N. Knoppers and J. G. McConville, eds., *Reconsidering Israel and Judah: Recent Studies on the Deuteronomistic History* (SBTS 8; Winona Lake, IN: Eisenbrauns, 2000) 276–318.

CHART 8. Basic Compositional Units of 1 Samuel 1–15

1 Sam. 1:1–4:1a	Samuel-Shiloh stories. The account of Samuel's birth in 1 Sam. 1 may have had to do originally with Saul.
1 Sam. 4:1b–7:2	*The Ark Narrative* (continues in 2 Sam. 6). Explains how the ark made its way from Shiloh to Jerusalem.
1 Sam. 9:1–10:16; 10:26–11:15; 13:2–14:46	*Saul Stories.* A cycle of stories that tell about Saul's battles and how he came to be king over Israel.
1 Sam. 7:3–8:22; 10:17–25; 12; 15	*The Samuel Narrative.* A continuous narrative that presents Samuel as the last of the judges who anointed Saul as the first king of Israel and then rejected him in favor of David.

There appear to be several clusters, or cycles, of stories involved.[2] We recognize the following.

The Samuel-Shiloh Stories (1 Sam. 1:1–4:1a). These stories associate the young Samuel with a temple at Shiloh where the old priest Eli and his two sons, Phinehas and Hophni, were in charge. They are told from an obvious anti-Elide perspective and seek to emphasize that the demise of the Elides was in accordance with Yahweh's will and justified because of the scandalous behavior of Eli's sons. As indicated above, at least the birth story in 1 Samuel 1 probably pertained originally to Saul rather than to Samuel.

The Ark Narrative (1 Sam. 4:1b–7:2 with continuation in 2 Sam. 6).[3] This narrative explains how the ark of Yahweh came to be transferred from the Elide priests of Shiloh into the hands of Levites at Beth-shemesh, from there to Gibeah ("the hill") near Kiriath-jearim, and eventually to Jerusalem. While this narrative must be recognized as independent of the Samuel-Shiloh stories, it reflects the same overriding theme: it explains that the demise of the Elides and the transfer of the ark from their hands to those of the priests in Jerusalem happened in accordance with a divine plan. According to the present form of the

---

2. Scholars have argued for seeing much of 1 Samuel as a combination of only two originally independent sources; see Halpern, *Constitution*, 149–74; idem, *David's Secret Demons: Messiah, Murderer, Traitor, King* (Grand Rapids: Eerdmans, 2001) 14–53, 263–66, and the chart on 277–79. For an attempt to consider the material as a unified presentation, see Iain Provan et al., *A Biblical History of Israel* (Louisville: Westminster John Knox, 2003) 193–99, 201–14.

3. On the Ark Narrative see A. F. Campbell, *The Ark Narrative (1 Sam. 4–6; 2 Sam. 6): A Form-critical and Traditio-historical Study* (SBLDS 16; Missoula, MT: SBL and Scholars Press, 1975); and P. D. Miller Jr. and J. J. M. Roberts, *The Hand of the Lord: A Reassessment of the "Ark Narrative" of 1 Samuel* (Baltimore: Johns Hopkins University Press, 1977). For doubts about the independence of this material, see J. T. Willis, "An Anti-Elide Narrative Tradition from a Prophetic Circle at the Ramah Sanctuary," *JBL* 90 (1971) 288–308; idem, "Cultic Elements in the Story of Samuel's Birth and Dedication," *ST* 26 (1972) 33–61; and idem, "Samuel versus Eli: I Sam. 1–7," *TZ* 35 (1979) 201–12. A survey of the issues can be found in K. A. D. Smelik, "The Ark Narrative Reconsidered," in A. S. van der Woude, ed., *New Avenues in the Study of the Old Testament* (OtSt 25; Leiden: Brill, 1989) 128–44.

narrative, the ark remained in the hands of the Philistines throughout the reign of Saul. Jerusalem priests are the likely ones to have perpetrated such a view.

The Ark Narrative may preserve distant memories of actual historical events—a disastrous battle with the Philistines at Aphek, and transfer of the ark of Yahweh from its original home at Shiloh to Jerusalem. But whatever memories the narrative preserves are probably very distant indeed and terribly garbled. It is surely more than coincidence that other traditions in 1 Samuel also mention Aphek and Ebenezer as the scenes of major battles with the Philistines, but presuppose different contexts and feature Samuel or Saul rather than Eli. The Samuel narrative (see below and 1 Sam. 7:3–14) has Samuel naming Ebenezer after a battle with the Philistines at Mizpah. In 29:1–5 the Philistines are camped at Aphek near Mount Gilboa on the eve of the disastrous battle in which Saul and Jonathan were killed. We suspect that the Ark Narrative and the account of Saul's death hark back to the same historical battle, and that the story of Saul's death in 1 Samuel 29 is probably closer to the actual historical circumstances.

The Saul Stories (1 Sam. 9:1–10:16; 10:26–11:15; 13:2–14:46).[4] When isolated from their present context, these stories focus on Saul and, in an earlier form, presented him in an essentially favorable light. The original sequence of these stories probably was 9:1–10:16 . . . 13:2–14:46 . . . 10:26–11:15, thus relating the following sequence of events.[5] The young Saul, in search of his father's asses, encountered an anonymous prophet in the land of Zuph. The prophet anointed him prince (*nagid*), predicted certain circumstances that would occur as Saul returned home, and instructed him to proceed to Gibeath-elohim, where there was a Philistine garrison and where he was to "do whatever your hand finds to do, for God is with you." The story picks up again in 13:2–14:46 with the scene at Gibeah, and is somewhat difficult to follow at that point, since it apparently telescopes two versions of a single incident. One of the versions seems to presuppose that Saul attacked the Philistine garrison at Gibeah (see especially 13:4), whereupon the Philistines moved a larger military force to Michmash (across the valley from Gibeah) and began to raid the surrounding countryside. The other version credits Jonathan with the raid and has him attacking the Philistine garrison at Michmash. The end result, presumably according to both versions, was that Saul chased the Philstines out of southern Ephraim and established himself with a small army at Gibeah. Thus the story in 10:26–11:15 begins with Saul and his soldiers in place at Gibeah and describes how he responded to an urgent call for help from the people of Jabesh in Gilead. Their city was under Ammonite siege at the time and unable to hold out much longer. Saul mustered a large army (in addition to his private soldiers), defeated the Ammonites, and in the wake of the victory was proclaimed (or reaffirmed) king over Israel.

Samuel and the Gilgal episode (10:8; 13:8–15) have been written into this narrative complex at some secondary stage of transmission. Also, in the process of

---

4. See J. M. Miller, "Saul's Rise to Power: Some Observations Concerning 1 Samuel 9:1–10:16; 10:26–11:15 and 13:2–14:46," *CBQ* 36 (1974) 157–74.

5. For a different assessment see R. P. Gordon, "Who Made the Kingmaker? Reflections on Samuel and the Institution of the Monarchy," in A. R. Millard et al., eds., *Faith, Tradition and History: Old Testament Historiography in Its Near Eastern Context* (Winona Lake, IN: Eisenbrauns, 1994), 255–69.

compiling the final Genesis–2 Kings account, the story in 1 Sam. 13:2–14:46 has been transposed to its present position (rather than following in sequence after 9:1–10:16), introduced with the formulaic introduction to Saul's reign (13:1), and concluded with further notes regarding Saul's deeds in office (14:47–52).

The Samuel Narrative (1 Sam. 7:3–8:22; 10:17–25; 12; 15). These passages form a continuous narrative that focuses on Samuel. They present him as the last of the judges, an authentic spokesman for Yahweh who instituted the monarchy in Israel and anointed Israel's first king. Although this Samuel narrative seems to be based on old traditions, these traditions have been largely recast to serve the interests of the late compilers of Genesis–2 Kings. As a judge, Samuel is credited with a victory over the Philistines at Ebenezer and discredited by his two sons whom he installed as judges at Beer-sheba. As a kingmaker, Samuel is depicted first as opposing the institution of a monarchy and warning the people of the many ways in which future kings would take advantage of them. Nevertheless, under divine guidance, he is reported to have selected Saul by lot, explained the rights and duties of kingship, and written these in a book to be laid up before Yahweh. Finally, 1 Samuel 15 has Samuel rejecting Saul and anticipates the shift of divine favor to David.

The Stories about David's Rise to Power (1 Sam. 16–2 Sam. 5:5). Beginning with the account of Samuel's anointing of David in 1 Samuel 16 and concluding with the account of David's conquest of Jerusalem in 2 Samuel 5, one encounters a miscellaneous collection of stories that focus on David. Samuel, Saul, and Saul's descendants are mentioned from time to time when they are relevant to David's career, but otherwise remain very much in the background. Some of these stories seem contradictory and some seem to be duplications, but they all tend to have a common theme—David's rise to power and his rightful claim to the throne. We will explore these stories in more detail in chapter 6, although it will be necessary to draw on them to a certain extent in this chapter's treatment of Saul's reign and the collapse of his kingdom.

Problem Areas for the Historian

If the analysis provided above is even close to the mark, then the materials in 1 Samuel are insecure grounds for saying anything at all about the historical Eli, Samuel, or Saul. We are inclined to suppose that many of these stories contain at least a kernel of historical truth, but concede that there is no way to determine for certain what is historical kernel, what is garbled memory, and what is legendary elaboration. That the compilers of Genesis–2 Kings were not so interested in Saul's reign as in David's is an added problem. We are told very little about Saul's career, and much of what we are told is embedded in the stories about David. Even the matter of establishing approximate dates for Saul is problematic. First Samuel 13:1, the verse that introduces Saul's reign (see above), has been corrupted or deliberately distorted during the process of transmission. Literally it reads: "Saul was a year old when he began to reign; and he reigned two years over Israel." Chronological data provided in 1–2 Kings and to be discussed in chapter 8 place Solomon's death within a decade or so of 925 B.C.E. We are told also that Solomon and David reigned forty years each (1 Kgs.

2:11; 11:42), the "forty years" to be regarded as symbolic or round numbers in both cases. So about the only thing that we can say, very tentatively, is that Saul's career occurred approximately 1000 B.C.E.

Finally, some topographical uncertainties have a bearing on one's interpretation of the Eli, Samuel, and Saul narratives. Particularly problematic is the appellative "Gibeah," with variant forms "Gibeath," "Geba," and "Gibeon," all of which mean "the hill." This name appears time and again in the early biblical narratives. Clearly more than one place by that name is involved, but it is impossible to say for certain how many different places are spoken about, and which biblical texts refer to which place.[6]

As a working hypothesis, we recognize four Gibeahs in the hill country north of Jerusalem: (1) Gibeah of Phinehas (or "Phinehas's hill"), probably somewhere in the immediate vicinity of Shiloh (Josh. 24:33); (2) Gibeah (or "the hill") near Kiriath-jearim where, according to the Ark Narrative, the ark was temporarily placed during its transfer from Shiloh to Jerusalem (1 Sam. 7:1–3; 2 Sam. 6:1–3); (3) Gibeon, the Hivite city with which Saul apparently had unpleasant dealings (2 Sam. 21) and where David's troops skirmished with Saul's forces after the latter's death (2 Sam. 2:12–17). Later, according to 1 Kings 3:4–15, Solomon would sacrifice at Gibeon and have his famous dream there. Kiriath-jearim (present-day Deir el-Azar) and Gibeon (el-Jib) were situated on opposite sides of a very prominent height (present-day Nebi Samwil). Possibly this was the common denominator between the two names. Nebi Samwil would have been the Gibeah ("hill") near Kiriath-jearim, and Gibeon would have received its name from its proximity to this hill; (4) Gibeah (with the alternate form "Geba," present-day Jaba), sometimes called Gibeah/Geba of Benjamin and sometimes Gibeah/Geba of Saul. This village played a crucial role in the tribal war with Benjamin (Judg. 19–21) and in Saul's early wars (1 Sam. 13:2–14:46), and became Saul's capital (1 Sam. 22:6; 23:19; etc.). Gibeath-elohim ("the hill of God" in 1 Sam. 10:5) may have been the same place, or perhaps more specifically the crest of the hill on the side of which Gibeah/Geba was situated.

The place name Aphek presents a similar situation. This name appears in two different contexts in 1 Samuel, and in both cases it is the site of the Philistine camp prior to a major battle in which the Israelites were defeated. According to the Ark Narrative, the Philistines camped at Aphek before the battle in connection with which Eli and his sons were killed and the ark was captured. This context would seem to suggest that the Aphek involved was somewhere on the frontier between Israelite territory and Philistia. According to 1 Samuel 29:1, on the other hand, the Philistines camped at Aphek prior to the battle in which Saul and his son Jonathan were killed, and the context places this Aphek somewhere in the vicinity of Mount Gilboa. One possibility, the one generally assumed, is that these were two different battles involving two different Apheks. As indicated above, however, we view the Ark Narrative as a fanciful and biased account (pro-Jerusalem, anti-Elide) that, to the extent that it is based

---

6. See Joseph Blenkinsopp, *Gibeon and Israel: The Role of Gibeon and the Gibeonites in the Political and Religious History of Early Israel* (Cambridge: Cambridge University Press, 1972); idem, "Did Saul Make Gibeon His Capital?" *VT* 24 (1974) 1–7; J. M. Miller, "Geba/Gibeah of Benjamin," *VT* 25 (1975) 145–66; P. M. Arnold, *Gibeah: The Search for a Biblical City* (JSOTSup 79; Sheffield: JSOT Press, 1990); and S. D. Walters, "Saul of Gibeon," *JSOT* 52 (1991): 61–76.

31. *Geba/Gibeah of Saul.* The present-day village of Jaba, about ten miles northeast of Jerusalem's Old City, is probably to be identified with Geba/Gibeah of Saul, also called Geba/Gibeah of Benjamin.

32. *Gibeon.* Present-day el-Jib, about ten miles northwest of Jerusalem and west of Jaba (Geba/Gibeah of Saul), is the site of ancient Gibeon.

on historical reality, strays rather far from the actual chronology and geography of events. Thus we suspect that it preserves a distant and garbled memory of the same battle of Aphek that occurred in the vicinity of Mount Gilboa at the end of Saul's reign and in which he and Jonathan were killed. This means that we need search for only one Aphek in connection with the 1 Samuel narratives, and that this Aphek would have been located somewhere in the vicinity of Mount Gilboa at the southeastern end of the Jezreel Valley.

Shiloh and the Elides

What role did Shiloh and the Elide priests who served the Yahwistic sanctuary there play in the history of early Israel?[7] Two different impressions emerge from the Genesis–2 Kings History. On the one hand, the late compilers would have the reader believe that the people of Israel assembled at Shiloh soon after their entry into Palestine, and from that time forward Shiloh served as the chief political and cultic center for the tribes. The "tent of meeting" was set up at Shiloh and the ark installed there. Eleazar son of Aaron served as priest until followed in this office by his son Phinehas (Josh. 14:1; 17:4; 19:51; 22:13, 31–32; 24:33). On the other hand, the stories in the book of Judges give quite a different impression. Except for one isolated verse, likely a scribal gloss, there is not the slightest suggestion in any of these stories that Shiloh was, or ever had been, an important political and cultic center for the Israelites. The verse in question, Judges 21:12, belongs to the story of the tribal war with Benjamin and has the Israelites returning to their camp at Shiloh after a raid on Jabesh-gilead. As the narrative unfolds, however, we find that the Israelites, rather than being camped at Shiloh, decide to conduct a raid on Shiloh. Moreover, it is clearly the assumption of the story that the camp from which they conducted the raid was not even near Shiloh, because we hear the elders instructing the warriors as to how to find the place. "So they said, 'Look, the yearly feasting of Yahweh is taking place at Shiloh, which is north of Bethel, on the east of the highway that goes up from Bethel to Shechem, and south of Lebonah'" (Judg. 21:19).

Whatever interpretation one places on the narrative, it seems out of keeping with the idea that Shiloh was an important center for the early Israelite tribes. Neither does it prepare one for the opening chapters of 1 Samuel, where we find Eli and his two sons, Phinehas and Hophni, officiating before the ark in a temple at Shiloh (1 Sam. 1:24; 3:3; note, however, the one reference to "the tent of meeting" in 2:22).

The two different impressions are not necessarily in conflict. One could surmise that Shiloh served early on as the chief political and cultic center for the Israelite tribes (as reflected in the book of Joshua), then declined in importance (as seems to be the situation in the Judges narratives), gained prominence again

---

7. See M. A. Cohen, "The Role of the Shilonite Priesthood in the United Monarchy of Ancient Israel," *HUCA* 36 (1965) 59–98; and D. G. Schley, *Shiloh: A Biblical City in Tradition and History* (JSOTSup 63; Sheffield: Sheffield Academic Press, 1989). Excavations at the site of ancient Shiloh (present-day Seilûn) reveal a small Iron I settlement that was destroyed sometime during Iron I. While it is tempting to attribute this destruction to the Philistines and relate it to one or another of the biblical stories about Eli, Samuel, and Saul, nothing about the archaeological remains either suggests or prohibits this. On the excavations at Shiloh see Israel Finkelstein et al., *Shiloh: The Archaeology of a Biblical Site* (Tel Aviv: Institute of Archaeology of Tel Aviv University, 1993).

briefly at the time of Eli (opening chapters of 1 Samuel), and then, with the loss of the ark at the first battle of Aphek (as described in the Ark Narrative), had ceased to function for all practical purposes by the time Saul appeared on the scene. Eli and his son Phinehas would have been direct descendants of Phinehas son of Eleazar son of Aaron. At some point they presumably built a temple alongside the tent of meeting, and somehow one of their descendants contemporary with Saul gained temporary possession of the ark.

However, we propose an alternate scenario, which is admittedly speculative but which we think better takes into account the surprising attitude toward Shiloh reflected in Judges 19–21, compensates for the strong anti-Elide bias that pervades the opening chapters of 1 Samuel, and provides an explanation as to why an Elide priest contemporary with Saul would have been in possession of the ark. Shiloh, in our opinion, was one of the numerous local shrines that dotted the Palestinian hill country during the early tribal period. Its priests, the Elides, were Yahwistic and served before an ark that represented Yahweh's presence. But Shiloh was probably never regarded as a particularly important "Israelite" cultic center before Saul's day. There seems to have been some sort of supportive relationship between Saul and the Elides; and it was during his time, we suspect, that the Shiloh sanctuary began to figure prominently in Israelite affairs and Shiloh's ark became a "national" religious symbol. If so, Shiloh's heyday was brief and ended with the disastrous battle near Aphek in which Saul and his sons were killed.

This battle and Saul's death also opened the way for David's rapid rise to power and the ascendancy of the Jerusalem cult, whose priests would eventually claim authority over all others in Israel and Judah. The ark was brought to Jerusalem (possibly after a checkered history that may have involved its capture by the Philistines during Saul's last disastrous battle with them), where it continued to serve as a national religious symbol. Later, the whole chain of events— the disaster at Aphek, the decline of the Shiloh cult, and the transfer of the ark to Jerusalem—came to be regarded in Jerusalem as the unfolding of Yahweh's will. This is the point of view reflected in the opening chapters of 1 Samuel, as we have seen, and also in Psalm 78.

> He abandoned his dwelling at Shiloh,
>   the tent where he dwelt among mortals,
> and delivered his power to captivity,
>   his glory to the hand of the foe.
> He gave his people over to the sword,
>   and vented his wrath on his heritage. . . .
> He rejected the tent of Joseph,
>   he did not choose the tribe of Ephraim;
> but he chose the tribe of Judah,
>   Mount Zion, which he loves.
> He built his sanctuary like the high heavens,
>   like the earth, which he has founded forever.
> He chose his servant David,
>   and took him from the sheepfolds;
> from tending the nursing ewes he brought him
>   to be the shepherd of his people Jacob,
>   of Israel his inheritance.
>   (Ps. 78:60–62, 67–71)

The seventh-century prophet Jeremiah almost lost his life to an angry Jerusalem mob when he warned that God would reject Jerusalem as he had rejected Shiloh (Jer. 7:12–14; 26:6–9). Still later, the compilers of Genesis–2 Kings projected the ark back into the wilderness period, represented Shiloh as the chief cultic center of their idealized Israel under Joshua, and provided the Elides with a genealogy traced back to Aaron.

The "Historical" Samuel

Samuel is much like Moses and Joshua in that, while the biblical materials assign him a major role at a crucial turning point in Israel's history, he remains an elusive figure. Indeed, three quite different Samuels emerge from the stories about him: there is Samuel the priest-prophet at Shiloh (1 Sam. 1:1–4:1a); Samuel the local "seer" from the land of Zuph (9:1–10:16); and Samuel of Ramah, the last of the judges, the kingmaker and king rejecter (7:3–8:22; 10:17–25; etc.). This threefold picture of Samuel results, in our opinion, from the fact that Samuel has been introduced secondarily into stories and contexts that did not originally involve him—particularly the Samuel-Shiloh stories in 1 Samuel 1–4 and the Saul stories in 9:1–10:16; 10:26–11:15; 13:2–14:46. Samuel does not appear at all in the Ark Narrative, and rarely appears in the stories about David's rise to power in 1 Samuel 16 and following. By process of elimination, therefore, the Samuel narrative in 7:3–8:22; 10:17–25; 12; and 15 is our only hope of catching even a fleeting glimpse of the "historical" Samuel. And this narrative strand, while possibly based on old traditions, is largely the work of the late compilers of Genesis–2 Kings who wished to depict Samuel as the last of the great judges.[8]

Between the lines of their idealized presentation, the Samuel who emerges seems to have been a local cultic leader from Ramah in southern Ephraim/Benjamin who went on a yearly circuit to Bethel, Gilgal, and Mizpah (all three places close to Ramah). He is described as "judging Israel," which may be the compilers' terminology, and reminds one in this regard of Deborah. She likewise is said to have judged Israel "between Ramah and Bethel in the hill country of Ephraim" (see Judg. 4:4–10). The claim that Samuel installed his two sons at Beer-sheba, where they took advantage of the office, is questionable on at least two grounds. First, the literary motif of the righteous old priest with two wayward sons is one that we encounter also in connection with Eli. Second, it seems unlikely that a local Ephraimite priest would have had influence as far south as Beer-sheba; yet this is the sort of thing that the compilers of Genesis–2 Kings would have wished to claim for Samuel. Perhaps there was another Beer-sheba in the more immediate vicinity of Ramah. But more likely, in our opinion, the whole matter of the two sons judging at Beer-sheba is editorial embellishment of a floating folk motif. We have reservations about the story of the victory over the Philistines at Ebenezer during Samuel's judgeship on the same grounds. Here again the whole thing sounds like a highly editorialized

8. For differing views on the historical Samuel, see Gordon, "Who Made the Kingmaker?"; and J. L. McKenzie, "The Four Samuels," *BR* 7 (1962) 1–16.

version of a folk story about how the place called Ebenezer ("the stone of help") got its name.

One motif that persists in the stories about Samuel, however, and cannot be explained away easily, is that of the conflict between Samuel and Saul. If Samuel was a local priest who played some role in the official recognition of Saul's rule, it is quite plausible that he might have done so under popular pressure rather than in accordance with his own wishes. Saul's emerging strength could only have diminished Samuel's own leadership authority. Nor is there any reason to doubt that what may have been coolness on the part of Samuel toward Saul from the beginning soon developed into open conflict. Less convincing is the explanation given for the break between the two. Samuel was supposedly angry because Saul failed on two occasions to follow precisely Yahweh's instructions as conveyed by Samuel. Yet one has to suspect that more was involved than matters of ritual detail. Possibly the conflict had to do with Saul's close alignment with the Elides of Shiloh. Samuel may have resented that this new leader based at Gibeah, the next village over the mountain from his own Ramah, looked increasingly to the Elide priests of Shiloh for support.

Saul, an Early Israelite Chieftain

The cycle of Saul stories represents at best a mixture of folk memory and legend. Yet read in proper sequence (1 Sam. 9:1–10:16 . . . 13:2–14:46 . . . 10:26–11:15), it is our opinion that these stories probably bring us nearer to an accurate glimpse of the historical Saul than we have been able to attain for any of the earlier characters of biblical history.[9] (1) In contrast to the Samuel stories, for example, where whatever old traditions are preserved have been thoroughly recast by the late compilers of Genesis–2 Kings, the secondary editorial elements in the Saul stories can be separated out with somewhat more confidence. (2) When these elements are removed, the material that is left is noticeably free of the anti-Saul and antimonarchical bias that otherwise pervades 1 Samuel. Indeed, these stories seem to be told from a "northern" perspective according to which Saul was remembered in a favorable light. (3) The glimpse of Saul that one attains from these stories fits well with the occasional references to him elsewhere in the Samuel materials, particularly in the stories about David's rise during Saul's reign.

However, the Saul that emerges from these and the other stories in 1 Samuel 1–16 is not a "king," certainly not in any medieval or modern sense of the word, and his realm is hardly a "kingdom" comparable even to the later kingdoms of "Israel" and "Judah." Using anthropological terminology, we might

---

9. See Joseph Blenkinsopp, "The Quest of the Historical Saul," in J. W. Flanagan and A. W. Robinson, eds., *No Famine in the Land: Studies in Honor of John L. McKenzie* (Missoula, MT: Scholars Press, 1975) 75–99; Nadav Na'aman, "The Pre-Deuteronomistic Story of King Saul and Its Historical Significance," *CBQ* 54 (1992) 638–58; V. P. Long, "How Did Saul Become King? Literary Reading and Historical Reconstruction," in Millard et al., eds., *Faith, Tradition, and History*, 271–84; and M. White, "Searching for Saul: What We Really Know about Israel's First King," *BRev* 17/2 (2001) 22–29, 52–53.

refer to Saul's realm more appropriately as a "chiefdom."[10] His administration remained largely a family affair, for example; and in visualizing the extent of his domain, one should think in terms of a loosely defined area of military activity rather than a territorial state with precisely defined boundaries. At the core of Saul's chiefdom was southern Ephraim/Benjamin, his own home territory. Beyond that, especially after the Jabesh-gilead victory, his authority would have come to be recognized throughout Ephraim and the neighboring tribes closely associated with Ephraim. Before the end of his career, Saul seems to have subdued at least some of the "non-Israelite" cities in the north-central hill country (e.g., Gibeon), made his presence felt among the clans and villages of the southern hill country, and perhaps extended his military reach into Transjordan north of Gilead. Beyond the Ephraim-Benjamin-Gilead zone, however, Saul's rule probably consisted of little more than temporary military forays, with local loyalty lasting only as long as he or his troops were present, or as long as the people needed to rely on him for protection against other threats. The following is our admittedly speculative profile of Saul's career.

Saul's Rise to Power

Saul seems to have been from a prominent and relatively wealthy family (1 Sam. 9:1–2) whose ancestral home was the village of Zela in southern Benjaminite territory (2 Sam. 21:14; cf. Josh. 18:28; Zelza in 1 Sam. 10:2 may be a variant of the same name[11]). We have noted that the story in 1 Samuel 1, which describes the unusual circumstances of Samuel's birth, may have originally had to do with Saul. If so, it is to be regarded as a "royal legend." The people of the later kingdom of Israel probably thought of Saul as the founder of their nation, and it was not uncommon for rulers in ancient times, particularly founders of kingdoms, to be credited with unusual births.

Saul came to the fore at a time when the Philistines dominated the central hill country and made a name for himself by attacking a Philistine garrison in the Gibeah-Michmash vicinity (or challenging their authority in some fashion)

10. See J. W. Flanagan, "Chiefs in Israel," *JSOT* 20 (1981) 47–73, who is dependent on the work of E. R. Service, *Primitive Social Organization* (2d ed.; New York: Random House, 1962); and idem, *Origins of the State and Civilization* (New York: Norton, 1975). The concept and terminology were already used by Johannes Pedersen, *Israel* (4 vols.; London: Oxford University Press, 1926–1940) III–IV: 32–106; on Saul as a chief see pp. 45–46. Some variation of the following classification of societies, originally proposed by Service, is widely accepted by anthropologists: band, tribes, chiefdoms, and states. Tribes, according to the scheme, are egalitarian, multicommunity societies bound together by kinship and usually sustained by agricultural-pastoral economies. Chiefdoms are organized around kinship as well—clan and tribal relationships do not disappear—but the people tend to have unequal or "ranked" positions within the sociopolitical organization. This ranking is often determined by birth. Also, chiefdom economy involves some accumulation and redistribution of goods, usually by the chief. States, including kingdoms, exhibit a significant amount of ethnic plurality and/or societal differentiation. Also they are governed by central political bureaucracies that are usually seated in one or more urban centers and tend, as far as governance is concerned, to overshadow kinship relations. For critiques of Service's work as too simplistic and evolutionary, see Raz Kletter, "Chronology and United Monarchy: A Methodological Review," *ZDPV* 120 (2004) 13–54, esp. 13–21.

11. Zela is probably to be identified with present-day Khirbet es-Salah in close geographical proximity to Gibeon (Josh. 18:25–28). Also two genealogical references connect Saul's family with Gibeon (1 Chr. 8:33–40; 9:39–44). Some have speculated further that Saul made Gibeon his capital city (see works by Blenkinsopp in n. 6 above). This seems unlikely in our opinion, and it would require that some of the references to Gibeah in the stories about Saul be interpreted as references to Gibeon.

and then successfully expelling the Philistines from southern Ephraim/ Benjamin. The narrative that reports the initial victory (1 Sam. 13:2–14:46) telescopes two versions of the incident, one featuring the young Saul, while the other features the young Jonathan. The result, in any case, was that Saul, having expelled the Philistines from the area, established himself at Gibeah-Michmash with a small standing army. Note that 1 Samuel 13:2 does not describe the situation at the beginning of the Gibeah-Michmash battle but, in typical biblical narrative style, introduces the account of the battle by summarizing its outcome: "Saul chose three thousand men of Israel; two thousand were with Saul in Michmash and the hill country of Bethel, and a thousand were with Jonathan in Gibeah of Benjamin; the rest of the people he sent home, every man to his tent." (This biblical estimate, 3,000 men, is surely an exaggeration.)

Gibeah and Michmash were situated on opposite sides of a steep valley (present-day Wadi es-Suweinit) that cuts into the hill country from the Jordan Valley. Together they were strategically located for dominating southern Ephraim/Benjamin. Michmash, on the northern bank, had access to the territory north of the valley ("the hill country of Bethel"), while Gibeah had corresponding access to the territory southward. At the same time, Michmash and Gibeah were in visual communication with each other and together controlled the valley crossing. It is not surprising that the Philistines would have established some sort of outpost in one or both of these villages, or that Saul, having chased the Philistines from the area, would have chosen these twin villages for his own military base.

This is the situation presupposed at the beginning of the Jabesh-gilead affair (1 Sam. 10:26–11:15).[12] Saul is residing with a band of soldiers at Gibeah, where presumably he and his men have received gifts from the local population, who now look to them for protection. This is implied by the reference in 10:27 to certain ones who, apparently regarding the Philistine victory as "beginner's luck," doubted Saul's ability to handle a serious military challenge and thus refused to provide any support: "But some worthless fellows said, 'How can this man save us?' They despised him, and brought him no present. But he held his peace."[13]

In the meantime the people of Jabesh in Gilead found themselves in a desperate situation. The Ammonites were attacking Jabesh, and clearly the city would soon fall. When the Jabeshites appealed to the Ammonite ruler Nahash for a peace settlement, he offered impossible terms: "On this condition I will make a treaty with you, that I gouge out all your right eyes, and thus put disgrace upon all Israel" (11:2). Thereupon, as a last resort, the people of Jabesh sent messengers across the Jordan to Saul at Gibeah. For three reasons this would have been the logical place for them to turn. (1) The Gileadites were among the tribes closely aligned with Ephraim. (2) There may have existed some special kinship relationship between Gibeah and Jabesh-gilead, as suggested by the account of the tribal war with Benjamin (Judg. 21:8–12). (3) Word would have spread to Gilead that Saul had defeated the Philistines and

---

12. D. V. Edelman, "Saul's Rescue of Jabesh-Gilead (I Sam. 11:1–11): Sorting Story from History," *ZAW* 96 (1984) 195–209.

13. Note the NRSV addition after 1 Sam. 10:27, which is based on the reading of a single Qumran scroll and Josephus, *Ant.* 6.68–71. For a critique of this textual addition, see Alexander Rofé, "The Acts of Nahash according to 4QSamª," *IEJ* 32 (1982) 129–33.

33. *Rocky crags between Jaba and Mukhmas.* A rugged valley (Wadi es-Suweinet) separates the present-day villages of Jaba and Mukhmas, almost certainly to be identified with ancient Geba/Gibeah and Michmash, respectively. According to 1 Sam. 14:4–6, Jonathan and his armor-bearer had to negotiate rocky crags when they crossed over from Geba to attack a Philistine garrison at Michmash.

expelled them from the Ephraimite hill country. Perhaps this new Ephraimite/Israelite military leader would extend his protection to Gilead as well.

Saul acted immediately. Butchering a yoke of oxen, he sent pieces of the carcass with messengers throughout the countryside with a call to arms and a stern warning: "Whoever does not come out after Saul and Samuel [the reference to Samuel here is probably an editorial addition], so shall it be done to his oxen!" (1 Sam. 11:7). Not surprisingly, there was an ample muster of troops. They crossed the Jordan under Saul's leadership, and he achieved with their help a second major victory of his career: first the Philistines expelled from the hill country, now the Ammonite siege of Jabesh lifted.

If the scenario offered above is even approximately correct, Saul emerged on the scene as a regional warlord—essentially the same type of leader as Jephthah, Abimelech, and David. All three of these men, according to the stories about them, entered the picture as military leaders with private armies that they used to rule and protect their home regions. Jephthah, we are told, was an outcast from the Gileadites around whom "worthless fellows" collected and they raided together (Judg. 11). Later, when threatened by the Ammonites, the Gileadites appealed to Jephthah for help. Jephthah and his men came to their aid and defeated the Ammonites, but on the advance agreement that he would rule Gilead thereafter: "If you bring me home again to fight with the Ammonites, and Yahweh gives them over to me, I will be your head" (Judg. 11:9). Abimelech solicited funds from the people of Shechem with which he hired an army and established himself as "king" of that vicinity (Judg. 9:6). As it turned out, the

Shechemites themselves were the ones who later brought about his downfall. David, as we shall see below, commanded a renegade army in the Judean wilderness during his early career, with which he posed as "protector" of the local people, collected "presents" from them, conducted raids on their enemies, and eventually may have taken the title "king" in Hebron (2 Sam 2:4; 5:3).

Saul may have taken the title "king" also at some point, and the story in 1 Samuel 10:20–24 may hark back to an occasion when he was acclaimed thus by popular assembly presided over by a reluctant Samuel. Some initial opposition from Saul's countrymen is understandable, as would have been a more unified and enthusiastic affirmation after the Jabesh-gilead victory. Yet this story about Saul's selection by lot does seem rather far-fetched, and it has clearly been shaped by the interests of the compilers of Genesis–2 Kings, who wished to emphasize divine guidance and Samuel's role in the selection process. Moreover, whatever titles were applied to Jephthah, Abimelech, Saul, and even David, they can best be described as regional warlords or chieftains.

The Territorial Extent of Saul's Chiefdom

Saul's strongest base of support, the core of his chiefdom, was the Ephraim-Benjamin-Gilead zone. On the frontiers of that zone, his administrative authority would have consisted of occasional military excursions, and local loyalty would have depended largely on whether his protection was needed against some other enemy. Two passages call for particular attention—the overview in 2 Samuel 2:8–9 of the "kingdom" that fell to Ish-bosheth after Saul's death, and the summary of Saul's wars in 1 Samuel 14:47–48.

According to 2 Samuel 2:8–9, the domain inherited by Ish-bosheth consisted of "Gilead and the Ashurites and Jezreel and Ephraim and Benjamin and all Israel."[14] One expects to find Gilead, Ephraim, Benjamin, and "all Israel" included here. Jezreel comes as no surprise either, although Saul's influence there was probably confined to the southeastern end of the valley. The only unexpected item in the description, therefore, is the reference to the "Ashurites." The term usually refers to the Assyrians, which would be totally out of place in this context. Some ancient versions read "Asher," apparently with reference to the Galilean tribe of that name, while others read "Geshur," which was the name of a locale approximately east or northeast of the Sea of Galilee. "Geshur" makes better historical sense, on the assumption that Saul expanded his influence beyond Gilead into northern Transjordan. No texts associate Saul in any way with Galilee. And why would the tribe of Asher be singled out and the other Galilean tribes ignored?

Note finally that the passage does not mention any territory in the southern hill country or Negeb, although 1 Samuel 15 describes a raid led by Saul against the Amalekites who roamed the Negeb. This was supposedly punishment to the Amalekites because they had harassed the Israelites during the exodus from Egypt. Be that as it may, the Amalekites probably presented a

---

14. See D. V. Edelman, "The 'Ashurites' of Eshbaal's State (2 Sam. 2.9)," *PEQ* 117 (1985) 85–91; and Nadav Na'aman, "The Kingdom of Ishbaal," *BN* 54 (1990) 33–37; repr. in *AIHH* 18–22.

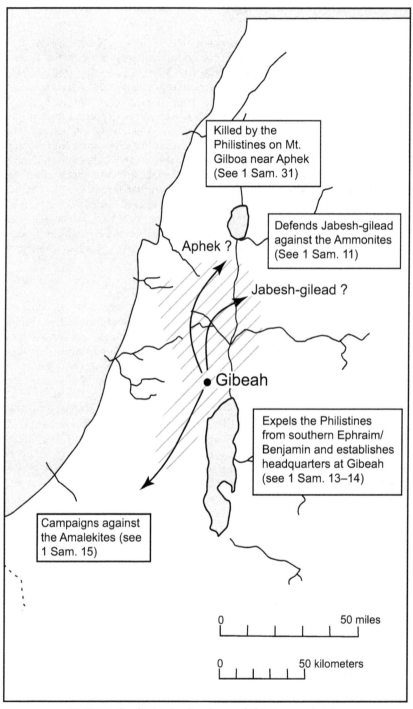

MAP 14. Saul's Major Battles and the Approximate Extent of His Chiefdom

constant problem for the clans and villages in the southern hill country (1 Sam. 30:1–3), which raises the possibility that the villagers may have called on Saul for protection against the Amalekites in the same way that the people of Jabesh-gilead had appealed to him for help against the Ammonites. If so, the Kenites may have taken the lead in this matter. We are told that Saul gave the Kenites advance warning of the raid so that they could remove themselves from danger, and that, having defeated the Amalekites, he set up a victory stela (or a monument of some sort, a *matstsib*) in Carmel, a town southeast of Hebron. Such a monument would have signaled Saul's claim to political authority in the area. Later we hear of Saul moving freely with his army throughout the southern hill country in search of David, while the local people are pictured reporting to Saul from time to time on David's whereabouts (23:6–14; 24:1; 26:1).

It is difficult to know what to make of the broadly sweeping summary of Saul's victorious wars in 1 Samuel 14:47–48. Almost certainly this is to be attributed to the compilers of the Genesis–2 Kings History. Yet its positive assessment of Saul's military career contrasts with their otherwise negative treatment of him. "He fought against all his enemies on every side—against Moab, against the Ammonites, against Edom, against the kings [or 'king,' so some Hebrew manuscripts and the Greek] of Zobah, and against the Philistines; wherever he turned he routed them. He did valiantly, and struck down the Amalekites, and rescued Israel out of the hands of those who plundered them."

First among Saul's enemies, of course, were the Philistines. Probably they did not attempt any permanent occupation of the hill country, but were satisfied to establish outposts at various points and to undertake plundering raids from time to time (1 Sam. 10:5; 13:17; 14:1). Also, they apparently sought to control in some fashion the presence of weapons in that area (13:19–22). Saul's first major military accomplishment, as we have seen, was his expulsion of the Philistines from the Ephraim/Benjamin area. Unfortunately this was only the beginning of his struggles with them. Conflicts with the Philistines continued throughout Saul's reign (see 17:1–2; 18:20–30; 19:8), and he died in battle fighting them.

We have discussed the narrative about how Saul came to the defense of Jabesh-gilead against the Ammonites. But we hear nothing in any of the Saul narratives about warfare with Zobah, Moab, or Edom. Zobah was located somewhere in the vicinity of present-day Homs in Syria, and will turn up again in the biblical materials relating to David. It apparently dominated southern Aram at the time, presumably with influence extending into northern Transjordan. If Saul fought against Zobah, therefore, he may have done so in behalf of Gileadite (and perhaps Geshurite) settlements in that area. Any battles with the Moabites or Edomites would have been frontier skirmishes or temporary eruptions of violence resulting from plundering raids. Similar to Saul's Israel, the Ammonites and Moabites were tribal societies with emerging chiefdoms at this time. Edomite territory seems to have had little settled occupation.[15]

---

15. See the essays in Piotr Bienkowski, ed., *Early Edom and Moab: The Beginning of the Iron Age in Southern Jordan* (Sheffield Archaeological Monographs 7; Collis in Association with National Museums and Galleries on Merseyside, 1992).

Administrative Affairs

Command of Saul's military forces probably remained largely a family affair throughout his career. His son Jonathan and cousin Abner are seen performing leading roles, for example, with Abner identified as commander of the army (1 Sam. 14:50; 26:5; 2 Sam. 2:8). The occasional references to Saul's servants ("officials") generally make little if any distinction between military and other types of servants (see 1 Sam. 18:5, 22, 30; 22:6; etc.). One of his servants, Doeg the Edomite (or Aramaean according to some ancient versions), is identified as "the chief of Saul's herdsmen" (21:7; see 22:9). However, one need not assume that Doeg's responsibilities were limited to, or even primarily related to, cattle raising. Often in ancient times, as well as in modern, the name of an office does not correspond exactly to the actual responsibilities of the post (for example, a "chamberlain" in connection with British government or the papacy). It is tempting to speculate on the fact that Saul had an Edomite among his officials, but perhaps not too much should be made of that either in view of the heterogeneous character of Palestine's population and the fluid sociopolitical situation of the period.

Saul's army and nascent administrative system required financial support. This would have come primarily in the form of "presents" from the villagers whom he protected (1 Sam. 10:27; and cf. 1 Sam. 25, where David attempts to extract such support from Nabal). While there may not have been any systematic program of taxation or military conscription under Saul, neither the "presents" nor general musters of troops for battle would have been entirely voluntary matters. In addition to the "presents" that Saul received from the villagers whom he protected, there would have been spoils from raids (1 Sam. 15:9) and perhaps from warfare. Second Samuel 4:1–4 identifies two brothers from Beeroth as "captains of raiding bands" in the service of Ish-bosheth. They were apparently leaders of hit-and-run squads operating for pillage and spoil. Such squads and actions seem to have been common features of the unstable times. The Amalekites operated such bands (1 Sam. 30:1) and, as we shall see, David and his men represented such a group while in the service of the Philistines (1 Sam. 27:8–12). Joab is reported to have led raiding forays for David even after the latter had set up his rule in Hebron (2 Sam. 3:22).

The words attributed to Saul in his attempt to dissuade his inner circle of Benjaminite supporters of sympathy for David suggest that he had redistributed landholdings to them: "Hear now, you Benjaminites; will the son of Jesse [David] give every one of you fields and vineyards, will he make you all commanders of thousands and commanders of hundreds?" (1 Sam. 22:7). The two "captains of raiding bands" in the service of Ish-bosheth mentioned above are identified as Benjaminite residents of Beeroth, one of the cities of the Hivite enclave from which the earlier population had been forced to flee: "For Beeroth is considered to belong to Benjamin. (Now the people of Beeroth had fled to Gittaim and are there as resident aliens to this day)" (2 Sam. 4:2–3). Saul's policy of land redistribution may have been the background of this Hivite displacement.

Saul and Yahwism

The biblical traditions preserve no detailed description of Saul's religious practices or policies. He is pictured throughout as a staunch Yahwist, however, and we have suggested that he had special connections with the Elide priests of Shiloh. Apparently Saul fought his battles under the banner of Yahweh. We read of his erecting an altar to Yahweh in time of battle, for example, and of his extreme concern for sacrificial purity (1 Sam. 14:31–35). First Samuel 28:3 notes the incongruity of Saul's visit to the witch of Endor, since he "had put the mediums and the wizards out of the land" (28:3, 9). Even Samuel's condemnations of Saul (13:13–14; 15:17–30), which reflect at least in part the anti-Saulide bias of later editors, never accuse him of infidelity to Yahweh but only of failure to follow all of Samuel's specific directives. To speak of a state religion under Saul would be inappropriate. Nonetheless, his reign and his pro-Yahwistic inclination must be seen as moving Yahwism nearer to center stage in Israelite cultic affairs.

Opposition to Saul

As one would expect for any political leader, Saul faced opposition. David emerged as the leader of this opposition, and we will look more closely at his career in the next chapter. At this point it is sufficient to note that David also came to the fore as a Philistine fighter, apparently in the service of Saul. Later he commanded a renegade army along the fringes of the southern hill country. "When his brothers and all his father's house heard of it, they went down there to him. Everyone who was in distress, and everyone who was in debt, and everyone who was discontented gathered to him; and he became captain over them. Those who were with him numbered about four hundred" (1 Sam. 22:1b–3).

The favoritism Saul showed to his Benjaminite relatives and his redistribution of land to them typify chiefdom society. But the land grants made to his inner circle of Benjaminite supporters, and perhaps to others as well, had to be made at someone's expense. We may suppose, therefore, that among the "discontented" that gathered around David were persons whom Saul had dispossessed of their lands. And of course his encroachment upon non-Israelite cities, such as Gibeon, won him especially bitter enemies (2 Sam. 21:1–2).

Saul's Last Battle

Saul's career ended as it had begun, fighting against the Philistines. The circumstances that led up to his last battle remain vague—the passages that pertain to the incident are less concerned with the broader political situation than with describing David's activities and attempting to justify the fact that he was allied with the Philistines at the time rather than with the Israelite army (1 Sam. 28–31). The scene of the battle was the southeastern end of the Jezreel Valley, at the foot of Mount Gilboa (31:1). Apparently the Philistines controlled the valley itself and camped first at Shunem and then at Aphek. They routed Saul's army, which fled for cover on Mount Gilboa (31:1). Saul and his three sons—Jonathan, Abinadab, and Malchishua—were all killed.

According to 1 Samuel 31:1, Saul himself committed suicide by falling on his sword after being mortally wounded in combat. Second Samuel 1:1–16 provides a slightly different version, with an Amalekite claiming to have delivered the coup de grace at the wounded monarch's request. The Philistines exhibited the bodies of Saul and his sons on the walls of Beth-shean, we are told, and

34. *Beth-shean.* The tell of ancient Beth-shean, where the Philistines exposed the bodies of Saul and Jonathan after their deaths on Mt. Gilboa, looms in the distance. In the foreground is the entrance to a Roman period theater.

presumably would have left them there to rot had it not been for certain daring men from Jabesh-gilead. Remembering that Saul had come to their city's aid at a crucial and desperate time, they rescued the bodies in a nighttime raid so that they could be given a proper burial in Jabesh (1 Sam. 31:11–13). Later Saul and Jonathan's bones would be transferred to Saul's home in Benjamin (2 Sam 21:14).

Something of Saul's popularity, heroism, and the significance of his reign from an early Israelite perspective is indicated by a lament recorded in 2 Samuel 1:17–27.

> From the blood of the slain,
>   from the fat of the mighty,
> the bow of Jonathan did not turn back,
>   nor the sword of Saul return empty.
> Saul and Jonathan, beloved and lovely!
>   In life and in death they were not divided;
> they were swifter than eagles,
>   they were stronger than lions.
> O daughters of Israel, weep over Saul,
>   who clothed you with crimson in luxury,
> who put ornaments of gold on your apparel.
>   How the mighty have fallen
> in the midst of the battle!
>
> (2 Sam. 1:22–25a)

These verses are attributed to David, and a second stanza focuses on David's love for Jonathan (vv. 25b–27). Yet Davidic authorship seems unlikely (or at best self-serving) in view of the fact that David had apparently thrown in his lot with the Philistines by the time of Saul's and Jonathan's deaths.

Whoever the author, the words no doubt embodied the sentiment of many Israelites.

Abner and Ish-bosheth

Although it reflects many of the folk story characteristics and editorial biases that we have observed elsewhere, the continuation of the Genesis–2 Kings History into the opening chapters of 2 Samuel offers a plausible picture of the circumstances and unfolding events that may have followed Saul's death. The following scenario depends entirely on the biblical narrative.

After the disastrous defeat at Gilboa, which would have left Saul's Israelite chiefdom in disarray and without strong leadership, an inner core of his followers recognized Ish-bosheth as Saul's successor and fled with him to Mahanaim in Transjordan. Mahanaim was in Gileadite territory and, as we have seen, the Gileadites had special reasons for loyalty to Saul's house. Ish-bosheth may have claimed authority over all the areas that Saul had ruled (see 2 Sam. 2:8–9), but west of the Jordan he obviously could not ensure the defense even of Gibeah in the heart of Benjaminite territory.

We are told very little about Ish-bosheth (called Eshbaal in 1 Chr. 8:33 and 9:39). He is identified as a son of Saul in 2 Samuel 2:8, 12, but not named among Saul's sons in other 1 Samuel passages. (Specifically, 1 Sam. 14:49 identifies Saul's sons as Jonathan, Ishvi, and Malchishua, while 31:2 reports the death of "Jonathan and Abinadab and Malchishua, the sons of Saul.") According to 2 Samuel 2:10, Ish-bosheth was "forty years old when he began to reign over Israel, and he reigned two years." The forty years is to be understood as a symbolic number, of course, and the two years at best a rough estimate. That Ish-bosheth is not mentioned along with Saul's other sons even in connection with Saul's last battle suggests that he may have been a minor when Saul was killed, or possibly a grandson rather than a son. If the former, this would help explain also why he was so easily dominated by Abner (see 2 Sam. 2:8–9).

Abner, Saul's cousin and chief military officer, seems to have orchestrated both the selection of Ish-bosheth and the retreat to Mahanaim; and he remained the real power behind Ish-bosheth in Mahanaim. The Philistines, meanwhile, had free run of the central hill country. David was allied with the Philistines, and had been using his position during the last years of Saul's reign to build support among the clans and tribes in the southern hill country, principally Judah. Now he moved into Hebron with his private army and began to rule from there over the tribe of Judah.

Second Samuel 3:1 reports that "there was a long war between the house of Saul and the house of David; and David grew stronger and stronger, while the house of Saul became weaker and weaker." Only one battle is actually reported, which apparently began with some sort of ritual engagement at Gibeon between Israelite troops under Abner and David's troops under Joab (2 Sam. 2:12–32). Three items are noteworthy about this encounter as it is described. First, that it occurred at "the pool of Gibeon" suggests that David had encroached deep into former Saulide domain. Second, it illustrates the important role of family ties in political and military affairs at that time. Abner

35. *Pool of Gibeon*. Entrance to an ancient water reservoir at el-Jib, ancient Gibeon. This reservoir may be the pool of Gibeon mentioned in 2 Sam. 2:13.

was Saul's cousin, and the prominent Judeans mentioned—Joab, Abishai, and Asahel—were nephews of David, sons of his sister Zeruiah (1 Sam. 26:6; 2 Sam. 2:18; 1 Chr. 2:13–16; see also 2 Sam. 21:11 for reference to another nephew of David). Abner killed Asahel during the battle, and that, as we shall see, was to have significant later political consequences. Third, the account distinguishes between the Benjaminites who fell in battle (accounting for most of the casualties) and Abner's men. Apparently we have to do here with Benjaminite loyalists to the house of Saul who fought alongside Abner's soldiers.

Conflict between Abner and Ish-bosheth was perhaps inevitable. Abner was the real power behind Ish-bosheth, and Ish-bosheth must have feared that Abner would eventually displace him altogether. Thus when Ish-bosheth accused Abner of relations with one of Saul's concubines, more was at stake than the concubine's reputation (2 Sam. 3:7–11). Ish-bosheth, as Saul's successor, would have inherited his father's harem. Indeed, this would have been one of the symbols confirming that he was Saul's successor. By the same measure, he may have interpreted Abner's taking access to the harem as an initial step toward displacing him. Abner reacted angrily to the accusation, according to the narrative, although apparently without actually denying the charge, and began negotiations with David toward shifting Israelite allegiance from Ish-bosheth to David.

Perhaps Abner had recognized by this time the inevitability of David's triumph and hoped to negotiate while he could bargain from a position of strength. The success of his maneuver depended on whether he could deal with two rather delicate matters. First, David demanded that Michal, Saul's daughter whom David supposedly had married while still an officer in Saul's court, be returned to him (1 Sam. 18:17–27; 2 Sam. 3:13). Such a decision would have to be made by Ish-bosheth, at least officially. Surprisingly, when David sent messages to Ish-bosheth requesting Michal, Ish-bosheth agreed—probably on the advice of, or under pressure from, Abner, and certainly without knowledge of Abner's and David's intentions. The second barrier to Abner's maneuver to shift Israelite allegiance from Ish-bosheth to David was the opposition to be expected from staunch loyalists to the house of Saul, particularly the Benjaminites. In addition to the kinship connection with Saul, the Benjaminites had already suffered heavy casualties from David's men. It is not surprising, therefore, that 2 Samuel 3:17–19 has Abner giving the Benjaminites special attention as he conferred with the elders of Israel.

Abner was reportedly able to persuade the Benjaminites also, or was confident that he could orchestrate the shift of Israel's allegiance from Ish-bosheth in spite of their opposition. Thus he came to David at Hebron, sealed the agreement, and had begun the return journey when Joab assassinated him (2 Sam. 3:20–30). Joab claimed that this was vengeance for his brother Asahel, whom Abner had slain during the skirmish at Gibeon (2:18–23). An additional factor might have been Joab's realization that Abner was about to become a very influential figure in David's administration and thus a challenge to Joab's own influence.

Ish-bosheth's days were numbered in spite of Abner's death. Perhaps there was already significant momentum among the elders of Israel toward shifting their allegiance to David. The issue was forced when two brothers from Beeroth, both "captains of raiding bands" in the service of Ish-bosheth, brutally assassinated him (2 Sam. 4:1–4). Possibly taking advantages of their irregular contact with Ish-bosheth, they gained access to his quarters and decapitated him (4:5–7a; the original reading of v. 6 is uncertain). Then, no doubt expecting a reward, they hastened by night and delivered Ish-bosheth's head to David at Hebron (4:7b–8).

With both Abner and Ish-bosheth dead, representatives of the elders of Israel came to David at Hebron and arranged a covenant that involved recognizing him as ruler over Israel as well as Judah. They were mindful, no doubt, that expediency favored their voluntary submission to David rather than attempting to defend against him. This was the end of the early Israelite chiefdom. As we shall see, however, the Israelites remained a distinctive group during the years of Davidic and Solomonic rule, and reemerged as the core of the kingdom of Israel following Solomon's death.

General Bibliography

Among the numerous studies that treat from various perspectives the issues explored in this chapter, the following deserve special mention: D. M. Gunn, *The Fate of King Saul* (JSOTSup 14; Sheffield: JSOT Press, 1980); Baruch Halpern, *The Constitution of the Monarchy in Israel* (HSM 25; Chico, CA: Scholars, 1981); F. S. Frick, *The Formation of the State in Ancient Israel: A Survey of Models and Theories* (SWBA 4; Decatur, GA: Almond, 1985); V. P. Long, *The Reign and Rejection of King Saul: A Case for Literary and Theological Coherence* (SBLDS 118; Atlanta: Scholars Press, 1989); D. V. Edelman, *King Saul in the Historiography of Judah* (JSOTSup 121; Sheffield: Sheffield Academic Press, 1991); Karel van der Toorn, "Saul and the Rise of Israelite State Religion," *VT* 43 (1993) 519–42; Volkmar Fritz and P. R. Davies, eds., *The Origins of the Ancient Israelite States* (JSOTSup 228; Sheffield: Sheffield Academic Press, 1996); Sarah Nicholson, *Three Faces of Saul: An Intertextual Approach to Biblical Tragedy* (JSOTSup 339; London: Sheffield Academic Press, 2002); and Simcha Shalom Brooks, *Saul and the Monarchy: A New Look* (Society of OT Monograph Series; Aldershot: Ashgate, 2005); and C. S. Ehrlich and M. C. White, eds., *Saul in Story and Tradition* (FAT 47; Tübingen: Mohr Siebeck, 2006).

6. David

The "house of David" ruled in Jerusalem for over four centuries. Even after Jerusalem fell to the Babylonians in 586 B.C.E., which ended the long line of Davidic kings, the people of Jerusalem and Judah (including many scattered abroad by that time) continued to hope for a restoration of the days of old when the house of David was secure on the throne. Thus it is not surprising that the founder of the dynasty, David, receives so much attention in the biblical materials or that there was such an obvious effort on the part of the ancient Judean compilers of these materials to present him in a favorable light.

The Genesis–2 Kings History, compiled sometime after the fall of Jerusalem, devotes forty-two chapters to David and seeks to portray him as Yahweh's chosen, the true and righteous king. The Chronicler's History, after hurrying quickly over the time before David, devotes twenty chapters to his reign. For the Chronicler, David was an ideal hero, God's man who could do no wrong. Finally, tradition associates David with the book of Psalms, which connects thirteen of the individual psalms by their superscriptions with particular moments in his career.

A nonbiblical reference to the "house of David" appears on an inscription, actually three fragments of a single inscription, discovered recently at Tel Dan in northern Israel.[1] The inscription is in Aramaic, and because of its fragmentary condition only parts of thirteen separate lines can be read, and no complete sentences. The parts that can be read, along with the archaeological context in which the fragments were discovered, suggest that the inscription commemorated a successful Aramaean attack on the kingdom of Israel during the latter half of the ninth century B.C.E. We will discuss this inscription in more detail in chapter 10, having to do with the ninth century. For the moment it is relevant to note that one of the broken lines includes the phrase *byt dwd*, which almost certainly is to be translated "house of David."

8. king of Israel, and . . . killed . . . iahu son of . . .
9. . . . of the house of David. And I set . . .
10. their land. . . .

One must keep in mind that the inscription refers to the "house of David," not to David himself, and dates from approximately a century and half after David would have lived. Moreover, while the dynastic name *byt dwd* presup-

---

1. For accounts of the discoveries see Avraham Biran and Joseph Naveh, "An Aramaic Stela Fragment from Tel Dan," *IEJ* 43 (1993) 81–98; idem, "The Tel Dan Inscription: A New Fragment," *IEJ* 45 (1995) 1–18.

poses a dynastic founder named David, its appearance in an ancient inscription does not necessarily confirm the historical accuracy of the biblical stories about David. If anything, it is the other way around. If scholars had not already known about David and the Davidic dynasty from the Bible, they would probably be much less confident that *byt dwd* should be translated "house of David," and certainly there would have been no reason to connect the "house of David" with Jerusalem.[2] (Otherwise the expression could have been translated as a place name or a reference to a temple.)

The other archaeological data present a similar situation. Gradually, during the course of Iron I, some of the small hill country settlements grew into villages. This process must have been well under way by the early tenth century, the approximate time that David would have lived. But it is difficult to obtain precise dates for the stages of this gradual process, and no certain connection can be made between any particular occupational phase of any particular settlement and David.[3] Jerusalem is no exception, as we shall see below.

David as Presented in the Biblical Materials

Ultimately, therefore, whatever is to be said about the historical David depends on what information can be extracted from the biblical materials. We turn our attention first to the Genesis–2 Kings History, specifically 1 Samuel 16–1 Kings 2. David is anticipated already in 1 Samuel 13:13–14 and 15:27–28, where Samuel proclaims that Yahweh has rejected Saul and selected another to rule over Israel. But David first appears by name in 1 Samuel 16, and from that point on, until Solomon gains the throne in 1 Kings 1–2, David dominates the Genesis–2 Kings narrative. We begin, therefore, with a summary of 1 Samuel 16–1 Kings 2.

Summary of 1 Samuel 16–1 Kings 2

Having denounced Saul a second time and proclaimed that Yahweh had chosen another to rule in Saul's stead, Samuel was sent by Yahweh to Bethlehem, to the house of Jesse, where he was to anoint this future ruler. Guided by Yahweh, Samuel anointed David, even though David was the youngest of Jesse's

2. For suggestions that "house of David" should also be read in the Mesha Inscription, see André Lemaire, "'House of David' Restored in Moabite Inscription," *BAR* 20/3 (1994) 30–37; and A. F. Rainey, "Following upon the Ekron and Mesha Inscriptions," *IEJ* 50 (2000) 116–17. This view has been challenged on the basis of a reexamination of the original squeeze by Pierre Bordreuil, "A propos de l'inscription de Mesha' deux notes," in P. M. Michèle Daviau et al., eds., *The World of the Aramaeans: Studies . . . in Honour of Paul-Eugène Dion* (3 vols.; JSOTSup 324–326; Sheffield: Sheffield Academic Press, 2001) 3:158–67. For the possibility that the expression "the heights of David" occurs in Shishak's list of Palestinian place names, see K. A. Kitchen, "A Possible Mention of David in the Late Tenth Century BCE, and Deity *Dod as Dead as the Dodo?" *JSOT* 76 (1997) 29–44.

3. If one begins with the biblical profile of David as a successful warrior, it is tempting to credit him with destructions at certain sites that apparently occurred about the time he would have lived, e.g., at Megiddo, Tel Masos, Ashdod, and Tel Qasile. Nothing about the archaeological evidence itself at these sites, however, warrants attributing the destructions to David. The same must be said for crediting him with some Early Iron Age fortified enclosures in the Negeb. For the view that this is a likely possibility nevertheless, see Amihai Mazar, *Archaeology of the Land of the Bible, 10,000–586 B.C.E.* (ABRL; New York: Doubleday, 1990) 390–96.

sons (1 Sam. 16:1–13). Yahweh's spirit "came mightily upon David from that day forward," while an evil spirit from Yahweh began to torment Saul. When a search was made throughout the land for a musician to play before Saul and soothe his tormented mind, David again was selected. Thus he came to Saul's court, where he entered service as Saul's personal musician and armor-bearer (16:14–23). On one occasion when the Israelite and Philistine armies were camped over against each other anticipating battle, Jesse sent David from Bethlehem to the battlefront with food for David's older brothers. When David arrived on the scene, a Philistine giant, Goliath, was challenging anyone from the Israelite camp to come out and face him in single combat. David accepted the challenge, killed Goliath, and became a hero. Saul sent to inquire who the young lad was who had killed the giant and "took him that day and would not let him return to his father's house" (17:1–18:2).

As a member of Saul's court, David became a close friend of Jonathan, Saul's son. In fact, Jonathan gave David his own robe, armor, and weapons. Also Michal, Saul's oldest daughter, loved David. David continued to fight the Philistines with much success, to the extent that his fame as a military hero began to exceed that of Saul. As a result, Saul in jealousy attempted on more than one occasion to kill him. In connection with one such attempt, Saul promised to give Michal to David in marriage, with the understanding that David would give a hundred Philistine foreskins as the marriage present. David produced two hundred foreskins and married Michal (1 Sam. 18:3–30).

Eventually the conflict between Saul and David became so great that David was forced to flee Saul's court. He was aided in his escape by Jonathan, Michal, Samuel, and Ahimelech of the priests of Nob (1 Sam. 19:1–21:9). David went first to Achish, the Philistine king of Gath, and then to the vicinity of Adullam. There he was joined by kinsmen and others who were on the run for one reason or another, so that he became the commander of a renegade army. When Saul learned that David was in Keilah, one of the cities in the Adullam vicinity, and began preparations to march against the city, David moved with his men to the Wilderness of Ziph. Finally, after several narrow escapes from Saul as he and his men roamed in that area, David returned to Achish and placed his army in Achish's service. Achish gave the city of Ziklag to David, from which base David and his men conducted raids against the Amalekites and other tribal groups in the Negeb (21:9–27:12).

David was still in the service of Achish when the Philistines routed Saul's army at Mount Gilboa and killed Saul and his sons. David and his men did not fight in the battle, however, because the Philistines feared that they might switch sides during the fighting. Thus David returned to Ziklag with his army, where he found that the city had just been raided by the Amalekites. They overtook the Amalekite raiders, massacred them, and shared the spoil with some of the elders of Judah. The deaths of Saul and Jonathan were reported to David by an Amalekite who claimed to have delivered the coup de grace to Saul. David executed the Amalekite and mourned Saul and Jonathan with a psalm (1 Sam. 28–2 Sam. 1).

Then David, with divine instructions, moved to Hebron and vicinity with his army, whereupon the men of Judah came and anointed him as their king. He sent messengers to the people of Jabesh-gilead indicating that they should take note of what had transpired. There was continued warfare between David's soldiers and those of Ish-bosheth, Saul's son now ruling at Mahanaim over the remnant of Saul's kingdom, with David becoming increasingly stronger. Six sons were born to David while he ruled from Hebron, including Amnon, Absalom, and Adonijah (2 Sam. 2:1–3:5).

Abner, Saul's general, began negotiations with David toward shifting the Israelite allegiance from Ish-bosheth to David. But when the negotiations were virtually completed, Joab killed Abner. Then two men of Beeroth, "captains of raiding bands," assassinated Ish-bosheth. With both Abner and Ish-bosheth dead, the elders of Israel came to David at Hebron, made a covenant with him, and anointed him as their king (2 Sam. 3:6–5:5).

Next David conquered Jerusalem and made it his capital. His reign was recognized on the international scene by Hiram king of Tyre. David took more wives and concubines, who bore him more sons and daughters. The Philistines began to attack when they heard that he had been made king of Israel, but he defeated them also (2 Sam. 5:6–6:25). Then he transferred the ark from Kiriath-jearim (see 1 Sam. 7:1–2) to the house of Obed-edom, a Gittite, and from there to Jerusalem. David's ritual dance before the ark was offensive to his wife, Michal. David responded to her in anger, and she bore him no children (2 Sam. 6).

Having been given rest by Yahweh from all his enemies and having built a palace for himself in Jerusalem, David proposed to build also a temple for Yahweh. Nathan the prophet, speaking for Yahweh, declined the proposal but promised that Yahweh would give David rest from all his enemies and establish his dynasty forever. David prayed to Yahweh for continued blessing (2 Sam. 7).

David defeated the enemy on every side: the Philistines, the Moabites, the Zobahites, the Ammonites, the Amalekites, and the Edomites. And he reigned over all Israel and administered justice and equity to all his people (2 Sam. 8). He restored Saul's family estate to Mephibosheth, a lame son of Jonathan, but placed Ziba, a former servant of Saul, in charge of the estate and specified that Mephibosheth was to remain in Jerusalem and eat at the king's table (2 Sam. 9).

David's troops, now commanded in the field by Joab while David himself remained in Jerusalem, fought against the Ammonites. These Ammonite wars were the context also of battles with the Zobahites (Aramaeans) and of David's affair with Bathsheba. When Bathsheba became pregnant, David arranged for her husband's death and married her himself. The baby died, but Solomon was born to her later. The Ammonites were eventually defeated (2 Sam. 10–12).

Amnon raped Tamar, his half sister, whereupon her brother Absalom killed Amnon. David then exiled Absalom to Geshur, but later allowed Absalom to return to Jerusalem, where eventually the two of them reconciled (2 Sam. 13–14). Still later Absalom led an uprising against David, which was temporarily successful. David fled to Mahanaim in Transjordan, and Absalom ruled in Jerusalem for a time. After attacking David in Transjordan, Absalom's army was defeated, Absalom was killed, and David was restored to the throne. Absalom's rebellion was followed by another less successful rebellion instigated by Sheba, a Benjaminite (2 Sam. 15–20).

David executed Saul's male descendants in connection with a famine (2 Sam. 21:1–14). There was further warfare with the Philistines (vv. 15–22). David composed psalms of praise because Yahweh had delivered him out of the hands of his enemies and of Saul (22:1–23:7). Yahweh incited David to make a census of his realm and then punished David for doing so. The punishment consisted of three days of pestilence on the kingdom (2 Sam. 24).

When David reached old age, was failing in health, and no longer potent, Adonijah proceeded to assume the throne. Nathan brought the matter to Bathsheba's attention and together they influenced David to designate Solomon as his successor instead of Adonijah. Solomon was crowned in a ceremony orchestrated by Nathan and Zadok (1 Kgs. 1–2).

Observations Regarding the Genesis–2 Kings Account of David's Reign

Three observations that we have made in earlier chapters about the nature of the Genesis–2 Kings History need to be reemphasized and applied more specifically to this David section. (1) The Genesis–2 Kings account is composite, and the various traditions that have been combined and intertwined to produce this David section can best be described, with some exceptions, as folk legends. They are certainly not to be read as historical records. (2) Most of the individual traditions that make up this David section of the Genesis–2 Kings History, and especially the compilers' editorial contributions, reflect a definite pro-Davidic and pro-Solomonic bias. (3) Not only the selection and the tone but also the arrangement of these materials has been determined to a significant degree by the theological interests of the late Judean compilers. Let us explore each of these three points in further detail.

Compilation of Folk Legends. The composite nature of the Genesis–2 Kings presentation of David's career is apparent from the beginning. First we are told that David was brought to Saul's court as a musician to play before Saul and soothe his tormented mind. Once there, he became Saul's armor-bearer as well (1 Sam. 16:14–23). But then the scene changes and we find David still at home in Bethlehem, from which he is sent to take food to his brothers serving in Saul's army. Having reached the battlefront, David accepts Goliath's challenge and kills the giant, whereupon Saul inquires who the father of the lad is.

> When Saul saw David go out against the Philistine, he said to Abner, the commander of the army, "Abner, whose son is this young man?" And Abner said, "As your soul lives, O king, I do not know." The king said, "Inquire whose son the stripling is." On David's return from killing the Philistine, Abner took him and brought him before Saul with the head of the Philistine in his hand. Saul said to him, "Whose son are you, young man?" And David answered, "I am the son of your servant Jesse the Bethlehemite." (1 Sam. 17:55–58)

At least three details in the Goliath story suggest that originally it was told independently of the preceding story and of the materials that follow. (a) If David had previously entered service as Saul's personal musician and armor-bearer, why then was he not already with Saul at the beginning of the Goliath episode rather than back home in Bethlehem? And why does Saul not know who David is? (b) First Samuel 17:54 states that David took Goliath's head to Jerusalem. According to 2 Samuel 5:6–10, however, Jerusalem would not yet have been in Israelite hands. (c) In contrast to this delightful story that relates

CHART 9. Basic Compositional Units of 1 Samuel 16–1 Kings 2

1 Sam. 16–2 Sam. 5	A collection of stories pertaining to David's rise to power, from his anointment by Samuel to the establishment of his rule in Jerusalem.
2 Sam. 6:1–23	The continuation and conclusion of the Ark Narrative, the main part of which is to be found in 1 Sam. 4:1–7:2.
2 Sam. 7	A chapter essentially from the hands of the compilers of Genesis–2 Kings that emphasizes Yahweh's affirmation of David and his dynasty.
2 Sam. 8:1–15	A summary of David's military accomplishments and administrative officials.
2 Sam. 9–20; 1 Kings 1–2	An essentially continuous narrative that describes various problems faced by David during his reign and explains how it happened that Solomon, rather than any of the older brothers, succeeded David to the throne.
2 Sam. 21–24	Miscellaneous materials relevant to David's reign.

how the lad David killed Goliath, 2 Samuel 21:19 credits another Bethlehemite, Elhanan the son of Jaareoregim, with killing Goliath.[4]

Conflicting items such as these are noticeable throughout the 1 Samuel 16–1 Kings 2 presentation of David's career. They remind us that this segment of the Genesis–2 Kings History is, like the remainder of the work, composed of various originally independent traditions. The basic compositional units that we recognize in this David section of the Genesis–2 Kings History are summarized in Chart 9.

Folk themes, such as the lad killing the giant with a sling stone (1 Sam. 17) and the young hero winning the hand of the king's daughter in marriage by overcoming impossible odds (1 Sam. 18:20–29), remind us also that we are dealing with largely legendary materials. This is particularly true of the collection of stories about David's rise to power (1 Sam. 16–2 Sam. 5).[5] Admittedly, the other large block of material that comprises this David section of the Genesis–2 Kings

---

4. On the various versions of the Goliath story, see Dominique Barthélemy et al., *The Story of David and Goliath: Textual and Literary Criticism* (OBO 73; Fribourg: Éditions Universitaires, 1986); Emanuel Tov, "The David and Goliath Saga: How a Biblical Editor Combined Two Versions," *BRev* 2/4 (1986) 34–41; and J. C. Trebolle Barrera, "The Story of David and Goliath (1 Sam. 17–18): Textual Variants and Literary Composition," *Bulletin of the International Organization for Septuagint and Cognate Studies* 23 (1990) 16–30. See also Alexander Rofé, "The Battle of David and Goliath: Folklore, Theology, Eschatology," in Jacob Neusner et al., eds., *Judaic Perspectives on Ancient Israel* (Philadelphia: Fortress, 1987) 117–51; as well as Arie van der Kooji, "The Story of David and Goliath: The Early History of Its Text," *ETL* 68 (1992) 118–31. The Goliath story and his armor have been seen as reflecting later Greek influence; see Israel Finkelstein, "The Philistines in the Bible: A Late-Monarchic Perspective," *JSOT* 27 (2002) 131–67, and Azzan Yadin, "Goliath's Armor and Israelite Collective Memory," *VT* 54 (2004) 373–95.

5. For discussion and bibliography regarding this block of material, see R. P. Gordon, *1 & 2 Samuel* (OTG; Sheffield: JSOT Press, 1984) 61–70.

History, the essentially continuous narrative in 2 Samuel 9–20–1 Kings 1–2,[6] is surprisingly free of obvious legendary elements and overt theological commentary. Indeed, it gives the appearance of having been written by someone who was rather close to the royal family and who recorded their ups and downs dispassionately. Upon close examination, however, one begins to notice items in even this source that are more suggestive of the storyteller's art than of historical record. The reader is allowed to listen in on private conversations, for example, and to witness bedroom scenes. This is not the sort of information that would have been readily available even to persons close to the royal court.

Included with the legends and stories are occasional miscellaneous items such as psalms, lists, and brief reports. Some of these have a ring of authenticity—for example, the list of David's officials in 2 Samuel 8:16–18. Others do not, such as the psalms attributed to him in 2 Samuel 1:19–27 and 22:2–23:7. Finally, certain key passages are clearly the product of the late compilers of the Genesis–2 Kings History and are intended to convey what they regarded to be the significance of David's reign in Israel's history. Consider 2 Samuel 7, for example, where Nathan, in a style very similar to the farewell addresses of Moses, Joshua, and Samuel, pronounces Yahweh's blessing on David's kingdom and promises that the Davidic dynasty will last forever.[7] In the same way that Joshua's farewell address concludes the era of conquest in the compilers' perception of Israel's past and Samuel's last address concludes the era of the great judges, so also Nathan's dynastic oracle informs the reader that the true king and the true dynasty are finally in place. In effect, Nathan's oracle expresses the same Davidic-Jerusalemite theology presupposed in Psalms 89 and 132. It was on the basis of this royal theology that the Davidic dynasty claimed perpetual right to the throne. The roots of this theological claim may go back to David's reign, but the full expression of it, such as one finds in Nathan's oracle and the psalms, belongs to a later day.

Pro-Davidic and Pro-Solomonic Slant. If the biblical account summarized above is anywhere close to the actual sequence of historical events, the route by which David gained access to the combined crown of Israel and Judah, and the process by which Solomon instead of one of David's older sons inherited the throne, would have raised serious questions about the legitimacy of their respective reigns and, by extension, the legitimacy of the whole Davidic line. No doubt this legitimacy issue was still very much alive in the exilic and early postexilic periods—the time of the final compilation of the Genesis–2 Kings History. Its Judean compilers would have hoped for a restoration of Jerusalem and the reunion of Israel and Judah under a revived Davidic dynasty. Others of the day, the Samaritans in particular, however, would have held no such allegiance to either the house of David or Jerusalem. Accordingly, the so-called Ark Narrative embedded in 1 Samuel 16–2 Samuel 7 serves as an apology for

---

6. For decades many have treated this material as an originally independent source and designated it as either the "throne succession story" or "court history." For discussion of the issues and bibliography, see Gordon, *1 & 2 Samuel*, 81–94; Serge Frolov, "Succession Narrative: A 'Document' or a Phantom?" *JBL* 121 (2002) 81–104 (with bibliography); Albert de Pury and Thomas Römer, *Die Sogenannte Thronfolgegeschichte Davids: Neue Einsichten und Anfragen* (OBO 176; Freiburg: Universitätsverlag 2000).

7. See D. J. McCarthy, "II Samuel 7 and the Structure of the Deuteronomic History," *JBL* 84 (1965) 131–38.

David's actions toward Saul and his descendants and functions as authenticating tradition to legitimate both the Davidic dynasty and the preeminence of Jerusalem in the life of the people and the plan of Yahweh. This section opens with the story of David's divine election and concludes with Yahweh's promise that David's dynasty will rule securely in Jerusalem forever.[8]

The concern to legitimize David's actions toward Saul and his descendants is especially obvious in the passages that emphasize Jonathan's deference to David. Consider the scene described in 1 Samuel 18:4, for example, where Jonathan "stripped himself of the robe that he was wearing, and gave it to David, and his armor, and even his sword and his bow and his belt." The text comes close to portraying Jonathan's deed as an act of abdication to any claim to the throne (see also 23:15–18). While there may have existed a close relationship between David and Jonathan, one must suspect that this theme has been intentionally magnified in the traditions as we have received them in order to justify the fact that David and his descendants ended up with the throne.[9] Similarly, the passages that emphasize David's unwavering loyalty to Saul on the grounds that Saul was "Yahweh's anointed" (1 Sam. 26, especially v. 9) anticipate that David will replace Saul in this capacity. In effect, therefore, these passages call for the same unqualified loyalty to David and his descendants that David is depicted giving to Saul.

Literary Structure. Not only the selection and tone of the folk materials assembled in this segment of the Genesis–2 Kings History, but also the literary structure of the resulting composite account of David's reign, are determined to a certain degree by the theological concepts that the compilers wished to convey. Second Samuel 8, which describes David's domain and provides a list of his cabinet officers, serves as the centerpiece of the presentation of his career. What precedes tells how David replaced Saul, established his own rule, acquired and turned Jerusalem into the center for his kingdom, and received from Yahweh the dynastic blessing and promise. What follows (with the exception of 2 Sam. 20–24, which contains various miscellaneous items relevant to David's reign but not integrated into the story line) concerns the fate of the rule of David and how that rule was transferred to Solomon. Broadly speaking, then, we are presented first with a victorious David on the rise and then a David troubled by political and family problems; first a David under the blessing and then a David under the curse.[10]

---

8. On royal apology and propaganda in the ancient Near East and the Bible, see H. A. Hoffner Jr., "Propaganda and Political Justification in Hittite Historiography," in Hans Goedicke and J. J. M. Roberts, eds., *Unity and Diversity: Essays in the History, Literature, and Religion of the Ancient Near East* (Baltimore: Johns Hopkins University Press, 1975) 49–62; Hayim Tadmor, "Autobiographical Apology in the Royal Assyrian Literature," in Hayim Tadmor and Moshe Weinfeld, eds., *History, Historiography, and Interpretation* (Jerusalem: Magnes, 1984) 36–57; P. K. McCarter Jr., "The Apology of David," *JBL* 99 (1980) 489–504; repr. in G. N. Knoppers and J. G. McConville, eds., *Reconsidering Israel and Judah: Recent Studies on the Deuteronomistic History* (SBTS 8; Winona Lake, IN: Eisenbrauns, 2000) 260–75; and M. B. Dick, "The 'History of David's Rise to Power' and the Neo-Babylonian Succession Apologies," in B. F. Batto and K. L. Roberts, eds., *David and Zion: Biblical Studies in Honor of J. J. M. Roberts* (Winona Lake, IN: Eisenbrauns, 2004) 3–19.

9. See David Jobling, "Jonathan: A Structural Study in 1 Samuel," in *The Sense of Biblical Narrative: Three Structural Analyses in the Old Testament* (JSOTSup 7; Sheffield: JSOT Press, 1978) 4–25.

10. See R. A. Carlson, *David the Chosen King: A Traditio-Historical Approach to the Second Book of Samuel* (Uppsala: Almqvist & Wiksell, 1964).

David's wars with the Philistines are reported after his conquest of Jerusalem, and in that context seem intended to illustrate the military successes of the divinely chosen king now firmly established in the divinely chosen capital (2 Sam. 5:17–25). One has to suspect, however, that the Philistines would have reacted to David's maneuvers long before he conquered Jerusalem, and in fact the passage in question connects the beginning of the Philistine wars with David's acceptance of rule over Israel rather than with his conquest of Jerusalem (see v. 17). In short, David would probably have had to deal with Philistine hostilities before he transferred from Hebron to Jerusalem.[11]

Absalom's and Sheba's rebellions are reported near the end of the Genesis–2 Kings presentation of David's career, leaving the impression that these incidents occurred fairly late in his reign, during the time of "David under the curse." Yet it makes more sense to suppose that such challenges to David's authority would have occurred earlier in his reign, while he may have been less secure on the throne. Note also that when David fled from Absalom's army and arrived in Transjordan, he was greeted and aided by Shobi son of the Ammonite king Nahash. This is the sort of response one might expect before, but certainly not after, Nahash's death and David's ensuing war against the Ammonites (2 Sam. 10:2–3; 17:27–29).

A similar case can be made regarding David's execution of Saul's descendants, reported among the miscellaneous items at the end of 2 Samuel. Surely David would have had to deal with this potential threat early in his reign. Three additional arguments may be marshaled: (a) There would probably not have been a long time lapse between Saul's offense against the Gibeonites and the famine that was attributed to the offense and served as the pretext of David's action (21:1–6). (b) The account of David's dealings with Mephibosheth presupposes that he was the only remaining descendant of Saul, the others presumably having already been executed (2 Sam. 9; 21:7). (c) The arrangements regarding Mephibosheth, on the other hand, were already in place at the time of Absalom's rebellion (16:1–4).

The Chronicler's Presentation of David's Reign

Although the Chronicler's History begins with Adam, it provides little more than genealogical lists for the time from Adam to Saul (1 Chr. 1–9). Only occasionally are tidbits of nongenealogical information interspersed among the lists (see, e.g., 1 Chr. 4:38–43; 5:23–26). Moreover, some of the lists actually pertain to the period after the Babylonian exile (see, e.g., the list of royal descendants in 1 Chr. 3:17–24 and the list of returnees from exile in 1 Chr. 9). For all practical purposes, therefore, the Chronicler's narrative account begins with Saul's death in chapter 10.

From that point forward, the Chronicler's History overlaps the Samuel–Kings segment of the Genesis–2 Kings History. There is often conspicuous verbal overlap. Compare the Chronicler's description of Saul's death on Mount Gilboa in

---

11. For the view that David continued his close alliance with the Philistines throughout his reign, see Baruch Halpern, *David's Secret Demons: Messiah, Murderer, Traitor, King* (Grand Rapids: Eerdmans, 2001) 144–56. On the status and role of David's supporter, Ittai of Gath, see Nadav Na'aman, "Ittai the Gittite," *BN* 94 (1998) 22–25.

chapter 10, for example, with the description in 1 Samuel 31. Apparently the Chronicler had access to the material of Samuel–Kings in essentially its present form and relied heavily upon it. Indeed, one might describe the Chronicler's History as a more theologized version (a midrash) of Samuel–Kings. The Chronicler was more attentive to cultic and religious affairs than the compilers of Genesis–2 Kings. He gives special attention to the life, organization, and personnel of the Jerusalem temple. Especially he highlights the role of the Levites in the Jerusalem cult. Also the Chronicler was more narrowly focused on the Davidic dynasty and the kingdom of Judah than were the compilers of Genesis–2 Kings. Affairs of the northern Israelite kingdom are virtually ignored.

Since the Chronicler's treatment depends so heavily on Samuel–Kings, it shares also in the limitations and difficulties of the latter for the historian's purposes.[12] Moreover, comparison of parallel texts in Samuel–Kings and Chronicles reveals that the Chronicler often took extreme liberties with the Samuel–Kings material. Numbers are exaggerated, miraculous features are introduced into the stories, religious aspects are emphasized, unedifying features about the prominent heroes are downplayed or bypassed, and the evils of antiheroes are stressed.

The Chronicler's tendentious use of the Samuel–Kings material is especially obvious in his treatment of David. One does not get the impression from the Chronicler's History, for example, that David had any struggles in his rise to power. There is no substantial description of the conflict between Saul and David. It is hardly mentioned that David was in the service of the Philistines at the time of the battle of Gilboa, that Ish-bosheth ruled after Saul until assassinated, or that David was crowned first by the elders of Judah and only later by the Israelites. Instead, the Chronicler emphasizes that David received widespread support while at Ziklag, Mount Gilboa, and Hebron, and leaves the reader to infer that the crown was passed on to David almost routinely immediately following Saul's death (1 Chr. 10–12).

Perhaps the most characteristic feature of the Chronicler's presentation of David is that he credits David with being the real organizer of the temple cult, its staff, and especially of the Levitical functionaries associated with the temple and the ark (1 Chr. 15–16; 23–26). Indeed, the Chronicler would have us suppose that David planned the entire construction of the temple and passed along the plans and provisions to Solomon (1 Chr. 28–29). This is in striking contrast to the Genesis–2 Kings History, which allows David a much less significant role in the organization of the Jerusalem cult. It is noticeable, finally, that the Chronicler mentions none of the troubles of David's reign—the Bathsheba affair, Absalom's and Sheba's rebellions, the struggles between Adonijah and

12. On the issues relating to the historicity of material in Chronicles, see Sara Japhet, "The Historical Reliability of Chronicles: The History of the Problem and Its Place in Biblical Research," *JSOT* 33 (1985) 83–107; M. Z. Brettler, "Chronicles as a Model for Biblical History," in *The Creation of History in Ancient Israel* (London: Routledge, 1995) 20–47; M. P. Graham et al., eds., *The Chronicler as Historian* (JSOTSup 238; Sheffield: Sheffield Academic Press, 1997); and Isaac Kalimi, *The Reshaping of Ancient Israelite History in Chronicles* (Winona Lake, IN: Eisenbrauns, 2004). For a comparison of the materials in Genesis–2 Kings and 1–2 Chronicles, see J. C. Endres et al., *Chronicles and Its Synoptic Parallels in Samuel, Kings, and Related Biblical Texts* (Collegeville, MN: Liturgical Press, 1998); and W. R. Brookman, *A Hebrew-English Synopsis of the Old Testament: Samuel, Kings, and Chronicles* (Peabody, MA: Hendrickson, 2003). On the figure of David in 1 Chronicles, see J. W. Wright, "The Founding Father: The Structure of the Chronicler's David Narrative," *JBL* 117 (1998) 45–59.

Solomon. The transition to Solomon's rule is made under David's supervision and without incident (1 Chr. 23:1; 29:22). In short, the Chronicler presents us with a highly idealized David who was a great warrior, who was the founder of the temple with its associated religious orders and institutions, and whose reign was virtually free of internal conflicts from beginning to end.

The Chronicler also introduced material that has no parallel in Samuel–Kings. Much of this supplementary material amounts to theological exposition. But some are items of substance that may have been derived from other sources the Chronicler had at hand. In connection with David, for example, the Chronicler provides lists of:

- Men who came to David at Ziklag (1 Chr. 12:1–7)
- Men who deserted Saul and joined David at the time of the battle at Mount Gilboa (12:19–22)
- Fighting men who came to Hebron to crown David king (12:23–40)
- Levitical heads of families charged with attending the ark and other cultic responsibilities (15:2–27; 23:3–26:32)
- Military officers, tribal chiefs, overseers of the king's treasuries and possessions, and so on (chap. 27)

In light of the obviously tendentious way in which the Chronicler used the Samuel–Kings materials, serious questions must be raised about the trustworthiness of these materials supplied in Chronicles but without parallels in Samuel–II Kings. It is not a question just of whether the Chronicler had access to sources no longer available today but of whether he also used whatever other sources he had at hand in the same tendentious fashion that he used the Samuel–Kings material.

David and the Psalms

David is associated by tradition with the book of Psalms, and in fact the superscriptions of seventy-three of the psalms (in the Masoretic Hebrew manuscripts) include the notation *ledawid*. This is usually translated "of David"—that is, with the inference that David composed these particular psalms. In thirteen of these "Davidic" psalms, moreover, the superscriptions report the circumstances under which David supposedly wrote or sang the psalm (Pss. 3; 7; 18; 34; 51–52; 54; 56–57; 59–60; 63; 142). If we do indeed have at hand psalms written by David, then this amounts to another source of information about his life and even his attitudes. Unfortunately the situation is not so simple.

In the first place, the preposition *le* of *ledawid* may be translated in other ways ("for," "concerning," "dedicated to," etc.) that would not necessarily suggest authorship. The term *dawid*, on the other hand, which is not even necessarily to be taken as a proper name, may refer to the Davidic dynasty in general rather than specifically to David himself (see Ezek. 34:23–24; 37:24–25). Thus *ledawid* in the superscriptions could mean simply that these particular psalms were connected in some way with the Davidic court, with the Jerusalem temple (which was the Davidic chapel par excellence), with royal usage, or perhaps with a special royal collection of the psalms.

Second, while David may have had musical ability and may have played some role in establishing the personnel and procedures of the Jerusalem cult (see 1 Sam. 16:14–22; Amos 6:5), it seems clear that his image as a musician and cultic innovator did not blossom until fairly late in Judean history. We have already noted this as one of the ways in which the Chronicler's presentation of David differs from that of Genesis–2 Kings. While the latter has little to say about David's involvement with music or the cult, for the Chronicler this was the most important aspect of David's career. The final compilation of the Psalter belongs to the Chronicler's era or later, so it is not surprising that David is given pride of place in the editorial superscriptions to the Psalms. Moreover, the later the version, the more numerous the psalms assigned to David. In fact, one of the Psalms manuscripts discovered among the Dead Sea Scrolls (11QPs^a) credits David with having written 4,050 psalms and contains previously unknown "autobiographical" psalms of David.[13]

In short, the superscriptions that presuppose Davidic authorship of many of the psalms and seek to explain the circumstances under which he composed them represent late speculative attempts to relate the feelings of trouble and distress reflected in the psalms to episodes in David's life. Even if it could be established that David wrote the *ledawid* psalms and that the superscriptions are authentic, the Psalter would still provide relatively little specific information about David's career. The psalms are poetry and generally speak in metaphorical, typical, and generalized language that provides few or no specific historical details.

The Biblical David and the Historical David

While the Bible has much to say about David, it will be obvious from the preceding observations that none of the biblical material pertaining to him submits easily to critical historical inquiry.[14] By the same measure, any attempt to describe the "historical" David necessarily involves a great deal of subjective judgment, and our attempt below is no exception. Perhaps it will be useful to identify in advance some of the interpretative principles that we employ and also to provide a thumbnail sketch of the historical David as we suspect him to have been.

1. We are mindful that any speculation regarding the historical David must depend heavily on the biblical traditions. The Dan Inscription seems to confirm that the founder of Jerusalem's ruling dynasty was named David, but it tells us nothing about this David. Neither is archaeology of much help for understanding any of the specifics of David's career. Perhaps the most important thing we learn from archaeology is that Jerusalem was a very modest settlement during the time that David and Solomon would have lived.

13. See J. A. Sanders, *The Dead Sea Psalms Scroll* (Ithaca, NY: Cornell University Press, 1967); and A. M. Cooper, "The Life and Times of King David According to the Book of Psalms," in R. E. Friedman, ed., *The Poet and the Historian: Essays in Literary and Historical Biblical Criticism* (HSS 20; Chico, CA: Scholars Press, 1983) 117–31.

14. For the view that David and Solomon are about as historical as King Arthur, see P. R. Davies, "'House of David' Built on Sand: The Sins of the Biblical Maximizers," *BAR* 20/4 (1994) 54–55. See also N. P. Lemche, "Is It Still Possible to Write a History of Ancient Israel?" *SJOT* 8/2 (1994) 165–90. For a popular press description of the issues, see C. Shea, "Debunking Ancient Israel: Erasing History or Facing the Truth?" *Chronicle of Higher Education* 44/13 (21 November 1997) A12–A14.

2. Our treatment of David will favor the Samuel–Kings account of his career over the Chronicler's account. Particularly, items unique to the Chronicler will be regarded with extreme caution, especially where it appears that they were introduced to support the Chronicler's characteristic views.

3. Most of the materials that constitute the Samuel–Kings account of David's reign are folk traditions that have been transmitted, shaped, and editorialized by pro-Davidic, Judean circles. We think that many, perhaps most, of these traditions are based ultimately on historical persons and events. But this is a judgment call that cannot be proved, and any attempt to separate the historical from the legendary and editorial is a highly subjective process. Consequently, the David described in the remainder of this chapter must be understood as nothing more than our best-guess scenario for the historical figure who may lurk behind the folk traditions.

4. We see David as one who emerged on the scene as a military figure, a local warlord in the tradition of Jephthah, Abimelech, and Saul. He managed to displace Saul, establish a chiefdom of his own centered in Jerusalem, and dominate the interior of western Palestine and northern Transjordan.

5. Jerusalem seems to have been a small settlement, centered around a stronghold, with a mixed population including people of Amorite, Hurrian, and Hittite stock. In the immediate vicinity of Jerusalem were Gibeon and other Hivite villages. During the course of his reign, David probably secured control also over some of the old Bronze Age cities that had continued on as modest settlements during Iron I (such as Shechem, Megiddo, and Hazor). There is no reason to suppose, on the other hand, that his realm included Philistia or southern Transjordan.

6. David's realm also included the Judahites, his own tribe of origin, and the remnants of Saul's Israelite chiefdom. David may have taken some measures—such as bringing the ark to Jerusalem—to symbolize that his regime was a continuation of Saul's Israel. Yet the Israelites were only one of the population groups under David's rule, their initial acceptance of his authority was not entirely voluntary, and they were never among his most loyal supporters. The concern to depict David as the divinely ordained successor to Saul and the first really legitimate "king of Israel" is to be attributed primarily (if not entirely) to the late Judean compilers of the Genesis–2 Kings History and the Chronicler's History.

7. Whether one should think of David as a chieftain or as a king is unclear. We think that "king" is probably the appropriate term, at least for his later career after he established himself in Jerusalem. Jerusalem had a tradition of kingship, and the pluralistic population over which David ruled would have required a more complex administrative structure than Saul had employed.

David in Saul's Court[15]

David's father, Jesse, is referred to both as a Bethlehemite (1 Sam. 16:1, 18) and as an Ephrathite (17:12; see also Ruth 1:2). The name of their village, Bethlehem

---

15. See R. P. Gordon, "David's Rise and Saul's Demise: Narrative Analogy in I Samuel 24–26," *TynBul* 31 (1980) 37–64.

("temple of Lehem"), would have derived from a local sanctuary, while Ephrath was presumably the name of the dominant local clan. Apparently David came to Saul's court as a young professional soldier and made a name for himself as a gallant and successful warrior in skirmishes against the Philistines (1 Sam. 18:5, 30; 19:8). Soon, we are told, his fame as a Philistine fighter began to surpass even that of Saul.

> As they were coming home, when David returned from killing the Philistine, the women came out of all the towns of Israel, singing and dancing, to meet King Saul, with tambourines, with songs of joy, and with musical instruments. And the women sang to one another as they made merry,
>
> > "Saul has killed his thousands,
> > and David his ten thousands."
> > (1 Sam. 18:6–7)

In addition to his general popularity in Saul's court, David is pictured as having an intimate and favored relationship with Saul's own family. Specifically, we are told that there was a strong bond of friendship between David and Saul's son Jonathan (1 Sam. 18:1–4, 20; 23:16–18), and that Saul's daughter Michal loved David and was given to him in marriage (18:20–27). Perhaps there is a kernel of truth to this family connection, but the matter has probably been overplayed in the effort to emphasize that David was an appropriate successor to Saul. The reader is to understand that (1) David was innocent of any designs on the throne, (2) that Saul's own son and daughter were satisfied that David was to have the throne, and (3) David was practically a member of the family anyway. As for the marriage between David and Michal, consider the manner in which the story is told, with the folkloric motif of the young man who acquires the king's daughter by performing a seemingly impossible deed and in spite of the monarch's machinations (18:17–19). If there was such a marriage, the story almost certainly plays loose with the actual historical circumstances.[16]

The stress in the biblical materials on David's military success, his popularity among the people, and his close relationship with Saul's family contrasts noticeably with the negative fashion in which Saul is depicted. On the one hand, we are presented with a humble, obedient, and even naive but highly successful David. On the other hand, we encounter Saul as a melancholic paranoid who was suspicious of the success of his own soldier. To substantiate this, in good literary fashion but with doubtful historical basis, the narrators appeal to what Saul personally thought and felt (1 Sam. 18:8–12), record his blundering attempts to kill David (18:10–11; 19:8–10) or to get him killed (18:17–29), and report the content of secret and private conversations (18:20–26; 19:1–6).

Here again one must suspect that the biblical traditions as they have been handed down to us rather overdo it. Saul probably did become jealous and greatly concerned as the young David's popularity increased. Saul's own authority depended on military prowess, and he would have been well aware that any other exceedingly successful and popular military hero posed a threat,

---

16. See D. J. A. Clines and Tamara Eskenazi, eds., *Telling Queen Michal's Story: An Experiment in Comparative Interpretation* (JSOTSup 119; Sheffield: Sheffield Academic Press, 1991).

if not to his own rule, then certainly to Jonathan's chances of succeeding him. But while it is reasonable to suppose that Saul's jealousy and concern for Jonathan's future were factors in the Saul-David conflict, one senses that David's ambitions were also a contributory cause. This is suggested, if for no other reason, by the fact that the narrators of the stories in 1–2 Samuel seem so concerned to convince the reader otherwise.

Eventually David left Saul's court and organized a rebel army that operated along the fringes of the southern hill country. Again the narrators of the biblical account insist that it was Saul's blind jealousy that forced David to flee and emphasize that the escape was aided by Michal, Jonathan, Samuel, and the priests at Nob (1 Sam. 19:11–23; 20; 21:1–9). But once more one must wonder, as Saul apparently did, whether this was a calculated move on David's part.

David the Renegade

Having withdrawn from the royal court, David apparently spent a period of time as a renegade on the run from Saul (see Map 15). This phase of his career is treated in 1 Samuel 19:11–2 Samuel 1. Although the narratives that make up these chapters do not necessarily represent the exact chronology of events, they do seem to suggest the following four stages:

1. David escapes from Saul's court (1 Sam. 19:11–21:15)
2. David hides in the vicinity of Adullam and is joined by others (22:1–23:14)
3. David and his band roam at large in the southern wilderness east of Ziph, Carmel, and Maon (23:15–26:25)
4. David places himself and his army in the service of the Philistines (1 Sam. 27–2 Sam. 1)

Escape from Saul's Court

First Samuel 19:11–21:9 is composed of essentially four narratives that feature, respectively, Michal, Samuel, Jonathan, and Ahimelech of the priests of Nob, and describe how each of these persons aided David in his flight from Saul's court. The story of how Michal stalled Saul's soldiers while David escaped through a window (19:11–17) and the one about how David received provisions at Nob (21:1–9) are somewhat more convincing than the ones that involve Samuel and Jonathan (19:18–20:42). All four of the stories find their setting at Gibeah (present-day Jaba) or in the immediate vicinity. The follow-up narrative (21:10–15), which has David going over to the Philistines at this point, is obscure, probably a confusion of two separate traditions: the one about David and Ahimelech of Nob (note that the superscription to Ps. 34 has David playing the madman before Abimelech [= Ahimelech]) and the other about David's later alliance with the Philistines (1 Sam. 27ff.). Our guess is that David slipped away from Gibeah with Michal's help, received provisions from Ahimelech of Nob without the latter realizing that he was on the run, and headed straight for the tribal territory of Judah.

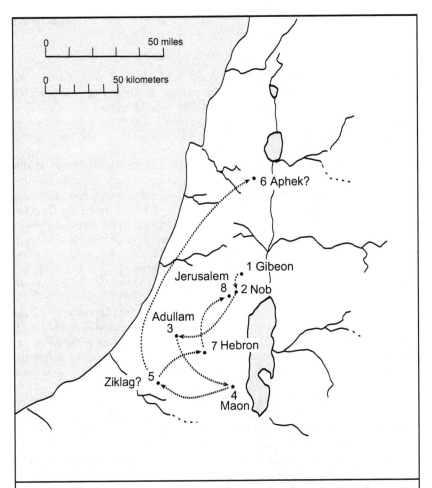

1. David in Saul's Court.

2. David escapes with the help of the priests of Nob.

3. David hides in the vicinity of Adullam. Others join him.

4. Saul learns David's position. David escapes to the "wilderness" east of Carmel and Maon.

5. With Saul close on his trail, David goes over to Achish, the Philistine ruler of Gath. Achish assigns the city of Ziklag to David and his men.

6. David marches with the Philistines to Aphek, where they defeat Saul and the Israelite army. Unsure of David's loyalties, the Philistines do not allow David to join them in batttle.

7. With Saul and Jonathan dead, David and his men move into Hebron, where the Judahites crown him king. Later the remnant of Saul's Israelite chiefdom accept David as their king also.

8. After ruling at Hebron for seven years. David conquers Jerusalem and makes it his capital.

**MAP 15. David's Moves from Saul's Court
to the Conquest of Jerusalem**

David in Adullam and Vicinity

Saul apparently did not pursue David immediately, giving David time to transfer his parents to Moab for their safety and secure himself at Adullam (Tell
Sheikh Madhkur in the Shephelah; read "stronghold" rather than "cave" in
1 Sam. 22:1). There he was joined by individuals of various sorts—kinsmen,
opponents of Saul, other persons on the run for one reason or another—so that
soon he was in command of a small private army (22:1–2).

Two religious functionaries also reportedly joined David's troop at this
stage. One was the prophet Gad, a shadowy figure, who is pictured offering
David advice about strategy (1 Sam. 22:5) and who apparently remained with
David throughout their careers (see 2 Sam. 24:11–14). Gad convinced David to
remove himself and his men from Adullam and camp in the forest of Hereth.
While the location of this forest is uncertain, it must have been in the same general vicinity. The new campsite would have had a double advantage. It was less
conspicuous—a forest rather than a known fortification—and it was in the territory of Judah, David's own tribe. Adullam was apparently outside Judean
territory (see 1 Sam. 22:5).

The other religious functionary reported to have joined David at this stage
was Abiathar, sole survivor of a ruthless massacre of the priests of Nob. As it
turned out, David had been seen at Nob by Doeg, an Edomite in the service of
King Saul. Doeg reported this to Saul, who jumped to the conclusion that the
Nob priests were in conspiracy with David and ordered their execution
(22:6–23).

Soon Saul learned that David was in the Adullam area as the result of an
incident reported in 23:1–5. Philistine raiders were robbing the threshing floors
of the people of Keilah (present-day Khirbet Qila, also near Adullam), whereupon David and his men came and chased the Philistines away. This was a daring move, and the text suggests that some of David's men regarded it as bad
judgment: "But David's men said to him, 'Look, we are afraid here in Judah;
how much more then if we go to Keilah against the armies of the Philistines?'"
(v. 3). Having chased away the Philistine raiders, therefore, David now faced a
double danger, especially if he and his men remained in Keilah. The Philistines
could be expected to return in force; and Saul, who now knew David's whereabouts, began preparing a campaign against the city. Much depended upon
whether David and his men could trust the people of Keilah.

> Saul summoned all the people to war, to go down to Keilah, to besiege David
> and his men. When David learned that Saul was plotting evil against him, he
> said to Abiathar the priest, "Bring the ephod here." Then David said, . . . "Will
> the men of Keilah surrender me and my men into the hand of Saul?" Yahweh
> said, "They will surrender you." Then David and his men, who were about
> six hundred, set out and left Keilah; they wandered wherever they could go.
> When Saul was told that David had escaped from Keilah, he gave up the
> expedition. David remained in the strongholds in the wilderness, in the hill
> country of the Wilderness of Ziph. Saul sought him every day, but God did
> not give him into his hand. (23:8–14)

This text makes clear that David and his band could not rely upon the support
of the citizens of Keilah and vicinity.

36. *Judean wilderness.* Barren slopes of the Judean wilderness, where David and his men sought refuge from Saul. The stories in 1 Sam. 23:15–26:25 have their setting in this desolate region.

Roaming the Wilderness of Ziph

Fleeing Keilah, David and his men sought refuge in the barren southeastern slopes of the southern hill country, primarily the area between the villages of Ziph, Carmel, and Maon (present-day Tell Zif, Khirbet el-Kirmil, and Tell Ma'in) and the Dead Sea. This was on the southeastern fringe of Saul's area of influence. Saul had set up a monument for himself in Carmel (1 Sam. 15:12), and, as we shall see below, persons such as Nabal of Maon seem to have recognized Saul's authority in the area. David's army is reported to have numbered six hundred fighting men by this time, but this seems excessive. It is difficult to see how he would have maintained such a number in this desolate "wilderness" region with Saul in close pursuit and without support from the local people. Yet the stories that pertain to this phase of his career (23:15–26:25) reflect precisely these two themes: David's narrow escapes from Saul, and the lack of support that David received from the local people in the areas where he and his men roamed.

Three of the stories about this period follow essentially the same pattern (1 Sam. 23:19–29; 24; and 26). Each begins with the local people (Ziphites in two of the instances) reporting David's location to Saul. Then Saul arrives on the scene with a large army and it appears that David and his men will surely be captured. The three stories diverge from that point, but with essentially the same result in each case—Saul withdraws voluntarily, leaving David and his men at large. These stories may represent three versions of a single incident, in which case we regard the one in 23:19–29 as the more convincing. The other two are more novelistic in their style, their scenarios as to how David spared Saul's life are hardly plausible, and their emphases on David's loyalty to Saul in his capacity as "Yahweh's anointed" sound too much like pro-Davidic propaganda.

The story about Nabal in 1 Samuel 25:1–42 further illustrates that the local inhabitants of the region regarded David as a nuisance. In the story Nabal, a Calebite rich in sheep and goats, lived in Maon but often grazed his flocks at nearby Carmel. On one occasion when Nabal was in Carmel for sheepshearing, David sent ten men with the following message: "I hear that you have shearers; now your shepherds have been with us, and we did them no harm, and they missed nothing, all the time they were in Carmel. . . . Therefore let my young men find favor in your sight; for we come on a feast day. Please give whatever you have at hand to your servants and to your son David" (25:7–8). In short, David suggested that payment was due in return for protection that he and his men had provided. Nabal responded with incredulity: "Who is David? Who is the son of Jesse? There are many servants today who are breaking away from their masters" (25:10). Upon receiving Nabal's reply, David repeated the claim that he had been providing Nabal with a significant service and threatened to take drastic action. "Now David had said, 'Surely it was in that I protected all that this fellow has in the wilderness, so that nothing was missed of all that belonged to him; but he has returned me evil for good. God do so to David and more also, if by morning I leave so much as one male of all who belong to him'" (25:21–22).

At that point, we are told, Nabal's wife Abigail took matters into her own hands and sent David a caravan of supplies that included "two hundred loaves, two skins of wine, five sheep ready dressed, five measures of parched grain, one hundred clusters of raisins, and two hundred cakes of figs" (25:18). Now it was Nabal's turn to be angry, and he seems to have died a rather mysterious death soon thereafter: "his heart died within him; he became like a stone. About ten days later Yahweh smote Nabal; and he died" (25:37–38). The story ends with David marrying Abigail.[17]

David with the Philistines

Apparently realizing that he would not be able to elude Saul indefinitely, David took a drastic step. He and his band of followers entered the service of Achish, the Philistine king of Gath (1 Sam. 27:1–4). On the one hand, Achish would have known of David's recent activities and recognized the opportunity to formalize the split in Saul's ranks. On the other hand, as a vassal of the Philistine ruler, David secured what previously had eluded him, a stable base of operations beyond the reach of Saul. Specifically, Achish gave David the city of Ziklag, whose exact location is unknown, but it was clearly somewhere in the southern Shephelah or western Negeb—that is, on the frontier between

---

17. The tendency in much modern scholarship is to blame David for complicity in many of the killings reported in the stories of his rise and reign. See J. D. Levenson, "I Samuel 25 as Literature and History," *CBQ* 40 (1978) 11–28; idem and Baruch Halpern, "The Political Import of David's Marriages," *JBL* 99 (1980) 507–18; J. C. VanderKam, "Davidic Complicity in the Deaths of Abner and Eshbaal: A Historical and Redactional Study," *JBL* 99 (1980) 521–39; Meir Malul, "Was David Involved in the Death of Saul on the Gilboa Mountain?" *RB* 103 (1996) 517–45; and Halpern, *David's Secret Demons*, 73–94.

Philistine territory and the southern hill country. Ziklag would remain crown property for the Davidic dynasty in years to come (27:5–7).

David's commitment to Achish was probably threefold. He would have been responsible for protecting this part of the Philistine frontier. In case of Philistine mobilization his troops would have been expected to fight under Philistine banners (see 29:1–2). Finally, he would have been expected to engage in raids on the enemies of the Philistines, particularly the Judahite, Jerahmeelite, and Kenite villages in the nearby hill country and the Negeb. We are told that David remained in the service of Achish for a year and four months, presumably until the death of Saul on Mount Gilboa (27:7), and that throughout that period he systematically deceived Achish by raiding farther south.

> Now David and his men went up, and made raids upon the Geshurites, the Girzites, and the Amalekites . . . on the way to Shur and on to the land of Egypt. . . . When Achish asked, "Against whom have you made a raid today?" David would say, "Against the Negeb of Judah," or "Against the Negeb of the Jerahmeelites," or, "Against the Negeb of the Kenites." David left neither man nor woman alive, to be brought back to Gath, thinking, "They might tell about us, and say, 'David has done so and so.'" . . . Achish trusted David, thinking, "He has made himself utterly abhorrent to his people Israel; therefore he shall always be my servant." (27:8–12)

In short, this text claims that while serving under the Philistines David never preyed on his own people. The narrative in 1 Samuel 30 suggests that he even used his vassal service to protect them and that on at least one occasion he shared the spoils of a victory with certain Judahite, Jerahmeelite, and Kenite villages. Only about half of the villages listed (see 30:27–31) can be located with any degree of certainty. Those that can be identified were situated south and southeast of Hebron.

When the Philistine troops massed at Aphek for a major confrontation with Saul, David and his troops were on hand with Achish ready to fight with the Philistines against the Israelites. However, the other Philistine rulers were leery of "these Hebrews," fearing that in battle they might shift sides, as had the Hebrews at the battle of Michmash (29:1–10; cf. 14:21). Thus David was dismissed from the battlefield and saved from what could only have been an embarrassment, if not an impediment, in his later career.

David Rules from Hebron

Saul emerged on the scene as a fighter of Philistines, as we have seen in chapter 5, and his chiefdom consisted of a loosely defined and administered territory whose inhabitants looked to him for protection. With the Philistine victory at Mount Gilboa and the deaths of Saul and his sons, even Saul's strongest supporters would have been left in a state of shock. Ish-bosheth withdrew to Mahanaim in Transjordan, presumably for security reasons, leaving the hill country villages west of the Jordan open to Philistine raiding and plundering. There was nothing to prevent the Philistine vassal David from returning with his troops to the Judean hill country on a permanent basis.

After David had sufficiently and publicly lamented the deaths of Saul and Jonathan (2 Sam. 1:17–27), therefore, he and his followers, "every one with his household," moved into and occupied the city of Hebron and its surrounding villages (2:1–3). Thereupon, probably with little choice, "the people of Judah came [to Hebron], and there they anointed David king over the house of Judah" (2:4). Although none of the details of the occasion is reported, three observations should be made. First, "Judah" at this stage is to be understood as the individual tribe of Judah composed of clans settled in the vicinity of Mount Judah, not the compilers' "Greater Judah" (see chapter 4). Second, by anointing David the Judahites formally recognized his authority, but "anointing" in this context did not necessarily imply any notions of divine designation as it does in the Samuel stories (1 Sam. 10:1; 16:1–13; see also 1 Kgs. 1:39; 2 Kgs. 11:12; 23:30). Third, we need to keep in mind that "king" (*melek*) is the compilers' terminology. At this stage of his career David was an emerging regional chieftain with Philistine backing. One can speculate that the arrangement between David and the Judahites involved some understanding (possibly even negotiations) regarding the rights and responsibilities of the two parties (see 1 Sam. 10:25), although the Judahites seem to have had little choice in the matter one way or another.

David is reported to have ruled in Hebron seven years and six months (2 Sam. 5:4–5; 1 Kgs. 2:11 rounds this off to an even seven years). Presumably he maintained good relations with the Philistines at least for a time, and used the time to expand his authority throughout the southern hill country. It would have been during this Hebron phase of his career also that David made an alliance with Nahash, the king of Ammon and an old enemy of Israel and Saul (1 Sam. 11; 2 Sam. 10:1–2; 17:27), and that he made overtures to the people of Jabesh-gilead. According to the biblical narrative, he commended the latter for their heroic gallantry in rescuing Saul's body and informed them that the Judahites had anointed him king (2 Sam. 2:4b–7). The implication was obvious. Perhaps the Jabeshites should consider shifting their allegiance to him as well.[18] Finally, the narrative in 2 Samuel 2:12–32 implies that David began to encroach on Benjaminite territory, with the situation summed up as follows at the end of the narrative: "There was a long war between the house of Saul and the house of David; and David grew stronger and stronger, while the house of Saul became weaker and weaker" (3:1).

By the time Abner began negotiations with David regarding the transfer to him of Saul's chiefdom, therefore, David was already encroaching on Israelite territory. Then, as a final blow, both Abner and Ish-bosheth were assassinated. Given these circumstances, it is not surprising that the "elders of Israel" came to David at Hebron and submitted to his rule. Second Samuel 5:3 reports the event in a minimum of words: "King David made a covenant with them at Hebron before Yahweh, and they anointed David king over Israel." The terms of the covenant are not even hinted at; but again, as had been the case with the Judahites, the elders of Israel were not in a strong bargaining position.

---

18. Note also that David's marriage to Maacah, daughter of Talmai king of Geshur, Absalom's mother, occurred during the Hebron phase of his career (2 Sam. 3:3). If we read "Geshurites" rather than "Ashurites" in 2 Sam. 2:9, it would appear that David allied himself through marriage with this, another of the regions claimed by Ish-bosheth.

The Philistines, meanwhile, must have sensed that David was outgrowing vassal status. Now that he had secured the allegiance of Israel as well as Judah, with the responsibility of defending Israel, they appropriately regarded him as an enemy. The two Philistine skirmishes reported in 2 Sam. 5:17–25 probably belong to this period, that is, to the time shortly after "the Philistines heard that David had been anointed king over Israel" (v. 17). The setting of the two skirmishes was the Valley of Rephaim, the upper branches of the Sorek Valley that descend from the hill country near Jerusalem to the plain below. This was a logical entrance to the hill country for the Philistines and an area that David would have to control if he was to keep them out of Israelite territory. David is credited with success on both occasions.

David, King of Jerusalem

Surely the most important move of David's career was his conquest of Jerusalem and choice of this site for his residency. Jerusalem was one of the old Bronze Age cities that lingered on as a modest settlement during the Early Iron Age. The name "Jerusalem" (*yerushalim*) means something like "founded by Shalem," Shalem being a Canaanite god best known from the Ugaritic texts. (Solomon's name may also derive from this god's name.) From the Amarna Letters, we know the name of one of the kings who had ruled Jerusalem during the Late Bronze Age.[19] This king's name, Abdi-Heba, suggests that he may have been of Hurrian stock. Ezekiel preserves a tradition that the people of Jerusalem were of Hittite and Amorite stock: "Your mother was a Hittite and your father an Amorite" (Ezek. 16:45). According to 2 Samuel 5:6–8, David took the city from the Jebusites, identified otherwise only as "the inhabitants of the land." The Jebusites were apparently a local group whose name was derived from Jebus, a landmark somewhere in the immediate vicinity of Jerusalem.[20]

Saul had incorporated Gibeon and the associated Hivite cities into his realm, so Jerusalem represented the last alien town of consequence separating Israelite and Judean territory. Situated on the central north-south watershed, Jerusalem had undoubtedly been a disruptive feature for Saul's chiefdom. By the same measure, it was ideal for David's purposes.[21] It was located in the frontier zone between Israel and Judah, thus unencumbered by previous ties with either. It offered a defendable position. And there was a good water source—the Gihon Spring.

The Jerusalem of David's day was a modest settlement probably confined to Ophel, the knoll immediately south of what is known today as the Temple

---

19. The six texts (nos. 285–90) written from Jerusalem to the Egyptian court are translated in W. L. Moran, *The Amarna Letters* (Baltimore: Johns Hopkins University Press, 1992) 325–34. On parallels between Late Bronze and Early Iron Age Jerusalem, see Nadav Na'aman, "The Contribution of the Amarna Letters to the Debate on Jerusalem's Position in the Tenth Century B.C.E.," *BASOR* 304 (1996) 17–27; repr. in *AIHH* 1–17.

20. See J. M. Miller, "Jebus and Jerusalem: A Case of Mistaken Identity," *ZDPV* 90 (1974) 115–27.

21. For arguments that Jerusalem at the time of David could not have been the center of a territorial state, see D. W. Jamieson-Drake, *Scribes and Schools in Monarchic Judah: A Socio-Archeological Approach* (JSOTSup 109; SWBA 9; Sheffield: Sheffield Academic Press, 1991); and Israel Finkelstein, "State Formation in Israel and Judah: A Contrast in Context, a Contrast in Trajectory," *NEA* 62 (1999) 35–52. For a rejoinder see A. F. Rainey, "Stones for Bread: Archaeology versus History," *NEA* 64 (2001) 140–49.

37. *Jerusalem "stepped structure."* This unusual "stepped structure," excavated on the eastern slopes of Ophel, may have supported the foundations of a building from approximately the time of David and Solomon. (Zeev Radovan, Jerusalem)

Mount and Haram esh-Sharif. Ophel was surrounded on all sides except the north by valleys, and the Gihon Spring is located near the base of the Kidron Valley on its eastern side. Archaeological excavations on Ophel have revealed segments of a Middle Bronze Age fortification wall, more than ten feet thick, higher up the slopes of Ophel from the spring, which itself was protected by a Middle Bronze Age tower system. It is possible, although by no means certain, that some of the Middle Bronze Age fortification continued in use through the Late Bronze Age and into the Iron Age. Otherwise archaeological remains from the Late Bronze and Iron I ages are meager and difficult to date. We should probably think in terms of a small settlement centered around a stronghold that may or may not have reutilized some surviving portion of the Bronze Age fortification.[22]

22. On the general, popular debate over the archaeological remains from Jerusalem during the time of David and Solomon, see Nadav Na'aman, "Cow Town or Royal Capital? Evidence for Iron Age Jerusalem," *BAR* 23/4 (1997) 43–47, 67; Margreet Steiner, "David's Jerusalem, It's Not There: Archaeology Proves a Negative," *BAR* 24/4 (1998) 26–33, 62–63; J. M. Cahill, "David's Jerusalem: It Is There: The Archaeological Evidence Proves It," *BAR* 24/4 (1998) 34–41, 63; idem, "Jerusalem in David's and Solomon's Time," *BAR* 30/6 (2004) 20–31, 62–63; and Eilat Mazar, "Did I Find King David's Palace?" *BAR* 32/1 (2006) 16–25, 70. More detailed descriptions with bibliography can be found in J. M. Cahill, "Jerusalem at the Time of the United Monarchy: The Archaeological Evidence"; A. E. Killebrew, "Biblical Jerusalem: An Archaeological Assessment"; and Margreet Steiner, "The Evidence from Kenyon's

An interesting stepped stone structure on the eastern slope of Ophel, possibly a retaining wall or rampart of some sort, apparently dates from the very end of the Late Bronze Age or early Iron I. Remains of another large stone structure immediately to the north and dating from the same time frame may be related. We are told that David constructed a palace for himself in Jerusalem with the aid of the Phoenician king Hiram of Tyre (2 Sam. 5:11), and it is intriguing to speculate that both of these structures may have related in some way to David's palace. However, the archaeological situation is not such that this can be verified.

The same must be said of the notion that a particular tunnel (Warren's Shaft) associated with the Gihon Spring provided David's soldiers entry to the Jebusite fortification. Until recently it was generally accepted that this tunnel had been constructed to provide underground access to the spring from inside a stronghold. Supposedly David's men discovered the shaft, gained surprise entry to the stronghold through it, and captured the place without any prolonged siege or assault. Although the meaning of *tsinnor* in the passage below is uncertain, note that the NRSV renders it "water shaft."[23]

> The king and his men marched to Jerusalem against the Jebusites, the inhabitants of the land, who said to David, "You will not come in here, even the blind and the lame will turn you back"—thinking, "David cannot come in here." Nevertheless David took the stronghold of Zion, which is now the city of David. David had said on that day, "Whoever would strike down the Jebusites, let him get up the water shaft (*tsinnor*) to attack the lame and the blind, those whom David hates." . . . David occupied the stronghold, and named it the city of David. David built the city all around from the Millo (*hammillo'*) inward. (2 Sam. 5:6–9)

The term *millo'*, usually simply transliterated "Millo" without any attempt at translation, may refer to a system of retaining walls that enabled the inhabitants of Jerusalem to expand the settlement down the slopes of Ophel.

How long David ruled from Jerusalem cannot be determined—the forty years ascribed to him in 1 Kings 2:11 is probably a symbolic figure. But he ruled there long enough for the city to become eternally associated with his name. We are told that David constructed a palace for himself in Jerusalem with the aid of the Phoenician king Hiram of Tyre, which may be true; but the archaeological situation is not such that this can be verified (2 Sam. 5:11).[24]

Excavations in Jerusalem: A Response Essay," in A. G. Vaughn and A. E. Killebrew, eds., *Jerusalem in Bible and Archaeology: The First Temple Period* (SBLSymS 18; Leiden: Brill, 2003) 13–80, 329–45; 347–63. On the size of Jerusalem and its population at the time, see A. G. Auld and Margreet Steiner, *Jerusalem I: From the Bronze Age to the Maccabees* (Cities of the Biblical World; Macon, GA: Mercer University Press, 1996) 33–38.

23. For the problem see Terence Kleven, "The Use of *ṣnr* in Ugaritic and 2 Samuel V 8: Hebrew Usage and Comparative Philology," *VT* 44 (1994) 195–204.

24. Hiram and David may have reigned contemporaneously for several years. See A. R. Green, "David's Relations with Hiram: Biblical and Josephan Evidence for Tyrian Chronology," in C. L. Meyers and M. P. O'Connor, eds., *The Word of the Lord Shall Go Forth: Essays in Honor of David Noel Freedman in Celebration of His Sixtieth Birthday* (Winona Lake, IN: Eisenbrauns, 1983) 373–97. On early Israel-Phoenician relations see Herbert Donner, "The Interdependence of Internal Affairs and Foreign Policy During the Davidic-Solomonic Period (with Regard to the Phoenician Coast)," in Tomoo Ishida, ed., *Studies in the Period of David and Solomon and Other Essays* (Winona Lake, IN: Eisenbrauns, 1982) 205–14.

Dealing with Opposition

David's rise to power and his Jerusalem-centered administration were not without opposition. Jerusalem's central role would have resulted in a corresponding loss of influence and prestige for other cities, especially Hebron, while the official status of the Jerusalem-Nob priesthood will have had a similar effect in cultic affairs. The administration of affairs from the new capital must have produced some sense of alienation as well on the part of clan and tribal elders, particularly of Ephraim/Israel. Saul had been a popular ruler in many circles, especially among his Benjaminite kinsmen, and those loyal to the Saulide family must have regarded David with some disdain. Three incidents reported for David's reign illustrate the level of opposition that he faced and how he dealt with it: the execution of Saul's descendants, a rebellion led by David's son Absalom, and another rebellion led by Sheba.

It is impossible to establish when in David's reign these developments occurred. Indeed, we do not know how long his reign lasted or, as with all the stories about David, whether we can trust the reports. Yet it seems more likely that these incidents would have occurred during the earlier years while David was still in the process of securing his authority, rather than nearer the end of his reign as is implied by the present arrangement of the materials in 2 Samuel.

The Execution of Saul's Descendants

According to 2 Samuel 21:1–4, David authorized the execution of several members of Saul's family in an effort to remove bloodguilt and famine from the land; but obviously it also would have removed a potential threat to David's rule. Saul, we are told, had attempted to annihilate the Gibeonites "in his zeal for the people of Israel and Judah" (21:1–2) and presumably in violation of a long-standing covenant relationship between Gibeon and the Israelites (see Josh. 9:3–21). This supposedly resulted in bloodguilt, which in turn was identified as the cause of the famine. Thus David, having consulted with the Gibeonites, ordered the ritual execution and public exposure of the corpses of seven of Saul's sons and grandsons. "The king took the two sons of Rizpah daughter of Aiah [see 2 Sam. 3:7], whom she bore to Saul, . . . and the five sons of Merab daughter of Saul . . . ; and he gave them into the hands of the Gibeonites, and they impaled them on the mountain before Yahweh" (21:8–9).[25]

Also, perhaps in conjunction with these executions, David appropriated Saul's family estate. Later, when the crippled son of Jonathan, Mephibosheth (called Meribbaal in 1 Chr. 8:34), turned up in Lo-debar, a place somewhere in Transjordan, David restored the estate to Mephibosheth. Yet there were strings attached. Mephibosheth was required to eat "at the king's table" from that time forward—that is, take up residence in Jerusalem, where his activities could be scrutinized. The property itself was placed in the custody of a certain Ziba, a servant of the house of Saul, who was to till the land and "bring in the produce, so that your master's grandson [Mephibosheth] may have food to eat" (2 Sam. 9:1–13).[26]

---

25. Most Hebrew manuscripts read "Michal" rather than "Merab"; see NRSV's footnote.

26. See Zafrira Ben-Barak, "Meribaal and the System of Land Grants in Ancient Israel," *Bib* 62 (1981) 73–91.

Absalom's Rebellion

Absalom's rebellion is described in great detail in the Genesis–2 Kings History (five full chapters; 2 Sam. 15–19).[27] This extended narrative, plus the fact that its details connect with other details in other parts of the Genesis–2 Kings presentation of David's reign, press again the question that we have struggled with all along: to what extent do the narratives collected and edited by the compilers of Genesis–2 Kings represent authentic memory of circumstances in early Israel, and to what extent do they represent generations of vivid storytelling imagination? In this case we are inclined to think that it is a substantial mixture of both—that there is a significant element of historical memory involved in the account of Absalom's rebellion; that the circumstances described are not entirely fictitious; and that, even though we cannot separate historical memory from storyteller's imagination, a close look at the details will give us at least some sense of the internal dynamics of David's reign. Two factors come through loud and clear. (1) There was conflict among David's sons and, already before his death, attempts to displace and succeed him on the throne. (2) David did not enjoy the full loyalty and support of his subjects, certainly not of all the Israelites and Judahites.

Absalom is identified earlier in the biblical narrative as the son of Maacah, an Aramaean princess from Geshur (2 Sam. 3:3). Born during David's rule at Hebron, Absalom is the only one of David's sons explicitly said to have inherited royal blood from his mother's line. Immediately preceding the account of Absalom's rebellion, and really to be considered a part of it, is a narrative that describes how Amnon, Absalom's eldest half brother, raped Tamar, Absalom's sister (2 Sam. 14). Absalom plotted revenge, had Amnon killed, and, fearing their father's wrath, fled into exile. Taking refuge with his grandfather in the kingdom of Geshur, Absalom remained absent from Jerusalem for three years until Joab intervened with David on Absalom's behalf (14:28–33). With Amnon dead, Absalom was apparently now David's oldest living son. He began to play the role of the royal heir and to appeal to popular grievances.

> After this Absalom got himself a chariot and horses, and fifty men to run ahead of him. Absalom used to rise early and stand beside the road into the gate; and when anyone brought a suit before the king for judgment, Absalom would call out, and say, "From what city are you?" When the person said, "Your servant is of such and such a tribe in Israel," Absalom would say, "See, your claims are good and right; but there is no one deputed by the king to hear you." Absalom said moreover, "If only I were judge in the land! Then all who had a suit or cause might come to me, and I would give them justice." Whenever people came near to do obeisance to him, he would put out his hand, and take hold of them, and kiss them. Thus Absalom did to every Israelite who came to the king for judgment; so Absalom stole the hearts of the people of Israel. (15:1–6)

---

27. See Jacob Weingreen, "The Rebellion of Absalom," *VT* 19 (1969) 263–66; M. A. Cohen, "The Rebellions During the Reign of David: An Inquiry into Social Dynamics in Ancient Israel," in Charles Berlin, ed., *Studies in Jewish Bibliography, History, and Literature in Honor of I. Edward Kiev* (New York: Ktav, 1971) 91–112; and Charles Conroy, *Absalom Absalom! Narrative and Language in 2 Sam 13–20* (AnBib 81; Rome: Biblical Institute Press, 1978).

The reference to "no one deputed by the king to hear you" implies grievances over David's administration, while the diverse elements that supported Absalom's conspiracy indicate that these grievances were widespread. Both Israelites and Judahites joined the movement. Moreover, Absalom's backers included some who might have been considered David's own close supporters: important members of David's administration, the counselor Ahithophel, and a nephew, Amasa.

Absalom initiated the rebellion, according to the biblical account, by having himself proclaimed king in Hebron, the heartland of Judah and David's earlier capital. This was coordinated with proclamations of his kingship in other centers, particularly in Ephraim/Israel (2 Sam. 15:7–12). As support for the rebellion mounted, especially in Ephraim/Israel, David fled Jerusalem, accompanied by his inner core of supporters and mercenaries (15:13–31). Before leaving he instructed the priests Zadok and Abiathar to remain behind and send him secret reports regarding developments. Also he left his counselor Hushai as a plant and pretended supporter of Absalom (15:32–37; 17:15–22).

The biblical description of David's departure reflects the range of sentiments that one would expect. Ziba, whom David had appointed custodian of the Saulide estate recently restored to Mephibosheth, rushed to David's side and accused Mephibosheth of supporting the rebellion. On the spot, David declared Ziba himself the new owner of the estate. Shimei, a Benjaminite member of the house of Saul, cursed and threw stones at the fleeing king, denouncing him for having shed the blood of Saul's family (2 Sam. 16:5–14; see 21:1–6). Once across the Jordan and at Mahanaim, various prominent persons from that area came to David's support (17:27–29). These included Shobi, a son of Nahash the Ammonite king; Machir of Lo-debar who earlier had sheltered the young Mephibosheth (9:4); and Barzillai, a wealthy Gileadite whose name suggests that he may have been an Aramaean (see 19:31–38).

David deployed his forces under Joab and Abishai, his nephews, and under Ittai a Gittite (18:1–3). Ittai was apparently the head of a contingent of six hundred Philistine mercenaries who had recently arrived with their families from Gath (15:18–22). (This suggests that David continued good relations with at least some of the Philistines.) Absalom, on the other hand, placed his cousin Amasa in charge of his forces. Yet he delayed in coming after David. Instead, after occupying Jerusalem, and on the advice of Ahithophel, Absalom made a public show of taking over David's harem. This would have been intended to emphasize his replacement of David and to demonstrate that the break was irrevocable (16:15–23). Ahithophel, of course, would have been particularly concerned to ensure that Absalom's policy left no room to abort the coup. David and Absalom were, after all, father and son, and might conceivably be reconciled again as they had after the Tamar affair. But for Ahithophel and other prominent persons like him who had chosen to side with Absalom, there could be no turning back. He had gambled both his career and his life on the success of the rebellion.

By the same measure, it was a devastating blow to Ahithophel when Absalom rejected his advice in deference to that of Hushai, and failed to take best advantage of the military situation with a speedy attack on David's retreating forces (17:1–14). Instead, Absalom wasted time rallying a large force and gave David's troops time to organize. Ahithophel, no doubt sensing that he would

38. *Mountains of Gilead.* David and his supporters retreated to the mountains of Gilead (in present-day Jordan) when Absalom seized Jerusalem. This photograph views the vicinity of Ajlun with Rabad Castle on the western horizon. The exact location of Mahanaim, where David made his headquarters (2 Sam. 17:24–19:8), remains uncertain.

continue to be disregarded in the new government and that the rebellion was probably doomed to failure in any case, committed suicide (17:23).

The eventual encounter between David's and Absalom's forces took place in Gilead in the forest of Ephraim (18:6). David's troops, with their prior deployment, had the advantage and were victorious. Absalom's forces, which seem to have consisted primarily of Israelites rather than Judeans, were severely beaten but were spared from slaughter by Joab. Joab killed Absalom, on the other hand, in spite of David's earlier admonition to "deal gently" with his son (18:5–16).

The collapse of Absalom's rebellion did not mean that everyone was ready to reinstate David. The Israelites in particular were reluctant (19:8b–10). While they deliberated, David, still in Transjordan, sent a message to Zadok and Abiathar instructing them to encourage the elders of Judah to take the lead in restoring him. After all, he pointed out, "you are my kin, you are my bone and my flesh." Also he promised to retain Amasa, who had commanded Absalom's army—a move probably intended to ease the fears of all those who had supported Absalom by signaling that they would receive clemency. Thus Judah rallied in support of David and came to meet him at Gilgal, situated near a crossing of the Jordan (19:11–15).

Once the Judeans had declared themselves in favor of restoring David to the throne and begun the process of bringing him back to Jerusalem, the Israelites could delay their decision no longer. Their only choice was to support his return or to prepare for civil war—a war they would have little chance of winning. They decided to support his return, therefore, and sent their representatives to Gilgal as well.

The description of the scene at Gilgal (2 Sam. 19:16–43) illustrates the disparate elements and internal tensions that must have characterized David's realm. The main contingent of Israelites appeared at Gilgal late, after the Judeans had escorted David across the Jordan. Israelite and Judean animosities surfaced immediately, with the Israelite representatives charging that the Judeans had acted precipitously and were being favored in spite of Israel's larger size. The Israelite representatives claimed, moreover, that it was they rather than the Judeans who had made the first moves toward restoring David to the throne (19:41–43). Also at Gilgal was Shimei, now repentant in the light of changed circumstances, offering his submission and support along with a thousand other Benjaminites. Even the lame Mephibosheth came to Gilgal to show his loyalty. David granted clemency to Shimei and restored half of Mephibosheth's estate (19:24–30). This entire scenario, in which Israel and Judah act independently, presupposes that the two groups, and perhaps the Benjaminites as a third (see 19:16–17), still understood themselves as separate entities.

Sheba's Revolt

As one might expect, and as described in the biblical narrative, there was opposition especially among the Israelites to David's return. Among those opposed was Sheba, also a Benjaminite. Possibly while David was still meeting with Israelite and Judean leaders at Gilgal, Sheba was calling for a break with the house of David: "We have no portion in David, and no share in the son of Jesse! Everyone to your tents, O Israel!" (2 Sam. 20:1).[28] After arriving back in Jerusalem, therefore, David moved quickly to put down Sheba's rebellion before it could mushroom: "or he will find fortified cities for himself, and escape from us" (20:6b). David's original plan was for Amasa to muster Judean troops and deal with Sheba. Amasa delayed beyond the time that David had designated for the beginning of the campaign, however, possibly because of slow response on the part of the Judeans. Whatever the reason, by the time Amasa appeared on the scene with his troops David had already turned the affair over to his professional soldiers—specifically to Abishar, Joab, the Cherethites, and the Pelethites. Thereupon Joab killed Amasa, his temporary replacement as commander of the army, and pursued Sheba to Abel of Beth-maacah (Tell Abil, at the sources of the Jordan River in the extreme north of Palestine) with a combined force of professional troops and loyal volunteers (20:8–13). With their city under siege, the citizens of Abel decapitated Sheba and tossed his head over the wall to a waiting Joab (20:14–22).

David's Administration

The compilers of the Genesis–2 Kings History wished to present David as the legitimate successor to Saul, and Jerusalem as the legitimate heir to Israel's cul-

---

28. The text goes on to say that "all the men of Israel withdrew from David, and followed Sheba," but this is no doubt exaggeration, as is the statement in 2 Sam. 19:41 that asserts that "all the men of Israel" met David at Gilgal. The subsequent account of Sheba's venture suggests that his following was rather limited (see esp. 20:14, where he seems to have been supported only by his own clan).

tic traditions. How much this was a concern for David is less clear, but he is reported to have taken at least one step that would have implied continuity between Saul's Israel and Davidic Jerusalem: David brought the ark, the old religious symbol of the Shilonite cult and the Elide line, to Jerusalem and had it placed in a special tent erected for that purpose (2 Sam. 6:17).

While David's transference of the ark to Jerusalem may have suggested continuity with Saul's Israel, his regime clearly represented quite a new development for the clans and villages that had looked to Saul for protection. The difference had largely to do with the role of Jerusalem. David and his professional army had conquered Jerusalem, so it became crown property. Regardless of whether the Judahites and Israelites were acting voluntarily when they came to him at Hebron, therefore, and whether their acceptance of his rule had followed negotiations or involved stipulations of any sort, this would not have been the case with the Jerusalemites. David was their king and they his subjects by conquest. Autocratic monarchy would have been in keeping with their Bronze Age heritage, of course, and other cities eventually incorporated into his realm would have had this heritage as well—Shechem, Megiddo, possibly Hazor, and others.

David apparently drew heavily on his family and an inner circle of loyalists for his chief officials. For secondary levels of administration he seems to have turned to groups whose allegiance would have been directed more toward the crown than toward clan and tribal structures. His military, for example, included foreign mercenaries, even Philistine units. Nathan and Gad appear as prophets at the court (2 Sam. 12; 24:11), while the national cult was in the hands of the indigenous priestly lines of Jerusalem and nearby Nob. For the general administration of government policies, especially in outlying territories, David may have relied heavily on Levites from his hometown Bethlehem and paid them with land grants in the territories where they were stationed.

The "High Officials"

Second Samuel 8:15–18 (= 1 Chr. 18:14–17) and 2 Samuel 20:23–26 are variant versions of a list supposedly of David's high officials (see Chart 10). Whether this is an authentic list from David's time or an artificially constructed one from some later period is impossible to say. Authentic or not, the offices mentioned represent basic administrative functions that a fledgling kingdom would have required.[29] The priests were in charge of religious affairs. The recorder would have been responsible for records and documents both economic and administrative. The secretary probably handled the routine activities of the king and court and perhaps diplomatic correspondence as well. Joab was chief commander over the whole military, a position that he had not been willing to share earlier with either Abner or Amasa. The Cherethites and the Pelethites appear to have been royal mercenaries under their own commanders. The names of these two mercenary groups remain unexplained. Perhaps they denote Cretans and Philistines, the former perhaps also to be associated with

---

29. N. S. Fox, *In the Service of the King: Officialdom in Ancient Israel and Judah* (HUCM 23; Cincinnati: Hebrew Union College Press, 2000), contains a discussion of all the official titles in the Hebrew Bible.

CHART 10. High Officials under David

2 Sam. 8:16–18 (= 1 Chr. 18:15–17)

Over the army	Joab son of Zeruiah
Recorder	Jehoshaphat son of Ahilud
Priests	Zadok son of Ahitub; Ahimelech son of Abiathar
Secretary	Seraiah (Shavsha in 1 Chr. 18:16)
Over the Cherethites and Pelethites	Benaiah son of Jehoiada
Priests	David's sons (1 Chr. 18:17 identifies David's sons as "chief officials in the service of the king")

2 Sam. 20:23–26

Over the army of Israel	Joab
Over the Cherethites and Pelethites	Benaiah son of Jehoiada
Over the forced labor	Adoram
Recorder	Jehoshaphat son of Ahilud
Secretary	Sheva
Priests	Zadok and Abiathar
David's priest	Ira the Jairite

the Sea Peoples (see 1 Sam. 30:14). Second Samuel 15:18 mentions Gittites among David's mercenaries, and 23:8–39 refers to "the three" and "the thirty" as if they were special groups or honor guards, perhaps also military in function. Most of David's "warriors" were from Judah, especially the Bethlehem area, which illustrates the strong kinship/clan basis of his administration. The "forced labor" over which Adoram had charge would have been conscripted for public and royal projects (see 2 Sam. 12:31; Judg. 1:28, 30, 33, 35).

The Zadokites and the Priests of Nob

David seems to have retained the indigenous Jerusalem priesthood, the Zadokites, and allowed the Jerusalem cult to become, in effect, incorporated into the state cult. Unfortunately the crucial passages that have most bearing on the identity of David's priestly officials are problematic. Second Samuel 8:17 names his two main priests as "Zadok the son of Ahitub and Ahimelech the son of Abiathar." However, the account of Saul's massacre of the Nob priests in 1 Samuel 22 identifies Abiathar as the son of Ahimelech rather than the other way around, and identifies Abiathar-Ahimeleh as descendants of Ahitub. Finally, to take the problem a step farther back, 1 Samuel 14:3 connects Ahitub with the house of Eli. Supposedly, then, both of David's top priests, Zadok and Ahimelech (Abiathar), would have belonged to the Elide line.

Yet this seems to conflict with the sense of the Ark Narrative, which goes to such lengths to explain how the Elide line came to an end before the ark found its way to Jerusalem. Also the texts of 1 Samuel 14:3 and 2 Samuel 8:17 have undergone some editorial tampering, in our opinion, probably intended precisely for the purpose of connecting David's two chief priests with the Elide line. We suspect that the reference to "Ahitub, Ichabod's brother," has been introduced secondarily into 1 Samuel 14:3, so that originally the passage would have read simply "Ahijah . . . son of Phinehas, son of Eli." Second Samuel 8:17, on the other hand, would have read something like "Zadok and Abiathar the sons of Ahimelech." If these two passages are corrected accordingly, David's two chief priests would have been Zadok and Abiathar; and we are left to suppose that they represented local priestly families of Jerusalem and nearby Nob (Mt. Scopus, which overlooks Jerusalem on the northeast).

That Zadok represented the indigenous Jerusalem priesthood is suggested also by two other passages, both admittedly obscure, that associate pre-Davidic Jerusalem with persons whose names include the same root as *Zadok* as an element. Genesis 14:18–20 has Abraham paying a tithe to *"Melchizedek* king of Salem." "Salem" here is probably an abbreviated form of "Jerusalem." Joshua 10:1–5 mentions an *"Adoni-zedek* king of Jerusalem."[30]

The Levites

According to the schematic twelve-tribe genealogy advanced by the compilers of the Genesis–2 Kings History, the Levites were one of the original twelve tribes and that was designated to be a tribe of priests for all Israel. But traditions embedded in the Genesis–2 Kings History strongly suggest otherwise. More likely, in our opinion, they originated as a local priestly line in the southern hill country, associated especially with Bethlehem, and gained national prominence under David, who used them in his administration.[31]

1. The Judges narratives presuppose that Levitical groups were in existence before the rise of the monarchy, and that they had close connections with the south, especially with David's hometown, Bethlehem (Judg. 17:7–8; 19).

2. Genesis 49:5–7 depicts the Levites as fierce, zealous, and scattered among the tribes. Our suggestion is that this zealousness involved special loyalty to the Davidic regime, and that their scattering was due at least in part to their role in David's administration.

3. According to 1 Kings 12:31, one of the first acts of Jeroboam I after the northern Israelite kingdom broke away from Jerusalem and Judah at Solomon's death was to appoint new priests who were not Levites. This would have been a reasonable move if the Levites were known to have a special loyalty to the house of David.

---

30. See H. H. Rowley, "Zadok and Nehushtan," *JBL* 58 (1939) 113–41. For the view that Zadok had non-Jerusalemite origins, see S. M. Olyan, "Zadok's Origins and the Tribal Politics of David," *JBL* 101 (1982) 177–93.

31. See C. E. Hauer, "David and the Levites," *JSOT* 23 (1982) 33–54.

4. Joshua 21:1–42, paralleled by 1 Chronicles 6:54–81, provides a highly schematic list of Levitical cities. As it stands now, the list conforms to the artificial twelve-tribe scheme, with forty-eight cities distributed evenly among the twelve tribes. Note, however, that the cities are not evenly scattered geographically. Instead, they tend to be clustered outside the central hill country and in areas that probably would have been on the frontiers of David's realm. The received schematic list may be based on an older one that identified the cities from which the Levites administered David's policies. Scattered throughout his realm, but especially in non-Israelite and non-Judean areas annexed by David, they would have been a means for maintaining control and enforcing policies.[32]

The Extent of David's Rule and His Frontier Wars

The core of David's direct rule would have been Jerusalem and the central hill country. Beyond that, he apparently exercised some degree of authority over the Jezreel Valley, Galilee, and northern Transjordan. But nothing suggests that his realm included Philistia, and it is unlikely that he ever controlled any of Transjordan south of the Arnon River.

Determining the Extent of David's Direct Rule

Three texts come into consideration for determining the extent of David's direct rule: the account of David's census in 2 Samuel 24 (= 1 Chr. 21:1–27), the list of Levitical cities in Joshua 21:1–42 (= 1 Chr. 6:54–81), and the list of "unconquered cities" in Judges 1:27–33. The geographical coverage of the census is described in very general fashion, seems incomplete, and is not entirely intelligible. Beginning at the Arnon (present-day Wadi el-Mujib) in Transjordan, the surveyors are said to have proceeded northward to a point near Dan at the foot of Mount Hermon and then westward across Upper Galilee approaching the Phoenician cities of Sidon and Tyre. A second arm of the survey is said to have covered the Negeb of Judah to Beer-sheba. There is no mention of the hill country west of the Jordan. Perhaps the census, or at least the geographical description, pertained specifically to certain outlying territories, the frontiers of David's rule.

A similar hypothesis was advanced above regarding the Levitical city list. Although the list is highly schematic in its present form, with the cities supposedly distributed evenly among the eleven non-Levitical tribes, most of the Levitical cities are located outside the central hill country and in what would probably have been frontier areas of David's realm.

Finally, Judges 1:27–33 lists cities that were incorporated into the Israelite monarchy at some point but whose indigenous, non-Israelite populations were allowed to remain in place. Several of these, like Jerusalem, were old Bronze Age settlements that had survived into the Iron Age, for example, Beth-shean,

---

32. On the various problems associated with the Levitical city list and the dating of the text, see A. G. Auld, "The 'Levitical Cities': Texts and History," *ZAW* 91 (1979) 194–206; and J. R. Spencer, "Priestly Families (or Factions) in Samuel and Kings," in S. W. Holloway and L. K. Handy, eds., *The Pitcher Is Broken: Memorial Essays for Gösta W. Ahlström* (JSOTSup 190; Sheffield: Sheffield Academic Press, 1995) 397–400 (with bibliography).

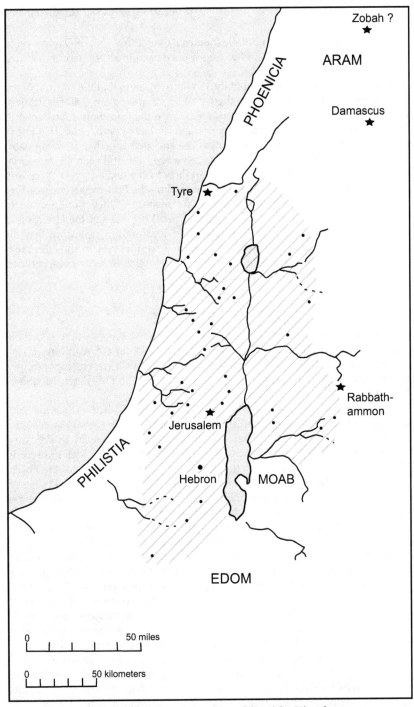

MAP 16. Approximate Extent of David's Kingdom
and the Configuration of the Levitical Cities

Taanach, Megiddo, Gezer, and Beth-shemesh. One thinks first of David's reign as the likely time when these cities might have been incorporated under such circumstances.

It would be an overstatement of the evidence to claim that the account of the census, the Levitical city list, and the list of unconquered cities all presuppose essentially the same territorial boundaries, since the information provided in each case is neither detailed nor firm enough for close comparison. It is fair to say, however, that the three are compatible and that together they highlight what one suspects on other grounds to have been the approximate territorial extent of David's direct rule. Note that all three of the texts suggest expansion into Upper Galilee, approaching but not including the Phoenician cities of Tyre and Sidon. According to the census text, for example, "they went around to Sidon, and came to the fortress of Tyre and to all the cities of the Hivites and Canaanites" (2 Sam. 24:6–7). The only other information regarding David's relations with the Phoenicians is the note in 2 Samuel 5:11 to the effect that "King Hiram of Tyre sent messengers to David, along with cedar trees, and carpenters and masons who built David a house."

David's Frontier Wars

In addition to the Phoenician cities of Tyre and Sidon, these texts would seem also to exclude from David's realm Philistia, Rabbath-Ammon of the Ammonites, and the region south of the Arnon. Other texts, correspondingly, report David's warfare (frontier skirmishes) against the Philistines, Moabites, Edomites, Ammonites, and Aramaeans.

Philistines. David gained popularity as a fighter of Philistines, we are told, then allied himself with the Philistines for a time, and then again is depicted fighting against them. The second shift, from Philistine vassal to Philistine enemy, probably occurred relatively soon after he established himself in Hebron. That stage of his career, in any case, is the likely context of the Philistine battle reported in 2 Samuel 5:17–25, and probably of most of the Philistine-related items reported in 2 Samuel 23. Possibly there were frontier skirmishes later on as well, with the frontier being approximately the Shephelah.

Moabites. The meager information provided regarding David's dealing with Moab invites speculation with no promise of satisfying results. On the one hand, there is the tradition that David himself was of Moabite ancestry and the statement that he took his parents to Moab for safety while he was on the run from Saul. On the other hand, 2 Samuel 8:2 reports that he defeated the Moabites and was particularly brutal to them. "He also defeated the Moabites, making them lie down on the ground, measured them off with a cord; he measured two lengths of cord for those who were to be put to death, and one length for those who were to be spared. And the Moabites became servants to David and brought tribute." "Moab" in these passages would refer to the tableland north of the Arnon. Moab proper, south of the Arnon, was never easily accessible to Israelite and Judean kings. Even if David conducted a campaign south of the Arnon with any success, he would hardly have been able to establish any permanent control there.

Edomites. The report that David slew eighteen thousand Edomites in the Valley of Salt and put garrisons throughout all Edom (2 Sam. 8:13–14) is echoed in 1 Kings 11:15–16. "For when David was in Edom, and Joab the commander of the army went up to bury the slain, he killed every male in Edom (for Joab and all Israel remained there six months, until he had eliminated every male in Edom)." Here again one recognizes hyperbole, especially if Edom is to be understood as it is usually depicted in modern biblical atlases—as an expansive nation south of Moab in southern Transjordan. There is very little archaeological evidence of sedentary occupation in southern Transjordan (south of Wadi el-Hesa) during Iron I. Also, "Edom" seems to have been a rather loose geographical designation, and in some biblical texts clearly refers to territory southwest of the Dead Sea (Num. 34:3; Josh. 15:1–4). If David subjected Edom and secured it with garrisons, therefore, the Edom involved was probably the Negeb area on his southern frontier, home of "Edomite" tribes such as the Kenizzites and the Amalekites.[33]

Ammonites. Rabbah of the Ammonites (present-day Amman), situated on an upper branch of the Jabbok River at the edge of the desert, was apparently the center of an Ammonite chiefdom during the time of Saul and David and was the most developed region in Transjordan in the Early Iron Age. Earlier narratives in the Genesis–2 Kings History have reported Ammonite attacks on the Gileadites that prompted Gileadite appeals first to Jephthah and later to Saul. David seems to have formed an alliance with the Ammonite ruler Nahash that remained in effect until Nahash died and was succeeded by his son Hanun. Hostilities between Jerusalem and Rabbah erupted at that point, and seem to have continued off and on for some time. Joab is usually depicted carrying the fight to the Ammonites while David remained in Jerusalem. It was on one such occasion, while Joab and his troops were ravaging the Ammonites and besieging Rabbah, that David is reported to have had his affair with Bathsheba (2 Sam. 11). Rabbah was eventually taken, we are told; David was called to the scene in time to participate in the victory; and the Ammonites were consigned to forced labor (2 Sam. 12:26–31).[34]

Aramaeans. Three passages come into consideration for understanding David's relations with the Aramaeans or Syrians: 2 Samuel 10:6–19; 8:3–12; and 1 Kings 11:23–25. The first two passages are garbled accounts of a military conflict between David and Hadadezer, king of Zobah. The third describes a situation in Damascus during Solomon's reign. "God raised up another adversary against Solomon, Rezon son of Eliada, who had fled from his master, King Hadadezer of Zobah. He gathered followers around him and became leader of a marauding band, after the slaughter by David; they went to Damascus, settled there, and made him king in Damascus. He was an adversary of Israel all the days of Solomon" (1 Kgs. 11:23–25).

One can only guess at the historical circumstances behind these three passages. Our guess is as follows: Under attack from David's army, the Ammonites appealed to Hadadezer king of Zobah for help. Zobah, a city-state

---

33. On Moab and Edom in the Early Iron Age, see the essays in Piotr Bienkowski, ed., *Early Edom and Moab: The Beginning of the Iron Age in Southern Jordan* (Sheffield Archaeological Monographs 7; Sheffield: Collis, 1992).

34. See L. G. Herr, "Whatever Happened to the Ammonites?" *BAR* 19/6 (1993) 26–35, 68; and R. C. Bailey, *David in Love and War: The Pursuit of Power in 2 Samuel 10–12* (JSOTSup 75; Sheffield: JSOT Press, 1990).

located somewhere in the vicinity of present-day Homs in Syria, apparently dominated southern Aram at the time. Hadadezer probably regarded Galilee and northern Transjordan as belonging to his realm as well, and responded to the Ammonite appeal with troops from various Aramaean cities. David defeated Hadadezer decisively in two resulting battles, one before the gates of Rabbah and one at Helam, somewhere in Transjordan. Hadadezer then withdrew from Transjordan, abandoning the region to David. He also lost control of Damascus—apparently not to David, but to a marauding band led by Rezon son of Eliada. Naturally Toi of Hamath, a long-standing enemy of Hadadezer, was pleased with the turn of events. He sent his son to David with congratulations and gifts.

Whether, or the extent to which, David encroached militarily on Aramaean territory is unclear.[35] The crucial passage is rather sweeping, possibly from the hand of the compilers of Genesis–2 Kings, and in any case is ambiguous. "Then David put garrisons among the Aramaeans of Damascus; and the Aramaeans became servants to David and brought tribute. Yahweh gave victory to David wherever he went. David took the gold shields that were carried by the servants of Hadadezer, and brought them to Jerusalem. From Betah and from Berothai, towns of Hadadezer, King David took a great amount of bronze" (2 Sam. 8:6–8). The statement that David "put garrisons in Aram of Damascus," if it is to be trusted, would not necessarily mean that David controlled the city of Damascus itself, only that he placed garrisons within some portion of the territory generally associated with Damascus. And are we to understand that he conducted raids on Betah (read "Tibhath" with 1 Chr. 18:8) and Berothai, both probably located in the Lebanese Bekaa Valley? Regardless, there is no reason to suppose that David actually conquered Zobah or exercised any sort of permanent rule over Aram proper.

The summary of David's military activities provided in 2 Samuel 8:1–14 is reminiscent of the summary of Saul's conquests in 1 Samuel 14:47–48. Both kings are credited with sweeping victories and having subdued all their enemies on every side.

General Bibliography

Two recent scholarly biographies of David are S. L. McKenzie, *King David: A Biography* (New York: Oxford University Press, 2000); and Baruch Halpern, *David's Secret Demons: Messiah, Murderer, Traitor, King* (Grand Rapids: Eerdmans, 2001). McKenzie sets out to interpret the biblical account of David "against the grain" (p. 45), and Halpern seeks to "contemplate David as his enemies saw him" (p. xv). Stanley Isser, *The Sword of Goliath: David in Heroic Literature* (SBLStBL 6; Atlanta: Society of Biblical Literature, 2003) surveys the treatments of David from a literary perspective. Other works on David are D. M. Gunn, *The Story of King David: Genre and Interpretations* (JSOTSup 6; Sheffield: JSOT Press, 1978); M. J. Steussey, *David* (Columbia: University of South Carolina Press, 1999); Robert Alter, *The David Story: A Translation*

35. David's relationship to the Aramaean states is discussed in Edward Lipiński, *The Aramaeans: Their Ancient History, Culture, Religion* (OLA 100; Leuven: Peeters, 2000) 330–43. See also Nadav Na'aman, "In Search of Reality behind the Account of David's Wars with Israel's Neighbors," *IEJ* 52 (2002) 200–224; repr. in *AIHH* 38–61, who sees the reflection of later historical events in the accounts.

with Commentary of 1 and 2 Samuel (New York: Norton, 1999); and Keith Bodner, *David Observed: A King in the Eyes of His Court* (Sheffield: Sheffield Phoenix, 2005).

A survey of issues related to the quest for the historical David is R. P. Gordon, "In Search of David: The David Tradition in Recent Study," in A. R. Millard et al., eds., *Faith, Tradition, and History: Old Testament Historiography in Its Near Eastern Context* (Winona Lake, IN: Eisenbrauns, 1994) 285–98. The development of monarchic politics and ideology are discussed in Tomoo Ishida, *The Royal Dynasties in Ancient Israel: A Study on the Formation and Development of Royal-Dynastic Ideology* (BZAW 142; Berlin: de Gruyter, 1977); and John Day, ed., *King and Messiah in Israel and the Ancient Near East* (JSOTSup 270; Sheffield: Sheffield Academic Press, 1998).

General archaeological matters are discussed in Gabriel Barkey, "The Iron Age II-III," in Amnon Ben-Tor, ed., *The Archaeology of Ancient Israel* (New Haven: Yale University Press, 1992) 302–73; J. S. Holladay, "The Kingdoms of Israel and Judah: Political and Economic Centralization in the Iron IIA-B (ca. 1000–750 B.C.E.)," in T. E. Levy, ed., *The Archaeology of Society in the Holy Land* (New York: Facts on File, 1995) 368–98; and L. G. Herr, "The Iron Age II Period: Emerging Nations," *BA* 60 (1997) 114–83. For additional archaeological discussions, especially on Jerusalem, see above, n. 22; and archaeological reports on excavations in Jersalem: Yigal Shiloh et al., *Excavation at the City of David* (6 vols.; Qedem 19, 30, 33, 35, 40, 41; Jerusalem: Institute of Archaeology, Hebrew University of Jerusalem, 1984–2000) and Margaret Steiner, *Excavations by Kathleen M. Kenyon in Jerusalem 1961–1967*, vol. 3: *The Settlement in the Bronze and Iron Ages* (Copenhagen International Series 3; Sheffield: Sheffield Academic Press, 2001).

Important essays are found in Volkmar Fritz and P. R. Davies, eds., *The Origins of the Ancient Israelite States* (JSOTSup 228; Sheffield: Sheffield Academic Press, 1996), and Israel Finkelstein and Nadav Na'aman, eds., *From Nomadism to Monarchy: Archaeological and Historical Aspects of Early Israel* (Washington, DC: Biblical Archaeology Society, 1994).

The "historical" and the "legendary" David are discussed in Israel Finkelstein and N. A. Silberman, *David and Solomon: In Search of the Bible's Sacred Kings and the Roots of the Western Tradition* (New York: Free Press, 2006).

7. Solomon

Solomon's reign was a "golden age"—or at least that is what one would conclude from a casual reading of the Bible. The compilers of the Genesis–2 Kings History depicted Solomon as an exceedingly wise, exceptionally wealthy, and extremely powerful ruler whose empire stretched from the Euphrates River in the north to the Egyptian frontier in the south. The Chronicler pressed these claims even further, neutralizing all negative aspects of Solomon's reign and elaborating on his role as temple builder and cofounder with David of the Jerusalem cult. The introductions to the books of Proverbs, Ecclesiastes, and Song of Songs appear to credit him for their wisdom. Not surprisingly, Solomon's reign came to be regarded as the epitome of splendor, opulence, and wise government (see Luke 12:27).

A closer examination of the biblical materials, however, probing beneath the sweeping claims and editorial generalizations, raises doubts about the extent of Solomon's glory. We read, for example, that the "wealthy" Solomon developed cash flow problems that required him to concede twenty cities in Galilee to the Phoenician king of Tyre (1 Kgs. 9:10–14). The "powerful" Solomon, who supposedly "ruled over all the kingdoms from the Euphrates to the land of the Philistines and to the border of Egypt" (4:21), was troubled by adversaries much nearer home—Hadad of Edom, Rezon of Damascus, and Jeroboam of Ephraim (11:14–40). The "wise" Solomon apparently so exploited his people through forced labor and other despotic practices that the bulk of the kingdom chose to break away from Jerusalem at his death rather than to continue under his policies (12:1–20).

When we consider that Solomon is not mentioned in any ancient written sources apart from the Bible, the golden age envisioned by the biblical narrators becomes even less convincing. One can dismiss the fact that Saul and David find no mention in contemporary written sources on the grounds that they lived during a transitional period, a time from which virtually no written records have survived. But the Solomonic empire with its extravagant and splendid court as envisioned by the compilers of Genesis–2 Kings would have been a dramatic aberration for the international situation of his age. Indeed, if such an empire actually existed, and especially if it lasted anywhere near the forty years attributed to Solomon in the Bible, then the times were not really transitional. At least some written records or royal inscriptions should have survived somewhere from Solomon's empire itself.[1]

---

1. K. A. Kitchen has argued that even during the transitional period (1200–900 B.C.E.), there were four mini-empires in the Levant: Tabal, Carchemish, Aram-Zobah, and Israel. See "The Controlling Role

The archaeological evidence is even more ambivalent, as we shall see, and equally problematic for the biblical claims. Perhaps the most glaring discrepancy has to do with the supposedly international character of Solomon's reign. We are told that Solomon engaged in international trade and brought luxury goods to Jerusalem from distant lands. Yet the material culture of Early Iron Age Palestine, including the tenth century during which Solomon would have lived, is characterized more by the absence of trade items from abroad than by the presence of such items.[2]

When all of the above is taken into account, it is difficult to escape the conclusion that the Solomon we encounter in the Hebrew Bible is an idealized figure and that the golden age envisioned in the biblical materials is highly rhetorical at best. How then did Solomon achieve such prominence in Jewish legend? Why did the compilers of Genesis–2 Kings depict his reign as a golden age? And why did the Chronicler make so much of it? One reason may be that there is a core of truth to the legend—David the warrior was followed by Solomon the administrator and builder, who upgraded the royal office, made the fledgling Jerusalem city-state look more like a real kingdom, and enjoyed more visibly the benefits of the crown. But the main reason probably has to do with Solomon's association with the Jerusalem temple. Over the coming centuries, as the temple became increasingly central to Judahite ideology, the one credited with building the temple was transformed in Judah's folk memory from a Jerusalemite king of some local fame into a world-class emperor who presided over a golden age.

Scholarly opinion regarding the historical Solomon is widely divided. Views range from those on the one side who are prepared to take the biblical profile essentially at face value,[3] to those on the other side who question whether Solomon was an historical character at all.[4] We propose a mediating position between these two extremes. Without denying that the biblical portrait of Solomon is legendary, often unrealistic, and probably modeled after Neo-Assyrian and Neo-Babylonian rulers in the biblical narrators' recent memory, we see Solomon as an historical person who ruled in Jerusalem after David and probably did build the temple. Before exploring this middle road, let us review the biblical materials related to Solomon and the archaeological data relevant for understanding the tenth century B.C.E. during which he would have lived.

---

of External Evidence in Assessing the Historical Status of the Israelite Monarchy," in V. P. Long et al., eds., *Windows into Old Testament History: Evidence, Argument, and the Crisis of "Biblical Israel"* (Grand Rapids: Eerdmans, 2002) 111–30; and idem, *On the Reliability of the Old Testament* (Grand Rapids: Eerdmans, 2003) 98–101.

2. For a general archaeological survey of the period, see L. G. Herr, "The Iron Age II Period: Emerging Nations," *BA* 60 (1997) 114–83, esp. 114–32; and the older work of Amihai Mazar, *Archaeology of the Land of the Bible, 10,000–586 B.C.E.* (ABRL; New York: Doubleday, 1990) 368–402.

3. See Iain Provan et al., *A Biblical History of Israel* (Louisville: Westminster John Knox, 2003) 239–58; Kitchen, *Reliability*, 107–58; and the earlier essays of C. L. Meyers, "The Israelite Empire: In Defense of King Solomon," in D. N. Freedman and M. P. O'Connor, eds., *Backgrounds for the Bible* (Winona Lake, IN: Eisenbrauns, 1987) 181–98; and A. R. Millard, "Text and Archaeology: Weighing the Evidence: The Case for King Solomon," *PEQ* 123 (1991) 19–27.

4. See J. A. Soggin, *An Introduction to the History of Israel* (3d ed.; London: SCM, 1993) 32; he asks: "So is it possible that the reference to David and Solomon and to their empire is simply a later artificial construction, tending to glorify a past which never existed to compensate for a present that is dull and gray?"

Solomon in the Biblical Materials

Both the Genesis–2 Kings History and the Chronicler's History provide accounts of Solomon's reign. In addition, Solomon is closely associated with the so-called wisdom books of the Hebrew Bible: Proverbs, Ecclesiastes, Song of Songs, as well as the apocryphal Wisdom of Solomon.

The Genesis–2 Kings Presentation of Solomon's Reign

While the Genesis–2 Kings presentations of Saul and David are composed for the most part of numerous, previously independent folk legends that have been combined and superimposed with an editorial veneer, its presentation of Solomon is more thoroughly editorial. First Kings 1–2 provides the transition from David's reign to Solomon. Then, for the next nine chapters, until Solomon's reign is concluded at the end of 1 Kings 11, the narrator or narrators expound on Solomon's piety, wisdom, wealth, and international prestige. Various items are incorporated into the exposition by way of illustration: occasional stories (3:16–28; 10:1–10, 13), descriptions (chap. 6; 7:13–51), lists (4:1–19), and so on. But these items are not always well integrated into the narration or interrelated with one another, which leaves the impression in some places of a disjointed assemblage of odds and ends. Toward the end, the reader is referred to a "Book of the Acts of Solomon" (11:41). Presumably some of the 1 Kings presentation was drawn directly or indirectly from that source, but it is difficult to determine exactly what.[5]

Because it tends to be more exposition with illustrating odds and ends than story line, it is difficult to summarize the Solomon section of the Genesis–2 Kings history. The main sequence of events as narrated is essentially the following.

Summary of 1 Kings 1–11

When David grew old, was failing in health and no longer potent, Adonijah proceeded to exalt himself as king. This move was supported by Joab (the chief commander of the army) and Abiathar (one of the two chief priests), but not by Nathan the prophet, Zadok (the other chief priest), or Benaiah (who commanded the Cherethite and Pelethite mercenaries). Nathan reported the matter to Bathsheba, and together they influenced David publicly to designate Solomon as his successor instead of Adonijah. Solomon was crowned in a surprise ceremony orchestrated by Nathan, Zadok, and Benaiah.

Before dying, David instructed Solomon to deal favorably with the descendants of Barzillai, who had come to his aid at the time of Absalom's rebellion, but to execute Shimei the Benjaminite, who had supported the rebellion, and Joab, the infamous commander of David's army. Solomon did as instructed, although he waited until there was some provocation before ordering the executions. Also he executed Adonijah and exiled Abiathar to Anathoth, a village

5. On this work see Jacob Liver, "The Book of the Acts of Solomon," *Bib* 48 (1967) 75–101.

just north of Jerusalem. The provocation in the case of Joab, Adonijah, and Abiathar was that Adonijah requested a maiden from David's harem for his wife (the same Shunammite maiden who had been brought to the court to assist David in overcoming his impotency). Solomon interpreted this as a calculated move on Adonijah's part to recover the crown (1:1–2:46a).

"So the kingdom was established in the hand of Solomon" (2:46b), and his royal status was recognized internationally. He entered into a marriage alliance with the pharaoh of Egypt and brought the pharaoh's daughter to live in Jerusalem (3:1–2; see 7:8; 9:16, 24; 11:1).

No temple had yet been built for Yahweh in Jerusalem, so the people sacrificed at high places. Solomon was a pious king and went to the great high place at Gibeon to offer a thousand burnt offerings. Yahweh appeared to him in a dream there and called on him to "ask what I should give you." Solomon requested "an understanding mind to govern your people, able to discern between good and evil; for who can govern this your great people?" This request pleased Yahweh, who granted it and promised riches and honor as well. Solomon awoke and returned to Jerusalem, where his ability as a wise judge was manifested in a case that involved two prostitutes, both of whom claimed to be the mother of the same child (3:3–28).

Solomon's high officials are listed next (4:1–6) and also the twelve officers in charge of providing food for the king's table and his household (4:7–19). There follow sweeping claims regarding the extent of Solomon's realm, the splendor of his court, and his international renown as a wise king:

> Solomon was sovereign over all the kingdoms from the Euphrates to the land of the Philistines, even to the border of Egypt; they brought tribute and served Solomon all the days of his life.
>
> Solomon's provision for one day was thirty cors of choice flour, and sixty cors of meal, ten fat oxen, and twenty pasture-fed cattle, one hundred sheep, besides deer, gazelles, roebucks, and fatted fowl. For he had dominion over all the region west of the Euphrates from Tiphsah to Gaza, over all the kings west of the Euphrates; and he had peace on all sides. . . . Solomon also had forty thousand stalls of horses for his chariots, and twelve thousand horsemen. . . .
>
> God gave Solomon very great wisdom, discernment, and breadth of understanding as vast as the sand on the seashore, so that Solomon's wisdom surpassed the wisdom of all the people of the east, and all the wisdom of Egypt. He was wiser than anyone else . . . ; his fame spread throughout all the surrounding nations. He composed three thousand proverbs, and his songs numbered a thousand and five. . . . People came from all the nations to hear the wisdom of Solomon. (4:21–34)

Solomon began preparations for building the temple. Hiram king of Tyre agreed to supply building materials and skilled workmen, while Solomon raised a levy of forced labor for the project. Construction began in the fourth year of Solomon's reign, which was the 480th year after the people of Israel had come out of the land of Egypt. There is an elaborate description of the temple, which itself was completed in seven years (1 Kgs. 5–6). Thirteen years were required to build Solomon's palace and associated royal buildings (including a house for the pharaoh's daughter), which are described in less detail (7:1–12). In addition, Solomon engaged a bronzesmith from Tyre, also named Hiram, to cast bronze fixtures and furnishings for the temple (7:13–50). When all the work was completed, Solomon stored the things that David had dedicated (silver, gold, and vessels) in the treasuries of the temple (7:51).

Then Solomon assembled all the dignitaries of his realm in Jerusalem and dedicated the temple to Yahweh. The dedication ceremony included (1) a ritual transfer of the ark into the temple; (2) a long prayer by Solomon in which he called upon Yahweh to reconfirm his promise to David of a permanent dynasty, to bless the temple with his special presence, and to forgive the people when they repented of their wrongdoings; (3) elaborate sacrifices and peace offerings; and (4) a great feast. When all the people had returned to their homes, Yahweh appeared to Solomon a second time and assured him that his prayer would be answered, depending on the king's faithfulness (8:1–9:9).

At this point several items are appended that pertain in one way or another to the completion of the building program. Solomon gave twenty cities to Hiram king of Tyre in payment for the latter's contributions to the various projects. There is a clarification of Solomon's policies regarding forced labor. The pharaoh's daughter was moved to her own house. Solomon built the Millo. With the temple and altar in place, Solomon began a schedule (three times a year) of burnt offerings and peace offerings (9:10–25).

Finally, a series of items further illustrates Solomon's wealth, wisdom, and international prestige. He built a fleet of ships at Ezion-geber and engaged in a shipping venture with the Phoenician king (9:26–28; 10:11–12, 22). The queen of Sheba, hearing of Solomon's fame, came to test his wisdom. They exchanged costly gifts (10:1–13). Solomon had an abundance of silver and gold as well as a huge chariotry with imported horses and chariots. "The whole earth sought the presence of Solomon to hear his wisdom, which God had put into his mind. Every one of them brought a present, objects of silver and gold, garments, weaponry, spices, horses, and mules, so much year by year" (10:25).

But Solomon loved many foreign women. In addition to the pharaoh's daughter, he had Moabite, Ammonite, Edomite, Sidonian, and Hittite women—totaling seven hundred wives-princesses and three hundred concubines—and these women turned his heart after other gods. Indeed, he built sanctuaries for Chemosh and Molech, the gods of the Moabites and the Ammonites, respectively, on the mountain ridge east of Jerusalem (11:1–13). Thus Yahweh became angry with Solomon and sent adversaries. Three of these adversaries are named: Hadad of Edom (11:14–22), Rezon of Damascus (11:23–25), and Jeroboam of Ephraim (11:26–40). Jeroboam was an able and industrious young man whom Solomon placed in charge of the forced labor of the house of Joseph. Ahijah, a prophet from Shiloh, confronted Jeroboam on one occasion, announced that Solomon's kingdom would be torn apart in the future, and predicted that Jeroboam would receive the major portion of it. Jeroboam escaped to Egypt, where he remained until Solomon died. Solomon's reign lasted forty years, and he was buried in the city (or royal quarter) of his father in Jerusalem (11:43).

Composition and Structure of 1 Kings 1–11[6]

This Genesis–2 Kings presentation of Solomon is characterized throughout by editorial exaggeration. A cautious historian might be inclined to ignore the account altogether if there were any other more convincing source of information available. Unfortunately there is none. We have observed already that Solomon does not appear in any known ancient inscriptions, and we will see below that the other biblical materials are similarly problematic as historical sources and that the archaeological evidence is ambivalent. If we are to catch any glimpse of the "historical" Solomon, therefore, it will have to come from the materials included and so thoroughly editorialized in 1 Kings 1–11. As a first step in that direction, it is necessary to distinguish and evaluate some of the different kinds of material involved.

First, of course, there is the account in 1 Kings 1–2 that describes the palace intrigue surrounding Solomon's accession to the throne. This account may be read as the conclusion to the narrative of David's rule in Jerusalem and of the troubles that plagued his reign, discussed in chapter 6. As we observed there, this narrative invites more confidence as a source for historical information than much of the other material pertaining to David; yet it also has certain novelistic features more suggestive of a storyteller's skill than of historical record. Moreover, especially as we reach the conclusion of this narrative, its propagandistic intention becomes increasingly obvious.[7] It explains how Solomon, who was not one of David's older sons in line for the crown, happened to make it to the throne nevertheless, and seeks to justify Solomon's palace coup and subsequent executions. It was David himself, the narrator assures us, who designated Solomon as his successor and who instructed Solomon to execute Joab and Shimei. Adonijah's execution was his own fault. His request for the Shunammite maiden demonstrated that he still had designs on the throne.

A second large block of material consists of detailed descriptions of Solomon's cultic activities: the theophany at Gibeon (3:2–15), his building program in Jerusalem with primary attention given to the temple and its furnishings (chaps. 5–7), the dedication ceremony (chap. 8), and Yahweh's second theophany (9:1–9). The interests and intentions of the Judahite editors of the Genesis–2 Kings account are obvious in this block of material. These descriptions of Solomon's cultic activities emphasize that (1) Jerusalem is the appropriate center of Yahweh worship; (2) a new age in history was inaugurated

---

6. On the structure and content of the Solomonic material in 1 Kings, see Bezalel Porten, "The Structure and Theme of the Solomonic Narrative (1 Kings 3–11)," *HUCA* 38 (1967) 93–128; M. Z. Brettler, "The Structure of I Kings 1–11," *JSOT* 49 (1991) 87–97; A. Frisch, "Structure and Its Significance: The Narrative of Solomon's Reign (1 Kings 1–12.24)," *JSOT* 51 (1991) 3–14; and J. D. Hays, "Has the Narrator Come to Praise Solomon or to Bury Him? Narrative Subtlety in 1 Kings 1–11," *JSOT* 28 (2003) 149–74. For the view that 1 Kgs. 1–2 did not belong to the so-called Succession Narrative, see J. W. Flanagan, "Court History or Succession Narrative? A Study of 2 Samuel 9–10 and 1 Kings 1–2," *JBL* 91 (1972) 172–81. Variations between the Greek and Hebrew versions of the reign of Solomon are discussed in P. S. F. van Keulen, *Two Versions of the Solomon Narrative: An Inquiry into the Relationship between MT 1 Kgs. 2–11 and LXX 3 Reg. 2–11* (VTSup 104; Leiden: Brill, 2005).

7. On royal apology in ancient Near Eastern sources and the Bible see the literature in chapter 6 above, n. 8; and on the succession of Solomon see the essays by Timoo Ishida in the section "The Succession Narrative in Historical Perspective," in *History and Historical Writing in Ancient Israel: Studies in Biblical Historiography* (SHCANE 16; Leiden: Brill, 1999) 102–85.

when Solomon began work on the temple, 480 years after the exodus from Egypt; (3) Solomon himself, who erected and dedicated the temple, was a pious and righteous king who ruled at a time when Israel had peace on all sides and dwelt in safety; (4) Yahweh confirmed the dedication of the temple, with the promise of his special presence in years to come; and (5) Yahweh also reconfirmed, in connection with the dedication, his commitment to the permanence of the Davidic dynasty.

Yet there is also a note of qualification in Solomon's long prayer and Yahweh's response.[8] Solomon raises the possibility that the people might sin in future years, so that Yahweh would give them into the hand of an enemy who in turn would carry them captive into a foreign land:

> If they sin against you—for there is no one who does not sin—and you are angry with them and give them to an enemy, so that they are taken away captive to the land of the enemy, far off or near; yet if they come to their senses in the land to which they have been taken captive, and repent, and plead with you in the land of their captors, . . . then hear in heaven your dwelling place their prayer and their plea, maintain their cause and forgive your people. (1 Kgs. 8:46–50)

Yahweh's response to Solomon's prayer includes a warning that unfaithfulness would indeed result in an end to Jerusalem with its temple, foreign captivity for its people, and even an end to the Davidic dynasty:

> As for you, if you will walk before me, as David your father walked, with integrity of heart and uprightness, doing according to all that I have commanded you, and keeping my statutes and my ordinances, then I will establish your royal throne over Israel forever, as I promised your father David. . . . If you turn aside from following me, you or your children, and do not keep my commandments and my statutes that I have set before you, but go and serve other gods and worship them, then I will cut Israel off from the land which I have given them; and the house that I have consecrated for my name I will cast out of my sight; and Israel will become a proverb and a taunt among all peoples. (1 Kgs. 9:4–7)

In short, these passages anticipate, interpret theologically, and offer hope in the face of circumstances that for Solomon's day were still in the distant future but that for the compilers of Genesis–2 Kings were recent past: the Babylonian capture of Jerusalem, the exile of many of its people, the destruction of the temple, and the end of the Davidic line. This happened, the compilers want us to understand, because the rulers who followed Solomon, and even he himself in his later years, were unfaithful to Yahweh and led the people astray. But theirs was also a message of hope, if the exilic community would repent: "if they come to their senses in the land to which they have been carried captive, and repent . . ."

Although these passages that focus on Solomon's cultic activities clearly were formulated long after Solomon's day and address theological concerns of

---

8. See G. N. Knoppers, "Prayer and Propaganda: The Dedication of Solomon's Temple and the Deuteronomistic Program," *CBQ* 57 (1995) 229–54; repr. in G. N. Knoppers and J. G. McConville, eds., *Reconsidering Israel and Judah: The Deuteronomistic History in Recent Thought* (SBTS 8; Winona Lake, IN: Eisenbrauns, 2000) 370–96.

the exilic community, they may include some elements of authentic historical memory. There is no reason to doubt that Gibeon was an important worship center during Solomon's reign, for example, or that Solomon himself worshiped there. The description of the temple and its furnishings also seems realistic enough, if not entirely understandable at every point. The temple remained standing until the sixth century B.C.E. If the description is misleading in any way, therefore, possibly it tends (1) to depict the temple as it existed after four centuries of use (and perhaps after numerous modifications) rather than as it was when Solomon first built it, and (2) to exaggerate the richness of the original furnishings.

The report of Yahweh's appearance to Solomon in a dream while he slept in the Gibeon sanctuary finds close parallels in stories associated with other kings of the ancient world (see, for example, Herodotus 2.141). The historicity of the "pharaoh's daughter," mentioned five different times (1 Kgs. 3:1–2; 7:8; 9:16, 24; 11:1), is doubtful on similar grounds. She also turns up in Arabic lore. The story about Solomon's wise judgment of the two prostitutes and the one about the visit of the queen of Sheba are probably just that and nothing more—good stories that emerged long after Solomon's day and play on the theme of his wisdom and wealth. Any attempt to identify the pharaoh who gave his daughter to Solomon in marriage[9] or speculation on the political and commercial implications of the queen of Sheba's visit[10] simply misunderstands the fanciful nature of the material. The same goes for the sweeping editorial claims regarding Solomon's daily food supply (ten oxen, twenty cattle, a hundred sheep, etc.), the broad expanse of his dominion (from the Euphrates to the Egyptian frontier), his forty thousand stalls of horses, his three thousand proverbs, his seven hundred wives and three hundred concubines, and so on.[11] All of this belongs to the idealized Solomon of legend.[12]

Some of the items included in the Genesis–2 Kings treatment of Solomon have a more authentic ring, however, suggested if for no other reasons than that (1) they supply details of a sort not characteristic of idealized propaganda or editorial hyperbole, and (2) they point to a Solomonic reign of more modest and realistic proportions than the editors of the Genesis–2 Kings account wished to convey. Belonging to this category are the lists of Solomon's high

9. On arguments for identifying Siamun of the Twenty-first Egyptian Dynasty as Solomon's Egyptian father-in-law, see A. R. Green, "Solomon and Siamun: A Synchronism between Dynastic Israel and the Twenty-First Dynasty of Egypt," *JBL* 97 (1978) 353–67; and Kitchen, *Reliability*, 108–12.

10. See the essays in J. B. Pritchard, ed., *Solomon and Sheba* (New York: Praeger, 1974); and for arguments favoring the historicity of the queen's visit, see Kitchen, *Reliability*, 116–20.

11. On the issue of highly exaggerated numbers in Near Eastern literature, see Marco de Odorico, *The Use of Numbers and Quantifications in the Assyrian Royal Inscriptions* (SAAS 3; Helsinki: Neo-Assyrian Text Corpus Project, 1995); and on their use in biblical narrative, see K. L. Younger Jr., "The Figurative Aspect and the Contextual Method in the Evaluation of the Solomonic Empire," in D. J. A. Clines et al., eds., *The Bible in Three Dimensions: Essays in Celebration of Forty Years of Biblical Studies at the University of Sheffield* (JSOTSup 98; Sheffield: JSOT Press, 1990) 157–75.

12. On the problems of the legendary versus the historical Solomon, see G. J. Wrightman, "The Myth of Solomon," *BASOR* 277/278 (1990) 5–22; M. M. Gelinas, "United Monarchy—Divided Monarchy: Fact or Fiction?" in S. W. Holloway and L. K. Handy, eds., *The Pitcher Is Broken: Memorial Essays for Gösta W. Ahlström* (JSOTSup 190; Sheffield: JSOT Press, 1995) 227–37; J. M. Miller, "Separating the Solomon of History from the Solomon of Legend," in L. K. Handy, ed., *The Age of Solomon: Scholarship at the Turn of the Millennium* (SHCANE 11; Leiden: Brill, 1997) 1–24; and G. N. Knoppers, "The Vanishing Solomon: The Disappearance of the United Monarchy from Recent Histories of Ancient Israel," *JBL* 116 (1997) 19–44.

officials (1 Kgs. 4:1–6), of the officers in charge of providing food for his household (4:7–19), and of the cities he built (fortified) with forced labor (9:15–19).
Also to be considered in this regard are the occasional items that provide some
specific detail about his international involvements: his dealings with Hiram
the king of Tyre, particularly the shipping venture (9:26–28; 10:11–12, 22); the
sources and costs of his horses and chariots, although not the excessive size of
the chariotry attributed to him (10:28–29); and the conflicts with Hadad of
Edom and Rezon of Damascus (11:14–25). Finally, the episode involving Jeroboam of Ephraim (11:26–40) must be taken seriously, since it conflicts so obviously with the portrait of Solomon that the compilers of Genesis–2 Kings
wished to convey and since it anticipates the rebellion that occurred at
Solomon's death (see 1 Kgs. 12:1–20).

The conflict noted at the beginning of this chapter between the sweeping
claims about Solomon's wisdom, wealth, and power, on the one hand, and bits
of information that seem to undercut these claims, on the other, was noticeable
also to the compilers of Genesis–2 Kings. They dealt with this conflict by distinguishing between the first and main part of Solomon's reign, during which
they depict him as the faithful ruler who achieved "the golden age" (1 Kgs.
3–10), and his last years during which they depict him as one led astray by foreign women.[13] Accordingly, the negative items reported for Solomon's reign,
such as Jeroboam's opposition to the forced-labor policies and his escape to
Egypt, are all placed in the last years. We have encountered the same pattern
in connection with David—David under the blessing followed by David under
the curse—and will see it later in the biblical presentations of other Judean
kings. Needless to say, this is an artificial editorial arrangement of the material.

Also artificial and schematic are the chronological notations provided. The
temple, we are told, was begun in the fourth year of Solomon's forty-year
reign, which was also the four hundred and eightieth year after the exodus
from Egypt. Solomon's building projects required exactly half of his reign,
twenty years, and seven years of that time were devoted to the building of the
temple (1 Kgs. 6:1, 37–38; 7:1; 11:42). These are symbolic numbers—four, forty,
multiples of forty, and seven—not to be taken literally. For example, Moses is
said to have lived for a hundred and twenty years, which were divided into
three forty-year periods. Many of the judges served for forty years and were
separated by forty-year intervals of peace. David ruled for forty years, seven of
which he resided at Hebron, and on and on. We have no way of knowing how
long either David's or Solomon's reign lasted. It does appear, for reasons that
will be discussed in chapter 9, that Solomon's reign ended in approximately
925 B.C.E.

The compilers of the Genesis–2 Kings History concluded their presentation
of Solomon's reign with reference to a source from which, presumably, they
derived some of their material. "Now the rest of the acts of Solomon, and all
that he did, and his wisdom, are they not written in the Book of the Acts of
Solomon?" (1 Kgs. 11:41). This pattern will be repeated for each of the later
Israelite and Judean kings. That is, for the "rest of the acts" of each of the

---

13. On women as villainous in the biblical historical books, see G. N. Knoppers, "Sex, Religion, and
Politics: The Deuteronomist on Intermarriage," *HAR* 14 (1994) 121–41.

Israelite kings the reader will be referred to "the Book of the Annals of the Kings of Israel" and for the "rest of the acts" of each of the Judean kings to "the Book of the Annals of the Kings of Judah" (14:29; 15:7, 23, 31; etc.). These books of "Annals" or "Chronicles" of the kings of Israel and Judah are not to be confused with the canonical books of 1–2 Chronicles, of course, which refer the reader to still other sources, such as "the records/chronicles of the seer Samuel," "the records/chronicles of the prophet Nathan," and "the records/chronicles of the seer Gad" (1 Chr. 29:29). Scholars have generally supposed, although it cannot be proved, that the books to which the compilers of Genesis–2 Kings referred were annalistic-like accounts based ultimately on court records. That this was the case as well with "the Book of the Acts of Solomon," "the records/chronicles of the Seer Samuel," "the records/chronicles of the prophet Nathan," and so on, seems less likely. In any case, it is impossible to determine which material in the Genesis–2 Kings presentation of Solomon derived from "the Book of the Acts of Solomon."

The Chronicler's Presentation of Solomon

The Chronicler's treatment of Solomon (2 Chr. 1–9) follows the same pattern as his treatment of David. It depends heavily upon, and largely reproduces, the corresponding section of the Genesis–2 Kings History but modifies the latter in a noticeably tendentious fashion.[14]

1. The questionable circumstances surrounding Solomon's accession to the throne disappear in the Chronicler's version. David designates Solomon as his successor and actually crowns him even before assigning the Levites their special responsibilities (1 Chr. 23:1). Later, after completing his total organization of the cultic and civil administration and as he approaches death, David turns the throne over to Solomon, who receives unanimous approval. "They made David's son Solomon king a second time; they anointed him as Yahweh's prince, and Zadok as priest. Then Solomon sat on the throne of Yahweh as king, succeeding his father David as king; he prospered, and all Israel obeyed him. All the leaders and the mighty warriors, and also all the sons of King David, pledged their allegiance to King Solomon" (1 Chr. 29:22b–24).

2. When describing the actual reign of Solomon, the Chronicler omits or recasts any items that might be taken to suggest less than ideal circumstances. Thus, for example, the brief report in 1 Kgs. 9:10–14 about Solomon's concession of twenty cities to Hiram of Tyre is turned around to suggest that it was the Phoenician king who gave the cities to Solomon (2 Chr. 8:1–2). We hear nothing of the troubles with Hadad of Edom or Rezon of Damascus. There is silence as well about Jeroboam's role in Solomon's forced-labor program and Ahijah's prediction that Jeroboam would receive ten parts of the kingdom (although Jeroboam's escape to Egypt is presupposed later in the Chronicler's account; 2 Chr. 10:2–3).

3. The Chronicler assigns even greater prominence to Solomon's cultic activities than does the Genesis–2 Kings History and elaborates on the details of the

14. See R. B. Dillard, "The Chronicler's Solomon," *WTJ* 43 (1980) 289–300; idem, "The Literary Structure of the Chronicler's Solomon Narrative," *JSOT* 30 (1984) 85–93.

ceremonies. Of the nine chapters that the Chronicler devotes to Solomon, six have to do with the building and dedication of the temple. Occasionally the Chronicler introduces supernatural elements into the ceremonies, as at the end of Solomon's prayer: "Fire came down from heaven and consumed the burnt offering and the sacrifices, and the glory of Yahweh filled the temple. The priests could not enter the house of Yahweh, because the glory of Yahweh filled Yahweh's house. When all the people of Israel saw the fire come down and the glory of Yahweh upon the temple, they bowed down" (2 Chr. 7:1–3).

Most of the Chronicler's elaboration of the ceremonies, however, has to do with the various orders of Levites who are depicted fulfilling the cultic functions that, according to the Chronicler, David had assigned them.

Solomon and the "Wisdom" Books

In addition to undertaking building projects and engaging in international commerce, the powerful rulers of the ancient world also sponsored learning and literature. Particularly the collection and transmission of instructional and proverbial literature, the sort of thing one finds in the biblical books of Ecclesiastes and Proverbs, appear to have been largely a royal endeavor in the ancient Middle East.[15] The king—or pharaoh, since our best examples come from Egypt—was the patron, while royal scribes conducted the actual literary activity. It is not surprising, therefore, that the idealized Solomon whom we encounter in the Hebrew Bible, patterned as he was after the powerful rulers of the day, would have been credited with proverbs and wise sayings. In the same way that David, known as the patron of Israel's cultic music, came to be credited with many psalms that he almost certainly did not compose, so also Solomon, envisioned as the wealthy and powerful potentate of the golden age, came to be associated with books pertaining to wisdom and love that were written or compiled long after his day. Specifically, Solomon is associated with the books of Proverbs, Ecclesiastes, Song of Songs, and Wisdom of Solomon.

We have no way of knowing, of course, whether Solomon sponsored such activities, or whether any of the proverbs and wise sayings that found their way into these books date back to Solomon's day. The latter seems a more likely possibility in the case of the book of Proverbs than Ecclesiastes or Wisdom of Solomon. The subtitles in the book of Proverbs suggest that the book incorporates older collections of proverbs, two of which are associated with Solomon (Prov. 10:1 and 25:1). The second of these subtitles reads: "These are other proverbs of Solomon that the officials of King Hezekiah of Judah copied." Presumably the compilers of the book of Proverbs drew on older collections that they, for some reason, associated with Solomon.

Solomon's connection with the Song of Songs, a collection of love poetry, can be dismissed out of hand. Since Solomon was said to have had many wives, it was natural to fantasize that he must have been a great lover. Thus it seemed reasonable for the compilers of Song of Songs, or a later copyist, to identify the male character in the love poetry as Solomon.

---

15. K. I. Parker, "Solomon as Philosopher King? The Nexus of Law and Wisdom in I Kings 1–11," *JSOT* 53 (1992) 75–91.

The Biblical Solomon and Historical Reconstruction

The preceding discussion of the biblical materials pertaining to Solomon leads to three conclusions. First, the Genesis–2 Kings History must serve as our primary source of information about his reign, as it has for the earlier periods of biblical history. The Chronicler's account is of no significant help. Nor is there anything of consequence to be learned about Solomon from any of the other biblical sources. Second, the Genesis–2 Kings presentation of Solomon's reign consists largely of extended descriptions of Solomon's cultic activities and sweeping, generalized claims regarding his great wisdom, wealth, and international prestige. Third, which will become more apparent below, when one attempts to probe beneath these sweeping, generalized claims for specific information about Solomon's reign, the results are disappointing and the few specifics provided suggest that Solomon's kingdom was of rather modest extent and local consequence.

Solomon and Archaeology

As explained earlier in this volume, most of the Palestinian cities that had managed to survive through the Middle and Late Bronze ages were destroyed or abandoned during the widespread disturbances that brought the Late Bronze Age to a close and marked the beginning of Iron I. Modest settlements, sometimes of squatters, lingered on at some of the old city sites, however, and some of the sites were resettled during the course of Iron I. Meanwhile, peoples with Mycenaean-related material culture (apparently the biblical Philistines) established cities along the Palestinian coast, and small agricultural settlements emerged in the highlands of the Palestinian interior. The highland settlements, with which the early Israelites and Judahites are probably to be associated, appeared later and less densely in some areas than in others. The appearance of settlements in the south-central or Judean highlands seems to have lagged behind this development in the northern or Ephramite highlands, for example; and in Transjordan, settlement south of the Arnon (Wadi el-Mujib), and especially south of the Zered (Wadi el-Hesa), lagged behind settlement north of the Arnon. Gradually, over a span of some two or three hundred years and in step with the remainder of the Levant, Palestine began to enter a new phase of urbanization. Many of the small squatter and agricultural settlements grew into towns, a few of the towns grew into modest cities, public buildings began to appear, and some of the cities were fortified.

Archaeologists refer to this new phase as Iron II. Earlier archaeologists tended to date the transition from Iron I to Iron II at approximately 1000 B.C.E., or about the beginning of David's reign as calculated on the basis of biblical chronology. The more recent trend is to lower the date toward 900 B.C.E., or about the end of Solomon's reign, again according to biblical chronology. More crucial for our purposes than agreeing upon a specific date for the transition, which would have been a gradual process in any case, is the question of whether any particular archaeological remains can be dated specifically to Solomon's reign. The answer depends on two potential correlations: (1) between 1 Kings 9:15–19

39. *Sheshonq relief from Karnak.* This triumphant relief of Sheshonq I on the outer wall of the temple of Amun at Karnak commemorates his military campaign into Syria-Palestine during the latter half of the tenth century B.C.E. Almost certainly Sheshonq is the Shishak who, according to 1 Kgs. 14:25–27, threatened Jerusalem five years after Solomon's death. Stylized figures beneath Sheshonq's feet represent conquered cities.

40. *Stylized figures from Sheshonq's relief.* Close-up of some of the stylized figures from Sheshonq's triumphal inscription on the walls of the temple of Amun at Karnak. Each figure represents a defeated city.

and fortification systems excavated at Megiddo, Hazor, and Gezer;[16] and (2) between Pharaoh Shishak's campaign into Palestine reported in 1 Kings 14:25 and destruction levels at several Palestinian sites including Megiddo and Gezer. Both of these correlations gained wide acceptance during the 1960s and continue to find strong support. Both also, for more than a decade now, have encountered serious challenges.

According to 1 Kings 9:15–19, Solomon built (or fortified) several cities, including Hazor, Megiddo, and Gezer. Archaeological excavations in the ruins of these three cities reveal that all three were fortified with strong walls and similar city gates at about the time of the transition from Iron I to Iron II. A characteristic feature of the city gates is that one enters through a sequence of piers—four on each side, forming four entryways and three chambers on each side, six chambers in all. In light of the relatively large scale (by Early Iron Age standards) and similar designs of the fortifications, it was argued that all three cities must have been fortified as part of a centralized, royally sponsored building program. Naturally, in view of the biblical profile of Solomon and especially 1 Kings 9:15–19, it is tempting to attribute this royally sponsored building program to Solomon. That being the case, the pottery styles associated with the fortification systems in question came to be regarded as "Solomonic," dated to the tenth century with biblical chronology, and regarded as indicators of Solomonic/tenth-century strata at other Palestinian sites.

According to 1 Kings 14:25, "King Shishak of Egypt came up against Jerusalem" in the fifth year of Solomon's successor, Rehoboam. Shishak almost certainly is to be identified with Sheshonq, founder of Dynasty 22, who commemorated a campaign into Palestine with an inscription on the walls of the great temple of Amun at Karnak (to be discussed further in the next chapter). Also, among the ruins at Megiddo and possibly to be associated with a destruction of the city phase that featured the four-entry/six-chambered gate mentioned above, archaeologists discovered a fragment of a monumental stela erected by Sheshonq.[17] Thus it is tempting to conclude that the Megiddo city phase that featured a four-entry/six-chambered gate was destroyed by Shishak/Sheshonq, which would mean in turn that the pottery styles associated with the destruction can be dated to the late tenth century and used to identify late-tenth-century/post-Solomonic strata at other sites. The situation at Gezer seemed to confirm this line of reasoning—that is, the city phase that

16. Megiddo has been excavated by several major expeditions: Gottlieb Schumacher and the German Society for Oriental Research (1903–5), the Oriental Institute of the University of Chicago (1924–39), Yigael Yadin (1960s and 1970s), and currently Tel Aviv University in cooperation with Pennsylvania State University (from 1994). Hazor has been excavated by expeditions led by John Garstang in 1928, then by Yigael Yadin in 1955–59 and 1968–70, and Ammon Ben-Tor in 1987, 1990–2000. Gezer was first excavated by R. A. S. Macalister in 1902–9 and Alan Rowe in 1934; then by expeditions led by W. G. Dever in 1964–74, 1984, and 1990. For the correlation between 1 Kgs. 9:15–19 and the fortifications at these three sites see especially Yigael Yadin, "Solomon's City Wall and Gate at Gezer," *IEJ* 8 (1958) 80–86; W. D. Dever, "Late Bronze Age and Solomonic Defenses at Gezer: New Evidence," *BASOR* 26 (1986) 9–34; idem, *Recent Archaeological Discoveries and Biblical Research* (Seattle: University of Washington Press, 1990) 87–117; idem, *What Did the Biblical Writers Know and Why Did They Know It? What Archaeology Can Tell Us about the Reality of Ancient Israel* (Grand Rapids: Eerdmans, 2001) 131–38.

17. The Shishak Stela fragment was actually recovered by the Chicago expedition in one of Schumacher's dumps and thus unstratified.

41. *Four-entryway/six-chambered gate at Hazor.* Note the plan of the gate and associated walls in the upper left corner of the photograph with an arrow indicating the direction from which the photograph was taken.

featured the four-entry/six-chambered gate was followed by a destruction often attributed to Shishak/Sheshonq.

In short, the pottery styles associated with the six-chambered gates at Megiddo, Hazor, and Gezer came to be recognized by archaeologists as characteristic of Solomon's reign and have been used to identify Solomonic strata at other sites, while the supposedly Shishak/Sheshonq destructions and associated pottery styles at Megiddo and Gezer were seen as marking the end of the Solomonic era. Following this line of reasoning, archaeologists identified Solomonic/tenth-century strata at sites throughout Palestine—Megiddo, Gezer, Hazor, Tel Batash, Tell el-Mazar, Tell el-Hama, Tell el-Sa'idiyeh, Tell Abu Hawam, and so on.

The archaeological picture of Solomon's realm achieved in the fashion described above has been enhanced by studies that focus on parallels between Solomon's temple, as described in 1 Kings 6 and Ezekiel 41, and other temples from the Bronze and Iron ages. Rather much has been made of the tripartite plan of Solomon's temple, for example, and a small eighth-century B.C.E. chapel excavated at Tell Ta'yinat (east of Antakya in southern Turkey) is often cited as a close parallel.[18] Recent attention is given also to a larger temple excavated at

18. See C. J. Davey, "Temples of the Levant and the Buildings of Solomon," *TynBul* 31 (1980) 107–46; Amihai Mazar, "Temples of the Middle and Late Bronze Ages and the Iron Age," in Aharon Kempinski and Ronny Reich, eds., *The Architecture of Ancient Israel: From the Prehistoric to the Persian Periods* (Jerusalem: Israel Exploration Society, 1992) 161–87. See also V. A. Hurowitz, *I Have Built You an Exalted House: Temple Building in the Bible in Light of Mesopotamia and Northwest Semitic Writings* (JSOTSup 115; Sheffield: JSOT Press, 1992).

'Ain Dara, about fifty miles to the northeast of Ta'yinat (on the Syrian side of the Turkish-Syrian border).[19] The 'Ain Dara temple may date as early as the tenth century B.C.E., thus roughly contemporary with Solomon, and is decorated with spectacularly sculptured sphinxes (cherubim) and other exotic figures. One finds additional parallels between the iconography and furniture of the temple described in the Bible and those of other public buildings of the ancient Middle East.[20] Solomon is reported to have made five hundred shields of beaten gold, for example, and "put them in the House of the Forest of Lebanon" (1 Kgs. 16–17). The practice of decorating royal buildings with metal shields is well attested.[21] These parallels are sometimes proffered as evidence of the historical accuracy of the biblical description of Solomon's temple and, by extension, the essential accuracy of the whole biblical account of Solomon's reign.

Although still widely accepted, the traditional archaeological picture of Solomon's reign described above has come under heavy attack. Prominent archaeologists, including the directors of the most recent excavations at Megiddo (Israel Finkelstein and David Ussiskin), now challenge both the Solomonic dating of the four-entry/six-chambered gates and the association of the subsequent destructions with Shishak/Sheshonq. They argue that (1) the archaeological strata are not as clearly defined at Megiddo and Gezer as one might hope; (2) the attribution of the six-chambered gates to Solomon is based less on archaeological evidence than on the biblical vision of Solomon as a great ruler who undertook building projects; (3) Shishak/Sheshonq would hardly have erected a stela at Megiddo if he had destroyed the city; and (4) his Karnak inscription does not mention several of the cities that archaeologists have credited him with destroying, most notably Gezer.[22] Having challenged the Solomonic and Shishak/Sheshonq connections, they propose to lower the date of the four-entry/six-chambered gates and associated pottery styles from the

19. John Munson, "The New 'Ain Dara Temple: Closest Solomonic Parallel," *BAR* 26/3 (2000) 20–35, 67; and Ali Abu-Assaf, *Der Tempel von 'Ain Dara* (Damaszener Forschungen 3; Mainz: Philipp von Ozabern, 1990).

20. See V. A. Hurowitz, "Inside Solomon's Temple," *BRev* 10 (1994) 24–37, 50; L. E. Stager, "Jerusalem and the Garden of Eden," *ErIsr* 26 (1999) 13*–94*; idem, "Jerusalem as Eden," *BAR* 26/2 (2000) 36–47.

21. A. R. Millard, "King Solomon's Shields," in M. D. Coogan et al., eds., *Scripture and Other Artifacts: Essays on the Bible and Archaeology in Honor of Philip J. King* (Louisville: Westminster John Knox, 1994) 286–95.

22. See especially the symposium papers published by Wightman, Ussishkin, and Finkelstein in *BASOR* 277/278 (1990) 5–22, 71–91, 109–19. On the partial nature of the Chicago expedition's publication of the material related to Stratum VI and the content of the unpublished material, see T. P. Harrison, "The Battleground: Who Destroyed Megiddo? Was It David or Shishak?" *BAR* 29/6 (2003) 28–35, 60, 62, 64; and idem, *Megiddo 3: Final Report on the Stratum VI Excavations* (OIP 127; Chicago: Oriental Institute, 2004). Harrison argues that Stratum VI was destroyed by David and that Stratum VA/IVB was Solomonic and destroyed by Shishak. See also Israel Finkelstein, "The Stratigraphy and Chronology of Megiddo and Beth-shan in the 12th-11th Century B.C.E.," *TA* 23 (1996) 170–84. Regarding Gezer see Finkelstein, "Gezer Revisited and Revised," *TA* 29 (2002) 262–96; and W. D. Dever, "Visiting the Real Gezer: A Reply to Israel Finkelstein," *TA* 30 (2003) 259–82. Other relevant studies include David Milson, "The Design of the Royal Gates at Megiddo, Hazor, and Gezer," *ZDPV* 102 (1986) 87–92; Douglas Esse, "The Collared Pithos at Megiddo: Ceramic Distribution and Ethnicity," *JNES* 51 (1992) 81–103; Amnon Ben-Tor and Dror Ben-Ami, "Hazor and the Archaeology of the Tenth Century B.C.E.," *IEJ* 48 (1998) 1–37; and Dror Ben-Ami, "The Iron Age I at Tel Hazor in Light of Recent Excavations," *IEJ* 51 (2001) 148–70.

42. *'Ain Dara temple.* Remains of an Iron Age temple excavated at 'Ain Dara in northwest Syria. Probably dedicated to the goddess Ishtar, it may have been an approximate contemporary of the Jerusalem temple and exhibits a number of parallels. Note the plan in the upper left corner of the photograph with an arrow indicating the direction from which the photograph was taken.

43. *'Ain Dara sphinx.* Sphinx guarding the entrance to the 'Ain Dara temple. The cherubim of the temple in Jerusalem would have been similar creatures.

tenth to the ninth century B.C.E.[23] Solomon's reign, therefore, rather than having occurred at the transition between Iron I and Iron II and beeing characterized by monumental building projects, would recede deeper into the unimpressive Iron I phase that preceded the fortifications at Megiddo, Hazor, and Gezer.

In any case, while the fortification walls at Megiddo, Hazor, and Gezer are impressive by Early Iron Age Palestinian standards, they are not in a class with the royal architecture that has survived from the major empires of the ancient world. Neither should one press too far the argument that they presuppose a centralized building program, and by extension some sort of centralized government. Certainly nothing in the archaeological evidence suggests that Megiddo, Hazor, and Gezer were subject to a king resident in Jerusalem. Jerusalem, in fact, remains an enigma. What we have said about it already in connection with David applies as well for Solomon. Occupational remains from Early Iron Age Jerusalem, including the tenth century when Solomon would have lived, are meager and difficult to interpret.

As for the parallels between Solomon's temple and other temples of the ancient Middle East, one must keep in mind that these are parallels that relate to *the biblical description* of Solomon's temple—nothing has survived or has been excavated of the temple itself—and that the features involved (tripartite plan, sphinxes, shields, etc.) occur throughout the Bronze and Iron ages, not just the tenth century. Thus the biblical narrators may have been describing the Jerusalem temple as it appeared very late in Judah's history, or describing it as it was remembered long after the Babylonians had destroyed it. In either case, to the same extent that they probably modeled their description of Solomon after the Neo-Assyrian and Neo-Babylonian rulers of more recent memory, so also they may have modeled their description of Solomon's temple after the Assyrian and Babylonian or even Persian temples of their own day.[24]

In the final analysis, one's interpretation of the archaeological evidence depends heavily upon the degree of confidence that one places in the biblical profile of Solomon. If one begins with the biblical vision of Solomon as a powerful ruler and great builder, then it makes sense to credit him with the fortifications at Megiddo, Hazor, and Gezer, along with roughly contemporary architectural remains at other Palestinian sites, and to see these as cities, towns,

---

23. The most prominent advocate of what has come to be called the "low chronology" is Israel Finkelstein. Among his articles see the following: "The Date of the Settlement of the Philistines in Canaan," *TA* 22 (1995) 213–39; "The Archaeology of the United Monarchy: An Alternative View," *Levant* 28 (1996) 177–87; "Biblical Archaeology or Archaeology of Palestine in the Iron Age? A Rejoinder," *Levant* 30 (1998) 167–74; "Hazor and the North in the Iron Age: A Low Chronology Perspective," *BASOR* 314 (1999) 55–70; "State Formation in Israel and Judah: A Contrast in Context, a Contrast in Trajectory," *NEA* 62 (1999) 35–52; and with N. A. Silberman, *The Bible Unearthed: Archaeology's New Vision of Ancient Israel and the Origin of Its Sacred Texts* (New York: Free Press, 2001). Lowering the archaeological horizon by several decades at various sites was already argued by G. J. Wightman; see his "Megiddo VIA-III: Associated Structures and Chronology," *Levant* 17 (1985) 117–29; and "The Myth of Solomon," *BASOR* 277/278 (1990) 5–22; as well as David Ussishkin, "Was the 'Solomonic' City Gate at Megiddo Built by King Solomon?" *BASOR* 239 (1980) 1–18.

24. See John Van Seters, "Solomon's Temple: Fact and Ideology in Biblical and Near Eastern Historiography," *CBQ* 59 (1997) 45–57. Finkelstein contends that the tripartite (*bit hilani*) temple plan known from Tell Ta'yinat and 'Ain Dara was not introduced into Israel and Judah until the century following Solomon, the time of the Omride dynasty: "The Rise of Jerusalem and Judah: The Missing Link," in A. G. Vaughn and A. E. Killebrew, eds., *Jerusalem in Bible and Archaeology* (SBLSymS 18; Leiden: Brill, 2003) 81–101.

and villages as belonging to a Jerusalem-centered government. Likewise, in spite of the meager archaeological evidence from Jerusalem, the parallels between the biblical description of Solomon's temple and the architecture, furniture, and iconography of other ancient structures are evidence enough that Solomon conducted a splendorous building program in Jerusalem. On the other hand, if one is not convinced in advance by the biblical profile, then there is nothing in the archaeological evidence itself to suggest that much of consequence was going on in Palestine during the tenth century B.C.E., and certainly nothing to suggest that Jerusalem was a great political and cultural center.

The one thing that cannot be interpreted in either direction is the relative absence of international trade goods in either Iron I or early Iron II contexts. This fact seems to constitute a strong argument against the biblical vision of Solomon as a wealthy potentate who engaged in international commerce and brought luxury items to his court from distant lands.

Possible Glimpses of the Historical Solomon

Solomon is not mentioned in any of the written sources that have survived from ancient times, except for the Hebrew Bible. The biblical account of his reign, as we have suggested, presents us with an idealized golden age as envisioned by Judean compilers active a half millennium or more after Solomon would have lived. The archaeological evidence can be interpreted in different ways, but even interpreted in the most positive light it offers little support for the biblical vision of Solomon's grandeur. So what can be said with absolute certainty about Solomon? Nothing! Indeed, as mentioned above, some scholars have suggested that he may be an entirely fictional character. We are inclined nevertheless to think that Solomon was an historical person, and offer below some cautious thoughts as to what might have been the circumstances of his reign.

Solomon's Accession to the Throne

Allowing for the fact that the account of Solomon's accession to the throne is the work of a storyteller with pro-Solomonic inclinations, we nevertheless can draw some probable conclusions from this material. The overriding conclusion, of course, is that Solomon was not the heir apparent but gained the throne by a surprise palace coup.[25] The coup apparently occurred after David had reached old age and was no longer effective as a ruler. Thus it was not really David whom Solomon displaced, but Adonijah. The narrative presupposes that Adonijah had already begun to function as king to some degree but that his support was not unanimous.

---

25. 1 Chr. 3:5 ("These were born to him [David] in Jerusalem: Shisa, Shobah, Nathan, and Solomon, four by Bath-shua [= Bath-sheba] daughter of Ammiel [= Eliam in 2 Sam. 11:3]") seems to imply that Solomon was the fourth son of Bath-sheba. For the view that Solomon was actually the offspring of Uriah, see Timo Veijola, "Solomon: Bathsheba's Firstborn," in Knoppers and McConville, eds., *Reconsidering Israel and Judah*, 340–57; and Baruch Halpern, *David's Secret Demons: Messiah, Murderer, Traitor, King* (Grand Rapids: Eerdmans, 2001) 401–3.

Now Adonijah the son of Haggith exalted himself, saying, "I will be king"; he prepared for himself chariots and horsemen, and fifty men to run before him. His father had never at any time displeased him by asking, "Why have you done thus and so?" He was also a very handsome man; and he was born next after Absalom. He conferred with Joab the son of Zeruiah and with the priest Abiathar; and they supported Adonijah. But the priest Zadok, and Benaiah the son of Jehoiada, and the prophet Nathan, and Shimei, and Rei, and David's own warriors did not side with Adonijah. (1 Kgs. 1:5–8)

It may be significant to note that Adonijah and Solomon were each supported by a leading priest and a leading military figure, and that in both instances the one who had been with David the longest supported Adonijah. Joab, of course, was the commander of the army who had killed both Abner and Amasa when it appeared that they might pose a challenge to his supreme command. Abiathar, from the priests of Nob, had joined David when they both were fugitives from Saul.

One can only speculate on the reason for the division within the court between those who supported Adonijah's move and those who did not. At least three possibilities present themselves: (1) There may have been some ideological difference between the two parties. (2) Those who "were not with Adonijah" may have felt that it was premature for Adonijah to begin to play the role of king while David was still alive. (3) Adonijah may have turned only to Joab and Abiathar for support and ignored the others. Fearful that they would have a diminished role in his new administration, therefore, they may have organized against him. One can only speculate as well about whether David had promised Bathsheba that her son Solomon would inherit the throne, whether she and Nathan simply convinced David that he had made such a promise, or whether the whole bedroom scene described in 1 Kings 1:11–37 is the storyteller's fiction designed to authenticate Solomon's coup by explaining that it had David's approval.[26] The same kind of uncertainty surrounds the report of David's last instructions to Solomon, which claims that David himself approved the executions of Joab and Shimei.

In any case, David's commands and instructions were presumably all given behind the scenes and reported by those who supported the coup, rather than announced publicly by the old man himself. Moreover, Solomon's hasty coronation seems to have been conducted in semisecrecy, with only a select and controlled audience, and without any consultation with, or participation of, the elders of Israel or Judah.

So the priest Zadok, the prophet Nathan, and Benaiah son of Jehoiada, and the Cherethites and the Pelethites, went down and had Solomon ride on King David's mule, and led him to Gihon. There the priest Zadok took the horn of oil from the tent and anointed Solomon. Then they blew the trumpet, and all the people said, "Long live King Solomon!" And all the people went up following him, playing on pipes and rejoicing with great joy, so that the earth was split by their noise. (1 Kgs. 1:38–40)

26. For the view that David had earlier designated Solomon, see Provan et al., *Biblical History*, 236–37; and Halpern, *David's Secret Demons*, 391–406.

Saul and David, and even Absalom, had probably been crowned in public ceremonies with some semblance of representative participation, including strong support from outside Jerusalem. Solomon's coronation seems to have been an act of appointees to office with the acclamation of a Jerusalem crowd.

Finally, we learn from the opening chapters of the book of 1 Kings that Solomon removed Adonijah and his two prominent supporters from the scene following David's death. The official explanation again presupposed an incident that occurred in private and involved Bathsheba. Adonijah supposedly came to Bathsheba with a rather precipitous and daring request: "Please ask King Solomon—he will not refuse you—to give me Abishag the Shunammite as my wife" (2:17). Abishag was the young maiden who had been brought in to comfort David in his old age and now resided in the royal harem. Taking access to the king's harem may have been regarded as a symbolic action, perhaps tantamount to claiming the crown itself. We have seen, for example, that Absalom made a public show of entering the harem when he seized Jerusalem (2 Sam. 16:21). Whatever the actual implications, Solomon accused Adonijah of still having designs on the crown and sent Benaiah to execute both him and Joab. Abiathar was exiled to his estate at the village of Anathoth, a short distance northeast of Jerusalem.[27]

The Extent of Solomon's Kingdom and International Relations

The claim in 1 Kings 4:24, "For he [Solomon] had dominion over all the region west of the Euphrates from Tiphsah [on the Euphrates] to Gaza [at the border of Egypt], over all the kings west of the Euphrates," may be dismissed. This is an editorial generalization, a summarizing hyperbole pertaining to the idealized Solomonic golden age that never existed. More likely, Solomon's realm remained essentially what he inherited from David—the bulk of western Palestine (but excluding most of the Mediterranean coast) and some of northern Transjordan (see Map 17). Note that the cities Solomon is said to have fortified all fall within the territorial limits suggested above, as do the cities/areas from which his twelve officers collected produce. It is difficult to imagine how Solomon would have expanded his frontiers beyond what he inherited from David. Even the sweeping editorial claims about Solomon's wealth and power do not credit him with military conquests. Some have suggested that he expanded his territories with marriage alliances. But it is difficult to see how this would have worked out in terms of specific territories, especially when we consider the surrounding peoples each in turn.

Philistia. As we observed in chapter 6, nothing suggests that David ever subjugated the Philistines, and certainly nothing suggests that Solomon expanded Jerusalem's influence in their direction. On the contrary, one of the purposes in fortifying Gezer (1 Kgs. 9:15) would presumably have been to secure the western

---

27. Anathoth was situated just north of the Mount Scopus ridge, which further supports the view that the Nob sanctuary, with which Abiathar was associated before he joined David, was on Mount Scopus. The editors of the Genesis–2 Kings account (or perhaps a later copyist) connected the Nob priests with the Elide line and interpreted Abiathar's exile as the fulfillment of predictions that the Elide line would come to a disastrous end (cf. 1 Sam. 2:27–36; 14:3; 22:20; 1 Kgs. 2:27). But this is an artificial connection, as we observed and explained in chap. 5; see also Chart 7.

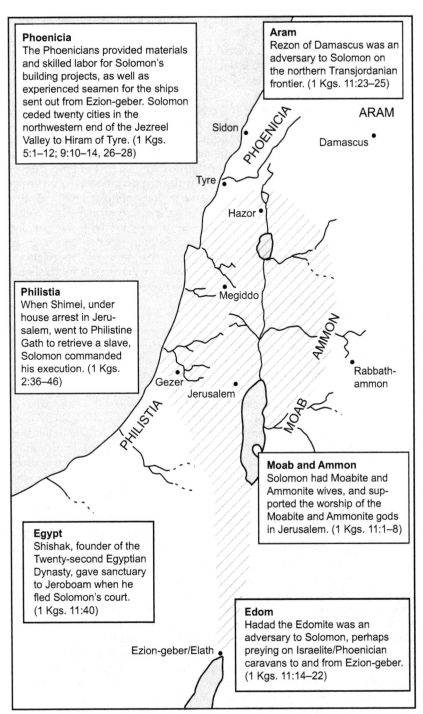

Phoenicia
The Phoenicians provided materials and skilled labor for Solomon's building projects, as well as experienced seamen for the ships sent out from Ezion-geber. Solomon ceded twenty cities in the northwestern end of the Jezreel Valley to Hiram of Tyre. (1 Kgs. 5:1–12; 9:10–14, 26–28)

Aram
Rezon of Damascus was an adversary to Solomon on the northern Transjordanian frontier. (1 Kgs. 11:23–25)

ARAM

Sidon

PHOENICIA

Damascus

Tyre

Hazor

Philistia
When Shimei, under house arrest in Jerusalem, went to Philistine Gath to retrieve a slave, Solomon commanded his execution. (1 Kgs. 2:36–46)

Megiddo

AMMON

PHILISTIA

Gezer

Jerusalem

Rabbath-ammon

MOAB

Moab and Ammon
Solomon had Moabite and Ammonite wives, and supported the worship of the Moabite and Ammonite gods in Jerusalem. (1 Kgs. 11:1–8)

Egypt
Shishak, founder of the Twenty-second Egyptian Dynasty, gave sanctuary to Jeroboam when he fled Solomon's court. (1 Kgs. 11:40)

Edom
Hadad the Edomite was an adversary to Solomon, perhaps preying on Israelite/Phoenician caravans to and from Ezion-geber. (1 Kgs. 11:14–22)

Ezion-geber/Elath

MAP 17. Approximate Extent of Solomon's Kingdom

frontier and commerce route against Philistine encroachment. According to 9:16, the Egyptian pharaoh had taken and burned Gezer before presenting it to Solomon. The Egyptians also may have been attempting to stifle Philistine control of commerce in the region.

Egypt. Egypt was relatively weak at the time—the Third Intermediate Period—but it would have been approximately during Solomon's reign that Sheshonq founded the Twenty-second Dynasty. We have encountered Sheshonq already, and he will require more attention below. Sheshonq was a Libyan mercenary commander who established his rule first in Lower Egypt (with a capital at Bubastis) and from there expanded his influence, soon bringing all Egypt under control. He conducted a military campaign into Palestine and left a commemorative record of it on the walls of the great temple of Amun at Karnak. Sheshonq is almost certainly to be equated with the pharaoh Shishak who is reported to have invaded Palestine during the reign of Solomon's successor Rehoboam (1 Kgs. 14:25). We decline to speculate on which pharaoh gave his daughter to Solomon in marriage and presented Solomon with Gezer as dowry (9:16), since we regard the whole "pharaoh's daughter" theme as suspect.

Aram. Our only information about the politics of cities in southern Aram at this time comes from the Hebrew Bible. Damascus, earlier one of the cities of Hadadezer of Zobah, was presumably ruled now by Rezon. And Rezon, we are told, "was an adversary of Israel all the days of Solomon, making trouble as Hadad did; he despised Israel and reigned over Syria" (1 Kgs. 11:25).

Ammon, Moab, and Edom. Solomon's relations with the Ammonites and Moabites were presumably peaceful and, we are told, secured by his marriage to Ammonite and Moabite princesses. The Ammonites and Moabites were probably also making the transition at this point from chieftain societies to fledgling kingdoms. Edom remained sparsely settled during the tenth century, however, and we are told that an Edomite prince Hadad gave Solomon problems of some sort. One may speculate that Hadad was a tribal sheikh who preyed on Solomon's caravans moving to and from Ezion-geber.

Phoenicia. The Phoenician cities were actively engaged in maritime trade, particularly Tyre under Solomon's contemporary Hiram. Both David and Solomon benefited from the more advanced technology and craftsmanship of the Phoenicians. We will suggest below that the joint shipping venture was really a Phoenician undertaking in which Solomon was allowed to participate because he controlled access to the Gulf of Aqabah. Certainly none of the information provided about Solomon's dealings with Hiram suggests that Solomon was ever regarded as the senior partner or that he expanded his territorial realm at Phoenician expense. Indeed, it may have been the other way around. Consider in this regard the Greek text of 3 Kingdoms 5:1 (= 1 Kgs. 5:1): "King Hiram of Tyre sent his servants to anoint Solomon as king in place of his father David because Hiram had always loved [= was an ally of] David." This wording suggests that Solomon was in some sense subordinate to Hiram; and one can understand why later scribes, uncomfortable with this suggestion, might have altered the text to read as it does now in the Hebrew: "Now King Hiram of Tyre sent his servants to Solomon, when he heard that they had anointed him king in place of his father; for Hiram had always been a lover [ally] to

David." But it is difficult to think of a motive for changing it the other way around. If the Phoenicians were in fact the dominant partner in Israel-Tyre relations, then they may have had a hand in the city constructions at Hazor, Megiddo, and Gezer. As administrative and military posts guarding the main trade route between Egypt and the north, these sites would have been as important to the Phoenicians as to the Israelites.[28]

In return for Hiram's contributions to Solomon's building program, and perhaps also because of imbalance in their commercial arrangements, Solomon ceded to Hiram a considerable portion of territory in the northwestern Jezreel Valley.

> At the end of twenty years, in which Solomon had built the two houses, the house of Yahweh and the king's house, King Hiram of Tyre having supplied Solomon with cedar and cypress timber and gold, as much as he desired, King Solomon gave to Hiram twenty cities in the land of Galilee. But when Hiram came from Tyre to see the cities that Solomon had given him, they did not please him. Therefore he said, "What kind of cities are these which you have given me, my brother?" So they are called the land of Cabul [good for nothing?] to this day. But Hiram had sent to the king one hundred and twenty talents of gold. (1 Kgs. 9:10–14)

"The land of Cabul" would have been in the vicinity of the town Cabul, approximately ten miles east-southeast of Acco. One must conclude, therefore, that the Mediterranean coast from Mount Carmel northward plus a sizable portion of the Jezreel Valley were considered Phoenician territory by the end of Solomon's reign.

Solomon and International Commerce

The passages that relate to Solomon's commercial involvements were intended less to explain his commercial endeavors than to emphasize and illustrate the luxury and wealth of his court. The reader is to understand that silver, gold, and exotic goods flowed into Jerusalem from all corners of the world: tribute from merchants and governors; presents from other rulers, such as the queen of Sheba; shiploads of gold, silver, precious stones, and exotica from Ophir; the finest horses and chariots from Kue (Que) and Egypt. As with the whole Genesis–2 Kings presentation of Solomon, it is difficult to know where realistic description ends and exaggeration begins. Moreover, the few passages that provide details to support the sweeping claims are beset with textual problems that preclude confident interpretation.

Overland Commerce. Solomon's main asset, as far as the potential for deriving profit from commerce was concerned, was the geographical position of his kingdom. Two international thoroughfares passed through Palestine: (1) "the Way of the Sea," which originated in Egypt, passed through the coastal plain until it turned inward at the Carmel ridge through the Megiddo pass into the

---

28. See J. K. Kuan, "Third Kingdoms 5.1 and Israelite-Tyrian Relations during the Reign of Solomon," *JSOT* 46 (1990) 34–46; and E. A. Knauf, "King Solomon's Copper Supply," in Eduard Lipiński, ed., *Phoenicia and the Bible* (Studia Phoenicia 11; Leuven: Peeters, 1991) 167–86. On the history of Tyre see the essays in M. S. Joukowsky, ed., *The Heritage of Tyre: Essays on the History, Archaeology, and Preservation of Tyre* (Dubuque, IA: Kendall/Hunt, 1992).

Jezreel Valley, and joined at that point the main roads to northern Transjordan, to the Aramaean cities of Damascus and Hamath, and to the Phoenician coast; and (2) the north-south route through Transjordan that connected western Arabia and the Red Sea, specifically the Gulf of Aqabah, with Damascus. Solomon would presumably have been able to control the traffic along the Way of the Sea from cities such as Gezer, Megiddo, and Hazor. He might also have controlled a segment of the Transjordanian highway, as well as the route through the Arabah from southern Judah to the Gulf of Aqabah.

There would have been ways for Solomon to derive profit from commercial traffic through his realm without undertaking commercial ventures of his own, by imposing customs duties, for example, and by taxing transit traffic. One is tempted to read this sort of thing between the lines of 1 Kings 10:14–15, which states literally: "The weight of gold that came to Solomon in one year was six hundred sixty-six talents [about 20 tons] of gold, besides that which came from the traders and from the business of merchants, and from the kings of Arabia and the governors of the land." However, the exact meaning of this text is unclear and the income seems greatly exaggerated. Typical of the sweeping and generalized editorial statements of this Solomon section of Genesis–2 Kings, the terminology is vague and the description based on later fantasies about Jerusalem's "golden age." Who were "the traders and merchants" or "the kings of Arabia"? The expression translated "governors of the land" (*pachoth ha'arets*) derives from the later political vocabulary of the period of Assyrian domination in Palestine.

The one passage that some interpret to mean that Solomon had his own merchants who engaged in overland commerce also is ambiguous. Literally, 1 Kings 10:28–29 reads: "Solomon's trade in horses was from Egypt, and from Kue [on the Cilician coast of Asia Minor] the merchants of the king took—from Kue for a price. A chariot went up and came out from Egypt for six hundred shekels of silver, and a horse for one hundred fifty; and thus to all the kings of the Hittites, and to the kings of Aram, by their hand they delivered." This passage has been taken to mean that Solomon's merchants were middlemen, enjoying somewhat of a monopoly on the horse and chariot trade between Egypt and Asia Minor. Yet the whole passage is ambiguous at best, and it may say nothing more than that Solomon imported his horses and chariots from Egypt and Kue, paying the same standard price for them that the kings of the Hittites and of Aram paid.[29] The point, in other words, is not to explain Solomon's business procedures, but to provide further illustration of his wealth (his purchasing power). Possibly the commerce that passed along the highways through Solomon's kingdom did involve some trade in horses and chariots. But to suppose that Solomon's merchants became deeply involved in this particular business is difficult to imagine since the Israelites heretofore had such little experience with either horses or chariots. David is said to have hamstrung horses taken in war (2 Sam. 8:4), which suggests that he had no use for them. Also, it makes no sense for the Hittite and Aramaean kings to have received horses from Kue via Israel, since they were located much nearer to the Cilician source.

---

29. See D. G. Schley, "1 Kings 10:26–29: A Reconsideration," *JBL* 106 (1987) 595–601; and, for a more traditional view, Yutaka Ikeda, "Solomon's Trade in Horses and Chariots in Its International Setting," in Tomoo Ishida, ed., *Studies in the Period of David and Solomon and Other Essays* (Winona Lake, IN: Eisenbrauns, 1982) 215–38.

A Shipping Venture with the Phoenicians. The Phoenicians, whose merchant ships were planting colonies across the north African coast at the time, no doubt wished to open markets along the east African and Arabian coasts as well. The Red Sea gulf was the only viable sea route to these ports. Thus they may have allowed Solomon some participation in the Red Sea trade in return for transit permission through his kingdom and access to the gulf. Solomon's involvement in the shipping venture is reported briefly in three slightly different versions. First we are told that Solomon himself built a fleet of ships at Ezion-geber and sent them out with Phoenician seamen to Ophir, from which they brought great amounts of gold (1 Kgs. 9:26–28). A few verses later we read that the fleet belonged to the Phoenician king Hiram and that they returned with almug wood and precious stones as well as gold (10:11–12). Finally it is explained that Solomon had a fleet of ships that went out with Hiram's ships, and that they returned every three years bringing gold, silver, ivory, apes, and peacocks (10:22).

Regardless of who actually owned the fleet or fleets, the passages assume that both Hiram and Solomon contributed to the viability of the venture. Hiram would have provided the maritime knowledge: shipbuilders to direct the construction of the fleet at Ezion-geber, sailors to command the ships at sea, and merchants experienced in opening markets on distant shores. Solomon would have provided access to the Red Sea (perhaps not without difficulty if Hadad the Edomite preyed on his caravans), laborers and supplies for the shipbuilding, and inexperienced sailors.

The exact location of Ezion-geber and even the general locale of Ophir are unknown. One suspects that the description of costly goods imported is exaggerated, and one wishes to know what sort of trade items Solomon exported in exchange. No ancient texts, biblical or otherwise, suggest that Solomon had mines. This is pure speculation of modern vintage.

Solomon's Administration

The occasional items of information provided regarding Solomon's administrative arrangements suggest an increase in bureaucracy over David's arrangements. This is only suggestive, however. The information provided may not be historically authentic, or it may have been garbled during the process of transmission through the centuries; in any case it is not adequate to reconstruct either David's or Solomon's administrative system in any comprehensive fashion. The following texts, or groups of texts, are relevant to Solomon's administration: (1) the list in 1 Kings 4:1–6 of Solomon's "high officials"; (2) the list in 4:7–19 of the twelve (or thirteen?) officers (*nitstsabim*) "over all Israel, who provided food for the king and his household"; (3) the several texts pertaining to Solomon's practice of extracting forced labor for his construction projects; and (4) the account of the Shechem assembly where Solomon's son Rehoboam is called on to decide whether he will continue Solomon's harsh policies (12:1–20).

Solomon's "High Officials." The list of Solomon's high officials (*sarim*) recorded in 1 Kings 4:1–6 (see Chart 11) corresponds to the list of David's chief officers provided in three versions (2 Sam. 8:16–18; 20:23–26; 1 Chr. 18:15–17; cf.

CHART 11. Solomon's High Officials (1 Kgs 4:1–6)

The priest	Azariah the son of Zadok
Secretaries	Elihoreph and Ahijah the sons of Shisha
Over the army	Benaiah the son of Jehoiada
Priests	Zadok and Abiathar (?)
Over the officers	Azariah the son of Nathan
Priest and king's friend	Zabud the son of Nathan
Over the palace	Ahishar
Over the forced labor	Adoniram the son of Abda

chart 10, above). Presumably these represent the "cabinet," the inner circle of advisers and chief administrators of David and Solomon, respectively.[30]

The entry for Zadok and Abiathar as priests in Solomon's list is probably a secondary scribal addition intended to take into account that Zadok and Abiathar were the chief priests at the very beginning of Solomon's reign. But this would not have applied after Abiathar was exiled to Anathoth and after the sons of Zadok and Nathan assumed office. If we presume this entry to be secondary, the original list would have represented the situation later in Solomon's reign, after both Abiathar and Zadok had passed from the scene. We can make two further observations: (1) Benaiah and Nathan were apparently rewarded for their role in securing the throne for Solomon. Benaiah has taken Joab's place as supreme commander over the military, and two of Nathan's sons hold "cabinet positions." (2) The chief administrative offices are becoming hereditary.

Officers "Who Provided for the King." The officers over whom Azariah had charge were presumably the twelve *nitstsabim* listed in 1 Kings 4:7–19 "who provided food for the king and his household" (see Chart 12). This passage has been interpreted as an authentic document from the time of Solomon that reveals how his kingdom was divided for administrative purposes into twelve districts reminiscent of the twelve tribes. Such an interpretation seems forced, however, because of the strange assortment of place names and the seemingly haphazard way they are scattered throughout Palestine. Thus it remains unclear exactly what these officers did. Their function is described as twofold: (a) to supply provisions on a rotating monthly basis for the royal court, and (b) to provide barley and straw for the horses of Solomon's chariots (4:7, 27–28). But how did they collect the produce? Were they in effect tax collectors who assessed the citizens in their assigned cities/areas? Or were they in charge of crown properties scattered throughout the kingdom, thus serving in a capacity similar to that of Ziba, whom David placed in charge of Saul's estate, and to

---

30. See T. N. D. Mettinger, *Solomonic State Officials: A Study of the Civil Government Officials of the Israelite Monarchy* (ConBOT 5; Lund: Gleerup, 1971), and N. S. Fox, *In the Service of the King: Officialdom in Ancient Israel and Judah* (HUCM 23; Cincinnati: Hebrew Union College Press, 2000).

CHART 12. Officers Who Provided for the King (1 Kgs. 4:7–19)

Ben-hur	In the hill country of Ephraim
Ben-deker	In Makaz, Shaalbim, Beth-shemesh, and Elon-beth-hanan
Ben-hesed	In Arubboth (to him belonged Socoh and all the land of Hepher)
Ben-abinadab	In all Naphath-dor (he had Taphath the daughter of Solomon as his wife)
Baana son of Ahilud	In Taanach, Megiddo, and all Beth-shean and from Beth-shean to Abel-meholah, as far as the other side of Jokmeam
Ben-geber	In Ramoth-gilead (he had the villages of Jair the son of Manasseh, which are in Gilead, and he had the region of Argob, which is in Bashan, sixty great cities with walls and bronze bars)
Ahinadab son of Iddo	In Mahanaim
Ahimaaz	In Naphtali (he had taken Basemath the daughter of Solomon as his wife)
Baana son of Hushai	In Asher and Bealoth
Jehoshaphat son of Paruah	In Issachar
Shimei son of Ela	In Benjamin
Geber son of Un	In the land of Gilead, the country of Sihon king of the Amorites and of Og king of Bashan

"And there was one officer in the land [of Judah]"

that of the stewards who, according to the Chronicler, managed David's own properties (1 Chr. 27:25–31)? Solomon would presumably have had some means of doing both, collecting taxes as well as managing the royal estates.[31]

Forced Labor. Already under David, we are told, there was an official in charge of forced labor (2 Sam. 20:24). Under Solomon the employment of forced-labor gangs seems to have become a more significant policy of state. Moreover, while David was active and successful in military affairs, thus producing foreign prisoners for his labor gangs, Solomon seems to have placed

31. See D. B. Redford, "Studies in Relations Between Palestine and Egypt During the First Millennium B.C.: I—The Taxation System of Solomon," in J. W. Wevers and D. B. Redford, eds., *Studies in the Ancient Palestinian World* (Toronto: University of Toronto Press, 1972) 141–56; P. S. Ash, "Solomon's? District? List," *JSOT* 67 (1995) 67–86; R. S. Hess, "The Form and Structure of the Solomonic District List in I Kings 4:7–19," in G. D. Young et al., eds., *Crossing Boundaries and Linking Horizons: Studies in Honor of Michael C. Astour on His Eightieth Birthday* (Bethesda, MD: CDL, 1997) 279–92; and Nadav Na'aman, "Solomon's District List (1 Kings 4:7–19) and the Assyrian Province System in Palestine," *UF* 33 (2002) 419–36; repr. in *AIHH* 102–9.

this burden on his own subjects. Solomon's preparations for his building program are reported as follows:

> King Solomon conscripted forced labor out of all Israel; the levy numbered thirty thousand men. He sent them to the Lebanon, ten thousand a month in shifts; they would be a month in the Lebanon and two months at home; Adoniram was in charge of the forced labor. Solomon also had seventy thousand laborers and eighty thousand stonecutters in the hill country, besides Solomon's three thousand three hundred supervisors who were over the work, having charge of the people who did the work. (1 Kgs. 5:13–16)

The figures provided in this passage must be regarded as editorial exaggerations. Also attributable to the compilers of Genesis–2 Kings is the statement in 1 Kings 9:15–23 clarifying that only foreigners had to serve in the labor gangs:

> All the people who were left of the Amorites, the Hittites, the Perizzites, the Hivites, and the Jebusites, who were not of the people of Israel—their descendants who were still left in the land, whom the Israelites were unable to destroy completely—these Solomon conscripted for slave labor, and so they are to this day. But of the Israelites Solomon made no slaves; they were the soldiers, they were his officials, his commanders, his captains, and the commanders of his chariotry and cavalry. (9:20–22)

In addition to the fact that this comment presupposes the late editors' idealized view of Israel's origins, it is contradicted by the Jeroboam-Ahijah affair described in 11:26–40. Specifically, Jeroboam is introduced as an Ephraimite officer whom Solomon had placed in charge "over all the forced labor of the house of Joseph." The "house of Joseph" would have been essentially the Ephraim/Israel group of tribes so prominent in the narratives of the book of Judges and forming the core of Saul's chiefdom. In short, while there may have been exemptions to Solomon's forced-labor program and to whatever other means he had of extracting wealth from his kingdom—relatives and friends of the king if no one else—there appears to have been no exemption for the Israelites.

Solomon the Builder

Solomon is reported to have built a palace and temple in Jerusalem (1 Kgs. 5–7), six named cities outside Jerusalem (Hazor, Megiddo, Gezer, Lower Beth-horon, Baalath, and Tamar), and other store-cities and enclosures for his horses and chariots (9:15–19). As we have seen, archaeology has not been very helpful for verifying this, or for clarifying the extent of his buildings. Either the available archaeological evidence for the Early Iron Age is very meager, as in the case of Jerusalem, or it is open to differing interpretations, as in the cases of Hazor, Megiddo, and Gezer.

Bronze Age Jerusalem and the Early Iron Age settlement that David conquered was probably confined to Ophel, the slope that extends south of what is known today as the Temple Mount or the Haram esh-Sharif. Presumably Solomon built his palace-governmental complex on the unexcavated Temple Mount itself, which means that the emerging city was expanded northward. David may have already done some building there, as he apparently had

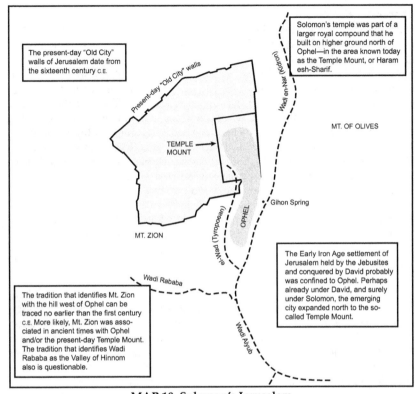

The present-day "Old City" walls of Jerusalem date from the sixteenth century C.E.

Present-day "Old City" walls

Wadi en-Nar (Kidron)

Solomon's temple was part of a larger royal compound that he built on higher ground north of Ophel—in the area known today as the Temple Mount, or Haram esh-Sharif.

MT. OF OLIVES

TEMPLE MOUNT

Gihon Spring

MT. ZION

al-Wad (Tyropoean)

OPHEL

Wadi Rababa

The tradition that identifies Mt. Zion with the hill west of Ophel can be traced no earlier than the first century C.E. More likely, Mt. Zion was associated in ancient times with Ophel and/or the present-day Temple Mount. The tradition that identifies Wadi Rababa as the Valley of Hinnom also is questionable.

The Early Iron Age settlement of Jerusalem held by the Jebusites and conquered by David probably was confined to Ophel. Perhaps already under David, and surely under Solomon, the emerging city expanded north to the so-called Temple Mount.

Wadi Ayub

MAP 18. Solomon's Jerusalem

already begun work on the Millo (2 Sam. 5:9). If so, and if Solomon expanded the city wall northward to include the newly built-up area on the Temple Mount, perhaps this is what is meant when we are told in 1 Kings 11:27 that Solomon "closed up the breach of the city of his father David."[32]

Since the temple was included in the palace-governmental complex situated on what is known today (for that reason) as the Temple Mount, and in view of the fact that many of the psalms associate the Temple closely with Mount Zion, it is tempting to conclude that ancient Mount Zion and the so-called Temple Mount are one and the same. Be that as it may, the name Mount Zion has been associated since the Byzantine period with another hill that overlooks Ophel from the west.

Outside Jerusalem, Solomon is reported to have built Hazor, Megiddo, Gezer, Lower Beth-horon, Baalath, and "Tamar in the wilderness, in the land [of Judah]," as well as unnamed warehouses and enclosures for his horses and

32. For discussion and bibliography pertaining to archaeology and Davidic-Solomonic Jerusalem, see chap. 6, n. 22, and esp. David Ussishkin, "Solomon's Jerusalem," Vaughn and Killebrew, eds., *Jerusalem in Bible and Archaeology*, 103–15.

chariots (1 Kgs. 9:15–19). The first four of the named cities can be identified with present-day Tell el-Qedah, Tell el-Mutesellim, Tell Jezer, and Beit 'Ur et-Tahta, respectively. Baalath and Baalah are variant forms of a common name used for several different places in ancient Palestine. Since it is mentioned with Lower Beth-horon in this context, one thinks of the Baalah near (or identical with) Kiriath-jearim (see Josh. 15:9–10). Tamar (meaning "palm tree") was probably located somewhere in the Judean wilderness, although the qualifier "of Judah" is not supplied in the Hebrew (Masoretic) manuscripts. Note that the parallel passage in 2 Chronicles 8:1–4 reads "Tadmor in the wilderness" (Tadmor usually identified with Palmyra in the Syrian Desert) and has Solomon conquering Hamath-zobah and building his store-cities in that vicinity. This is that same fanciful passage which has Hiram giving Solomon the twenty cities rather than the other way around.

In regard to the four cities mentioned in the 1 Kings version that can be located with confidence, we make four observations. (1) None of these was an entirely new city founded by Solomon. In each case he was building on, or refortifying, a site that had been occupied earlier. (2) Each of these cities was strategically located to control traffic (military and commercial) through Solomon's realm (see Map 17). Hazor, in northern Palestine, was situated at the juncture of the main roads to Hamath and Damascus and at the place where the road to Damascus crossed the Jordan. Megiddo guarded the pass through which the coastal highway, or the Way of the Sea, crossed from the Sharon Plain into the Jezreel Valley. Gezer and Beth-horon dominated the most direct approaches to Jerusalem from the west. (3) As explained above, excavations at three of these cities—Hazor, Megiddo, and Gezer—have produced remains from approximately the time that Solomon would have lived, but archaeologists disagree regarding which particular strata and structures should be associated with Solomon's reign.[33]

First Kings 9:19, which speaks of Solomon's "storage-cities," "cities for his chariots," and "cities for his cavalry," sounds like editorial generalization, although one might presume that Solomon had storage depots and military units distributed throughout the land both for normal operations and in case of military emergencies.

Solomon and the Cult

The "Great High Place" at Gibeon. Solomon's sacrifices at the high place at Gibeon and his patronage of foreign gods in Jerusalem presented a theological problem for the compilers of Genesis–2 Kings.[34] Such acts were inappropriate for the builder of Yahweh's temple and the king whom Yahweh blessed above all others. They resolved the problem by placing the Gibeon incident at the beginning of Solomon's reign, before the temple would have been available for worship, and by placing Solomon's involvement with foreign cults at the end of his reign after he supposedly had fallen under the influence of foreign wives.

---

33. See references in n. 24 above.
34. On Solomon and Gibeon see D. M. Carr, *From D to Q: A Study of Early Jewish Interpretation of Solomon's Dream at Gibeon* (SBLMS 44; Atlanta: Scholars Press, 1991).

This is an artificial and anachronistic arrangement; sacrifices elsewhere than at the Jerusalem temple and royal patronage of foreign gods would probably not have been regarded as religious apostasy in Solomon's day. Yahweh had emerged as the chief god of the Israelites already under Saul and must have figured prominently in David's Jerusalem. Yahweh's status as the national god of the land seems to have been formalized by Solomon, then, when he included a temple dedicated to Yahweh in the royal building complex at Jerusalem. But the concept of exclusive Yahwistic monotheism was still many years, even centuries, in the future. Given the religious perceptions and practices of the Early Iron Age, plus the still heterogeneous character of the population that Solomon ruled, it would have been regarded as altogether appropriate for him to provide shrines in Jerusalem for other persons of the court (not just wives) who looked to other gods. Moreover, the Gibeon high place may have had its own special role in the Yahwistic cult.

According to 1 Samuel 7:1 and 2 Samuel 6:2–3 (from the so-called Ark Narrative discussed in chapter 5 above), the ark resided for a time at Gibeah ("the hill") in the vicinity of Kiriath-jearim before David brought it to Jerusalem. We suggested above that this Gibeah/"hill" may have been Nebi Samwil, a prominent hill situated between the sites of ancient Kiriath-jearim and Gibeon. Now we hear of Solomon going to "the great high place" at Gibeon to offer sacrifices (1 Kgs. 3:4). The Gibeon sanctuary would not necessarily have been in the village itself but more likely, it seems to us, on Nebi Samwil, which overlooked the village. In other words, Solomon may have continued to worship at the same place where the ark had resided before David transferred it to Jerusalem. (According to the Chronicler, in fact, the "tent of meeting" was still there when Solomon went to offer his sacrifices. See 2 Chr. 1:6.)

Construction of the Temple. Solomon's construction of the temple is given pride of place among his accomplishments by the compilers of Genesis–2 Kings and by the Chronicler. As observed above, the description provided may be both anachronistic and idealized; that is, it may describe the temple as it was known or remembered centuries later, and it may be modeled after other major temples of the Neo-Assyrian or Neo-Babylonian realm. In any case, the temple plan, decorations, and furnishings were fairly typical of the Iron Age, and eclectic. This is what one would expect, of course, for a sacred precinct constructed and decorated by Phoenician craftsmen. According to the description, moreover, the temple was but part of a more extensive royal complex constructed by Solomon, and by no means the largest building in the complex.

The temple, we are told, was built in tripartite form, with the dimensions provided for the three main sections requiring a total space of 70 cubits long by 20 cubits wide by 30 cubits high. Calculated on the basis of a royal cubit of 21 inches, this would be approximately 122 by 35 by 52 feet. Such a building was obviously not intended for the use of the general public but as a "house" for Yahweh (1 Kgs. 6:1) and a royal chapel for the king and senior priests. A precise plan cannot be reconstructed in spite of the detail of the biblical description or historical parallels. It is unclear from the various dimensions provided, for example, how to allow for the width of the walls. Two cherubim, winged guardian figures, each with a wingspan of some 20 feet, were placed in the inner sanctuary. The ark itself was deposited beneath their wings. Flanking the entrance to the temple were two freestanding, highly decorated columns, which with their bronze capitals stood 23 cubits (or about 40 feet) high. These bore the names, still unexplainable, Jachin and Boaz. The general worship of the people and public cultic activity would have taken place in the courtyard, where were situated the altar of sacrifice and an enormous basin, the "molten sea" (7:23–26; for some reason the account omits any description of the altar).

Development of the Royal Zion Theology. Nathan's oracle in 2 Samuel 7:8–17, the psalm attributed to David in 2 Samuel 23:1–7, Solomon's prayer in 1 Kings 8:46–53 with Yahweh's response in 9:2–9, and a number of the psalms in the book of Psalms (e.g., Pss. 89 and 132) reflect what some refer to as "royal Zion theology." The primary elements of this theology were the related claims (1) that Yahweh chose Jerusalem as the place of his own special presence and as the chief city of his people, and (2) that Yahweh designated David and David's descendants to rule from Jerusalem in perpetuity. Secondary elements included (3) the cultic centrality of the Jerusalem temple, (4) the special intermediary role of the Davidic king between Yahweh and the people, and (5) the qualification that Yahweh's protection of Jerusalem and the continuance of the Davidic dynasty depended on the faithfulness of the king and people to Yahweh.

Several of the psalms depict Jerusalem, particularly the Temple Mount, as a cosmic mountain where Yahweh himself actually reigned as king over all of his created order. Thus in a very special way Yahweh protected the city against its enemies (Pss. 46; 48; 76). Also there emerged the concept of a special covenant relationship between Yahweh and the Davidic rulers (2 Sam. 23:5; Ps. 89:19–37). The king might even be referred to as "the son of God" (2 Sam. 7:14; Ps. 2:7). As the representative of Yahweh and the embodiment of the community, the person of the king was a channel of Yahweh's blessings and the source of the life and fertility for the people (2 Sam. 23:2–4; Ps. 72).

While this royal Zion theology may have already begun to emerge under David, the elaborated form summarized above and reflected in the passages cited would have developed over time. It was probably under Solomon that this royal theology received its first clear and strong articulation.[35] This seems likely on at least three grounds: (1) Solomon was the first of the Davidic kings whose claim to the throne was based purely on the dynastic principle. David was crowned by the people of Judah and Israel in ceremonies that involved covenant arrangements, and he claimed Jerusalem by conquest. But Solomon's claim to authority over the land was in effect the royal Zion theology. Yahweh had chosen David and his descendants to rule, and David had chosen Solomon to be his successor. (2) The Jerusalem temple, built by Solomon, is a prominent element in the Zion theology. (3) The passages listed above, although composed long after Solomon's day, seem to point particularly to him as the focus of the dynastic promise. Note, for example, the wording of Nathan's oracle:

---

35. See J. J. M. Roberts, "Solomon's Jerusalem and the Zion Tradition" (with bibliography), in Vaughn and Killebrew, eds., *Jerusalem*, 163–70; and for a contrary view see S. L. McKenzie, "The Typology of the Davidic Covenant," in J. A. Dearman and M. P. Graham, eds., *The Land that I Will Show You: Essays on the History and Archaeology of the Ancient Near East in Honour of J. Maxwell Miller* (JSOTSup 353; Sheffield: Sheffield Academic Press, 2001) 152–78. On the importance of 2 Sam. 7 see W. M. Schniedewind, *Society and the Promise to David: A Reception History of 2 Samuel 7:1–17* (New York: Oxford University Press, 1999).

"Moreover Yahweh declares to you that Yahweh will make you a house. When your days are fulfilled and you lie down with your ancestors, I will raise up your offspring after you, who shall come forth from your body, and I will establish his kingdom. He shall build a house for my name, and I will establish the throne of his kingdom forever" (2 Sam. 7:11b–13).

Internal Conflict

Clearly all was not happiness and bliss under Solomon's rule. Externally, Israel was confronted by Edom and Damascus,[36] but these probably represented less of a crisis situation than the growing internal tensions. If Solomon's forced-labor policies were anything like what is reported, for example, the Israelites must have felt especially alienated. So whether or not the narrative regarding Jeroboam's flight to Egypt in 1 Kings 11:26–40 is historically accurate in other regards, it portrays the sentiment that must have existed. Solomon had placed Jeroboam in charge of the forced labor of the house of Joseph, we are told. But Jeroboam, encouraged by the prophet Ahijah of Shiloh, "lifted up his hand against the king" and escaped to Egypt. Ahijah predicted that the kingdom would be divided into two unequal parts and that Jeroboam would become king of the larger part, and as the narrative continues in 1 Kings 12 it recounts how the kingdom did split following Solomon's death. We will look more closely at this narrative in the next chapter. For the moment it is sufficient to mention it as an indication of the discontent that must have existed among Solomon's subjects and to note that the friction in this particular case centered on the house of Joseph, that is, on the Ephraimite/Israelite tribes who had represented the core of Saul's kingdom. Jeroboam was an Ephraimite and the prophet Ahijah was from Shiloh, the Elide sanctuary that had enjoyed prominence under Saul.

General Bibliography

The twenty-four essays in L. K. Handy, ed., *The Age of Solomon: Scholarship at the Turn of the Millennium* (SHCANE 11; Leiden: Brill, 1997), discuss, from various perspectives, most of the issues covered in this chapter. The more traditional treatment of Solomon is represented by E. W. Heaton, *Solomon's New Men: The Emergence of Israel as a National State* (London: Thames & Hudson, 1974). Many of the essays in Volkmar Fritz and P. R. Davies, eds., *The Origins of the Ancient Israelite States* (JSOTSup 228; Sheffield: Sheffield Academic Press, 1996), treat topics related to the Solomonic period. For a literary-theological examination see Walter Brueggemann, *Solomon: Israel's Ironic Icon of Human Achievement* (Studies on Personalities of the Old Testament; Columbia: University of South Carolina Press, 2005).

General treatments of the archaeological evidence can be found in J. S. Holladay, "The Kingdoms of Israel and Judah: Political and Economic Centralizations in the

---

36. See J. R. Bartlett, "An Adversary Against Solomon: Hadad the Edomite," *ZAW* 88 (1976) 205–26; Nadav Na'aman, "Israel, Edom, and Egypt in the 10th Century B.C.E.," *TA* 19 (1992) 71–93; repr. in *AIHH* 120–38; and D. V. Edelman, "Solomon's Adversaries Hadad, Rezon and Jeroboam: A Trio of 'Bad Guy' Characters Illustrating the Theology of Immediate Retribution," in Holloway and Handy, eds., *Pitcher Is Broken*, 166–91.

Iron II A-B," in T. E. Levy, ed., *The Archaeology of Society in the Holy Land* (New York: Facts on File, 1995) 368–98; and Gabriel Barkay, "The Iron Age II-III," in Amnon Ben-Tor, ed., *The Archaeology of Ancient Israel* (New Haven: Yale University Press, 1992) 302–19. Preliminary reports on the recent Jerusalem excavations can be found in J. M. Cahill, "Jerusalem at the Time of the United Monarchy: The Archaeological Evidence"; A. E. Killebrew, "Biblical Jerusalem: An Archaeological Assessment"; and Margreet Steiner, "The Evidence from Kenyon's Excavations in Jerusalem"; all in A. G. Vaughn and A. E. Killebrew, eds., *Jerusalem in Bible and Archaeology: The First Temple Period* (SBLSymS 18; Leiden: Brill, 2003) 13–80, 329–45, 347–63; and Eilat Mazar, "Did I Find King David's Palace?" *BAR* 32/1 (2006) 16–27, 70.

Several older essays, in English translation for the first time, can be found in Hershel Shanks, ed., with archaeological commentary by Ronny Reich, *The City of David: Revisiting Early Excavations* (Washington, DC: Biblical Archaeological Society, 2004).

Issues related to the "low" and "high" chronologies for the archaeological and other data concerning the united monarchy are surveyed, with full bibliography, in Raz Kletter, "Chronology and the United Monarchy: A Methodological Review," *ZDPV* 120 (2004) 13–54.

Both Israel Finkelstein and N. A. Silberman, *David and Solomon* (New York: Free Press, 2006), and P. A. Torijano, *Solomon, the Esoteric King: From King to Magus, Development of a Tradition* (JSJS 75; Leiden: Brill, 2002), trace the development of the legend of Solomon.

8. Separate Kingdoms

Having concluded its account of Solomon's reign in 1 Kings 11, the Genesis–2 Kings History goes on to describe how the northern tribes rebelled against Solomon's successor, Rehoboam, and established a separate kingdom centered in the north-central hill country. The Ephraim/Israel tribes formed the core of this northern kingdom, and eventually Samaria became its capital. Consequently, the kingdom came to be called "Israel," and sometimes "Ephraim" or "Samaria." Meanwhile, Rehoboam and his successors continued to rule from Jerusalem over Judah and other tribal elements in the southern hill country. This southern kingdom was to be called "Judah."

The remainder of the Genesis–2 Kings History recounts the parallel and intertwined stories of the two kingdoms—Israel in the north and Judah in the south—and provides basic chronological information for the rulers of both kingdoms. This chronological information enables an attentive reader to compile king lists and work out relative chronologies for both Israel and Judah. Moreover, beginning with Omri, who reigned during the ninth century B.C.E., there are occasional references to Israelite kings in the inscriptions of neighboring peoples. During the following century, Judean kings find some mention as well. These epigraphical references, particularly those provided by Assyrian and Babylonian sources, enable scholars to correlate the biblically derived kings lists and relative chronologies for Israel and Judah with Assyrian and Babylonian chronology, and ultimately to calculate reasonably precise dates for the Israelite and Judean kings in terms of our modern calendar.

Admittedly, some chronological problems and uncertainties will require attention below. But for the moment, it is sufficient to say that the two kingdoms existed alongside each other for approximately two centuries—from Solomon's death toward the end of the tenth century B.C.E. until the 720s B.C.E. when the Assyrians conquered Samaria and annexed Israel's territory. Judah managed to survive a little more than a century after Israel's demise, until 586 B.C.E., when the Babylonians sacked and destroyed Jerusalem. Thus the period of the separate kingdoms of Israel and Judah corresponds to the mid-centuries (late tenth to the early sixth) of what archaeologists refer to as the Iron Age.

From a casual reading of the biblical account, one might get the impression that Israel and Judah figured prominently in international affairs of the day. In fact, they both were rather modest monarchies that, were it not for the Hebrew Bible, would probably receive little notice in modern history books. The next eight chapters will explore their unfolding stories, first those of the two kingdoms side by side and then of Judah alone. The purpose of this chapter is to set

CHART 13. Chronological Outline of the Kings of Israel and Judah

Judah	Israel	Four Decades of Hostilities (927–879 B.C.E.)

Four Decades of Hostilities
(927–879 B.C.E.)

Judah	Israel	
Rehoboam (926–910)	Jeroboam (927–906)	Solomon's death and the Israelite rebellion against Rehoboam's rule resulted in two minor kingdoms—Israel in the north
Abijam/Abijah (909–907)		and Judah in the south. Hostilities between the two kingdoms drained their
Asa (906–878 [866])	Nadab (905–904)	strength, and the effective domain of both kingdoms combined probably consisted
	Baasha (903–882 [880])	of little more than the hill country west of the Jordan. Sheshonq, biblical Shishak
	Elah (881–880)	and founder of Egyptian Dynasty 22, conducted a military campaign into
	Zimri (seven days)	Syria-Palestine early in Rehoboam's reign. Phoenician sailor-merchants were exploring the Mediterranean shores.

The Omride Era (879–840 B.C.E.)

	Omri (879–869)	Israel emerged strong under Omri and Ahab and enjoyed a period of prosperity and international prominence that
Jehoshaphat (877–853)	Ahab (868–854)	probably exceeded that of Solomon. Good commercial relations with the Phoenicians were enhanced by Ahab's
Jehoram (852–841)	Ahaziah (853–852)	marriage to Jezebel, daughter of the king of Sidon. Judah under Jehoshaphat
	Jehoram (851–840)	was a close ally of Israel—possibly little
Ahaziah (840)		more than a vassal. Assyria began to expand westward under Ashurnasirpal and Shalmaneser III.

The Jehu Dynasty (839–748 B.C.E.)

Athaliah (839–833)	Jehu (839–822)	Related palace coups brought new rulers to the thrones of both Israel and Judah
Joash/Jehoash (832–803 [793])	Jehoahaz (821–805)	and initiated a period of mutual weakness. Urartu emerged strong, extended its
Amaziah (802–786 [774])	Joash (804–789)	domain into northern Syria, and even threatened Assyria. Momentarily free of
Uzziah/Azariah (785–760 [734])		Assyrian pressure, Aramaean kings of Damascus, Hazael and Ben-hadad, made
Jotham (759–744)	Jeroboam II (788–748)	deep inroads into Israelite and Judean territory. Assyrian armies were active in the region again toward the end of the 9th century, during the reign of Adad-nirari III but probably led by the energetic Assyrian governor Shamshi-ilu. Both Israel and Judah enjoyed a brief period of recovery during the reign of Jeroboam II. It was at this time also that the Cushite Dynasty 25 came to power in Egypt.

Judah	Israel	
	Zechariah (six months)	***Under Assyrian Rule*** ***(745–627 B.C.E.)***
	Shallum (one month)	Under Tiglath-pileser III (744–727), Assyria entered a new phase of con-
Jehoahaz/Ahaz I (743–728)	Menahem (746–737)	quest and consolidation of the resulting empire. By the end of his reign, all of the
	Pekahiah (736–735)	peoples of Syria-Palestine, including Israel and Judah, were under the Assyr-
	Pekah (734–731)	ian yoke. Tiglath-pileser's immediate successors continued the momentum,
	Hoshea (730–722)	and eventually overpowered even the Cushite dynasty in Egypt. Attempts to
Hezekiah (727–699)		rebel against Assyrian rule resulted in the annihilation of Israel and annexa-
Manasseh (698–644)	*Fall of Samaria* *(722)*	tion of its territories. Judah managed to survive as an Assyrian vassal through
Amon (643–642)		the reign of Ashurbanipal (668–627), at which time a close alliance existed
Josiah (641–610)		between Assyria and Egypt, and Egypt gradually assumed administrative con-

trol of Syria-Palestine. For a brief period following the death of Ashurbanipal, Egypt alone controlled Syria-Palestine.

Under Babylonian Rule
(605–586 B.C.E.)

Judah	
Jehoahaz II (three months)	The Assyrian Empire declined rapidly after Ashurbanipal's death, while Baby-
Jehoiakim (608–598)	lon emerged strong under the energetic rule of Nabopolassar. The Babylonians
Jehoiachin (three months)	and Medes joined forces to conquer the Assyrian capital Nineveh in 612, and the
Zedekiah (596–586)	Assyrians made a last unsuccessful stand at Carchemish in 605. Soon the Babyloni-
	ans were masters of Syria-Palestine.
Destruction of Jerusalem (586)	Judean resistance led eventually to the Babylonian destruction of Jerusalem and the exile of King Zedekiah in 586.

the stage by (1) reviewing the international scene during the mid-centuries of the Iron Age, (2) introducing our sources of information about the two kingdoms, and (3) discussing some of the interpretational issues that emerge from these sources. Chart 13 will serve as a convenient reference.

The International Scene during the Mid-Centuries of the Iron Age

In earlier chapters we identified various peoples of the Bronze Age—Amorites, Canaanites, Hurrians, Hittites, and so on—and observed that, as the Bronze Age drew to a close, Mycenaean civilization flourished around the shores of the eastern Mediterranean Sea and the Egyptian and the Hittite empires dominated the Middle East. Mycenaean civilization fragmented and both empires collapsed after about 1200 B.C.E., and there followed, during the opening centuries of the Iron Age, a period of turbulence and urban decline.[1] Although circumstances varied from region to region and there were notable exceptions, one might speak of these opening centuries of the Iron Age as a dark age, at least in terms of our understanding today of what was going on.

The situation began to change during the tenth and ninth centuries B.C.E. Firsthand written information becomes more abundant at that point, and again it is possible to obtain a reasonably clear picture of the international scene. Much had changed in the meantime. In place of the Mycenaean, Hittite, and Egyptian zones of political influence, we encounter a wide array of emerging cities, city-states, tribal confederations, and modest territorial kingdoms. By the mid-ninth century another important development had occurred: the rise of the Assyrian Empire. Assyria was to be the first of three eastern empires—Assyria, Babylon, and Persia—that would dominate the Fertile Crescent and surrounding regions until the end of the Iron Age.

The various peoples of the eastern Mediterranean seaboard, including the two small kingdoms of Israel and Judah, shared much the same historical experience. For a time they lived alongside one another, sometimes at peace, sometimes at war, but enjoying a degree of local autonomy. During the ninth century, as Assyrian armies penetrated deeper and deeper into Syria-Palestine, local kingdoms managed to resist with some success. But by the late eighth century, one after another they had all submitted to Assyria. Some, such as Israel, were annexed to Assyria; others, such as Judah, survived as Assyrian satellite states. When the Assyrian empire collapsed in 612 B.C.E., the Chaldean rulers of Babylon stepped into the breach and quickly secured control of most of the former Assyrian realm. Thus Judah and her neighbors became Babylonian subjects; and when Judah attempted to resist one time too many, the Babylonians destroyed Jerusalem (586 B.C.E.).

In short, much of the history of the separate kingdoms of Israel and Judah is that of two provincial states struggling to survive under the shadow of the Assyrian and Babylonian empires. To set the stage, let us begin with a tour

---

1. For a convenient summary see Hayim Tadmor, "The Decline of Empires in Western Asia ca. 1200 BCE," in F. M. Cross, ed., *Symposia: Celebrating the Seventy-fifth Anniversary of the Founding of the American Schools of Oriental Research* (Cambridge: American Schools of Oriental Research, 1979) 1–14.

around the ancient world identifying some of the other peoples of the day who also felt the impact, directly or indirectly, of Assyria and Babylon.[2]

Peoples of the Iron Age

Phoenicians.[3] Along the northeastern coast of the Mediterranean Sea, especially the rugged stretch of coastline where the Lebanon Mountains reach the water, were the Phoenician cities of Tyre, Sidon, Byblos, Arvad, and others. The Phoenicians would have thought of themselves as Canaanites, but typically would have identified themselves in terms of their city of origin. It was the Greeks who called them Phoenicians. The Phoenicians were seafarers and merchants whose ships ranged the full extent of the Mediterranean Sea and explored even beyond Gibraltar. They established trade centers along the North African coast, in southern Spain, and in western Sicily. Some of the Phoenician trade centers became important cities and established other colonies of their own. The most notable of these was Carthage, probably founded during the late ninth century B.C.E. Along with their trade, the Phoenicians served as a cultural interface between the east and west, and it was largely through the Phoenicians that the interior kingdoms of Israel and Judah had access to the Mediterranean world. Israelite and Judean artistic styles were much influenced by the Phoenicians, whose own tastes, not surprisingly, were eclectic. Egyptian influence is especially noticeable. Phoenician seafarer merchants competed with Greek and Etruscan counterparts until the fourth century B.C.E. when Rome emerged powerful. Competition between Rome and the Phoenicians, especially Carthage, resulted eventually in the Punic Wars. ("Punic" is the Latin form of "Phoenician.")

Greeks.[4] Greek-speaking peoples were concentrated around the shores of the Aegean Sea. Among their cities on mainland Greece were Thebes, Athens, and Megara; on the Peloponnese were Corinth and Sparta; on the western and southern shores of Anatolia were Smyrna, Ephesus, Miletos, and Halicarnassus; and on the Aegean islands were Chalcis (on Euboea) and Nexos. While the

---

2. General histories for the period include H. W. F. Saggs, *Civilization before Greece and Rome* (New Haven: Yale University Press, 1989); Amélie Kuhrt, *The Ancient Near East, c. 3000–330 B.C.* (2 vols.; New York: Routledge, 1995); W. W. Hallo and W. K. Simpson, *The Ancient Near East: A History* (2d ed.; Fort Worth: Harcourt Brace, 1998); Sabatino Moscati, *The Face of the Ancient Orient: Near Eastern Civilizations in Pre-Classical Times* (repr. Mineola, NY: Dover, 2001); and Marc van de Mieroop, *A History of the Ancient Near East, ca. 3000–322 B.C.* (Blackwell History of the Ancient World; London: Blackwell, 2004).

3. See Eric Gubel and Edward Lipiński, eds., *Phoenicia and Its Neighbors* (Studia Phoenicia 3; Leuven: Peeters, 1985); Edward Lipiński, ed., *Phoenicia and the East Mediterranean in the First Millennium B.C.* (OLA 22; Leuven: Peeters, 1987); idem, *Phoenicia and the Bible* (Studia Phoenicia 11; Leuven: Peeters, 1991); Sabatino Moscati et al., *The Phoenicians* (New York: Abbeville, 1988); G. E. Markow, *Phoenicians* (Peoples of the Past; Berkeley: University of California Press, 2000); and M. E. Aubet, *The Phoenicians and the West: Politics, Colonies, and Trade* (2d ed.; Cambridge: Cambridge University Press, 2001).

4. Peter Green, *Ancient Greece: A Concise History* (London: Thames & Hudson, 1973); Walter Burkert, *The Orientalizing Revolution: Near Eastern Influence on Greek Culture in the Early Archaic Age* (Cambridge: Harvard University Press, 1992); G. R. Tsetskhladze and Franco De Angelis, eds., *The Archaeology of Greek Colonisation: Essays Dedicated to Sir John Boardman* (Oxford University School of Archaeology Monograph 40; Oxford: Short Run, 1994); W. R. Biers, *The Archaeology of Greece* (2d ed.; Ithaca, NY: Cornell University Press, 1996); J. C. Waldbaum, "Early Greek Contacts with the Southern Levant, ca. 1000–600 B.C.: The Eastern Perspective," *BASOR* 293 (1994) 53–66; idem, "Greeks in the East or Greeks and the East? Problems in Definition and Recognition of Presence," *BASOR* 305 (1997) 1–17; and W. D. Niemeier, "Greek Mercenaries at Tel Kabri and Other Sites in the Levant," *TA* 29 (2002) 328–31.

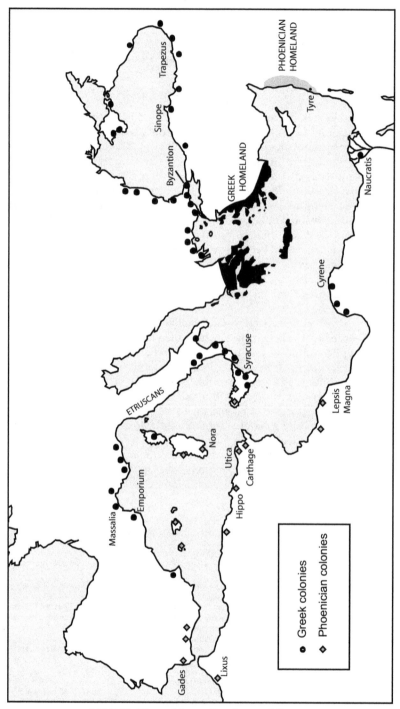

MAP 19. Phoenicians, Greeks, and Etruscans

Phoenicians were planting trade colonies across North Africa, these Greek cities were establishing colonies in southern Italy (Pithekoussai, Rhegion, Croton, Tarentum), eastern Sicily (Nexos, Megara Hyblaia, Syracuse), North Africa (Cyrene), through the Bosporus (Byzantium), and along the shores of the Black Sea (Trapezus). Wherever the Greeks went, they spread Hellenic culture. By the mid-eighth century the Greeks had adopted and modified for their purposes the Canaanite/Phoenician alphabet. The *Iliad* and *Odyssey* were probably written down about that time, and the Greek poet Hesiod lived about 700 B.C.E. The traditional date of the first Olympic Games is 776 B.C.E.—about the time of the Israelite king Jeroboam II.

Etruscans.[5] Stimulated by contact with the Phoenicians and especially the Greeks, Etruscan cities began to emerge in northwestern Italy (Etruria; present-day Tuscany) during the late eighth century B.C.E. Their wealth and influence peaked during approximately the sixth century, and they continued to flourish independently until they fell under the shadow of Rome during the fourth century and following. The Etruscans spoke a language quite different from the Indo-European languages of their immediate neighbors (Umbrians, Latins, Samnites, etc.), and they wrote it with an alphabet adapted from the Greek alphabet (which the Greeks had borrowed in turn from the Phoenicians). Herodotus claimed that the Etruscans emigrated to Etruria from Lydia, but archaeological evidence suggests that they were indigenous to Etruria.

Phrygians.[6] The Phrygians were a horse-rearing, military aristocracy who invaded Anatolia from Thrace and Macedonia in successive waves after about 1200 B.C.E. The earliest waves may have been part of the so-called Sea Peoples movements. They settled in and around Gordion in north-central Anatolia during the mid-ninth century, and a century later Gordion was the political center of what appears to have been a loose confederation of Phrygian tribes. (Gordion was supposedly founded by a king named Gordias who was succeeded by his son Midas, whence the "Gordion knot" and Midas's "golden touch.") One might think of Phrygia as the successor to the Hittite Empire, and the Phrygians continued Hittite customs and traditions. Cimmerians sacked Gordion at the beginning of the seventh century, and although the city survived thereafter, its political power was eclipsed by Lydia.

Lydia.[7] The kingdom of Lydia, with its capital at Sardis situated in the fertile plain of the River Hermus in western Anatolia, emerged strong during the seventh century under Gyges (680–652 B.C.E.). Cimmerians overran Lydia toward the end of Gyges's reign, but Sardis managed to withstand the threat and emerged even stronger thereafter. Sardis was an exceedingly wealthy city

5. Larissa Bonfante, ed., *Etruscan Life and Afterlife: A Handbook of Etruscan Studies* (Detroit: Wayne State University Press, 1986); Graeme Barker and Tom Rasmussen, *The Etruscans* (London: Blackwell, 1998); Sybille Haynes, *Etruscan Civilization: A Cultural History* (Los Angeles: J. Paul Getty Museum, 2000); and Mario Torelli, ed., *The Etruscans* (New York: Rizzoli, 2000).

6. R. D. Barnett, "Phrygia and the Peoples of Anatolia in the Iron Age," *CAH* 2/2:417–42; Kenneth Sams, "Midas of Gordion and the Anatolian Kingdom of Phrygia," *CANE* 2:1147–59; and M. M. Voight and R. C. Hendrickson, "Formation of the Phrygian State: The Early Iron Age at Gordion," *AnSt* 50 (2000) 37–54.

7. G. M. A. Hanfmann, *Sardis from Prehistoric to Roman Times: Results of the Archaeological Exploration of Sardis 1958–1975* (Cambridge: Harvard University Press, 1983); Janet Tassel, "The Search for Sardis," *Harvard Magazine* (March–April 1998) 51–95; C. H. Greenewalt Jr., "Croesus of Sardis and the Lydian Kingdom of Anatolia," *CANE* 2:1173–83.

44. *Phoenician ship and sailors.* This fragmentary relief from the walls of Sennacherib's palace at Nineveh shows a Phoenician ship at sea, being rowed by its crew. Solomon's shipping ventures (1 Kgs. 9:26–28; 10:11–12, 22) would have involved Phoenician sailors and ships such as this. (*British Museum*)

45. *Temple of Zeus at Cyrene.* Cyrene in North Africa was colonized by Greeks from Thera, present-day Santorini, in the seventh century B.C.E.

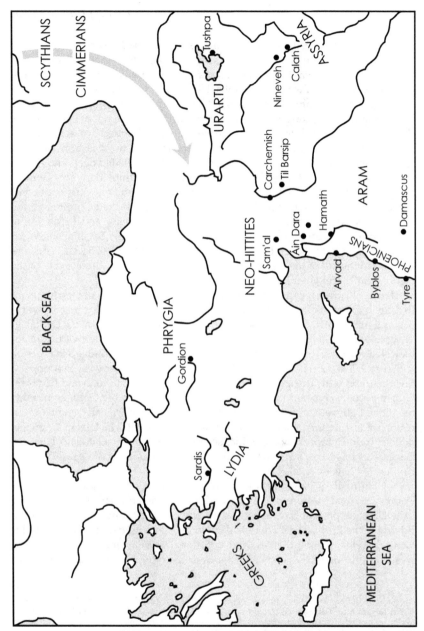

MAP 20. Iron Age Peoples of Anatolia

because of gold deposits on Mount Timolus that washed down into the Pactolus, a tributary to the Hermus River. King Croesus (563–546 B.C.E.), the last of the kings of Sardis, was the richest ruler of his day ("rich as Croesus") and controlled virtually all of western Anatolia. Herodotus describes how Croesus misinterpreted the Delphic oracle, crossed the Halys River to attack Cyrus the Persian, and lost his kingdom. Although the Lydians were not of Greek origin, they used the Greek alphabet and were very much influenced by Greek culture.

Cimmerians and Scythians.[8] These two peoples from northeastern Anatolia, the Caucasus, and the northern shores of the Black Sea, raided deep into Anatolia and Mesopotamia during the seventh century. The Cimmerians are "Gomer" in the Hebrew Bible, and it is from them that the Crimean Peninsula derived its name. During the first half of the seventh century they sacked Gordion, raided Urartu, clashed with the Assyrians (in the Taurus Mountains) and, before losing momentum, overran Lydia in approximately 652 B.C.E. The Scythians were on the move later in the seventh century, especially during 630–625 B.C.E., and contributed to the fall of the Assyrian Empire. They may be the "Ashkenaz" of the Hebrew Bible and Jeremiah's "foe from the north" (Jer. 6:22)

Urartu.[9] Known mostly from Assyrian records, the peoples of Urartu inhabited the highlands of eastern Anatolia. They were highly skilled bronze workers and renowned for their horsemanship. A kingdom with its capital at Tushpa (on the outskirts of present-day Van, on the eastern shore of Lake Van) took shape during the ninth century and reached its apogee under King Menua (ruled ca. 800 B.C.E.). Urartu exerted political influence as far west as Aleppo at this time, and with Tushpa less than a hundred miles from Calah and Nineveh, Urartu posed a constant threat to Assyria. In addition to the Cimmerian raids mentioned above, Sargon II (721–705) claims to have devastated the Urartian countryside, but not actually to have taken Tushpa itself. The Urartu language, neither Indo-European nor Semitic, seems to have been related to Hurrian. Genesis 8:4 has Noah's ark coming to rest on the mountains of "Ararat" (a corruption of "Urartu").

Neo-Hittites.[10] Several cities in southern Anatolia and northern Syria—for example, Sam'al (present-day Zinçirli), Carchemish in present-day Turkey, and 'Ain Dara in present-day Syria—show cultural continuity with the Hittite Empire of the Bronze Age. This is indicated by the continuation of Hittite architectural styles, artistic themes, and occasional Luwian inscriptions. Luwian was a Hittite dialect written with its own hieroglyphic characters. Some of

8. Tadeusz Sulimirski, "The Cimmerian Problem," *Bulletin of the Institute of Archaeology* 2 (1959) 45–64; Tamara Rice, *The Scythians* (London: Thames & Hudson, 1957); E. M. Yamauchi, *Foes from the Northern Frontier: Invading Hordes from the Russian Steppes* (Grand Rapids: Baker, 1982); and Renate Rolle, *The World of the Scythians* (London: Batsford, 1989).

9. Boris Piotrovsky, *The Ancient Civilization of Urartu* (New York: Cowles, 1969); Guitty Azarpay, *Urartian Art and Artifacts: A Chronological Study* (Berkeley: University of California Press, 1968); Charles Burney and D. M. Lang, *The Peoples of the Hills: Ancient Ararat and Caucasus* (New York: Praeger, 1972); P. E. Zemansky, *Ecology and Empire: The Structure of the Urartian State* (Chicago: Oriental Institute, 1985); idem, "An Urartian Ozymandias," *BA* 58 (1995) 94–100.

10. See J. D. Hawkins, "The Political Geography of Northern Syria and South-East Anatolia in the Neo-Assyrian Period," in Mario Liverani, ed., *Neo-Assyrian Geography* (Rome: University of Rome Press, 1995), as well as idem, "The Neo-Hittite States in Syria and Anatolia," *CAH* 3/1:372–441.

46. *Urartian fortress.* Ruins at Çavuştepe, an Urartian fortress near present-day Van in eastern Turkey.

these Neo-Hittite cities were situated in Aramaean areas, and a Luwian inscription has been discovered as far south as Hamath (present-day Hama) in Syria.[11] We should probably think in terms of a Neo-Hittite aristocracy living among a largely Aramaean population. In 2 Kings 7:6 an Aramaean king of Damascus is heard to say: "The king of Israel has hired against us the kings of the Hittites and the kings of Egypt to fight against us." The Hittites at this stage of history would be the Neo-Hittites of southern Anatolia and northern Syria.

Aramaeans.[12] Aram is the earlier name for Syria, and the people who inhabited the interior of Aram were known as Aramaeans. Although originally a nomadic people, several important Aramaean cities emerged early on in the Iron Age: Haran, Til Barsip, Arpad, Hamath, Damascus, and others. The Aramaeans posed a constant threat to the Assyrians, when the Assyrians were not themselves campaigning westward across the Euphrates into Aramaean territory. The closest Aramaean city to Israel and Judah was Damascus, and the Aramaean kings of Damascus (Hazael, Ben-hadad, Rezin) figure prominently in Israelite and Judean history. Indeed, the Genesis stories presuppose that Israel's ancestors emigrated from Aram to Canaan, and Deuteronomy 26:5 refers to Jacob as "a wandering Aramean." The Aramaic language was a Semitic language closely akin to the various Canaanite dialects such as Phoenician, Hebrew, and Moabite.

11. Known Luwian inscriptions have been published by J. D. Hawkins and Halet Cambel, *Corpus of Hieroglyphic Luwian Inscriptions* (2 vols. in 4; Studies in the Indo-European Language and Culture New Series 8; Berlin: de Gruyter, 1999–2000).
12. See Giorgio Buccellati, *Cities and Nations of Ancient Syria: An Essay on Political Institutions with Special Reference to the Israelite Kingdoms* (Rome: Istitutio di Studi del Vicino Oriente, 1967); Horst Klengel, *Syria, 3000 to 300 B.C.: A Handbook of Political History* (Berlin: Akademie Verlag, 1992); Edward Lipiński, *The Aramaeans: Their Ancient History, Culture, Religion* (OLA 100; Leuven: Peeters, 2000); and P. M. Michèle Daviau et al., eds., *The World of the Aramaeans: Studies . . . in Honor of Paul-Eugène Dion* (3 vols.; JSOTSup 324–326; Sheffield: Sheffield Academic Press, 2001).

Philistines.[13] Several groups of Sea Peoples intruded upon Anatolia, the Levant, and Egypt during the turbulent times at the close of the Late Bronze Age. Among them were the Philistines, who settled primarily along the southern Palestinian coastal plain. The Philistines seem to have assimilated quickly in terms of language and material culture with the indigenous Palestinian population, but maintained their separate identity throughout the Iron Age. They had five main cities (Gath, Ekron, Ashdod, Ashkelon, and Gaza), which tended to be larger and more impressive than those of the interior (i.e., those of Israel, Judah, Ammon, Moab, and Edom). The name "Palestine" derives from "Philistine."

Ammonites, Moabites, and Edomites.[14] Israel and Judah, as we have seen, were centered in the north-central and south-central Palestinian hill country, respectively. Across the Jordan, from north to south, lived the Ammonites, Moabites, and Edomites. The chief Ammonite city was Rabbath-ammon, situated at the source of the Jabbok River, where water was available, but along the zone where inhabitable land gives way to desert. The Moabites occupied the rolling plateau east of the Dead Sea. This plateau is severed into two unequal parts by the steep Arnon River canyon (present-day Wadi el-Mujib). Most of the Moabite towns and villages known to the Israelites and Judahites were situated north of the Arnon (Heshbon, Medeba, Dibon, and probably Kir-hereseth). But the name "Rabbah-Moab," known from Greek and Latin sources and preserved in that of present-day Rabba south of the Arnon, suggests that the Moabites regarded it as their chief city. Edom, a vaguely defined zone that extended from south of the Zered River (present-day Wadi el-Hesa) westward below the Dead Sea and into the eastern Negeb, apparently remained largely nomadic well into the eighth century or later. Its chief city at that point was Bosrah (present-day Buseirah in southern Jordan). The Ammonites, Moabites, and Edomites spoke languages very similar to Hebrew and Phoenician, all dialects of Canaanite.

Egypt.[15] The opening turbulent centuries of the Iron Age correspond to Egypt's Third Intermediate Period. Egypt was fragmented at this time with

13. See Trude Dothan, *The Philistines and Their Material Culture* (New Haven: Yale University Press, 1982); J. F. Brug, *A Literary and Archaeological Study of the Philistines* (British Archaeology Reports International Series 265; Oxford: British Archaeology Reports, 1985); Trude Dothan and Moshe Dothan, *People of the Sea: The Search for the Philistines* (New York: Macmillan, 1992); Trude Dothan, "Tel Miqne-Ekron: An Iron Age I Philistine Settlement in Canaan," in N. A. Silberman and D. B. Small, eds., *The Archaeology of Israel: Constructing the Past, Interpreting the Present* (JSOTSup 237; Sheffield: Sheffield Academic Press, 1997) 96–106; Israel Finkelstein, "The Date of the Settlement of the Philistines in Canaan," *TA* 22 (1995) 213–39; idem, "The Philistine Countryside," *IEJ* 46 (1996) 225–42; idem, "The Philistines in the Bible," *JSOT* 27 (2002) 131–67; Seymour Gitin, "The Philistines: Neighbors of the Canaanites, Phoenicians, and Israelites," in D. R. Clark and V. H. Matthews, eds., *One Hundred Years of Archaeology in the Middle East* (Boston: ASOR, 2004) 57–85; idem, "Excavating Ekron," *BAR* 31/6 (2005) 40–56.

14. See J. R. Bartlett, *Edom and the Edomites* (JSOTSup 77; Sheffield: Sheffield Academic Press, 1989); Piotr Bienkowski, ed., *Early Edom and Moab: The Beginning of the Iron Age in Southern Jordan* (Sheffield Archaeological Monographs 7; Sheffield: Collis, 1992); *BA* 60/4 (1997) is devoted to Moab; D. V. Edelman, ed., *You Shall Not Abhor an Edomite For He Is Your Brother: Edom and Seir in History and Tradition* (SBLABS 3; Atlanta: Scholars Press, 1995); Burton MacDonald and R. W. Younker, eds., *Ancient Ammon* (SHCANE 17; Leiden: Brill, 1999); and B. E. Routledge, *Moab in the Iron Age: Hegemony, Polity, Archaeology* (Philadelphia: University of Pennsylvania Press, 2004).

15. D. B. Redford, *Egypt, Canaan, and Israel in Ancient Times* (Princeton: Princeton University Press, 1992); K. A. Kitchen, *The Third Intermediate Period in Egypt (1100–650 BC)* (2d ed.; Warminster: Aris & Phillips, 1996); and Karol Myśliwiec, *The Twilight of Ancient Egypt: First Millennium B.C.E.* (Ithaca, NY: Cornell University Press, 2000).

47. *Ammonite figure.* This standing Ammonite figure (83 cm. high), dating from the mid-eighth century B.C.E., was recovered from the Citadel of present-day Amman in Jordan. The Citadel is the tell of ancient Rabbath-ammon, capital city of the Ammonites. (*Amman Archaeological Museum*)

competing dynasties (Dynasties 21–24) sometimes overlapping chronologically and ruling in different parts of the land. A notable pharaoh of this Third Intermediate Period was Sheshonq, who founded Dynasty 22. He conducted a military campaign into Palestine around 925 B.C.E., an event noted in 1 Kings 11:41. Eventually, during the eighth and the first half of the seventh century B.C.E., a Kushite dynasty (25) from Napata near the fourth cataract of the Nile in present-day Sudan reunited most of Egypt under its rule.[16] This begins the so-called Late Dynastic Period of ancient Egypt's history. Egypt enjoyed a renaissance under the Cushites, but the Assyrians were also expanding at the time and eventually Assyrian armies were on Egyptian soil. Ashurbanipal's sack of Thebes in 664/663 B.C.E. meant the end of Cushite rule, replaced by a pro-Assyrian dynasty (26) that ruled from Sais. It was one of these Saite pharaohs, Neco II, who executed the Judean king Josiah (2 Kgs. 23:29). The Saite dynasty came to an end in 525 B.C.E. when the Persian king Cambyses II conquered Egypt and annexed it to the vast Persian Empire. Cambyses and his Persian

16. See László Török, *The Kingdom of Kush: Handbook of the Napatan-Meriotic Civilization* (Handbook of Oriental Studies: The Near and Middle East 31; Leiden: Brill, 1997); and J. D. Hays, "The Cushites: A Black Nation in the Bible," *BSac* 153 (1996) 396–409.

successors (Dynasty 27) dominated the land until Alexander the Great reached Egypt in 332 B.C.E. Toward the end of the Persian period, however, and under the Persian shadow, three "resistance dynasties" (28–30) managed to rule parts of the land. Clearly the Egypt contemporary with the kingdoms of Israel and Judah was no longer the powerful force that it had been during the Late Bronze Age. But it was a regional power to be reckoned with, and one that constantly meddled in Syro-Palestinian affairs.

Medes.[17] The Medes, known primarily through Assyrian and Babylonian records, were an Indo-European people who occupied the Zagros Mountains. Their capital was Ecbatana (present-day Hamadan in Iran), itself situated on a major route from the upper Tigris (Assyria) to the Iranian plateau. A Median state emerged early in the seventh century and reached its peak under Cyaxares (625–583 B.C.E.). Cyaxares joined with the Chaldean rulers of Babylon to overthrow Assyria.

Persians.[18] Settled further south in the Zagros Mountains, in an area traditionally ruled by Elamites from their capital Susa (present-day Shush near the modern city of Disful in western Iran), were the Persians. The Persians burst suddenly on the scene of recorded history under Cyrus II (Cyrus the Great) who, in the course of twenty years (550–530 B.C.E.), conquered more extensive territories than had ever before been united under a single crown. First Cyrus conquered Ecbatana and Media; next Croesus's Lydian kingdom in Anatolia; and then, in 539, he defeated a Babylonian army at Opis. It remained for his son Cambyses II (530–522) to conquer Egypt. For the next two centuries, until Alexander the Great marched east in 334–333 and more than matched Cyrus's military accomplishments, the Middle East was part of the Persian Empire.

The Neo-Assyrian Empire[19]

The homeland of the Assyrians was the fertile plain along the middle Tigris River where it is joined by the Greater and Lesser Zab tributaries. Today this is in northern Iraq and largely Kurdish territory. The Assyrians enjoyed periods of political and military strength during the Bronze Age. Also, while there was a brief period of decline, a royal line of kings continued at Ashur through the turbulent times that brought the Bronze Age to a close. One of these kings, Tiglath-pileser I (1114–1076 B.C.E.), conducted military excursions against Aramaean tribes along the Euphrates and beyond. Because of these earlier periods of strength, it is customary to refer to the later Iron Age phase of Assyrian expansion as the Neo-Assyrian Empire.

Three ancient cities, all situated along the banks of the Tigris, figured prominently during the Neo-Assyrian period. The Assyrians derived their name from Ashur (present-day Qalat Sharqat, about twenty miles north of where the Lesser Zab joins the Tigris). Further upstream, near the juncture of the Greater Zab, was Kalkhu, usually spelled "Calah" in English (present-day Nimrud). On the

17. D. T. Potts, *The Archaeology of Elam: Formation and Transformation of an Ancient Iranian State* (Cambridge: Cambridge University Press, 1999); and M. W. Waters, *A Survey of Neo-Elamite History* (SAAS 12; Helsinki: Neo-Assyrian Text Corpus Project, 2000).
18. For a bibliography on the Persians see the general bibliography to chap. 16.
19. On the Neo-Assyrians see the general bibliography to chap. 12.

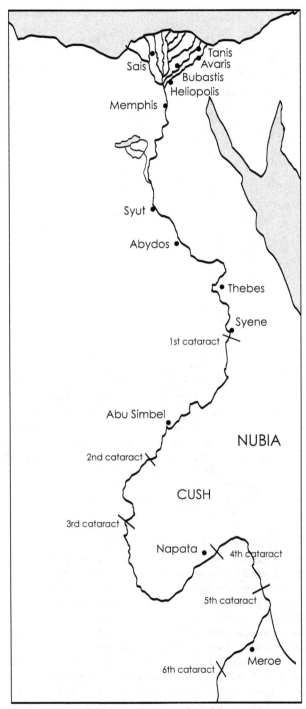

MAP 21. Egypt and Nubia

48. *Ashurbanipal killing a lion.* Assyrian king Ashurbanipal killing a lion. Detail from a hunt scene on the walls of Ashurbanipal's palace in Nineveh. (*British Museum*)

outskirts of present-day Mosul was Nineveh (Tell Kuyunjik and Nebi Yunus). Less ancient, but also important for the Neo-Assyrian period, was Dur Shar-rukin (Khorsabad, about twenty miles northeast of Mosul). Sargon II founded Dur Sharrukin, or "Fort Sargon," and it served as his capital for about five years.

Assyrian culture was essentially Babylonian. For example, the Assyrians spoke a dialect of Akkadian, the same language as the Babylonians. Also the Babylonian god Marduk was almost as important for the Assyrians as their own god Ashur. Yet Assyria was a more militaristic society than Babylon, and the Assyrian kings prided themselves on their ruthless treatment of defeated peoples. Assyrian palaces were decorated with sculptured reliefs depicting gruesome battle scenes in which Assyrian victories were followed up by atroc-ities. Conquered peoples were made to pay heavy tribute and defaulters were crushed mercilessly.

The Neo-Assyrian phase may be said to have begun in the ninth century with Ashurnasirpal II (883–859 B.C.E.) and his successor Shalmaneser III (858–824). Ashurnasirpal conducted numerous military campaigns west of the Euphrates as far as the Mediterranean Sea. Thereby he collected tribute from Aramaean and Phoenician cities, which he used to rebuild Calah as his capital. Apparently Ashurnasirpal did not campaign deep enough into Syria-Palestine to threaten the southern Aramaean cities of Hamath and Damascus or to threaten Israel. Shalmaneser III continued the western thrusts, however, focusing at first on the Neo-Hittite and Aramaean regions of northern Syria, but eventually reaching southern Aram and Israel. In 853 he was met and apparently halted momentar-ily by a coalition of Syro-Palestinian kings led by Irhulenu of Hamath and including Ahab of Israel. But Shalmaneser returned with his armies again and again until eventually, in 841, he reached the city of Damascus and marched through Israelite territory, collecting tribute from the Israelite Jehu.

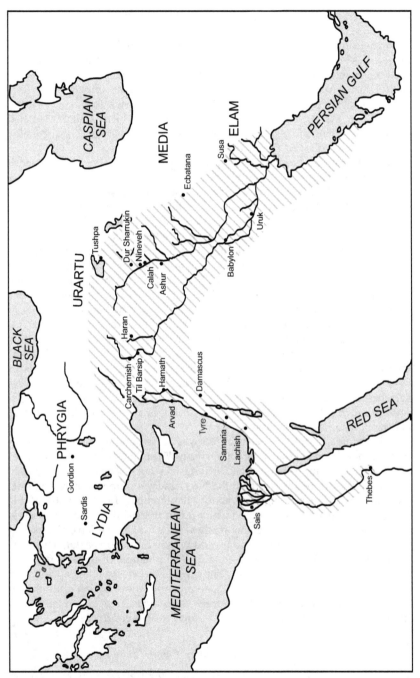

MAP 22. Assyrian Empire at Its Greatest Extent

Homeland revolts at the end of Shalmaneser's reign broke the momentum of Assyria's westward expansion, and his immediate successors were relatively weak kings who had their hands full with the Babylonians, Medes, and especially Urartu. Adad-nirari III (810–783) reports western campaigns and lists Joash of Israel among those who paid him tribute. As we shall see, however, Shamshi-ilu, the Assyrian governor of Til Barsip (which Shalmaneser had renamed Kar-Shalmaneser) may have been the one who actually conducted the campaigns and collected the tribute.

A revolt in Calah brought to the throne Tiglath-pileser III (744–727), and it is with his reign, after a half century of decline, that the Neo-Assyrian Empire truly began. Tiglath-pileser expanded and consolidated Assyrian rule throughout the whole Fertile Crescent and into Anatolia. For the next hundred years, through the reigns of the next five Assyrian kings, a Pax Assyrica remained in place. Relatively little is known about the first of these five kings, Shalmaneser V (726–722), but he apparently subdued the city of Samaria, leaving his successor Sargon II (721–705) to complete the task of provincialization. Sargon restored order in Babylon, which had been seized by Chaldeans under the leadership of Merodach-baladan, and built the fabulous palace-fort at Dur Sharrukin (Khorsabad). Sennacherib (704–681) put down several revolts in Babylon and finally sacked the city. Also he moved the Assyrian capital to Nineveh, and depicted on the walls of his palace there a campaign into Palestine where he put down another revolt in which the Judean king Hezekiah was involved. Esarhaddon (680–669) began the subjugation of the Cushites in Egypt, which was completed by Ashurbanipal (668–627). Ashurbanipal is perhaps best remembered for the royal library that he sponsored in Nineveh. Discovered among the ruins at Nineveh in 1853, this archive provides valuable information about ancient Assyria.

Ashurbanipal's sack of Thebes in 663 was an astounding military achievement. It ended Cushite rule in Egypt (Dynasty 25) and marked the beginning of a period of close rapprochement between Assyria and a Saite dynasty (Dynasty 26). But with Ashurbanipal's reign the Neo-Assyrian Empire was reaching its own end. One hears nothing more about Ashurbanipal after 630, so he, at this point, may have abdicated. Subsequently political instability rendered Assyria vulnerable to its enemies. Chief among these were the Cimmerians, Medes, and the Chaldeans under the command of a leader named Nabopolassar, who managed to take over Babylon four years after Ashurbanipal disappears from the scene. A Median army conquered Ashur in 614. Nineveh fell to a combined Median and Babylonian force in 612. A remnant of the Assyrian army fled to Haran where they were joined by their Egyptian allies. Then Haran fell in 609, and an attempted last Assyrian stand at Carchemish failed in 605.

The Neo-Babylonian Empire[20]

Situated further downstream from Ashur, where the Tigris and Euphrates rivers flow near each other and about sixty miles southwest of present-day Baghdad,

20. See J. A. Brinkman, *A Political History of Post-Kassite Babylonia 1158–722 B.C.* (AnOr 43; Rome: Biblical Institute Press, 1968); idem, *Prelude to Empire* (Occasional Publications 7; Philadelphia: University Museum, 1984); and Grant Frame, *Babylonia 689–627 B.C.: A Political History* (Leiden: Nederlands Historisch-Archaeologisch Instituut te Istanbul, 1992).

was the city of Babylon. Babylon also had enjoyed periods of grandeur during the Bronze Age, thus the rubric "Neo-Babylonian" for the Iron Age phase of the city's history. Assyria dominated Babylon through the reign of Ashurbanipal, but not without constant resistance, much of it instigated by Elamites from the Zagros Mountains east of Babylon and Chaldean tribes (probably related to the Aramaeans) who inhabited the lowlands south of the city.

Under the command of a Chaldean leader named Nabopolassar, four years after Ashurbanipal abdicated in 630 B.C.E., the Babylonians successfully defended their city against an Assyrian army. Nabopolassar was crowned king soon after the battle, thus beginning a Chaldean dynasty that was to reinvigorate Babylon for a short time. Allied with the Medes, Nabopolassar and his son Nebuchadrezzar conquered Assyria in short order. Nebuchadrezzar commanded the Babylonian army at the battle of Carchemish in 605. Nabopolassar died while the battle was under way, Nebuchadrezzar followed him to the throne, and it was under Nebuchadrezzar's rule (604–562) that the Neo-Babylonian Empire reached its apogee.

Nebuchadrezzar followed up his Carchemish victory with campaigns into Syria-Palestine and soon controlled virtually all of the former Assyrian territories, excluding Egypt. He beautified Babylon and built monumental structures there such as the famous Ishtar Gate. Nebuchadrezzar's successors were weaker kings, and in less than a quarter of a century Babylon submitted to Cyrus and the Persians. The last of Babylon's Chaldean line was Nabonidus (555–539), the Neo-Babylonian Empire having lasted only about a half century. Yet it was a very important half century for the people of Judah. During the reign of Nebuchadrezzar, for example, they witnessed the destruction of Jerusalem, the end of their royal line of kings, and the exile of their leading families to distant lands.

Sources of Information about the Two Kingdoms

As is the case for earlier periods, we have three main sources of information about the separate kingdoms of Israel and Judah—the Hebrew Bible, epigraphy, and archaeology. But now the situation improves for the historian in all three categories. As the Genesis–2 Kings History moves nearer in its coverage to the time that it was compiled, the narrative becomes, on the whole, more credible from the perspective of modern historiography. Also it provides more references to people and events that are known from epigraphical sources. After the mid-ninth century, the epigraphical sources make occasional references to Israelite and Judean kings and even some key events in Israelite history (such as Sennacherib's siege of Lachish and the Babylonian sack of Jerusalem). With more informative written sources at hand, it is possible to make tighter correlations between the written sources and the archaeological record.

The Hebrew Bible

Let us turn our attention first to the Genesis–2 Kings History, specifically to 1 Kings 12–2 Kings 25, which provides the primary biblical account of the two kingdoms from Solomon's death to the destruction of Jerusalem and the

Babylonian exile.[21] This segment of the Genesis–2 Kings History is paralleled and partially duplicated by 2 Chronicles 10–36. Certain of the prophetical books, such as Isaiah and Jeremiah, are also relevant.

Continuation of the Genesis–2 Kings History. After reporting Solomon's death, the Genesis–2 Kings narrative continues, describing how Solomon's son Rehoboam followed him to the throne in Jerusalem, but met with resistance when he went to Shechem to be crowned by Israel. The leaders of Israel, we are told, inquired of Rehoboam whether he intended to continue Solomon's harsh policies. Rehoboam considered the matter for three days, sought advice first from the older men of his court, then from the younger men, and finally, following the advice of the younger men, said that he intended to be even more harsh than his father: "My father made your yoke heavy, but I will add to your yoke; my father chastised you with whips, but I will chastise you with scorpions" (1 Kgs. 12:14). Upon hearing his response, the people of Israel rejected Rehoboam and crowned instead Jeroboam, who meanwhile had heard of Solomon's death and returned from Egypt.

As the narrative continues, we are told that Jeroboam built (fortified?) Shechem, made it his residence, and undertook certain cultic measures intended to render Israel's separation from Jerusalem and Judah permanent. Specifically, he also built (restored?) Penuel, erected golden calves at Dan and Bethel, appointed priests who were not Levites, and instituted a new cultic calendar that called for annual celebrations at Bethel rather than at Jerusalem. It is in connection with these cultic changes that the Judean slant of the compilers of the Genesis–2 Kings History becomes most obvious. Making these changes was a great sin in their eyes, and one that doomed the breakaway kingdom of Israel.

With the separate kingdoms in place—Rehoboam on the throne in Jerusalem and Jeroboam ruling in Shechem—the Genesis–2 Kings History proceeds to narrate the parallel and intertwined histories of both kingdoms. It follows a set pattern throughout. The rulers of both Israel and Judah are introduced each in turn, in chronological order according to their respective accessions to the throne regardless of which kingdom they represent. Brief notes are provided for each king that give certain specifics about his reign— family connections, building activities, length of reign, and so forth. Supplementing these notes are evaluations of each king's reign and interpretative statements that explain theologically the overall flow of events. Each king's reign is concluded, finally, with a reference to either of two sources, one for the kings of Israel and the other for the kings of Judah—"the Book of the Annals of the Kings of Israel" and "the Book of the Annals of the Kings of Judah." The presentation of Abijam's reign is typical:

> Now in the eighteenth year of King Jeroboam son of Nebat, Abijam began to reign over Judah. He reigned for three years in Jerusalem. His mother's name was Maacah daughter of Abishalom. He committed all the sins that his father did before him; his heart was not true to Yahweh his God, like the heart of his father David. Nevertheless for David's sake Yahweh his God gave him a

---

21. See G. N. Knoppers, *Two Nations under God: The Deuteronomistic History of Solomon and the Dual Monarchies* (2 vols.; HSM 52–53; Atlanta: Scholars Press, 1993–94).

lamp in Jerusalem, setting up his son after him, and establishing Jerusalem; because David did what was right in the sight of Yahweh, and did not turn aside from anything that he commanded him all the days of his life, except in the matter of Uriah the Hittite. The war begun between Rehoboam and Jeroboam continued all the days of his life. The rest of the acts of Abijam, and all that he did, are they not written in the Book of the Annals of the Kings of Judah? There was war between Abijam and Jeroboam. Abijam slept with his ancestors; and they buried him in the city of David. Then his son Asa succeeded him. (1 Kgs. 15:1–8)

The notations, evaluations, and interpretative passages described above represent the basic framework of 1 Kings 12–2 Kings 25. Occasionally there are extended interpretative passages such as 2 Kings 17. Also, narratives of essentially two sorts have been inserted into this framework where the compilers considered them pertinent or illustrative. Some of the narratives focus on key events, usually with a noticeable intention to provide a specific theological or political interpretation of the events. Examples of such narratives are the account of the assembly at Shechem (1 Kgs. 12:1–19) and the story of the coup led by Jehu (2 Kgs. 9:1–10:27). Other narratives feature the prophets and emphasize their role in Israelite and Judean life, for example, the stories about Elijah and Elisha (1 Kgs. 17–19; 21; 2 Kgs. 2; 3:4–8:15; 13:14–21).

There are several reasons to believe that the basic outline of the history of the separate kingdoms as reported in 1–2 Kings is essentially accurate. (1) The pattern and content of the information provided suggests that at least some of it derived directly or indirectly from official records. (2) The reference to Sheshonq/Shishak's campaign (1 Kgs. 14:25), and the fact that the narrators placed it in an approximately accurate chronological context, is further indication that they had at least some grasp of the chronology of events going back to the beginning of the period of the separate kingdoms. (3) This is even more obvious for the mid-ninth century and forward when Israelite and Judean kings begin to turn up in epigraphical sources. The sequence in which they appear in the biblical account fits with the sequence in which they appear in the inscriptions. (4) Allowing for the agendas of the narrators and the historical assumptions of their day, the story that unfolds seems altogether reasonable—the sort of thing one would expect of two minor kingdoms playing out their histories among their similar neighbors and amid the succession of major empires.

On the basis of the Genesis–2 Kings History, therefore, as it continues through 1–2 Kings, it is possible to (a) reconstruct a sequential list of the kings of both Israel and Judah, (b) calculate reasonably close relative dates for these kings, (c) determine some of their individual deeds, (d) recognize political and social trends that unfolded during the centuries of the separate kingdoms, and (e) establish some correlations between developments in Israel and Judah and the international scene.

This is not to suggest that the Genesis–2 Kings History, which up to this point has presented us with an idealized and theologically driven vision of Israel's past, now suddenly becomes a fully trustworthy source of historical information. On the contrary, this last segment of the long narrative that began with creation in Genesis 1 is perhaps the most theologically driven part of all. It is here that the compilers set about to explain why—after Yahweh had chosen David and his descendants to rule, and had heaped such wisdom, wealth, and power on Solomon—things went so badly after Solomon. One must keep in mind that, by the time the compilers of the Genesis–2 Kings History were doing their work, the northern Israelite kingdom had been gone for more than a century, Jerusalem was in ruins, and Jehoiachin, the last of the line of Davidic rulers, was in Babylonian exile. How could this be?

Their answer, which is the unifying theme of this last segment of the Genesis–2 Kings History, is that Yahweh's people, led by their kings, were unfaithful to Yahweh and that Yahweh thus allowed them to be destroyed. The northern Israelite kingdom, having rebelled from Davidic rule and split away from the Jerusalem cult, had no redeeming qualities. Thus it was the first to be abandoned to an enemy, the Assyrians. Yahweh was more patient with Judah because of David, the man after his own heart. Also, not all of the Judean kings were totally evil. Yet finally, especially because of the unfaithfulness of Manasseh, Yahweh abandoned Jerusalem and all Judah to the Babylonians.

From the compilers' perspective, moreover, the unfaithfulness was primarily cultic. In their view, the security and prosperity of the kingdoms at any given time depended upon the religious fidelity of the current king. Accordingly, they tended to make rather much of the successes and to play down the failures of those kings whom they judged to be faithful, while de-emphasizing the successes and magnifying the failures of those judged to be unfaithful. Their primary criterion for evaluating each king's faithfulness was the extent to which the ruler was loyal to the royal cult in Jerusalem and used monarchical powers to eradicate worship of any sort, Yahwistic or otherwise, at sanctuaries outside that city. Thus Jeroboam and all of the successor kings of Israel who patronized northern sanctuaries over against Jerusalem were judged to be unfaithful. Most of the Judean kings were condemned as well, in varying degrees, because they too allowed sanctuaries and priesthoods to exist outside Jerusalem. (This is not surprising, of course, because the notion that the Jerusalemite sanctuary and its priesthood had exclusive claims to Yahwistic worship probably did not emerge even in Judah until the late eighth century.)

The imbalance of attention given to Omri and Josiah is a prime example of the perspective described above. Omri, a northern king and founder of what the compilers of the Genesis–2 Kings History considered to be an exceedingly evil dynasty, is allowed only thirteen verses, most of which have to do with events prior to his actual reign (1 Kgs. 16:16–28). If one compares this with their lengthy treatment of the Judean king Josiah, whom they regarded to be a truly faithful king and credited with a royal program designed to destroy all sanctuaries outside Jerusalem, one might get the impression that Israel was a minor kingdom of little international consequence under Omri, while Judah under Josiah played a leading role in international affairs. Actually the situation was exactly the reverse, as we shall see in later chapters.

In addition to the theological bias, the information provided in 1–2 Kings is very selective—the names of the kings, basic chronological data about their reigns, a few notes about their wars and building activities, stories about the exploits of certain prophets, and so forth. Even the compilers of this material were conscious of their selectivity and for further information refer the reader again and again to "the Book of the Annals of the Kings of Israel" and "the

Book of the Annals of the Kings of Judah." Modern historians, aware that factors pertaining to economics, sociology, and international politics must have had considerable bearing on the history of the two kingdoms, are given hardly enough information about those sorts of things even to speculate. Moreover, the fact that the biblical narrative focuses so specifically on Israelite and Judean history leaves the mistaken impression that Israel and Judah were the only kingdoms of consequence in Palestine at the time. One is tempted to think of Phoenicia, Philistia, Ammon, Moab, and Edom as having been marginal kingdoms by comparison, reduced to narrow strips of territory along the sea coast and the desert fringe. This may have been the case at times when Israel and Judah were strong (under the Omrides, for example). At other times, however, the domains of the Israelite and Judean kings were reduced to little more than an embattled foothold in the central hill country.

The narratives interspersed throughout 1 Kings 12–2 Kings 25 have their own individual theological (and sometimes propagandistic) intentions that the historian must take into consideration. A more serious problem with the narratives, however, is that the compilers seem to have placed some of them out of proper historical context. This is particularly obvious with the Elisha narratives that appear in the context of the reign of Jehoram but clearly presuppose the sociopolitical circumstances of the later period of the Jehu dynasty. The same is probably true, as we shall see, of the three battle accounts in 1 Kings 20 and 22:1–38.

Finally, the compilers may have misunderstood their sources and created unnecessary problems for modern historians in connection with certain kings who had identical or similar names. At one point we are presented with contemporary Israelite and Judean kings, both named Jehoram, both descended from Omri, both reigning approximately the same number of years, and both meeting their death about the same time. Israel and Judah were very closely aligned at the time politically, which raises the possibility that Jehoram of Judah and Jehoram of Israel were in fact the same person—a single ruler over both kingdoms. Assuming that the official records of the Israelite and Judean kings were kept separately, one can see how later editors might have inferred that the Jehoram who appeared in the Judean records was distinct from the Jehoram who appeared in the Israelite records and treated them as separate kings.

Continuation of the Chronicler's History. Our second biblical source of information for the period of the separate kingdoms is the Chronicler's History, specifically 2 Chronicles 10–36.[22] As was the case with the Chronicler's treatment of David and Solomon, much of the Chronicler's material is found already in 1–2 Kings. Moreover, as we have observed, the Chronicler occasionally adjusts and elaborates on this material so that it will serve his theological purposes more effectively. Compare, for example, 2 Chronicles 20:35–37 with 1 Kings 22:47–50 and note that the details of the account of Jehoshaphat's shipping venture as presented in 1 Kings have been conspicuously revised by the Chronicler, so that the failure of the venture is attributable to Jehoshaphat's alliance with the unfaithful king of Israel.

22. See M. P. Graham et al., eds., *The Chronicler as Historian* (JSOTSup 238; Sheffield: Sheffield Academic Press, 1997); and Isaac Kalimi, *The Reshaping of Ancient Israelite History in Chronicles* (Winona Lake, IN: Eisenbrauns, 2004).

The Chronicler apparently had access to other ancient sources in addition to the 1–2 Kings materials; and one must presume that he likewise adjusted the information derived from these other sources. Examples of supplemental material provided by the Chronicler are the report that Jehoshaphat had garrisons "in the cities of Ephraim which Asa his father had taken" (2 Chr. 17:2) and the account of Yahweh's miraculous protection of Judah when Jehoshaphat was attacked by Moabites, Ammonites, and Meunites (2 Chr. 20). Obviously these supplementary materials must be used with extreme caution, especially where it is apparent that the Chronicler's political or theological interests are involved. For example, the claim that Jehoshaphat placed garrisons "in the cities of Ephraim" appears to be part of the Chronicler's effort to present Jehoshaphat as a strong ruler, at least comparable to his Israelite contemporary, Ahab. The very way in which the battle and victory are reported in 2 Chronicles 20—without Jehoshaphat and his army even having to take the field—marks the narrative as pious fiction. But is the account totally fictitious? Did the Moabites, the Ammonites, and the Meunites actually attempt to invade Judah during Jehoshaphat's reign and perhaps meet with some disaster? There is no way to know with certainty.

One other disadvantage with using the Chronicler's account as a source for reconstructing the history of the period of the separate kingdoms is that the Chronicler was interested almost exclusively in the southern kingdom, the Judean monarchs, and the temple and cult in Jerusalem. Matters pertaining to the northern kingdom are mentioned only insofar as they have some bearing on Judean affairs.

Other Biblical Sources. Other biblical sources also provide data relevant to the history of the separate kingdoms. For example, the prophetical books of Amos, Hosea, Micah, Isaiah, and Jeremiah provide considerable insight into the life and times of the eighth and seventh centuries B.C.E. All of these prophets addressed the political situation of their day and sought to persuade their compatriots of what they regarded to be the divine course of affairs. Thus one catches frequent glimpses in their pronouncements, even if only indirectly, of the inner dynamics of Israelite and Judean politics. Indeed, some of these prophets, particularly Isaiah and Jeremiah, were themselves involved in politics. The prophets' scathing denunciations of the religiosity, the economic injustices, and the religious and civil leadership of their day provide insight into sociocultural matters—at least from the prophets' perspectives. The prophetic oracles against foreign nations extend the historian's vision beyond domestic to international affairs.

Epigraphical Evidence

The Merneptah Inscription provides an early reference to "Israel," as we have seen, but it is difficult to know what to make of this reference other than that the name "Israel" was in use in Palestine toward the end of the thirteenth century B.C.E. Sheshonq's late-tenth-century inscription on walls of the Karnak temple is perplexing as well. He reports a military campaign into Palestine during the late tenth century, almost certainly to be equated with Shishak's invasion mentioned in 1 Kings 14:25 and dated there to the fifth year of

Rehoboam's reign. Yet the Karnak inscription makes no mention of either Solomon, who presumably would have died only five years earlier, or the two kingdoms that presumably would have been in place when Sheshonq conducted the campaign. For all practical purposes, therefore, the epigraphical trail of ancient Israel begins in the ninth century. From that point forward, we find occasional references in nonbiblical written sources (mostly royal inscriptions) that verify the presence of the separate kingdoms. We will examine these documents as they become relevant in the chapters that follow. At this point it will be useful to review the kinds of written materials available and identify some of the especially important texts.

Canaanite and Aramaic Inscriptions. The languages spoken by these various peoples who lived along the eastern Mediterranean seaboard—Phoenician, Hebrew, Ammonite, Moabite, and Edomite—are all dialects of what contemporary scholars refer to as Canaanite. Aramaic, very similar to Canaanite, was spoken by the Aramaeans who inhabited the regions of the Upper Euphrates and between the Euphrates and the seaboard. Several Canaanite and Aramaic inscriptions have been discussed that have bearing on general circumstances in Syria-Palestine during the time of the Israelite and Judean kingdoms. The following three are of special interest and will be discovered in detail in subsequent chapters.

- *Mesha Inscription,* also called the Moabite Stone. Discovered in 1868 at the site of the ancient Moabite city of Dibon, the Mesha Inscription reports the royal accomplishments of King Mesha, who ruled Moab from Dibon in the ninth century B.C.E (see Text 4). Among his accomplishments reported was Mesha's successful struggle to rid Moab of Israelite domination, and the inscription identifies Omri as the Israelite king who had subjected Moab in the first place. This same King Mesha figures in the narrative of 2 Kings 3:4–28, which reports how Jehoram, Omri's grandson, attempted unsuccessfully to restore Israelite control over Moab.
- *Tel Dan Fragments.* These three joining fragments discovered in 1993 and 1994 were apparently part of a stela erected at Dan by one of the Aramaean kings of Damascus to commemorate a victory over Israel and Judah. No complete lines are preserved, so it is difficult to make sense of the inscription. However, it clearly refers to "the king of Israel" and probably to "the house [or dynasty] of David." Also preserved are parts of what appear to be the name of the king of Israel involved and possibly a king of Judah. Likely reconstructions of these names are [Jeho]ram and [Ahaz]iah.
- *Siloam Inscription.* This brief inscription was discovered at Jerusalem in 1880, in a tunnel hewed out of solid rock for the purpose of transferring water from the Gihon Spring to the Siloam Pool. Certainly to be attributed to the reign of Hezekiah (see 2 Chr. 32:30), the inscription commemorates the completion of the tunneling project.

Royal Assyrian and Babylonian Chronicles and Inscriptions. Assyria and Babylon, the major powers of the day, provide the most important records for reconstructing international events in the Middle East during the time of the dual kingdoms. Their records are in the Akkadian language, written in cuneiform script. Especially crucial for working out the chronology of the kings of Israel and Judah are two categories of documents: Assyrian *limmu* lists, also called Assyrian Eponym Chronicles, and the so-called Babylonian Chronicles.

As a means of keeping a year-by-year record of their kings, dating contracts, and important events, the Assyrians devised a method of chronological reckoning whereby each year was named after a different court official. That official served as the *limmu* for the year; lists were kept of the *limmu*s in the order that they served; and events were dated in terms of the month and *limmu* year in which they occurred.[23] The following example is from a treaty of King Esarhaddon: "Eighteenth day of the month Iyyar [April–May], limmu of Nabu-belu-usur, governor of Dur-Sar-rukku. The treaty which Esarhaddon, king of Assyria, concluded on behalf of Ashurbanipal, the great crown prince of Assyria, and Shamash-shum-ukin, the crown prince designate of Babylon."

Several copies, all fragmentary, of the *limmu* lists are now known, so that it is possible to reconstruct a composite but reasonably full list covering several hundred years—beginning in the tenth century and continuing into the seventh century. In addition to the names of the *limmu*s and their official positions, some of the lists supply an additional note for each year—some prevailing condition at the time, some significant event of the year, and/or the location of the main Assyrian army at the end of the year.[24] The following is an example: "*Limmu* of Bur-sagale (governor) of Guzana. Revolt in the city of Ashur. In the month of Simanu an eclipse of the sun occurred." Astronomers are able to calculate the date for this particular eclipse as June 15, 763 B.C.E. And with a firm date for Bur-sagale's *limmu* year, it is possible to calculate dates as well for the *limmu* years that preceded and followed.

In short, because of the *limmu* lists we have accurate dates for the Assyrian kings and many other events in Assyrian history. These Assyrian dates serve as benchmarks, in turn, for working out the chronology of the other peoples of the day, such as the kings of Israel and Judah. Indeed, our only absolutely certain date in Egyptian history during the Iron Age is 663 B.C.E., the year that Ashurbanipal sacked Thebes. One must keep in mind, however, that the Assyrian year did not correspond exactly to ours. Specifically, the *limmu* year of an official extended from the end of one New Year (*akitu*) Festival till the same festival a year later, and the *akitu* festivals were held in the opening days of the spring month of Nisan (corresponding to our March–April).[25]

"Babylonian Chronicles" is a loose designation for a group of texts of various shapes and sizes also written in Akkadian cuneiform. They provide annalistic-

23. A. R. Millard, *The Eponyms of the Assyrian Empire 910–612 B.C.* (SAAS 2; Helsinki: Neo-Assyrian Text Corpus Project, 1994), provides a complete study of the *limmu* lists. See also J. K. Kuan, *Neo-Assyrian Historical Inscriptions and Syria-Palestine* (Jian Dao Dissertation Series 1; Hong Kong: Alliance Bible Seminary, 1995) 7–18; hereafter abbreviated *NAHI*.

24. The locations given in the lists normally pertain to the military headquarters of the main Assyrian army, not to the king himself as is commonly assumed. This is apparent from the facts that (a) the *limmu* lists occasionally provide a second location for the king, and (b) Shalmaneser III remained in the capital city and did not accompany the military into battle during the years 832–824 B.C.E., while the *limmu* lists provide locations that can have applied only to the army headquarters.

25. On the *akitu* festival see J. A. Black, "The New Year Ceremonies in Ancient Babylon: 'Taking Bel by the Hand' and a Cultic Picnic," *Religion* 11 (1981) 39–59; Karel van der Toorn, "The Babylonian New Year Festival: New Insights from the Cuneiform Texts and Their Bearing on Old Testament Study," in J. A. Emerton, ed., *Congress Volume, Leuven 1989* (VTSup 43; Leiden: Brill, 1991) 331–39; and M. E. Cohen, *The Cultic Calendars of the Ancient Near East* (Bethesda, MD: CDL, 1993) 433–40.

like treatments of the Babylonian kings and, until the Babylonians were able to shake free of the Assyrian yoke, of their Assyrian overlords.[26] Different texts cover different periods, and a text may cover a range of several kings. Those that pertain to earlier periods are less useful than those relating to the early seventh century and following, when the information provided is more detailed. Events are dated in terms of the regnal years of the Babylonian kings. One of the Babylonian Chronicles reports Nebuchadrezzar's conquest of Jerusalem in his seventh year on the second day of the month of Addaru (March 597 B.C.E.).

Complementing *limmu* lists (the Eponym Chronicle) and Babylonian Chronicles are inscriptions and documents of various sorts commissioned by the Assyrian and Babylonian kings to commemorate their deeds.[27] Several of the Assyrian inscriptions are particularly relevant for understanding the fortunes of Israel and Judah and working out the chronology of the Israelite and Judahite kings.

- Shalmaneser III (858–824 B.C.E.) claims in his Monolith Inscription (see Text 3) to have defeated a coalition of Syro-Palestinian kings that included "Ahab of Israel." The battle, fought at Qarqar on the Orontes River in Syria, is reported for Shalmaneser's sixth year, which would have been 853. Other inscriptions from later in Shalmaneser's reign report that he conducted several more western campaigns and, in 841–840, collected tribute from "Jehu the son of Omri" (see Text 5).

- Adad-nirari III (810–783 B.C.E.) claims in one inscription to have received tribute from "the land of Omri" (see RIMA 3:213) and in another to have received tribute from "Joash of the land of Samaria" (see RIMA 3:211).

- Tiglath-pileser III (744–727 B.C.E.) reports receiving tribute from Menahem of the land of Samaria and claims to have confirmed Hoshea on the throne in Samaria after the people overthrew the rebellious King Pekah (see *COS* 2:285, 287; cf. 2 Kgs. 15:19–20, 29–31). Jehoahaz, also listed among the local Palestinian rulers who paid tribute to Tiglath-pileser III, is the first Judean king named in the ancient epigraphical sources (see *COS* 2:289; cf. 2 Kgs. 16:7–9).[28]

- Sargon II (722–705 B.C.E.) claims to have conquered Samaria, exiled much of its population, and resettled the city with exiles from other places (see Text 10; cf. 2 Kgs. 17:5–6).

- Sennacherib (704–681 B.C.E.) provides in three annalistic prisms almost duplicate accounts of his invasion of Palestine and siege of Jerusalem in 701 (see Text 12; cf. 2 Kgs. 18:9–19:37).

- Both Esarhaddon (680–669 B.C.E.) and Ashurbanipal (668–627 B.C.E.) report receiving tribute from Judah, Edom, and Moab (see *ANET* 289–301).

26. J.-J. Glassner, *Mesopotamian Chronicles* (SBLWAW 19; Atlanta: Society of Biblical Literature, 2004), provides a convenient English translation of all the texts. Transliterated cuneiform texts with an English translation are also given in the standard work, A. K. Grayson, *Assyrian and Babylonian Chronicles* (Texts from Cuneiform Sources 5; Locust Valley, NY: Augustin, 1975; repr. Winona Lake, IN: Eisenbrauns, 2000), hereafter abbreviated *ABC*.

27. All of these inscriptions are being published in English translation with transliterated Akkadian texts in the series *Royal Inscriptions of Mesopotamia* by the University of Toronto Press.

28. The one possible exception is Ahaziah, who, as noted above, may be mentioned in the Tell Dan Inscription.

Ostraca, Seals, and Seal Impressions from Palestine.[29] Ancient scribes sometimes wrote records and letters on potsherds or fragments of stone. These are known as ostraca, and three important groups of ostraca have been found at Palestinian sites. Discovered among the ruins at ancient Samaria (present-day Sebastiyeh) are approximately sixty ostraca bearing administrative records concerning dispatches of wine and oil (for a selection see *ANET* 321). These Samaria ostraca include no references to known persons or events that enable scholars to date them with certainty. But the archaeological context of their discovery, the script, and certain clues from their content suggest that they derive from the time of the Jehu dynasty (late ninth to early eighth century B.C.E.). Two other important ostraca groups have been uncovered among the ruins of ancient Arad and Lachish (Tell Arad and Tell ed-Duweir, respectively). Both groups contain letters apparently sent to military commanders at these two places in the seventh and sixth centuries B.C.E.[30]

Various seals that would have been used to denote ownership and for signing important documents have been discovered, as well as seal impressions on clay, including bullae. Bullae are patties of clay stamped with seals that would have been used to secure the binding of important documents. Noteworthy among the seals is one discovered in the ruins at Megiddo and bearing the inscription: "belonging to Shema, servant of Jeroboam." More intriguing for the historian's purposes are a large number of seal impressions found on jar handles at many sites in Judah bearing a two- or four-winged symbol of the sun along with the inscription *lmlk* ("of the king").

Mention should be made finally of various short inscriptions scratched on vessels and of graffiti scratched on the walls of tombs. Surely the most interesting items of this category are several large jars discovered at a site we have already noted, Kuntillet Ajrud in the northeastern Sinai Peninsula. Kuntillet Ajrud seems to have been a caravan stop with a small sanctuary for travelers. The jars have drawings painted on them in rather primitive fashion reflecting common religious themes and motifs of the day (lions, ibexes, tree of life). One of these jars may show the Egyptian god Bes along with a seated half-nude female playing a lyre and an inscription that reads: "I bless you by Yahweh of Samaria and by his Asherah."

The Archaeology of Iron II Palestine

One would not necessarily conclude from the archaeological evidence alone that there were two kingdoms centered in the Palestinian hill country, one with

---

29. The ostraca inscriptions can be found in G. I. Davies, *Ancient Hebrew Inscriptions: Corpus and Concordance* (2 vols.; Cambridge: Cambridge University Press, 1991, 2004); Johannes Renz and Wolfgang Röllig, *Handbuch der althebräischen Epigraphik* (3 vols. in 4; Darmstadt: Wissenschaftliche Buchgesellschaft, 1995–2003); and F. W. Dobbs-Allsop et al., *Hebrew Inscriptions: Texts from the Biblical Period of the Monarchy with Concordance* (New Haven: Yale University Press, 2004). See also K. A. D. Smelik, *Writings from Ancient Israel: A Handbook of Historical and Religious Documents* (Louisville: Westminster/John Knox, 1991); and P. K. McCarter, *Ancient Inscriptions: Voices from the Biblical World* (Washington, D.C.: Biblical Archaeological Society, 1996). On the seals and stamp impressions see Nahman Avigad and Benjamin Sass, *Corpus of West Semitic Stamp Seals* (Jerusalem: Israel Academy of Sciences and Humanities, Israel Exploration Society, and Institute of Archaeology, Hebrew University, 1997). On the identity of persons mentioned on seals and inscriptions see L. J. Mykytiuk, *Identifying Biblical Persons in Northwest Semitic Inscriptions of 1200–539 B.C.E.* (SBL Academia Biblica 12; Atlanta: Society of Biblical Literature, 2004).

30. Most of these letters appear in J. M. Lindenberger, *Ancient Aramaic and Hebrew Letters* (2d ed.; SBLWAW 14; Atlanta: Society of Biblical Literature, 2003).

its capital at Samaria and the other with its capital at Jerusalem, during Iron II. But the archaeological evidence is compatible with this scenario. There was a trend toward increased urbanization, for example, and several sites feature city fortifications, reasonably impressive public buildings, water systems, and such.[31] At the same time, the archaeological scene is not exactly what one would have expected from the biblical account. Clearly the compilers of the Genesis–2 Kings History preferred to think of Israel as a breakaway kingdom from Judah, which before the rupture had enjoyed a fabulous golden age under Solomon. However, archaeological surveys indicate that the region of Judah lagged significantly behind that of Israel in terms of population density and urbanization. Also the evidence for public (presumably royal) building projects occurred first and more impressively at northern sites (Samaria, Hazor, Megiddo, and Jezreel) and somewhat later in southern sites (Lachish, Jerusalem, and Ramat Rahel). Some have suggested that Judah, until the late eighth century, was little more than a hinterland to the more developed northern state.[32]

The overall character of the material culture of the two kingdoms—architecture, domestic utensils and tools, religious and cultic paraphernalia, arts and crafts—was much like that of neighboring peoples of the day. It was eclectic, with strong Phoenician, Egyptian, and Syrian influences, much of the Egyptian and northern Syrian influence probably having been mediated by the Phoenicians. Israel's capital city Samaria will serve as an example.

Samaria was a walled city of approximately 150 acres. Crowning the highest point of the city was a royal-administrative quarter with its own internal defensive walls. Monumental capitals adorned the entrance to this royal quarter. Along with other administrative buildings in the quarter was a splendid palace constructed with well-dressed ashlar stones laid in header-stretcher fashion. Both the city layout and the palace architecture find parallels in northern Syria, for example, at Sam'al (present-day Zinçirli in what was historically northern Syria but now is Turkey). The construction work finds even closer parallels in Phoenician architecture. One suspects, as was claimed for Solomon's palace and temple, that much of the building project was subcontracted to Phoenician architects and workers.

The Phoenician influence is even more obvious in pieces of carved ivory discovered among the acropolis ruins. These are apparently the remnants of inlays and decorations that enhanced the palace walls and furniture. While the style and carving techniques are clearly Phoenician, the iconography is general Middle Eastern with a strong Egyptian flavor—bulls, lions, sphinxes (or cherubs), lotus blossoms, and palmettes. These designs and motifs were popular throughout the Mediterranean world. Similar ivories have been discovered in northern Syria (Arslan Tash, Til Barsip) and at the Assyrian capital Nineveh. The palmette design possibly represents a stylized "tree of life" and is featured again on the capitals mentioned above.

31. See Volkmar Fritz, *The City in Ancient Israel* (Sheffield: Sheffield Academic Press, 1995); and Ze'ev Herzog, *Archaeology of the City: Urban Planning in Ancient Israel and Its Social Implications* (Sonia and Marco Nadler Institute of Archaeology Monograph Series 13; Tel Aviv: Emery and Claire Yass Archaeology Press of the Institute of Archaeology, Tel Aviv University, 1997).

32. See Israel Finkelstein and N. A. Silberman, *The Bible Unearthed: Archaeology's New Vision of Ancient Israel and the Origin of Its Sacred Texts* (New York: Free Press, 2001) 149–62.

The architectural styles and iconographical motifs of Samaria's royal quarter were repeated at other monumental public buildings in the region. Similar capitals adorned entrances at Hazor and Megiddo, for example, as well as at Jerusalem and Ramat Rahel in Judah and Medeba in Moab. Because they seem to anticipate the Ionic (or Aeolic) capitals of classical Greek archaeology, they have been called "proto-Ionic" or "proto-Aeolic" capitals.

Naturally these royal buildings do not reflect the lifestyle of ordinary people. But archaeology sheds light on the general population as well, and here again the main observation to be made is that the material culture of the ordinary Israelites and Judahites was very similar to that of their neighbors. This is true, moreover, contrary again to what one might assume from the biblical materials, with regard to religion and cult. Everything suggests that the people of Israel and Judah shared in many of the common beliefs and practices of the day.

Regarding archaeology and the history of the two kingdoms, a few reasonably certain correlations can be drawn between specific events known from written sources and the stratified remains at key Palestinian sites. These correlations serve in turn as benchmarks for working out the overall archaeological phasing of Iron II Palestine. As one might expect, however, some of the correlations that have been proposed are less secure than others, and thus debated among archaeologists.

An Omride "Golden Age." First Kings 16:24 reports that King Omri of Israel founded a new capital city on a hill that he bought for that purpose, and that he named his new city "Samaria" after the name of the previous owner of the hill. Excavations at present-day Sebastiyeh, the site of ancient Samaria, reveal that its first major building phase occurred early in Iron II. Thus it seems reasonable to attribute this first building phase to Omri, who reigned during the first half of the ninth century B.C.E. A similar argument can be made for the single-phase palace compound excavated at Jezreel where, according to 2 Kings 9:6–26, Jehoram and Jezebel were in residence at the time of Jehu's coup. As explained in chapter 7, the earliest Iron Age building phases of relatively monumental scale at Hazor, Gezer, and Megiddo—characterized by six-chambered gates—are usually attributed to Solomon. This would mean that the next building phases at Hazor, Gezer, and Megiddo—actually more impressive than the Solomonic phases—would probably belong to the Omride dynasty. Omride Hazor, in this case, would have been almost double the size of Solomonic Hazor.

Yet a recent proposal also discussed in chapter 7 lowers the dates of the supposedly Solomonic phases at Hazor, Gezer, and Megiddo to the ninth century. According to this proposal, the six-chambered gates and contemporary structures at Hazor and Gezer are Omride rather than Solomonic. At Megiddo, where the stratigraphy has always been problematic, distinction is made between the six-chambered gate phase and another phase that preceded it. This preceding phase—consisting of a smaller gate, two palaces, and various other buildings—is attributed to the Omrides, leaving the six-chambered gate and the famous Megiddo stable-like structures to the eighth century, probably the reign of Jeroboam II.

Whatever one's position on the dating of the early Iron II remains at these three key northern sites, it seems clear that Israel's Omride dynasty (Omri, Ahab, Ahaziah, Jehoram) have a much better claim than Solomon to a "golden age" of

49. *Ivory plaque of striding sphinx.* This plaque of a striding sphinx (8.7 cm. high) was among the ivory decoration fragments recovered from the ruins at Sebastiyeh, ancient Samaria. (*Israel Museum*)

50. *Proto-Aeolic capitals.* Proto-Aeolic capitals enhanced the architecture of public buildings in ancient Israel. The capital at the top was excavated from the ruins at Samaria, the one in the middle at Megiddo, and the one at the bottom at Hazor. Similar capitals have been recovered from sites in ancient Judah and Moab.

royal wealth and building accomplishments. This fits well with the epigraphical evidence. As we have seen, Omri and Ahab are the first of the kings of either Israel or Judah to find mention in the surviving writings of neighboring peoples.

Assyria's Conquest and Annexation of Israel. Tiglath-pileser III of Assyria first campaigned down the Syro-Palestinian coast in 738 B.C.E. and subdued everyone in his path. Yet Rezin of Damascus and Pekah of Samaria, whose kingdoms were not in his immediate path, dared to resist. So Tiglath-pileser and Assyrian forces returned in 734–731, sacked Damascus, executed Rezin, and confirmed Hoshea to rule on the Israelite throne. All of this we know from Assyrian records and from 2 Kings 15:29–30; 16:1–9. Destruction levels ending Hazor V and Beth-shean V should perhaps be attributed to Tiglath-pileser, and Megiddo III probably represents the administrative capital of the Assyrian province of Magiddu. Shalmaneser V and Sargon II returned a little over a decade later to reduce and resettle Samaria. Although the excavations at Samaria shed no light on the military action, there are evidences among the ruins of Assyrian presence.

Hezekiah's Rebellion and Sennacherib's Response. Israel's demise was paralleled by, and indeed probably contributed to, a burst of population growth and prosperity in Jerusalem and Judah. But then Hezekiah involved Judah in an Egyptian-supported rebellion against Assyria, whereupon Sennacherib marched down the coast toward Egypt, besieged and captured Lachish, devastated many of the towns and villages of Judah, and threatened Jerusalem. In addition to Sennacherib's own account of this campaign, and the biblical account in 2 Kings 18:13–19:37, the siege of Lachish is depicted on a wall of Sennacherib's palace in Nineveh. Two archaeological features of Jerusalem are almost certainly to be interpreted as expansion and strengthening of the city's defenses during the last two decades of the eighth century: the water tunnel mentioned above in connection with the Siloam Inscription, and a new defensive wall that incorporated part of the western hill. The tunnel transported water from the Gihon Spring to the Siloam reservoir, and water still flows through it. A segment of the new wall has been excavated in the Jewish Quarter in the Old City of Jerusalem. The *lmlk*-stamped jar handles noted above may connect here as well; that is, they may have marked jars of grain or other supplies stored throughout the country in anticipation of an inevitable attack. Finally, Lachish III is firmly established now as the phase of that city conquered by Sennacherib. Destruction levels at several other sites have been attributed to the Assyrians as well: Tell Batash, Tell Beit Mirsim, Gerar (Tel Haror), Mareshah, Azekah, Tell Judeideh, and Tell es-Safi.

The End of Judah. With Lachish III dated before Sennacherib (eighth century), it follows that Lachish II belongs to the seventh century. And the end of Lachish II is almost certainly to be attributed to Nebuchadrezzar's attacks, which ended with the destruction of Jerusalem in 586 B.C.E.

Matters of Interpretation

Two issues require attention before we proceed with a period-by-period treatment of the separate kingdoms.

Origins of the Separate Kingdoms

There is clearly enough correlation between the three categories of information reviewed above—the Hebrew Bible, epigraphical sources, and archaeology— to establish the existence of the separate kingdoms of Israel and Judah beyond any reasonable doubt. Yet we are dependent largely on the Hebrew Bible for most of the details about the two kingdoms. It will be instructive to consider, for example, what historians would know about ancient Israel and Judah if there were no biblical account and we were solely dependent upon the epigraphical and archaeological evidence.

In the first place, when names are carried over from one language to another, they often take on slightly different pronunciations—Hebrew "Jezreel" becomes Greek "Esdraelon," German "Köln" becomes English "Cologne," and so on. Add to that the difficulty of reproducing names phonetically with different writing systems—the difficulty, for example, of expressing Semitic names in Egyptian hieroglyphics. Without prompting from the biblical story about Israel's early Egyptian origins, therefore, it is at least questionable whether modern scholars would agree that the name rendered by Merneptah's scribes in hieroglyphics is precisely "Israel" (rather than some other similar-sounding name, perhaps "Jezreel"), or that it is the same name that turns up more than three centuries later in Old Canaanite script (Mesha Inscription) and Akkadian cuneiform (Shalmaneser's Monolith Inscription). Otherwise there would be no reason to suppose that an entity known as Israel, and certainly not a kingdom by that name, existed before Omri, the earliest Israelite king mentioned in any of the inscriptions. On the contrary, historians would probably assume that the kingdom of Israel was founded in the ninth century B.C.E. by Omri himself. As we have seen, the Assyrian scribes typically referred to Israel as "Bit-Omri," and continued to do so long after Omri had passed from the scene.

It would be known from Shalmaneser's inscriptions that Ahab was on the throne in 853, and that Jehu, whom the Assyrian scribes identified as a son of Omri, was on the scene in 841–840. Three subsequent Israelite kings from the third quarter of the eighth century would be known by name—Menahem, Pekah, and Hoshea—all three of whom felt the strong hand of Tiglath-pileser (744–727). Finally, it would be known that Sargon II (721–705) conquered Samaria and deported many of its inhabitants in 720–719.

With such limited information gleaned from the inscriptions, would scholars be able to locate Omri's Israel on the map and identify Sebastiyeh as the site of its capital Samaria? Postbiblical sources might help, but the connection between Sebastiyeh and Samaria would probably remain tentative. The connection between Omri and the relatively impressive ninth-century phase of that city would remain tentative for the same reason, and, by extension, his connection with the corresponding phases at other sites in the north-central hill country.

Regarding Judah, there would be no reason, without prompting from the Hebrew Bible, to associate the phrase *byt dwd* in the Tel Dan fragments with a royal family in Jerusalem, and no reason even to suppose the existence of a kingdom called Judah before the reign of Tiglath-pileser, to whom Jehoahaz (Ahaz) paid tribute. The approximate location of the land of Judah, the identity of its capital city as Jerusalem, and the name of a second Judahite king, Hezekiah, could be surmised from Sennacherib's account of his 701 campaign to Syria-Palestine. A third Judean king, Manasseh, would be known by name because he, along with other local Syro-Palestinian rulers, supplied laborers for Esarhaddon. And it would be known that Nebuchadrezzar conquered Jerusalem in 597. Jerusalem itself would be known from Bronze Age sources, but nothing about its meager archaeological remains would suggest that it was an active Iron Age city until about the time of Hezekiah and Manasseh. In short, our hypothetical historians with no knowledge of the Hebrew Bible would probably see Judah as another minor kingdom that emerged during the eighth century B.C.E., about the time of Israel's demise, and managed to survive first as an Assyrian and then as a Babylonian satellite.

A few scholars have argued recently that the impression one gets from the epigraphical and archaeological sources alone is accurate—that there was no Davidic monarchy, no kingdom of Israel before Omri founded it in the ninth century, and no kingdom of Judah before the eighth century. We take a less extreme approach, although fully aware of our heavy dependence on the Hebrew Bible, and at the same time departing significantly from the biblical account. As explained in previous chapters, we regard David and Solomon to have been historical rulers, but rulers of rather local importance. David might better be described as a tribal chieftain than a king; and although Solomon may have taken on more of the symbols of kingship, his realm was at best a modest city-state centered in Jerusalem. The Ephraim/Israel tribes were never fully (or at least not happily) integrated into Davidic rule. They had their own tribal traditions and memories of autonomous rule going back to Saul. So at Solomon's death they simply realigned themselves with the Shechemites and others in the north-central hill country. The result was two fledgling states, Israel in the north and Judah in the south. We will continue the story of these two states in the next chapter.

Establishing Dates for the Kings of Israel and Judah

A Babylonian Chronicle reports the first surrender of Jerusalem to Nebuchadrezzar's army in 597 B.C.E. as follows: "Year 7, month Kislimu: The king of Akkad moved his army into Hatti land, laid siege to the city of Judah . . . and the king took the city on the second day of the month Addaru. He appointed in it a (new) king of his liking, took heavy booty from it and brought it into Babylon" (*ANET* 564). This is one of the few firmly dated events in the history of the separate kingdoms, and the only one that can be dated to the very month and almost to the day. The second day of Addaru in the seventh year of Nebuchadrezzar would have been 15 or 16 March 597 B.C.E. The uncertainty as to the specific day has to do with the fact that the Babylonians calculated their days from evening to evening rather than from midnight to midnight. In other words, one must presume from the chronicle that Jerusalem fell sometime between sundown 15 March and sundown 16 March.

The difficulty otherwise of establishing firm and precise dates for the rulers of the separate kingdoms and for events during their respective reigns is not due to lack of chronological information. As explained above, 1–2 Kings generally provides for each of the Israelite and Judean kings (1) a synchronistic date (that is, each king's accession to the throne is dated in relation to the reign of his contemporary on the throne of the other kingdom) and (2) the length of the king's reign. Occasionally the Chronicler adds further chronological data. Compare the following excerpts pertaining to Asa of Judah and Baasha of Israel.

> In the third year of King Asa of Judah, Baasha son of Ahijah began to reign over all Israel at Tirzah; he reigned twenty-four years. (1 Kgs. 15:33)

> In the twenty-sixth year of King Asa of Judah, Elah son of Baasha began to reign over Israel in Tirzah; he reigned two years. But his servant Zimri, commander of half his chariots, conspired against him. . . . Zimri came in and struck him down and killed him, in the twenty-seventh year of Asa king of Judah, and succeeded him. (1 Kgs. 16:8–10)

> In the twenty-seventh year of King Asa of Judah, Zimri reigned seven days in Tirzah. (1 Kgs. 16:15)

> In the thirty-sixth year of the reign of Asa, King Baasha of Israel went up against Judah, and built Ramah. (2 Chr. 16:1)

Utilizing these chronological data provided in 1–2 Kings, one can work out reasonably accurate relative dates for the rulers of the separate kingdoms. However, both of the qualifiers—"relative" and "reasonably accurate"—must be emphasized. The dates derived from the Hebrew Bible are relative in that the kings are dated in relation to one another rather than in terms of a standard calendar with absolute dates. They can be regarded as only reasonably accurate because of problems and uncertainties associated with the biblical chronological data.

From Relative Dates to Absolute Dates. As explained above, it is possible with the aid of the *limmu* lists and Babylonian Chronicles to establish absolute dates—dates that can be recalculated in terms of our modern calendar—for the Neo-Assyrian and Neo-Babylonian rulers and for many important events in Assyrian and Babylonian history. Fortunately also, a few "benchmark correlations" can be made between events in Assyrian and Babylonian history and the kings of Israel and Judah. It can be established that:

- Ahab was on the throne in Israel in 853 B.C.E. when Shalmaneser III fought against a coalition of Syro-Palestinian kings, including Ahab, at Qarqar.
- Jehu paid tribute to Shalmaneser III when the latter campaigned through northern Palestine during an 841–840 campaign.
- Jehoash's reign overlapped with that of Adad-nirari III (810–783), and Jehoash paid tribute to Adad-nirari sometime between 806 and 796.
- Menahem of Israel and Jehoahaz (Ahaz) of Judah paid tribute to Tiglath-pileser III in the latter's eighth year (738) and twelfth year (734), respectively.
- Tiglath-pileser III either replaced Pekah with Hoshea, or designated Hoshea to be king of Israel, in Tiglath-pileser's fourteenth or fifteenth year (732–731 or 731–730)
- Sargon II conquered Samaria and deported much of its population in his second year, 720–719.

- Hezekiah of Judah was on the throne in 701 when Sennacherib conquered Lachish and marched against Jerusalem.
- Nebuchadrezzar conquered Jerusalem and replaced Jehoiachin with Zedekiah in March of 597.

If the Bible provides us with a sequential list of the kings of Israel and Judah, reports the length of each king's reign, and even synchronizes the reigns of the Israelite and Judean kings, why should we not be able (1) to work out a comprehensive (although relative) chronology for the rulers of both kingdoms and (2) with that task completed, and with the aid of the "benchmark correlations" with the Assyrian and Babylonian kings who can be dated absolutely, work out absolute dates for the Israelite and Judean kings? The problem here is that none of the "benchmark correlations" before the Babylonian destruction of Jerusalem in 597 B.C.E. can be correlated with a specific regnal year of an Israelite or Judean king. We know from Shalmaneser's Monolith Inscription that Ahab was on the throne of Israel in 853, for example, and 1 Kings 16:29 reports that Ahab ruled twenty-two years, but was 853 the first year of Ahab's reign, the last year of his reign, or sometime in between? Other factors internal to biblical chronology seem to require that 853 was near the end of his reign, but exploring these other factors raises additional uncertainties.

Reasonably Accurate Dates. The following characteristics of the biblical figures and related uncertainties limit us to reasonably accurate dates at best for the kings of Israel and Judah. (1) The chronological figures provided in 1–2 Kings are integral to the overall chronological structure of the Genesis–2 Kings History, which, as we saw in chapter 3, seems to presuppose an artificially schematic view of history. Even if the biblical figures were derived originally from official records, therefore, some of them have probably been adjusted to fit the requirements of the compilers' chronological schema. (2) These figures were apparently somewhat fluid in earlier stages of the transmission of the biblical materials, as is evidenced by the numerous variant readings in early manuscripts and versions of 1–2 Kings. (3) There are internal discrepancies, moreover, in all of the manuscript traditions and versions. The figures do not add up. (4) The "biblical figures" require more time than the occasional "benchmark correlations" with the Assyrian and Babylonian chronology allow. We learn from the Assyrian records that Menahem paid tribute to Tiglath-pileser III in 738, for example, and that Hoshea was confirmed on the throne in Samaria perhaps as early as 732. In other words, the Assyrian records allow a maximum of six to eight years between the end of Menahem's reign and the beginning of Hoshea's. Yet 2 Kings credits Pekahiah and Pekah, who ruled between Menahem and Hoshea, with regnal periods totaling twenty-two years.

In addition to the difficulties described above, there are several crucial unknowns. What kind of calendar or calendars were in use in the two kingdoms—would a normal full year have been calculated from fall to fall or spring to spring? What method or methods were used to reckon the length of a king's reign? When a king died in midyear, for example, was the incomplete year ascribed to his reign, to his successor's reign, or to both? Were there coregencies or joint rules other than the one recorded for Uzziah and Jotham in 2 Kings

15:5? If so, how are they calculated in the biblical figures? To what extent have accidental errors and changes been introduced into the biblical figures during the process of transmission, or intentional changes introduced in an effort to clear up apparent inconsistencies?

Many scholars have researched these issues, and produced almost as many different sets of dates for the kings of Israel and Judah, all of which require at least some "adjustment" to the biblical figures. (The author of one important study, for example, provides a set of dates that, by his estimate, reconciles approximately 90 percent of the biblical and external data.[33]) While different authorities give different dates for the biblical kings, however, the proposed dates are typically not very far apart—usually no more than a decade difference for the earlier kings, and no more than a year for some of the later ones. Dates calculated for Solomon's death and the first year of Rehoboam and Jeroboam, for example, range from 932 to 922 B.C.E. Dates calculated for Omri's accession to the throne range from 886 to 876; dates proposed for Hezekiah's first year range from 727 to 715; and dates given to the second and final fall of Jerusalem are either 587 or 586. The dates provided for the Israelite and Judean kings in Chart 13 at the beginning of this chapter and in the chapters that follow are those worked out by Hayes and Hooker.[34]

General Bibliography

In addition to the general works noted in n. 2, see Wolfram von Soden, *The Ancient Orient: An Introduction to the Study of the Ancient Near East* (Grand Rapids: Eerdmans, 1994); D. C. Smith, *Life in the Ancient New East, 3100–332 B.C.* (New Haven:

33. Gershon Galil, *The Chronology of the Kings of Israel and Judah* (Leiden: Brill, 1996). Other relatively recent studies of chronology are: Jeremy Hughes, *Secrets of the Times: Myth and History in Biblical Chronology* (JSOTSup 66; Sheffield: Sheffield Academic Press, 1990); W. H. Barnes, *Studies in the Chronology of the Divided Monarchy of Israel* (HSM 48; Atlanta: Scholars Press, 1991); E. R. Thiele, *The Mysterious Numbers of the Hebrew Kings* (rev. ed.; Grand Rapids: Zondervan, 1994); J. S. Rogers, "Synchronism and Structure in 1–2 Kings and Mesopotamian Chronographic Literature" (PhD diss., Princeton Theological Seminary, 1992); Hayim Tadmor, "The Chronology of the First Temple Period: A Presentation and Evaluation of the Sources," in J. A. Soggin, *An Introduction to the History of Israel and Judah* (2d ed.; Valley Forge, PA: Trinity Press International, 1993) 394–417; and M. C. Tetley, *The Reconstructed Chronology of the Divided Kingdoms* (Winona Lake, IN: Eisenbrauns, 2004).

34. J. H. Hayes and P. K. Hooker, *A New Chronology for the Kings of Israel and Judah and Its Implications for Biblical History and Literature* (Atlanta: John Knox, 1988). This chronology is based on the following conclusions: (1) regnal years for both kingdoms until the time of Josiah were calculated from the main autumn festival, the 15th of Tishri in Judah and a month later, the 15th of Marheshvan, in Israel (see 1 Kgs. 12:32–33 and J. H. Hayes, "The Beginning of the Regnal Year in Israel and Judah," in J. A. Dearman and M. P. Graham, eds., *The Land that I Will Show You: Essays on the History and Archaeology of the Ancient Near East in Honour of J. Maxwell Miller* [JSOTSup 343; Sheffield: Sheffield Academic Press, 2001] 92–95). Regardless of when a king ascended the throne, his official regnal period began with the first autumn (New Year) festival of his reign. Thus the year in which a king died was credited to him even if he reigned only a short period after the autumn festival. The king whose rule did not include the time of the festival had his reign simply stipulated in days or months rather than years. (During the reign of Josiah, the beginning of the year was shifted from the fall to the spring.) (2) The years assigned to the reign of a monarch included the time from his first regnal year until the king's death. Some kings, because of injury or illness that rendered them incapable of functioning in the cult, abdicated the throne (see, e.g., Uzziah; 2 Kgs. 15:1–5). The years from his abdication and including the year of his death were included in the total years of his reign. (3) Numbering regnal years served practical business, economic, and contractual as well as royal purposes.

Yale University Press, 1997); K. A. Kitchen, "'In Media Res'—The Era of the Hebrew Kingdoms," in *On the Reliability of the Old Testament* (Grand Rapids: Eerdmans, 2003) 7–64, 502–14; and various articles in D. N. Freedman, ed., *The Anchor Bible Dictionary* (6 vols.; New York: Doubleday, 1992); J. M. Sasson, ed., *Civilizations of the Ancient Near East* (4 vols.; New York: Scribner, 1995; repr. in 2 vols.; Peabody, MA: Hendrickson, 2000); and E. M. Meyers, *The Oxford Encyclopedia of Archaeology in the Near East* (5 vols.; New York: Oxford University Press, 1997).

9. Four Decades of Hostilities

The first four decades after Solomon's death were apparently a time of hostilities between what remained of the Davidic state—the villages and clans of Ephraim/Israel having broken away—and the newly established kingdom of Israel. The hostilities seem to have consisted mostly of border skirmishes fought on Benjaminite terrain. Except for Sheshonq's depiction of his Palestinian campaign, we are dependent entirely on the Hebrew Bible for our information about this period. The following reconstructions, therefore, are our best hypotheses, based on the biblical account, as to what transpired between Solomon's death and the rise of the Omride dynasty.

Sources for the Period

For the first time, we possess an example of nonbiblical epigraphic material whose contents can be correlated with an episode described in the biblical traditions. Only with the rise of the Neo-Assyrian period in the following century does such twofold testimony become somewhat abundant.

The Biblical Materials

The majority of the biblical material on the split of the Solomonic state and the early days of the two kingdoms consists of prophetic legends. Such legends often defy credulity, apparently having been constructed to illustrate and substantiate theological positions and political claims. In the Genesis–2 Kings story line, the division of the kingdom is prepared for by an account of Solomon's apostasy in his old age. The king's infidelity is depicted as the basis for the loss of the northern tribes (1 Kgs. 11:1–13). According to 1 Kings 11:26–39, Ahijah, a prophet from Shiloh, symbolically presented to Jeroboam ten pieces of a new, shredded garment predicting the severance of ten tribes from the Davidic house. The coming breakup of the kingdom is presented as the will of Yahweh with a promise to Jeroboam of an enduring rule if he is obedient to the divine will. All of this occurs before the death of Solomon.

First Kings 12:1–24 reports how Rehoboam, the Solomonic heir apparent, was rejected at Shechem and Jeroboam crowned as the king of the north (see below). Some Greek manuscripts (Codex Vaticanus and related texts as well as manuscripts of the so-called Lucianic recension) present the narrative as found in the Hebrew text but subsequently add a long section following 1 Kings 12:24

(numbered as 12:24a-z) that differs considerably from previous material, even contradicting earlier statements contained in the Greek.[1] (The major points will be noted below.)

The events of Jeroboam's reign are briefly noted in 1 Kings 12:25–33, a highly polemical text.[2] The remainder of the material about him (13:1–14:18) are further prophetic legends. In one of these, the destruction of Bethel's altar by Josiah (642–610 B.C.E.) is predicted with the later Judean king noted by name (13:2)![3] All of the legends assure the reader that Jeroboam was an evil ruler and that the northern kingdom was doomed to the judgment of Yahweh. Whether the condemnation of the king by the prophet Ahijah reflects some historical occurrence remains uncertain and depends upon how one evaluates the prophet's role in the rise of Jeroboam.

The Chronicler reports the division of the kingdom in terms very close to those found in the Genesis–2 Kings narrative (cf. 2 Chr. 10 with 1 Kgs. 12:1–24). Since the Chronicler does not discuss the kings of the north, except when they are connected in some specific fashion with Judean monarchs, the author provides no narrative of Jeroboam's reign.

The material on the actual reign of Rehoboam, the first ruler of the new kingdom of Judah, in 1 Kings is very sparse (14:21–31), consisting primarily of generalities—the religious condition in Judah (14:21–24) and a summary of his reign (14:29–31). Only one specific event is noted—the campaign of Pharaoh Shishak into the region (14:25–28). His is the first reign of a Judean king described in typical formulaic fashion: name, age at accession, length of reign, mother's name, Deuteronomistic evaluation, reference to sources, concluding formula, and reports of some events of the reign interspersed.

In comparison the Chronicler provides a more expansive narrative (2 Chr. 11:5–12:16).[4] Rehoboam is said to have constructed defense cities throughout his kingdom (11:5–12), a fact not reported in 1 Kings. The Chronicler divides his reign into a three-year period of fidelity to "the way of David and Solomon," notes his numerous wives (eighteen) and concubines (sixty), and ascribes significant importance to the Levites during this period (11:13–23). The remainder of his reign, however, was a period of abandonment of "the law of Yahweh" (12:1–12). The invasion of Shishak is placed in this period of disobedience, and the Egyptian campaign is presented as punishment for the king's infidelity. Shemaiah the prophet is introduced into the narrative to confirm the connection. Nonetheless, the Chronicler here has Rehoboam and Jerusalem saved through the king's humbling of himself (12:6–8, 12). According to the Chronicler, further accounts of Rehoboam's reign were recorded in "the

---

1. Many studies have been written on this addition, apparently originally composed in Hebrew, then translated into Greek. The following recent works discuss the text, the issues it raises, and evaluate its historicity as well as provide full bibliographic data: S. L. McKenzie, *The Trouble with Kings: The Composition of the Book of Kings in the Deuteronomistic History* (VTSup 42; Leiden: Brill, 1991) 29–40; Zipora Talshir, *The Alternative Story of the Division of the Kingdom: 3 Kings 12:24a-z* (Jerusalem Bible Studies 6; Jerusalem: Simor, 1993); and C. S. Shaw, "The Sins of Rehoboam: The Purpose of 3 Kingdoms 12.24a-z," *JSOT* 73 (1997) 55–64.

2. For the view that this text was composed to undermine Bethel's importance in the exilic period, see Juha Pakkala, "Jeroboam's Sin and Bethel in 1 Kings 12:25–33," *BN* 112 (2002) 86–94.

3. The "man of God from Judah" narratives in 1 Kgs. 13 are often assumed to be based on the career of Amos; see the commentaries.

4. See G. N. Knoppers, "Rehoboam in Chronicles: Villain or Victim?" *JBL* 109 (1990) 423–40.

records of the prophet Shemaiah and of the seer Iddo" (12:15), but these writings are otherwise unknown.

The Genesis–2 Kings narrative provides little information about Rehoboam's successor Abijam other than the usual elements: synchronism with the northern king, length of reign, mother's name, and (negative) evaluation of his reign (1 Kgs. 15:1–8). Note is taken of the warfare between Israel and Judah but no specifics are given. The Chronicler, on the other hand, turns Abijam, called Abijah, into a Yahwistic preacher and a war hero (2 Chr. 13). The Judean king is presented at the head of a 400,000-man army fighting an Israelite force of twice that number and slaughtering half a million picked men! Such figures greatly exceed what would have been the total population of the two kingdoms. The Chronicler's presentation sounds like an imaginary creation based on 1 Kings 15:6.

Asa, Abijam's successor, is succinctly treated in 1 Kings 15:9–24 as a righteous king who reformed the cult, deposed his mother from the office of queen mother, and fought against Israel, eventually purchasing the intervention of Damascus against Baasha, the northern king. The Chronicler, on the other hand, devotes three chapters (2 Chr. 14–16) to Asa and presents him as a great reformer (14:1–5) who even removed the high places from throughout Judah (cf. 14:5 and 1 Kgs. 14:15) and as a king who fortified Judean cities and led an army of 580,000 Judeans and Benjaminites (2 Chr. 14:6–8). Asa is said to have warded off an attack by a million-man army of Cushites (2 Chr. 14:9–15) and to have extended his authority into the hill country of Ephraim (15:8). The king is presented as supported by the prophet Azariah son of Obed and as concluding, in his fifteenth year, a covenant in which the people, including aliens from Ephraim, Manasseh, and Simeon residing in the south, promised to seek Yahweh (15:1–15). For thirty-five years Judah and Asa had peace, but in the thirty-sixth year Asa was confronted by the Israelite king Baasha. The Judean king's appeal to Damascus for assistance was denounced by the prophet Hanani, whose protests led to his imprisonment and to Asa's punishment by God (16:1–14).

For a number of reasons, the Chronicler's material not found in 1 Kings appears dubious. (1) The numbers of troops attributed to Asa defy credulity. (2) There is no evidence of any early ninth-century Cushite (Ethiopian) invasion of Palestine. (3) The scheme of good years of reign and blessing followed by bad years and punishment is a rather typical organizational pattern of the Chronicler. (4) The chronological calculations clash head-on with those of 1 Kings. According to 1 Kings 16:8, Elah had succeeded to the Israelite throne in the twenty-sixth year of Asa. According to 2 Chronicles 16:1, Baasha the father of Elah invaded Judah in Asa's thirty-sixth year, ten years after the 1 Kings account has him replaced on the throne.

Sheshonq's Inscription

The invasion of Palestine by the Egyptian pharaoh Sheshonq/Shishak is noted in 1 Kings 14:25–28 and 2 Chronicles 12:1–12. Shishak I, the Libyan founder of the Twenty-second Dynasty, left an inscription concerning this exploit on a wall relief in a temple at Karnak dedicated to the god Amun (see photographs

39–40).[5] Originally consisting of about 150 place names, the text makes no mention of the kingdoms of Israel or Judah nor any reference to kings Rehoboam and Jeroboam.[6] Many of the place names mentioned can be identified with sites in Palestine, but no statement is made about whether the places surrendered or were captured or destroyed. A portion of a stela of Shishak was excavated at the site of ancient Megiddo, and the city appears as one of the toponyms in the Karnak relief. Various destruction levels unearthed at Palestinian sites have been associated with Shishak's campaign, but such associations remain uncertain.[7]

The value of the Egyptian relief lies not so much in any specific information it provides but rather in its general confirmation of the biblical claims that "in the fifth year of King Rehoboam, King Shishak of Egypt came up against Jerusalem" (1 Kgs. 14:25), even though no reference to Jerusalem is found in the surviving portion of the inscription.

The Shechem Assembly and Its Aftermath

Rehoboam, Solomon's son and the offspring of Naamah, an Ammonite (1 Kgs. 14:21), was the heir designate. The Jerusalemites were presumably willing to confirm him as their new king without hesitation. Jerusalem was, after all, the personal domain of the Davidic dynasty, having been conquered by David. Officials there would have been appointed by and owed allegiance to the Davidic family, while the royal Zion theology perpetrated under David and Solomon called for an eternal rule of the Davidic dynasty over Jerusalem. Judah at the time was probably inclined toward loyalty to the Davidic family also. After all, the dynasty was Judean in origin.

Rehoboam's confirmation was obviously not a matter of course among the Ephraimite/Israelite clans and villages or in the key northern city of Shechem, since we read of Rehoboam making a journey to Shechem and appearing before "the assembly of Israel" there (1 Kgs. 12). Why was this journey necessary? David had been confirmed by "all the tribes of Israel," with the elders of Israel coming to him at Hebron for that purpose (2 Sam. 5:1–3). There is no indication that Solomon went to Shechem for any sort of "double crowning" or that this would have been a normal expectation for his successors. There were apparently pressing political reasons for Rehoboam to go to Shechem to negotiate the matter of kingship. Probably the people of the north had already given signals of disloyalty to Jerusalem and disenchantment with the house of David.

5. Of the many studies of this relief, see most recently (with bibliography), J. D. Currid, *Ancient Egypt and the Old Testament* (Grand Rapids: Baker, 1997) 173–202; K. A. Kitchen, *On the Reliability of the Old Testament* (Grand Rapids: Eerdmans, 2003) 32–34; and K. A. Wilson, *The Campaign of Pharaoh Shosheng I into Palestine* (FAT 2/9; Tübingen: Mohr Siebeck, 2005).

6. Israel Finkelstein has used these absences to argue that there were no major Judean and Israelite kingdoms at the time; see "The Campaign of Shoshenq I to Palestine: A Guide to 10th Century BCE Polity," *ZDPV* 118 (2002) 109–35.

7. For a discussion of these destruction levels, see Amihai Mazar, *Archaeology of the Land of the Bible, 10,000–586 B.C.E.* (ABRL; New York: Doubleday, 1990) 396–98.

The Constituency of the Shechem Assembly

The assembly of Shechem was probably an ad hoc convocation of voices that represented two not entirely distinct but essentially different groups. On the one hand, there would have been representatives of the old cities such as Shechem, Tirzah, and Megiddo, that had probably been brought under Jerusalem's political influence by David and Solomon. Possibly some of these cities had even retained much of their independence and autonomy during their reigns. These old cities had a history of being ruled by others, notably by the Egyptians. The foreign rule, however, had been rather loose, allowing a degree of local autonomy. Such cities could not have been expected to cooperate or offer their submission to an autocratic king in Jerusalem unless this was to their advantage or could not be avoided.

Shechem in particular was an important city with ancient traditions and no doubt much pride. Contrary to the implications of Judges 8:30–35 and Joshua 24, which represent late editorial elements, Shechem seems not to have succumbed to Israelite domination during premonarchical times. One wonders, in fact, whether the account of the Shechem assembly reported in Joshua 24[8] might not have as its actual historical basis the same post-Solomonic assembly reported in 1 Kings 12, the event having been retrojected back to the period of the "conquest." If Judges 8:30–35 and Joshua 24 are to be taken as authentic evidence of Israelite involvement in cultic activity at Shechem prior to the time of the monarchy, the cult would probably not have been that of the Baal/El-berith temple in the city but of another sacred place, the oak of Moreh (Gen. 12:6), somewhere outside the city.

Others among those who confronted Rehoboam at Shechem would have represented the sentiments of the clans, tribes, and small villages of the northern hill country, that is, essentially the constituency of the old Ephraim/Israel tribal group.[9] These would have had special reasons for disenchantment with the house of David, beyond Solomon's harsh treatment of his subjects. In the first place, David's family home and tribal connections were with Judah, and he ruled from Jerusalem, having displaced the house of Saul, whose home and tribal connections were with Ephraim/Israel. Second, the cultic places and priestly lines of Ephraim/Israel had apparently been de-emphasized under David and Solomon in deference to those of Jerusalem. Indeed, as we have seen, there may have been a deliberate effort to co-opt some of the old Ephraimite/Israelite cultic relics, priests, and traditions to support the cultic primacy of Jerusalem. The ark had been taken to Jerusalem. Jerusalemite court propaganda emphasized that Samuel, a Benjaminite prophet, had anointed David to rule in place of Saul (2 Sam. 16:1–13). Especially the old sanctuary at Shiloh and its priesthood had been eclipsed by the Jerusalem cult. It is not at all surprising, therefore, that a Shilonite, Ahijah, is credited with predicting and helping to precipitate the north's break with Jerusalem (1 Kgs. 11:29–39).

Acting alone, these small clans and villages, representative of the old Ephraimite/Israelite interests, would have been powerless to challenge Rehoboam. In cooperation with the people of Shechem and other northern

---

8. Many Greek manuscripts of the OT place Joshua's assembly at Shiloh rather than Shechem (see Josh. 18:1).

9. See Baruch Halpern, "Sectionalism and the Schism," *JBL* 93 (1974) 519–32.

cities, however, they were in a position to resist. The extent to which the Shechem assembly was broadly representative is unclear. Which cities other than Shechem actually participated? Were representatives of the Galilean tribes present? Nothing is said of these groups, but one could have expected them to follow the lead of Shechem and Ephraim/Israel.

Rehoboam's Rejection

Whatever chances Rehoboam had of holding together the Davidic state were dashed at Shechem. He was confronted with the demand to alter Solomon's harsh policies: "Your father made our yoke heavy. Now therefore lighten the hard service of your father and his heavy yoke that he placed on us, and we will serve you" (1 Kgs. 12:4). The reader is led to conclude that state forced labor was the primary concern of the north, but other elements of the despotism of the house of David may have been involved: taxation inequities, political favoritism, defense measures or lack thereof against Damascus, and the surrender of Israelite territory (Cabul) to Phoenicia. Following the advice of his younger and perhaps less-experienced advisers,[10] Rehoboam chose not to negotiate but to threaten even more repressive measures: "My father made your yoke heavy, but I will add to your yoke; my father disciplined you with whips, but I will discipline you with scorpions" (perhaps some special form of whip) (12:14). In response to this recalcitrant attitude and the deterioration of negotiations, the northerners raised the old cry of rebellion that had rung through the hills of Israel already during David's reign:

> What share do we have in David?
> We have no inheritance in the son of Jesse.
> To your tents, O Israel!
> Look now to your own house, O David.
> (1 Kgs. 12:16; see 2 Sam. 20:1)

To handle matters, Rehoboam delegated Adoram, probably identical with the Adoniram who had begun service as state supervisor of compulsory labor under David (2 Sam. 20:24; 1 Kgs. 4:6; 12:17–18). No doubt Adoram had long experience in dealing with David and Solomon's subjects, and for the northerners he embodied the policies of state that they sought to have redressed. The rebels stoned Adoram to death while Rehoboam fled to Jerusalem in his chariot (1 Kgs. 12:17–18).

Back in Jerusalem, Rehoboam is said to have assembled an army of Judeans and Benjaminites, but then decided against any immediate military attempt to recover the northern territories. The biblical account states that this decision was made on the advice of Shemaiah, a "man of God" (1 Kgs. 12:21–24). Rehoboam may have realized as well that even Judah and the other southern territories were not entirely secure in his hands.

---

10. The identity of these groups, especially "the young men" and whether they were a new cabinet, Rehoboam's male siblings, or youthful hotheads, has been much debated. See Abraham Malamat, "Organs of State in the Israelite Monarchy," *BA* 28 (1965) 34–65; C. D. Evans, "Rehoboam's Advisers at Shechem and Political Institutions in Israel and Sumer," *JNES* 25 (1966) 273–79; and N. S. Fox, "Royal Officials and Court Families: A New Look at the *yĕlādîm* in 1 Kings 12," *BA* 59 (1996) 225–32.

The Role of the Tribe of Benjamin

The Benjaminites, settled in the hill country immediately north of Jerusalem, were caught in the middle of the struggle between Israel and the house of David. On the one hand, they had been part of the old Ephraim/Israel alliance. Indeed, Saul himself was a Benjaminite whose power base included Ephraim. We have noted some indications, on the other hand, that suggest occasional conflicts between the Ephraimites and the Benjaminites during earlier times. Also, since the Benjaminites were situated in such close proximity to Jerusalem they could expect to suffer first and most from any Jerusalemite military action directed against the north.

The biblical account of the Shechem assembly does not indicate whether Benjaminites were represented, as they had been in the original negotiations between Israel and David (2 Sam. 3:17–19), or, if they were present, what role they played. According to 1 Kings 12:21, which seems, however, to contradict the preceding verse, at least some Benjaminites remained loyal to Rehoboam. In any case, the tiny tribal territory of Benjamin became a frontier between the two kingdoms and thus the scene of intermittent warfare during the coming decades.

Jeroboam at Shechem

The north apparently never gave any consideration to reverting to a non-monarchical form of government. Kingship had become an established tradition. Not surprisingly, the rebel kingdom took the old name "Israel," and Jeroboam, the Ephraimite from Zeredah who earlier had fled to Egypt in opposition to Solomon's forced-labor policies, was selected as the first king. The course of Jeroboam's earlier career, his role, if any, in the negotiations at Shechem, and the details of his rise to kingship are uncertain. The problem is not so much a lack of information as the fact, which we have already noted, that the Hebrew and Greek versions of the pertinent biblical passage (1 Kgs. 11:26–12:33) differ significantly.

According to the Hebrew version, Jeroboam was one of Solomon's officials who had been given "charge over all the forced labor of the house of Joseph" (11:28). Yet he "rebelled against the king" (11:26) and then was confronted by the prophet Ahijah from Shiloh, who predicted that Jeroboam himself would become king over the northern tribes (11:29–39). Specifically, we are told that Ahijah at Shiloh dramatized the forthcoming split of Solomon's kingdom by tearing Jeroboam's garment into twelve parts (representing the twelve tribes) and presenting him with ten of these. When Solomon sought to kill Jeroboam, the latter took refuge with Pharaoh Shishak in Egypt (11:40). Later, following Solomon's death, Jeroboam returned and presumably participated in the Shechem assembly, although, there seems to be some internal contradiction in the Hebrew version on this latter score (compare 12:3, 12 with 12:20).

The Greek version duplicates most of the Hebrew account but then adds a supplement that reiterates some of the Hebrew version and expands upon it. Jeroboam, we are told, was the son of a harlot named Sarira. As Solomon's "lash master" over the levies of the house of Joseph, he built the city of Sarira (= Zeredah?) for the king. He possessed three hundred chariots, built the Millo, and fortified the city of David, but aspired to the kingship. When Solomon sought to kill Jeroboam, he fled to Shishak the king of Egypt. In Egypt he married the pharaoh's sister-in-law, who bore him a son, Abia (Abijah). After Solomon's death, Jeroboam returned to Sarira and fortified the city. When his son became ill, Jeroboam's wife visited the prophet Ahijah of Shiloh, who pronounced doom upon Jeroboam's family. It was Jeroboam, according to the Greek version, who assembled the tribes in Shechem; and it was at the Shechem assembly, before the negotiations with Rehoboam had begun, that the prophet Shemaiah (rather than Ahijah) tore a new garment into twelve pieces and presented ten of these to Jeroboam.

While the Hebrew and Greek versions thus present us with two differing accounts of Jeroboam's early career and rise to kingship, both support the following scenario: Jeroboam, probably from an important and established family, was, in his early career, an official in the Solomonic bureaucracy. Specifically, he was an overseer of some sort in connection with forced laborers drafted from northern (Ephraimite/Israelite) territory. At some point, however, he defied Solomon with a mutinous act that is specified only as "lifting his hand against the king" (11:26). This does not necessarily mean that Jeroboam proposed to overthrow the monarchy or to have himself crowned king. He may have simply protested Solomon's treatment of his Israelite subjects, a protest that eventually could have led to Jeroboam's fortifying his own hometown against Solomon. Jeroboam thus gave expression to widespread anti-Solomonic sentiment and would have received the support of various disaffected groups. Among these, no doubt, were religious and prophetic figures such as Ahijah of Shiloh. Moreover, the very fact that a "wanted" governmental official such as Jeroboam could flee the country may suggest complicity on the part of other high-level officials. The pharaoh who gave Jeroboam shelter in Egypt was Shishak, the founder of the Twenty-second Dynasty. When the negotiations with Rehoboam failed and full-scale rebellion developed, it was only natural that attention should turn to Jeroboam.

Differences between the Kingdoms

There now were two kingdoms, Israel in the north and Judah in the south, where formerly one had existed. From a casual reading of 1 Kings and 2 Chronicles, one might get the idea that these two kingdoms were roughly equal in size and strength, or perhaps even infer that Judah was the superior power and Israel only a breakaway fragment. The Israelites, no doubt, saw the situation quite the other way around. For them, the Davidic-Solomonic years represented an unfortunate episode in "Israelite" history, the true founder of which was Saul, and Judah was the fragment state. This Israelite perspective is more in keeping with the archaeological evidence and almost certainly nearer to the historical realities.

Territorial Size and Strength

Archaeological surveys in the central Palestinian hill country indicate that the Iron Age trend toward population density and urbanization occurred earlier in the north-central hill country, where the kingdom of Israel was centered, and only later in Judahite territory. Likewise, the northern sites such as Samaria, Jezreel, Hazor, and Megiddo present the earliest evidences of public building projects on a monumental scale. This is not surprising. Israel was better situated than Judah for participation in international trade. Also in terms of size and military strength, Israel was probably the dominant kingdom.

Traffic along the major coastal road, "the Way of the Sea," could bypass Judah altogether but had to negotiate through at least a corner of the hill country of Israel. Most of this traffic would have crossed the Mount Carmel ridge near Megiddo or passed farther to the southeast through the Dothan plain. Also there was little east-west traffic through Judah, since the Dead Sea formed a barrier along the eastern side. For Israel, on the other hand, the Dothan plain and the Shechem pass were major east-west thoroughfares.

When the Israelites were able to control the Sharon and Jezreel plains, Galilee, and northern Transjordan, as was apparently the case later under the Omrides and Jeroboam II, they had direct access to the Mediterranean Sea, close communications with Phoenicia and Damascus, and a stake in the north-south trade through Transjordan. Thus Israel was able to share in and profit from international trade much more so than Judah.[11] Accordingly, largely because of its more strategic geographical position, the northern kingdom included more cities of significant size.

Regarding the relative military strength of the two kingdoms, we have seen that Rehoboam backed down from making any immediate move to recover control of the northern territories. Subsequent skirmishes initiated by Judah during the early period of the separate kingdoms were never serious threats to Israel but merely attempts on the part of the Judean kings to establish a buffer zone of reasonable depth north of Jerusalem. Later, in the ninth and eighth centuries when Israel and Judah established a cooperative alliance, Israel was clearly the dominant partner. On one occasion when the Judean king Amaziah challenged his northern counterpart Jehoash "to look each other in the face," Jehoash scoffed at the idea that Amaziah would consider himself an equal, and then proceeded to crush the Judean army (2 Kgs. 14:8–14).

Instability of the Northern Kingdom

In comparison with Judah, where the Davidic family remained in power for more than three centuries except for one brief interlude, Israelite political life appears to have been extremely unstable. We will see that the situation may not always have been as stable even in Judah as the biblical records seem to imply. Nevertheless, of the two kingdoms, it is clear that Israel had a far more turbulent political history. Seven of its kings were assassinated or executed (eight if we count the pretender Zimri), each time resulting in a dynastic change. There were probably several reasons for this political instability.

No doubt the plurality and diversity of the people who made up the northern kingdom were contributing factors to its instability. As noted above, Israel

---

11. See Moshe Elat, "The Monarchy and the Development of Trade in Ancient Israel," in Edouard Lipiński, ed., *State and Temple Economy in the Ancient Near East* (2 vols.; OLA 5–6; Leuven: Peeters, 1991) 2:527–46.

included several cities of reasonable size. These, with their more cosmopolitan inhabitants and their own cultic centers, self-interests, and pride existed side by side with the little villages of the hill country, Transjordan, and Galilee. The latter also had their self-interests and pride, of course, not to mention their own political and cultic traditions grounded in clan structures. The economic base of both city and village was agriculture and small handcraft industries. Yet the economy of the cities incorporated other components as well, such as income from trade and from services rendered to the central government. Any ruler would have been hard-pressed to satisfy both of these diverse groups.

Israel's location astride the main Syro-Palestinian trade routes meant that the kingdom was particularly vulnerable to outside influences, including military pressures from other nations wishing to control these routes. This was another contributing factor to instability in the north. Struggles between Egyptian and Mesopotamian powers quickly drew Israel, much more so than Judah, into the maelstrom of international politics and meant that foreign governments exerted enormous influence on Israel's domestic affairs.

Still another cause of instability in Israel was the lack of a generally accepted royal theology that could help sustain a dynasty on the throne during difficult times—through the reign of a weak king, for example, or one whose policies met with widespread disfavor among the populace. No doubt the northern kings attempted to develop something similar to the royal Zion theology of Jerusalem. This was never successfully achieved, however, and would have been difficult, since each ruling family, beginning with Jeroboam, had come to power by rejecting the dynastic claims of their predecessors.

Finally, political activism on the part of the Yahwistic prophets must be mentioned among the contributing factors to instability in the north. Admittedly, the importance of their political involvement may have been overemphasized somewhat by the compilers of the books of Kings and Chronicles. Nevertheless it is clear that the prophets did play some particular role as "king rejecters" and "kingmakers" in the history of the northern kingdom, and one of the practical results of this role seems to have been that they were a constant source of antiroyal subversion.

These last two factors, the absence of a sustaining royal theology in the north and the political involvement of Yahwistic prophets, require further comment.

Absence of a Sustaining Royal Theology

The people of the north obviously did not accept the royal Zion theology that emerged in Jerusalem and claimed that Yahweh had granted the exclusive right to rule his people to a Judean dynasty founded by David and centered in Jerusalem. On the contrary, the voices at the Shechem assembly made clear that they were thoroughly disenchanted with Solomon's policies and felt no binding commitment to either the house of David or the city of Jerusalem. This does not mean, as some suppose, that the people of the northern kingdom possessed a special political ideology of their own that rejected in principle the very concept of dynastic rule.[12] The northern cities already had a well-established tradition of dynastic kingship, and even the clans and villages of Ephraim/Israel had accepted some sort of dynastic concept in the cases of Abimelech and Saul. Nor is there any reason to suppose that the concept of dynastic rule would have been considered an encroachment on Yahweh's kingship or incompatible with the view that Yahweh delegated this authority to individuals confirmed by prophetic word. The royal Zion theology itself illustrates how these two concepts could be combined in the view that Yahweh delegated his authority by the word of a prophet to a permanently ruling family rather than to a single individual.

The action of the Shechem assembly and the subsequent history of the northern kingdom demonstrate, on the other hand, that while the people of the north did not necessarily reject the dynastic concept in principle, neither did the population at large have any strong commitment to the dynastic principle, or at least not to any particular dynasty. The assembly dismissed any obligations to Rehoboam, who came with unquestionable hereditary credentials, and opted instead for Jeroboam, who had made a name for himself opposing the royal family and who had been proclaimed by the prophet Ahijah as Yahweh's "next man."

A similar pattern would repeat itself again and again in the northern kingdom for the next two centuries: the old king would die; he would be succeeded on the throne by his son; the son would then be put to death and the entire royal family annihilated; the leader of the rebellion would become the new king. The new king would usually be supported in his seizure of the throne by the military or some element in the military, and there is usually some indication that he received prophetic support. When Israel eventually fell to the Assyrians, only two of its royal families, those of Omri and Jehu, had been able to hold the throne beyond a second generation.

With the Omrides, prophetic opposition led by Elijah surfaced already in the second generation, that is, during Ahab's reign. Ahab was sufficiently strong to withstand opposition, but within a decade of his death the family line was eliminated by Jehu, who himself was apparently supported by the prophet Elisha. The Jehu dynasty lasted until the fifth generation, although during much of this time Israel was subject to Damascus. Once the kingdom had recovered, particularly under Jeroboam II, Yahwistic prophets, including Amos and Hosea, began to oppose the Jehu dynasty also. When Jeroboam II died and his son Zechariah ascended the throne, he was put to death, and never again in Israel was a son able successfully to follow his father to the throne.

The Role of Prophets in Northern Politics

Conflict between prophet and king is a recurring theme in the biblical materials pertaining to the northern kingdom. The compilers of Genesis–2 Kings

---

12. Albrecht Alt argued that kingship in Israel was charismatic/prophetic-based and thus basically anti-dynastic by nature; see "The Monarchy in Israel and Judah," in *Essays on Old Testament History and Religion* (New York: Doubleday, 1967) 239–59 (German original published in *VT* 1 [1951] 116–34). This view was called into question by Giorgio Buccellati, *Cities and Nations of Ancient Syria: An Essay on Political Institutions with Special Reference to the Israelite Kingdoms* (Rome: Istitutio di Studi del Vicino Oriente, 1967). Alt's radical position is no longer generally followed.

CHART 14. From Solomon's Death to the Assassination of Elah

Judah	Israel	Contemporary Rulers
Rehoboam (926–910)	Jeroboam (927–906)	Shishak of Egypt invades in the fifth year of Rehoboam
Abijam/Abijah (909–907)		
Asa (906–878 [866])	Nadab (905–904)	
	Baasha (903–882 [880])	Ben-hadad of Damascus,
	Elah (881–880)	son of Tabrimmon, was a contemporary of Asa and Baasha

attribute this to apostasy on the part of the kings. Jeroboam I, it is claimed, led the whole kingdom astray when he instituted places and procedures of worship in competition with the Jerusalemite cult. The northern kings are charged further with supporting the worship of Baal in varying degrees.

Admittedly some of the prophets did specifically oppose the cultic practices at certain of the northern sanctuaries. Nevertheless, the charge that Jeroboam committed religious apostasy when he revived the northern cults must be attributed largely to the Judean bias of the biblical compilers. The second charge, that the northern kings supported Baal worship in varying degrees, has some historical basis but surely represents an oversimplification. There does seem, especially under the Omrides, to have been some competition and conflict between the supporters of Yahwism and those of Baalism, with each side vying for support from the royal family. The issues would have been more complex than merely a religious clash between the worshipers of two different deities. Indeed, many of the people of Israel and Judah at that time probably saw nothing wrong with worshiping more than one god. Yahwism versus Baalism would have been but the tip of an iceberg, an obvious embodiment of a much more complex and deeply rooted fracture within the pluralistic kingdom.

Possibly another aspect of this fracture was tension between the inhabitants of the cities, such as Shechem and Samaria where the royal family resided, and the rural folk, who may have been more firmly rooted in clan and tribal structures, particularly those who looked back to Ephraim/Israel as their heritage. Since the prophets seem to have been strongest in their opposition when the monarchy itself was strongest, it may be that they functioned as a sort of check over and against the kings and the centralization of power. In any case, we probably can assume some mutuality between the conservative stance and revolutionary actions of the Yahwistic prophets and the old clan/village/tribal interests and religious affiliations.

Rehoboam, Abijam, and Asa of Judah

Rehoboam. Although reported to have already been forty-one years old when he became king (but only sixteen according to the Greek; 1 Kgs. 12:24g), Rehoboam, the son of Naamah an Ammonite, is credited with a reign of seventeen years (14:21).[13] First Kings provides few specifics about his reign except for the account of his actions in connection with the northern rebellion, the report of Shishak's invasion (14:25–28), and the note that there was constant warfare between Rehoboam and Jeroboam. The Chronicler adds two other noteworthy items: a list of fifteen "cities of defense" that Rehoboam built in Judah (2 Chr. 11:5–12), and the observation that Rehoboam "distributed some of his sons through all the districts of Judah and Benjamin, in all the fortified cities; and he gave them abundant provisions, and found many wives for them" (2 Chr. 11:23).

Although these last two items are included only by the Chronicler, we are inclined to regard them as authentic for three reasons: (1) The city list is more detailed than editorial fiction would have required. (2) Neither this list nor the report that Rehoboam distributed his sons around the kingdom in fortified cities serves any obviously ulterior motive in the Chronicler's work. (3) On the contrary, these two items make sense when understood as a coordinated move on Rehoboam's part to secure his control over the clans and villages of the southern hill country.[14]

One need not assume that the people of the southern hill country, except possibly for Jerusalem and some elements in Judah, were any more strongly committed to the Davidic dynasty than the people of the north had been. No doubt there were those even among the Judean clans and villages who felt no strong loyalty to the royal family or to Jerusalem. It is noteworthy that when Rehoboam's "cities of defense" are plotted on the map, they turn out to have been scattered throughout the southern hill country rather than along what would have been the kingdom's frontier. (See Map 23.) This suggests that they were not intended solely, if at all, as defense against foreign invaders. On the contrary, placing loyal family members at key places throughout the realm, particularly in fortified cities with abundant supplies and with the procurement of local wives, may have been a move on Rehoboam's part to strengthen Jerusalem's hold on the southern hill country, lest it follow the actions of the rebel north. Even the Chronicler seems to connect the fortified cities with internal security: "So he held Judah and Benjamin" (2 Chr. 11:12b).

We have taken the position above that it was David who established the network of Levitical cities (listed in Josh. 21 and 1 Chr. 6) and that the Levitical

---

13. Later synchronisms suggest that Rehoboam's first regnal year began a year after that of Jeroboam. This can be accounted for by assuming that Solomon died after the Judean New Year Festival (15 Tishri) but that Jeroboam ascended the throne shortly before or at the Israelite New Year Festival (15 Marheshvan).

14. For support of this view see J. M. Miller, "Rehoboam's Cities of Defense," in L. G. Perdue et al., eds., *Archaeology and Biblical Interpretation: Essays in Memory of D. Glen Rose* (Atlanta: John Knox, 1987) 273–86. For a date of the fortresses to the reign of Hezekiah, see Nadav Na'aman, "Hezekiah's Fortified Cities and the *LMLK* Stamps," *BASOR* 261 (1986) 5–21; repr. in *AIIN* 153–78; for a date in the reign of Josiah see Volkmar Fritz, "The List of Rehoboam's Fortresses in 2 Chr 11:5–12—A Document from the Time of Josiah," *ErIsr* 15 (1981) 46*–53*.

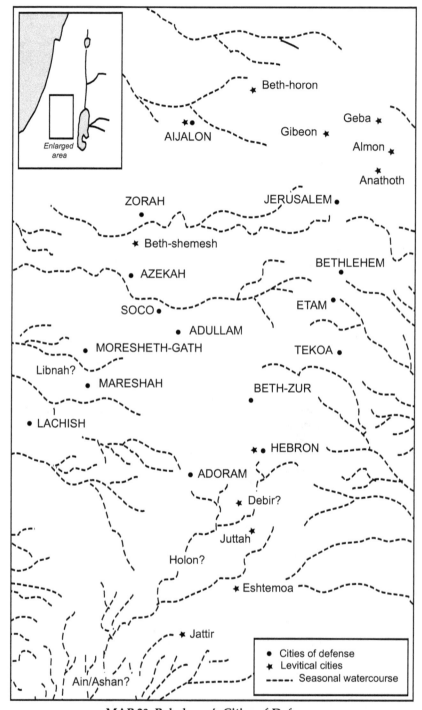

MAP 23. Rehoboam's Cities of Defense

families whom he placed in these cities would have remained staunch loyalists to the crown. Presumably Rehoboam could still count on the support of these Levitical cities, which, however, tended to be located in outlying areas, possibly territories that David had added to his kingdom secondarily by conquest. It is noteworthy, therefore, that Rehoboam's "cities of defense" tended to complement (by filling the space in between) rather than overlap the geographical coverage of the Levitical cities. No doubt this was intended.

Abijam. Rehoboam's successor, Abijam (= Abijah in Chronicles), is credited with a reign of only three years (1 Kgs. 15:1–8; 2 Chr. 13:1–21). This short reign, plus the unusually long reign ascribed to his successor, Asa (forty-one years), who in turn was remembered for having taken action against the queen mother, invites speculation: (1) that Abijam died an early, untimely death; (2) that Asa was still a minor when he became king; and (3) that the queen mother served as regent during Asa's early years.

There seems to be some confusion within the biblical records, however, regarding the precise identity of this queen mother.[15] First Kings 15:9–10, paralleled by 2 Chronicles 15:16, identifies her as Maacah daughter of Abishalom (Absalom, the son of David?). One might presume, therefore, that Maacah was Asa's mother and Abijam's wife except that 1 Kings 15:2 records this same Maacah as Abijam's mother. Second Chronicles 11:20–22 elaborates further that Maacah was Rehoboam's favorite wife and that he passed over other sons to designate her son Abijam as crown prince. Finally, complicating matters all the more, 2 Chronicles 13:2 records the name of Abijam's mother as Micaiah daughter of Uriel of Gibeah.

Any solution to this genealogical problem must be conjectural and take liberties with the biblical text. Two obvious possibilities present themselves: (1) Micaiah daughter of Uriel and Maacah daughter of Abishalom were two different persons who have become confused. It was the former whom Rehoboam favored over all his other wives; the latter was Abijam's wife and the mother of Asa. (2) There was only one Micaiah/Maacah involved. Abijam and Asa were brothers rather than father and son. Micaiah/Maacah had gained such a political position during Rehoboam's reign that even when her first son, Abijam, died she was able to secure the throne for a second son, Asa.

The Chronicler would have one believe that Abijam was a powerful king who achieved a crushing victory over Jeroboam of Israel. Yet the account of the battle (2 Chr. 13:3–20) is typical Chronicler midrash. Moreover, even if the story is based on an actual historical incident, the few real details provided indicate that the battle was a border skirmish at most (see below).

Asa. As successor to Abijam, Asa is assigned a reign of forty-one years.[16] He is also credited with performing several acts of cultic reform and is one of the

---

15. See Susan Ackerman, "The Queen Mother and the Cult in Ancient Israel," *JBL* 112 (1993) 385–401; Ktziah Spanier, "The Queen Mother in the Judean Royal Court: Maacha—A Case Study," in Athalya Brenner, ed., *A Feminist Companion to Samuel and Kings* (Sheffield: Sheffield Academic Press, 1994) 186–95; and E. K. Solvang, *A Woman's Place Is in the House: Royal Women in Judah and Their Involvement in the House of David* (JSOTSup 349; Sheffield: Sheffield Academic Press, 2003).

16. Our chronology presumes that Asa abdicated the throne in his twenty-ninth year (878–877 B.C.E.) but continued to live until 866–865. The reason for such an abdication is indicated in 1 Kgs. 15:23: "in his old age he was diseased in his feet [= his genitals]." Such a disease would have rendered him incapable of participation in worship services in the temple.

very few kings following David and Solomon whom the editors of Kings and Chronicles counted as having done "what was right in the sight of Yahweh" (1 Kgs. 15:11–15; 2 Chr. 14:2). Maacah may have served as regent during Asa's early years, as indicated above, and the biblical editors saw it as significant that he eventually removed her from being the queen mother, "because she had an abominable image made for Asherah" (1 Kgs. 15:13).

Among the other reforming acts credited to Asa in 1 Kings were that (1) he put away the *qodeshim* (sacred males?) from the land;[17] (2) he removed all the idols his father had made; and (3) he brought the votive gifts of his father and his own votive gifts into the temple of Yahweh. On the negative side, the editors of 1 Kings report that the local cultic shrines were not taken away (15:14a).

The Chronicler introduces further information, mostly negative, about Asa's reign. Also, in an obvious effort to deal with the theological problem of a cult-reforming king who nevertheless did evil and suffered tragedy, the Chronicler reverts to the pattern we have observed already in connection with David and Solomon: he places all the negative aspects of Asa's reign in his last years, indicating that these occurred after a long and successful reign and were brought on by the king's unfaithfulness to Yahweh in his old age.

Specifically, the Chronicler allows Asa thirty-five good years, during which he is presented as an active cultic reformer with successes on every side— major building activities, a huge army, and victory over Zerah the Ethiopian (2 Chr. 14–15).[18] But then, during his last six years, Asa became an evil king whose rule turned sour. The turning point apparently was when, in his thirty-sixth year, Asa appealed to Ben-hadad of Syria for help against Israel (1 Kgs. 15:16–22; 2 Chr. 16:1–10), a move that the Chronicler clearly regarded as a breach of faith in Yahweh. Asa supposedly was confronted at that time by a prophet, Hanani the seer (2 Chr. 16:7–10), just as earlier he had been confronted by the prophet Azariah (2 Chr. 15:1–7). This second time, however, Asa responded negatively, put Hanani in stocks, and inflicted cruelties on the people in general (2 Chr. 16:7–10). Eventually, in his thirty-ninth year when he was afflicted in his feet, Asa went so far as to consult physicians rather than Yahweh (2 Chr. 16:11–12). For reasons already noted, this schematization seems unhistorical overall.

Jeroboam, Nadab, Baasha, and Elah of Israel

Jeroboam.[19] First Kings provides only minimal information about the first four decades of the northern kingdom. Moreover, much of the space devoted to affairs in Israel during this early period has to do with Jeroboam's religious

17. Scholars have usually understood this as referring to "male temple prostitutes," but some recent scholars have called into question the existence of cultic prostitution; see P. A. Bird, "The End of the Male Cult Prostitute: A Literary-Historical and Sociological Analysis of Hebrew *qādēš-qĕdēšîm*," in J. A. Emerton, ed., *Congress Volume, Cambridge 1995* (VTSup 66; Leiden: Brill, 1997) 37–80.

18. On Zerah see J. D. Hays, "The Cushites: A Black Nation in the Bible," *BSac* 153 (1996) 396–409.

19. On Jeroboam and his treatment in the Bible, see C. D. Evans, "Naram-Sin and Jeroboam: The Archetypal *Unheilsherrscher* in Mesopotamian and Biblical Historiography," in W. W. Hallo et al., eds., *Scripture in Context II* (Winona Lake, IN: Eisenbrauns, 1983) 97–125; and P. S. Ash, "Jeroboam I and the Deuteronomistic Historian's Ideology of the Founder," *CBQ* 60 (1998) 16–24.

51. *Bull Statuette.* Although of bronze, rather than gold, and presumably smaller (about 5 in. high) than the golden calves erected by Jeroboam I at Dan and Bethel, this statuette nevertheless gives an idea of how Jeroboam's calves may have looked. (*Israel Museum*)

activities, which, not surprisingly, are seen in a negative light by the Judean compilers. The Chronicler ignores the first four Israelite kings completely except where they are directly involved with the Judean kings.

Jeroboam's Cultic Reformation. As observed earlier, the northern rejection of Rehoboam implied also a rejection of the royal Zion theology centered in the Jerusalem cult. Jeroboam followed through on this implication by renovating and upgrading the ancient sanctuaries at Bethel and Dan (erecting calf or bull images at both places), installing new priests in some of the northern sanctuaries, and revising the cultic calendar (1 Kgs. 12:26–33). To the Judean compilers of 1–2 Kings who lived long after the northern kingdom was no more, Jeroboam's actions were rank apostasy. Jeroboam and his contemporaries saw it, no doubt, as cultic reform and renewal, a movement back to old traditions uncontaminated by the ideas of the Jerusalemite and Davidic ideologies.

Both Bethel and Dan were old sanctuaries. Bethel figures prominently in the patriarchal stories (Gen. 12:8; 28:18–22; 35:1–15) and had associations with Samuel (1 Sam. 7:16). Dan claimed a priestly line that traced its ancestry back to Moses (Judg. 18:30). The golden calves set up by Jeroboam were probably not intended as idols any more than were the cherubim in Solomon's temple. They, like the cherubim, were common features in the religious iconography of the day and would have served as symbols of the divine presence or as pedestals on which the Deity stood or sat invisibly. The difference between the cherubim and the bull images was primarily one of religious iconography rather than theology (see photograph 53).

Naturally the separation of the kingdoms would have called for a change in priestly personnel in the northern shrines, if nothing more than an ousting of priests who had been installed in office by David and Solomon and/or who had pro-Davidic leanings. It is perhaps significant in this regard that Jeroboam is said to have installed priests who were not "Levites" (1 Kgs. 12:31). If, as we proposed in chapter 6, the early Levites were particularly loyal to David, who had placed them at key places throughout the kingdom, then Jeroboam would have been a fool not to remove them from the sanctuaries now within his realm. One can imagine that many refugees from the north were returning to the south after the partition—people who for various reasons were closely identified with the administration of David and Solomon (see 2 Chr. 11:13–17; 13:9; 15:9).

Jeroboam's cultic reformation was apparently oriented to Aaronite priestly lines, traditions, and iconography. This is suggested by the parallels between the way Aaron is depicted in Exodus 32 and Leviticus 10 and the way Jeroboam is depicted in 1 Kings 12. Both Aaron and Jeroboam are said to have constructed a golden calf on advice from the people (Exod. 32:1–4; 1 Kgs. 12:28a); both proclaim that the god worshiped was the one who had brought Israel up out of the land of Egypt (Exod. 32:4; 1 Kgs. 12:26–33); and both have two sons with essentially the same names—Nadab and Abihu/Abijah (Lev. 10; 1 Kgs. 14:1, 20). At an earlier stage, the tradition or traditions behind these related passages in Exodus–Leviticus and 1 Kings may have presented both Aaron and Jeroboam in a favorable light. The passages as they stand now, however, clearly show the imprint of anti-Aaronite circles that were hostile to both. As the likely source for such hostility, one thinks first of southern, Jerusalemite, cultic circles committed to Zadokite and Levitical priestly interests.[20]

The charge that Jeroboam set up a new festival dated to the fifteenth of the eighth month (15 Marheshvan) found in 1 Kings 12:32–33 recognzes that Judah and Israel operated on two different calendars.[21] In all probability, however, a New Year Festival was already observed in the north one month later than in the south. Thus, in this matter, Jeroboam was more a traditionalist than an innovator.

While Jeroboam's cultic moves are probably to be understood as an intentional effort to revive Aaronite traditions and priestly interests in certain of the old northern sanctuaries, especially Bethel, he seems to have passed over the Elide sanctuary at Shiloh. This is noteworthy especially in view of the tradition that it was a Shilonite prophet, Ahijah, who had predicted Jeroboam's rise to power. Actually there may have been little left at Shiloh to revive. Archaeological excavations have revealed that the village was destroyed sometime during

---

20. See Moses Aberbach and Leivy Smolar, "Aaron, Jeroboam, and the Golden Calves," *JBL* 86 (1967) 129–40.

21. See Shemaryahu Talmon, "Divergences in Calendar-Reckoning in Ephraim and Judah," *VT* 8 (1958) 58–74; repr. in his *King, Cult, and Calendar in Ancient Israel: Collected Essays* (Jerusalem: Magnes, 1986) 113–39.

52. *Present-day Nablus.* This photograph, taken on Mount Gerizim, looks down upon the present-day city of Nablus. Nablus incorporates Tell Balatah, the site of ancient Shechem, where Israel rejected Rehoboam and crowned Jeroboam as their king instead.

the eleventh century B.C.E. This destruction has been attributed to the Philistines, although there are no biblical indications that the Philistines ever attacked Shiloh, and no clear archaeological evidence that they were the perpetrators. As far as the biblical account is concerned, the Elide priestly line simply fades into the background after the death of Saul, whom they had supported, and with the transfer of the ark to Jerusalem. If Ahijah hoped for a revival of the Shiloh cultic center, he was disappointed. We hear of him last when, as a blind old man, he predicts the downfall of Jeroboam's dynasty (1 Kgs. 14:1–16).

Bethel and Dan were also frontier sanctuaries, possibly intended to mark the northern and southern limits of the newly established Israelite kingdom. Consequently they changed hands from time to time, Bethel perhaps falling occasionally into Judean hands and Dan into Syrian hands (for example, during the military conflict between Asa, Baasha, and Ben-hadad, which will be discussed below). Jeroboam's rebuilding of Penuel in Transjordan (1 Kgs. 12:25) represented the renovation of another old sanctuary city (see Gen. 32:22–30) and affirmed Israelite control over Gileadite territory. Gilead, of course, had been aligned with Ephraim/Israel during the days of the judges and had belonged to Saul's chiefdom.

Shechem itself was another old sanctuary center that received new life under Jeroboam. Archaeological excavations at Shechem (Tell Balatah in present-day Nablus) have revealed a major Bronze Age temple that went through several building phases and continued in use into the Early Iron Age. This may have been the temple of Baal-berith mentioned in Judges 9:4. One is tempted to attribute the last destruction of this temple, during the twelfth century, to Abimelech (Judg. 9:46–49), but this of course cannot be established with certainty. Nothing like a temple has been found in the less imposing remains from the later Iron Age; however, there must have been some continuation of the city's old religious traditions.

Political Life in Israel. First Kings 12:25 indicates that Jeroboam dwelt in Shechem and then went out from there and fortified Penuel. Tirzah, a few miles northeast of Shechem, is mentioned as the royal residence in 14:17, however, and apparently served as the capital until Omri moved to Samaria. Tirzah may have been the seat of government from the beginning, with such texts as 12:25 meaning only that the kings resided in various cities such as Shechem and Penuel while overseeing construction work (compare 15:17 and 21).

The dynastic instability in Israel is well illustrated by the first four kings. Two of these kings (Jeroboam and Baasha) were usurpers for all practical purposes. Emerging with prophetic and, one would assume, popular support, they seized the throne in spite of the credentials of their predecessors. They are credited with reigns of twenty-two and twenty-four years, respectively.[22] The other two, Nadab and Elah, sons of Jeroboam and Baasha, respectively, ascended the throne by virtue of dynastic inheritance but were quickly assassinated and their families massacred.

Nadab had ruled only two years when he was put to death by Baasha from the tribe of Issachar. Baasha's coup occurred, we are told, while "all Israel" (the generally mustered army?) was laying siege to Gibbethon of the Philistines. This suggests that the coup was supported, if not initiated, by the troops in the field. Elah, on the other hand, was still in his second year of reign when Zimri, a commander in the Israelite chariot corps, rose up against him. Zimri immediately encountered serious difficulties of his own, as we shall see below.

Jeroboam had been designated for the throne and was subsequently denounced by the prophet Ahijah of Shiloh. Baasha was first supported, it seems, and then denounced by the prophet Jehu son of Hanani (1 Kgs. 16:1–14). Both prophetic denunciations, although perhaps heavily edited in their present forms, are violent pronouncements of judgment that call for regicide and massacre of the reigning families without benefit of burial: "Anyone belonging to . . . who dies in the city the dogs shall eat; and anyone who dies in the open country, the birds of the air shall eat." No doubt these daring and stern pronouncements contributed to, if they did not trigger, the ensuing conspiracies (compare 14:10–16; 15:27; 16:1–4, 9).

Shishak's Invasion

In the fifth year of the reign of Rehoboam (922–921 B.C.E.), according to 1 Kings 14:25–28 and 2 Chronicles 12:1–12, Pharaoh Shishak of Egypt invaded Palestine.[23] Rehoboam offered no resistance, according to the biblical account. In fact, the

22. Apparently Baasha also abdicated the throne, in his twenty-second year. (1) According to 1 Kgs. 16:8, Elah his son began to reign in Asa's twenty-sixth year (881–880 B.C.E.). Zimri put Elah to death in Asa's twenty-seventh year (1 Kgs. 16:10). These facts suggest that his two years overlapped the twenty-four assigned to Baasha. (2) In 16:3, 7, 8–13, Zimri is said to have killed off Baasha and his house, implying that Baasha was still living at the time Elah was killed (see, however, 16:6).

23. The dates of Egyptian rulers for the time are somewhat uncertain and Shishak's relief is not dated, though his campaign probably occurred late in his reign.

Chronicler describes Shishak's invasion as divine punishment for Rehoboam's apostasy and has the prophet Shemaiah instructing Rehoboam to submit.

As already noted, Shishak is to be equated with Sheshonq, a Libyan and founder of the Twenty-second Egyptian Dynasty. Sheshonq's capital was Bubastis in the Nile Delta, but Thebes was still an important city. Following the lead of the great pharaohs of Dynasties 19 and 20, therefore, Sheshonq adorned a section of the wall of the great temple of Amun at Thebes with a battle scene and an inscription commemorating his military exploits. The inscription includes a list of distant places that Sheshonq claims to have conquered. Some of the place names are no longer legible, and of those that are, only about twenty can be identified geographically with reasonable certainty. There is no doubt that the inscription pertains to a Palestinian campaign. Less clear is whether the place names are listed in any consistent geographical order.

Contrary to what one might suppose from the biblical record, moreover, the place names recorded seem to indicate that Israel rather than Judah received the main thrust of Sheshonq's military action. Megiddo is among the northern cities listed, and a fragment of a stela left by Sheshonq indicates the presence of the Egyptian army at the site. Sheshonq seems virtually to have bypassed Judah, presumably because Rehoboam chose to ransom the kingdom with the temple treasury. Another reason may have been that the villages and towns of Judah were poorer and had less booty to offer than those of Israel.

Sheshonq's invasion was probably a blitzkrieg affair intended to give stature to his regime, collect booty, and perhaps reassert Egyptian influence on Arabian trade. No doubt his campaign wreaked havoc in the area and demonstrated how vulnerable the Palestinian kingdoms were to outside invasion. Sheshonq's expedition probably had little lasting impact, however, certainly not in terms of continuing Egyptian domination of Palestine. Destruction layers at numerous sites—Gezer, Megiddo, and Beth-shean, for example—have been attributed to Sheshonq's invasion, but one can never be sure of such associations. Many of the cities that fell to Sheshonq may have submitted without a fight, as apparently did Jerusalem. Indeed, that he erected a victory stela at Megiddo suggests that he may not have destroyed the city.

The Chronicler reports one further international incident during this period: a battle between Asa and Zerah the Cushite (or Ethiopian) (2 Chr. 14:9–15). This is another of the Chronicler's stories that may be based on some historical event but that is presented in such midrashic form that the historian hardly knows what to do with it. Zerah is unknown from any other ancient source. The figures describing the Cushite force—one million men and three hundred chariots—are as weird as they are exaggerated. Whatever Zerah's Ethiopian connection, the incident seems at most to have involved frontier raiding between Judah and certain inhabitants of the western Negeb.

Conflicts between the Kingdoms

When 1 Kings 14:30 reports that "there was war between Rehoboam and Jeroboam continually," this does not necessarily mean that there was constant open warfare between the two kings. More likely one should think in terms of a general state of hostilities with occasional frontier skirmishes. First Kings 12:21–33 suggests that Rehoboam put aside any thought of recovering the north, while Jeroboam's policies are said to have been designed to halt religious traffic between his newly established kingdom and Jerusalem, with no apparent thought of invading Judah. After all, both kings had Sheshonq to deal with, first his invasion and then their recovery. At the most, then, we can presume that minor skirmishes occurred along the frontier between the two kingdoms—which itself was probably an ill-defined zone between Bethel and Jerusalem.

The same condition would have continued during Abijam's brief rule, even though the Chronicler recounts a major battle between Abijam and Jeroboam that supposedly ended in an overwhelming Judean victory (2 Chr. 13). If there is any historical kernel to the Chronicler's story about the battle, it probably concerned a border skirmish around Bethel, Jeshanah, and Ephron, the last two places probably near or just north of Bethel. Moreover, this would have been only a temporary Judean success. Note that Asa, who followed Abijam, was hard-pressed to defend a frontier in the area of Mizpah and Geba—only about ten miles north of Jerusalem (1 Kgs. 15:22).

The account of the military conflict between Asa and Baasha, which came to involve also King Ben-hadad of Damascus, has a much more authentic ring and represents a step beyond a border skirmish (1 Kgs. 15:16–22; 2 Chr. 16:1–6). The Israelite king Baasha initiated the incident, we are told, when he undertook to fortify Ramah (present-day er-Ram), "to prevent anyone from going out or coming in to King Asa of Judah" (1 Kgs. 15:17). This was not just an attempt to halt religious traffic between Israel and Jerusalem, which the editors present as Jeroboam's concern and which the Chronicler would have us believe reached mammoth proportions under Asa (2 Chr. 15:9–10). A military garrison based at a fortified Ramah could also control commercial traffic into Jerusalem from the west, via the Aijalon Valley, and would pose a constant threat to the Judean capital itself. Asa was fully aware that, with Israelite forces in Ramah, troubles were at Jerusalem's door. (See Map 24.)

Asa appealed to Ben-hadad of Syria, who at that point was allied with Baasha. The Judean king wanted Ben-hadad to break the Syro-Israelite alliance and to apply military pressure to Israel's northern flank, thus forcing Baasha to withdraw troops from the Judah-Israel frontier. Encouraged by gifts, Ben-hadad broke with Baasha, moved against Israel's northern frontier, and "conquered Ijon, Dan, Abel-beth-maacah, and all Chinneroth, with all the land of Naphtali" (1 Kgs. 15:20).[24] The three towns noted here were all located along the upper reaches of the Jordan River between the southern slopes of the Lebanon and Anti-Lebanon mountains. Meanwhile Asa pushed northward from Jerusalem, dismantled Ramah, and used the building materials to fortify Mizpah and Geba. The last two sites, probably to be identified with present-day Tell en-Nasbeh and Jeba, would have been obvious positions for fortification.

---

24. For attempts to associate some destruction levels at northern sites with Ben-hadad's attack, see Amnon Ben-Tor and Dvor Ben-Ami, "Hazor and the Archaeology of the Tenth Century B.C.E.," *IEJ* 48 (1998) 1–37.

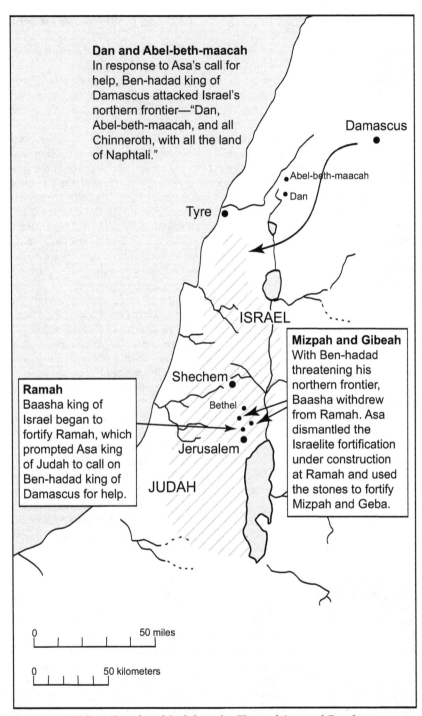

Dan and Abel-beth-maacah
In response to Asa's call for help, Ben-hadad king of Damascus attacked Israel's northern frontier—"Dan, Abel-beth-maacah, and all Chinneroth, with all the land of Naphtali."

Damascus

Abel-beth-maacah

Dan

Tyre

ISRAEL

Mizpah and Gibeah
With Ben-hadad threatening his northern frontier, Baasha withdrew from Ramah. Asa dismantled the Israelite fortification under construction at Ramah and used the stones to fortify Mizpah and Geba.

Shechem

Bethel

Ramah
Baasha king of Israel began to fortify Ramah, which prompted Asa king of Judah to call on Ben-hadad king of Damascus for help.

Jerusalem

JUDAH

0   50 miles

0   50 kilometers

MAP 24. Israel and Judah at the Time of Asa and Baasha

Mizpah protected Jerusalem from Israelite advancement along the main north-south watershed road through the central hill country and also guarded the route leading westward to the Mediterranean Sea. Geba guarded the only easy crossing of the Wadi es-Suweinit northeast of Jerusalem—that is, the second main route along which an army could advance on Jerusalem from the north (cf. Isa. 10:27b–32; see above, Map 13).

The affair between Asa, Baasha, and Ben-hadad raises the issue of the overall territorial extent of the two kingdoms during this early phase of mutual hostilities and their relationships with neighboring states. The domain of the first three Judean kings is perhaps best indicated by the spread of the Levitical cities, augmented now by Rehoboam's "cities of defense." Basically, they ruled over Jerusalem, the surrounding vicinity, and the southern hill country. Note that Asa's battle with Zerah the Ethiopian supposedly occurred near Mareshah, less than thirty miles southwest of Jerusalem. The sanctuary cities of Dan and Bethel represented the approximate northern and southern limits of the northern kingdom, while Penuel across the Jordan represented Israel's foothold among the Ephraim/Israel clans and villages in that area.

The Philistines, who apparently had remained independent under the shadow of David and Solomon, reemerged now as a constant threat. Two texts refer to battles between the Israelites and the Philistines at Gibbethon on the Philistine frontier (1 Kgs. 15:27; 16:15). Northern Moab, the rolling plains surrounding Medeba, would be conquered by Omri during the coming years, which confirms that it was not under Israelite or Judean control at this time.

When Asa of Judah sought the aid of Ben-hadad of Damascus against Baasha of Israel, he is reported to have alluded to a prior treaty between his own father and Ben-hadad's father. If this is to be taken literally, along with information provided earlier in the Genesis–2 Kings History about relations between Solomon and the kings of Damascus, one must assume several reversals in the foreign relations between Judah and Damascus—a state of hostility between Rezon and Solomon (1 Kgs. 11:23–25), followed by a Jerusalem-Damascus alliance negotiated by Abijam and Tabrimmon (the fathers of Asa and Ben-hadad, respectively), a collapse of this alliance in deference to an Israel-Damascus alliance that was in effect when Baasha began to build Ramah, and now a reinstatement of the Jerusalem-Damascus pact (1 Kgs. 15:19; 2 Chr. 16:3). Perhaps the references to "my father" and "your father" in 1 Kings 15:19 should be taken as merely formulaic language, in which case the following, less dramatic, scenario presents itself. Rezon, Solomon's old enemy, would have been pleased, no doubt, with the course of affairs following Solomon's death. Indeed, he may have encouraged the rebellion that broke out at Shechem and have stood ready to come to Israel's aid had Rehoboam decided to take military action. Within this context the Syro-Israelite alliance would have been formed, and probably provided the basis for good relations between Israel and Damascus through the early years of Baasha's reign. Under Baasha, however, the situation may have begun to change. Israel was on its feet now and posed a potentially more serious threat to Damascus than did Judah. Thus, when Asa offered to pay Ben-hadad to apply pressure on Israel's northern frontier, Ben-hadad may have needed little urging.

General Bibliography

Several works focus on Jeroboam and the division of the kingdom: see W. I. Toews, *Monarchy and Religious Institutions under Jeroboam I* (SBLMS 47; Atlanta: Scholars Press, 1993); and Roland Boer, *Jameson and Jeroboam* (Semeia Studies; Atlanta: Scholars Press, 1996). Literary and other issues are treated in G. N. Knoppers, *Two Nations under God: The Deuteronomistic History of Solomon and the Dual Monarchies* (2 vols.; HSM 52–53; Atlanta: Scholars Press, 1993), which treats the reign of Solomon, the rise of Jeroboam, and the reign of Jeroboam. Early Israelite relations with Damascus are discussed in W. T. Pitard, *Ancient Damascus: A Historical Study of the Syrian City-State from Earliest Times until Its Fall to the Assyrians in 732 B.C.E.* (Winona Lake, IN: Eisenbrauns, 1987), esp. 107–14.

On the role of Shechem in north-central highland politics, see Israel Finkelstein and Nadav Na'aman, "Shechem of the Amarna Period and the Rise of the Northern Kingdom of Israel," *IEJ* 55 (2005) 172–93.

The treatment of Jeroboam and northern kingship in the various biblical sources is discussed in Mark Leuchter, "Jeroboam the Ephratite," *JBL* 125 (2006) 51–72.

10. The Omride Era

The ninth century witnessed a major revival of political and economic activity throughout Mesopotamia and the eastern Mediterranean. After some decades of slow progress and economic-political stability, Assyria once again became a dominant power. The Assyrian king Ashurnasirpal II (883–859 B.C.E.)[1] was the first major ruler of what is known as the "Neo-Assyrian" period, which lasted until the last years of the seventh century. Ashurnasirpal undertook extensive building projects in Assyria and conducted numerous military campaigns. On several occasions he and his army crossed the Euphrates and campaigned throughout northern Syria and Phoenicia, receiving gifts of tribute from several rulers in the region. The following is from one of his inscriptions describing events of the year 878–877:

> At that time I made my way to the slopes of Mount Lebanon and went up to the Great Sea of the land Amurru [the Mediterranean]. I cleansed my weapons in the Great Sea and made sacrifices to the gods. I received tribute from the kings of the sea coast, from the lands of the people of Tyre, Sidon, Byblos, Mahallatu, Maizu, Kaizu, Amurru, and the city Arvad which is (on an island) in the sea—silver, gold, tin, bronze, a bronze casserole, linen garments with multi-coloured trim, a large female monkey, a small female monkey, ebony, boxwood, ivory. . . . They submitted to me. I climbed up to Mount Amanus and cut down logs of cedar, cypress, juniper. . . . I made a memorial to my valour and erected it therein. (RIMA 2:218–19)

The extensive building projects of Ashurnasirpal and his successors required not only finances and building materials (especially timber, almost totally absent from Mesopotamia proper) but also laborers. In his account of the rebuilding of the city of Calah, the king noted:

> The ancient city . . . had become dilapidated; it lay dormant. I rebuilt that city. I took people which I had conquered from the lands over which I had gained dominion, from the land Suhu, the city Sirqua, which is at the crossing of the Euphrates, the entire land Laqu, the entire land of Zamua, from Bit-Adini and the land Hatti, and from Liburna, the Patinu. I settled them therein. (RIMA 2:227)[2]

---

1. Dates given for Assyrian kings are those of their regnal years, which were calculated beginning with the first New Year Festival of their reign. In Assyria and Babylonia this fell in the spring month of Nisan (March–April). When a king succeeded to the throne prior to Nisan, this period of his rule was considered the accession year (year 0) and was not calculated in the number of years of his reign.

2. The nature and extent of Assyrian deportation of foreigners are described in Bustenay Oded, *Mass Deportations and Deportees in the Neo-Assyrian Empire* (Wiesbaden: Reichert, 1979). The center of the

Some conquered territories were placed under direct Assyrian control: "In the lands over which I gained dominion I always appointed my governors. They performed servitude and I imposed upon them corvée" (RIMA 2:222).

The needs, appetites, and splendor of the Assyrian court and the demands it placed upon subject states can be seen in Ashurnasirpal's account of the dedication of his new palace in Calah. He notes that thousands of fat oxen, calves, sheep, lambs, deer, ducks, geese, other birds, and fish, as well as thousands of skins of wine, and containers of grains, fruits, and vegetables, were consumed in the celebrations (see RIMA 2:292–93). The following concerns the guest list:

> When I consecrated the palace of Calah, 47,074 men and women who were invited from every part of my land, 5,000 dignitaries and envoys of the lands Suhu, Hindanu, Patinu, Hatti, Tyre, Sidon, Gurgumu, Malidu, Hubushkia, Gilzanu, Kummu, and Musasiru, 16,000 people of Calah, and 1500 *zariqu* of my palace, all of them—altogether 69,574 including those summoned from all the lands and the people of Calah—for ten days I gave them food, I gave them drink, I had them bathed, I had them anointed. Thus did I honor them and send them back to their lands in peace and joy. (RIMA 2:293)

In addition to noting the campaigns and conquests, receipt of gifts, exploitation of conquered lands, deportation of foreigners, and extensive building projects in the homeland, his texts also refer frequently to the brutality of his actions against non-Assyrians: the flaying of captives, the gouging out of eyes, the piling up of human heads, the massacring of the common population, and the looting, razing, and burning of conquered towns. From the time of the reign of Ashurnasirpal, the kingdoms of Syria-Palestine would live for over two and a half centuries under the shadow of the Assyrians and the threat of their exploitive and oppressive policies.

Along with the resurgence of Assyria, with its appetite for wealth and power, the ninth century also witnessed the political and economic development of significant monarchial states in Syria-Palestine. Among these were kingdoms centered around such cities as Arpad and Carchemish in the north, Hamath in central Syria, the Phoenician ports of Arvad and Tyre on the coast, and Damascus and Samaria in the south.[3]

According to the biblical narratives (2 Kgs. 16:8–22), Omri,[4] a contemporary of King Ashurnasirpal of Assyria, became king of Israel during a period of major civil strife. Whether this social unrest may have in some way been triggered by the trauma of Assyrian resurgence cannot be determined. Zimri, a commander in Israel's chariotry, assassinated Elah of the house of Baasha while the latter was participating in a drinking bout. This was the second occasion on which an Israelite king had succeeded his father to the throne according

---

empire Assyria proper, put constant economic, personnel, and material demands on peripheral states; see Michael Rowlands et al., eds., *Centre and Periphery in the Ancient World* (New Directions in Archaeology; Cambridge: Cambridge University Press, 1987); and J. N. Postgate, *Taxation and Conscription in the Assyrian Empire* (Studia Pohl, Series Major 3; Rome: Pontifical Biblical Institute, 1974).

3. At the time, Arpad, Carchemish, and Hamath were still ruled by dynasties of Anatolian (or neo-Hittite) origin and produced inscriptions written in hieroglyphic Luwian.

4. The name "Omri" is an unusual Hebrew form, which has led scholars to assume he may have been of Arabic or Phoenician background; see J. K. Kuan, "Was Omri a Phoenician?" in M. P. Graham et al., eds., *History and Interpretation: Essays in Honour of John H. Hayes* (JSOTSup 173; Sheffield: Sheffield Academic Press, 1993) 231–44.

to dynastic succession only to be put to death shortly thereafter. Zimri was unable to hold the throne and ruled for only seven days. The army commander Omri was acclaimed king by his troops and attacked Zimri in the capital city, Tirzah. Zimri burned the palace down upon himself in a suicidal defiance. Israelites then split into two factions, one supporting Omri and the other backing (the otherwise unknown) Tibni. Four years of civil strife ensued before Omri emerged as the unchallenged ruler. The biblical text provides no overt clue as to the internal causes of this national conflict. One can only speculate that it may have involved different elements in the military—perhaps the general militia versus the chariot forces.

Omri and his house ruled for almost three decades and were the first Israelite royal family to achieve dynastic succession beyond the second generation. Under Omri and his son Ahab, Israel enjoyed a prosperity probably unexcelled in the kingdom's history and became a major participant in Syro-Palestinian politics. During the period, Judah under King Jehoshaphat became, for all practical purposes, a vassal to the northern kingdom but shared in the benefits of Omride rule.

Sources for the Period and Their Problems

Information relevant to the Omride era derives from the Hebrew Bible, ancient inscriptions, and archaeology. The most important inscriptions date from the reigns of King Mesha of Moab and King Shalmaneser III of Assyria. The key archaeological sites for understanding this period are Hazor, Jezreel, Megiddo, and Samaria. The Genesis–2 Kings History and the Chronicler's History continue as the main biblical sources. Specifically, 1 Kings 16:15–2 Kings 8:27 and 2 Chronicles 17–20 pertain to the Omride kings.

The Omride Era as Presented in 1–2 Kings

In terms of its literary structure, the 1–2 Kings presentation of the Omride era consists of the usual summations of the kings' reigns, a number of prophetical narratives that the compilers introduced into the summaries at points where they regarded them as relevant, and the account of Jehu's coup (2 Kgs. 9:1–10:31) with which they concluded their treatment of the Omride era.

Summations of the Kings' Reigns. The perspective of the compilers is to be seen most clearly in their summations of the reigns of the individual kings (1 Kgs. 16:21–34; 22:39–53; 2 Kgs. 1:1, 17–18; 3:1–3; 8:16–29). The most important point to be made about the Omrides, in their opinion, especially Ahab, was that these rulers patronized the worship of the god Baal to an unprecedented degree. The very idea that the Omrides might have been successful monarchs conflicted with one of the main theological principles that the compilers wished to illustrate in Genesis–2 Kings—that Yahweh granted success only to those rulers who remained faithful to him and gave exclusive support to the Yahwistic cult in Jerusalem. No achievements are recorded for the Omrides, therefore, except for the notations that Omri founded the city of Samaria (1 Kgs. 16:24) and that Ahab's projects included "the ivory house that he built, and all the cities that he built" (22:39). One would conclude from the summa-

CHART 15. The Omride Era

Asa (906–878 [886])

Nadab (905–904)
Baasha (903–882 [880])
Elah (881–880)
Omri (879–869)

Jehoshaphat (877–853)	Ahab (868–854)		Ashurnasirpal (883–859)
		Hadadezer (?–?)	Shalmaneser III* (858–824)
	Ahaziah (853–852)		
Jehoram (852–841)			
	Jehoram (851–840)		
Ahaziah (840)	Jehu (839–822)	Hazael (ca. 843–?)	
Athaliah (839–833)			

*Shalmaneser conducted military campaigns into Syria-Palestine in 853, 849, 848, 845, 841, and 838 B.C.E. His inscriptions mention Ahab and Hadadezer in connection with the 853 campaign, Jehu and Hazael in connection with the 841 campaign.

---

tion of Jehoshaphat's reign that he too was a second-rate ruler with no successes worthy of mention. He is reported only to have continued Asa's policies regarding cultic matters, "made peace with the king of Israel," and failed in a maritime venture (22:41–50).

The Prophetical Narratives. Most of the material in the Omride section of 1–2 Kings consists of narratives that apparently circulated independently before being incorporated into the Genesis–2 Kings account and that, at least in their present form, focus on the deeds of Yahwistic prophets. These prophetical narratives may be classified into the following groupings (see also Chart 16):

The Elijah Stories (1 Kgs. 17–19; 2 Kgs. 1:2–16)
The Stories of Three Battles with the Syrian King Ben-hadad (1 Kgs. 20; 22:1–38)
The Naboth Vineyard Story (1 Kgs. 21)
The Elisha Stories (2 Kgs. 2; 4:1–8:15)
The Story of Jehoram's Moabite Campaign (2 Kgs. 3:4–27)

These prophetical narratives, especially the Elijah and Elisha stories, abound with folk themes and describe miraculous circumstances that modern historians find difficult to accept—a jar of meal and a cruse of oil that never emptied (1 Kgs. 17:8–16); fire from above that consumed Elijah's offering, the wood and stone of the altar, and even the dust and water surrounding the altar (1 Kgs. 18:30–40); the Syrian general whose skin ailment[5] was cured when he bathed in the Jordan (2 Kgs. 5); and so on. Since these narratives are primarily interested

5. It is now widely recognized that leprosy (Hansen's Disease) was not known in ancient Israel (see Modern Bible Dictionary entries). The Hebrew term *tsara'ath*, usually translated "leprosy," covered a wide variety of skin afflictions.

in the deeds of the prophets, they provide few tangible details that are not related directly to the prophets' actions. The king or kings of Israel are rarely identified by name in the Elisha stories and in the accounts of the three battles with Ben-hadad; and the references were probably entirely anonymous at an earlier stage in the transmission of these materials. For the historian's purposes, therefore, perhaps the most one can expect to learn from these prophetical narratives is something of the general social, religious, and political circumstances of the time from which they come. Particularly noteworthy in this regard, as we shall see in more detail below, the narrative groupings do not all presuppose a background of the same historical circumstances. The Elijah stories, for example, presuppose a time in which the kings of Israel ruled supreme from Samaria, the royal family was closely associated with Baalism, and there was sharp conflict between the royal family and the Yahwistic prophets. The Elisha stories and the stories of the three battles with Ben-hadad, on the other hand, depict the kings of Israel as international weaklings hard-pressed to defend Samaria from the Syrians, yet strong supporters of Yahwism and on good terms with the Yahwistic prophets.[6]

Some of these prophetical narratives show evidence of having been modified and expanded during the process of transmission. This is particularly true of the stories of the three battles with Ben-hadad and the story of Jehoram's Moabite campaign. Close analysis reveals essentially three stages in the process of their transmission. (1) At the first stage, these narratives appear to have been straightforward battle reports: three battles in which the king of Israel challenged Ben-hadad of Syria, and one in which Jehoram attempted to restore Israelite control over Moab. (2) Later these battle reports were expanded to give Yahwistic prophets center stage. An anonymous prophet predicted success for the king of Israel's challenge to Syria, provided the strategy for the first two battles, and then (another prophet?) denounced the king of Israel for allowing Ben-hadad to live and predicted that the king of Israel would pay with his own life (1 Kgs. 20:13–43). The prophet Micaiah repeated this prediction as the king of Israel made ready for the third battle against Syria, and the prediction was fulfilled when the king of Israel was killed in the third battle (1 Kgs. 22:13–36). As Jehoram's army approached Moab, it found itself without water and thus facing certain defeat. Elisha entered the story at that point and saved the day (2 Kgs. 3:9–27). (3) Finally, probably after these narratives had found their way into Judean hands, the two battle stories that involved the king of Judah were modified still further. Specifically, the king of Judah who appears in the third of the stories of the three battles with Ben-hadad (that is, the story of the Ramoth-gilead campaign; 1 Kgs. 22:1–38) and in the story of Jehoram's Moabite campaign (2 Kgs. 3:4–27) was identified as Jehoshaphat, and both stories were expanded to emphasize Jehoshaphat's loyalty to Yahwism.

There is reason to doubt that some of these prophetical narratives pertain to the Omride period at all. The Elisha stories and the stories of the three battles with Ben-hadad presuppose social, religious, and political circumstances quite different from the Elijah stories. This contrast will become even more apparent

6. For further analysis of these biblical sources, see J. M. Miller, "The Elisha Cycle and the Accounts of the Omride Wars," *JBL* 85 (1966) 441–54; idem, "The Rest of the Acts of Jehoahaz (I Kings 20; 22:1–38)," *ZAW* 80 (1968) 337–42.

as we explore the other sources of information for the Omride era. The best explanation for this situation, in our opinion, is that the stories of the three battles with Ben-hadad and the Elisha stories pertain to circumstances and events of a later period. We will return to this matter below.

The Naboth vineyard story is of a character different from the other narratives discussed above.[7] In contrast to the Elijah stories, for example, which presuppose that the reader will be familiar with Elijah, Ahab, and Jezebel, the Naboth vineyard story carefully introduces each of these figures as if they belong to a distant time and place. Also, the Naboth affair as recounted in this story does not square exactly with a reference to the incident in the account of Jehu's coup. According to the latter account, after assassinating Jehoram, Jehu said to Bidkar his aid:

> Lift him up, and throw him on the plot of ground belonging to Naboth the Jezreelite; for remember, when you and I rode side by side behind his father Ahab how Yahweh uttered this oracle against him: "For the blood of Naboth and for the blood of his children that I saw yesterday, says Yahweh, I swear I will repay you on this very plot of ground." Now therefore lift him out and throw him on the plot of ground, in accordance with the word of Yahweh. (2 Kgs. 9:25–26)

The Omride Era according to the Chronicler

The Chronicler, having no interest in Israelite affairs, mentions the Omrides only when they figure in the treatment of Jehoshaphat: (1) The first deed that the Chronicler records for Jehoshaphat is that he "strengthened himself against Israel" (2 Chr. 17:1). (2) The third of the stories of the three battles with Ben-hadad (that is, the account of the Ramoth-gilead campaign in 1 Kgs. 22:1–38) is repeated but expanded to give it a different context (a wedding feast), to emphasize Jehoshaphat's riches and honor, and to censure Jehoshaphat for having dealings with the wicked Israelite king (2 Chr. 18:1–19:3). (3) The brief report of Jehoshaphat's unsuccessful maritime venture in 1 Kings 22:47–50 is repeated also, but restated to say that Jehoshaphat *did* take Ahaziah on as a partner in the venture and that this in itself was the reason that the venture failed (2 Chr. 20:35–37). (4) Jehoram, who succeeded Jehoshaphat to the throne of Judah, is depicted as a wicked king whose wickedness derived from his Omride connection: "He walked in the way of the kings of Israel, as the house of Ahab had done; for the daughter of Ahab was his wife" (2 Chr. 21:6).

Otherwise the Chronicler elaborates extensively on the reigns of both Jehoshaphat and Jehoram, depicting the former as one of the truly great kings of Judah and the latter as totally unsuccessful. Jehoshaphat is depicted as loyal to Yahweh—walking "in the earlier ways of his father" Asa (2 Chr. 17:3). He sent princes and Levites to teach "in Judah, having the book of the law of Yahweh with them" (17:9). He had "great riches and honor" (17:5; 18:1), built fortresses and store-cities, and had abundant stores in the cities (17:12–13a). His

---

7. In addition to the commentaries on 1 Kgs. 21, see F. I. Andersen, "The Socio-Juridical Background of the Naboth Incident," *JBL* 85 (1966) 46–57; and Alexander Rofé, "The Vineyard of Naboth: the Origin and Message of the Story," *VT* 38 (1988) 89–104.

CHART 16. Prophetical Narratives Associated with the Omride Era

The Elijah Stories (1 Kgs. 17–19; 2 Kgs. 1:2–16)

A recounting of the deeds of Elijah from Tishbi (in northern Transjordan), who opposed, among other things, Omride patronage of Baalism. Ahab is depicted as an autocratic ruler; but Jezebel is the chief villain in the stories because of her active support of Baalism and persecution of the Yahwistic prophets. These are folk stories that abound with miraculous scenes.

The Stories of the Three Battles with Ben-hadad (1 Kgs. 20; 22:1–38)

A recounting of a sequence of three battles between a king of Israel and Ben-hadad of Damascus. The first account describes how the king of Israel successfully defended Samaria against Ben-hadad's attack (20:1–25). The second describes how the king of Israel and his pitifully small army defeated Ben-hadad's army at Aphek (20:26–43). The third describes a campaign initiated by the king of Israel to restore Israelite control over Ramoth-gilead (22:1–38). These narratives show evidence of having been modified during the process of transmission. At an earlier stage of their telling, both the king of Israel and the king of Judah (who appears only in the third battle) were probably anonymous. In their present form, and in keeping with their present context, the two kings are identified as Ahab and Jehoshaphat, respectively. Both identifications are problematic. These three accounts seem to belong to the same setting as the Elisha stories—that is, to the later period of the Jehu dynasty.

The Naboth Vineyard Story (1 Kgs. 21)

While most of the Elijah stories are typical folktales, the Naboth vineyard story seems to be more on the order of historical fiction. The three most colorful characters of the Omride period and one of the most memorable events of the era have been worked together into a story that probably bears little resemblance to the actual circumstances of the Naboth incident. Note that the account of Jehu's coup seems to place the Naboth incident soon before the coup—that is, during Jehoram's reign (2 Kgs. 9:25–26).

The Elisha Stories (2 Kgs. 2; 4:1–8:15)

A recounting of the deeds of another Yahwistic prophet from Transjordan (Abel-meholah) who was the recognized successor to Elijah. Elisha is remembered for the same sort of miraculous deeds as Elijah. In fact, some of the same deeds are credited to both. Yet these Elisha stories reflect a situation quite different from the Elijah stories: the Elisha stories presuppose close, positive relations between the "king of Israel" and the Yahwist Elisha. There are no references to Jezebel or to a Yahwism-Baalism conflict. Also, these stories presuppose a political situation in which the king of Israel is dominated by Ben-hadad of Damascus. The compilers of Genesis–2 Kings placed these Elisha stories in the context of the reign of Jehoram of Israel, which implies that Jehoram was the "king of Israel" who figures in them. More likely, they belong to the post-Omride period, and the anonymous king of Israel who appears in them was one of the rulers of the Jehu dynasty. Note that a concluding story which reports Elisha's death does appear in this latter context—that is, during the reign of Joash, Jehu's grandson (2 Kgs. 13:14–19).

The Story of Jehoram's Moabite Campaign (2 Kgs. 3:4–27)
This narrative shows striking similarities to the third of the stories about the three battles with Ben-hadad—that is, the story of the Ramoth-gilead campaign (1 Kgs. 22:1–38). (1) It seems to have undergone modifications during the process of transmission. Specifically, the story has been recast to give a Yahwistic prophet (Elisha in this case) and the king of Judah a prominent role. (2) The king of Judah has been identified, again secondarily and probably incorrectly, as Jehoshaphat. (3) Finally, the story as it stands now emphasizes Jehoshaphat's piety in contrast to that of Jehoram—specifically Jehoshaphat is depicted again, as in the Ramoth-gilead story, insisting that a Yahwistic prophet be consulted before proceeding with the campaign.

---

impressive wealth came not only from Judean tribute (17:5) but also from surrounding peoples (Philistines, Arabs; 17:11). He appointed judges throughout the land with instructions to judge "not on behalf of human beings but on Yahweh's behalf" (19:4–7), and designated certain priests and Levites in Jerusalem to make decisions in disputed cases (19:8–11). "He had soldiers, mighty warriors, in Jerusalem," numbering some 1,160,000 (17:13b–19), plus soldiers garrisoned at fortified cities throughout the land (17:2, 19).

These mighty men of valor, however, seem to fade into the background in the one battle scene reported by the Chronicler for Jehoshaphat's reign (that is, aside from the Chronicler's revised rendition of the Ramoth-gilead campaign). Jehoshaphat, we are told, overwhelmed with great fear when a coalition of Ammonites, Moabites, and men from Mount Seir marched on Jerusalem, assembled all Judah for fasting and prayer to Yahweh. The day was saved, as it turned out, without any need of an army. Yahweh set an ambush against the enemy so that they began to fight among themselves and completely destroyed one another. None escaped (2 Chr. 20:24). Clearly the Chronicler had led us deep into the realm of midrash.

Royal Inscriptions of Moab, Assyria, and Syria

The Mesha Inscription. Also called the Moabite Stone, this commemorative stela was discovered in 1868 near the ruins of ancient Dibon (present-day Dhiban, east of the Dead Sea).[8] The inscription appears on a large freestanding basalt column carved to contain the text. The stela represents one of the first royal inscriptions set up by Syro-Palestinian kings, probably in imitation of the practice of Assyrian monarchs. Unfortunately the stela was broken to pieces soon after its discovery, but later was reconstructed almost completely and the inscription can be translated with only a few uncertainties (see Text 4). One

---

8. On the Moabite Stone see J. M. Miller, "The Moabite Stone as a Memorial Stela," *PEQ* 106 (1974) 9–18; J. A. Dearman, ed., *Studies in the Mesha Inscription and Moab* (SBLABS 2; Atlanta: Scholars Press, 1989); K. A. D. Smelik, "The Literary Structure of King Mesha's Inscription," *JSOT* 46 (1990) 21–30; and A. F. Rainey, "Mesha' and Syntax," in J. A. Dearman and M. P. Graham, eds., *The Land that I Will Show You: Essays on the History and Archaeology of the Ancient Near East in Honour of J. Maxwell Miller* (JSOTSup 343; Sheffield: Sheffield Academic Press, 2001) 287–307.

learns from the content of the inscription that the stela was commissioned by King Mesha of Moab, apparently late in his reign and in connection with the dedication of a sanctuary to the Moabite god Chemosh. The text, looking back over Mesha's career, reports what he regarded to be the main accomplishments of his reign. He was especially proud of having brought Israelite dominance over Moab to an end and of recovering from Israel the Moabite territory north of the Arnon, that is, the plains surrounding the ancient city of Medeba.

Shalmaneser III's Inscriptions.[9] Assyrian texts from the reign of Shalmaneser III report military campaigns into Syria-Palestine for his sixth, tenth, eleventh, fourteenth, eighteenth, twenty-first, and twenty-second regnal years. It is possible, on the basis of the eponym lists (see above, p. 246), to calculate the dates of these campaigns as 853, 849, 848, 845, 841, 838, and 837 B.C.E., respectively. The first campaign (853 B.C.E.) is described in some detail in the so-called Monolith Inscription, engraved on a stela with the figure of Shalmaneser in relief, discovered in the mid-1800s (at Nimrud in present-day Iraq; see Text 3). The Monolith Inscription notes that a coalition of Syro-Palestinian kings fought against Shalmaneser and apparently halted his march in the vicinity of Qarqar, a city in northern Syria on the Orontes River. "Ahab the Israelite" is listed among the defending kings and is credited with deploying two thousand chariots in the battle. (See Map 25.)

The Monolith Inscription, composed fairly early in Shalmaneser's reign, does not cover his later western campaigns. For these we must turn to other inscriptions, especially the so-called Bull and Black Obelisk inscriptions (both discovered at Nimrud, ancient Calah, in 1845), which record Shalmaneser's deeds through his eighteenth and thirty-first years, respectively. The entries in these two inscriptions for Shalmaneser's next three western campaigns (849, 848, and 845 B.C.E.) are brief. Shalmaneser was apparently met again on each of these three campaigns by the same coalition of Syro-Palestinian kings, and while he claims to have achieved crushing victories, this seems unlikely, since he always turned back at the Orontes River rather than pushing farther south. Hadadezer of Damascus is mentioned by name in connection with the campaigns of 849, 848, and 845, but we can only speculate as to whether Jehoram, who would have been on the throne in Samaria during those years, continued to support the resistance.

The Black Obelisk provides our fullest report of Shalmaneser's 841 campaign (see Text 5). Apparently he reached Damascus with no serious opposition this time, ravaged the area around the city (but does not claim to have taken it), and then marched into northern Palestine, where he received tribute from Jehu and the Phoenician cities of Tyre and Sidon. The Black Obelisk is also the best source for Shalmaneser's 838 campaign, which of course takes us still farther beyond the Omride era.

The Tel Dan Inscription. Portions of an Aramaic inscription were discovered in the excavations at Tel Dan, site of ancient Dan (see Text 6 and Photograph 58). The inscription was erected by a Syrian king who claimed victory over Israel and the house of David.

9. All of Shalmaneser III's inscriptions are translated in A. K. Grayson, *Assyrian Rulers of the Early First Millennium BC, II (858–745 BC)* (RIMA 3; Toronto: University of Toronto Press, 1996) 5–179.

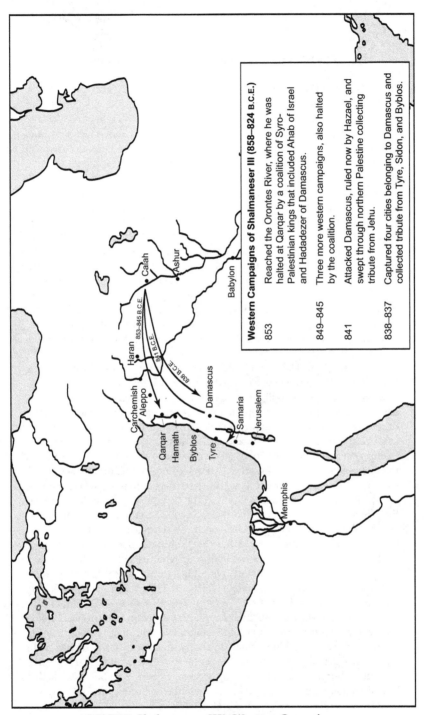

Western Campaigns of Shalmaneser III (858–824 B.C.E.)

853   Reached the Orontes River, where he was halted at Qarqar by a coalition of Syro-Palestinian kings that included Ahab of Israel and Hadadezer of Damascus.

849–845   Three more western campaigns, also halted by the coalition.

841   Attacked Damascus, ruled now by Hazael, and swept through northern Palestine collecting tribute from Jehu.

838–837   Captured four cities belonging to Damascus and collected tribute from Tyre, Sidon, and Byblos.

MAP 25. Shalmaneser III's Western Campaigns

TEXT 3. Excerpts from the Monolith Inscription

In the *limmu* of Dayan-Aššur [853–852], in the month of Iyyar [April–May],
the fourteenth day, I departed from Nineveh, crossed the Tigris and
approached the cities of Giammu on the river Balikh. They became afraid of
the terror of my sovereignty and the splendor of my fierce weapons, and
killed Giammu their master with their own weapons. I entered the towns of
Sahlala and Til-sa-Turahi, brought my gods into his palaces, and established
the *tasiltu*-festival in his palaces. I opened the treasury and saw his wealth. I
took as booty his possessions and his property and brought it to my city
Assur. I departed from Sahlala and approached Kar-Shalmaneser. I crossed
the Euphrates at its flood for the second time in goat-skin boats. The tribute
of the kings on the other side of the Euphrates—of Sangura the Carchem-
ishite, of Kundaspi the Kummuhite, of Arame the (A)gusite, of Lalli the
Melidean, of Hayani the Gabarite, of Qalpardua the Pattinean, and of Qal-
paruda the Gurgumite—silver, gold, tin, copper, and copper vessels, at
Assur-uttir-asbat, on the other side of the Euphrates, on the river Sagur,
which the people of Hatti call Pitru, I received. I departed from the Euphrates
and approached Halman (Aleppo). They were afraid to fight and seized my
feet. I received silver and gold as their tribute and offered sacrifices before the
god Adad of Halman.

I departed from Halman and approached the two cities of Irhulenu the
Hamathite and captured the cities of Adinnu and Barga, and Argana his royal
city. I brought out his spoil, his property, and the possessions of his palaces
and set fire to his palaces. I departed from Argana and approached Qarqar. I
destroyed, devastated, and burned with fire Qarqar his royal city. 1,200 chariots, 1,200 cavalry, and 20,000 soldiers of Adad-idri of the land of Imerisu
[Aram-Damascus], 700 chariots, 700 cavalry, and 10,000 soldiers of Irhulenu
the Hamathite, 2,000 chariots and 10,000 soldiers of Ahab the Israelite, 500
soldiers of the Gueans [or Byblians], 1,000 soldiers of the Musreans [or Egyp-
tians], 10 chariots and 10,000 soldiers of the Irqanateans, 200 of Matinu-ba'il
the Arwadite, 200 soldiers of the Usanateans, 30 chariots and soldiers and
10,000 soldiers of Adunu-ba'il the Sianean, 1,000 camels of Gindibu' the Arabian, [ ], 000 soldiers of Ba'sa the (Bit-)Ruhubite, the Ammonite—these
twelve kings he brought to his help. They marched against me for battle and
combat. I fought with them with the mighty forces which Assur, my lord,
gave me and the powerful weapons which Nergal, my leader, presented me.
I accomplished their defeat from Qarqar to Gilzau. I slew 14,000 of their soldiers with the sword. Like Adad, I rained destruction upon them. I made
their corpses sufficient and filled the entire plain with their wide spreading
armies. I made their blood flow down the *hur-pa-lu* of the district with
weapons. The plain was too small to let their bodies fall, the vast field was
used up in burying them. I spanned the Orontes with their bodies as with a
bridge. In that battle I took away from them their chariots, their cavalry, and
their horses broken to the yoke. (*NAHI* 30–31)

Archaeological Evidence

Corresponding to the extrabiblical records which indicate that the Omrides played a significant role in international affairs, the artifactual remains at key northern sites suggest an extensive post-Solomonic building phase, which must be dated approximately to the Omride era and no doubt is to be attributed to them. Chief among the sites to be considered in this regard are Samaria, Megiddo, Hazor, and Jezreel. Megiddo and Hazor along with Gezer were already discussed in chapter 7. There we noted some of the uncertainties and differing views among professional archaeologists regarding the dating of the Iron Age strata, that is, which stratum belongs to the Solomonic and which to the Omride era.

Samaria and Jezreel began to play a role in the biblical narratives only at the time of the Omrides. Samaria, modern Tell Sebastiyeh, lay in a strategic location in the heartland of the Ephraimite hill country. Located just west of the central watershed, Samaria was near the major east-west and north-south highways. To the east, roads led to Shechem and the Jordan Valley, to the west lay the coastal land and Phoenicia, to the north was Megiddo and the Jezreel Valley, and to the south was Jerusalem. Built on a hill rising about three hundred feet from the valley floor on the north, west, and south, the site sat atop the summit of a sloping ridge facing eastward. Extensive remains at the site, discussed below, can confidently be assigned to the Omride period.

Jezreel (Modern Zer'in), located on the northwestern slope of Mount Gilboa at the eastern end of the broad east-west Esdraelon Valley, lay in the territory of the tribe of Issachar (Josh. 19:18; 1 Sam. 29:1) and about ten miles east of Megiddo. The slightly elevated site commands a good view of the valley and enjoys a moderate temperature and cooling breezes, features that made it attractive for a royal residence. Excavations at the site in the 1990s uncovered the remains of a large "royal" enclosure surrounded by a casemate wall enclosing the top of the original hill. The enclosure provided a podium for what could have been an Omride palace. The remains and architectural features share some similarities with the remains from Samaria.

How the remains and stratigraphy from Samaria and Jezreel correlate with those from Megiddo, Hazor, and Gezer has become a subject of archaeological controversy. The Omride origin of Jezreel and Samaria materials remains unchallenged. Some of the Megiddo, Hazor, and Gezer remains, once universally assigned to the Solomonic period, have been reclassified by some archaeologists as Omride (see below).

Conflicts in the Sources

The General Political Circumstances of the Omride Period. One would conclude from the biblical summations of the reigns of the Omride kings, the Elijah stories, the account of Jehu's coup, the Mesha Inscription, and the Assyrian records that the Omrides (particularly Omri and Ahab) were relatively powerful kings who ruled over an independent kingdom. (1) The summary notes speak of their extensive building activities, marriage alliance with Phoenicia, and domination of Moab (see 1 Kgs. 16:24, 31; 22:39; 2 Kgs. 3:4). (2) The Elijah

TEXT 4. The Mesha Inscription

I am Mesha, son of Chemosh[yatti] king of Moab, the Dibonite. My father reigned over Moab thirty years and I reigned after my father. And I built this high place for Chemosh at Qarhoh [. . .] because he saved me from all the kings and caused me to triumph over all my adversaries. Omri, king of Israel, humbled Moab many days because Chemosh was angry at his land. And his son succeeded him, and he also said, "I too will humble Moab." In my days he said this, but I have triumphed over him and over his house and Israel has perished for ever. Omri had conquered the land of Medeba and he ruled over it during his days and half the days of his son, forty years, but Chemosh returned it in my days. And I built Baal-meon and I made in it a reservoir and I built Qaryaten.

And the men of Gad had dwelt in the land of Ataroth from of old and the king of Israel fortified Ataroth, but I fought against the town and took it. And I slaughtered all the people and the town became the property of Chemosh and Moab. And I brought from there the *ariel dodo* ("the royal altar" or "its davidic altar hearth"?) and I dragged it before Chemosh in Kerioth and I settled in it men of Sharon and men of Maharoth.

And Chemosh said to me, "Go, take Nebo from Israel." And I went by night and fought against it from the break of dawn until noon and I took it and I slaughtered all seven-thousand men and boys and women and maidens and slave girls because I had devoted it to Ashtar-Chemosh. And I took from there the *ariels* ("altar hearths"?) of Yahweh and I dragged them before Chemosh.

And the king of Israel had fortified Jahaz and dwelt in it while fighting me, but Chemosh drove him out from before me. And I took from Moab two-hundred men, all of them noblemen, and established them in Jahaz; thus I took possession of it to attach it to (the district of) Dibon. And I built Qarhoh, the wall of the parkland and the wall of the citadel, and I built the gates and I built its towers and I built a royal palace and I made both of its reservoirs for water inside the town. And there was no cistern in the town at Qarhoh, and I said to all the people, "Let each of you make a cistern for himself in his house." And I cut beams for Qarhoh with captives from Israel. And I fortified Aroer and I made the highway in the Arnon and I built Beth-bamoth, for it had been destroyed. And I built Bezer because it lay in ruins [   ] so men of Dibon, because all Dibon was loyal to me. And I ruled [. . .] one-hundred towns which I added to the land and I built [. . .] and Beth-diblathen and Beth-baal-meon and I placed there [. . . . . .] the land.

And as far as Hauronen, there dwelt in it [. . . . .].* Chemosh said to me, "Go down, fight against Hauronen." And I went down and I fought [   ]. Chemosh ruled there in my time [   ]. (Cf. *ANET* 320–21; see photograph on p. 301.)

---

*For the suggested reading "the house of David dwelt in it," see André Lemaire, "'House of David' Restored in Moabite Inscription," *BAR* 20/3 (1994) 30–37 and A. F. Rainey, "Following upon the Ekron and Mesha Inscriptions," *IEJ* 50 (2000) 116–17.

stories depict Ahab as an autocratic king in full control of his kingdom. (3) The Mesha Inscription confirms that Omri and Ahab dominated Moab. (4) The Assyrian records witness to the fact that Israel was a military power of some consequence under Ahab and acted in concert with other Syro-Palestinian states. (5) The account of Jehu's coup presupposes that the Omrides still claimed control over much of Transjordan at the end of Jehoram's reign. Jehu is said to have made his move when the Israelite army was "on guard" at Ramoth-gilead, defending against Syrian encroachment (2 Kgs. 9:14b). Thus Israel's holdings in Transjordan presumably still extended as far north as Ramoth-gilead (present-day Tell er-Ramith). Conflict between king and prophet is another strong motif in the summary notes, the Elijah stories, and the account of Jehu's rebellion.

In contrast to these sources, which presuppose that the Omrides were strong rulers over an autonomous kingdom and in hostile relations with the Yahwistic prophets, the stories of the three battles with Ben-hadad and the Elisha stories presuppose quite a different situation. Both of these narrative groups, associated by context with Ahab and Jehoram, respectively, depict the king or kings of Israel as international weaklings, bullied by the Syrian king of Damascus, and often hard-pressed to exercise authority outside the precincts of Samaria. At the same time these narratives, especially the Elisha stories, presuppose a close supportive relationship between the "king of Israel" and the Yahwistic prophets.

Most commentators and historians deal with this situation in either of two ways. Some conclude that the Omride era was a period of sharp contrasts. The Omrides had moments of greatness interspersed with moments of disaster; times when they dominated the surrounding nations interrupted by times when they could hardly defend their own royal city; periods of conflict with the Yahwistic prophets and other periods when they enjoyed the warm support of these Yahwistic champions. Others conclude, and it is our position, that the stories of the three battles with Ben-hadad (1 Kgs. 20; 22:1–38) and the Elisha stories (2 Kgs. 2; 4:1–8:15) do not pertain to the Omride period in the first place, but pertain to the following period of the Jehu dynasty when the conditions presupposed in these narratives did in fact apply. In short, we discount the narratives in question as valid sources of information for the Omride era but will draw upon them as sources for the Jehu period. Consequently, we view the Omride kings as strong rulers, after Omri's defeat of Tibni, who were in full charge of the Israelite kingdom.

The Sequence of Syrian Kings. Interrelated issues, also debated among historians, are the identity and the proper order of the kings of Damascus contemporary with the Omrides. Prior to the Omride period, we have encountered two Damascus kings: Rezon, Solomon's contemporary (1 Kgs. 11:23–25), and Ben-hadad, the contemporary of Asa and Baasha (1 Kgs. 15:18–20). The next mention of a king of Damascus in our sources occurs in connection with Ahab's last years. As seen above, the Monolith Inscription has Ahab fighting along with Hadadezer of Damascus against Shalmaneser III in 853, a date that must have been near the end of Ahab's reign. According to the Black Obelisk, this Hadadezer was still on the scene in 845 but had been replaced by the usurper Hazael by 841. It would appear from an Ashur fragment of an inscription of

53. *Relief of an Assyrian god.* Mesopotamian deities are frequently depicted astride the backs of animals. Israelites may have assumed that Yahweh stood atop the bull figure just as Yahweh was assumed to travel atop the ark. 47 cm. high, 34 cm. wide. (*Vorderasiatische Museen, Berlin*)

Shalmaneser III that Hazael followed immediately after Hadadezer, with no interim ruler. "Hadad-ezer (Adad-idri) passed away (and) Hazael, son of a nobody, took the throne. He mustered his numerous troops (and) moved against me to wage war and battle. I fought with him (and) defeated him. I took away from him his walled camp. He fled to save his life (and) I pursued (him) as far as Damascus his royal city" (RIMA 3:118).

This information conflicts, of course, with the biblical stories of the three battles with Ben-hadad as well as with the Elisha stories—if one assumes that these two narrative groups are in proper context. That is, if the stories of the three battles with Ben-hadad actually pertain to the last years of Ahab (note that the king of Israel is killed in the third story) and the Elisha stories actually pertain to Jehoram's reign, then we have a Ben-hadad on the throne of Syria followed by Hazael (see especially 2 Kgs. 8:7–15) rather than a Hadadezer followed by Hazael.

Again historians part ways. Those who hold that the narratives in question are in proper historical context conclude that Ben-hadad and Hadadezer were the same person.[10] Presumably the Assyrians knew him as Hadadezer, while the Israelites knew him as Ben-hadad, possibly a throne name. (For the purposes of clarity we have used Hebrew forms throughout this discussion. The Akkadian form of "Hadadezer" used in Shalmaneser's inscriptions is "Adad-idri." The Aramaic form of "Ben-hadad" that appears in various inscriptions is "Bar-hadad.") Those inclined to believe that the narratives in question are not in proper historical context see the Ben-hadad/Hadadezer discrepancy as further evidence supporting their position. Indeed, the references to Ben-hadad in

---

10. See F. M. Cross, "The Stela Dedicated to Melcarth by Ben-Hadad of Damascus," *BASOR* 205 (1972) 36–42; D. J. Wiseman, "Hadadezer," *RLA* 4 (1972–75) 38; and Mordechai Cogan, *I Kings* (AB 10; New York: Doubleday, 2000) 472–74.

the stories of the three battles with Ben-hadad and in the Elisha stories serve as one of several clues that these narratives belong instead to the period of the Jehu dynasty. Hazael, as it turns out, was followed on the throne by a Ben-hadad who continued Hazael's policy of harassing Israel (2 Kgs. 13:3–5, 14–25).

We will return to this matter below in our discussion of the Jehu dynasty. For the moment it is necessary only to make clear that we follow the second option indicated above and, accordingly, reconstruct the sequence of Damascus kings as follows:

Rezon	Solomon's contemporary
[Tabrimmon]	Whether Ben-hadad I was a commoner, or whether his father Tabrimmon ruled before him, is unclear.
Ben-hadad I	Son of Tabrimmon, contemporary of Asa and Baasha
Hadadezer	Contemporary with Ahab's last years and through most of Jehoram's reign
[Ben-hadad]	See 2 Kings 8:7–15
Hazael	Usurped the throne of Damascus sometime between 845 and 841—that is, near the end of Jehoram's reign. It is possible that another insignificant Ben-hadad held the throne briefly between Hadadezer and Hazael (see 2 Kgs. 8:7–15), but unlikely in our opinion.
Ben-hadad II	Son of Hazael; contemporary of Israelite kings Jehoahaz and Jehoash. This is probably the Ben-hadad of the Elisha stories and of the three battle accounts in 1 Kings 20; 22:1–38.

Chronological Issues

For the first time, Assyrian texts contain a reference in a context that makes it possible to assign a firm year and date to an Israelite king. Shalmaneser III reports that in the eponym of Dayan-Ashshur or in his sixth regnal year (= Nisan 853 to Nisan 852 B.C.E.) he fought against a coalition that included Ahab of Israel. Although the exact date during the year when this battle occurred cannot be determined, it was probably in the summer of 853. Thus Ahab was reigning in Israel at the time of the battle of Qarqar in 853.

Unfortunately, establishing a chronology for the remainder of the Omride dynasty confronts numerous problems. Among Israelite kings, Omri is assigned a reign of twelve years (1 Kgs. 16:23), Ahab of twenty-two years (16:29), Ahaziah of two years (22:52), and Jehoram of twelve years (2 Kgs. 3:1). Among the contemporary Judean kings, Jehoshaphat is assigned twenty-five years (22:42), Jehoram eight years (2 Kgs. 8:17), and Ahaziah one year (2 Kgs. 8:26). Some problems raised by the passages are the following. (1) Two kings named Jehoram ruled in Israel and Judah almost simultaneously, raising the question if they were one and the same person (see below). (2) Contradictions within the synchronisms in the Hebrew text present difficulties: according to 2 Kings 1:17 Jehoram became king of Israel in the second year of Jehoram of Judah, but 2 Kings 3:1 dates his accession to the eighteenth year of Jehoshaphat (cf. 1 Kgs. 22:51). (3) Differences exist between the Hebrew text and the Lucianic recension of the Greek. (4) How the chronological calculations reckon with the Omri-Tibni conflict remains uncertain. Zimri is said to have reigned for seven days in the twenty-seventh year of Asa (1 Kgs. 16:15), but Omri is said to have become king in the thirty-first year of Asa (16:23). This seems to suggest that Tibni, Omri's competitor, ruled for four years (16:21–22). (5) Many of the narratives dealing with the Omride era have been secondarily inserted and names for originally unidentified kings have been assigned. Some editorial harmonization of this material has thus perhaps led to secondary chronological adjustments.

Our suggested chronology assumes that Omri had been ruling for about four years when a reference from southern sources reports that he became king, at the death of Tibni, in the thirty-first year of Asa (876–875 B.C.E.; 1 Kgs. 17:23). Ahab became king in the thirty-eighth year of Asa (869–868 B.C.E.; 1 Kgs. 17:29). In order to allow time for rulers between Ahab and Jehu, we assume that Ahab's last year extended from the fall of 854 to the fall of 853. He thus died shortly after the battle of Qarqar. The twenty-two years assigned him may have originally referred to the end of his reign twenty-two years after the founding of Samaria in 875–874. Ahab's son Ahaziah succeeded him and reigned for two years, after which the southern Jehoram (son of Jehoshaphat) succeeded him during his second year as Judean king (851–850), probably at the fall festival in 851. First Kings 1:17 reports this fact but does not distinguish Jehoram as a son of Jehoshaphat: "Jehoram succeeded him [Ahaziah] as king, in the second year of King Jehoram son of Jehoshaphat of Judah, for he [Ahaziah] had no son" (NJPSV).

Israel at Its Zenith under Omri and Ahab

Omri's Rise to Power

The circumstances of Elah's assassination, which is the only information provided about his reign, would lead one to suspect that he was an inefficient or incompetent monarch not held in very high esteem by his compatriots. Although Israel's army was in the field at the time, fighting against the Philistines at Gibbethon, Elah was back at Tirzah "drinking himself drunk" in the house of one of his court officials. Moreover, Elah was assassinated by one of his own high-ranking professional soldiers, Zimri, commander of half the chariots. Perhaps Zimri recognized that Elah did not have the full support of the people. Indeed, he may have been responding to popular sentiment voiced by the prophet Jehu son of Hanani (1 Kgs. 16:7–10).

Zimri, having seized the throne, proceeded to massacre the royal family. When news of Zimri's coup reached Gibbethon, however, the troops proclaimed Omri, their field commander, as the new king and marched on Tirzah. Zimri soon recognized the futility of his position and committed suicide by burning down the palace over himself. Tirzah fell to Omri, therefore, who now faced opposition from a certain Tibni the son of Ginath. The biblical account of this Omri-Tibni phase of the struggle for the throne provides the reader with just enough information to whet the appetite for more: "Then the people of Israel were divided into two parts; half of the people followed Tibni son of Ginath, to make him king, and half followed Omri. But the people who followed Omri overcame the people who followed Tibni son of Ginath; so Tibni died, and Omri became king" (1 Kgs. 16:21–22).

54. *Mesha Inscription.* Discovered in 1868 and measuring 115 × 68 cm., the Mesha Inscription records the deeds of King Mesha of Moab, a contemporary of the Omride rulers of Israel (see Text 4). (*Louvre*)

It is tempting to speculate about Tibni's background, the source and strength of his support, the tactics by which Omri's party overcame Tibni's party, and above all the circumstances behind the curious statement, "So Tibni died."[11] There is, however, little basis for any speculation. The synchronisms in 1 Kings 16:15 and 23 suggest that civil war lasted for the first four years of Omri's reign.

Little is known about Omri, in spite of the fact that he is the earliest biblical character to be mentioned in ancient nonbiblical documents.[12] We are informed that Jeroboam was an Ephraimite, for example, and that Baasha was from Issachar (1 Kgs. 11:26; 15:27), but nothing is said of Omri's tribal origin. Possibly the village of Jezreel was his family home, since the Omrides apparently maintained an estate there in addition to the official residency at Samaria. If so, then it is tempting to speculate further that Omri was from the tribe of Issachar, which the book of Joshua associates with the general vicinity of Jezreel. Yet we cannot assume that he represented any one of the traditional twelve tribes (see above, n. 4).

Omri was clearly a successful military figure. He was commanding Israel's army against the Philistines at Gibbethon when Zimri assassinated Elah, for example, and it was he who conquered Moab. Otherwise, the only specific item recorded for Omri's reign is that he established Samaria as the new capital of

---

11. See J. M. Miller, "'So Tibni Died,'" *VT* 18 (1968) 392–94.

12. See Stephan Timm, *Die Dynastie Omri. Quellen und Untersuchung Zur Geschichte Israels im 9. Jahrhundert vor Christus* (FRLANT 124; Göttingen: Vandenhoeck & Ruprecht, 1982).

55. *The gateway from Hazor.* This gateway, reconstructed from the remains at Hazor, featured proto-Aeolic capitals. Similar capitals have been discovered at Judean and Moabite sites. (*Israel Museum*)

the northern kingdom. Much can be surmised, of course, about the Omride policies that introduced the new era of prosperity and international prestige. Yet it is difficult to distinguish Omri's contributions from those of Ahab. Probably the two construction phases at Samaria, if these are properly assigned (see below), represent the typical pattern: Omri made the beginning, but Ahab followed through in ways that far exceeded Omri's vision.

A New Capital at Samaria

Omri ruled from Tirzah during the first years of his reign, although the palace presumably had suffered damage in connection with Zimri's aborted takeover. Then Omri purchased a site for the construction of a new capital, which, according to 1 Kings 16:24, he named Samaria (Shomeron) after its previous owner, Shemer. (Note Judg. 10:1, however, which presupposes the existence of an Ephraimite village named Shamir already during the time of the Judges. Was this the same place? The pottery remains from the site indicate a small pre-Omride settlement.) Samaria would serve as Israel's capital for the next century and a half, until the city and kingdom eventually fell to the Assyrians.

Tirzah, the old capital (or royal residency, and thus the seat of government), is to be identified with present-day Tell el-Far'ah, in the Wadi Far'ah, whose perennial springs flow eastward into the Jordan River.[13] Stratum III of the ancient ruins excavated at the site probably represents the tenth- and early-ninth-century Israelite city. This stratum indicates a modest town with buildings that show evidence of numerous repairs and rebuilds. Foundations of unfinished structures built over a level with burned debris have been interpreted to mean that Omri started to rebuild the city after its destruction but

---

13. On the excavations at Tirzah see Roland De Vaux, "Tirzah," in D. W. Thomas, ed., *Archaeology and Old Testament Study* (London: Oxford University Press, 1967) 371–83.

then aborted the plan, presumably when he turned attention to Samaria. Obviously this interpretation depends more on the biblical account than on the rather meager artifactual evidence.

The hill of Samaria that Omri selected for his new capital, although not distinguished by its elevation (about fourteen hundred feet), stood well isolated from the surrounding terrain.[14] Thus its broad summit could be fortified to provide a formidable defense. Also, Samaria was much better located than Tirzah for international communication, particularly for contact with the north and west. Samaria was situated west of the highland watershed, thus much nearer to the main north-south route through Palestine, "the Way of the Sea," and overlooked a valley (present-day Wadi esh-Sha'ir), which provided the most direct east-west route from the Mediterranean coast to the interior of the hill country at Shechem. The best north-south route connecting Shechem with the Jezreel Valley (via Dothan) also passed near Samaria. That Omri is specifically said to have "purchased" the site for his new capital may be significant as well. Presumably the whole city would have had the status of royal property, thus rendering Omride rule within the capital less dependent upon popular support than elsewhere in the kingdom.

The first two building phases at Samaria (Sebastiyeh strata I and II) probably represent the work of Omri and Ahab, respectively. Stratum I, although not yet uncovered extensively, is represented by the remains of a modest palace on the summit of the hill. While this stratum I palace was still quite new, however, perhaps not even complete, work was begun on a second, more elegant, massive, and effectively defensive palace compound (stratum II) that would replace the first. This royal acropolis measures 89 by 178 meters. About five hundred ivory inlay pieces, intricately carved and probably manufactured in Phoenicia, were discovered among the debris at the site. Although these were not found specifically in the Stratum II context usually associated with Ahab, they do call to mind the reference to Ahab's "house of ivory" and suggest that this descriptive phrase had to do with the heavy use of ivory inlays in the palace decorations.

Omri and Ahab in International Affairs

Omride international policies involved a buildup of military strength and territorial annexation combined with a system of negotiated alliances, all conducted under the shadow of emerging Assyrian imperialism. (See Map 26.) Close relations with Phoenicia and Judah are indicated by the marriages between the royal families. Jezebel, the wife of Ahab, is identified in 1 Kings 16:31 as the daughter of Ethbaal king of the Sidonians. Josephus, writing in the first century C.E. and apparently following Menander of Ephesus, corrects this to "Ittobaal, the king of Tyre and Sidon" (*Ant.* 8.316–18; *Contra Apion* 1.116). Athaliah the daughter of either Omri or Ahab (compare 2 Kgs. 8:18 with 8:26)

---

14. Two major excavations were conducted at the site of ancient Samaria in the first four decades of the twentieth century (1908–10 and 1931–35). See now R. E. Tappy, *The Archaeology of Israelite Samaria, I: Early Iron Age through the Ninth Century BCE* (HSS 44; Atlanta: Scholars Press, 1992). Artifactual evidence indicates the presence of a tenth-century pre-Omride village on the site.

56. *Royal quarter at Samaria.* Remains of the southern wall of the Israelite royal quarter at Samaria and an example of header-stretcher stone masonry. Compare the plan of the royal quarter in the upper left with arrow pointing to the section of the wall in the photograph.

was given in marriage to Jehoram son of Jehoshaphat. Omride blood was thus destined to flow in Davidic veins.

For all practical purposes, the southern kingdom of Judah became a vassal state subservient to the Omrides. This is indicated by the following factors. (1) According to 1 Kings 22:4, Jehoshaphat placed his military, horses, and men at the disposal of Ahab. (2) In the Kings summation of his rule, Jehoshaphat is said to have made peace with the king of Israel (22:45). The verb used here, *sha-lam*, like its Akkadian counterpart *salamu*, can denote a condition of submission. Thus the NJPSV translates this verse as "Jehoshaphat submitted to the king of Israel." (3) Although Akkadian texts frequently refer to the kingdoms of southern Syria-Palestine in the vicinity of Judah, they do not mention Judah as a separate state until the time of Tiglath-pileser III, in 733 B.C.E., when the Davidic king Ahaz temporarily severed his loyalty to Samaria. Diplomatic relations with foreign powers during the Omride period would have been under Israelite control.

Omri subjugated Moab, we learn from the Moabite Stone, and the Moabites remained under Israelite domination through Ahab's reign (2 Kgs. 1:1; 3:4–5). Israel's actual military occupation in Moab was probably confined to the area north of the Arnon River where there were already "Israelite" elements among the population—"the men of Gad had dwelt in the land of Ataroth always" (Mesha Inscription; see Text 4). Gadite clans ranged with their sheep and goats in this area, and even certain villages had perhaps survived from a half century earlier when this area was controlled by David and Solomon. Either Omri or Ahab fortified Jahaz, located somewhere in the general vicinity of Dibon and probably situated on one of the northern tributaries of the Arnon. A military

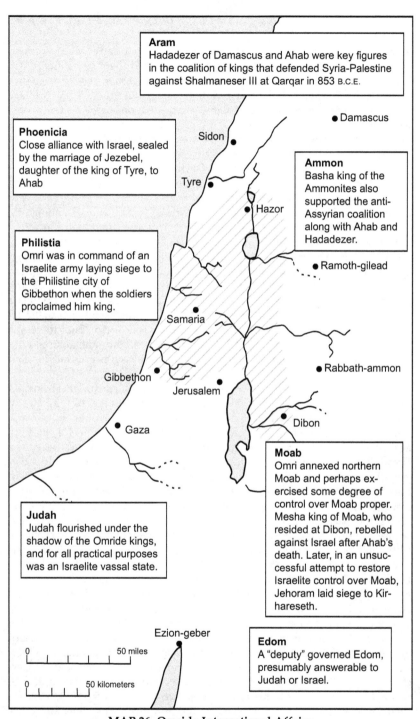

Aram
Hadadezer of Damascus and Ahab were key figures in the coalition of kings that defended Syria-Palestine against Shalmaneser III at Qarqar in 853 B.C.E.

Phoenicia
Close alliance with Israel, sealed by the marriage of Jezebel, daughter of the king of Tyre, to Ahab

Ammon
Basha king of the Ammonites also supported the anti-Assyrian coalition along with Ahab and Hadadezer.

Philistia
Omri was in command of an Israelite army laying siege to the Philistine city of Gibbethon when the soldiers proclaimed him king.

Damascus

Sidon

Tyre

Hazor

Ramoth-gilead

Samaria

Rabbath-ammon

Gibbethon

Jerusalem

Dibon

Gaza

Moab
Omri annexed northern Moab and perhaps exercised some degree of control over Moab proper. Mesha king of Moab, who resided at Dibon, rebelled against Israel after Ahab's death. Later, in an unsuccessful attempt to restore Israelite control over Moab, Jehoram laid siege to Kir-hareseth.

Judah
Judah flourished under the shadow of the Omride kings, and for all practical purposes was an Israelite vassal state.

Ezion-geber

0 ___ 50 miles

0 ___ 50 kilometers

Edom
A "deputy" governed Edom, presumably answerable to Judah or Israel.

MAP 26. Omride International Affairs

garrison positioned in that vicinity (at the site of present-day el-Medeiyineh on Wadi eth-Themed, for example) would have enabled them to maintain firm Israelite control over the rolling plateau north of the Arnon as well as control of the traffic, military and commercial, crossing the Arnon itself. Military strikes into the interior of Moab (between the Arnon and Zered canyons) would have been much more difficult, as illustrated by the narrative in 2 Kings 3:4–27. Note also that it is specifically the area north of the Arnon ("the land of Medeba") that Mesha claims to have recovered from Israel.

In addition to conquering Moab, the Omrides also reconquered land previously lost to Damascus. In association with the wars between Asa of Judah and Baasha of Israel, the Damascene king Ben-hadad I had fought against and captured the Israelite towns of "Ijon, Dan, Abel-beth-Maacah, and all Chinneroth, as well as the land of Naphtali" (1 Kgs. 15:20). This area would have included the territory of eastern Galilee, west of the Sea of Galilee, and extending southward to the Jezreel Valley. (The territory of Galilee, west of the Jordan, and of Gilead, east of the Jordan, were probably claimed by Syria and controlled from Damascus as often as they were by Israel.) No written sources provide any information about the recapture of this territory, but it must have occurred late in the reign of Omri or early in that of Ahab. The opening extant lines of the Tel Dan Stela seem to refer to Israelite action in the area (see Text 6). Thus there was a period of time when Israel and Damascus were military antagonists, with Israel apparently able to force a Syrian retreat from territory Damascus had seized from Israel.

Assyrian texts indicate that near the end of the reign of Ahab, Israel belonged to an anti-Assyrian coalition of kingdoms that included many of the states in southern Syria-Palestine. At this time, relations between Damascus and Samaria were cooperative; the two kingdoms united with others to protect themselves against a foreign intruder. Assyrian imperialistic expansion westward had already begun under Ashurnasirpal II, who ascended the throne only a few years before Omri came to power in Israel. His western campaigns, concentrated on northern Syria-Palestine, had several purposes: control of the crossing places of the Euphrates, the assertion of Assyrian claims along important trade routes, the establishment of Assyrian colonies, the acquisition of tribute, and luxury and building goods, as well as the procurement of captives to swell the labor force at home, where extensive construction projects were under way. His armies had reached the Mediterranean Sea as early as 878–877 B.C.E., when Phoenician states as far south as Tyre provided him with gifts. This Assyrian interruption of trade in the area of northern Syria may have stimulated Tyre's enlargement of its Red Sea and Arabian trade via its alliance with the Omrides.

Under Ashurnasirpal's successor, Shalmaneser III (858–828 B.C.E.), Assyrian activity in the west intensified and eventually involved the states of southern Syria-Palestine. In his first regnal year, Shalmaneser had crossed the Euphrates and fought against a Syro-Hittite coalition of four armies from Sam'al, Patin, Carchemish, and Bit-Adini; the last, located in the western bend of the Euphrates, was led by Ahunu, an old foe of his father (see the text in RIMA 3:9–10). He claims to have defeated and received tribute from them as well as four other kingdoms in northern Syria and southern Anatolia. Shalmaneser fought Ahunu "the man of Bit-Adini" on subsequent occasions in 856–855. In 856 he conquered

TEXT 5. Excerpts from the Black Obelisk

Assur, the great lord, king of all of the great gods; Anu, king of the Igigi and Anunnaki, the lord of lands; Enlil (Bêl), the exalted, father of the gods, the creator; Ea, king of the Deep (Apsu), who determines destiny; [Sin], king of the tiara, exalted in splendor; Adad, mighty, pre-eminent, lord of abundance (plenty); Shamash, judge of heaven and earth, director of all (things); Marduk, master of the gods, lord of law (omens); Urta, valiant (ruler) of the Igigi and the Anunnaki, the almighty god; Nergal, the ready (perfect), king of battle; Nusku, bearer of the shining scepter, the god who renders decisions; Ninlil, spouse of Bêl, mother of the [great] gods; Ishtar, first in heaven and on earth, who fills full the measure of bravery;—the great [gods], who ordain destiny (destinies), who have made great my kingdom, (I invoke).

Shalmaneser, king of all peoples, lord, priest of Assur, mighty king, king of all the four regions (of the world), sun of all peoples, despot of all lands; son of Assur-nâsir-pal, the high priest, whose priesthood was acceptable to the gods and who brought in submission at his feet the totality of the countries (of earth); glorious offspring of Tukulti-Urta, who slew all of his foes and overwhelmed them like a hurricane (deluge). . . .

In my eleventh year of reign [848–847] I crossed the Euphrates for the ninth time. Countless cities I captured. Against the cities of the land of Hamath, I descended. 89 cities I captured. Hadad-ezer of Aram (and) twelve kings of the land of Hatti stood by each other. I accomplished their overthrow. . . .

In my eighteenth year of reign [841–840] I crossed the Euphrates for the sixteenth time. Hazael of Aram (Damascus) came forth to battle. 1,121 of his chariots, 470 of his cavalry, together with his camp, I captured from him. . . .

(from the reliefs)

Tribute of Sûa, the Gilzânite. Silver, gold, lead, copper vessels, staves for the hand of the king, horses, camels, whose backs are two humps, I received from him.

Tribute of Iaua (Jehu), son of Omri (*mâr Humrî*). Silver, gold, a golden bowl, a golden beaker, golden goblets, pitchers of gold, lead, staves for the hand of the king, javelins, I received from him.

Tribute of the land of Musri. Camels, whose backs are two humps, a river-ox (buffalo), a *sakêa*, a *sûsu*, elephants, monkeys, apes, I received from him.

Tribute of Marduk-apal-usur of Suhi. Silver, gold, pitchers of gold, ivory, javelins, *bûia*, brightly colored (and) linen garments, I received from him.

Tribute of Karparunda, of Hattina. Silver, gold, lead, copper, copper vessels, ivory, cypress (timbers), I received from him. (*ARAB I*, §§555–56, 568, 589–93)

Til Barsip, the main city in Bit-Adini, and renamed it Kar-Shalmaneser. In the following year, Ahunu was captured, carried away to Assyria, and Bit-Adini was turned into a province under direct Assyrian administration.

> Ahunu, trusting in the might of his troops, came forth against me (and) drew up (his) battle line. I pointed the weapons of Assur, my lord, against them (and) defeated them. I cut off the heads of his warriors (and) dyed the mountain red with the blood of his fighting men. The multitudes of his (men) tumbled from mountain cliffs. I waged a mighty battle against his city. Fear of the brilliance of Assur, my lord, overwhelmed them (and) they came down (and) submitted to me. I took as my own Ahunu and his troops, chariots, cavalry, (and) rich palace property beyond measure. I transported (it) across the Euphrates [text reads "Tigris"] and brought (it) to my city, Assur. I regarded them as people of my land. (RIMA 3:22)

This aggressive policy of Shalmaneser triggered the formation of a major anti-Assyrian coalition in southern Syria-Palestine. Kingdoms in the region must have realized that acting independently they had no chance of protecting their territory, commerce, and vested interests against this Mesopotamian marauder. The Aramaean king Hadadezer of Damascus, the Neo-Hittite king Irhulenu of Hamath, and the Israelite king Ahab led in the creation of a major united front against Assyria. This anti-Assyrian Syro-Palestinian coalition met Shalmaneser in 853 in northern Syria at Qarqar on the Orontes River. The Monolith Inscription (see Text 3) provides the fullest account of the ensuing battle and indicates that Shalmaneser was either defeated or fought to a standstill, even though he claimed a great victory. The inscription notes the following coalition members and the numbers of their respective military contingents (following the reading of *NAHI*, 29–31):

States	Chariots	Cavalry	Soldiers	Camels
Aram-Damascus[15]	1,200	1,200	20,000	
Hamath	700	700	10,000	
Israel	2,000		10,000	
Byblos			500	
Egypt			1,000	
Irqanata	10		10,000	
Arvad			200	
Usanata			200	
Sianu	30		10,000	
Arabia				1,000
Beth-Rehob[16]			[ ],000	
Ammon				

15. Assyrian texts generally refer to the Syrian kingdom in Damascus (our Aram-Damascus) as *Imerishu* or *Sha-imerisuh*, which apparently means something like "donkey land"; see W. T. Pitard, *Ancient Damascus: A Historical Study of the Syrian City-State from Earliest Times until Its Fall to the Assyrians in 732 B.C.E.* (Winona Lake, IN: Eisenbrauns, 1987) 14–17.

16. This reading takes *ba-'a-sa mar ru-chu-bi* kur *a-ma-na-a-a* as referring to ba'sa of (bit) rehob with the name of the Ammonite ruler having been omitted. *A-ma-na-a-a* refers to Ammon rather than Amana in northern Syria. On the issue see G. A. Rendsburg, "Baasha of Ammon," *JANES* 20 (1991) 57–61; and Nadav Na'aman, "Hazael of 'Amqi and Hadadezer of Beth-rehob," *UF* 27 (1995) 381–94.

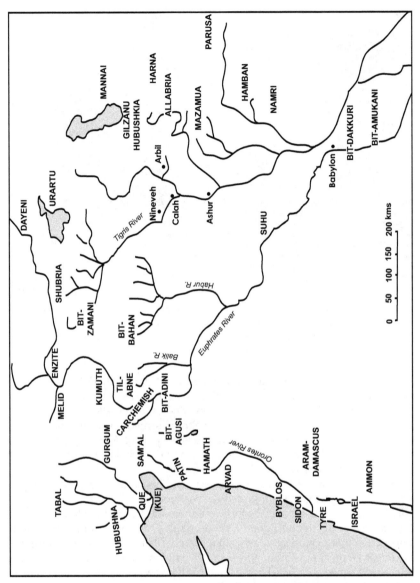

MAP 27. Upper Euphrates at the Time of Shalmaneser III

57. Scene of the battle of Qarqar. Tell Qarqur in the Orontes Valley (present-day Syria) preserves the name and probably represents the site of ancient Qarqar. Here in 853 B.C.E. Shalmaneser III was halted temporarily by a coalition of Syro-Palestinian kings including Ahab of Israel.

Note that "Ahab the Israelite" is credited with a larger chariot force than all of his allies combined. Some argue that there may be a scribal error, since "2,000" seems rather unreasonable.[17] Nevertheless, even allowing for scribal error or exaggeration, it is clear that Israel represented one of the major military powers of Syria-Palestine during the latter part of Ahab's reign. (Egypt, *msr*, may be a scribal error for Sumur, *smr*, in Syria. Scholars have pointed out over fifty errors in this carelessly written text.)

Judah, Moab, and Edom, as well as several Phoenician cities, are not listed among the kingdoms that supported the coalition. The absence of Moab is not surprising, since we know that Moab was subject to Israel at the time; but why the absence of Judah and Edom? One possibility, of course, is that Judah and Edom chose not to participate since they were farther removed from the Assyrian threat. Another possibility, however, is that Judah and Edom, like Moab, were so closely aligned with Israel at the time that their soldiers were simply counted as belonging to Ahab. None of the southern Phoenician states is mentioned in the text either. Some of these had offered gifts to establish good relationships with Assyria already during the reign of Ashurnasirpal, and Shalmaneser reports receiving gifts from the coastal cities in 856–855. They are not listed, however, among the states offering gifts to Shalmaneser during the 853 campaign but are noted as later providing tribute gifts in both 841 and 838 (see *COS* 2:268–69). If the southern Phoenicians had joined in or supported the coalition's efforts, they may have channeled their support through their ally Ahab.

17. See Moshe Elat, "The Campaigns of Shalmaneser III against Aram and Israel," *IEJ* 25 (1975) 25–35; and Nadav Na'aman, "Two Notes on the Monolith Inscription from Kurkh," *TA* 6 (1978) 68–90; repr. with revision as "Ahab's Chariot Force at the Battle of Qarqar," *AIIN* 1–12.

Assyrian armies were not active again in southern Syria-Palestine until 849 B.C.E. In that year and in 848 and 845, Shalmaneser again struggled with the coalition but was unable to overcome it, in spite of his claims to have defeated "the twelve kings on the shore of the sea" led by Hadadezer of Damascus and Irhulenu of Hamath. (On two rock inscriptions on the Upper Tigris, Shalmaneser refers to the "fourth time" he fought the coalition; see RIMA 3:94–96.) The Israelite king goes unmentioned in these later texts but was undoubtedly one of the twelve (see the texts in *COS* 2:265; and RIMA 3:95 which contain reference to "fifteen kings" in the coalition).

Omri and Ahab as Builders

Both Omri and Ahab are noted in 1 Kings for their building activities: Omri for founding and fortifying Samaria, and Ahab for building a temple of Baal in Samaria, an "ivory house," and other cities (16:24, 32; 22:39). We have noted already that Sebastiyeh I and II probably represent Omri's and Ahab's building phases at Samaria. Among the other cities probably built (actually expanded) by Ahab were Megiddo and Hazor, both already discussed in connection with Solomon. Since the mid-1990s, an intense debate has raged over the dating of archaeological strata and remains not only at Megiddo and Hazor but also at numerous other sites. As we have noted, proponents of a "low chronology" argue that what has traditionally been assigned to the second half of the tenth century—principally the "Solomonic" fortifications and related strata at Megiddo (VA–IVB), Hazor (X), and Gezer (VIII)—should be redated over fifty years later to the second quarter of the ninth century, and thus to the Omride era.[18] Part of the argument here involves the fact that no architectural remains comparable to Hazor and Megiddo have been found in Solomonic Jerusalem. How, it is asked, could the kingdom's capital city be devoid of parallel developed architecture when so much appears in outlying cities?

We do not adhere to this redating scheme for the following reasons.[19] (1) Ascribing such a large number of architectural remains at such a large number of sites to the Omride period seems unrealistic since the reigns of Omri and Ahab, after the collapse of Tibni, were only a little over two decades in length. Omri was preoccupied with civil strife for a considerable amount of time at the beginning of his reign, and Ahab's last years were preoccupied with Shalmaneser's threat. The intervening years do not seem sufficient for such widespread building activity. (2) Excavations at sites such as Samaria and Jezreel, clearly built or rebuilt by the Omrides, have not revealed the presence of any six-chambered gates in the outer defensive city walls, a distinctive feature of the "Solomonic" fortifications of Gezer, Hazor, and Megiddo. (3) Parallels and similarities between the pottery remains and architectural features in the

18. See Israel Finkelstein, "The Archaeology of the United Monarchy: An Alternative View," *Levant* 28 (1996) 177–87; idem, "Bible Archaeology or Archaeology of Palestine in the Iron Age? A Rejoinder," *Levant* 30 (1998) 167–74; idem, "Omride Architecture," *ZDPV* 116 (2000) 114–38; Finkelstein and N. A. Silberman, *The Bible Unearthed: Archaeology's New Vision of Ancient Israel and the Origin of the Sacred Texts* (New York: Free Press, 2001) 169–95, 340–44; and further references in n. 23 of chapter 7.

19. See further Amihai Mazar, "Iron Age Chronology: A Reply to I. Finkelstein," *Levant* 29 (1997) 155–65; and Baruch Halpern, *David's Secret Demons: Messiah, Murderer, Traitor, King* (Grand Rapids: Eerdmans, 2001) 427–78.

Omride strata at Samaria and Jezreel and the Solomonic strata at Megiddo and Hazor are insufficient to warrant assigning all the strata in question to the same decades. Pottery forms continued in usage over long periods of time, and the masonry work at all these sites may have been influenced by Phoenician style. During both the Solomonic and Omride periods, Phoenician influence was pervasive in Israel. (4) In continuously occupied and frequently rebuilt sites, such as Jerusalem, earlier remains are often almost totally obliterated. Solomonic structures in Jerusalem such as those at Gezer, Megiddo, and Hazor may have subsequently been totally dismantled. In addition, it is possible that during the united monarchy special attention and construction were focused on regional and strategic sites only recently incorporated into Israelite control. In spite of our resistance to the new "low chronology," we recognize, as emphasized already in the first edition of this history, that under the Omrides ancient Israel reached a level of economic and political strength unprecedented in its history.

At Omride Megiddo (following the traditional dating of the stratigraphy rather than the "low chronology"), a solid wall 3.6 meters thick built with insets and offsets replaced an earlier casemate wall.[20] The so-called Megiddo stables, which were probably storage depots of some sort or possibly stables for horses, also belong to the Omride phase, as do at least two palaces and the impressive tunneled water system that allowed access to the water source from inside the city fortifications. At Hazor, where Stratum VIII represents the Omride phase, the Solomonic city wall was also replaced with a more massive one that surrounded a larger area.[21] One of the buildings of this phase measures 21.5 by 25 meters with walls 2 meters thick. A second building (20 by 13 meters) was constructed probably as a storeroom or warehouse. A water shaft similar to the one at Megiddo, although penetrating downward to groundwater level rather than to a spring, provided access to water from inside the city.[22]

---

20. Meggido (Tell el-Mutesellim) was excavated by a German team in 1903–5 and by an American expedition in 1925–39. Small-scale excavations were undertaken in the 1980s and 1990s. New excavations are presently being conducted. See Yohanan Aharoni, "The Stratification of Israelite Megiddo," *JNES* 31 (1972) 302–11; G. I. Davies, *Megiddo* (Cambridge: Lutterworth, 1986); Aharon Kempinski, *Megiddo: A City-State and Royal Centre in North Israel* (Munich: Beck, 1989); R. S. Lamon, *The Megiddo Water System* (OIP 32; Chicago: Oriental Institute, 1935); and Yigael Yadin, "Megiddo of the Kings of Israel," *BA* 33 (1970) 66–96. On the most recent excavations see Israel Finkelstein et al., eds., *Megiddo III: The 1992–1996 Seasons* (2 vols.; Tel Aviv: Emery and Clair Yass Publications in Archaeology, Institute of Archaeology, Tel Aviv University, 2000); idem, *Megiddo IV: The 1998–2002 Seasons* (Tel Aviv: Emery and Clair Yass Publications in Archeology, Institute of Archaeology, Tel Aviv University, 2005); as well as H. M. Niemann, "Megiddo and Solomon—A Biblical Investigation in Relation to Archaeology," *TA* 27 (2000) 59–72.

21. Hazor (Tell el-Qedah) was first excavated in 1928 and then in 1955–58 and 1968–72 by an expedition led by Yigael Yadin and others. See Yigael Yadin et al., *Hazor I–V* (Jerusalem: Magnes, 1959–97); Yadin, *Hazor: With a Chapter on Israelite Megiddo* (Schweich Lectures 1970; London: Oxford University Press, 1972); idem, *Hazor: Rediscovery of a Great Citadel of the Bible* (New York: Random House, 1975); Amnon Ben-tor, "Tel Hazor, 1994," *IEJ* 45 (1995) 65–68; idem, "Solomon's City Rises from the Ashes," *BAR* 25/2 (1999) 26–37; and Ben-Tor and Dror Ben-ami, "Hazor and the Archaeology of the Tenth Century," *IEJ* 48 (1998) 1–37. Edward Lipiński has argued that Stratum VIII, traditionally considered Omride, reflects a Syrian building phase from the time of Hazael and that the town is to be identified with Malahu, known from Shalmaneser's inscriptions; see his *Aramaeans: Their Ancient History, Culture, Religion* (OLA 100; Leuven: Peeters, 2000) 350–51. see also Israel Finkelstein, "Hazor and the North in the Iron Age: A Low Chronology Perspective," *BASOR* 314 (1999) 55–70; idem, "Hazor XII–XI with an Addendum on Ben-tor's Dating of Hazor X–VII," *TA* 27 (2000) 231–47.

22. About a dozen subterranean water systems from this general period are known; see Yigal Shiloh, "Underground Water Systems in the Land of Israel in the Iron Age," in Aharon Kempinski and Ronny Reich, eds., *The Architecture of Ancient Israel from the Prehistoric to the Persian Periods* (Jerusalem: Israel Exploration Society, 1992) 275–93.

The Omrides, probably Ahab, were responsible for major construction at Jezreel (modern Zer'in).[23] Already noted in Joshua 19:18; 1 Samuel 29:1; and 1 Kings 4:12, Jezreel is said to have been the location of one of Ahab's palaces (1 Kgs. 21:1; see 18:45). Located in the eastern Jezreel Valley, the slightly elevated site enjoys pleasant weather and commands a good view of the valley and the surrounding hills. Excavations in the 1990s revealed the remains of a ninth-century palatial residence built on a platform of filled earth, surrounded by a casemate wall (constructed of field stones, not ashlar blocks as at Samaria), and encircled by a moat (about 25 feet wide and 15 feet deep) cut into bedrock. The remains at the site suggest a destruction in the ninth century without a lengthy period of major occupation.

Huge capitals, proto-Aeolic or palmette in style, have been discovered from this period at Samaria, Megiddo, and Hazor, as well as among roughly contemporary ruins in Judah (Ramat Rahel) and Moab (Medeba).[24] These were apparently typical architectural features of the day and probably represent a general eastern Mediterranean style adapted and employed by Phoenician craftsmen. All three sites seem to represent royal administrative centers. Little evidence has been unearthed of the residential and market settlements that must have surrounded these royal complexes or of normal townships of the day. Some have suggested that these Omride constructions witness to a "royal city" concept according to which the king and administration were isolated above and out of reach of the general citizenry. While this suggestion is probably an overinterpretation of the evidence, the Omride constructions clearly presupposed a considerable wealth at the king's disposal and required a large labor force.

Yahwism and Baalism under the Omrides

The compilers of Genesis–2 Kings regarded Ahab as the most evil of all the kings who had ruled to his day.

> And as if it had been a light thing for him to walk in the sins of Jeroboam the son of Nebat, he took for wife Jezebel daughter of King Ethbaal of the Sidonians, and went and served Baal, and worshiped him. He erected an altar for Baal in the house of Baal, which he built in Samaria. Ahab also made a sacred pole [Asherah]. Ahab did more to provoke the anger of Yahweh, the God of Israel, than all the kings of Israel who were before him. (1 Kgs. 16:31–33)

The Elijah stories in 1 Kings 17–19 and the Naboth vineyard story seem to support this evaluation of Ahab, placing most of the blame on Jezebel. The Elijah story in 2 Kings 1 and the story of Jehoram's Moabite campaign in 2 Kings 3:4–27 depict Ahaziah and Jehoram as apostate kings also.

23. On Jezreel and the excavations there see H. G. M. Williamson, "Jezreel in the Biblical Texts," *TA* 18 (1991) 72–92; idem, "Tell Jezreel and the Dynasty of Omri," *PEQ* 128 (1996) 41–51; the excavation reports by David Ussishkin and John Woodhead in *TA* 19 (1992) 3–56; *Levant* 26 (1994) 1–71; and *TA* 24 (1997) 6–72; David Ussishkin, "Jezreel, Samaria, and Megiddo: Royal Centres of Omri and Ahab," in J. A. Emerton, ed., *Congress Volume Cambridge 1995* (VTsup 66; Leiden: Brill, 1997) 351–64; Nadav Na'aman, "Historical and Literary Notes on the Excavations of Tel Jezreel," *TA* 24 (1997) 122–28; repr. in *AIHH* 139–46; and Dag Oredsson, "Jezreel—Its Contribution to Iron Age Chronology," *SJOT* 12 (1998) 86–101.

24. See Yigal Shiloh, *The Proto-Aeolic Capital and Israelite Ashlar Masonry* (Qedem 11; Jerusalem: Israel Exploration Society, 1979).

Several observations, however, must be made as a warning against taking too literally the image of the Omride rulers and the perception of the Yahwism-Baalism conflict reflected in these sources. First, there are the anachronistic and pro-Judean perspectives of the compilers of Genesis–2 Kings to be taken into account, particularly their tendency to project back into earlier times the concepts of exclusive Yahwism and the primacy of Jerusalem. It is doubtful in our opinion that even the most radical Yahwistic prophets of the ninth century B.C.E. would have called for the exclusive worship of Yahweh throughout the land, or even by the royal family. Second, as observed above, the Elijah stories are told from the perspective of the Yahwistic prophets and of groups that held these prophets in much awe. Thus they tend to oversimplify and exaggerate in their depiction of the Yahweh-Baal struggle. Third, as the Jehu dynasty began to lose popularity, there seems to have been an attempt to justify Jehu's coup and bloody massacre on the grounds that it was action taken in behalf of Yahweh. This apologetic theme is especially obvious in the account of Jehu's coup in 2 Kings 9:1–10:27. Finally, the emphasis on Jezebel as the aggressive champion of Baalism represents a tendency noticeable elsewhere in the Scriptures to see the queen, the queen mother, or foreign wives as the source of royal apostasy. (Compare the role of the foreign wives in the presentation of Solomon, for example, and of the queen mother in the presentation of Asa's reign; 1 Kgs. 11:1–8; 15:13.)

Nevertheless, while none of these sources can be regarded as an entirely objective witness to the religious scene during the Omride period, together they point unmistakably to some Yahweh-Baal conflict that apparently surfaced during Ahab's reign and that may have contributed to the eventual downfall of the dynasty. One presumes that the sanctuaries built (or revived) by Jeroboam I at Dan, Bethel, and Penuel were Yahwistic and, accordingly, that Israel's earlier kings had recognized Yahweh as the patron deity of the state. Quite a new situation seems to have developed with the Omrides. There was a new capital city, essentially private property of the royal family, and an impressive royal building complex under construction that would serve as the royal residence and administrative center of the land. In addition to, perhaps even instead of, a Yahwistic sanctuary (one is never noted in Samaria at this time), however, Ahab included in the new capital city a temple for Baal with all the associated furnishings. Since Israel, especially under Ahab, was part of a coalition of states engaged in commercial and political relations, it may have seemed only natural to provide non-Yahwistic devotees with a place of worship in Samaria, especially since Queen Jezebel was a non-Israelite. Ecumenical religious practices were probably an accompaniment to ecumenical politics.

A temple to Baal in the royal palace complex was a new direction, nevertheless, that probably brought protests from loyal Yahwists. Moreover, the religious conflict was probably but the surface of popular resentment toward Omride policies. The protests against Baalism, in other words, may have been part of a larger protest against the economic and social injustices that were attributed, correctly or not, to the Omrides.

One can ascertain only the faintest hints of social conditions during the Omride period. There was considerable prosperity, as we have already noted, especially in the better years during the reigns of Omri and Ahab. And certainly not all the wealth would have entered the royal treasury. Others in the kingdom will have benefited also from the active commerce made possible by the Omride successes in foreign policy, particularly the alliance of Phoenicia, Israel, and Judah. At the same time, the prosperity would not have spread to all. For most of the population of the land, certainly those in the rural villages, life must have continued at subsistence level. One of the results of Omride prosperity, therefore, would have been a substantial widening of the gap between the wealthy and the poor of the land.

In addition, the Omride rulers gained a reputation for self-serving high-handedness in their dealings with their subjects and as authors of unjust rules and regulations. This is illustrated by the Naboth vineyard story. While this story is probably historical fiction, authored long after the actual Naboth affair, it provides a glimpse of how the Omrides were remembered and typified in later years. Jezebel is depicted in the story using royal influence on local elders and nobles to pervert justice. More specifically, she employs the judicial system to destroy Naboth and allow the king to confiscate his family property in Jezreel. Micah 6:9–16 also recalls the Omride reputation for economic and social injustice. This text speaks of injustice, cheating, wicked scales, deceitful weights, violence, lies, and deceitful tongues, all of which it seems to equate with "the statutes of Omri, and all the works of the house of Ahab."

In short, the Yahweh-Baal struggle was probably only one aspect of a much more variegated rift that developed between the royal family and wealthy class on the one hand and the general population on the other. The former are to be associated primarily with the cities, such as Shechem and now Samaria, where autocratic rule was taken for granted and where foreign influences were strong. The latter are to be associated more with the rural villages, where the old clan structures applied and where Yahwism found its strongest and more conservative adherents. It is easy to see how Ahab's association with Phoenician Baalism, particularly his marriage to a foreign, Baal-worshiping wife and construction of a Baal temple in the capital city, became symbolic of all that was disliked about the Omride dynasty.

Whether Ahab constructed the Baal temple merely as a gesture to his Phoenician queen, as Solomon is said to have built sanctuaries for his foreign wives, or whether the cult played some role in the religion of the state is uncertain. (Note that both later rulers, Ahaziah and Jehoram, had Yahwistic names.) Regardless, prophetic groups led by Elijah are said to have called for destruction of the temple and annihilation of the royal family. The crown would have responded with repression, which explains the persecution of the Yahwistic prophets alluded to in the Elijah stories (see, for example, 1 Kgs. 18:4) as well as Elijah's enticement of the crowds to massacre the prophets of Baal (18:40; 19:1–3). One must be careful, however, not to read too much historical reality into these prophetic stories, since they tend to present life and faith in terms of do-or-die situations.

Ahab's Death and the Beginning of Decline under Ahaziah

The concluding summary of Ahab's reign in 1 Kings 22:39–40 states that Ahab "slept with his fathers," a phrase normally used in the Genesis–2 Kings account to refer to the burial of a person who died a natural death. This contrasts, of course, with the preceding and misplaced narrative (1 Kgs. 22:1–38; the third of the stories of the three battles with Ben-hadad), which describes the death of an Israelite king in battle. Ahab was succeeded by his son Ahaziah, for whom the Bible supplies only three items of information. According to 22:47–50 Jehoshaphat refused Ahaziah's request that Israelite merchants be allowed to participate in a maritime expedition that the former sent out from Ezion-geber. The Elijah story in 2 Kings 1:2–16 recounts how Ahaziah suffered an injury from which he never recovered, thus explaining his unusually short reign. Finally, it seems clear from 2 Kings 1:1; 3:4–5; and the Mesha Inscription that King Mesha seized upon Ahab's death and Ahaziah's incapacitation as occasion to challenge Israelite domination of Moab and to restore Moabite control over "the land of Medeba" (see Text 4).

In short, Ahaziah's reign was characterized by inactivity and ineffectiveness as well as by its brevity. Thus began a sharp decline in Omride fortunes. Before tracing this decline through Jehoram's reign to Jehu's coup, let us review developments in Judah under Jehoshaphat, who was contemporary with Ahab and Ahaziah.

Jehoshaphat of Judah

Developments in Judah during the Omride era were closely related to developments in Israel, to the extent that Judah's history at this time is virtually a mirror image of Israelite history. Judah clearly benefited from the international security and economic revival that resulted from Omride military strength and international policies. The two royal families became related by marriage during Jehoshaphat's reign, moreover, so that eventually the separate status of the two kingdoms may have become more a matter of formality than of fact. As we shall see, Ahab's death was a turning point for Judah as well as for Israel.

Jehoshaphat in the Shadow of Ahab

Information about Jehoshaphat's reign comes from three biblical sources: the brief summary of his reign in 1 Kings 22:41–50; the two narratives in which he is featured as a pious Yahwist in contrast to the king of Israel (that is, the third of the stories of the three battles with Ben-hadad [1 Kgs. 22:1–38] and the story of Jehoram's Moabite campaign [2 Kgs. 3:4–27]); and the Chronicler's elaborate description of Jehoshaphat's power, wealth, and great deeds (2 Chr. 17:1–20:37). The summary credits Jehoshaphat with very modest and not entirely successful accomplishments: some minor cultic reforms, peaceful relations with the king of Israel, and a maritime expedition that failed. The two narratives in question probably originally had nothing to do with Jehoshaphat, but illustrate in their present form how he was remembered by storytellers of later generations: as a Judean king loyal to Yahweh but extremely deferential to the king of Israel. "I am as you are; my people are your people, my horses are your horses" (1 Kgs. 22:4). Two themes thus emerge from both the summary and the two narratives—Jehoshaphat's strong Yahwistic leanings and his close supportive relations with the king of Israel. Both of these themes are magnified in

2 Chronicles, which depicts Jehoshaphat as an extremely successful monarch and energetic cultic reformer whose only flaw was that he became involved with the evil kings of Israel.[25]

Clearly the Jehoshaphat who emerges from the 1–2 Kings materials does not measure up to the aggressive, strong, and independent ruler one encounters in 2 Chronicles. Moreover, in the two instances where 1–2 Kings materials pertaining to Jehoshaphat are paralleled in 2 Chronicles, it is noticeable that these materials have been revised to support the image of Jehoshaphat that the Chronicler wished to convey.

The first of these instances involves the third of the stories of the three battles with Ben-hadad (compare 1 Kgs. 22:1–38 with 2 Chr. 18:1–19:3). The Chronicler's version follows 1 Kings virtually word for word, except that the Chronicler frames the narrative with a new introduction that emphasizes Jehoshaphat's great riches and honor, and with a second conclusion that has a Yahwistic prophet censure Jehoshaphat for giving military support to Israel.

> Now Jehoshaphat had great riches and honor; and he made a marriage alliance with Ahab. After some years he went down to Ahab in Samaria. Ahab slaughtered an abundance of sheep and oxen for him and for the people who were with him, and induced him to go up against Ramoth-gilead.

> King Jehoshaphat of Judah returned in safety to his house in Jerusalem. Jehu the son of Hanani the seer went out to meet him, and said to King Jehoshaphat, "Should you help the wicked and love those who hate Yahweh? Because of this, wrath has gone out against you from Yahweh. Nevertheless, some good is found in you, for you destroyed the sacred poles [Asherahs] out of the land, and have set your heart to seek God." (2 Chr. 18:1–2; 19:1–3)

The second passage that has been conspicuously revised in 2 Chronicles is the report of Jehoshaphat's unsuccessful maritime venture. According to 1 Kings, Jehoshaphat refused Ahaziah's request to participate in the venture. The Chronicler has Jehoshaphat granting Ahaziah's request, however, and then offers this as the reason that the venture failed.

> There was no king in Edom; a deputy was king. Jehoshaphat made ships of the Tarshish type to go to Ophir for gold; but they did not go, for the ships were wrecked at Ezion-geber. Then Ahaziah the son of Ahab said to Jehoshaphat, "Let my servants go with your servants in the ships," but Jehoshaphat was not willing. (1 Kgs. 22:47–49)

> After this King Jehoshaphat of Judah joined with King Ahaziah of Israel, who did wickedly. He joined him in building ships to go to Tarshish; they built the ships in Ezion-geber. Then Eliezer the son of Dodavahu of Mareshah prophesied against Jehoshaphat, saying, "Because you have joined with Ahaziah, Yahweh will destroy what you have made." And the ships were wrecked and were not able to go to Tarshish. (2 Chr. 20:35–37)

---

25. See Ray Dillard, "The Chronicler's Jehoshaphat," *Trinity Journal* 7 (1986) 17–22; and G. N. Knoppers, "Reform and Regression: The Chronicler's Presentation of Jehoshaphat," *BIB* 72 (1991) 500–524. On the possible impact of the Omrides on Judah and Jerusalem, see Israel Finkelstein, "The Rise of Jerusalem and Judah: The Missing Link," in A. G. Vaughn and A. E. Killebrew, eds., *Jerusalem in Bible and Archaeology: The First Temple Period* (SBLSymS 18; Leiden: Brill, 2003) 81–101.

Thus we are faced with the same dilemma encountered earlier in connection with the Chronicler's work. The Chronicler's treatment of Jehoshaphat is obviously not to be taken at face value. This is an ideal Jehoshaphat, a Jehoshaphat re-created in accordance with a distinctive theological perspective on Judah's history. But is the Chronicler's information to be disregarded altogether? Again, it is not just a question of whether the Chronicler had access to authentic sources unavailable to the compilers of 1–2 Kings but of whether information derived from such sources can be separated out from the Chronicler's imaginative editorial claims and whether, given the Chronicler's tendentious use of the Genesis–2 Kings materials, this information has been distorted also.

Granting that the Chronicler may have preserved authentic information about Jehoshaphat's reign in addition to what can be gleaned from 1–2 Kings, the following items about Jehoshaphat present themselves for consideration.

> He built fortresses and store-cities and laid up provisions in cities throughout Judah. (2 Chr. 17:12–13)

> He had soldiers and elite fighting men in Jerusalem . . . [officers are named, with fighting units totaling over a million men] and also in the fortified cities throughout Judah. (2 Chr. 17:2, 19)

> In the third year of his reign, he sent out five princes to teach in the cities of Judah; and with them nine Levites and two priests, Elishama and Jehoram. And they "taught in Judah, having the book of the law of Yahweh with them." (2 Chr. 17:7–9)

> He appointed certain Levites, priests, and heads of families in Jerusalem to "give judgment for Yahweh and to decide disputed cases." Regarding "matters of Yahweh," they were answerable to Amariah the chief priest; in all the king's matters they were answerable to Zebadiah the governor of the house of Judah. Also he appointed judges throughout the land, particularly in the fortified cities. (2 Chr. 19:5–11)

> He received presents and tribute from some of the Philistines and Arabs. (2 Chr. 17:11)

Whatever the accuracy of these details, one receives the impression of a ruler who looked to the security of his kingdom in terms both of its defensive posture and of its central administrative control. Of course, modern distinctions between church and state did not apply. Thus Jehoshaphat's administrative reforms were conducted in the name of, and largely through the mechanism of, the official Yahwistic cult.

Jehoshaphat's fortification of cities, buildup of a military force, and administrative reform would not have been incompatible with his establishment of peaceful relations with Ahab. On the contrary, as indicated above, it was the circumstances brought about by Omride military strength and foreign policies that enabled Jehoshaphat to do these things. Moreover, in spite of the Chronicler's efforts to convince the reader otherwise, one has to suspect that Jehoshaphat was at best a "junior partner" in the alliance with Ahab, sealed by the marriage of Athaliah, Ahab's sister (or daughter), to Jehoram, Jehoshaphat's son. This is suggested by at least two factors: (1) Judah goes unmentioned in the same non-biblical records that witness to Israel's military strength and international prestige at the time of Ahab and Jehoshaphat. (2) Jehoshaphat came to be remembered by tradition as the Judean king who gave unqualified support to Israel—"I am as you are; my people are your people, my horses are your horses." Only after Ahab's death, when Mesha of Moab also began to challenge Omride authority, do we hear of Jehoshaphat taking a more independent stance: he refused Ahaziah's request to send Israelite merchants on the shipping expedition from Ezion-geber.

Jehoshaphat's Maritime Venture

The brief report in 1 Kings 22:47–49 of Jehoshaphat's ill-fated maritime expedition (preferred over the Chronicler's version of the incident for reasons given above) is open to two different interpretations. Since there has been no mention in the biblical materials of Israelite or Judean maritime activity in the Gulf of Aqabah since Solomon's day, one might conclude that this was an essentially new venture undertaken by Jehoshaphat. Once again, after three-quarters of a century, a king of Jerusalem gained access to the Gulf of Aqabah and attempted to exploit the commercial advantage that this afforded. Yet it is difficult to believe that access would have been unavailable or the commercial advantage neglected earlier in the Omride period. With much of Transjordan in Israelite hands; with Phoenicia, Israel, and Judah joined by marriage alliances; and with a "deputy" (answerable to whom?) in Edom—nothing would have been more natural than to revive the commercial arrangements that had been in effect during Solomon's day, whereby the Red Sea port was connected by overland routes through Judah and Israel to Phoenician ports on the Mediterranean. Indeed, the alliance of Phoenicia, Israel, and Judah implied by the marriage of Jezebel to Ahab and Athaliah to Jehoram may have been essentially a commercial pact for this very purpose.

The other possibility, therefore, which seems more likely in our opinion, is that Jehoshaphat, rather than initiating a new shipping venture from Aqabah and refusing Ahaziah's permission to participate, had decided to seize the monopoly of a joint Phoenician, Israelite, and Judean shipping program that had already been under way for some time. Moreover, if Israel under Ahab had overshadowed and perhaps dominated Judah under Jehoshaphat, then Jehoshaphat's exclusion of Israelite merchants would have represented more than an economically motivated move. It would have been a signal asserting Judah's claim of independence from Omride domination.

The mention of an Edomite "deputy" in connection with Jehoshaphat's unsuccessful venture, plus a later statement in 2 Kings 8:20 to the effect that Edom rebelled against Judah during the reign of Jehoram (Jehoshaphat's son), could be taken to suggest that Jehoshaphat subjected Edom at some point. Yet the reference to the Edomite deputy is not introduced as an individual item about Jehoshaphat's reign, as if control of Edom was to be remembered among his deeds. Its purpose, rather, is to clarify how Jehoshaphat had thoroughfare across Edomite territory to a port on the Gulf of Aqabah. Also the notation seems unnecessarily vague if its intention was to imply that Jehoshaphat himself controlled Edom through a deputy. Even the Chronicler apparently did not draw that conclusion or he would surely have emphasized the point somewhere in the excessive claims about Jehoshaphat's greatness.

If, as suggested above, Israel dominated Judah as well as Moab during Ahab's reign, perhaps the Edomite deputy was also an Omride appointee. Ahab's death and Ahaziah's incapacitation would have left this deputy in a very insecure position. Possibly it was only then, therefore, if at all, that Jehoshaphat gained some degree of Judean authority over Edom. Another possibility, as we shall see below, is that Jehoram inherited control of Edom directly from Israel. One should not think in terms of total Judean (or Israelite) control over the whole of Edomite territory, in any case, but rather of some limited authority over the traditionally Edomite territory west of the Arabah—that part of Edom situated between Judah and the Gulf of Aqabah.

According to our chronology, Jehoshaphat was a contemporary of Omri, Ahab, and perhaps part of the short reign of Ahaziah of Israel, but he would have died in 853–852 B.C.E., sometime within a year after Ahab. This conflicts, we are well aware, with (1) the synchronisms provided in the texts (1 Kgs. 3:1 and 8:16) that have Jehoshaphat still on the throne of Judah for some time after Jehoram had ascended the throne of Israel, and (2) the story of Jehoram's Moabite campaign in 2 Kings 3:4–27, which *in its present form* has Jehoshaphat march with Jehoram against Moab. Our view on this matter is that the story did not involve Jehoshaphat originally, and the synchronisms represent secondary editorial revision, intended to accommodate the story. Once the story had been modified to identify the "king of Judah" as Jehoshaphat and incorporated into the Genesis–2 Kings corpus, then it was necessary also to revise the synchronisms so that Jehoshaphat would still be on the throne contemporary with Jehoram.

The Two Jehorams(?)

Jehoram (alternate form: Joram), son of Jehoshaphat and married to the Omride queen Athaliah, ascended the throne in Jerusalem during the brief reign of Ahaziah of Israel. Ahaziah, when he died, was also followed by a Jehoram, identified as "his brother" in some of the early versions of 2 Kings 1:17 but not in the Hebrew text: "So he died according to the word of Yahweh that Elijah had spoken. Jehoram [his brother] became king in his stead in the second year of Jehoram the son of Jehoshaphat, king of Judah, because Ahaziah had no son." For a time, therefore, several years according to our chronology, both Israel and Judah were ruled by kings with the same name. Only one other throne change is reported to have occurred before Jehu's coup: Jehoram of Judah is said to have been succeeded by his son Ahaziah shortly before the incident. Thus it was Jehoram king of Israel and Ahaziah king of Judah whom Jehu is said to have assassinated.

Who was this Jehoram who came to the throne in Samaria upon the earlier Ahaziah's death? One may assume that he was an Omride, and it is tempting to speculate with the early versions of 2 Kings 1:17 that he was Ahaziah's brother, another of Ahab's sons. That we have two Jehorams on the throne at the same time, however, and for approximately the same length of time, raises the possibility that they were the same person—that is, that Ahaziah of Israel who died without any sons was succeeded on the throne in Samaria by his brother-in-law (married to Athaliah, Ahaziah's sister), who was already king of Judah.[26] If so, then once again for almost a decade, Israel and Judah would have been united under a single crown, a Judean king married to an Omride queen.

Obviously the compilers of Genesis–2 Kings and the Chronicler did not understand it this way, and even report two different deaths for the two Jehorams (2 Kgs. 8:24; 9:21–26; 2 Chr. 21:18–20). Yet it is easy to see how they might have misunderstood the records at their disposal, and several irregularities in their summations of the reigns suggest that they did misunderstand. (1) The text of 2 Kings 1:17, which reports Jehoram's accession to the throne of Israel, presents several variant readings, such as the insertion of "his brother" in some of the versions. (2) The usual references to "the Book of the Annals of the Kings of Israel" and "the Book of the Annals of the Kings of Judah" are absent for Jehoram of Israel and Ahaziah of Judah. (3) The Lucianic system of synchronisms for the Omride period does not include synchronisms for Jehoram and Ahaziah of Judah. All of this suggests that the ancient records for the period may not have required as many separate kings as the compilers of Genesis–2 Kings inferred from them, and that even the early transmitters of the biblical texts sensed a degree of uncertainty about Jehoram of Israel's background.

In summary, there is reason to suspect that (1) only one Jehoram ruled both kingdoms, ascending the throne first in Jerusalem and later in Samaria. Thus (2) he was reported in different contexts in the official records—that is, his reign and deeds as king of Judah would have been recorded in the Judean records and his activities as king of Israel in the Israelite records. And (3) the compilers of Genesis–2 Kings inferred incorrectly that Jehoram of Judah and Jehoram of Israel were two different persons.

According to 2 Kings 8:17 Jehoram ruled for eight years in Jerusalem, and according to 2 Kings 3:1 Jehoram ruled for twelve years in Samaria. How is this possible if they were the same person? According to our chronology, Jehoram became king in Jerusalem in 852–851 B.C.E., and in Samaria in 851–850. His eighth year in Jerusalem would have been 845–844 and his twelfth year in Samaria 840–839. If there were only one Jehoram who died in 840–839, why would 845–844 have been his last year in Jerusalem? The following factors seem to explain this phenomenon. (1) Early in 845 Shalmaneser III crossed the Euphrates River at flood (early in the year) with 120,000 men and confronted the anti-Assyrian coalition led by Hadadezer of Damascus and Irhulenu of Hamath (RIMA 3:39) in which Jehoram and Israel-Judah probably participated. (2) Shortly thereafter Hadadezer died or may have been killed in battle, and Hazael usurped the throne in Damascus (see *ANET* 280; RIMA 3:118). (3) Hazael dissolved the anti-Assyrian coalition and began a program of conquest against Damascus's former allies, including Israel. (4) Preoccupied with the new Syrian threat, Jehoram did not return to Jerusalem for the fall festival to renew his kingship over Judah after the fall festival in 845, the beginning of his eighth year.

The hypothesis of only one Jehoram would explain several other rather curious matters reported in Kings and Chronicles. For example, there is the passing

---

26. See John Strange, "Joram, King of Israel and Judah," *VT* 25 (1975) 191–201. Some scholars who adopt the theory of a single Jehoram consider him to have been a northerner rather than a southerner; see John Rogerson and Philip Davies, *The Old Testament World* (Englewood Cliffs, NJ: Prentice-Hall, 1989) 146.

observation in 2 Chronicles 21:4 that Jehoram of Judah, once he was established on the throne, killed certain "princes of Israel" in addition to some sons of Jehoshaphat. It is understandable why a Judean king would have wanted to remove any other possible claimants to the Judean throne. But for what reason and on what authority would he have executed Israelite princes—unless he had inherited the throne of Israel also and needed to secure his position on it as well? The possibility also emerges that Jehoram's dominion over Edom presupposed in 2 Kings 8:20 came with the Israelite rather than the Judean crown.

Whether Jehoram of Judah and Jehoram of Israel were the same person or brothers-in-law, the years of his or their reign or reigns saw rapid decline for both kingdoms. The summary of the reign of Jehoram of Judah in 2 Kings 8:16–24 reports that both Edom and the Judahite city of Libnah revolted from Judah at that time. Moab, on the other hand, under King Mesha, and probably encouraged by Hazael as was Edom, was already in open rebellion against Israel. Mesha had succeeded his father as king of Moab approximately midway in Ahab's reign, and his inscription presents his accession to the throne as the turning point in Israelite-Moabite relations. (See Text 4.) It was probably not until Ahab's death, however, during Ahaziah's weak reign, that Mesha made his first moves to throw off the Israelite yoke (2 Kgs. 1:1; 3:5). Specifically, Mesha's "rebellion" consisted of his refusal to pay the annual tribute imposed by Omri and continued by Ahab, recovery of Moabite control over northern Moab ("the land of Medeba," approximately from Heshbon to the Arnon), and preparations to defend Moab against Israel's retaliatory attack, which could be expected as soon as an active ruler was established in Samaria.

In the process Mesha took some limited military action against Israelite settlements in the area north of the Arnon: he massacred the Israelite population of two towns situated on the western slopes of northern Moab, Ataroth and Nebo, and occupied Jahaz, near his own city of Dibon. The Israelite population at Ataroth belonged to the tribe of Gad, which had occupied the city "always," in Mesha's estimation. At Nebo, where there was a Yahwistic cult place, Mesha claims to have slaughtered seven thousand Israelites and dragged away for presentation before Chemosh some sort of cultic object associated with Yahweh. Both Ataroth and Nebo were resettled with Moabites, a measure intended no doubt to ensure the defense of the Medeba plateau from any Israelite retaliation from the northwest. Jahaz, which had been fortified by Omri or Ahab to facilitate military and administrative control of the area north of the Arnon, was apparently abandoned by the Israelites without a struggle. Without any mention of military action, Mesha claims to have placed his own officials in the city and attached it to the district of Dibon.

We hear nothing of any attempt on the part of Israel to restore control over Moab until Jehoram's reign. For Jehoram's unsuccessful attempt, we have only the story of his Moabite campaign in 2 Kings 3:4–27, which is beset with literary and interpretational problems. As indicated above, the parallels between this narrative and the third of the stories of the three battles with Ben-hadad (1 Kgs. 22:1–38) are particularly striking—both narratives appear to have been revised at some point to give a prominent role to the king of Judah, who is identified in turn as Jehoshaphat. Regardless of how one deals with the various uncertainties of this text, Jehoram's attempt to restore control over Moab was clearly unsuccessful. Apparently Jehoram marched on Moab around the southern end of the Dead Sea and laid siege to Kir-hareseth, probably located near Dibon and to be identified with Qarhoh of the Mesha Inscription.[27] The city was about to fall, according to the narrative, when Mesha in desperation sacrificed his oldest son on the wall. "And there came great wrath upon Israel; and they withdrew from him and returned to their own land" (2 Kgs. 3:27).

Shalmaneser remained a constant threat to Syria-Palestine for several years, and Israel presumably continued to support the anti-Assyrian coalition that had already successfully defended against him once near the end of Ahab's reign and did so again in 849, 848, and 845. Israel's continued involvement in the coalition cannot be verified, however, since the entries in Shalmaneser's inscriptions for these latter three campaigns are unfortunately brief and identify only two of the opposing kings by name (Irhulenu of Hamath and Hadadezer of Damascus). Typical is the following entry with its braggadocio and claims of complete victory for Shalmaneser's tenth year (849–848).

> At that time Hadad-ezer (Adad-idri) the Damascene, and Irhulenu the Hamatite, together with twelve kings on the shore of the sea, trusting in their united forces attacked me to wage war and battle. I fought with them and defeated them. I put to the sword 10,000 of their fighting men. I took from them their chariotry, cavalry, and military equipment. (RIMA 3:38)

The End of the Omrides in Israel

The biblical account of Jehu's coup (2 Kgs. 8:25–10:27) was clearly written from a pro-Jehu perspective, emphasizing his Yahwistic zeal. According to the account, Israel's army was in the field at Ramoth-gilead fighting against Syrian attack when Jehoram was wounded and returned to Jezreel to recover. This left Jehu, presumably Jehoram's chief of staff, in charge of the army. In the meantime, Ahaziah, either Jehoram's son (assuming one Jehoram) or the son of his brother-in-law (assuming two Jehorams), came to visit him at Jezreel, possibly to serve at least temporarily as ruler of Jehoram's kingdom.

Jehu at that point, according to the biblical narrative, urged on by the prophet Elisha, hastened to Jezreel, where he assassinated both Jehoram and Jezebel. Jehoram's body was left exposed for the animals and birds on the plot of ground belonging to Naboth, and Jezebel's body was devoured by dogs in the streets of Jezreel. Jezebel, we are told, faced death without flinching. Without sackcloth and ashes or begging for mercy, she prepared to meet her murderer dressed like a queen, with eyes painted and head adorned. Then she addressed Jehu as a traitor: "Zimri, murderer of your master." Holding her head aloof, this woman, no doubt now aged, played the role of queen to the very end (2 Kgs. 9:30–37).

Ahaziah attempted to escape but was overtaken only a few miles away (near Ibleam) and shot with an arrow, though he continued on to Megiddo, where he died. Next, Jehu sent letters to Samaria giving notice of his actions and challenging the officials of the city to select another Omride as their king and to prepare

27. See B. C. Jones, "In Search of Kir Haraseth: A Case Study in Site Identification," *JSOT* 52 (1991) 3–24.

58. *Tel Dan Inscription.* Fragments of an Aramaic inscription discovered in the excavations at Tel Dan in northern Israel. (*Israel Museum*) (See Text 6 for translation.)

to defend the government. "Now then, as soon as this letter comes to you, seeing your master's sons are with you, and there are with you chariots and horses, fortified cities also, and weapons, select the best and fittest of your master's sons and set him on his father's throne, and fight for your master's house" (2 Kgs. 10:2–3). The officials responded that they had no intentions of opposing Jehu, whereupon he sent further instructions with which they complied. "If you are on my side, and if you are ready to obey me, take the heads of your master's sons, and come to me at Jezreel tomorrow at this time" (2 Kgs. 10:6). Finally, we are told, Jehu came himself to Samaria and made a great feast for all the prophets and worshipers of Baal. When all were assembled in the Baal temple and guards stationed at the doors, he gave the signal that all were to be killed. The account ends with his demolishing the pillar of Baal and the temple itself.

This scenario for Jehu's rise to power has been called into question by the Tel Dan Stela (see Text 6).[28] As we shall see below, this inscription was probably erected by King Hazael of Damascus after he recaptured the region of Dan from Israel. The inscription opens with a statement about an Israelite king having encroached on Syrian territory. There follows a boast by the monarch who erected the stela that he had been made king and granted victories by the god Hadad. Further on, he claims to have killed ". . . rm, son of . . . king of Israel and . . . yhw son of . . . king of the house of David." The only Israelite king with a name ending in *rm* is Jehoram and the only Judahite ("house of David") king of the ninth century with a name ending in *yhw* is Ahaziah.[29]

28. See S. A. Irvine, "The Rise of the House of Jehu," in Dearman and Graham, eds., *Land*, 104–18; idem, "The Last Battle of Hadadezer," *JBL* 124 (2005) 341–47.

29. The Stela consists of three fragments containing portions of thirteen lines and was discovered in excavations at Tel Dan (Tell el-Qadi) in 1993 and 1994. See Avraham Biran and Joseph Naveh, "An Aramaic Stele Fragment from Tel Dan," *IEJ* 43 (1993) 81–98; idem, "The Tel Dan Inscription: A New Fragment," *IEJ* 45 (1995) 1–18. Our reading assumes that the various fragments found fit together. Others, however, assume that the two main sets of fragments come from different spots in a large inscription. Since the original publication, a plethora of articles on the stela have appeared: see the bibliography in Nadav Na'aman, "Three Notes on the Aramaic Inscription from Tel Dan," *IEJ* 50 (2000) 92–104; repr. in *AIHH* 173–86; and the study and reconstruction by George Athas, *The Tel Dan Inscription: A Reappraisal and a New Interpretation* (JSOTSup 360; Copenhagen International Seminar Series 12; Sheffield: Sheffield Academic Press, 2003). Athas places the two main fragmentary units at very different places in the text and argues that Ben-hadad, the son of Hazael, erected the stela; so also Gershon Galil, "A Re-arrangement of the Fragments of the Tel Dan Inscription and the Relations Between Israel and Aram," *PEQ* 133 (2001) 16–21.

TEXT 6. The Tel Dan Stela

. . . my father lay down [died], he went to . . . the king of Israel previously campaigned in the land of Abil [or "land of my father"]. [The god] Hadad made me king, me. And Hadad went in front of me . . . of my kingdom. And I killed two powerful kings who harnessed thousands of chariots and thousands of horsemen. [I killed Jeho]ram son of . . .* king of Israel and I killed [Ahaz]iah [his] son . . . of the house of David and I laid. . . . their land . . . (See *COS* 2:161-62.)

*One could here restore '*h'b* = Ahab or *yhspt* = Jehoshaphat.

Obviously, if Hazael killed Jehoram and Ahaziah, the biblical story of how Jehu killed them must be historically incorrect. Priority must be given to the Tel Dan Inscription over the biblical material, moreover, because the former is almost contemporary with the events under consideration, while the latter probably dates from the last years of the Jehu dynasty and is noticeably formulated to support the legitimacy and orthodoxy of that dynasty.[30] In short, the Omride era was brought to a close not only by an internal military revolt, but also by an external attack. The international circumstances surrounding this attack will be examined in the next chapter.

General Bibliography

The general history of the Neo-Assyrian empire is discussed in the following articles by A. K. Grayson: "Studies in Neo-Assyrian History: The Ninth Century B.C.," *BO* 33 (1976) 134–45; "Assyria: Ashur-dan II to Ashur-Nirari V (934–715 B.C.)," *CAH* 3/1:238–81; and "Assyrian Officials and Power in the Ninth and Eighth Centuries," *SAAB* 7 (1993) 19–52. The Assyrian royal inscriptions are collected and translated in his *Assyrian Rulers of the Early First Millennium BC, I (1114–859 B.C.)* and *II (858–745 B.C.)* (RIMA 2–3; Toronto: University of Toronto Press, 1987–1996).

Other important works on the relationships between Assyria and the west during the ninth century are: J. K. Kuan, *Neo-Assyrian Historical Inscriptions and Syria-Palestine:*

30. The problem of who killed Jehoram and Ahaziah has been handled in five ways. (1) J. W. Wesselius, "The First Royal Inscription from Ancient Israel: The Tel Dan Inscription Reconsidered," *SJOT* 13 (1999) 163–86, argues that the inscription was set up by Jehu. Thus no problem exists. (2) André Lemaire, "The Tel Dan Stela as a Piece of Royal Historiography," *JSOT* 81 (1998) 3–14, considers the stela to be royal propaganda and the claim of the Aramaean king as unhistorical. (3) Others propose some harmonization of the biblical and the stela texts. Shigeo Yamada, "Aram-Israel Relations as Reflected in the Aramaic Inscription from Tel Dan," *UF* 27 (1995) 611–25, argues that the term *qtl*, translated "kill," really means "defeat." W. M. Schniedewind, "Tel Dan Stela: New Light on Aramaic and Jehu's Revolt," *BASOR* 302 (1996) 75–90, thinks that Jehu was acting as a partner with Hazael when he assassinated the two kings. (4) Nadav Na'aman, "Three Notes on the Aramaic Inscription from Tel Dan," *IEJ* 50 (2000) 92–104, has argued that primacy must be assigned to the course of events described in the Tel Dan stela, namely that an Aramaean king (Hazael) killed Jehoram and Ahaziah, since the stela is a nearly contemporary document and the biblical stories about the rise of Jehu are later propagandistic and novelistic accounts. (5) A. F. Rainey reads the verbs in lines 7–8 as passive, "was killed," and thus the text makes no reference to who did the killing (Rainey and R. S. Notley, *The Sacred Bridge: Carta's Atlas of the Biblical World* [Jerusalem: Carta, 2006] 212–13).

Israelite/Judean-Tyrian-Damascene Political and Commercial Relations in the Ninth-Eighth Centuries B.C.E. (Jian Dao Dissertation Series 1; Hong Kong: Alliance Bible Seminary, 1995); Shigeo Yamada, *The Construction of the Assyrian Empire: A Historical Study of the Inscriptions of Shalmaneser III (859–824 B.C.) Relating to His Campaigns to the West* (SHANE 3; Leiden: Brill, 2000); Edward Lipiński, *The Aramaeans: Their Ancient History, Culture, Religion* (OLA 100; Leuven: Peeters, 2000); and W. T. Pitard, *Ancient Damascus: A Historical Study of the Syrian City-State from Earliest Times until Its Fall to the Assyrians in 732 B.C.E.* (Winona Lake, IN: Eisenbrauns, 1987).

Archaeological surveys of this period are provided by J. S. Holladay Jr., "The Kingdoms of Israel and Judah: Political and Economic Centralization in the Iron IIA-B (ca. 1000–750 BCE)," in T. E. Levy, ed., *The Archaeology of Society in the Holy Land* (2d ed.; London: Leicester University Press, 1998) 368–98; and Gabriel Barkay, "The Iron Age II-III," in Amnon Ben-Tor, ed., *The Archaeology of Ancient Israel* (New Haven: Yale University Press, 1992) 302–73. Israel Finkelstein and N. A. Silberman, *The Bible Unearthed: Archaeology's New Vision of Ancient Israel and the Origin of Its Sacred Texts* (New York: Free Press, 2001) 169–95, provide a history of the Omrides based on the "low chronology" archaeological perspective.

11. The Century of the Jehu Dynasty

Whatever the circumstances of Jehu's accession to the throne in Samaria—a matter to be explored in more detail below—it marked the end of an era. Israel and Judah fell under the shadow of more powerful states (Assyria and Damascus) at this time, and moments of national autonomy were to be the exception rather than the rule during the remainder of their respective histories. Jehu's accession to the throne in Samaria is also an important benchmark for chronological purposes. Jehu in Samaria and Athaliah in Jerusalem came to power in connection with the same political upheaval and at approximately the same time.

Jehu and his descendants were to rule in Samaria for almost a century, a record that is admittedly less impressive when one considers that the first two rulers of the dynasty (Jehu and Jehoahaz) were largely at the mercy of Damascus and exercised little authority outside the immediate vicinity of Samaria. Nevertheless, the era of the Jehu dynasty is the one period in the history of the separate kingdoms when political unrest and palace intrigue were more characteristic of Judah than of Israel.

It will be useful to divide the century of the Jehu dynasty into two parts. Roughly the first half—the reigns of Jehu and Jehoahaz in Israel contemporary with Athaliah and Joash (sometimes called Jehoash) in Judah—was the time of severe Syrian oppression at the hands of Hazael and Ben-hadad II of Damascus. At some point near the end of Jehoahaz's reign and/or early in the reign of Joash of Israel (the exact sequence of events is one of the issues to be explored below) Assyria again became active in the west. One result was that, at the hands of Assyria, the fortunes of Damascus took a turn for the worse, which allowed Israel and Judah a brief reprieve from Syrian oppression. During portions of the second half century of the Jehu dynasty, therefore, both kingdoms witnessed a relative moment of national restoration.

Sources of Information

The Biblical Materials

Although the Jehu dynasty held the throne of Israel twice as long as did the Omride dynasty, the compilers of Genesis–2 Kings devoted less than half as much space to the Jehu era. This is not surprising, since it was not a very impressive period in the history of the two kingdoms, certainly not of Judah. Moreover, the circumstances of this era were problematic for the compilers' theological perspective, particularly the view that Yahweh gave success to those kings who were faithful to him and especially those who supported his cult in Jerusalem. Jehu turned out to be powerless before Hazael. His great-grandson Jeroboam II, on the other hand, who was not remembered as a strong Yahwist, nevertheless was able to expand Israel's borders and clearly over-shadowed his Judean contemporary, Uzziah.

Thus the section of the Genesis–2 Kings corpus that has to do with the era of the Jehu dynasty—from the account of Jehu's coup (2 Kgs. 9:1–10:27) through 2 Kings 15—consists of little more than brief summations of the individual kings' reigns. There is a relatively full report of how the child Joash survived Athaliah's purge of the royal family, displaced her on the throne, and later arranged for repairs of the Jerusalem temple (11:1–12:16) and of the conflict between Joash of Israel and Amaziah of Judah that resulted in the sack of Jerusalem (14:8–14). Otherwise the only extended narrative in this section, comparable to the numerous prophetical narratives introduced by the compilers into the context of the reigns of the Omride kings, is another story pertaining to Elisha that the compilers placed in the context of the reign of Joash (Jehoash) of Israel (13:14–21). As we observed in chapter 10, most of the Elisha stories were inserted into the context of the Omride period (reigns of Ahab and Jehoram; 2 Kgs. 2; 4:1–8:15). Yet most of these Elisha stories, as well as the stories of the three battles with Ben-hadad II (1 Kgs. 20; 22:1–38), actually reflect conditions of the period of the Jehu dynasty and thus must be taken into account in this chapter.

The Chronicler's presentation of the era of the Jehu dynasty (2 Chr. 22:10–27:9) follows the now familiar pattern. The Israelite kings are ignored, except when they figure in Judean affairs. The information presented for the Judean kings essentially duplicates the summations that already appear in 2 Kings, but with expansions and modifications that often, but not always, reflect the Chronicler's particular interests and perspectives. For example, the Levites are given an important role in the coronation ceremony for Joash of Judah. There is a fuller account of Amaziah's victory over Edom. In the case of Joash, Amaziah, and Uzziah, there is the familiar pattern whereby a king's early years of rule, during which he was supposedly on good terms with the Yahwistic priests and prophets and led the kingdom to strength and prosperity, are contrasted with his later years when he turned against the Yahwistic leaders and met with various disasters.

Certain of the prophetical books come into consideration at this point in our survey of Israelite and Judean history. The superscriptions to the books of Amos and Hosea associate the careers of these two prophets with the reigns of Jeroboam II and Uzziah, for example, and Isaiah 1:1 places Isaiah's early career in the reigns of Uzziah and Jotham. Occasionally the oracles collected in these books contain rather specific references to the kings and the political circumstances of their reigns. Hosea 1 alludes to a bloody massacre by Jehu and predicts that his dynasty will receive its own punishment. Amos's oracles uttered at Bethel also included a strong denunciation of Jeroboam II. For the most part, however, like the Elijah and Elisha stories, the oracles collected in these books provide primarily general background information about the social, economic, and religious circumstances of the day from which they come.

Royal Assyrian and Syrian Records

Fortunately, although the epigraphical evidence is limited, there is enough to allow us to reconstruct the main outlines of Assyrian and Syrian (Aramaean) history during the century of the Jehu dynasty, and when placed against this backdrop, the also limited biblical materials pertaining specifically to this century take on more meaning. Especially useful for tracing the annual movements of the Assyrian army and its occasional forays into Syria-Palestine are the so-called Eponym Chronicles (or *limmu* lists) compiled by Assyrian scribes. These are frequently augmented by monumental inscriptions (in Akkadian) left by the Assyrian kings to commemorate their deeds. Also relevant for our consideration are some boundary markers placed by the Assyrians, as well as some inscriptions left by Assyrian governors in the west. In addition to these Akkadian texts, there are occasional Aramaic inscriptions left by local Aramaean rulers.

Shalmaneser's Last Two Western Campaigns. After an absence of three years (see chapter 10 for his earlier western campaigns in 853, 849, 848, and 845), Shalmaneser III returned to Syria-Palestine in his eighteenth regnal year (841–840). His inscriptions contain several accounts of this campaign; the following is a composite of statements drawn from three different texts.[1]

> Hadad-ezer passed away and Hazael, son of a nobody, took the throne . . . trusting in the might of his soldiers, he carried out an extensive muster of his troops. He fortified Mount Saniru, the mountain peak, which is before Mount Lebanon. I fought with him (and) defeated him. I put to the sword 16,000 of his fighting men (and) took away from him 1,121 of his chariots (and) took 470 of his cavalry with his military camp. To save his life he ran away (but) I pursued him. I confined him in Damascus, his royal city, (and) cut down his gardens. I marched to Mount Hauranu (and) razed, destroyed, (and) burned cities without number. I carried off more booty than could be counted. . . . I marched to Mount Ba'alira'asi, which is a cape (jutting out into the sea) before the land of Tyre, (and) erected my royal statue there. I received tribute from Ba'ali-manzeri of Tyre (and) from Jehu of the house of Omri. On my return I ascended Mount Lebanon (and) erected my royal statue with the statue of Tiglath-pileser (I), a strong king who preceded me. (RIMA 3:118, 48, 54)

This time Shalmaneser encountered a different political landscape in the region than he had during his earlier campaigns. Most notably, the anti-Assyrian coalition that had confronted him on four previous occasions was no longer in place, having disintegrated following the death of Hadadezer of Damascus sometime after 845. Also in connection with this campaign, both Jehu and his contemporary Hazael of Damascus make their first appearance in Assyrian records.

Not facing any unified resistance, the Assyrian army moved farther south into central Syria than ever before, passing through the territory of Hamath,

---

1. The three texts are from a fragmentary inscription engraved on a broken statue of Shalmaneser discovered by the German excavators in 1903 at the site of the ancient city of Ashur, the royal annals inscribed on two monumental bulls at Calah, and the royal annals inscribed on a stone tablet used in one of the walls of Ashur. Among the Akkadian texts, only the first inscription provides Shalmaneser's description of Hazael's takeover and only the third names the king of Tyre at the time.

59. *Jehu bows before Shalmaneser III.* Detail of the so-called Black Obelisk. *(British Museum)*

which had been an important city in the old anti-Assyrian coalition.[2] Tyre seems to have submitted quickly and renewed its pre-853 tributary relationship with Assyria. Hazael of Damascus made a temporary stand at Mount Saniru in the foothills of the Anti-Lebanon Mountains. He fled the field and took refuge in Damascus, while the Assyrian army ravaged southern Syria, the environs of Damascus, and the Hauran (Bashan) region east and southeast of the Sea of Galilee. Then the Assyrians turned west toward the Mediterranean where Shalmaneser set up a statue of himself at Ba'alira'asi (probably Ras en-Naqura on the present-day Israel-Lebanon border). By now it would have been early 840, and the Assyrian king returned home by way of Mount Lebanon in time for the spring *akitu* festival. At some point during his swing through northern Palestine from the Hauran to Ba'alira'asi, Shalmaneser received tribute from "Jehu the Omride."

Shalmaneser's sixth and last Syro-Palestinian campaign, conducted in 838–837, is reported on the Black Obelisk: "In my twenty-first regnal year I crossed the Euphrates for the twenty-first time and marched to the cities of Hazael of Damascus. I captured four cities and received tribute from the peoples of the land of Tyre, Sidon, and Byblos" (RIMA 3:67).

One of the panels (B) on the Black Obelisk is devoted to Jehu and depicts him bowing before the Assyrian king.[3] The accompanying epigraph reads as follows: "I received the tribute of Jehu (the man) of Bit-Humri: silver, gold, a golden bowl, a golden goblet, golden cups, golden buckets, tin, a staff of the

2. Although a member of the anti-Assyrian coalition for years, Hamath had apparently capitulated to or was earlier defeated by the Assyrians. The Assyrian king Sargon II later reported, after defeating Hamath in 720–719 B.C.E., that he imposed tribute on Hamath along with "gifts and corvée work, as my royal fathers had imposed on Irhulenu" (see *COS* 2:294), one of the leaders of the coalition that first fought Shalmaneser III at Qarqar in 853. The absence of any reference to subduing Hamath in Shalmaneser's inscriptions is surprising. Possibly, Hazael had broken Hamath's power between 845 and 841, or else Hamath chose voluntarily to submit to Assyria as did Jehu.

3. See C. C. Smith, "Jehu and the Black Obelisk of Shalmaneser III," in A. L. Merrill and T. W. Overholt, eds., *Scripture in History and Theology: Essays in Honor of J. Coert Rylaarsdam* (Pittsburgh: Pickwick, 1977) 71–105.

king's hand, (and) javelins" (*COS* 2:270; see RIMA 3:149). This reference to Jehu, like the other three in Shalmaneser's inscriptions, actually calls him *mar Humri*, "the son of Omri." The designation, however, should not be understood as an indication of his genealogical heritage.[4] (Note that according to 2 Kgs. 9:2 Jehu was the son of Jehoshaphat son of Nimshi.) It should be read instead as a gentilic—that is, Jehu was "the man of the house of [Bit] Omri." "Bit-Omri" was what the Assyrians frequently called Israel, apparently recognizing Omri as its founder.[5]

The term translated "staff," which is used also in panel A of the inscription pertaining to Sua the Gilzanean, perhaps should be interpreted as a symbolic item. That is, the transference of the staff would have indicated that Jehu was placing himself and his country under the protection of the Assyrian king.[6] In other words, Jehu is depicted offering the state he represented into the custodial care of Assyria.

We learn that Shalmaneser captured four of Hazael's cities during this 838–837 campaign, two of which are noted in the Eponym Chronicle—Malahu and Danabu. The Assyrians, however, seem not to have inflicted any extensive damage on Hazael's kingdom, although Malahu is called a "royal city." Moreover, there is no indication in the Assyrian records that either Shalmaneser or his successor Shamshi-Adad V (823–811) returned to southern Syria after 838–837. It is noteworthy that Shalmaneser did not accompany his army on their campaigns during the last nine years of his reign (832–824), but placed them instead under the command of his field marshal (*turtanu*). This may suggest a weakness or insecurity in the administration of his power. Also of the final four years of Shalmaneser's reign (827–824), and through the first three years of Shamshi-Adad's rule (823–821), the Eponym Chronicle gives other signals of political instability in Assyria, noting there was "revolt" in the land. An inscription of the latter king states that "twenty seven towns with their fortresses had rebelled against Shalmaneser" (RIMA 3:183).

Adad-nirari III and the West. Not until the reign of Adad-nirari III (810–783) did the Assyrians resume a vigorous policy in the west. The Eponym Chronicle reports a long and major campaign into Syria during the early years of his reign (805/804—802/801), and we possess three notable inscriptions that fill out the picture somewhat. The first is the Saba'a Stela inscription discovered in the desert south of the Sinjar hills (in present-day Iraq) in 1905. Between the

---

4. See T. J. Schneider, "Rethinking Jehu," *Bib* 77 (1996) 100–107, who argues that Jehu was a member of a secondary Omride line; and Nadav Na'aman, "Jehu Son of Omri: Legitimizing a Loyal Vassal by His Overlord," *IEJ* 48 (1998) 236–38 (repr. in *AIIN* 13–15), who argues that the title was honorarily supplied to legitimate Jehu as a member of the ruling family. The idiom "son" to mean "member/ruler" of a state or kingdom, however, is common in Akkadian, as is the reference to a kingdom as a "house" (*bit*). Thus "son of Omri" is shorthand for "member of the house of Omri"; see K. A. Kitchen, *The Reliability of the Old Testament* (Grand Rapids: Eerdmans, 2003) 523 n. 44; and for other similar designations (*mar Agusi*, etc.) see Simo Parpola, *Neo-Assyrian Toponyms* (AOAT 6; Neukirchen-Vluyn: Neukirchener Verlag, 1970) 75–92.

5. On the Assyrian designations for the northern kingdom, see B. E. Kelle, "What's in a Name? Neo-Assyrian Designations for the Northern Kingdom and Their Implications for Israelite History and Biblical Interpretation," *JBL* 121 (2002) 639–66.

6. See Moshe Elat, "The Campaigns of Shalmaneser III against Aram and Israel," *IEJ* 25 (1975) 25–35. On the depiction of Jehu and his courtiers on the Black Obelisk, see P. J. King and L. E. Stager, *Life in Biblical Israel* (LAI; Louisville: Westminster John Knox, 2001) 262–63.

introduction and conclusion, which are typical of the royal Assyrian inscriptions, the following items are reported.

> In the fifth year after I had ascended nobly the royal throne [that is, in 806–805], I mustered the land and commanded the extensive troops of Assyria to march to the land Hatti. I crossed the Euphrates in flood. The kings of the extensive [land Hatti] who, in the time of Shamshi-Adad [V], my father, had become strong and withheld their [tribute]—by the command of . . . the gods . . . (my) awesome radiance overwhelmed them and they submitted to me. (RIMA 3:208–9)

The second inscription appears on the Rimah Stela discovered in 1967 during the excavations at al-Rimah in Iraq (see Text 8 and Photograph 60). After the usual introduction, Adad-nirari claims to have conquered "the land of Amurru and the Hatti land" in a single year. Lines 6–8 of this inscription, which shifts from first person to third person, repeat Adad-nirari's claim to have received tribute from Mari' of Damascus and makes the same claim regarding the rulers of Tyre, Sidon, and "Iu'asu (= Joash), the Samarian" (RIMA 3:211; COS 2:276). *Mari'* is an Aramaic title, "lord," not the name of the king of Damascus. It was probably Bar (= Ben)-hadad II, son of Hazael, who had recently succeeded Hazael his father.

The third inscription, on the so-called Calah Slab, gives a slightly different version of the Damascus capitulation, mentioning that Mari' was confined in the city of Damascus, eventually submitted, and paid tribute in his royal palace. Also it provides a slightly different tribute list (see RIMA 3:313; COS 2:276).

At first glance, the reference to "(my) fifth year" in the Saba'a Inscription, combined with the claim that he conquered "the land of Amurru and the Hatti land" in a single year, seems to imply that Adad-nirari subdued the west and collected tribute from Joash all in his fifth year. But this does not necessarily follow. First, 805–804 was but the beginning of a long and major campaign that continued through 802–801. The main Assyrian army probably remained in the west throughout these years; only the king and his personal entourage would have returned to the capital city each year to celebrate the *akitu* festival. Second, the Saba'a and Rimah inscriptions, like the Mesha Inscription, are not annals but summary texts that report Adad-nirari's deeds over a period of years. Accordingly, the reference to Adad-nirari's fifth year in the Saba'a Inscription probably means only that it was in his fifth year that Adad-nirari began his military campaigns or, since these inscriptions summarize specifically his western campaigns, that it was in his fifth year that Adad-nirari began his conquest of the west.

Early on in the campaign, as we shall see below, the Assyrian army probably encountered opposition from an anti-Assyrian coalition. The resistance was probably led by Damascus, and the Assyrians may not actually have conquered the city. Yet Damascus clearly submitted, its role as the dominating power in Syria was eclipsed, and by the end of the long campaign Adad-nirari had received the submission of states farther to the south of Syria-Palestine than any previous Assyrian king.

Shamshi-ilu of Til Barsip. Naturally Adad-nirari claimed the credit, but much of Assyria's renewed military activity and political influence in the west should be attributed to his provincial governors. One in particular, his field marshal Shamshi-ilu, deserves special attention.[7] Shamshi-ilu was appointed field marshal (*turtanu*) about 807–806 and ruled essentially as a monarch of Til Barsip, the major city of the kingdom of Bit-Adini, for over fifty years (see Photograph 62).[8] The Eponym Chronicle identifies him as *limmu* for the years 780–779, 770–769, and 752–751, which means that he served under three different kings (Adad-nirari III, Shalmaneser IV, and Ashur-dan III). Adad-nirari III appears to have been a rather unimpressive ruler with provincial governors exercising major leadership roles. Shamshi-ilu in reality actually functioned as a reigning monarch over the western portion of the Assyrian Empire.[9]

The Assyrian army was usually occupied away from Syria-Palestine during the latter years of Adad-nirari and during the reigns of his two successors. Especially under Shalmaneser IV (782–773), the annual campaigns were conducted primarily against a new enemy that had appeared on the scene—Urartu. This kingdom, located around Lake Van in present-day Turkey, emerged under King Argishti I (ca. 786–764) as a major competitor with Assyria. Shalmaneser IV's army fought in Urartu during six of his ten years, and Shamshi-ilu, in one of his inscriptions, also reports battling Argishti (see *COS* 2:278; RIMA 3:232–33).

Shamshi-ilu was responsible for keeping the local rulers of Syria-Palestine, including Damascus, in check. The Eponym Chronicle records that the Assyrian army marched against Damascus in 773–772, and a recently (1990) published stela found in the Pararcik region of Turkey provides information on this campaign. The stela contains two inscriptions, one on the front and the other on the back.[10] One is from the time of Adad-nirari III and the other from the reign of Shalmaneser IV (782–773). The latter reports on a military campaign

7. See J. K. Kuan, "Šamši-ilu and the *Realpolitik* of Israel and Aram-Damascus in the Eighth Century B.C.E.," in J. A. Dearman and M. P. Graham, eds., *The Land that I Will Show You: Essays on the History and Archaeology of the Ancient Near East in Honour of J. Maxwell Miller* (JSOTSup 343; Sheffield: Sheffield Academic Press, 2001) 135–51.

8. That he was already *turtanu* before 805 B.C.E. is indicated by a boundary stela set up to settle a border dispute between the kingdoms of Arpad and Hamath along the Orontes River (see *COS* 2:272; RIMA 3:203–4). The stela unearthed in 1968 by a farmer near Antakya in Turkey reports that Adad-nirari and Shamshi-ilu settled the dispute in favor of Arpad. Since another boundary stone, unearthed in building the Pazarcik dam in Turkey (see the translation in n. 11 below), as well as the Eponym Chronicle, indicate that Arpad (along with eight allies) was in rebellion against Assyria by 805–804, Shamshi-ilu must have been serving as *turtanu* before the latter date; otherwise the rebellious Arpad would not have been treated favorably (see *COS* 2:273; RIMA 3:205).

9. Shamshi-ilu's own inscriptions seldom mention the Assyrian king and take the form of royal dedicatory texts; see François Thureau-Dangin, "L'inscription des lions de Til-Barsib," *RA* 27 (1930) 11–21. In one of his inscriptions, he describes himself as "the field marshal, the great herald, [the administrator of] temples, chief of the extensive army, governor of the land of Ḫatti (and) of the land of the Guti and all the land of Namri, conqueror of the mountains in the West, who lays waste . . . overthrows . . . who plunders his people, who devastates the lands' (RIMA 3:232; *COS* 2:278). On Bit-Adini, his primary territory, see David Ussishkin, "Was Bit-Adini a Neo-Hittite or Aramaean State?" *Or* 40 (1971) 431–37; and Edward Lipiński, *The Aramaeans: Their Ancient History, Culture, Religion* (OLA 100; Leuven: Peeters, 2000) 163–93.

10. The original stela with a single inscription from the time of Adad-nirari III had been taken to Damascus, probably by Hazael. Shamshi-ilu retrieved it on his campaign to the Syrian capital, inscribed the reverse side with a new inscription, and reerected it. For the publication of the stela, see Veysel Donbaz, "Two Neo-Assyrian Stelae in the Antakya and Kahramanmaras Museums," *Annual Review of the Royal Inscriptions of Mesopotamia Project* 8 (1990) 5–24; for a discussion of the previously unknown Syrian king Hadianu, see Stephan Timm, "König Hesion II. von Damaskus," *WO* 24 (1993) 55–84. English translation of the full inscriptions are given in RIMA 3:204–5, 239–40; *COS* 2:273, 283–84.

that Shamshi-ilu conducted against Damascus in 773–772, clearly the same campaign noted in the Eponym Chronicle.

When Shamshi-ilu, the *turtanu*, marched to Aram-Damascus, "the tribute of Hadianu of the Arameans of Damascus—silver, gold, copper, his royal bed, his royal couch, his daughter with her enormous dowry, the countless property of his palace—I received from him" (*NAHI* 115).[11]

Texts Related to Syrian Rulers. During the approximately three decades between the last western campaign of Shalmaneser III (838–837 B.C.E.) and renewed Assyrian campaigning in the west by Adad-nirari (805/804–802/801), Damascus emerged under the energetic leadership of Hazael as the dominant regional power in Syria-Palestine. Hazael's aggressive policies are well noted in the biblical materials (2 Kgs. 10:32–33; 13:3–25). He was followed by Bar-hadad II (biblical Ben-hadad), who apparently continued the same policies until eclipsed by the return to the west of the Assyrian armies under Adad-nirari in 805–804 and following.

Hazael's Booty Inscriptions. If King Hazael set up the Tel Dan Stela, discussed in the previous chapter, it constitutes the only significant firsthand inscription from his reign. Four smaller dedicatory inscriptions of his reign are known. Of these, two are very fragmentary. The other two were incised on pieces of horse gear unearthed at sites in Greece where they had later been taken as loot.[12] Apparently almost identical, the one-line Aramaic text reads: "That which (the god) Hadad gave to our lord Hazael from Amqi in the year our lord crossed the river" (see *COS* 2:162–63). The identity of "the river" in these inscriptions has been a matter of debate. Frequently, in the Bible and elsewhere, unspecified references to "the river" denote the Euphrates. That being the case, these texts could imply that Hazael controlled territory throughout northern Syria and even crossed the Euphrates to attack Assyrian home territory.[13] There is no support for such an attack in Assyrian records, so "the river" should probably be understood as the Orontes and the inscribed booty would have been from the region known in Assyrian texts as Umqi or Patinu, which lay between the Orontes River and the Mediterranean Sea.[14]

The Zakkur Inscription. The Eponym Chronicle locates the Assyrian army at Arpad in 805–804, and there are indications that the Assyrians were again encountering an anti-Assyrian coalition (as had Shalmaneser III in 853). A boundary stela notes that Adad-nirari defeated Atarshumki, king of Arpad, along with eight of his allies (*COS* 2:273; RIMA 3:205; and above n. 11).

Something of the internal Syro-Palestinian politics that will have preceded this encounter between the Assyrians and the coalition can be seen in the inscription on the so-called Zakkur Stela, discovered at Afis (ancient Hatarikka) near Idlib in northern Syria (see *COS* 2:155, and Text 7). Zakkur,

---

11. The obverse of the stela mentioned in the previous note contains the following claim: "I [Adad-nirari] fought a pitched battle with them—with Ataršumki, the son of Adrame, the Arpadite, together with eight kings who were with them at the city of Paqiraḥubuna. I took away from them their camp. In order to save their lives they ran away" (*COS* 2:273; RIMA 3:205).

12. See Israel Eph'al and Joseph Naveh, "Hazael's Booty Inscriptions," *IEJ* 39 (1989) 192–200; and François Bron and André Lemaire, "Les inscriptions araméenes de Hazaël," *RA* 83 (1989) 35–44.

13. This view is advocated by P. E. Dion, "Syro-Palestinian Resistance to Shalmaneser III in the Light of New Documents," *ZAW* 107 (1995) 482–89.

14. For this view, see Lipiński, *Aramaeans*, 386–90.

TEXT 7. The Zakkur Inscription

I am Zakkur, king of Hamat and Lu'ash. I am a man of 'Anah.* The Baal of
heaven [called me] and stood by me. The Baal of Heaven made me king over
Hatarikka [Hadrach].

Barhadad, the son of Hazael, king of Aram, united s[even]teen kings
against me: Barhadad and his army; Bargush [Arpad] and his army; the king
of Que and his army; the king of 'Amuq and his army; the king of Gurgum
and his army; the king of Sam'al and his army; the king of Melid and his
army. [All these kings whom Barhadad united against] me, seven[teen] kings
and their armies. All these kings laid siege to Hatarikka. They made a rampart higher than the wall of Hatarikka. They made a moat deeper than its
moat. But I lifted up my hand to the Baal of Heaven, and the Baal of Heaven
heard me. The Baal of Heaven [spoke] to me through seers and through *diviners.* The Baal of Heaven [said to me]: "Do not fear, for I made you king, and
I shall stand beside you and deliver you from all [these kings who] set up
a siege against you." [*The Baal of Heaven*] said to me: ["*I shall destroy*] all
these kings who set up [a siege against you and *made this moat*] and this *wall*
which. . . ." (See *COS* 2:155.)

*Zakkur was apparently a usurper from 'Anah on the Middle Euphrates.

who erected the stela, identified himself as king of Hamath and Lu'ash as well
as king of Hatarikka (Hazrach). He claims to have defended Hatarikka against
a coalition of kings organized by Bar(Ben)-hadad, son of Hazael, king of Aram.
It is perhaps noteworthy that Bar-hadad alone, of all kings identified in his
coalition, was from southern Syria-Palestine. The remainder were from northern Syria and eastern Anatolia, thus indicating the widespread influence of the
king of Damascus. This event probably occurred in anticipation of the Assyrian campaign, and the purpose of the siege would have been to force the pro-
Assyrian Zakkur to join the anti-Assyrian coalition.[15]

Archaeology

It is possible, as indicated in the preceding chapter, to identify with some
degree of certainty the Omride strata in certain key Palestinian sites. Evidences
of city destructions at numerous sites during approximately the late eighth
and early seventh centuries, on the other hand, can generally, although rarely
with certainty in specific cases, be attributed to Assyrian military activities in
Palestine at that time. Thus the strata in between would represent the era of the
Jehu dynasty. To be considered in this regard are Samaria/Sebastiyeh III–IV,
Megiddo/Tell el-Mutesellim IV A, Tirzah/Tell el-Far'ah II, Hazor/Tell el-Qedah

15. See Nadav Na'aman, "Forced Participation in Alliances in the Course of the Assyrian Cam-
paigns to the West," in Mordechai Cogan and Israel Eph'al, eds., *Ah, Assyria . . . ! Studies in Assyrian
History and Ancient Near Eastern Historiography Presented to Hayim Tadmor* (ScrHier 33; Jerusalem:
Magnes, 1991) 80–98; repr. in *AIIN* 16–39. On Hamath see Lipiński, *Aramaeans*, 249–318.

VII–V, Shechem/Tell Balatah VIII–VII, Gezer/Tell Jezer VI, Lachish/Tell ed-Duweir IV, Arad/Tell Arad X–IX, and Beer-sheba/Tell es-Seba' II. In general, the major building structures of the Omride period remained in use, often repaired and occasionally expanded with less careful construction and masonry. There is little evidence of royal or public building programs, certainly nothing to compare with those of the Omride period.

An interesting discovery among the ruins at Samaria are the so-called Samaria Ostraca, approximately sixty inscribed potsherds excavated in 1910 in what appears to have been a storehouse and assigned by the excavators to Stratum IV (see *ANET 321)*.[16] Typical are ostraca numbers 4 and 19, which bear the following inscriptions: "In the ninth year, from Kozah to Gaddiyau, jar of old wine. In the tenth year, from Yazith, to Ahinoam, jar of fine oil." These were obviously records concerning dispatches of wine and oil, possibly tax records of some sort, or records of wine and oil shipments from royal estates to Samaria. The apparent reference to a regnal year but without the name of the monarch is unexpected. One would have expected a text to have read something like, "in the ninth year of King X."

Mention should be made also of seals and seal impressions from the period, which indicate the spread of writing and literacy. One discovered at Megiddo, but whose whereabouts is now unknown, for example, identifies its owner as "Shema, the servant of Jeroboam" (see Photograph 61). That he is referred to as a "servant" of Jeroboam could mean that he was a royal official under King Jeroboam II (788–748).

Chronological Matters

Previously, we argued that Jehu made special gifts to Shalmaneser, buying the right to rule, probably in early 840 B.C.E. Since the year 840–839 seems to have been assigned to his predecessor King Jehoram (851–840), Jehu apparently did not secure the throne and control of the government in Samaria until after the fall festival in 840. Thus 839–838, in our chronology, was his first regnal year. Second Kings 10:36 assigns twenty-eight years to his reign. This passage, however, is unusual since it forms part of the concluding summary of his reign. Almost without exception, the length of a king's reign is noted elsewhere in the introduction to the reign. Also, to assign Jehu this many years clashes with those assigned subsequent kings. Perhaps this figure referred originally to the number of years between the first full regnal year of King Jehoram (851–850), who, if we assume there was only one Jehoram, would have had a southerner interrupting the succession of northern kings, and the last full regnal year of Jehu (823–822). Queen Athaliah's reign in Jerusalem also began in 839. She was succeeded by the seven-year-old Jehoash in Jerusalem in the seventh year of Jehu (832; 2 Kgs. 12:1–2).

Jehoash of Judah and his son Amaziah are assigned forty and twenty-nine years, respectively (2 Kgs. 12:2; 14:2). It is impossible, however, to include this

---

16. See A. F. Rainey, "The Samaria Ostraca in the Light of Fresh Evidence," *PEQ* 99 (1967) 32–41; and I. T. Kaufmann, "The Samaria Ostraca: An Early Witness to Hebrew Writing," *BA* 45 (1982) 229–39.

CHART 17. The Century of the Jehu Dynasty

Regnal Periods Recorded for the Kings of Judah

Athaliah	7 years
Joash (Jehoash)	40 years
Amaziah	29 years
Uzziah (Azariah)	52 years
Jotham	16 years

Regnal Periods Recorded for the Jehu Dynasty

Jehu	28 years
Jehoahaz	17 years
Joash	16 years
Jeroboam II	41 years
Zechariah	6 months

Tentative Chronology

Judah	Israel	Damascus	Assyria
			Shalmaneser III
Athaliah	Jehu	Hazael	(858–824)
(839–833)	(839–822)	(ca. 843–?)	
Joash/Jehoash			
(832–803 [793])	Jehoahaz		Shamshi-Adad V
	(821–805)		(823–811)
		Ben-hadad	Adad-nirari III
Amaziah		(?–?)	(810–783)
(802–786 [774])	Joash		
	(804–789)		Shalmaneser IV
Uzziah/Azariah			(782–773)
(785–760 [734])	Jeroboam II		
	(788–748)	Hadianu	Ashur-dan III
Jotham		(?–?)	(772–755)
(759–744)			Ashur-nirari V
	Zechariah		(754–745)
	(748)		

many successive years between the end of Athaliah's reign and the beginning of Azariah's (Uzziah's) reign, that is, between 832 and about 785. Both kings underwent unique experiences that may be germane to understanding the chronology of the period. According to 2 Kings 12:20–21, Jehoash was the subject of a plot and was wounded, probably rendering him incapable or unqualified to function as king. This occurred in the thirtieth year of his reign in 803–802, although he continued to live for ten additional years, until 793–792. Amaziah succeeded his father in the second year of Jehoash of Israel (803–802; 2 Kgs. 14:1) but was later captured and carried hostage to Samaria (14:13) before the last year of Jehoash's reign (789–788). Later released, perhaps by Jeroboam II, whose reign began in the fifteenth year of Amaziah (788–787; 2 Kgs. 14:23), the Judean king had been replaced by Azariah (Uzziah) in 785. Azariah (Uzziah) had to abdicate the throne because of *tsara'ath* (2 Kgs. 15:5) probably in 760–759, but lived until 734–733, the fifteenth year after the death of Jehoash of Israel (2 Kgs. 14:17). (Many of the biblical synchronisms related to the reigns of the kings during this period remain unexplainable [e.g., 13:1, 10] unless they were originally related in some way to the regnal years of King Hazael.)

Under Syrian Oppression and Recovery

For approximately three decades following Shalmaneser III's 838–837 campaign, Syria-Palestine was relatively free of Assyrian military activity. During this time, the Aramaean city of Damascus emerged under the rule of Hazael as a regional power.[17] Hazael may have assassinated his predecessor Hadadezer, but in any case seized the throne soon after the latter's death, about 845–844. The Assyrian texts refer to Hazael as "the son of a nobody," an Akkadian expression generally used to refer to someone who was an enemy of Assyria and who attained the throne illegitimately. The Hebrew Bible, on the other hand, has Hazael serving as right-hand man to the king of Damascus (whom it identifies incorrectly as Ben-hadad), and describes how Elisha prophesied that Hazael would decimate Israel (2 Kgs. 8:7–15). The Hebrew narrative does not actually state that Hazael assassinated his predecessor, but could imply as much (cf. NRSV): "He [Hazael] . . . dipped a netting in water and spread it over his [the king's] face [as an air-conditioning device?], but he died [an active, not a causative, form ("he killed") without a direct object] and Hazael reigned in his place" (8:15).

Hazael eventually extended his influence throughout Syria-Palestine. The exact chronological order and the nature of the conquests by which he came to dominance in the region cannot be determined with any certainty. In 845, Shalmaneser had confronted the Syro-Palestinian anti-Assyrian coalition for the last time. The Assyrian king reports that he raised an army of 120,000 troops (RIMA 3:39, 47), probably intent on eradicating the coalition once and for all. He confronted a force "too numerous to be counted," however, and his inscriptions claim victory in the most general of terms, not even noting the region

17. See André Lemaire, "Hazaël de Damas, roi d'Aram," in Dominique Charpin and Francis Joannès, eds., *Marchands, diplomats et empereurs. Études sur la civilisation mésopotamienne offertes à Paul Garelli* (Paris: Editions Recherche sur les Civilisations, 1991) 91–108; and Lipiński, *Aramaeans*, 384–400.

where the encounter occurred. The following year, his military campaigning was limited to a low-key expedition to the source of the Tigris. One could conclude that the coalition inflicted heavy casualties on the Assyrian army and greatly reduced Assyrian power in Syria-Palestine. Shortly thereafter Hazael came to the throne and was perhaps convinced that the need for the coalition was past and that Damascus could be the dominant power in the region.

Hazael may have quickly moved northward and across the Anti-Lebanon range into the territory of Hamath and even into Galilee before the Assyrians returned in 841 (see n. 2 above). When he crossed "the river" cannot be determined, but Damascene influence was felt throughout northern Syria and southern Anatolia into the reign of Adad-nirari. In his twenty-eighth year (831), Shalmaneser sent but did not accompany his army to put down a rebellion in Patinu (RIMA 3:69, 81–82) but otherwise stayed clear of Syria-Palestine.

Before Jehu assumed the throne, Hazael had moved to conquer Israelite territory in Transjordan (2 Kgs. 8:28). The whole region was eventually taken and annexed to Syria: "In those days Yahweh began to cut off parts of Israel. Hazael defeated them throughout the territory of Israel: from the Jordan eastward, all the land of Gilead, the Gadites, and the Reubenites, and the Manassites, from Aroer, which is by the Wadi Arnon, that is, Gilead and Bashan" (2 Kgs. 10:32–33).

Probably having already taken Galilee and the Jezreel Valley from Israel, Hazael moved southward down the Mediterranean coast. According to 2 Kings 12:17–18, he took the Philistine city of Gath and thereafter moved against Jerusalem.[18]

> At that time King Hazael of Aram went up, fought against Gath, and took it. But when Hazael set his face to go up against Jerusalem, King Jehoash of Judah took all the votive gifts that Jehoshaphat, Jehoram, and Ahaziah, his ancestors, the kings of Judah, had dedicated, as well as his own votive gifts, and all the gold that was found in the treasures of the house of Yahweh and of the king's house, and sent these to King Hazael of Aram. Then Hazael withdrew from Jerusalem.

This would have occurred sometime after 832, when Jehoash assumed the throne. In all likelihood, Hazael eventually controlled the entire length of the Via Maris through Palestine and thus the important trade along the route.

Also a case can be made that Hazael occupied Elath, the port and shipping outlet to the Red Sea via the Gulf of Aqabah. A century later, according to 2 Kings 16:6, the Syrian monarch Rezin "recovered Elath for Aram; he drove out the Judahites from Elath, and Edomites came to Elath and settled there" (NJPSV). The only previous Syrian king before Rezin who could have held Elath was Hazael. Hazael's takeover of Elath would have given him control over the port and shipping outlet to the Red Sea via the Gulf of Aqabah. Damascus now controlled all the major trade routes previously dominated by the Omrides.

Hazael was followed by his son Ben-hadad, Ben-hadad II by our reckoning. The Zakkur Inscription indicates that Ben-hadad had assumed the throne (ca.

---

18. For a discussion of this text see C. S. Ehrlich, *The Philistines in Transition: A History from ca. 1000–730 B.C.E.* (SHCANE 10; Leiden: Brill, 1996) 72–74, 150–53. On the history of Gath, see W. M. Schniedewind, "The Geopolitic History of Philistine Gath," *BASOR* 309 (1998) 69–77.

806–805?) with considerable influence and power in Syria-Palestine. Zakkur, the first king of Hamath to bear a Semitic rather than a Neo-Hittite name, was attacked by a coalition of seventeen kings led by Ben-hadad the son of Hazael. The six kingdoms named in the text as participants with Ben-hadad were all north Syrian or east Anatolian states far from Damascus. This indicates, first, that if Ben-hadad was not dominant over the entire eastern Mediterranean, he was certainly an influential figure, and, second, that he had assumed the role of organizer of resistance against Assyria in the region.

Jehu, Jehoahaz, and Joash of Israel

Jehu. A few years after Hazael, the "son of a nobody," seized the throne in Damascus, Jehu came to power in Samaria. Israel's fortunes had declined rapidly during the years following the death of Ahab. Thus Jehu ascended the throne of a kingdom already in trouble, and everything suggests that matters got worse during his reign. One of the things recalled about Jehu's reign in 2 Kings is that Hazael encroached on and annexed significant portions of Israelite territory (10:32–33; 12:17–18; both passages quoted above). If the Elisha stories reflect conditions in Israel during this period, as we have argued, then Jehu's reign was not merely a time of Syrian encroachment on Israelite territory—it was a time when Syrian oppression made life almost unbearable in Israel. In 8:12, for example, we hear Elisha declaring to Hazael: "I know the evil that you will do to the people of Israel; you will set their fortresses on fire, you will kill their young men with the sword, dash in pieces their little ones, and rip up their pregnant women."

The only deed attributed to Jehu in 2 Kings, aside from the circumstances of his seizure of the government and loss of territory to Hazael, is that he purged Israel of Baalism. Even in this regard Jehu is probably given more credit than he is due. Jehoram had probably already taken some measures to reduce the prominence of Baalism in Samaria (compare 3:3 with 10:26). If Jehu did take measures against Baalism, this would surely have displeased some elements of the kingdom even while ensuring him the support of others.

Second Kings 8–9 provides an extended account of how Jehu assassinated Jehoram, seized the government, and massacred the remainder of the Omrides, including King Ahaziah of Judah. When summarizing this account at the close of chapter 10, we observed that it has all the earmarks of political propaganda. The account attempts to present Jehu as one prophetically designated, a savior of Israel from Baalism, and holy war executioner of the Omride apostates. Moreover, this narrative conflicts with the Tel Dan Inscription, which unfortunately is also problematic because only fragments have survived (see n. 29 in chapter 10). The Tel Dan Inscription has been dated to the ninth century and was apparently erected by an Aramaean king to commemorate a victory in the vicinity of Tel Dan. The inscription opens with a statement about an Israelite king having encroached on Syrian territory. Further on, the one who commissioned the inscription claims to have killed ". . . rm, son of . . . king of Israel and . . . yhw son of . . . king of the house of David." The most likely Aramaean king to have challenged Israelite control of territory in the vicinity of Dan, and then been able to reclaim it, was Hazael. The only Israelite king of that era with a name ending in *rm* is Jehoram, and the only Judahite ("house of David") king of the ninth century with a name ending in *yhw* is Ahaziah. In short, whereas the propagandistic biblical account of Jehu's coup states that Jehoram and Ahaziah were assassinated in connection with the coup, the extremely fragmentary and at the same time propagandistic Tel Dan Inscription seems to require that Jehoram and Ahaziah were killed by an Aramaean king, probably Hazael.

Two possibilities come to mind as to what might have happened, neither of which can be argued to the exclusion of the other with much confidence. First, while the 2 Kings 8–9 account of Jehu's coup is clearly not to be taken at face value, it is difficult to dismiss it entirely. Second, the Tel Dan Inscription is fragmentary, the reconstruction of its text speculative, and the Aramaean king who left it would probably not have been beyond making his own false claims for propagandistic purposes.

Jehu seems, in any case, to have had to resort to violence in his rise to power. Hosea 1:4 speaks of the "blood of Jezreel" of which the house of Jehu was guilty (but without reference to any slaughter of reigning monarchs).[19] Also, excavations at the site of Jezreel indicate that the city suffered destruction only a few years after reaching the height of its prosperity.[20] Thus, even though the 2 Kings 9–10 account of Jehu's coup may not be historically trustworthy in its details, it may nevertheless report correctly that Jehu's move to secure the throne involved a massacre at Jezreel and perhaps the execution of both Jehoram and Ahaziah. (It should be noted, however, that Syria and Hazael were active in the region at the time and may have destroyed Jezreel.)

The other possibility is that Jehu's rise to power involved a longer struggle, and that the Omrides may not have disappeared from the scene so quickly, as the 2 Kings 9–10 account suggests. If so, then two events, not necessarily in the following sequence, would finally have secured the throne for Jehu: the deaths of Jehoram and Ahaziah, and Shalmaneser's campaign through Palestine. Jehoram and Ahaziah may have been wounded or killed in battle while defending Israel's northern frontier against Hazael—defending either Ramoth-gilead (see 1 Kgs. 22:3; 2 Kgs. 8:28) or the vicinity of Dan (Tel Dan Inscription). When Shalmaneser passed through northern Palestine, he accepted tribute from Jehu and sanctioned Jehu's rule over "the land of the house of Omri." Regarding the sequence, it is possible that Shalmaneser would have recognized Jehu as ruler over the land of Omri while members of the family of Jehoram were still alive and claiming the throne. Jehu may have rushed to Shalmaneser ahead of Jehoram, for example, and Shalmaneser may have perceived that Jehu, without any royal credentials, was more inclined to offer complete submission to Assyria. If Jehu was recognized as ruler by the Assyrian king early in 840, it may have taken some months before Jehu secured the capital city of Samaria and established his rule. Our chronology assumes 839–838 to have been his first regnal year.

Jehoahaz. The Hebrew Bible tells us even less about the reigns of Jehoahaz and Joash than it does about Jehu. Apparently the Syrian oppression became

---

19. See S. A. Irvine, "The Threat of Jezreel (Hosea 1:4–5)," *CBQ* 57 (1995) 494–503.
20. See the bibliography in n. 23 to chap. 10.

even more intolerable under Jehoahaz. Second Kings 13:3 reports that Yahweh gave Israel "repeatedly into the hand of King Hazael of Aram, then into the hand of Ben-hadad son of Hazael." Further on in the same chapter (13:7) we are told that Jehoahaz possessed an army of no more than "fifty horsemen, ten chariots and ten thousand footmen; for the king of Aram had destroyed them and made them like the dust at threshing."

Did the Syrians only raid Israelite towns and villages from time to time to collect booty and slaves? Or did they impose some sort of vassal relationship upon Jehu, Jehoahaz, and possibly Joash and reorganize the territory? First, the narrative in 1 Kings 20 may shed some light on this issue. Although the compilers of the Genesis–2 Kings history placed this narrative in the context of Ahab's reign and identified the Israelite king mentioned in it as Ahab, it is more likely, as we shall see below, that the narrative recalls circumstances from the end of Jehoahaz's reign. This narrative refers to "the young men who serve the district governors," which suggests that there were Israelite administrative districts with governors. Given the status of Israel during the time of Aramaean dominance, which 1 Kings 20 presupposes, it would be most unlikely that Israel had itself initiated a new political reorganization of districts with governors of which we hear nowhere else. (The Hebrew terminology used here is completely different from that used in describing Solomon's "districts" in 1 Kgs. 4:7–19.)

Second, two texts refer to the "king of Samaria" (1 Kgs. 20:1—"Ahab king of Samaria"; and 2 Kgs. 1:3—"[Ahaziah] king of Samaria"). This is an unusual expression. There is no statement in the Bible, for example, that refers to the "king of Jerusalem." The expression "king of Samaria" indicates the existence of a political entity called "Samaria," a district, province, or some other geographically demarcated region. Interestingly, when the Assyrian king, Adad-nirari III, mentions Josah in the Rimah Stela, he refers to him not as the king of Israel or Bit-Omri but as Joash "of the land of Samaria." All this indicates that during the period of Syrian domination under Hazael the king in Samaria ruled over only a minor political area that bore the name "land of Samaria," a reference to the city-state and immediately surrounding territory.

The Elisha stories (2 Kgs. 2; 4:1–8:15), which probably hark back to the years of Syrian oppression during the reigns of Jehu and Jehoahaz, provide further glimpses of Israel's dismal political situation. It would appear from these stories, highly dramatized no doubt, that Syrian raids into Israelite-held territory were an ordinary occurrence and often involved the taking of slaves (5:2). Israel's military tactic in response to such raids was simply to avoid the Syrians as far as possible (6:8–23). A letter from the Syrian king to the Israelite king requesting the aid of an Israelite prophet so frightened the Israelite king, we are told, that he tore his clothes. We hear of Samaria itself under siege on one occasion, and saved only by a "miracle" (6:24–7:20). Elisha is depicted in these stories as a trusted adviser of the Israelite king and Israel's real champion in the struggle for survival under Syrian oppression. He used his miraculous powers as a man of God to thwart Syrian actions against Israel (6:8–23), advised the king of Israel on matters of state, and could speak a word on others' behalf to the king or royal officials (4:13).

Finally, perhaps toward the end of Jehoahaz's reign, but certainly during the reign of Joash, relief came. We will return our attention below to the timing and nature of this relief. Eventually the situation began to change, and 2 Kings 13:3–5 seems to assume that already during Jehoahaz's reign something of significance occurred toward that end.

> The anger of Yahweh was kindled against Israel, so that he gave them repeatedly into the hand of King Hazael of Aram, then into the hand of Ben-hadad the son of Hazael. But Jehoahaz entreated Yahweh, and Yahweh heeded him; for he saw the oppression of Israel, how the king of Aram oppressed them. Therefore Yahweh gave Israel a savior, so that they escaped from the hand of the Arameans; and the people of Israel lived in their homes as formerly.

The catalyst for change was no doubt connected with the resurgence of Assyrian activity in the west. We have seen how Adad-nirari III (810–783) conducted a long and major campaign into Syria-Palestine in 805/804–802/801. Adad-nirari's *turtanu* Shamshi-ilu, who represented Assyria's interests and ruled practically as a monarch from Til Barsip, would have figured prominently in the preparations for and conduct of this campaign. Also, as we have seen, the Zakkur Stela may witness to Ben-hadad II's efforts to form an anti-Assyrian defensive front. This renewed Assyrian diplomatic and military activity in the west would have been at work before the end of Jehoahaz's reign (also in 805–804 by our chronology), and it may have been in connection with Ben-hadad's efforts to secure the defensive front that he intentionally, or by necessity, began to treat Israel less harshly. Israel's "savior" was probably the Assyrian army led by Shamshi-ilu.

Joash. As indicated above, the Rimah Stela identifies Joash among those who paid tribute to Adad-nirari III. Two further items are reported for Joash in 2 Kings 13:14–14:14. He defeated Ben-hadad three times in battle and regained possession of Israelite cities that Hazael had seized. Also he defeated Amaziah of Judah near Beth-shemesh in a battle instigated by the Judean king, after which he proceeded to capture Jerusalem, tear down a large section of the city wall, take hostages, and loot the temple and royal treasuries. We will return to this last episode below in connection with Amaziah's reign. For the moment let us examine more closely the respective roles of Jehoahaz and Joash in Israel's recovery from Syrian oppression.

Second Kings 13 consists of the summations of the reigns of Jehoahaz and Joash (13:1–9 and 13:10–13, respectively), followed by what amounts to an appendix to Joash's reign (13:14–25). This appendix consists, in turn, of the last of the Elisha stories (actually two episodes, 13:14–19 and 20–21) and some concluding summary notes about Syria's oppression of Israel and Joash's victories over Ben-hadad (13:22–25). A straightforward reading of the chapter invites the interpretation presented above: Israel received some relief from Syrian oppression before the end of Jehoahaz's reign, but it was Joash who actually defeated Ben-hadad in battle and recovered Israelite cities that had fallen into Syrian hands. At least three factors, however, suggest that the three battles may have occurred at the very end of Jehoahaz's reign and that the third battle resulted in his death.

1. The initial summations of the reigns of Jehoahaz and Joash (2 Kgs. 13:1–9 and 10–13, respectively), read without reference to the appendix materials that follow, would seem to indicate that Ben-hadad had succeeded Hazael to the throne and that Israel had recovered some independence already before

60. *Rimah Inscription*. The Rimah Inscription (129.5 cm. high), discovered in 1967, reports the deeds of Adad-nirari III (see Text 8). According to the inscription, Adad-nirari received tribute from Joash of Samaria. (*British School of Archaeology in Iraq*)

Jehoahaz's death. See especially 13:3–7 in the summation of Jehoahaz's reign and note that the summation of Joash's reign makes no reference to battles with Syria. It is specifically the appendix, in other words, which associates Israel's recovery from Syria (and also Ben-hadad's accession to the throne? see especially vv. 24–25) with Joash's reign.

2. The theme of three battles, three Israelite victories over Syria, surfaces twice in the appendix. The Elisha story anticipates three battles in which the king of Israel will defeat the king of Syria (2 Kgs. 13:17–19). Then it is explained in the concluding notes at the end of the appendix that "three times Joash defeated him [Ben-hadad] and recovered the cities of Israel" (13:25). One is reminded of the stories of the three battles with Ben-hadad that appear in the context of Ahab's reign (1 Kgs. 20; 22:1–38) but clearly do not belong there (see the discussion of these stories in chapter 10). Several factors suggest that these stories and the appendix to Joash's reign pertain to the same three battles. (a) The stories of the three battles assume a period in which Syria dominated Israel. The first of these stories begins, for example, with the Syrian king making exorbitant demands on Samaria that the king of Israel is reluctant to refuse. While it is difficult to imagine a Syrian king making such demands on Ahab, this squares very well with the situation of the early years of the Jehu dynasty. (b) Ben-hadad is the Syrian king defeated three times in the battle stories as well as in the appendix. (c) The battle stories locate Israel's main victory over Ben-hadad at Aphek, as does the Elisha story in the appendix. (d) Joash is said

in the appendix to have recovered cities from Ben-hadad that Hazael had taken from Israel earlier. The same claim is made in the battle stories for the king of Israel after the victory at Aphek, and with surprisingly similar wording: "And Ben-hadad said to him, 'The cities which my father took from your father I will restore; and you may establish bazaars for yourself in Damascus, as my father did in Samaria'" (1 Kgs. 20:34). (e) The king of Israel is killed in the third of the three battles, which would explain why the Elisha story anticipates only three victories and no more (1 Kgs. 22:29–38).

3. If the three battles mentioned in the appendix are the same three featured in the stories of the three battles with Ben-hadad, and if these stories preserve any accurate historical memory, then we must take into account certain factors that seem to point to Jehoahaz rather than to Joash as the king of Israel involved. (a) It was especially during Jehoahaz's reign, when Syrian oppression had reached its worst, that the conditions presupposed at the beginning of the three battle stories would have existed. Note in this regard the similarity between Israel's pitiful little army as described in the summation of Jehoahaz's reign and as described in the second of the battle stories (compare 1 Kgs. 20:27 with 2 Kgs. 13:7). (b) The king of Israel is killed in the third of the three battle stories, which means that the battles should be placed at the end of a king's reign. The end of Jehoahaz's reign, where Adad-nirari was beginning his western campaigns, would have been a propitious time for Israel to challenge Syrian authority. By the end of Joash's reign, on the other hand, Israel had apparently already long since regained both independence from Damascus and domination over Jerusalem. (c) In the third of the three battle stories, the king of Israel leaves his son, the crown prince, in charge of Samaria while the king himself leads Israel's army against Ben-hadad at Ramoth-gilead (1 Kgs. 22:26). The son is identified by name—Joash. This would fit Jehoahaz, who was followed on the throne by Joash, but not Joash, who was followed by Jeroboam.

Admittedly all of this is highly speculative, and there are counterarguments that cannot be ignored. The stories of the three battles show evidence of having undergone significant modifications during the process of transmission, for example, which serves as a warning in turn that they do not necessarily preserve accurate historical memory, certainly not in the details. This is especially true, as we have seen, of the third story, which recounts the Ramoth-gilead campaign and concludes with the king of Israel's death (1 Kgs. 22:29–38; see above, p. 288). It is possible that the ancient storytellers confused the circumstances of this third battle with those of an earlier conflict at Ramoth-gilead, the one in connection with which Jehoram may have been wounded or killed (2 Kgs. 8:28–29). Neither can we ignore that the compilers of Genesis–2 Kings (or whoever was responsible for the appendix to Joash's reign) clearly associated Elisha's death and the three victories over Ben-hadad with Joash rather than his father. Note also that it is recorded for both Jehoahaz and Joash that they "slept with the fathers," a phrase normally reserved for kings who died a natural death (1 Kgs. 13:9, 13).

To summarize, it seems safe to conclude, at the very least, that circumstances occurring near the end of Jehoahaz's reign and the beginning of Joash's reign resulted in the recovery of Israelite independence from Damascus. If we dare to speculate further along the lines indicated above, the following scenario emerges.

Near the end of the century, by which time Ben-hadad had succeeded Hazael on the throne, Damascus began to lose its grip on the surrounding kingdoms. Adad-nirari's western campaign was no doubt the factor involved. Local rulers such as Zakkur of Hamath and Jehoahaz of Samaria challenged Ben-hadad's authority and successfully defended against his attempts at reprisal. The three battle stories in 1 Kings 20 and 22:1–38 represent three stages in Jehoahaz's struggle to throw off the Syrian yoke.

The renewal of the Israelite struggle against Damascus began when Ben-hadad, along with a coalition of thirty-two kings, marched south with an army, established camp in the Jordan Valley, and sent demands to Samaria.[21] This siege of the city of Samaria, of which 2 Kings 6:24–7:19 may be a duplicate, was probably an effort, like the siege of Zakkur, to force pro-Assyrian Samaria into joining the anti-Assyrian coalition.

Jehoahaz and his supporters decided to defend their city and stay their course. This they did and were successful. The city was saved by the sound of an approaching (Assyrian?) army (2 Kgs. 9:6).

The following spring Ben-hadad marched south again. Jehoahaz and the Israelite army met the Syrians at Aphek. The exact location of Aphek is unknown, but this is presumably the same Aphek that witnessed Saul's last battle with the Philistines, that is, situated at the northern end of the central hill country where its slopes give way to the Jezreel Valley. Again Israel's army was victorious, in spite of overwhelming odds, and captured Ben-hadad himself. Jehoahaz allowed Ben-hadad to go free, but only after the latter agreed to relinquish all claims on Israel, return certain cities that Hazael had taken from Jehu, and allow Israelite merchants trading rights in Damascus.

Among the cities that Hazael had taken from Israel were those located in northern Transjordan (2 Kgs. 10:32–33), and three years later Jehoahaz is heard complaining that one of these cities, Ramoth-gilead, was still in Syrian hands. This occasioned the Ramoth-gilead campaign in which, as the story stands now, Jehoahaz was killed.

Joash, the crown prince who had remained in Samaria while Jehoahaz conducted the Ramoth-gilead campaign, now ascended the throne. Joash probably continued hostilities with Ben-hadad, which would help explain why the compilers of Genesis–2 Kings credited him with the victories. His father, Jehoahaz, however, deserves major credit for successfully challenging Syrian authority.

Assyria, meanwhile, under Adad-nirari III and Adad-nirari's *turtanu*, Shamshi-ilu, was reasserting its authority in the west, which perhaps was the main reason Ben-hadad lost his grip on Israel. According to the Rimah Stela, Joash presented tribute to Adad-nirari on behalf of the land of Samaria.[22] This stela also mentions voluntary tribute from Tyre and Sidon, but no other states. As we have seen, Tyre submitted to Assyria early on and thereby continued good relations with the conquerors. Perhaps Joash also ingratiated himself to

---

21. For an attempt to identify the thirty-two kings, see André Lemaire, "Joas de Samarie, Barhadad de Damas, Zakkur de Hamat. La Syrie-Palestine vers 800 av. J.C.," *ErIsr* 24 (1993) 148*–57*.

22. As a rule, Assyrian royal inscriptions refer to such tribute payment (or presentation gift) only when made under exceptional circumstances—when it was paid directly and personally to the king or received on campaign. The normal, routine annual tribute paid by vassal or cooperative states was sent directly to the Assyrian capital and is seldom referred to in royal inscriptions.

TEXT 8. The Rimah Stela of Adad-nirari III

I, Adad-nirari, the strong king, king of the universe, king of Assyria, son of Šamši-Adad, the king of the universe, king of Assyria, son of Shalmaneser, the king of the four corners, mobilized chariots, troops, and camps, and ordered a campaign against Hatti. In a single year I made Amurru and Hatti in its entirety kneel at my feet; I imposed tribute (and) regular tax for future days upon them. He received two thousand talents of iron, three thousand multi-colored garments and (plain) linen garments as tribute from Mari' of the land of Imerisu (= Aram-Damascus). He received the tribute of Joash of the land of the Samarians, of the land of the Tyrians, and of the land of the Sidonians. I marched to the great sea where the sun sets, and erected a stela of my royal self in the city of Arwad which is in the middle of the sea. I went up the Lebanon mountains and cut down timbers: one hundred mature cedars, material needed for my palace and temples. He received tribute from all the kings of Na'iri. (*NAHI* 79)

the Assyrian king early in the campaign and for the same reason, probably already in 804–803, shortly after Joash had acceded to the throne.

Damascus resisted, on the other hand, but eventually submitted and was forced to pay heavy tribute. The Rimah Stela describes the tribute: "He received 2,000 talents of silver, 1,000 talents of copper, 2,000 talents of iron, 3,000 linen garments with multi-coloured trim—the tribute of Mari' of the land of Damascus" (RIMA 3:211; *COS* 2:276).

On the Calah Slab, which unfortunately cannot be dated, Adad-nirari claims to have received the submission of the land of Hatti, the land of Amurru in its entirety, the land of Tyre, the land of Sidon, the land of Omri (Humri), the land of Edom, and the land of Palastu (= Philistia) (see *COS* 2:276; RIMA 3:213). Judah does not appear in the list, and whereas the Rimah Stela refers to "the land of Samaria," the Calah Slab speaks of the "land of Omri." Between the time interval of these two inscriptions, Joash appears to have expanded his holding beyond the province of Samaria and perhaps revived Israel's dominance over Judah (see below).

Athaliah, Joash, and Amaziah of Judah

Athaliah. Athaliah came to Judah as the bride of Jehoram son of Jehoshaphat. When Jehoram ascended the throne, he took the precaution, according to 2 Chronicles 21:4, of removing other possible claimants. Then when Jehoram himself died (or was killed, if he and Jehoram of Israel were the same person), and Ahaziah was killed, Athaliah herself seized the throne in Jerusalem. Again there was a purge of all others who might have some claim to the crown.

Nothing is recorded about Athaliah's reign except how she gained the throne and how she lost it. Supposedly Jehosheba, a daughter of Jehoram and sister of King Ahaziah, succeeded in hiding one of Ahaziah's sons, the remainder of whom were slain during Athaliah's purge. Jehosheba then cared for the

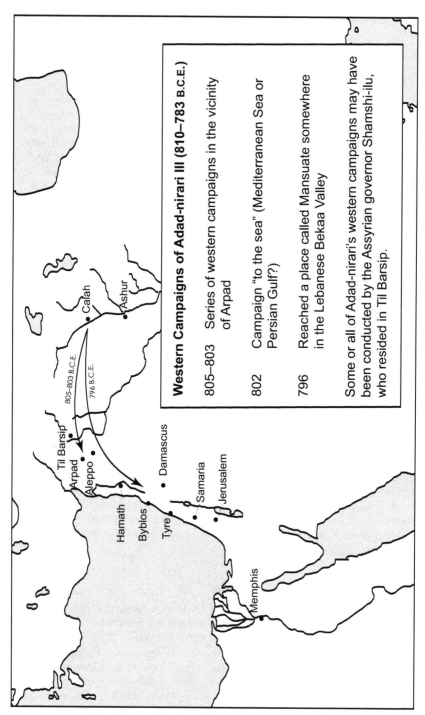

Western Campaigns of Adad-nirari III (810–783 B.C.E.)

805–803   Series of western campaigns in the vicinity of Arpad

802   Campaign "to the sea" (Mediterranean Sea or Persian Gulf?)

796   Reached a place called Mansuate somewhere in the Lebanese Bekaa Valley

Some or all of Adad-nirari's western campaigns may have been conducted by the Assyrian governor Shamshi-ilu, who resided in Til Barsip.

Til Barsip
Arpad
Aleppo
Calah
Ashur
Damascus
Hamath
Byblos
Tyre
Samaria
Jerusalem
Memphis

805–803 B.C.E.
796 B.C.E.

MAP 28. Adad-nirari III's Western Campaigns

child, Joash by name, until he was seven years old. At that point Jehoiada, a priest who was in on the secret, orchestrated a palace coup that resulted in the enthronement of Joash and the assassination of Athaliah.

The account of this episode in 2 Kings 11:4–20 provides a vivid glimpse of the personnel and ritual associated with the royal Judean palace and temple, even if all the details are not entirely clear. The ritual of the young king's coronation and investiture included the crowning, the presentation of the insignia, the proclamation, the anointment, the acclamation, and the enthronement (2 Kgs. 11:12, 19). Along with the temple officials and palace guard who participated in the coronation were others referred to collectively as "the people of the land." Encountered here for the first time in the Genesis–2 Kings account, these would have been adult, landowning males, possibly but not necessarily representing a particular faction in the government. They would come to play an important role in southern politics.

The Chronicler's version of the episode agrees with the 2 Kings account with only a few notable differences. For example, the Chronicler identifies Jehosheba as the wife of Jehoiada as well as the daughter of Jehoram. And it was the priests and the Levites who conducted the affair, according to the Chronicler, rather than the palace guard. Certain soldiers were involved, but their responsibility was to circulate through Judah and assemble the Levites and heads of families from all the cities. In the Chronicler's version, therefore, the displacement of Athaliah with Joash was a nationwide movement rather than an internal palace coup. Both 2 Kings and the Chronicler's version report that the crowd, after taking Athaliah out of the Yahweh temple for execution, proceeded to the Baal temple, looted it, and killed the solitary Baal priest.

Joash. Athaliah was executed in her seventh year of rule, according to the chronological data provided, and Joash was seven years old at the time. Who was this child whom Jehoiada presented as a royal heir and succeeded in placing on the throne? Clearly the final compilers of Genesis–2 Kings were satisfied that Joash was an authentic son of Ahaziah, presumably born the year of Ahaziah's death. In view of the circumstances as described, however, one can hardly avoid wondering whether Joash might have been an impostor whom Jehoiada used to get rid of Athaliah and bring his own influence to bear on the nation.

On the one hand, there are the strange circumstances of the affair. Why would it have been in the interest of Athaliah to kill her own grandchildren in the first place? It seems they would have been her best justification for seizing the throne and best insurance for holding it—that is, she would have posed as regent in their behalf. And is it likely, after the double purges of Jehoram and Athaliah, not to mention the episode described in 2 Chronicles 21:16–17, which states that Arabs and Philistines wiped out all of Jehoram's family "except Jehoahaz [?], his youngest son," that anyone with a remote claim to the crown had survived?

On the other hand, the priests and soldiers who participated in the coup, the compilers of Genesis–2 Kings, the Chronicler, and even we today are ultimately dependent upon the word of Jehosheba and Jehoiada as recorded in the Hebrew Bible that Joash was in fact Ahaziah's son. And both of these witnesses, of course, would have had good reason to seek Athaliah's downfall. Jehosheba, a sister of Ahaziah, had lost members of her family in Athaliah's purge. Jehoiada

would have wanted a ruler more favorably disposed toward Yahwism, and perhaps more susceptible to his own influence. No doubt many other temple and
palace officials and much of the population of Judah in general preferred to
believe that Joash was an authentic heir, or were prepared to accept him as such.

Jehoiada in any case does seem to have exercised significant influence over
Joash. According to 2 Kings 12:2, Joash "did what was right in the eyes of Yahweh all his days, because Jehoiada the priest instructed him." The Chronicler
expands on this, indicating that Jehoiada selected wives for the young king and
that Jehoiada's death brought to an end Joash's years of righteous rule. Thereafter, according to the Chronicler, Joash fell under the influence of the princes
of Judah, rejected the words of Zechariah Jehoiada's son, and even had
Zechariah stoned (2 Chr. 24:17–22).

A program of temple repair is the main item reported for Joash's reign in
both Kings and Chronicles. Joash commanded that certain categories of funds
brought into the temple be applied to repairs of the Yahweh temple and left the
matter in the hands of the priests. By the twenty-third year of his reign, however, no repairs had been made. The matter was apparently handled haphaz-
ardly, and, without any accountability, the collected funds had been misused or
embezzled. Thus Joash summoned Jehoiada and inaugurated new procedures
intended to reduce the graft and get the repairs under way. (1) All collected
funds were deposited in a secured box set beside the altar. (2) When the box
began to fill, the king's secretary and the high priest would open the box, count
the money, and place it in tied bags. (3) The bags were delivered then to the
workmen in charge of the repairs: "And they did not ask an accounting from
the men into whose hand they delivered the money to pay out to the workmen,
for they dealt honestly" (2 Kgs. 12:15). The implication of the text seems to be
that the contractors and overseers could be trusted better than the priests.

The other item reported for Joash's reign is Hazael's conquest of Gath and
his threat to sack Jerusalem. As in the case of the temple treasury, Joash is not
depicted as an assertive leader. He chose to ransom the city with the temple
treasury rather than attempt to defend it.

The Chronicler places the Syrian campaign immediately following the ston-
ing of Jehoiada's son, reports that there was a battle in which Judah was
defeated and Joash wounded, and explains that "his servants conspired against
him because of the blood of the son(s) of the priest Jehoiada, and they killed
him on his bed" (2 Chr. 24:25). Second Kings 12:20–21 literally reports about
Joash's end: "His servants plotted and formed a conspiracy and attacked Joash
at Beth-millo on the way down to Silla. His servants who attacked him were
Jozacar son of Shimeath and Jozabad son of Shomer. When he died they [the
people] buried him with his fathers in the city of David." The text does not say
that Joash was killed; the form of the verb is active and singular ("he died"),
not causative and plural ("they killed"). According to our chronology, Joash
had to abdicate the throne perhaps because of injuries received (in 803–802) but
survived for another ten years (until 793–792).

Amaziah. Joash was succeeded on the throne by his son, Amaziah, who took
action against his father's attackers, so the text declares, as soon as the royal
power was "firmly in his hand" (2 Kgs. 12:21; 14:5). It is tempting to speculate
on the fuller circumstances of the assault on Joash and the nature of the chal-

lenge or challenges that Amaziah had to overcome before power was "firmly in his hand." Joash had been placed on the throne, strongly influenced (possibly dominated) throughout most of his reign by the inner circle of priests and officials in Jerusalem. Was Joash attacked because he began to exert more independence or hold the priests and officials to closer accountability, as in the case of the funds collected for the temple repair? Did Amaziah have to establish his authority over against powerful figures in the court, or come to terms with them? Were there other claimants to the throne, perhaps candidates who raised questions about Joash's legitimacy? Possibly the inner circle of leadership in Jerusalem knew all along that Joash was an impostor and allowed him to rule as a figurehead until he began asserting too much independence. Whatever the circumstances, it is obvious that palace intrigue was involved.

Amaziah's reign overlapped that of Joash of Israel, which means that he witnessed the renewed Assyrian activity in the west and the decline of the power of Damascus under Ben-hadad II. The local kingdoms of Syria-Palestine that had been dominated by Damascus for several decades began to test their strength against one another. Amaziah defeated the Edomites in the Valley of Salt (possibly Wadi el-Milh east of Beer-sheba) and chased the fugitives to Sela, a huge rocky crag on the rugged slopes east of the Arabah (probably as-Sil' south of Tafileh). Apparently the fugitives climbed to the top of Sela and attempted to defend it. Somehow Amaziah's men were able to take the position and, according to the Chronicler, threw ten thousand Edomites from the summit to their deaths below (2 Kgs. 14:7; 2 Chr. 25:11–12). Defeating the Edomites meant renewed access to the Gulf of Aqabah. Thus we are informed that "he [Amaziah? Uzziah?] built Elath and restored it to Judah, after the king [?] slept with his fathers" (2 Kgs. 14:22).

Next Amaziah challenged Joash, possibly to assert Jerusalem's independence from Samaria. This turned out to be an unfortunate move. Second Kings 14:9–10 states simply that he challenged Joash to battle, to which Joash responded as follows: "A thorn bush on Lebanon sent to a cedar on Lebanon, saying, 'Give your daughter to my son for a wife'; but a wild animal of Lebanon passed by and trampled down the thorn bush. You have indeed defeated Edom, and your heart has lifted you up. Be content with your glory, and stay at home; for why should you provoke trouble so that you fall, you and Judah with you?" Amaziah pressed the challenge, however, and a battle occurred that resulted in overwhelming victory for Israel. Having routed the Judean army and captured Amaziah, Joash marched on Jerusalem, where he dismantled a large section of the city wall, emptied the temple treasury (which had already been drained by Hazael not many years earlier), and took additional hostages along with King Amaziah back to Samaria.

It is interesting to note that, although Amaziah was the one who supposedly insisted on war, the battle occurred in traditionally Judean territory. The two armies met near Beth-shemesh, which is in the Shephelah, almost directly west of Jerusalem. That the battle occurred near Judah's western frontier is also problematic for the Chronicler's explanation that Amaziah was seeking redress of an incident that occurred in connection with his Edomite campaign. Amaziah had hired one hundred thousand Israelite soldiers for this campaign, according to the Chronicler, but then discharged them before departure, presumably without pay. While Amaziah was fighting the Edomites, therefore, the discharged Israelite soldiers looted some Judean villages on their return home.

Whatever the specifics, the battle between Joash and Amaziah at Beth-shemesh reflects the power struggle between Israel and Judah. Amaziah had his ambitions, which did not involve any kind of secondary status or subjection to Israel. The location of the battle may suggest that Joash had already moved to annex traditionally Judean territory west of Jerusalem. Thus Amaziah's call for war would have involved more than adventurism on his part or determination to hold Israel accountable for the actions of some renegade soldiers. It was his signal to Samaria that he intended to resist Israelite dominance of Judean territory and to assert Judean independence.

Unfortunately for Judah, Amaziah had underestimated Israel's strength. Joash ridiculed his challenge, crushed the Judean army, and captured Jerusalem. In short, Joash reaffirmed Judah's vassal status. This situation, a strong Israel dominating Judah, reminiscent of the Omride period, continued throughout the reigns of Jeroboam II and Uzziah, the successors of Joash and Amaziah, respectively.

Amaziah was apparently taken to Samaria and held as a hostage. Eventually, in 785 according to our chronology, "All the people of Judah took Azariah (Uzziah), who was sixteen years old, and made him king to succeed his father" (2 Kgs. 14:21). This action by "all Judah" suggests that the succession was irregular. Normally only "the people of the land" interceded to assure succession. Amaziah lived for fifteen years after the death of Joash of Israel in 789–788 (or until 774–773; 2 Kgs. 14:17). Apparently after his release, Amaziah was involved in some political scheme, fled to Lachich, and there was put to death. (In 2 Kgs. 14:19 the verb is a plural causative: "they put him to death.")

National Restoration under Jeroboam II and Uzziah

During much of the second half of the century of the Jehu dynasty, beginning with the reign of Joash of Israel (804–789) but especially during that of Jeroboam II (788–748), Israel enjoyed a period of national restoration and expansion. Judah, under Uzziah and Jotham, who were roughly contemporary with Jeroboam II, enjoyed a period of recovery as well, although overshadowed by, and largely dependent upon, Israel. This time of national restoration for the two Hebrew kingdoms, however, had already faded before the accession of Tiglath-pileser III to the throne over Assyria early in 745.

Israel under Jeroboam

Jeroboam II "restored the border of Israel from Lebo-hamath [the entrance of Hamath] as far as the Sea of the Arabah" (2 Kgs. 14:25). The "entrance of Hamath" refers generally to the Bekaa Valley, the corridor between the Lebanon and Anti-Lebanon mountains. The southern entrance to the corridor, to which this passage probably refers, would be approximately at the city of Dan. The Sea of the Arabah, on the other hand, is the Dead Sea. Jeroboam also

61. *"Shema the servant of Jeroboam."* Found in the ruins at Megiddo, this seal (3.8 cm. long) bears an inscription reading *"lshm' 'bd yrb'm* ("belonging to Shema, servant of Jeroboam"). (*Israel Museum*)

apparently restored Israelite control over much of Transjordan, as presupposed by 1 Chronicles 5:17.

Naturally Jeroboam and his administration took pride in having restored Israel's boundaries to what they had been in earlier times. In fact this accomplishment is said in the 2 Kings summation of Jeroboam's reign (14:23–29) to have been predicted by Jonah the son of Amittai, a prophet from Gath-hepher later to become the chief character of the fictitious book of Jonah.

First Chronicles 5:17 alludes to a census conducted in Transjordan during Jeroboam's reign. Following genealogical material pertaining to Reubenite and Gadite clans settled in Gilead and Bashan, this text states: "all of these were enrolled by genealogies in the days of King Jotham of Judah, and in the days of King Jeroboam of Israel."

These passages that indicate that Jeroboam restored Israel's former frontiers do not prepare one, however, for the sweeping claim at the end of the 2 Kings summation of his reign: "The other events of Jeroboam's reign, and all his actions and exploits, how he fought and recovered Damascus and Hamath for Judah in Israel, are recorded in the Annals of the Kings of Israel" (14:28 NJPSV). This text makes extravagant claims for Jeroboam, that he made Damascus and Hamath into Israelite tributaries. In addition, the phrase "for Judah in Israel" is nonsensical. Various suggestions have been made about the original reading, as noted in commentaries on 2 Kings. The most that we can conclude from this text, other than the fact that it is corrupt, is that Jeroboam must have expanded his territorial holdings at the expense of both Hamath and Damascus. At the very most, one might suppose that the rulers of Hamath and Damascus were willing to pay Jeroboam some nominal tribute or allow the Israelites commercial concessions in their cities rather than risk facing him in battle.

Jeroboam's expansion and the state's new prosperity probably occurred during the first twenty-five years of his reign and were aided by friendship with Assyria and participation in the Assyrian economic realm. The last part of his career was a troublesome time, with his kingdom undergoing a rapid decline.[23] The success of Israel and Judah during this period was no doubt a reflection of the Assyrian presence in the region and particularly the influence of Shamshi-ilu. In 773–772 Shamshi-ilu had to campaign against Damascus, forced the

---

23. Menahem Haran, "The Rise and Decline of the Empire of Jeroboam ben Joash," *VT* 17 (1967) 266–97, argued that the expansion occurred in the last few years of Jeroboam's reign, after 755. On the last years of Jeroboam II see Nadav Na'aman, "Azariah of Judah and Jeroboam II of Israel," *VT* 43 (1993) 227–34, repr. in *AIHH* 228–35, who argues that the period was one of Judean-Israelite warfare.

62. *Til Barsip.* Tell Ahmar, situated near the Euphrates River in northern Syria, was ancient Til Barsip. Beginning with Shalmaneser III, who renamed the city Kar-Shalmaneser, it served as an important Assyrian administrative center. Among the Assyrian governors who resided there was Shamshi-ilu, during the reign of Adad-nirari III.

surrender of its king Hadianu, and received extensive tribute along with the king's daughter.

Hadianu was apparently the successor of Ben-hadad II, but when he became king is unknown. Shamshi-ilu probably had to take action against Hadianu when the latter attempted to reassert Syrian authority and expanded into neighboring states. There may be an allusion to this expansion by Damascus into Israelite territory in Isaiah 9:1:[24] "Like the time the former one [Hadianu] treated contemptibly the land of Zebulun and the land of Naphtali, so also the latter one [Rezin] has treated harshly the Way of the Sea, Beyond the Jordan, and Galilee of the Nations."[25] If this translation and the identifications are correct, then this passage would suggest that in the second decade of Jeroboam's reign there was a temporary setback when Damascus seized Israelite territory along the main Damascus-Egypt highway ("the land of Zebulun and the land of Naphtali"). Shamshi-ilu brought Damascus back under control for a time, allowing Israel to recover its prosperity temporarily.

The final years of Jeroboam II, which witnessed the activities of the prophets Hosea and Amos, were a time of rapid decline and internal trouble. A number of factors indicate the background and nature of this decline.

1. Assyria gradually slid into decline, and as a pro-Assyrian state Bit-Omri suffered as well. Under Shalmaneser IV (782–773), Assyrian campaigns were conducted annually but against Urartu to the north. By the middle of the reign

24. G. R. Driver has shown that this text refers to two different kings, "the former one" and "the latter one" ("Isaianic Problems," in Gernot Wiesner, ed., *Festschrift für Wilhelm Eilers* [Wiesbaden: Harrosowitz, 1967] 43–49); see the translation in NJPSV.
25. See Kuan, "Šamši-ilu and *Realpolitik*," 142, 151.

of Ashur-dan III (772–755), Assyrian campaigns to lands outside Mesopotamia had become sporadic. Revolts broke out in Assyria beginning in 762. The Assyrian army, probably led by Shamshi-ilu, was in northern Syria in 755–754 and 754–753, but this was the exception rather than the rule. Just as Israel had been strong while Assyria was strong and its military active in the west, so Israel's strength ebbed away with Assyria's decline.

2. Israel and Judah were confronted with hostility and aggression on all sides. In Amos's oracles against the nations (Amos 1:3–2:3) practically all the foreign neighbor kingdoms are condemned for atrocities against Israel and Judah or for acquisitions of their territory. Several of these enemy kingdoms would form the backbone of a later anti-Assyrian coalition. Israel and Judah, surrounded by opposition states, must have been shut off from the larger world of trade and commerce for the first time in several decades.

3. Jeroboam was confronted with prophetic opposition, which found incorporation in the books of Amos and Hosea. Both prophets predicted divine judgment on Jeroboam and the house of Jehu (Hos. 1:4–5; Amos 7:11). In the period of decline Jeroboam, the royal court, and the wealthy upper class apparently continued to live as they had in the more recent prosperous days, but now at the expense of their own citizenry. With the loss of Israelite and Judean territory, refugees must have been numerous and poor people plentiful. Amos spoke of how small Jacob was and about the ruin that had befallen the house of Joseph (Amos 6:6; 7:3, 5).

4. Israel and Judah were confronted with a rival kingdom swelling in their midst. The Israelite Pekah acting in concert with King Rezin of Damascus, the successor to Hadianu, was leading the growth of an anti-Assyrian movement in Israel and Judah, which would climax in his takeover of Samaria in 734 and his full participation in an anti-Assyrian revolt. The evidence for such a movement is the following.

a. Pekah, who was still reigning in Samaria when the Assyrian king Tiglath-pileser III withdrew from Syria-Palestine in 731–730, is assigned a twenty-year rule (2 Kgs. 15:27). If this represents Pekah's calculation, then he claimed kingship from 750. His kingdom probably had its roots in Transjordan but came to encompass much of the territory west of the Jordan except for the enclaves around Jerusalem and Samaria and the hill country lying between the two.[26]

b. According to 2 Kings 15:37, Rezin of Damascus and Pekah son of Remaliah were already carrying out raids against Judah during the reign of the Judean king Jotham (759–744). Although this text does not appear as part of a typical summation of a king's rule, and it claims that Yahweh was behind the attacks, there is no reason to doubt its historicity.[27]

c. Such texts as Hosea 5:5 refer to three political entities among the people. This text reads literally: "It will be humbled, the pride of Israel before his face; and Israel and Ephraim, they will stumble in their iniquity; Judah stumbles

---

26. See H. J. Cook, "Pekah," *VT* 14 (1964) 121–35. The view that Pekah organized a rival kingdom to the monarchs of Samaria and Jerusalem was first proposed by Carl Lederer, *Die biblische Zeitrechnung vom Auszuge aus Ägypten bis zum Beginne der babylonischen Gefangenschaft* (Speier: Kleeberger, 1888) 135–38.

27. See Ehud Ben-Zvi, "Tracing Prophetic Literature in the Book of Kings: The Case of II Kings 15:37," *ZAW* 102 (1990) 100–105.

also with them." The three entities noted in this text are Israel, Ephraim, and Judah. Ephraim here appears to denote the central northern hill country south of the Jezreel Valley. It would have corresponded to what we earlier noted as the reduced "land of Samaria." Interestingly, as we shall see below, the earliest inscriptions of Tiglath-pileser revert to the language of "land of Samaria" in referring to the domain of King Menahem. The name "Israel" appears to have been conscripted by Pekah and his supporters.[28]

In spite of the preaching of Hosea and Amos, which could have been interpreted as a call for the end of the dynasty of Jehu and the assassination of King Jeroboam, the latter apparently died a natural death (2 Kgs. 14:29). The events following Jeroboam's death speak for themselves. Zechariah, Jeroboam's son, took the throne but was put to death within six months. Never again in the northern kingdom was dynastic succession successfully accomplished. The northern kingdom would last only two chaotic decades more anyway.

Judah under Uzziah and Jotham

Uzziah, who came to the throne at the age of sixteen, is also called Azariah. Possibly "Uzziah" was a throne name and Azariah his personal name, although the difference between the two forms is not as great in Hebrew as in English. Uzziah and his son Jotham were roughly contemporary with Jeroboam II, with Jotham probably outliving Jeroboam by a few years. One would assume from the presentation of their reigns in the Genesis–2 Kings corpus that Uzziah and Jotham were ordinary rulers overshadowed, if not dominated, by Jeroboam. According to 2 Kings 14:22, Uzziah rebuilt and retook the port of Elath "after the king slept with his fathers." The unnamed king in this text was probably Joash of Israel rather than Amaziah of Judah (cf. NRSV), who died a violent death (2 Kgs. 14:19). The Judean recapture of the port was probably aided by Israel. Jotham is credited with adding a new gate to the temple compound in Jerusalem (15:35). Otherwise, aside from the usual formulaic evaluations of their cultic fidelity, we learn only that Uzziah contracted *tsara'ath* and had to turn over the affairs of government to Jotham (15:5).

Uzziah and Jotham are somewhat similar to Jehoshaphat, therefore, in that they ruled under the shadow of a powerful Israelite king, are passed over rather quickly by the compilers of Genesis–2 Kings, but depicted by the Chronicler as majestic and powerful rulers in their own right (2 Chr. 26–27). The Chronicler's effort to improve Uzziah's image is especially transparent. Moreover, as one could predict, the Chronicler emphasizes that Uzziah's accomplishments all occurred during the first part of his reign, when he was on good terms with the temple priests: "He set himself to seek God in the days of Zechariah, who instructed him in the fear of God; and as long as he sought Yahweh, God made him prosper" (2 Chr. 26:5). The turning point occurred, according to the Chronicler, when Uzziah presumed to enter the temple to burn incense on the altar. Challenged by the priests, who claimed this as a priestly prerogative, Uzziah became angry and broke out with *tsara'ath* (26:16–21).

---

28. Cook, "Pekah," has demonstrated that at this time "Israel" and "Ephraim" are never used as synonyms.

63. *Epitaph of Uzziah.* The marble plaque bears the inscription *lkh byty tmy 'wzyh mlk yhwdh wl' lmpth* ("here were brought the bones of Uzziah, king of Judah, and not to be moved"). Because he suffered from *tsara'ath* (see 2 Chr. 26:23), Uzziah may not have been buried in the royal necropolis. At some point, in any case, his remains were reburied, and this inscription marked the new burial spot. (*Israel Museum*)

The Chronicler's enumeration of the great deeds of Uzziah and Jotham probably represents a kernel of truth that is much exaggerated. Specifically, Uzziah is credited with building up Judah's army to 307,500 men; with victories over the Philistines, the Arabs, and the Meunites; with much building, including towers at key points on the walls of Jerusalem; and with extensive farms, vineyards, and herds throughout the land (2 Chr. 26:6–15). Jotham is said to have done more building on the Jerusalem (Ophel) wall and at other places in Judah, and to have defeated the Meunites (27:3–6). The references to Ammonites in 26:8 and 27:5 should be corrected to read "Meunites," which in Hebrew involves only reversing the first two consonants. One might expect Israel, which is known to have been expanding its territories in Transjordan under Jeroboam II, to come into conflict with the Ammonites, but not Judah. The Meunites, known also from Tiglath-pileser's inscriptions, were apparently a nomadic people who ranged to the southwest of Judah, from the vicinity of Wadi esh-Shari'ah toward Sinai.

With the above correction, and allowing for exaggeration, the only item reported by the Chronicler for Uzziah and Jotham that raises serious doubts is the claim that Uzziah captured Philistine Gath, Jabneh, and Ashdod (2 Chr. 26:6). The last activity reported in that general vicinity was Joash's defeat of Amaziah at Beth-shemesh. Perhaps it was the Israelite kings Joash and Jeroboam who went on to conquer the Philistine cities; and the Chronicler, who essentially ignores the existence of Israel during this period, has attributed the action to Uzziah.

Social and Religious Conditions

The prophetical literature and limited archaeological remains provide some insight into the general economic, social, and religious conditions of the period of the Jehu dynasty. The Elisha stories, as we have seen, pertain to the early years of the dynasty, that is, to the latter part of the ninth century B.C.E. when Damascus dominated Syria-Palestine. While these stories have to do specifically with Israel, which was nearer to Damascus and thus more vulnerable to Syrian harassment, the situation in Judah would not have been much better.

The early period of rule by the Jehu dynasty was a difficult time even for the royal family in Samaria, much less for villagers scattered throughout the land. Constant Syrian raids devastated the countryside, depleting the land of its agricultural produce and removing all accumulated wealth of any sort. There was famine, so severe that people are described as searching desperately for wild herbs, vines, and gourds for food (2 Kgs. 4:38–41). When a city dared to resist the Syrians and fell under siege, inflation and exorbitant prices prevailed (6:24–25). One story tells of a widow about to lose her children to slavery because of debts (4:1–7). We read of cannibalism even in Samaria, parents eating their children (6:24–31).

With the book of Amos, the scene shifts to the latter part of the period of the Jehu dynasty, that is, the mid-eighth century after Israel and Judah had enjoyed better times. Here again, while Amos speaks primarily to conditions in Israel, similar conditions must have prevailed in Judah. In fact, Judah continued as a vassal to Israel—which would help explain why Amos, from the Judean town of Tekoa, directed so much of his message to Israelite affairs.

Still there were natural calamities, such as earthquake and famine, which Amos interpreted as divine punishment and warnings of worse disasters to come (Amos 4:6–10; 7:1–9).[29] Israel under Jeroboam II had early on experienced a recovery. While most of the population consisted of poor farmers who had barely survived the long years of Syrian oppression, a wealthy and privileged upper class had emerged in the process of national restoration who lived in stark contrast to the ordinary citizens. Amos uttered stern maledictions against this wealthy upper class, who enjoyed their luxury while ignoring the dismal conditions of those around them.

> Alas for those who lie on beds of ivory,
> and lounge on their couches,
> and eat lambs from the flock,
> and calves from the stall;
> who sing idle songs to the sound of the harp,
> and like David improvise on instruments of music;
> who drink wine from bowls,
> and anoint themselves with the finest oils,
> but are not grieved over the ruin of Joseph!
>
> (Amos 6:4–5)

Not only did this upper class enjoy great advantage over the poor, but also Amos accuses them of increasing this advantage by unjust means. He speaks of their "selling" the poor and placing exactions upon them—presumably references to debt slavery and excessive taxation (2:6b–7a; 5:11). Amos also condemns the abuse of the judicial process and those who profited thereby (5:10–12), especially the inhabitants of Samaria (3:9–11). In short, Amos's oracles presuppose a social and legal situation in which even the governmental and judicial officials, those allegedly committed to preserving justice, were contributing to what the prophet considered an ungodly social imbalance.

---

29. W. G. Dever, "A Case-Study of Biblical Archaeology: The Earthquake of ca. 760 BCE," *ErIsr* 23 (1992) 27*–35*; and S. A. Austin et al., "Amos's Earthquake: An Extraordinary Seismic Event of 750 B.C.," *International Geology Review* 42 (2000) 657–71.

The superscription to the book of Hosea indicates a rather long time span for this prophet's career—from as early as the reigns of Jeroboam and Uzziah to as late as that of Hezekiah. This long time span is suggested also by the contents of the book, which alludes to the "sin of Jezreel" yet to be punished, along with references to Israel's political entanglements with Egypt and Assyria (Hos. 1:4–5; 5:13–14; 7:11–13; 8:8–10; 9:5–6; 11:10–11; 14:3). The prediction of judgment presupposes that the Jehu dynasty is still in power, while the alliance with both Egypt and Assyria suggests circumstances in foreign affairs after the end of the dynasty.

General Bibliography

W. T. Pitard (*Ancient Damascus: A Historical Study of the Syrian City-State from Earliest Times until Its Fall to the Assyrians in 732 B.C.E.* [Winona Lake, IN: Eisenbrauns, 1987]; and his "Arameans," in A. J. Hoerth et al., eds., *Peoples of the Old Testament World* [Grand Rapids: Baker, 1994] 207–30), provide a competent treatment of Syrian-Israelite relations in general agreement with the present volume. For a slightly different treatment, see Benjamin Mazar, "The Aramean Empire and Its Relations with Israel," *BA* 25 (1962) 97–120; repr. in E. F. Campbell and D. N. Freedman, eds., *The Biblical Archaeologist Reader,* 2 (Garden City, NY: Doubleday, 1964) 127–51; revised in Mazar, *The Early Biblical Period: Historical Studies* (Jerusalem: Israel Exploration Society, 1986) 151–72.

Assyrian relations with Philistia, Israel, and the Arabs are discussed in Hayim Tadmor, "Philistia under Assyrian Rule," *BA* 29 (1966) 86–102; W. W. Hallo, "From Qarqar to Carchemish: Assyria and Israel in the Light of New Discoveries," *BA* 23 (1960) 34–61; repr. in Campbell and Freedman, eds., *Biblical Archaeologist Reader,* 2:152–88; and Israel Eph'al, *The Ancient Arabs: Nomads on the Borders of the Fertile Crescent 9th-5th Centuries B.C.* (Jerusalem: Magnes, 1982).

The Assyrian perspectives on its conquests are discussed in Bustenay Oded, *War, Peace, and Empire: Justification for War in Assyrian Royal Inscriptions* (Wiesbaden: Reichert, 1992).

12. The Era of Assyrian Domination: The End of the Kingdom of Israel

The Late Bronze Age in the Middle East had been an era of empires. The disintegration of long-established cultures and powerful political centers occurring at the end of this age, in the thirteenth and twelfth centuries, inaugurated a lengthy period characterized by greatly reduced political entities—tribal groupings, city-states, and small kingdoms. This in turn was succeeded by a time of national states of limited size. The eighth century introduced a new age of empires that lasted well into the first millennium c.e. Assyria, Babylonia, Persia, Macedonia, and Rome took their places, each in turn, as the head of major and far-flung international empires.

The first of these large empires was the Assyrian, whose age of extensive dominance may be said to have begun with the rule of Tiglath-pileser III (744–727 b.c.e.) and to have ended with the fall of the Assyrian capital at Nineveh in 612. Thus for over a century the Assyrians, with their center of power on the Upper Tigris River and its tributaries, dominated the life and politics of the Middle East. From about 730 onward, Assyria, for all practical purposes, was master over the eastern Mediterranean seaboard and thus over the kingdoms of Israel and Judah.

Israel ceased to exist as an independent kingdom quite early in this period of major Assyrian domination. Israelite territory was incorporated subsequently into the Assyrian provincial system. Judah maintained its national identity throughout this period but was almost completely dominated by Assyria.

Israelite and Judean history throughout the eighth and seventh centuries must be viewed, therefore, as the history of a small corner of the Assyrian Empire. The course of events for both states was largely shaped by the ambitions and policies of Assyria, and most of their actions were largely reactions to the Assyrians.

Sources for the Period

Second Kings 15:8–17:41 and 2 Chronicles 28:1–15 are the primary biblical sources for this period of Israelite and Judean history. The latter, of course, because of its exclusive interest in Judean affairs, provides only incidental information on Israelite matters and then only when Israelite history impinged directly on that of Judah. For the last days of Israel, this was the case only in the reign of Ahaz.

We learn from the narrative in 2 Kings that of Israel's final six rulers, four were put to death by their own citizens, one died from nonviolent causes, and the other apparently ended life in Assyrian exile. More specifically, 2 Kings reports the following for the last years of Israel. (1) The dynasty of Jehu came to an end, after a rule of almost a century, when Zechariah the son of Jeroboam II was put to death (15:8–12). (2) Zechariah's attacker and successor, Shallum, was killed by Menahem after a rule of only one month (15:13–16). (3) Menahem ruled for ten years. At some point in his reign, the Assyrian king Pul (who bore the throne name Tiglath-pileser) aided Menahem's attempt to hold power at the price of a rather heavy payment (15:17–22). (4) Following Menahem's demise, his son Pekahiah was put to death by Pekah after a rule of two years (15:23–26). (5) Pekah, who is said to have reigned twenty years, was king in Samaria when Tiglath-pileser conquered portions of Syria-Palestine and deported people from the area (15:27–32). In reporting on Judean kings, the editors of 2 Kings provide additional information on Pekah, who in alliance with the Syrian ruler Rezin is said to have taken action against Judah during the reign of Jotham (15:37) and to have attacked Jerusalem during the reign of Ahaz. The latter is said to have sent presents to Tiglath-pileser to secure the Assyrian king's aid against Israel and Syria (16:5–9). (6) Pekah was put to death and succeeded on the throne by Hoshea, who was eventually attacked by the Assyrians when they found out he had betrayed them by appealing to Egypt for aid and by failing to pay tribute (17:4). Hoshea was captured, Samaria was taken, Israelites were deported, and foreigners were moved into the area, which was subsequently placed under direct Assyrian rule (15:30; 17).

Other biblical material directly related to this period is found in the prophetical books of Hosea and Isaiah. Hosea appears to have been active during as well as after the last years of the Jehu dynasty and to have witnessed the troublesome conditions produced by the internal power struggles within Israel and by the westward advance of the Assyrians. Isaiah, a Judean prophet, functioned in Jerusalem throughout most of the last half of the eighth century. Many of his oracles were concerned with Israel and the international affairs of the time. Isaiah 7–8 provides important material independent of the 2 Kings narrative about the attack on Jerusalem by Pekah and Rezin, including the fact that Israel and Syria sought to depose Ahaz and replace him on the Jerusalem throne.

Assyrian inscriptions from this period—during the reigns of Tiglath-pileser III, Shalmaneser V, and Sargon II—are quite numerous, and several refer directly to Israelite rulers and to Assyrian policy toward Israel or to general Assyrian activity in the eastern Mediterranean seaboard. Included in these sources are materials of diverse form—letters addressed from Assyrian officials to the royal court, inscriptions commemorating military campaigns, and summary annals reporting the events of the various kings' rule. The Assyrian texts, however, present historians with a number of problems. For the second of these rulers, Shalmaneser V, we possess no firsthand historical texts and thus have no direct information from the Assyrian perspective on the final revolt of Israel. The inscriptions of Sargon II, however, do provide information about the disposition of the northern kingdom and its final incorporation into the Assyrian

Empire.[1] The most strategic Assyrian inscriptions for the period are those of Tiglath-pileser, but unfortunately most of these are fragmentary and problematic.[2] Inscribed on stone slabs on the walls of his palace at Calah (Nimrud), his annals were removed by one of his successors and reused in a later palace. This plus the treatment the slabs received at the hands of their modern-day discoverers has left them severely damaged and disordered. Scholars often differ considerably on how breaks in the texts should be restored. Great caution must be exercised, therefore, in drawing conclusions on the basis of such restored texts. Fortunately, other nonannal inscriptions of Tiglath-pileser, although again frequently fragmentary, supplement and make possible partial reconstruction of the events of his reign noted in the damaged annals. References in the Assyrian texts, in spite of their textual problems and their propagandistic, idealized presentations, provide a general chronology for the period. Especially beneficial are the *limmu* lists (the Eponym Chronicle), which provide notations for each year of Tiglath-pileser's rule. In his accession year and the fourteen successive years, the Assyrian army was on campaign and its location is noted.

A new source for Near Eastern history from the time of Tiglath-pileser until the second century B.C.E. is the so-called Babylonian Chronicles. These texts, written on clay tablets in Akkadian cuneiform, provide entries following a chronological order and cover a period extending from the mid-eighth to the third century. They do not appear to have been the official state records of Babylon but may have been based on these.[3] Fortunately, these supply a few fragments of information about the reign of Shalmaneser V.

Some surviving Egyptian texts related to this period are also available. Of particular importance is the Victory Stela of Pharaoh Piye (Pianki), the first important ruler of the Twenty-fifth Ethiopian or Cushite Dynasty, that describes conditions in Egypt in the second half of the eighth century.[4]

In this and subsequent chapters, classical sources written in Greek or Latin become more relevant to the reconstruction of Near Eastern history. The most important of these are the writings of Herodotus and Josephus.

Herodotus, a fifth-century B.C.E. Greek historian, traveled throughout many Near Eastern countries collecting traditions and historical recollections.[5] These were incorporated into the nine books of his *Histories,* which concern relations between the Greeks and the oriental kingdoms to the early years of the fifth century. Herodotus often supplies materials on various historical matters not found in other sources.

1. See Andreas Fuchs, *Die Inschriften Sargons II. aus Khorsabad* (Göttingen: Cuvillier, 1994; hereafter abbreviated *ISK*) and his *Die Annalen des Jahres 711 v. Chr. nach Prismenfragmenten aus Ninive und Assur* (SAAS 8; Helsinki: Neo-Assyrian Text Corpus Project, 1998; hereafter abbreviated *AJ*), and the selections in *COS* 2:293–300.

2. All his known inscriptions are collected in Hayim Tadmor, *The Inscriptions of Tiglath-pileser III King of Assyria: Critical Edition, with Introductions, Translations and Commentary* (Jerusalem: Israel Academy of Sciences and Humanities, 1994; hereafter abbreviated *ITP*); and J. K. Kuan, *NAHI* 135–92.

3. For an edition of all the chronicle texts, see A. K. Grayson, *Assyrian and Babylonian Chronicles* (Locust Valley, NY: Augustin, 1975; repr. Winona Lake, IN: Eisenbrauns, 2000); hereafter abbreviated *ABC.*

4. See Miriam Lichtheim, *Ancient Egyptian Literature* (3 vols.; Berkeley: University of California Press, 1973–80) 3:66–88 (hereafter abbreviated *AEL*); reproduced in *COS* 2:42–55.

5. Herodotus's history is available in several English translations; see, e.g., the LCL version trans. A. D. Godly (4 vols.; Cambridge: Harvard University Press, 1990); and *The History: Herodotus,* trans. David Greve (Chicago: University of Chicago Press, 1987).

Josephus, a Jewish historian of the first century C.E., wrote three major works—*Jewish Antiquities, Jewish War, Contra Apion*—and an autobiography.[6] His *Antiquities* covers from the creation of the world until the outbreak of the First Jewish Revolt against Rome in 66 C.E. but consists primarily in a retelling of the biblical story. The *War* is a history of the Jews from the early second century B.C.E. until the time shortly after the First Jewish Revolt, which resulted in the destruction of the Jerusalem temple in 70 C.E. To defend his role in the Jewish war with Rome and the charge that he was a traitor to the Jewish cause, Josephus wrote his autobiography, actually an appendix for the *Antiquities*, which primarily describes and defends his actions as commander of the Jewish forces in Galilee. *Contra Apion* is a defense of Judaism against various pagan charges.

Two points should be noted about Josephus as a historical source. (1) Where his work and the biblical narrative overlap, he is fundamentally dependent on biblical materials. (2) At times, however, Josephus supplements the biblical narrative. Sometimes his material is drawn from Jewish homiletical and midrashic traditions, and at other times it is drawn from ancient and reliable sources. This means that such supplemental material must be carefully evaluated in every particular case with regard to historical reliability.

Syria-Palestine and the Assyrian Empire

Before discussing the particular history of Israel and Judah during the eighth and seventh centuries, the time of Assyrian domination, we should survey the general outline of the Assyrian conquest of the eastern Mediterranean seaboard (see Chart 18) and the empire's relationship to its conquered subjects.

The Assyrian Conquest of the Eastern Mediterranean Seaboard

Under Tiglath-pileser III (744–727 B.C.E.), who began his rule in the late spring of 745, usurping the throne at a time of revolt in the capital city of Calah, a highly successful program of Assyrian expansion and consolidation was accomplished. This program included the curtailment of power held by provincial Assyrian governors, the relocation of conquered populations, and the annexation of territories into the Assyrian provincial system, policies designed to ensure continued Assyrian domination of conquered areas. Before his death, Tiglath-pileser III had extended the Assyrian Empire to include practically the whole of the eastern Mediterranean seaboard as well as territory to the north, east, and south of Assyria proper.

Two goals lay behind the new initiatives and policies of Tiglath-pileser III in the west. First, he set out to reduce or eliminate Urartian influence in northern Syria and to consolidate Assyrian authority in this area. During the reigns of his three immediate predecessors, the kingdom of Urartu (biblical Ararat), to the north and northwest of Assyria proper, had expanded its presence and

---

6. Josephus's *Antiquities* is available in the LCL series, trans. H. S. J. Thackeray et al. (6 vols.; Cambridge: Harvard University Press, 1926–65).

TEXT 9. Correspondence of an Assyrian Official

To the king my lord your servant Qurdi-assur-lamur.

Concerning the ruler of Tyre, about whom the king said: "Talk nicely to him," all the wharves are at their disposal. His subjects enter and leave the warehouses at will, and trade. The Lebanon range is accessible to him; they go up and down at will and bring lumber down. On the lumber they bring down I impose a tax. I have appointed tax inspectors over the customs (houses) of the entire Lebanon range, (and) they keep the watch on the harbor. I appointed a tax-inspector (for those who) were going down into the customs houses which are in Sidon, (but) the Sidonians chased him away. Thereupon I sent the Itu'a contingent into the Lebanon range. They terrified the people, (so that) afterwards they sent a message and fetched the tax inspector (and) brought (him) into Sidon. I spoke to them in these terms: "Bring down the lumber, do your work on it, (but) do not deliver it to the Egyptians or Palestinians, or I shall not let you go up to the mountains." (H. W. F. Saggs, *The Nimrud Letters, 1952* [London: British School of Archaeology in Iraq, 2001] 156–57)

influence at Assyrian expense.[7] States in northern Syria had become cooperative with Urartu. Tiglath-pileser's immediate predecessor, Ashur-nirari V (754–745), had little success in controlling the empire. In an inscription the Urartian king Sardur II (ca. 764–735) claims to have defeated the Assyrians severely (RIMA 3:246). A treaty between Ashur-nirari V and Mati'el king of Arpad has survived but in fragmentary form (*ANET* 532–33).[8] This treaty must have been imposed in Ashur-nirari's first year, when the Eponym Chronicle reports that the Assyrian army was at Arpad. Shamshi-ilu had probably carried out the expedition. Mati'el was soon involved, however, in an anti-Assyrian coalition organized by Sardur, which included Melid, Gurgum, and Kummuh as well as Arpad (*ITP* 101, 125, 133). Shamshi-ilu, the embodiment of Assyrian authority in the west, seems to have died before 750, having served as *limmu* for the last time in 752–751. In campaigns that he led personally, Tiglath-pileser III was able to reassert control over the region directly.

Second, the Assyrian king wanted not only to secure Assyrian trade with the west but also to gain control of commerce throughout the eastern Mediterranean seaboard. By dominating the trade routes leading through northern Syria and into western Asia Minor, Urartu had deprived Assyria of such needed materials as foodstuffs, metals, timber, and horses. The resulting shortages in Assyria had produced widespread insurrections in the homeland from

---

7. Urartian history is discussed in the following works: B. B. Piotrovsky, *The Ancient Civilization of Urartu* (New York: Cowles, 1969); and P. E. Zimansky, *Ecology and Empire: The Structure of the Urartian Civilization* (SAOC 41; Chicago: Oriental Institute, 1985); idem, "The Kingdom of Urartu in Eastern Anatolia," *CANE* 2:1135–46.

8. Mati'el also appears as a treaty partner in the so-called Sefire Inscriptions, which refer to an Upper Aram (the north Syrian Aramean states) and a Lower Aram (the south Syrian Aramaean states). See *COS* 2:213–17; and J. A. Fitzmyer, *The Aramaic Inscriptions of Sefire* (2d ed.; BibOr 19a; Rome: Pontifical Biblical Institute, 1995).

CHART 18. The Period of Assyrian Domination

Judah	Israel	Assyria
Jotham (759–744)	Zechariah and Shallum (748) Menahem (746–737)	Tiglath-pileser III (744–727) reports payment of tribute by Menahem probably in 738/737; he campaigns along the coast of the eastern Mediterranean seaboard and collects tribute from Jehoahaz in 734 or shortly thereafter, conquers the interior of the seaboard and Damascus, and confirms Hoshea on the throne in 731. In the so-called Syro-Ephraimite War, Rezin of Damascus and Pekah had sought to depose Jehoahaz prior to Tiglath-pileser's 734–731 campaign.
Ahaz (Jehoahaz I) (743–728)		
	Pekahiah (736–735) Pekah (734–731)	
	Hoshea (730–722)	
Hezekiah (727–699)		Shalmaneser V (726–722) lays siege to Samaria, which fell in 722, about the time of his death.
	Fall of Samaria (722), after which the kingdom of Israel ceases to exist.	Sargon II (721–705) completes and reaffirms Assyrian control of Syria-Palestine with campaigns in 720, 716, and 712.
		Sennacherib (704–681) marches on Philistia and Judah in 701 and puts down a revolt in which Hezekiah plays a significant role.
Manasseh (698–644)		Esarhaddon (680–669) holds Syria-Palestine securely under control, collecting tribute from Manasseh. He conquered Memphis in 671 but dies in a follow-up Egyptian campaign.
Amon (643–642)		Ashurbanipal (668–627) recovers Memphis and sacks Thebes in 663, but the Assyrian Empire confronts numerous difficulties at the end of his reign.

about 760. Assyrian control over the trade routes from the west and the north was considered a necessity in order to secure needed supplies and satisfy Assyrian demands at home. Tiglath-pileser thus moved into southern Syria-Palestine in order to establish and expand Assyrian control over the entire interregional trade along the eastern Mediterranean seaboard and to redirect the flow of western commerce into Assyria proper.

After establishing his authority throughout Mesopotamia during his accession year, Tiglath-pileser carried out a short campaign to the east. The Eponym Chronicle notes that the Assyrian army was in northern Syria fighting the Urartian-led anti-Assyrian coalition from his second through his fifth regnal years (743–739). After an excursion to the east, at which time the so-called Iran Stela was set up (see *ITP* 91–110; *COS* 2:287), the Assyrian army returned to the west and captured Calno (Kullani; see Amos 6:2; Isa. 10:9) in northern Syria near Aleppo. After expeditions to the north and east against Urartian-influenced territory, the Assyrians moved into southern Syria-Palestine during Tiglath-pileser's eleventh through his thirteenth regnal year (734–731) where he extended Assyrian control to the border of Egypt and suppressed an anti-Assyrian coalition led by Damascus. Much of the remainder of his career was focused on affairs in southern Mesopotamia, where he assumed the throne of Babylon in his sixteenth year (729–728).

Tiglath-pileser III bequeathed to his successor an empire that included practically all of Mesopotamia and the mountainous region to the east and north, as well as eastern Anatolia, and all of the eastern Mediterranean seaboard. King Sargon II (721–705) and his successors continued the process of Assyrian expansion by consolidating Assyrian hegemony to the border of Egypt. Assyrian control of the trade and commerce in the eastern Mediterranean was given an especially significant boost when Sargon succeeded in establishing suzerainty over the island of Cyprus (by 709).

Naturally, the movement of Assyria into the eastern Mediterranean seaboard and its attempt to control the area's commerce precipitated a struggle between Egypt and Assyria for dominance in the area. Already on his Black Obelisk, Shalmaneser III had noted the receipt of exotic tribute from Egypt: "two-humped camels, a water buffalo, a rhinoceros, an antelope, female elephants, female monkeys, (and) apes" (RIMA 3:150; *COS* 2:270). When this gift was received and under what circumstances are unknown; it was probably simply an affirmation of goodwill. While Tiglath-pileser was expanding westward, the Twenty-fifth Dynasty, headquartered in Upper Egypt, was seeking to dominate Lower Egypt and the Delta and to extend its influence in the eastern Mediterranean.[9] Perhaps as early as the mid-eighth century, the Ethiopians/Egyptians were trying to influence powers in Syria-Palestine against Assyria. Competition between Assyria and the Ethiopian Twenty-fifth Dynasty greatly influenced the political and economic life of the eastern Mediterranean seaboard until well into the seventh century.

---

9. This dynasty was centered along the Nile, upstream (south) of Egypt proper. Called Cush in the Bible, the kingdom included what is modern Sudan, Ethiopia, and Eritrea. See W. Y. Adams, *Nubia, Corridor to Africa* (Princeton: Princeton University Press, 1977); idem, "The Kingdom and Civilization of Kush in Northeast Africa," *CANE* 2:775–89. For the chronology of the Twenty-fifth Dynasty, which is followed here, see Dan'el Kahn, "The Inscriptions of Sargon II at Tang-i Var and the Chronology of Dynasty 25," *Or* 70 (2001) 1–18.

64. *Assyrian chariot and team*. Relief from Nineveh, depicting an Assyrian chariot and team, from approximately the reign of Tiglath-pileser III. (*Vorderasiatische Museum, Berlin*)

Assyrian Administrative Policies

The Assyrians protected their vested interests and extended their influence and dominance through both political and military means. Politically, they utilized various forms of treaty relationships with other kingdoms. These agreements ranged from "peace and friendship" treaties and nonaggression pacts in which Assyria and the other parties were treated as equals to vassal arrangements imposed upon weaker and submissive states. As a major superpower, Assyria was generally able to establish terms in its favor even in treaties where the second party was declared an equal. Militarily, Assyria sought to dominate those powers that it considered to be a threat or that hindered the development of their national interests.

Beginning with Tiglath-pileser III, one can discern a particular pattern in Assyria's dealings with weaker, subordinate, and conquered peoples. It is possible to distinguish various types of relationships between Assyria and its subject states, such as Israel and Judah, although it must be recognized that the distinction among the types should not be rigidly drawn or seen as necessarily consecutive stages.

1. In some cases relations with Assyria were based upon voluntary submission by local rulers. When the Assyrian army made its show of force in an area and subjected the region to psychological as well as actual warfare, many rulers chose not to offer opposition but to submit voluntarily to Assyrian overlordship and to become what might be called Assyrian satellites or puppet

states. This meant that they accepted Assyrian authority, offered special presentation gifts to the Assyrian king when he was in the area, agreed to pay
annual tribute, and supported Assyrian military operations as well as construction and other projects when called upon. The Assyrians interfered little or
only minimally in the social, religious, and administrative life of such states so
long as political allegiance was maintained, economic obligations fulfilled, and
Assyrian interests respected. An intelligence system based on spying reports
helped the Assyrians to keep informed of matters even in such satellite states
(see 2 Kgs. 18:22). Relations with the satellite states were concluded through
treaty arrangements. Stipulations and obligations of their relationship were put
down in writing and sworn to in the names of the gods of both Assyria and
those of the vassal states. These treaties contained numerous curses to fall upon
the satellite state should it prove disloyal and unreliable.[10]

2. When kingdoms, cities, or tribal groups refused to submit voluntarily or
showed disloyalty to Assyrian authority, they were conquered or forced into
submission by the Assyrian army. Payment of tribute and other requirements
were imposed, and the Assyrians took on a significant role in the state's political, military, and diplomatic life. In these situations Assyria assumed the role
of overlord and the subdued state that of a vassal. Assyrian officials were
sometimes stationed in the vassal states to oversee matters in which Assyrian
interests might be involved and to send reports about local conditions to the
royal Assyrian court. (For an example of such correspondence, see Text 9.) In
vassal states, members of the ruling family that had opposed the Assyrians
occasionally were allowed to continue their rule, provided they were willing to
offer allegiance to Assyria. Sometimes potential leaders of a state were carried
to Assyria to be reared at the royal court. Allegiance to Assyria was confirmed
through treaty renewals.

3. Rebellions by vassals, usually signaled by failure to pay the regular tribute, could be crushed mercilessly, and the rebel territory reduced to the status
of a province—that is, incorporated into the Assyrian provincial system and
placed under the control of an Assyrian military governor and a hierarchy of
officials. The Assyrian monarch had traveling personnel who investigated and
inspected the work of provincial officials and thus tended to oversee the overseers. As a further measure to maintain control over and stability in areas transformed into provinces, the Assyrians deported the "upper crust" and other
elements of the population and settled them elsewhere in the empire. In turn,
foreign populations from other countries could be resettled in the new
provinces. This mixing of populations through large-scale transplantations
was intended primarily to reduce moves toward nationalistic resurgence. Even
in conquered regions, Assyria sought to return the areas to normalcy and to
restore their economic base so that the provinces not only would be self-
sustaining but also could be a source of benefit for the Assyrian homeland.

This general pattern of political dominance was not a system rigidly followed, nor was it applied consistently throughout the empire. Local conditions
and the political and economic needs of the Assyrians—that is, ad hoc consid-

---

10. A collection of all known Neo-Assyrian treaties is available in Simo Parpola and Kazuko Watanabe, *Neo-Assyrian Treaties and Loyalty Oaths* (SAA 2; Helsinki: Helsinki University Press, 1988); hereafter abbreviated *NATLO*.

65. *Tiglath-pileser III.* Tiglath-pileser III (744–727) reorganized the Assyrian administrative bureaucracy and pursued an aggressive policy of control over the Phoenician and Palestinian seacoasts and trade routes. He was largely responsible for the resurgence of Assyrian strength in the mid-eighth century B.C.E. This depiction of him is from a wall relief of the Central Palace at Nimrud. (*British Museum*)

erations—often influenced the arrangement of relationships. The Assyrians seemed reluctant to reduce to provinces the territories and kingdoms in the southwestern tip of the Fertile Crescent, namely, the Phoenician and Philistine city-states, Judah, Ammon, Moab, Edom, and the Arabs. The Assyrians probably thought that it was advantageous to allow these regions to be governed as semi-independent states with some vested national interests. At least two geopolitical factors seem to have contributed to this situation. Some of these states—especially the Phoenician, Philistine, and Arab and other nomadic kingdoms—were important components in ancient Near Eastern trade. Since the Assyrians sought to control the commerce in the region, they certainly did not wish to diminish its importance or radically disrupt the relations on which it was based. These states were also border kingdoms and thus important as buffer zones.

The stakes were high for the Assyrian satellites and vassal kingdoms of Syria-Palestine. On the one hand, the Assyrian burden was heavy, financially and otherwise. This burden frequently led the states to participate in coordinated alliances and rebellion and to look southward, to Egypt, for hope and help. On the other hand, the horrendous disaster that accompanied the Assyrian suppression of an unsuccessful insurrection was an ever-present reality that tempered nationalistic enthusiasm. Assyrian rulers, who could take pride in their atrocities, were always to be feared. Once under the shadow of Assyrian power, practically every Syro-Palestinian kingdom developed pro- and anti-Assyrian parties. Such parties, of course, were not ideological adherents or opponents of Assyrian politics but merely divisions between those who called for defiance of Assyrian domination and for nationalistic resurgence and those who thought it best to swallow the bitter pill and continue submission and acquiescence to Assyrian rule.

Chronological Issues

The chronology of the Israelite kings and the sequence of events between 748 and 720 B.C.E. are extremely problematic, and the evidence is ambiguous. From Assyrian records we know that Tiglath-pileser III completed his first series of western campaigns in 739. During these initial western campaigns, he suppressed rebellions and established Assyrian provinces in northern Syria. Also at that time, he received tribute from several rulers in Syria-Palestine. An inscription discovered in Iran, and probably set up during his 739–738 campaign to Ulluba on the Iranian-Iraqi border, reports on tribute that Tiglath-pileser established over several kingdoms probably after his four-year campaign in northern Syria. Among the southern kings mentioned at that time were Menahem of the land of Samaria, Rezin of Damascus (actually Sha-imerisu), and Tubail of Tyre (*ITP* 107–9; *COS* 2:287).

In 733–731, Tiglath-pileser was again in the west suppressing a major revolt in southern Syria-Palestine. He first swept down the coast in 734–733, probably late in 734 or early in 733, and followed this with a campaign against the interior, which concluded with the destruction of Damascus. The Assyrian army, according to the Eponymn Chronicle, was still in the land of Damascus in the spring of 731 and was probably still fighting the Syrians. During or just after his campaign against Damascus, Tiglath-pileser III confirmed Hoshea to assume the throne in Samaria (*ITP* 141; *COS* 2:288). Thus any reconstruction of Israelite chronology must have Menahem on the Israelite throne no later than 738 and Hoshea ruling in 731–730. This provides us with two firm chronological points.

Two Israelite kings ruled in Samaria between Menahem and Hoshea and thus have to be placed sometime between 738 and 730. These were Pekahiah and Pekah. Pekahiah is assigned a rule of two years or parts thereof (2 Kgs. 15:23). Pekah is said to have ruled twenty years (15:27; see 16:1). It is, of course, impossible to fit a reign of twenty years in Samaria by Pekah into the firm chronology established on the basis of the Assyrian inscriptions. If Menahem died in 737 and Pekahiah ruled for parts of two years, then Pekah would have come to the throne in Samaria in 734. This would have been prior to Tiglath-pileser III's 733–731 campaigns in Syria-Palestine, after which Hoshea was placed on the Israelite throne. This seems in clear conflict with the twenty years assigned to Pekah in the Bible. This problem and the similarity of names have led some scholars to propose that Pekah and Pekahiah may have been the same person. The vast majority of scholars simply reduce Pekah's reign to the number of years that can be accommodated. An alternative explanation, which we develop more fully below, is that Pekah was already ruling over a portion of Israelite territory before coming to the throne in Samaria and that the twenty years credited to him includes the earlier years of his partial rule.

The chronology of Judean kings also presents some problems. Hezekiah is said to have ruled for twenty-nine years (2 Kgs. 18:2; 2 Chr. 29:1). In Hezekiah's sixth year, Samaria was captured by Shalmaneser V according to 2 Kings 18:10. (The fall of Samaria as well as the date given in 2 Kgs. 18:13 will be discussed below.) This would make Hezekiah's first year begin at the fall festival of 727. His predecessor, Ahaz, is assigned sixteen years of rule (2 Kgs. 16:2; 2 Chr. 28:1). Thus his reign would have begun in 743 and overlapped part of the reign of Menahem, all the reigns of Pekahiah and Pekah, and part of the reign of Hoshea (see 2 Kgs. 17:1). Ahaz's predecessor, Jotham, is also assigned a rule of sixteen years; thus he would have become king in 759. Jotham's predecessor, Uzziah (Azariah), is assigned a reign of fifty-two years. Uzziah, however, was struck with *tsara'ath* and had to surrender the throne to his son, Jotham (2 Kgs. 15:5). According to 15:8, Zechariah ruled during Uzziah's thirty-eighth year; and, according to 15:13, 17, Shallum ruled and Menaham began his rule in the thirty-ninth year of Uzziah. This suggests that Uzziah became king of Judah in 785 since the Zechariah-Shallum-Menahem conflict occurred in 748–747. If Jotham became king of Judah in 759, this suggests that Uzziah abdicated the throne in 760, in his twenty-sixth year. The fifty-two years assigned Uzziah would thus include the twenty-six years he actually reigned as well as twenty-six years when he "lived in a separate house" (15:5). During these years he probably continued to exert considerable control over Judean affairs. Uzziah died in 734, about the time Pekah seized the throne in Samaria (15:27; see 15:23).

Rezin's "Greater Syria"

While Assyria was the dominant Middle Eastern power throughout the period surveyed in this chapter and overshadowed politics far and wide, Israel and Judah also had to contend during the early part of this period—from the mid-eighth century until the fall of Damascus in 731—with a less gigantic but more immediately neighboring power: the Syrian kingdom of Damascus. The Syrian monarch at the time was the ambitious Rezin, who apparently had usurped the throne in Damascus, since the Assyrian inscriptions list Hadara rather than Damascus as his hometown (*ITP* 81; *COS* 2:286). At any rate, Rezin and Damascus exerted significant influence among the local kingdoms of southern Syria-Palestine for almost two decades.

Rezin's direct involvement in Israelite and Judean affairs is clearly indicated in the biblical account of the so-called Syro-Ephraimite War (2 Kgs. 16:5–9; 2 Chr. 28:16–21; Isa. 7–8). This combines with several other items of evidence to suggest (1) that Rezin had already begun to encroach on surrounding nations, especially Israel and Judah, as early as the reigns of Jeroboam II and Menahem of Israel and Jotham of Judah; (2) that his influence and territorial control had reached such an extensive level by the time of Pekahiah, Pekah, and Ahaz that it is possible to speak of a "Greater Syria"; and (3) that when Tiglath-pileser III began his western campaign in 734–733, Rezin was the leader of a powerful anti-Assyrian movement supported by most of the nations of southern Syria-Palestine. Since the existence and policies of this coalition constitute the political background of the Syro-Ephraimite crisis, let us examine these three points in detail.

1. There is some evidence, admittedly open to different interpretations, to suggest that Rezin was already expanding southward and westward, exerting significant pressure among the Palestinian kingdoms, before and during the reign of Menahem (746–737). First, the oracle on Damascus in Amos 1:3–5 describes Syria, referred to as the "house of Hazael" as in some contemporary Assyrian inscriptions, as invading Gilead, traditionally Israelite territory in Transjordan. While this oracle cannot be dated precisely, the common tendency is to associate the career of Amos with the final years of Jeroboam II. In addition, Damascus seems to have been working cooperatively with Bit-Adini, now ruled by an anti-Assyrian king rather than Shamshi-ilu. (Note the reference to Beth-eden = Bit-Adini in Amos 1:5.) Second, the note in 2 Kings 15:37 has Rezin and Pekah threatening Judah already in the reign of Jotham. Pekah could not

yet have been on the throne in Samaria, given the chronological structures mentioned above. Pekah was already ruling at that time over some portion of Israelite territory and claiming kingship. Pekah would have been a puppet ruler, subject to Rezin, over territory probably originally in northern Transjordan and/or Galilee, which Rezin had already wrenched away from Israel. Finally, there is the note in 2 Kings 16:6 to take into account. This text reads in Hebrew: "At that time Rezin the king of Syria recovered Elath for Syria, and drove the men of Judah from Elath; and the Syrians [or 'Edomites,' according to the Masoretic correction of the Hebrew] came to Elath, where they dwell to this day." The textual context would seem to place Rezin's seizure of Elath in Ahaz's reign. When one considers that the organization of the material in 2 Kings is often more theological than chronological, however, the possibility emerges that this action also occurred during the reign of Jotham.

Rezin's expansion of Syrian influence was not unlike that of his predecessor, Hazael, a century earlier, and for the same reasons. Hazael conquered much of Transjordan and probably all of Galilee and extended his influence into Philistine territory, that is, along the Mediterranean coast. At that time, both Israel and Judah suffered from Syrian oppression (2 Kgs. 10:32–33; 12:17–18). Rezin seems to have been attempting, but without the same success, to duplicate this earlier Syrian mini-empire. Unlike the situation at the time of his immediate predecessor, Hadianu, there was now no Shamshi-ilu to thwart Syria's expansion at Israel's expense.

2. However early Rezin began to expand his realm and exert influence on Israelite and Judean politics he seems to have clearly established what might be called a "Greater Syria." Some of the evidence for this has been noted above (Amos 1:3–5; 2 Kgs. 15:37; 16:6). In addition, Isaiah 9:11–12 speaks of Israel's enemies eating up its territory—Syria from the east and Philistia from the west. After Assyria's triumph over Damascus in 731, Assyria brought to an end the Syrian kingdom. As part of the dismantlement of the state, Assyria incorporated Syrian territory into the Assyrian provincial system. In one of his inscriptions Tiglath-pileser speaks of making provinces out of territory belonging to "the extended domain of the house of Hazael," territory that joined the land of Omri (ITP 187; COS 2:291). Second Kings 15:27 probably speaks of the same events when it describes the incorporation of (formerly) Israelite territory into the Assyrian Empire.[11] The places noted in this text are in Transjordan and Galilee, regions probably under Syrian control, at the time the reason for their incorporation by Assyria. (The central coastal plain of Palestine, the region around Dor, between Phoenicia and Philistia, may also have been controlled by Syria, and this was the reason for its annexation by Assyria.) The extended domain of the house of Hazael ("Greater Syria") thus included large areas previously considered Israelite territory. Isaiah 9:1 speaks of this territory in describing the time when "the latter one [Rezin] treated harshly the Way of the Sea, Beyond the Jordan, and Galilee of the Nations."

3. Rezin, like his earlier predecessor Hadadezer in the 850s, had put together a major coalition of states in Syria-Palestine to oppose Assyrian authority in the

---

11. See S. A. Irvine, "The Southern Border of Syria Reconsidered," CBQ 56 (1994) 21–41; and Nadav Na'aman, "Rezin of Damascus and the Land of Gilead," ZDPV 111 (1995) 105–17; repr. in AIIN 40–55.

area, as Syria had done in the preceding century during the days of Shalmaneser III. The refusal of Israel under Menahem and of Judah under Ahaz to join forces with the anti-Assyrian movement, however, meant that a fully united front in Syria-Palestine had not been achieved by Rezin, as was the case when such a coalition confronted Shalmaneser III.

Two factors may appear to call into question Rezin's leadership and even the existence of such an anti-Assyrian coalition. First, why did Rezin, if his Damascus kingdom was a power to be reckoned with, voluntarily make presentation gifts to Tiglath-pileser III on several occasions in the 740s and early 730s as Assyrian inscriptions indicate? Second, why did he not challenge Tiglath-pileser III when the Assyrian king marched his forces down the eastern Mediterranean seaboard in 734–733? The answer in the first instance is that a challenge to Tiglath-pileser III would have been more trouble than it was worth and that the cost of a nominal presentation under the circumstances was a cheap way to buy time. Assyria's threat to Rezin's emerging little empire was still fairly distant, even if one assumes that the Assyrians may have put on a show of force in Palestine to aid Menahem (see 2 Kgs. 15:19). Better to pay a nominal tribute voluntarily to a distant power than possibly have to deal with a wrathful Assyria bent on forcing submission. The 734–733 Assyrian military movement down the Mediterranean coast was a different matter. During the years 737–736 to 735–734, the Assyrians had been campaigning far away in the north and east. During this period the coalition must have decided on a fight-or-die policy. It was no longer a matter of nominal tribute to stave off a distant threat but a matter of submitting or not. Even though Rezin had not yet finally maximized his coalition, as evidenced by the continuing effort to force Judah's participation, Rezin refused to submit: he did not rush to meet Tiglath-pileser III in 733 with proper assurances of loyalty confirmed by presentation gifts. Instead, he chose to fight, although not to attack. There are several indications, moreover, that Rezin was not alone in this regard—that is, he and a coalition of states and rulers in Syria-Palestine strongly resisted Tiglath-pileser III for three years of hard conflict.

The evidence for this coalition is as follows. (a) Rezin's movement against Elath, probably in association with the Edomites (2 Kgs. 16:6), suggests Edomite and other Transjordanian support for Rezin. (b) In Isaiah 9:11–12 Syria is depicted attacking Israel from the east with Philistines attacking from the west, which suggests a Philistine-Syrian coalition. Second Chronicles 28:18, which describes the Philistines invading Judean territory, could indicate Philistine pressure on Judah to join the coalition. (c) The so-called Syro-Ephraimite War, which we shall discuss further in this and the next chapter, was an attempt by Israel and Syria to force Judah into an anti-Assyrian coalition. (d) Mention is made in Tiglath-pileser's texts of his attacks and reprisals against several Syro-Palestinian states in 733–731. These include the Meunites to the south of Judah and Samsi, queen of Arabia. Hiram of Tyre, apparently a "son of Tubail," also cooperated with Rezin against Assyria, support noted in the Assyrian texts (*ITP* 177–79, 187–91; *COS* 2:290–92). (e) The nature of Tiglath-pileser's campaigns, first down the coast and then against the interior of Syria-Palestine, points to a coalition of coastal and internal powers in the area. The Syro-Palestinian opposition to Assyria was not isolated but concerted opposition, and not opposition formed on the spur of the moment but coordinated by Rezin, with his dreams of a united anti-Assyrian front led by "Greater Syria."

Tiglath-pileser's move down the Mediterranean coast to the border of Egypt may have had larger than merely Syro-Palestinian perspectives in view. In his twentieth year, Pharaoh Piye (753–721) invaded the Delta region to stabilize Ethiopian/Cushite control over the area where a number of minor kinglets were struggling with one another for power and challenging the pharaoh's authority (COS 2:42–55). Chief among these troublemakers was Tefnakht, ruler in Sais. Piye's invasion began early in 734 (on the chronology see Kahn in n. 9). Thus Ethiopian troops were moving into the Delta when Tiglath-pileser's troops left Urartu for their march to Philistia. Whether the Twenty-fifth Dynasty gave any indication of interfering in Assyrian affairs in the eastern Mediterranean seaboard we cannot determine, but the course of Tiglath-pileser's march indicates that he moved to block any Ethiopian-Egyptian incursion into the region. At the time, the prophet Isaiah speculated on the movement of both Assyrians and Ethiopians into the region. "On that day Yahweh will whistle for the fly that is at the sources of the streams of Egypt [the Ethiopians], and for the bee that is in the land of Assyria. And they will all come and settle in the steep ravines, and in the clefts of the rocks, and on all the thornbushes, and on all the pastures" (Isa. 7:18–19).

The Last Years of Israel

Having gained an overview of the general international circumstances, let us now focus attention specifically on political developments in the kingdom of Israel. During the last decade of the reign of Jeroboam II, Israel began a rapid decline in its political situation from which it never fully recovered. Jeroboam's son and successor, Zechariah, reigned only a few months before being put to death. Once more the old problem of dynastic insecurity surfaced in the north. Zechariah's was only the first in a series of regicides. Never again was there a successful and lasting succession to the Israelite throne.

In addition to its monarchical instability, Israel was confronted with a reinvigorated Damascus kingdom. No doubt there were strong pro- and anti-Assyrian parties in Israel as well as pro- and anti-Syrian sentiments and factions. The anti-Assyrian party would have appealed to nationalistic hopes, urged cooperation with Rezin, and cast expectant glances in the direction of Egypt. Rezin's grandiose designs and anti-Assyrian program could not help but affect political and social matters in Israel and intensify conflict between the pro- and anti-Assyrian factions.

These three factors—the instability in leadership, the policies of Rezin and the pressure of the Syro-Palestinian anti-Assyrian coalition, and the existence of pro- and anti-Assyrian parties—played their roles in the precipitous decline of the northern kingdom. A fourth element, sectional and political rivalry, developed, and competing claimants to the throne arose (see Isa. 8:14; 9:21; and Hos. 5:5, with their implications of competing realms in the north). All these contributed significantly to the downfall of Israel and its ultimate defeat at the hands of Assyria.

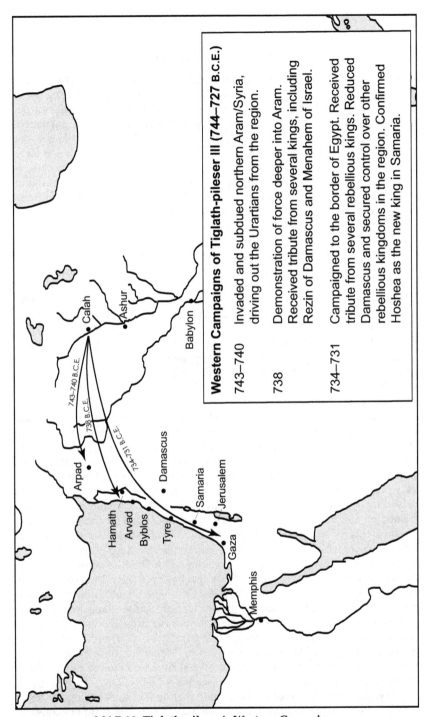

Western Campaigns of Tiglath-pileser III (744–727 B.C.E.)

743–740	Invaded and subdued northern Aram/Syria, driving out the Urartians from the region.
738	Demonstration of force deeper into Aram. Received tribute from several kings, including Rezin of Damascus and Menahem of Israel.
734–731	Campaigned to the border of Egypt. Received tribute from several rebellious kings. Reduced Damascus and secured control over other rebellious kingdoms in the region. Confirmed Hoshea as the new king in Samaria.

MAP 29. Tiglath-pileser's Western Campaigns

Shallum and Menahem

In an effort to obtain the throne, Shallum conspired against and had put to death Zechariah, the legitimate heir, and presumably the entire reigning house of Jehu. Zechariah had ruled for only six months (2 Kgs. 15:8–10). His murder and the extermination of the Jehu dynasty probably received encouragement from the prophetic denunciations of Amos (see Amos 7:10–17) and Hosea (see Hos. 1:4–5), whose pronouncements of judgment on the royal house served as calls to action and assassination. Shallum assumed the kingship, but nothing is said in the 2 Kings account about the basis of his support, which proved to be insufficient to keep him in power. In all likelihood, Shallum was backed by an anti-Assyrian faction that sought to reverse the pro-Assyrian policy that was characteristic of the entire Jehu dynasty. After one month he was slain by Menahem (2 Kgs. 15:14). Menahem is described as having come up from Tirzah, the old Israelite capital, to attack Shallum in Samaria. He may have been a military leader of some sort and thus a carryover from the Jehu dynasty. The Zechariah, Shallum, and Menahem affair had many parallels with the earlier episode of Elah, Zimri, and Omri, which brought an end to an earlier Israelite ruling family (1 Kgs. 16:8–22). In both cases the ruling dynasty was eliminated by a usurper who could not hold the throne, and civil strife accompanied the struggle for power. Shallum is said to have ruled (literally) "a month of days" (2 Kgs. 15:13b). He was apparently not on the throne at the fall festival of 747. Nor had Menahem begun his reign. Thus the year 747–746 went unassigned to any Israelite king but would have been considered Menahem's accession year.

Second Kings 15:16 notes that Menahem took some vicious action against Israelite citizens, either when taking over the throne or else following his accession: "At that time Menahem sacked Tiphsah, all who were in it and its territory from Tirzah on; because they did not open it to him, he sacked it. He ripped open all the pregnant women" (see 2 Kgs. 8:12; Hos. 13:16; Amos 1:13). Two problems about this text stand out: the identification of Tiphsah and the reason for Menahem's atrocity. The only Tiphsah known from antiquity was located on the Euphrates River, which clearly does not fit the geographical requirements of this text. Perhaps the Lucianic recension of the Greek of 2 Kings 15:16, which reads "Tappuah," should be followed. Tappuah was an Ephraimite town about fourteen miles southwest of Tirzah, the latter located in the territory of Manasseh (Josh. 17:8). It also has been hypothesized that "son of Jabesh" in describing Shallum (see 2 Kgs. 15:13–14) should be understood as "son of [the place] Jashib." Jashib was another Ephraimite village located in the general vicinity of Tirzah and only about two miles from Tappuah. If Shallum was from the Tappuah area, perhaps the local citizenry had supported him and opposed Menahem. This could explain why Menahem, once he gained the throne, treated them with such ferocity. Tribal rivalries between Ephraim and Manasseh may also have played a role (see Isa. 9:18–21).

Other than this reference to the trouble that he had establishing his reign, only one item is reported about Menahem (apart from his death notice). Both the biblical and Assyrian texts report that he made payments voluntarily to

Tiglath-pileser III (= Pul) and, one assumes, remained a loyal subject until his death (2 Kgs. 15:17–22). Menahem's name appears both in the annals and on a stela inscription of Tiglath-pileser III (*ITP* 197, 69; *COS* 2:287, 285).

The Eponym Chronicle shows that the Assyrian army was headquartered in northern Syria around Arpad for four years beginning in 743–742. Arpad under Mati'el had organized a major coalition against Assyria in cooperation with Urartu. Something of this coalition of "upper Aram" is reflected in the so-called Sefire Inscription containing a treaty between Bar-ga'yah of Kittik, a kingdom west of Carchemish,[12] and Mati'el, ruler of Arpad and the surrounding kingdom of Beth-Gush (for the treaty see *COS* 2:213–17). During this period the Eponym Chronicle reports that Urartu was defeated (in the region of Kummuh in eastern Anatolia according to the annals; *ITP* 125), thereby suggesting that the Assyrian military campaigned widely during this period and did not simply spend the four years encamped against Arpad.

Tiglath-pileser probably also came to the aid of Menahem during this time in the west. Second Kings 15:19–20 reports: "In his days, Pul [= Tiglath-pileser], king of Assyria, came into the land, and Menahem gave Pul a thousand talents [an exaggerated figure?] of silver to help him confirm his hold on the royal power. Menahem paid out the silver on behalf of Israel because of all the warriors to give to the king of Assyria, fifty shekels of silver per man. The king of Assyria then left and did not remain in the land."[13] This text indicates that Tiglath-pileser intervened directly and personally to support the pro-Assyrian Menahem and to preserve his hold on the throne. In addition, Menahem was supplied with mercenary troops at the price of fifty shekels per soldier. Menahem was apparently having great difficulty retaining his rule based on a pro-Assyrian policy against the rival anti-Assyrian King Pekah. In his inscriptions Tiglath-pileser refers to "Menahem of the land of Samaria," not "of Israel" or "of Bit-Omri." This indicates that Menahem was in control only of the city of Samaria and the surrounding district (what the prophet Hosea refers to as Ephraim; see also Isa. 7:9a). Probably Menahem held the central hill country from Samaria south to the border of Jerusalem-held territory in the region of the tribe of Benjamin.

Menahem died a natural death: "he slept with his fathers" (2 Kgs. 15:22), the last Israelite king about whom this could be said.

Pekahiah

The son of Menahem, Pekahiah, ascended the throne in Samaria with dynastic credentials (2 Kgs. 15:23–26). His rule was short-lived, for he was quickly attacked and put to death by Pekah, who had the support of the anti-Assyrian faction and the advocates of cooperation with Syria. The burden of Assyrian tribute had probably convinced many Israelites to support Pekah's coup and to favor Rezin's anti-Assyrian activities.

---

12. See Edward Lipiński, *The Aramaeans: Their Ancient History, Culture, Religion* (OLA 100; Leuven: Peeters, 2000) 222–31.

13. For this understanding of the text see T. R. Hobbs, *2 Kings* (WBC 13; Waco: Word, 1985) 199; and Kuan, *NAHI* 143–46.

Pekah

Second Kings 15:25 relates how Pekah conspired against Pekahiah and with a contingent of Gileadites attacked and put to death the king in the citadel of the royal palace in Samaria. Pekah's revolt was probably either directly inspired or at least strongly supported by Rezin. This is suggested by several considerations. (1) That men from Gilead, an area probably already under Syrian domination, participated in the takeover of the Israelite throne points to Syrian complicity. (2) Pekah and Rezin had already carried out cooperative actions against Judah during the reign of Jotham (2 Kgs. 15:37). (3) Pekah came to the throne in Samaria in the early fall of 734, when anti-Assyrian fervor under Rezin's influence would have been at its peak in Syria-Palestine. (4) In the biblical statements about Pekah and Rezin, the latter is always mentioned first and seems definitely to have been the dominant figure in the Syro-Ephraimite alliance against Ahaz (see, for example, Isa. 7:1). Isaiah 7:2 says, literally, "when Aram [Damascus] had come to rest on Ephraim," implying that Pekah's takeover was actually Rezin's seizure of the region.

Acting in partnership, Rezin and Pekah, and probably other members of the Syro-Palestinian anti-Assyrian coalition that had crystallized during Tiglath-pileser's absence from the region, turned their efforts to the south and Judah, hoping to increase the strength, proximity, and size of their coalition by including Judah in their program. Negotiations between Judah and Syria, even before Pekah secured the throne in Samaria, may have already taken place but with Ahaz refusing to join the movement. Second Chronicles 28:7 suggests that at some point there was an unsuccessful attempt, apparently externally inspired, to remove Ahaz from the throne through assassination: "Zichri, a mighty warrior of Ephraim, killed the king's [Ahaz's] son Maaseiah, Azrikam the commander of the palace, and Elkanah the next in authority to the king." Ahaz was also apparently under strong pressure from many of his own people to yield and join the coalition.

The Syro-Ephraimite Attack on Jerusalem

Rezin and Pekah marched in a blitzkrieg against Jerusalem to achieve through military force what they had not acquired through other means—a ruler in Judah who would join, support, and contribute to the anti-Assyrian coalition. This engagement, frequently called the Syro-Ephraimite War,[14] probably took place shortly after Pekah had usurped the throne and solidified his authority in Samaria just before the major fall festival in 734. Numerous biblical texts (such as 2 Kgs. 15:29–30, 37; 16:5–9; Isa. 6:1–12:6; 2 Chr. 28:5–21), as well as several inscriptions of Tiglath-pileser III, are relevant and related either to the specifics of this invasion or to the events that constitute the larger background. As we learn from Isaiah 7:6, the intention of Rezin and Pekah was to replace

---

14. Numerous studies on this episode in history have been published. A survey of the issues with bibliography and a reconstruction of the course of events are provided by S. A. Irvine, *Isaiah, Ahaz, and the Syro-Ephraimitic Crisis* (SBLDS 123; Atlanta: Scholars Press, 1990).

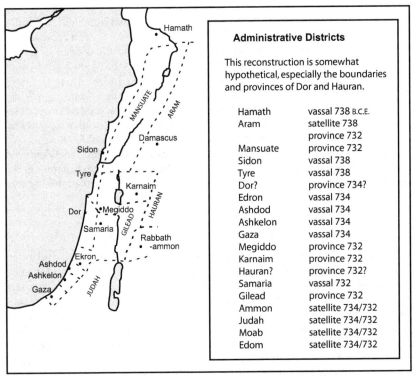

**MAP 30. Approximate Assyrian Administrative Districts
by the End of Tiglath-pileser III's Reign**

Ahaz on the Judean throne with a ruler who would support the anti-Assyrian fraternity. Ahaz had become king of Judah during the reign of Menahem. Menahem, of course, had remained submissive to Assyria throughout his reign, refusing to join the anti-Assyrian coalition. When Israel's policy toward Assyria changed with Pekah's assumption of the throne in Samaria, Pekah may have demanded that Ahaz join the coalition since Judah had basically functioned for years as a vassal state to Israel. With the encouragement of the prophet Isaiah, Ahaz refused to support the new Israelite policy, however, which could be seen from an Israelite perspective as the action of a renegade vassal. Isaiah publicly welcomed Ahaz's break with Israel, declaring that "the people who walked in darkness have seen a great light" (Isa. 9:2). Thus Ahaz's dethronement would have been a punitive action by Pekah against a rebellious subordinate. Syria, Israel, and Tyre, the leaders in the coalition, had agreed on a replacement for Ahaz, the unnamed "son of Tabeel" (Isa. 7:6),[15] perhaps the Phoenician Hiram, or one of his brothers, a member of the ruling family of Tyre

15. For a discussion of the problem of "the son of Tabeel," see J. A. Dearman, "The Son of Tabeel (Isaiah 7.6)," in S. B. Reid, ed., *Prophets and Paradigms: Essays in Honour of Gene M. Tucker* (JSOTSup 229; Sheffield: Sheffield Academic Press, 1996) 33–47.

whose king Tubail (= Tabeel) is mentioned in the so-called Iran Stela of Tiglath-pileser (*ITP* 107; *COS* 2:287), probably set up during the Assyrian campaign to Ulluba in 739–738. (If Jezebel was the wife of Ahab and the mother of Queen Athaliah [see 1 Kgs. 16:31; 2 Kgs. 8:16–18; but cf. 2 Kgs. 8:26], then relatives of a Phoenician royal family had previously ruled over Judah. This may have been a factor in choosing to place a Tyrian ruler on the Jerusalem throne.) Widespread support for the Israelite-Syrian policy even among the Judean population seemed to make the plan feasible. The Hebrew text of Isaiah 8:6 notes that "this people delight in Rezin and the son of Remaliah [Pekah]."

The scheme of Rezin and Pekah was unsuccessful. Ahaz and Jerusalem held out against their efforts (this will be discussed further in the next chapter in the section on Ahaz). The anti-Assyrian coalition was demolished in Tiglath-pileser's three-year campaign to the west.

Tiglath-pileser III's 734–731 Campaign

Between 738–737 when he received gifts from Rezin, Menahem, and other western rulers and 734–733 when the Assyrian army left the east and marched down the Mediterranean coast, Tiglath-pileser III was engaged in warfare against Urartu in the north and Media in the east and thus far from Palestine. When he had settled matters in these regions, the Assyrian king moved into southern Syria-Palestine, intent on securing control of the eastern Mediterranean commerce, on blocking movement into the region by the Egyptian Twenty-fifth Dynasty, and on suppressing the anti-Assyrian coalition, composed of many disloyal states that had shortly before offered him tacit submission only to crystallize opposition when his presence was elsewhere. By the spring of 733 the Assyrian army was located, as the Eponym Chronicle notes, "at Philistia." (See Map 29.) Fragmentary texts (see *ITP* 139–43, 187–91; *COS* 2:287–92) mention Assyrian military actions against Phoenician cities as well as the Philistine cities of Gaza, Ashkelon, and Gezer. In addition, Tiglath-pileser III fought and defeated the Meunites in the northern Sinai and probably other groups in the area (*ITP* 179). His forces penetrated to "the city of the Brook of Egypt" (Wadi Besor just south of Gaza), where he set up a stela indicating the southern boundary of the Assyrian Empire. It was probably at this time that he installed the Idibilu (apparently an Arabian tribe, possibly the Abdeel of Gen. 25:13) as a warden of marches on the border of Musur (Egypt) (*ITP* 142–43, 168–69, 202–3). The Idibilu tribesmen were probably made responsible and remunerated for supervision of the border region between Assyrian-dominated territory and Egypt. Land traffic and trade between Egypt, the Arabian desert, and the areas to the north may also have been placed under their control. Such Assyrian association with nomadic Arab groups would have been seen as creating a loyal buffer group at the southwestern boundary of the empire.

Hanunu, the king of Gaza, fled to Egypt before the city fell to the Assyrian forces. The Assyrians set up a statue of Tiglath-pileser in his royal palace. Hanunu, however, was allowed to return and was later reinstated in office. Mitinti, king of Ashkelon, who initially offered submission and paid tribute, apparently died or was killed by the Assyrians, perhaps as late as 732, and was replaced on the throne by his son Rukibtu. The coastal plain to the north of

Philistia, at this time certainly not under Israelite but under Philistine, Phoenician, or, more likely, Syrian control, appears to have been made into an Assyrian province called Dor. Gaza was turned into an Assyrian trading center and custom station. A stela was set up at the Brook of Egypt demarcating the boundary between Assyrian- and Egyptian-controlled territory.

One of Tiglath-pileser's lists of tribute payers gives the name "Jehoahaz [= Ahaz] of the land of Judah," the first reference to Judah in extant Assyrian texts (*ITP* 171; *COS* 2:289). The absence of the names Rezin of Damascus, Pekah of Israel, Hiram of Tyre, and Queen Samsi of Arabia in this list indicates that the tribute was offered early in the Assyrian campaign while Damascus, Samaria, Tyre, and Arabia were still Assyrian foes, probably in late 734 or early 733, more likely the latter. (For this inscription, *ITP* and *COS* 2 restore a reference to Hiram but probably erroneously.)

The Assyrian king's campaign down the eastern Mediterranean coast and against powers on the border of Egypt was not only a movement to acquire control of the maritime commerce and the seaports and the terminal stations of Arabic trade in the region but also a restraining action against possible Ethiopian/Egyptian support for the anti-Assyrian coalition. (For Assyrian efforts to control commerce between the seaboard and Egypt, see Text 9.)

The Twenty-fifth Dynasty with its capital in Upper Egypt at Napata was headed at the time by Piye. (Amos was already familiar with the Ethiopians or Cushites, as was his audience; see Amos 9:7.) In nominal control of Lower Egypt or the Delta, Piye sailed north on the Nile to assert his authority against budding revolts in the Delta. His Victory Stela (see *COS* 2:42–51) narrates his activities and proclaims his success. Although the Egyptian chronology for this period is somewhat uncertain, 734 is a feasible date for this military manuever, which occurred in Piye's twentieth year. This date coincides with the year of Tiglath-pileser's movement from the east to position his army in Philistia by spring 733. The route down the coast may have been taken to ward off any movement into Syria-Palestine by the Ethiopians. Interestingly, an oracle of Isaiah for this time speaks of the coming of "the fly that is at the sources of the streams of Egypt, and . . . the bee that is in the land of Assyria" (Isa. 7:18).

Before the Syro-Ephraimite War, King Ahaz controlled only a rump state of Judah, primarily Jerusalem and its environs and territory north of the capital city extending to Samaria-held territory. (Hosea 5:8–6:6 reflects struggles over attempts to control this corridor.) Much of Judah was pro-Pekah and favored participation in the anti-Assyrian coalition. Some of the cities in southwestern Judah may have opposed Tiglath-pileser's advance into the area and thus have been destroyed by the Assyrians. Such sites as Tell Beit Mirsim, Tel Halif, Tel Beersheba, Tel 'Eton, Tel 'Erani, and Tel Lachish show signs of destruction that predate the campaign and destruction levels of Sennacherib in 701.[16]

In 732–731 the Assyrians turned their attention inland, moved across the Galilean region, and campaigned "against the land of Damascus," as the Eponym Chronicle notes, for two years. Fragmentary texts refer to the taking

---

16. See J. A. Blakely and J. W. Hardin, "Southwestern Judah in the Late Eighth Century B.C.," *BASOR* 326 (2002) 11–64. For an alternative interpretation of the archaeological evidence, see Israel Finkelstein and Nadav Na'aman, "The Judahite Shephelah in the Late 8th and Early 7th Centuries BCE," *TA* 31 (2004) 60–79, who date much of the destruction to 701 and the invasion of Sennacherib.

of captives from places that can be located in Galilee, but whether these were considered to be part of Israel or Syria remains uncertain. Reference to "sixteen districts" in the texts suggests that Syria, not Israel, was in control of the area (contra *ITP* 80–84; *COS* 2:286). Rezin and his supporters apparently offered strong resistance but were no match for the Assyrians. One Assyrian text describes some of the warfare against Rezin but not the final siege or capture of Damascus or the rebel's death.

> That one [Rezin], in order to save his life, fled alone, and he entered the gate of his city [like] a mongoose. I impaled alive his chief ministers; and I made his country behold (them). I set up my camp around the city for 45 days; and I confined him like a bird in a cage. His gardens . . . orchards without number I cut down. . . . I destroyed 591 cities of the 16 districts of Damascus like mounds of ruin after the Deluge. (*ITP* 79–81; *COS* 2:286)

The consequences of Tiglath-pileser's three-year campaign were fourfold.

1. Damascus was destroyed, Rezin killed, and territory controlled by Syria was incorporated into the Assyrian provincial system (2 Kgs. 15:29; 16:9). (See Map 30.) This territory became the provinces of Megiddo, Gilead, Karnaim, Damascus, and perhaps Dor and Hauran. Much of these regions had once been under Israelite control but had been taken over earlier into "Greater Syria" or, as Tiglath-pileser III called it, "the extended domain of the house of Hazael." The Assyrian incorporation of this former Israelite territory is noted in 2 Kings 15:29, a text that does not claim, however, that the places were taken from Israel: "In the days of King Pekah of Israel, King Tiglath-pileser of Assyria came and captured Ijon, Abel-beth-maacah, Janoah, Kedesh, Hazor, Gilead, and Galilee, all the land of Naphtali; and he carried the people captive to Assyria" (cf. 1 Kgs. 15:20; see 1 Chr. 5:26).

2. Israel, which had already been reduced by Rezin to the central hill country of Mount Ephraim, does not seem to have suffered severely from Tiglath-pileser III's campaign, although some Israelites were apparently deported. A state of vassaldom was reimposed on the kingdom and a new ruler recognized. The Assyrian king reports that the Israelites "overthrew their king Pekah" and that he recognized Hoshea as his replacement. Second Kings 15:30, however, says that Hoshea conspired against Pekah and put him to death, without any reference to Assyria. At any rate, the pro-Assyrian party in Samaria seems to have regained the upper hand and to have removed Pekah. Hoshea became the new king in Samaria.

3. Many of the kingdoms in southern Transjordan submitted or were restored to Assyrian control. References are made in Assyrian inscriptions to the receipt of tribute from Sanipu of Ammon, Salamanu of Moab, Kaush-malaku of Edom, and Samsi queen of Arabia, the last offering stiff resistance to Assyria before capitulating.

4. Judah continued as a kingdom but was reabsorbed into the larger Bit-Omri. Tiglath-pileser apparently held a conference in Damascus during which he established new political conditions in the west that provincialized much of the area. King Ahaz of Judah met with the Assyrian king (2 Kgs. 16:10), and it may have been at this time that Hoshea was designated as the new king for Bit-Omri (*ITP* 141; *COS* 2:288). The Eponym Chronicle notes that the Assyrian

army was still in the land of Damascus in the spring of 731; thus Tiglath-pileser probably completed military operations in the late spring and settled matters in the summer or fall of that year after the capture of the city of Damascus. Subsequently Hoshea and his pro-Assyrian supporters, with the aid of Ahaz, captured Samaria and had Pekah put to death. Hoshea then sent tribute to Tiglath-pileser, now in southern Babylonia at Sarrabani, where he campaigned after leaving Damascus (*ITP* 189; *COS* 2:291). Hosea 1:10–11 hints at the cooperation of Ahaz and King Hoshea in taking Samaria: "The people of Judah and the people of Israel shall . . . appoint for themselves one head [Hoshea]; and they shall campaign [against Samaria] from the land [of Judah]" (v. 11). (One should note in this regard the mildly favorable and exceptional evaluation of the northern king Hoshea in 2 Kgs. 17:2.) In all his inscriptions describing the postwar conditions in the west, Tiglath-pileser always refers to Bit-Humri, not to the land of Samaria, Israel, or Judah, indicating the reconstitution of the old political entity of the house of Omri, but now greatly reduced from its Omride heyday (*ITP* 139, 187).

Hoshea and the Fall of Samaria

King Hoshea, assigned a reign of nine years, began his first regnal year in the fall of 730. Tiglath-pileser's inscriptions seem to imply that Pekah was put to death by his own citizens (*ITP* 141; *COS* 2:288), not by the Assyrians. Indeed, the Assyrians seem deliberately to have bypassed Samaria in their movement from Philistia to Damascus and did not attack the city (*ITP* 203; *COS* 2:292).

According to the biblical presentation, Hoshea organized a conspiracy against Pekah, attacked him in Samaria, and had him put to death (2 Kgs. 15:30). One cannot imagine this happening without the involvement of much of the nation in civil strife. According to 2 Kings 17:1, Hoshea began his reign in the twelfth year of Ahaz (732–731). This probably refers to the time when he was designated king by Tiglath-pileser, but Samaria still had to be captured and Pekah overthrown.

Hoshea's early years overlapped the last years of Tiglath-pileser. The Eponym Chronicle reports that the Assyrian army was in southern Babylonia, at Shapiya, in the spring of 730. The capture of Sarrabani probably took place on this campaign (*ITP* 123), and during its siege ambassadors from Hoshea presented tribute/payment for Tiglath-pileser's designation. In the spring of 729 the Assyrian army was "in the land," at home. Matters in Babylonia soon led to Tiglath-pileser's direct intervention, and at the *akitu* festival in the spring of 728 he "took the hand of Bel," that is, he assumed the kingship over the old and sacred city of Babylon, becoming the first Assyrian ruler in centuries to reign over Babylonia directly. Tiglath-pileser died in his eighteenth year of rule, in Tebet (December–January) 727–726 (*ABC* 72–73). The fragmentary Eponym Chronicle indicates that the Assyrian army, in the spring of 726, was on campaign, but neither a reference to the destination nor the location of the army has survived. No inscriptions of Shalmaneser V (726–722), who succeeded Tiglath-pileser early in 726, have survived or are known. The only source in Akkadian for his reign is the Babylonian Chronicles, which report the following:

The second year: Tiglath-pileser died in the month of Tebet.
For <*eighteen*> years Tiglath-pileser ruled Akkad [Babylonia] and
Assyria. For two of these years he ruled in Akkad.
On the twenty-fifth day of the month Tebet [in 726] Shalmaneser ascended
  the throne in Assyria <*and Akkad*>. He ravaged Samaria.

The fifth year [722–721]: Shalmaneser died in the month Tebet. For five years
Shalmaneser ruled Akkad [Babylonia] and Assyria. On the twelfth day of the
month Tebet Sargon ascended the throne in Assyria. In Nisan Marduk-aplu-
iddina [Merodach-baladan] ascended the throne in Babylon. (*ABC* 72–73;
COS 1:467)

The one event reported for Shalmaneser V's reign is that "he ravaged Samaria."
The horizontal section line in the text indicates that this occurred before his
fifth year (722–721).

The course of Shalmaneser's actions against Samaria is uncertain. The Jewish historian Josephus, relying he says on the writing of the Greek Menander
(ca. 341–291 B.C.E.), reports a long description of Shalmaneser's relationship to
Tyre, which can be of assistance in understanding Samaria's fate:

And the king of Assyria came with an army and invaded Syria and all of
Phoenicia. Now the name of the king is recorded in the Tyrian archives, for
he marched upon Tyre in the reign of Elulaios. This is also attested by Menander, the author of a book of Annals and translator of the Tyrian archives into
the Greek language, who has given the following account: "And Elulaios, to
whom they gave the name of Pyas, reigned thirty-six years. This king, upon
the revolt of the Kitieis (Cyprians), put out to sea and again reduced them to
submission. During his reign Selampasas [Shalmaneser], the king of Assyria,
came with an army and invaded all Phoenicia and, after making a treaty of
peace with all (its cities), withdrew from the land. And Sidon and Arke and
Old Tyre and many other cities also revolted from Tyre and surrendered to
the king of Assyria. But, as the Tyrians for that reason would not submit to
him, the king turned back again and attacked them after the Phoenicians had
furnished him with sixty ships and eight hundred oarsmen. Against these the
Tyrians sailed with twelve ships and, after dispersing the ships of their
adversaries, took five hundred of their men prisoners. On that account, in
fact, the price of everything went up in Tyre. But the king of Assyria, on retir-
ing, placed guards at the river and the aqueducts to prevent the Tyrians from
drawing water, and this they endured for five years, and drank from wells
which they had dug." This, then, is what is written in the Tyrian archives concerning Salmanessēs, the king of Assyria. (*Ant.* 9.283–87)

This text describes Shalmaneser's actions against Tyre as two-staged. There
was an initial attack by the Assyrian army and a subsequent withdrawal.
Assyrian forces later returned and laid Tyre under siege for five years but without taking the city.

The biblical material on Hoshea is limited to statements about Hoshea's
relationship with the Assyrians and about the fall of Samaria (2 Kgs. 17:1–6).[17]

---

17. 2 Kgs. 17:3–6 has been divided into two separate sources (vv. 3–4 and 5–6) or considered the
result of editorial activity: see Hugo Winckler, *Alttestamentliche Untersuchungen* (Leipzig: Pfeiffer,
1892) 23–24; Nadav Na'aman, "The Historical Background to the Conquest of Samaria (720 BCE)," *Bib*
71 (1990) 206–25; repr. in *AIIN* 76–93; and M. Z. Brettler, *The Creation of History in Ancient Israel* (London: Routledge, 1995) 115–19. We do not follow this procedure.

A second account of the capture of Samaria appears in the narratives about the reign of Hezekiah (18:9–12).[18] The following events are noted in the biblical account. (1) Shalmaneser campaigned against Hoshea, who became his vassal and paid tribute (v. 3). (2) Hoshea sent messengers to King So of Egypt[19] and ceased paying tribute to the Assyrian king (v. 4). (3) The Assyrian king, discovering the treachery, took Hoshea prisoner and confined him (v. 4). (4) The king of Assyria then invaded the land and besieged Samaria for three years before it was captured (v. 5; see 18:9–10). (5) Some Israelites were exiled and settled in other lands (v. 6; see 18:11).

The course of events leading to the capture and provincialization of Samaria is uncertain for two reasons: no records of Shalmaneser exist, and his successor Sargon II (721–705) claims to have captured Bit-Omri and the city of Samaria and exiled thousands of the population. When looked at in its totality, the Assyrian and biblical evidence combined indicates that there were two major Assyrian assaults on Samaria followed by two deportations of part of the populace. These belong to the years 722–721 (the ninth year of Hoshea, the fifth year of Shalmaneser, and the sixth year of Hezekiah) and 720–719 (the second year of Sargon and the eighth year of Hezekiah). In addition, Shalmaneser "ravaged Samaria," according to the Babylonian Chronicles, sometime prior to his final year of reign, probably in 726–725. The following is our reconstruction of events with supporting evidence.

1. Hoshea was made to submit to Shalmaneser V probably early in the latter's reign: "Shalmaneser of Assyria came up [campaigned] against him; Hoshea became his vassal, and paid him tribute" (2 Kgs. 17:3). This movement of Shalmaneser into the region of Syria-Palestine early in his rule is also indicated in Menander's reference, quoted by Josephus (see above), to the first stage of Assyrian action against Tyre. This may have occurred between Shalmaneser's assumption of kingship on the 25th of Tebet and the time of the *akitu* festival a little over two months later in the following Nisan. Shalmaneser had apparently become king when Tiglath-pileser died on campaign. The evidence supporting such a campaign are the fragmentary reference in the Eponym Chronicle indicating that the army was on campaign in the spring of 726, and some of Tiglath-pileser's inscriptions that mention trouble late in his reign with the kingdoms of Tyre and Tabal (*ITP* 171, 191; *COS* 2:289, 292).

2. During Shalmaneser's first regnal year (726–725), revolt broke out again in the west involving at least Tyre and Israel. The Eponym Chronicle notes that the main Assyrian army was "in the land" in the spring of 725. Second Kings 17:4

---

18. A number of studies on the fall of Samaria have been written with different approaches to the evidence. See Hayim Tadmor, "The Campaigns of Sargon II of Assur: A Chronological-Historical Study," *JCS* 12 (1958) 22–40, 77–100; Nadav Na'aman, "The Historical Background to the Conquest of Samaria (720 BC)," *Bib* 71 (1990) 206–25; repr. in *AIIN* 76–93; J. H. Hayes and J. K. Kuan, "The Final Years of Samaria (730–720 BC)," *Bib* 72 (1991) 153–82; Bob Becking, *The Fall of Samaria: An Historical and Archaeological Study* (SHANE 2; Leiden: Brill, 1992); K. L. Younger, "The Fall of Samaria in Light of Recent Research," *CBQ* 61 (1999) 461–802; M. C. Tetley, "The Date of Samaria's Fall as a Reason for Rejecting the Hypothesis of Two Conquests," *CBQ* 64 (2002) 59–77; and B. E. Kelle, "Hoshea, Sargon, and the Final Destruction of Samaria: A Response to M. Christine Tetley with a View Toward Method," *SJOT* 17 (2003) 226–44.

19. Since there was no known pharaoh of Egypt with the name "So," various suggestions have been made concerning the identity of this ruler. A survey of all the options is provided by Pnina Galpaz-Feller, "Is That So? (2 Kings XVII 4)," *RB* 107 (2000) 338–47. Most likely the text as it now reads should be understood as an error for "king of Egypt in Sais." The ruler was probably Tefnakht, who assumed the titular of kingship after Piye's withdrawal from the Delta and ruled for eight years (733–726/725).

TEXT 10. Sargon's Descriptions of the Capture
and Resettlement of Samaria

I besieged and conquered Samaria . . . , led away as booty 27,290 inhabitants of it. I formed from among them a contingent of 50 chariots and made remaining (inhabitants) assume their (social) positions. I installed over them an officer of mine and imposed upon them the tribute of the former king. (*ANET* 284–85)

Ia'ubidi from Hamath, a commoner without claim to the throne, a cursed Hittite, schemed to become king of Hamath, induced the cities Arvad, Simirra, Damascus . . . and Samaria to desert me, made them collaborate and fitted out an army. I called up the masses of the soldiers of Ashur and besieged him and his warriors in Qarqar, his favorite city. I conquered (it) and burnt (it). Himself I flayed; the rebels I killed in their cities and established (again) peace and harmony. (*ANET* 285)

[The Sa]marians with a king [hostile to] me consorted not to do service and not to bring tribute and they did battle. In the strength of the great gods, my lords I clashed with them, [2]7,280 people with their chariots and the gods they trust, as spoil I counted, 200 chariots (as) my royal muster I mustered from among them. The rest of them I caused to take their dwelling in the midst of Assyria. The city of Samaria I restored, and greater than before I caused it to become. People of lands conquered by my two hands I brought within it; my officer as prefect over them I placed, and together with the people of Assyria I counted them. (See *Iraq* 16 [1954] 180)

The tribes of Tamud, Ibâdid, Marsimanu, and Haiapâ, distant Arabs, who inhabit the desert, who know neither high nor low officials, and who had not brought their tribute to any king,—with the weapon of the god Assur, my lord, I struck them down [in 716 B.C.E.], the remnant of them I deported and settled them in Samaria. (*ARAB* II §17; cf. *ANET* 286; for a selection of Sargonic texts see *COS* 2:293–300)

notes that Hoshea sent messengers to Egypt to secure aid and "offered no tribute to the king of Assyria, as he had done year by year," that is, since 730. As a consequence, "the king of Assyria confined him and imprisoned him." It was probably after imprisoning Hoshea that the Assyrian army returned to campaign in Phoenicia. A significant issue involves how Shalmaneser captured Hoshea. Having not paid the annual tribute and having broken treaty agreements by seeking military assistance from Egypt, Hoshea seems unlikely simply to have surrendered voluntarily. He may have been captured when Shalmaneser "ravaged Samaria" (*ABC* 72–73) in about 725 before he advanced on Tyre.

3. In spite of the incarceration of King Hoshea, the Israelites appear to have continued their rebellion, perhaps in concert with Tyre: "the king of Assyria invaded all the land and came to Samaria" (2 Kgs. 17:5a); "in the fourth year of King Hezekiah, which was the seventh year of King Hoshea [724–723] . . . King Shalmaneser of Assyria came up against Samaria, [and] besieged it" (2 Kgs. 18:9); "the king [Shalmaneser] turned back again and attacked them [the Tyri-

ans]" (*Ant.* 9.28). The question of who was governing the city of Samaria after the arrest of Hoshea cannot be answered with certainty.[20] Hosea 8:4a may refer to the designation of a replacement for the imprisoned Hoshea: "They have made a king but not from me; they have made an officialdom that I do not acknowledge."[21] Samaria held out for three years before being captured or capitulating. The siege had apparently begun before Tishri (September–October) 724, the beginning of Hezekiah's fourth year and ended between Marheshvan (October–November) 722, the beginning of Hoshea's ninth year, and the twelfth of Tebet (December–January) 722/721, when Sargon succeeded to the throne (*ABC* 73). Shalmaneser is said to have deported Israelites, which may have occurred during the course of the siege as well as following its capture (2 Kgs. 17:6). (The late text in 2 Kgs. 17:7–41 probably reflects several deportations to Samaria.)

4. In eight different inscriptions Sargon II (721–705) describes his capture of Samaria and the Assyrian disposition of the area.[22] His texts place this event in either his accession year, his first, or his second regnal year.[23] That Sargon captured Samaria three times in three successive years seems highly unlikely for the following reasons. (a) When details are provided about the conquest the statements are practically identical indicating multiple accounts of the same event (compare the late Khorsabad annals [*COS* 2:293], the Calah Prism [*COS* 2:295], and the Summary Inscription from Khorsabad [*COS* 2:296]). (b) Sargon was apparently not the heir apparent to the throne and had to struggle to gain control of the kingdom, which prevented decisive action in his accession and first regnal years. (c) The Borowski Stela shows that Sargon faced an uprising among his own military upon his seizure of the throne. The stela declares: "I pardoned 6,300 guilty Assyrians; and showed mercy on them; and I settled them in Hamath" (see *COS* 2:295). (d) The conquest of Samaria is associated with a western campaign that involved putting down a major Syro-Palestinian rebellion led by Hamath as well as a military encounter with an army from Egypt. Sargon's texts date this campaign to his second regnal year and following a battle in Der with King Humbanigash of Elam that Sargon claims to have won but that the Babylonian Chronicles declare he lost (*ABC* 73), assuming that the texts refer to one and the same encounter. (e) The Ashur Charter, one of the earliest of Sargon's inscriptions,[24] places Sargon's attack against Hamath in his second regnal year following the Assyrian-Elamite clash and mentions the rebellion of other western areas, including Samaria.

The following would appear to be the most plausible course of events with regard to Sargon's reconquest of Samaria. (a) Shalmaneser's death and the

---

20. Tadmor, *JCS* 12 (1958) 37, raised the possibility "that a king whose name was unrecorded neither in the Bible nor in the Assyrian Inscriptions reigned until 722 or 720."

21. All modern translations read "they have made kings," but there is no reference to a plurality of monarchs in the text. Older translations properly read the text; for example, the Geneva Bible (1560) translated: "They have set up a king but not by me: they have made princes and I knew it not."

22. See the summary in *ISK* 457–58; and K. L. Younger Jr., "Recent Study on Sargon II, King of Assyria: Implications for Biblical Study," in M. W. Chavalas and K. L. Younger Jr., eds., *Mesopotamia and the Bible: Comparative Explorations* (JSOTSup 341; Sheffield: Sheffield Academic Press, 2002) 289–312.

23. For an explanation of this in terms of enhancing his reign, see Tadmor, *JCS* 12 (1958) 31–32.

24. See H. W. F. Saggs, "Historical Texts and Fragments of Sargon II of Assyria. I. The 'Aššur Charter,'" *Iraq* 37 (1975) 11–20.

Assyrian capture of Samaria occurred very near in time, and when Sargon assumed the throne precipitating civil disorder and military rebellion, the Assyrian army returned home withdrawing from Samaria and Tyre. Whether Shalmaneser had already declared Samaria an Assyrian province, either in 725–724 at the time of Hoshea's capture, or in 722–721 with his capture of the city, remains uncertain, but the former seems likely. Sargon's references to "the Samarians" rather than to a ruler over the city implies that the area had already been declared a province. (b) With the withdrawal of the Assyrian army and rebellion among Sargon's forces Samaria joined with the kingdoms of Hamath and Gaza and the provinces of Arpad, Simirra, and Damascus in a rebellion supported by Egypt (*COS* 2:296). (c) In his second regnal year (720–719), and probably late in the year (in 719) since he fought the Elamites in Der before moving west, Sargon marched into the eastern Mediterranean and defeated the king of Hamath at Qarqar, conquered Hanunu of Gaza, and defeated an Egyptian force at Raphia (see *COS* 2:296). (d) The city of Samaria was taken or capitulated.[25] (See Text 10.) The Nimrud Prism reports the following:

> The Samarians, who with a king hostile to me, not to offer servitude and not to deliver tribute, came to an agreement and they offered battle. I fought against them with the power of the great gods, my lords. I counted as spoils 27,280 people, together with their chariots and their gods in which they trusted. I formed a unit with 200 chariots for my own royal force. I settled the rest of them in the midst of Assyria. I made the population of Samaria greater than before. I appointed my eunuch as governor over them and I counted them as Assyrians. (See *COS* 2:295–96)

The Assyrian Province of Samerina

The activity of Sargon II in Syria-Palestine during 720–719 brought an end to the northern kingdom of Israel. Its territory was incorporated into the Assyrian provincial system.

Deportation and Resettlement

The inscriptions of Sargon II provide us with a number of statements about the Assyrian treatment of Samaria (see Text 10). Several features of Assyrian administration and the treatment of rebellious states are reflected in these texts.

1. The city of Samaria was rebuilt; Sargon claims that it was better and more populous than it had been. The restoration of the capital city was part of the effort to return the area to economic and social health so that the population could "assume their social positions," that is, their normal lifestyles and occupations.

---

25. Samaria was apparently not taken until after Sargon had moved down the coast. The prophet Hosea in 8:13 and 9:3 could still speak of Ephraim returning to Egypt (in flight), but in 11:5 declares that Ephraim "shall not return to Egypt but Assyria will rule over him," probably because the way to Egypt was now blocked by Assyrian forces. (The NRSV completely ignores the negative in v. 5 and offers no rationale for its translation: "they shall return to the land of Egypt.") On archaeological matters related to Samaria at this time, see R. E. Tappy, *The Archaeology of Israelite Samaria*, vol. 2: *The Eighth Century* (HSS 50; Winona Lake, IN: Eisenbrauns, 2001).

2. The area was organized as a province with an appointed governor. Those living in the province were classified as Assyrian citizens and were required to contribute to the state treasury, that is, pay taxes. For Samaria the provincial assessment was the same as Shalmaneser had required of Hoshea as tribute. The Assyrian texts make no distinction between the native population that remained in the area and those resettled there, and there were probably no economic or social distinctions between the two groups. New settlers would, of course, have been provided with land and property, perhaps that of those who had been deported.

3. Segments of the surviving military were absorbed into the Assyrian army. Sargon II notes that he formed a contingent of two hundred chariots (a variant version says fifty) from Samaria, which then became a component in the Assyrian chariot corps.[26]

4. A significant portion of the population was deported, along with the cultic paraphernalia of the Israelite Deity.[27] One of the goals of deportation, in addition to punishment for rebellion, was to remove those in leadership and thus to lessen the likelihood of nationalistic uprisings in the future. A second goal was to supply populations for use in other areas of the empire. Deportees were utilized in various ways by the Assyrians—as settlers in sparsely populated areas, especially in depopulated urban centers and in rural areas needing agricultural improvements, as skilled workers in various crafts, and as general laborers throughout the empire. According to 2 Kings 17:6 (= 18:11), the Israelites were resettled "in Halah, and on the Habor, the river of Gozan, and in the cities of the Medes."

5. Foreign populations over a period of time were resettled in Samaria.[28] According to 2 Kings 17:24 (see 18:34), Samaria was resettled with people from Babylon (where the Assyrians had constant trouble with the Chaldeans), Cuthah (generally identified with Tell Ibrahaim, northeast of Babylon), Avva (site unknown), Hamath (in northern Syria; it had been one of Sargon's primary objectives in his 720–719 campaign), and Sepharvaim (listed among the Syrian cities noted in 2 Kgs. 18:34 and 19:13; see Ezek. 47:16, where it is spelled Sibriam and located on the border between Damascus and Hamath). Samaria continued to be the recipient of new settlers for years (2 Kgs. 17:7–41 is a reflection looking back over several importations into the region). After a campaign in 716 in which Sargon II received gifts from Egypt and Queen Samsi of Arabia, he settled "distant Arabs" in Samaria (*COS* 2:293). Further transfer of population may have occurred in the region after 712 when Sargon II had to campaign against Ashdod, where a usurper had seized the throne and was attempting to stir up rebellion in the surrounding kingdoms. According to Ezra 4:2, 10, Samaria received further settlers as late as the reigns of Esarhaddon

---

26. See Stephanie Dalley, "Foreign Chariotry and Cavalry in the Armies of Tiglath-Pileser III and Sargon II," *Iraq* 47 (1985) 31–48.

27. Reference to "their gods" in the Assyrian texts does not mean that the Israelites were polytheistic. Since the Assyrians were polytheists, they assumed others were in noting that they took away the religious artifacts of the people. On the problem of those exiled see K. L. Younger Jr., "The Deportations of the Israelites," *JBL* 117 (1998) 201–27; idem, "Recent Study on Sargon II," 294–312.

28. See Nadav Na'aman and Ran Zadok, "Sargon II's Deportations to Israel and Philistia (716–708 BCE)," *JCS* 40 (1988) 36–46; and Na'aman, "Population Changes in Palestine Following Assyrian Deportations," *TA* 20 (1993) 104–24; repr. in *AIIN* 200–219.

(680–669) and Ashurbanipal (668–627). (Osnapper is generally identified with Ashurbanipal, since it was he who captured Susa/Elam in 646.)

Of Lions and Priests

Second Kings 17:7–41 contains a judgmental, editorial explanation of why the northern kingdom fell (vv. 7–23, 34b–40) and a narrative describing conditions after the settlement of foreigners in the region (vv. 24–34a, 41). The theological explanation of Israel's downfall blames the people for apostasy and for failure to pay heed to the prophets. The narrative describing conditions in the province after resettlement is characterized by folkloristic features: all the native people were carried away, the newcomers were plagued with fierce animals (lions) because they did not know the law of the god of the land, and a single priest was returned to teach the citizens of the province and thus ward off the attacks of lions. (On lions as instruments of judgment, see 1 Kgs. 13:24–28; 20:36.) Such features in the narrative obviously cannot be the basis for historical reconstruction. What does seem to have been characteristic of the religious situation in the Assyrian province of Samerina are the following:

1. We should not assume that either Yahwism, the priesthood, or cultic places for the worship of Yahweh totally disappeared from the north. The sanctuary places south of Samaria, such as Bethel, Mizpah, and Gilgal, may have been little disturbed by the final campaigns of Shalmaneser V and Sargon II, which centered on the capital city. The sanctuary at Bethel, later said to have been profaned by Josiah, had presumably continued in use throughout the eighth and seventh centuries (2 Kgs. 23:15).

2. The new settlers brought their own gods, religious traditions, and customs to their new home. At the same time they would have joined, at least to some extent, in the worship of Yahweh, the god of the land in which they now lived. Also, in such an Assyrian province as Samerina, official Assyrian religion would certainly have been given a prominent role.

3. Some of the northern population may have fled south to avoid deportation. Many northern traditions may have been brought south also, eventually to find their way into the Hebrew Scriptures. Among such traditions may have been some form of the royal annals, an early form of Deuteronomy, and prophetical narratives such as the Elijah and Elisha stories.

General Bibliography

General Assyrian and Urartian history during this period are treated in A. K. Grayson, "Assyria: Ashur Dan II to Ashur-nirari (934–745 B.C.)," in *CAH* 3/1:238–81; idem, "Assyria: Tiglath-pileser III to Sargon II (744–705 B.C.)," *CAH* 3/2:71–102; and R. D. Barnett, "Urartu," *CAH* 3/1:314–71. Israelite and Judean relations with Assyria are discussed by Morton Cogan, *Imperialism and Religion: Assyria, Judah, and Israel in the Eighth and Seventh Centuries B.C.E.* (SBLMS 19; Missoula, MT: Scholars Press, 1974); and J. W. McKay, *Religion in Judah Under the Assyrians, 732–609 BC* (SBT 2/26; London: SCM, 1973).

Simo Parpola and Kazuko Watanabe, *Neo-Assyrian Treaties and Loyalty Oaths* (SAA 2; Helsinki: Helsinki University Press, 1988), XV–XXV, provide an excellent introduction to Assyrian international politics. An inside view of Assyrian warfare and imperialism is provided in Bustenay Oded, *War, Peace, and Empire: Justification for War in Assyrian Royal Inscriptions* (Wiesbaden: Reichert, 1992).

Chronological problems and political history for Syria-Palestine are discussed by Nadav Na'aman, "Historical and Chronological Notes on the Kingdoms of Israel and Judah in the Eighth Century BCE," *VT* 36 (1986) 71–92; repr. in *AIHH* 235–54; idem, "Province System and Settlement Pattern in Southern Syria and Palestine in the Neo-Assyrian Period," in Mario Liverani, ed., *Neo-Assyrian Geography* (Rome: University of Rome Press, 1995) 103–15; repr. in *AIIN* 220–37.

13. The Era of Assyrian Domination: Judean History from Ahaz to Amon

For well over a century Judean life and politics were inexorably intertwined with those of Assyria. In 733 B.C.E. Ahaz, acting independently from Israel, paid tribute to Tiglath-pileser III and his name was recorded in an Assyrian list of contributors (*ITP* 171; *COS* 2:289). For a short time after Assyrian settlement of matters in the west, Judah again became part of Bit-Omri. With the rebellion of King Hoshea, the fall of Samaria, and the Assyrian provincialization of the region, Judah was left to its own design. Until the decline of Assyria in the last quarter of the seventh century, Judah existed as one among many small powers dominated by Assyria. Unlike Israel, Judah seems to have offered no major sustained resistance to Assyria during the reigns of Tiglath-pileser III (744–727), Shalmaneser V (726–722), and Sargon II (721–705). For a time, during the early years of Sennacherib (704–681), the aggressive Judean king Hezekiah participated in a widespread revolt in Syria-Palestine against Assyrian rule. The revolt, although well planned, was quickly suppressed by Sennacherib (in 701). The failure of Hezekiah's rebellion inaugurated a long period of Judean submission and vassaldom to Assyria during the lengthy reign of Manasseh (698–644).

Throughout this period, extending from the final decades of the eighth century to the final decades of the seventh century, the relationship among Assyria, the Delta Egyptians, and the Ethiopians was highly significant for all of southern Syria-Palestine, including the state of Judah. Several dynasties, the Twenty-second, the Twenty-third, the Twenty-fourth, and the Twenty-fifth, struggled for control of Egypt early in this period. The Twenty-fifth Dynasty eventually came to prominence. A nonnative family whose primary support was in Upper Egypt, the Twenty-fifth Dynasty became a competitor with Assyria for control of the commerce on the eastern Mediterranean seaboard and therefore for influence over the southern Syro-Palestinian states. Thus the period of ascendancy for this dynasty, which was finally broken in 664/663, was a time of conflict. With the rise of the Twenty-sixth Dynasty to prominence, after 663, friendly and cooperative relationships between Egypt and Assyria that had been the Assyrian goal since Sargon II were finally realized. Eventually the two powers shared control of the states of southern Syria-Palestine. Accordingly Judean politics came to be dominated by this Assyrian-Egyptian alliance.

The biblical material for the reigns of the Judean kings of this period—Ahaz, Hezekiah, Manasseh, and Amon—is rather extensive, although beset by numerous problems for interpreters. Second Kings 16–21 (partially paralleled by Isa. 36–39) and 2 Chronicles 28–33 contain the biblical narratives about this period. In addition to these sources, much of the material in Isaiah 1–33 originated during the reigns of Ahaz and Hezekiah. Isaiah, whose career spanned the reigns of Uzziah, Jotham, Ahaz, and Hezekiah (Isa. 1:1), was significantly involved in Judean politics. Thus the material in Isaiah 1–33 that can be related to events and conditions during the prophet's career provides useful information for the historian.

The presentation of the material on Ahaz, Hezekiah, and Manasseh in Kings is strongly influenced by an editorial scheme in which the reign of a bad king is made to alternate with that of a good king.[1] The rulers are represented as the epitome of either evil (Ahaz and Manasseh; see 2 Kgs. 16:2b–4 and 21:2, 9) or good (Hezekiah and, later, Josiah; see 18:3–5; 22:2; 23:2–5). This patternization has probably affected not only the method of depicting the monarchs but also what has been told about them. Anything good known about Ahaz and Manasseh would have been omitted by the editors and anything bad about Hezekiah omitted or toned down. In the case of both the good and the bad rulers, the editors have presented us with idealized portraits. The nature of the particular biblical traditions about Ahaz, Hezekiah, and Manasseh will require more detailed comment when we discuss their individual reigns.

During the reigns of Ahaz, Hezekiah, Manasseh, and Amon in Judah, the Assyrian empire was ruled over by six kings: Tiglath-pileser III, Shalmaneser V, Sargon II, Sennacherib, Esarhaddon, and Ashurbanipal. We possess historical inscriptions from all of these rulers except Shalmaneser V. The inscriptions of Tiglath-pileser, while abundant, are fragmentary. Those of Sargon II and Sennacherib provide a reasonably full depiction of their reigns in chronological order. The inscriptional material for Esarhaddon and Ashurbanipal is abundant, but the inscriptions of Esarhaddon do not present the events of his reign chronologically; while those of Ashurbanipal, in addition to not always following a chronological scheme, were edited and reedited on several occasions. In spite of these problems, the Assyrian records augment greatly the biblical materials and are especially important for providing background information on the lengthy rule of Manasseh.

The Babylonian Chronicles at times provide enormously important data on international affairs. Egyptian involvement in Syro-Palestinian affairs during the last centuries of the Davidic kingdom is occasionally noted not only in Akkadian and Egyptian sources from ancient times but also in the works of Herodotus and other authors from the classical period.

Ahaz (Jehoahaz I)

According to 2 Kings 16:2, Ahaz, or Jehoahaz (743–728) as his full name is indicated in one of Tiglath-pileser III's inscriptions (*ITP* 171; *COS* 2:289), was the

---

1. See Hayim Tadmor and Mordechai Cogan, "Ahaz and Tiglath-pileser in the Book of Kings: Historiographic Considerations," *Bib* 60 (1979) 491–508; and P. R. Ackroyd, "The Biblical Interpretations of the Reigns of Ahaz and Hezekiah," in W. B. Barrick and J. R. Spencer, eds., *In the Shelter of Elyon: Essays on Ancient Palestinian Life and Literature in Honour of G. W. Ahlström* (JSOTSup 31; Sheffield: JSOT Press, 1984) 247–59. On editorial activity in the Ahaz narrative see K. A. D. Smelik, "The Representation of King Ahaz in 2 Kings 16 and 2 Chronicles 28," in J. C. de Moor, ed., *Intertextuality in Ugarit and Israel* (OtSt 40; Leiden: Brill, 1998) 143–85; and Nadav Na'man, "In Search of Reality behind the Account of the Philistine Assault on Ahaz in the Book of Chronicles," *Transeu* 26 (2004) 47–63.

son of King Jotham. He is said to have succeeded to the throne at the age of twenty. (Ahaz is one of only two Judean kings whose mother's name is not given in the regnal formulations, the other being Jehoram [see 2 Kgs. 8:17].) The mother of Hezekiah and the wife of Ahaz was Abi the "daughter of Zechariah" (18:2), who may have been the Israelite king of this name. If so, then this would be another case of intermarriage between the two kingdoms and could partially explain why Ahaz is said to have "walked in the way of the kings of Israel" (16:3).

According to our chronology, which relies heavily on the regnal periods given in the biblical text for the period following Jotham's death, Ahaz's sixteen-year reign would have begun in 743 and ended in 728. He was on the Judean throne during the crisis with Assyria in 734–731 precipitated by Rezin and his fellow anti-Assyrians. Although Uzziah had been forced to abdicate the throne in 760–759 because he contacted *tsara'ath* (2 Kgs. 15:5), he continued to live until 734 and was no doubt an important power during the reigns of Jotham and the early years of Ahaz, even though he could not function as monarch on worship occasions or other activities associated with the temple. The biblical descriptions of Ahaz's reign (2 Kgs. 16; 2 Chr. 28; Isa. 7:1–12:6) focus on the events associated with the Syro-Ephraimite crisis. Before we discuss what can be known about his rule, a further word is in order about the biblical sources related to his reign.

Ahaz as Depicted in the Biblical Sources

After the introductory formalities, 2 Kings 16 begins its presentation of Ahaz with an enumeration of his evil deeds (vv. 2–4). This is followed by a statement regarding his troubles (vv. 5–6). According to vv. 7–9, Ahaz secured the help of Tiglath-pileser by sending him a bribe. The Assyrian king responded by attacking Damascus, carrying away its people, and killing Rezin. More lengthy coverage is given to Ahaz's visit to meet Tiglath-pileser in Damascus, where he saw an altar, a copy of which was set up in the Jerusalem temple (vv. 10–16). Further alterations in the Temple are noted (vv. 17–18) before the statements about the conclusion of his reign (vv. 19–20).

Second Chronicles 28 makes Ahaz into an even more villainous ruler (vv. 1–4), punished by Yahweh, who gives him into the hand of Syrians and Israelites (vv. 5–7). The latter are reported to have carried away two hundred thousand Judeans but were convinced, by prophetic intervention, to return them (vv. 8–15). Ahaz is said to have sent to Tiglath-pileser for help against the Edomites and the Philistines, although even the Assyrian king ended up oppressing Ahaz (vv. 16–21). The chapter concludes with a denunciation of Ahaz, reporting his worship of Syrian gods, alteration of temple features, and establishment of altars throughout the city (vv. 22–25).

In Isaiah 7:1–12:6 the focus is on the prophet's advice and encouragement given to Ahaz, the house of David, and Jerusalem in the context of the anti-Assyrian coalition's move to involve Judah in its rebellion and to replace Ahaz on the throne. The advice offered by the prophet makes no mention of any appeal to Assyria by Ahaz and encourages the Judean king to continue the existing pro-Assyrian policies.

66. *Gihon Spring in the Kidron Valley.* The paved road marks the route of the Kidron Valley between Ophel on the right and present-day Silwan on the left. The Gihon Spring is at the base of Ophel, near the small building in the foreground to the right of the road.

Ahaz and the Syro-Ephraimite Crisis

During Ahaz's reign, Judah was hard-pressed on all sides by Rezin and his supporters in the anti-Assyrian coalition. (1) Rezin and Pekah seem to have encroached already on Judean territory even before Ahaz became king (see 2 Kgs. 15:37). (2) The Edomites expanded in the Arabah and the Negeb and occupied the seaport city of Elath, with Rezin's help (2 Kgs. 16:6; 2 Chr. 28:16). (3) The Philistines made raids on the Shephelah and the Negeb, taking "Beth-shemesh, Aijalon, Gederoth, Soco with its villages, Timnah with its villages, and Gimzo with its villages; and they settled there" (2 Chr. 28:18).

In addition to these external pressures, Ahaz ruled over a state in which much of the population favored joining the anti-Assyrian coalition and were supporters of the rival king, Pekah. Some of the opposition to Jerusalem and the rule of the Davidic house is reflected in, for example, the opening chapter of Micah.[2] Encouraged by the prophet Isaiah, and supported apparently by the people of Jerusalem, Ahaz was opposed to joining the anti-Assyrian coalition and favored the long-standing policy of pro-Assyrianism, although the Isaiah traditions indicate that the house of David had some doubts about whether joining or abstaining was the better decision (Isa. 7:13). The possible threat of

2. See C. S. Shaw, "Micah 1:10–16 Reconsidered," *JBL* 106 (1987) 223–29. Some of the pro-coalition, anti-Ahaz cities, in southwest and southern Judah, as noted in the last chapter, may have been destroyed by Tiglath-pileser in the early phase of his western campaign; see J. A. Blakely and J. W. Hardin, "Southwestern Judah in the Late Eighth Century B.C.E.," *BASOR* 326 (2002) 11–64. For an alternative interpretation of, and a later date for, the archaeological evidence, see Israel Finkelstein and Nadav Na'aman, "The Judahite Shephelah in the Late 8th and Early 7th Centuries BCE," *TA* 31 (2004) 60–79.

internal action by his own subjects to remove him from the throne as they had earlier toppled Athaliah must have caused Ahaz enormous unease.

The external threats and internal distress of Ahaz's kingdom reached their climax in the move that the Syro-Palestinian anti-Assyrian coalition made against Jerusalem. Shortly after Pekah occupied the Israelite throne in Samaria (in the year of Azariah/Uzziah's death; see 2 Kgs. 15:2, 27; and Isa. 6:1), he and Rezin and perhaps other members of the anti-Assyrian coalition marched against Jerusalem when Ahaz continued his refusal to join their anti-Assyrian escapade. Their intent was to depose the uncooperative king and replace him with the unnamed son of Tabeel (Isa. 7:6), apparently a member of the royal house ruling in Tyre, a son or relative of King Tubail (= Tabeel), mentioned in the Iran Stela of Tiglath-pileser (see *ITP* 107; *COS* 2:287). Since Tyre was one of the strong supporters of the anti-Assyrian coalition, the new ruler would have brought Judah into the group. The enthronement of this son of Tabeel would have involved not only the removal of Ahaz from power but also the slaughter of Ahaz and his family. The consequences of being a deposed ruler were no doubt vivid to Ahaz, since the family of Menahem/Pekahiah had been removed by Pekah only a short time earlier. An incidental reference in the Chronicler's History (see 2 Chr. 28:7) suggests that an unsuccessful effort was made to assassinate Ahaz either before or during the Syro-Ephraimite crisis. Indeed, not only Ahaz's life but also the lives of the entire reigning line of David would have been at stake. This explains why the "house of David" was so involved in the Syro-Ephraimite affair: "Now, when it was reported to the House of David that Aram [Syria] had allied itself with [literally 'alighted upon'] Ephraim, their hearts and the hearts of their people trembled as trees of the forest sway before a wind" (Isa. 7:2 NJPSV; see 7:15, 17). The prophet challenged Ahaz not to break with the policy of alignment with Assyria, that is, not to follow the lead of Pekah and Samaria, Rezin and Damascus, and certainly not to fear them (7:7–8a, 9a). Isaiah concluded his advice offered personally to Ahaz with the highly alliterative comment that may be translated with some poetical license as: "If you [pl. = house of David] do not stay the course [= remain loyal to Assyria] then you [pl. = house of David] will have no course to stay [= you will be conquered by the Assyrians]" (v. 9b). In offering encouragement to Ahaz to follow his independent path, the prophet Isaiah assured him that, if the king acted in faith and relied upon Yahweh, the still unborn son of the royal family could function as a sign (see 2 Kgs. 15:16 for reference to Menahem's slaughter of pregnant women). The child would not be threatened or slaughtered in its mother's womb; in fact, the prophet promised, while the child was still in its infancy, the lands of Ephraim and Syria would be devastated (Isa. 7:10–16).

Many, if not the majority, within Judah itself supported participation with Rezin and Pekah in the anti-Assyrian movement. This would suggest that the general Judean population had no do-or-die commitment to the Davidic dynasty.[3] Judean support for the anti-Assyrian alliance and thus lack of support for Ahaz are suggested in some of Isaiah's preaching:

---

3. On Judean opposition to the house of David, see S. A. Irvine, "Isaiah's *She'ar-Yashub* and the Davidic House," *BZ* 37 (1993) 78–88.

Yahweh spoke to me again: Because this people [those favoring the anti-Assyrian coalition] has refused the waters of Shiloah that flow gently [the Davidic dynasty], and rejoice in Rezin and the son of Remaliah [Pekah]; therefore, behold, Yahweh is bringing up against them the waters of the River [Euphrates], mighty and many, the king of Assyria and all his glory." (Isa. 8:5–7)

The cities denounced by the prophet Micah in the first chapter of his book were probably towns in the prophet's neighborhood that opposed Ahaz's stand and favored joining the anti-Assyrian coalition. The city of Lachish seems to have taken the lead in this opposition (Mic. 1:13). Possibly many, both Judeans and Israelites, were accusing Ahaz of conspiracy and treason against Israel, since Pekah as ruler in Samaria considered himself Judah's overlord. Ahaz's failure to support Israelite state policy and the anti-Assyrian coalition could have been seen as a conspiracy (see Isa. 8:11–15).

The prophet Isaiah advised Ahaz and Jerusalem not to panic in the light of the Syro-Ephraimite threat, promising that the fire produced by Pekah and Rezin, those two now smoldering stumps long past their fiery state, would be quickly extinguished by Assyria (Isa. 7:3–17; 8:1–4). The prophet thus recommended that Ahaz stay out of the Syrian-Assyrian fracas and, with faith in Yahweh to preserve his chosen (the Davidic) dynasty, merely defend Jerusalem against Syria and Israel, thus allowing Yahweh via Assyria to handle matters. (Isaiah does not mention payment to secure Assyria's aid as an option for Ahaz, who now surrounded by the enemy could have hardly penetrated their lines with messengers laden with gifts.) Indeed, he seems to have promised Ahaz that if he followed an independent policy and allowed Yahweh and the Assyrians to handle Israel and Syria without joining their coalition, then Ahaz and the Davidic house would stand a chance of regaining the old territory of Israel and restoring the glorious state of the two kingdoms under Davidic rule (see 7:17; the last phrase "the king of Assyria" is probably a later interpretative addition). The prophet celebrated Ahaz's declaration of Judah's independence from the north: "The people who walked in darkness have seen a great light; those who have lived in a land of deep darkness—on them light has shined" (9:2).

Israelite and Syrian forces moved south from Samaria (Isa. 10:27d–32)[4] and surrounded Jerusalem, besieging the city (2 Kgs. 16:5). If the Judean population at large favored joining Rezin and Pekah, these two kings and their forces may have moved to Jerusalem reasonably unmolested (note that 2 Kgs. 16:5 speaks only about waging war on Jerusalem). The route described in Isaiah 10:27d–32 was the more difficult but less defended eastern road from Samaria to Jerusalem (see Map 13). The Chronicler, in dramatic and theological fashion, describes the encounter as a major war (2 Chr. 28:5–15). The figures and descriptions, however, are incredulously suspect: Pekah slew 120,000 Judeans in one day, and the Israelites took 200,000 Judeans captive and brought them to

4. For a different understanding of this text that interprets it as a description of an Assyrian invasion, see M. A. Sweeney, "Sargon's Threat against Jerusalem in Isaiah 10, 27–32," *Bib* 75 (1994) 457–70; Nadav Na'aman, "The Historical Portion of Sargon II's Nimrud Inscription," *SAAB* 8/1 (1994) 17–20; repr. in *AIIN* 94–97; and K. L. Younger Jr. "Recent Study on Sargon II, King of Assyria: Implications for Biblical Studies," in M. W. Chavalas and K. L. Younger Jr., eds., *Mesopotamia and the Bible: Comparative Explorations* (JSOTSup 341; Sheffield: Sheffield Academic Press, 2002) 288–329.

Samaria (2 Chr. 28:6, 8). That some looting occurred and some captives were taken back to Samaria would be the minimum that one would surmise.

Ahaz's unwillingness to capitulate to Rezin and Pekah and the pressure of the anti-Assyrian coalition must have been supported by the citizens of Jerusalem and whatever personal forces the king commanded. For him, the appearance of Tiglath-pileser III and the Assyrian army in Syria-Palestine late in 734 or early in 733 must have been a godsend. The Eponym Chronicle notes that the Assyrian army had been in Urartu in the spring of 734 but had arrived in Philistia by the spring of 733. Ahaz probably voluntarily offered submission to Tiglath-pileser III on the first available occasion. Second Kings 16:7–9 reports on Ahaz's delivery of tribute to the Assyrian ruler put together by taking the gold and silver found in the temple and the royal treasury.

Several factors suggest that Ahaz made his presentation gift to Tiglath-pileser III after the latter arrived in Philistia in 733; that is, Ahaz's payment was a response to the Assyrian presence in the area rather than vice versa. (1) Since Ahaz had never previously submitted personally to Assyrian overlordship, he was not a subject who could have expected help from the Assyrians. The Assyrian monarch was no international mercenary waiting to pick up a few shekels as payment for rescuing beleaguered states. (2) Judah was surrounded by members of the anti-Assyrian coalition, and to have succeeded in sending an embassy carrying such a "present" destined for the Assyrian monarch through one of these nations seems highly unlikely. (3) Tiglath-pileser III mentions Ahaz's payment in a straightforward list as if it were merely a routine presentation, not a special bribe (see 2 Chr. 28:20–21). The Assyrian king makes no reference to any special appeal from Ahaz. (4) We hear of no return of Judean territory seized, for example, by the Philistines, which might have been the case if Ahaz were treated by the Assyrians with any exceptional favoritism. (5) The wording of the Kings report of the sending of the gift (2 Kgs. 16:7–8) uses terminology ("present," i.e., "bribe," and the biblically unparalleled "your servant and your son") that probably would not have been used in official annals or correspondence. (6) The Kings account has Ahaz send his present to the Assyrian ruler, who then marches against Damascus, takes it, and kills Rezin. This in no way parallels the account of the warfare reconstructed from Assyrian sources. The section is thus a literary construct of the biblical editors based on the knowledge that Ahaz paid tribute, but it is written so as to make Ahaz appear as the villainous king who "invited" the Assyrian troubles.[5]

Hoshea was ultimately designated by Tiglath-pileser as the new ruler of Bit-Omri. Ahaz and Judah aided in the capture of Samaria and the overthrow of Pekah. Judah once again became part of Bit-Omri.

Ahaz's Religious Practices

In addition to describing Ahaz's troubles with Rezin and Pekah, the compilers of Kings present Ahaz as an apostate king guilty of religious irregularities.

---

5. For an alternative view with texts which indicate that under certain circumstances such a present could and did buy Assyrian intervention, see S. B. Parker, "Stories of Appeal for Military Intervention," in *Stories in Scripture and Tradition: Comparative Studies in Northwest Semitic Inscriptions and the Hebrew Bible* (Oxford: Oxford University Press, 1997) 76–104.

How much of this is the product of theological bias remains uncertain; we should note that the contemporary prophet Isaiah nowhere condemns Ahaz for apostasy. The king is said to have sacrificed one of his sons (literally "made his son pass through the fire"; 2 Kgs. 16:3), presumably to Yahweh, and to have introduced cultic and ritual innovations. Perhaps the sacrifice of his son was occasioned by the Syro-Ephraimite siege of Jerusalem, and he took drastic action, as had Mesha king of Moab under similar circumstances on an earlier occasion (2 Kgs. 3:27).

According to 2 Kings 16:10–20, Ahaz introduced into the temple a new altar copied after one that he had seen at Damascus when he traveled there to meet with Tiglath-pileser III. The reader is tempted to conclude, as the Kings account could suggest, that this was actually an Assyrian altar, which had been installed in Damascus when the Assyrians took the city. The most natural reading of the 2 Kings narrative, however, points to a Syrian altar. Moreover, the Chronicler clearly specifies that Ahaz worshiped Syrian gods and dissociates this aspect of his reign altogether from the Assyrian invasion (2 Chr. 28:22–25). The introduction of such an altar into the temple seems not to have bothered the religious establishment. The priest Uriah, who supervised the construction of the new altar and cultic arrangements apparently without any protest (2 Kgs. 16:10), is also known to have served as a witness to one of Isaiah's symbolic acts at the time of the Syro-Ephraimite crisis (Isa. 8:2); that is, he appears to have been fully orthodox and Yahwistic.

Although there may be some evidence that the Assyrians sometimes required their vassals to practice Assyrian religion and thus, at least tacitly, to recognize the supremacy of the Assyrian gods over national deities, this does not seem to have been a factor in the case of Ahaz, since he was not an appointee of Tiglath-pileser III, and even after his submission to Assyria, Judah was a satellite state, not a vassal.[6] One aspect of Ahaz's religious changes, however, is connected by the editors of Kings with Assyrian domination: "The covered portal for use on the sabbath that had been built inside the palace, and the outer entrance for the king he removed from the house of Yahweh. He did this because of the king of Assyria" (2 Kgs. 16:18). What was at stake here is not clear, and the text presents numerous problems. (The last clause in the verse, "he did this because of the king of Assyria," may simply be a late gloss.) It could be that these changes within the sacred precinct had nothing to do with cultic matters per se. Ahaz may simply have had to melt down the bronze these items contained as part of his tribute payment to Assyria.

On the whole, to assume that Ahaz's cultic reforms and religious practices were significantly influenced by his position as an Assyrian subject would be misleading. Ahaz seems to have faced a desperate situation that persisted throughout his early reign. His kingdom, his life, and his family were all threatened. Texts frequently refer to his possible panic and distress (2 Chr. 28:22; Isa. 7:4). Except for Amaziah's ill-conceived adventure (2 Kgs. 14:8–14), Ahaz's action may have been the first time a Judean king had dared to act independently of and contrary to Israelite policies since the days of Omri. In the midst

6. See Mordechai Cogan, "Judah under Assyrian Hegemony: A Re-Examination of *Imperialism and Religion*," *JBL* 112 (1993) 403–14.

of anti-Assyrian nations, for Ahaz to follow an independent policy was indeed an act of faith. Isaiah appears to have been a persistent counselor to the king, who seems to have listened to and followed the prophet's advice.

Hezekiah

Under Hezekiah, Ahaz's successor, Judah recovered to the extent that the country eventually became involved in at least one widespread rebellion against Assyria. Hezekiah's years were recalled as highly significant in the history of Judah, and he was remembered as one of only a few good kings. Few reigns in the history of Israel and Judah, however, present the historian with as many problems of interpretation and reconstruction as that of Hezekiah. The problems are related not only to the biblical glorification of the king and his reign but also to issues of a chronological and literary nature.

Hezekiah as Depicted in the Biblical Sources

The biblical narratives about Hezekiah are extensive. They include 2 Kings 18–20; 2 Chronicles 29–32; and Isaiah 36–39. The material in 2 Kings 18–20 may be divided into the following episodes and sections:

A. General summary and evaluation (18:1–8)
B. Synchronism with Samaria's siege and capture (18:9–12)
C. The invasion of Sennacherib, Hezekiah's capitulation, and payment of the penalty placed on him by the Assyrian king (18:13–16)
D. The Assyrian Rabshakeh is sent by Sennacherib from Lachish with a large army to convince Jerusalem and Hezekiah to capitulate, but Hezekiah, after hearing of the speech about surrender, goes to the temple to pray. Isaiah the prophet responds to the visit of Hezekiah's officials, assuring the king that he should not be afraid, since Sennacherib will hear a rumor and will return home, where he will be killed. The Rabshakeh returns to Sennacherib, who is now at Libnah. The Assyrian hears that Tirhakah, the king of Ethiopia, has set out to fight him (18:17–19:9a).
E. Again messengers are sent to Hezekiah with a letter to convince him to capitulate, again he goes to the temple, and again the prophet Isaiah responds, giving assurance to Hezekiah and delivering a speech against Sennacherib announcing his defeat and containing promises to Hezekiah that Jerusalem will be saved. The city is spared when 185,000 Assyrians are killed in the night by the angel of Yahweh (19:9b–35).
F. Sennacherib departs, returns to Nineveh, and is killed by his sons (19:36–37).
G. Hezekiah becomes ill but is promised fifteen additional years of rule by Isaiah, who treats the king's malady with a poultice made from a cake of figs (20:1–11).
H. Hezekiah is visited by envoys of Merodach-baladan of Babylon who inspect Hezekiah's treasures and armory. Isaiah condemns Hezekiah for granting these visitors such privileges and announces that the posses-

sions of the king and his sons shall be carried to exile in Babylon (20:12–19).
I. Concluding summary (20:20–21)

The parallel material in Isaiah 36–39 is nearly identical, with the exception that the report in 2 Kings of Hezekiah's payment of indemnity to Sennacherib (2 Kgs. 18:13–16) has no parallel in Isaiah, and the thanksgiving prayer of Hezekiah in Isaiah 38:9–20 has no parallel in 2 Kings.

As on other occasions, the Chronicler parallels some of the material in Kings but deviates considerably.[7] The following are the significant sections and episodes in the Chronicler's account found in 2 Chronicles 29–32:

A. Opening summary (29:1–2)
B. Hezekiah and the Levites carry out a major purification of the temple and reinstitute proper worship (29:3–36).
C. Hezekiah holds a Passover in Jerusalem to which he invites all Israel from Beer-sheba to Dan, including the northern tribes, and some of the northerners attend (chap. 30).
D. Following the great Passover observance, the people move into the countryside and destroy the local shrines and cultic furniture (31:1).
E. Hezekiah regulates the various divisions of the priests and the Levites, and the people bring in many tithes and gifts, so that larger chambers have to be built to house them in the temple (31:2–21).
F. After these reforming activities and the people's religious responses, Sennacherib invades Judah, but Hezekiah makes preparation, encourages the people, and responds to the demands of Sennacherib's messengers and the letters he sent. Hezekiah and Isaiah pray together, and Yahweh sends an angel who kills the Assyrian mighty men. When Sennacherib returns home, he is killed by his sons (32:1–23).
G. Hezekiah becomes ill because of his pride. When he humbles himself, he and Jerusalem are spared (32:24–26).
H. A description of Hezekiah's wealth is followed by a cryptic reference to the matter of "the envoys of the princes of Babylon" (32:27–31).
I. Concluding summary (32:32–33)

Noticeably, the account in 2 Chronicles focuses on Hezekiah's religious reforms (2 Chr. 29:3–31:21), which 2 Kings notes explicitly only in its opening summary (2 Kgs. 18:4). The Chronicler makes no reference to the fact that Hezekiah rebelled against Sennacherib (see 2 Kgs. 18:7b, 20) but merely states that the Assyrian king wanted to take over the cities of Judah, "thinking to win them for himself" (2 Chr. 32:1). The Chronicler, like Isaiah, omits the account of Hezekiah's capitulation to Sennacherib (2 Kgs. 18:13–16). At the same time, Hezekiah is presented as a courageous leader who encourages his people and keeps his faith, unlike the Hezekiah in 2 Kings who relies upon Isaiah for encouragement (compare 2 Chr. 32:6–8, 20 with 2 Kgs. 19:1–2, 14). The Chronicler

---

7. See A. G. Vaughn, *Theology, History, and Archaeology in the Chronicler's Account of Hezekiah* (SBLABS 4; Atlanta: Scholars Press, 1999).

includes no speeches of Isaiah addressed either to Hezekiah (see 2 Kgs. 19:6–7, 20) or to Sennacherib (see 2 Kgs. 19:21–34) and no prayer of Hezekiah (see Isa. 38:9–20).

For the final compilers of 2 Kings, Hezekiah's rule was a good reign sandwiched between those of two horrible monarchs. The compilers' verdict on Ahaz, strongly biased to fit their theological schematization, is harshly acrimonious: "He did not do what was right in the sight of Yahweh his God, as his ancestor David had done, but he walked in the way of the kings of Israel" (2 Kgs. 16:2b–3a). Hezekiah's son, Manasseh, is described as even worse than his grandfather, for he "misled them [the people] to do more evil than the nations had done that Yahweh destroyed before the people of Israel" (2 Kgs. 21:9). Both Ahaz and Manasseh are depicted in extremely negative terms in order to serve as villainous and apostate antiheroes against whom the heroes, Hezekiah and Josiah, can stand out more sharply. In contrast to his predecessor and successor, Hezekiah is depicted as the ideal king:

> He did what was right in the sight of Yahweh just as his ancestor David had done. . . . He trusted in Yahweh the God of Israel; so that there was no one like him among all the kings of Judah after him, or among those who were before him. For he held fast to Yahweh; he did not depart from following him but kept the commandments that Yahweh commanded Moses. Yahweh was with him; wherever he went, he prospered. (2 Kgs. 18:3, 5–7a)

This idealization of Hezekiah, which was intensified in other biblical traditions (see Isa. 36–39; 2 Chr. 29–32) and in postbiblical interpretations, has no doubt greatly influenced not only what the compilers of the Kings materials recorded about Hezekiah but also how they have reported his reign.

What can be said regarding the biblical traditions about Hezekiah now that we have examined their contents? (1) In all of these accounts, religious concerns take precedence over political concerns. In 2 Kings and Isaiah, the focus is on the Assyrian threat to the sacred city of Jerusalem, the town's miraculous deliverance, and Yahweh's fidelity to his promises. In 2 Chronicles, the emphasis is on the religious reforms of Hezekiah. (2) 2 Kings and the book of Isaiah stress the role of the prophet Isaiah in the crisis, whereas 2 Chronicles focuses on the person of Hezekiah. (3) Even within 2 Kings, there appear to be duplicate accounts of the episode of Jerusalem's miraculous deliverance. Second Kings 18:17–19:9a + 19:36–37 tells one version of the story, and 19:9b–35 another version. (4) The episode of Jerusalem's miraculous deliverance in spite of great odds has many folkloric characteristics, and its themes appear in an Egyptian story, itself highly legendary, that also deals with the invasion of Sennacherib. The Greek historian Herodotus (2.141) tells a version that he learned in Egypt. The story reported that when Sennacherib, the "king of the Arabians and Assyrians," marched against Egypt, the Egyptian ruler enjoyed no support from his military, since he had recently deprived the soldiers of their traditional land grants. In his predicament the ruler went to a temple, where he bewailed the potential calamities confronting him. While lamenting, he fell asleep and received a divine vision promising that the god would let the king suffer nothing disagreeable from the attack but would send messengers to aid him. Awaking, he gathered what followers he could and set out for Pelusium on the northern Egyptian border. When they arrived there, a horde of field mice had invaded Sennacherib's camp and devoured the Assyrian forces' quivers and bows and the handles of their shields. On the morning of battle the Assyrians discovered that they were bereft of arms, and many were slain. Herodotus reports that the salvation of the Egyptian ruler was commemorated by a statue of the king with a mouse in his hand and an inscription saying, "Whoever looks on me, let him revere the gods." The similarity of this legend to the biblical story or stories of the deliverance of Hezekiah and Jerusalem is obvious and raises problems for any interpretation that would accept all the details of the biblical account at face value, especially those about an extraordinary deliverance. (5) The account of the visit of Merodach-baladan's envoys to Jerusalem, in its present form and place in the text of 2 Kings, functions to prepare the reader for the coming narrative on the fall of Jerusalem and the Judean exile. The episode with which this story about the Babylonian envoys is concerned probably occurred in Hezekiah's career before his revolt against Sennacherib.

Chronological Difficulties

Both the beginning and the end of Hezekiah's reign as well as the synchronisms between his reign and those of Israelite and Assyrian kings present unusual chronological problems. His first year is correlated with the third year of Hoshea (2 Kgs. 18:1), his fourth year with the beginning of the siege of Samaria by Shalmaneser V, and his sixth year with the fall of the city (18:9–10), while his fourteenth year is correlated with Sennacherib's invasion (18:13). Since Samaria fell to Shalmaneser V in the winter of 722–721 and Sennacherib's invasion of Judah occurred in 701, we are given the following impossible synchronisms for Hezekiah's reign: his sixth year = 722 and his fourteenth year = 701. The chronology that we propose, which assigns his rule to 727–699, is based on the twenty-nine years assigned him in the notation on regnal years (2 Kgs. 18:2) and is calculated by moving backward from the certain date of the first Babylonian capture of Jerusalem (16 March 597).

Hezekiah is said to have been twenty-five years old when he began his reign, although his father Ahaz is reported to have died at the age of thirty-six (2 Kgs. 16:2; 18:2). To believe that Ahaz fathered a child at the age of eleven is a bit difficult.[8] Some figures are undoubtedly wrong, and we earlier noted irregularities in the regnal statements about Ahaz. In addition, Hezekiah does not seem to have been Ahaz's oldest son. His father apparently sacrificed one of his sons (2 Kgs. 16:3), and another is said to have been killed in the attempt to overthrow Ahaz (2 Chr. 28:7; "king's son," however, may have been just an honorific title). Though it is nowhere said that the king sacrificed his oldest son, this could be assumed, since to offer the firstborn rather than a younger son would have been a greater expression of religious devotion. This issue, in addition to the problem of the synchronisms, raises further doubt about the reliability of some of the specific chronological references for Hezekiah.

---

8. On the possibility that Ahaz and Hezekiah were half brothers rather than father-son, see D. V. Etz, "The Genealogical Relationships of Jehoram and Ahaziah, and of Ahaz and Hezekiah, Kings of Judah," *JSOT* 71 (1996) 39–53, esp. 50–53; and W. B. Barrick, "Genealogical Notes on the 'House of David' and the 'House of Zadok,'" *JSOT* 96 (2001) 29–58, esp. 42–43.

In the narrative about Hezekiah's sickness (2 Kgs. 20; Isa. 38), the king is promised an additional fifteen years of life (2 Kgs. 20:6; Isa. 38:5). Since the narrative relates this episode to the time of Sennacherib's invasion, one would assume that Hezekiah should reign for fifteen years after 701. To extend his rule much beyond 700 is difficult, however, since it then would overlap with the regnal years assigned to Manasseh. Even the reference to Sennacherib's invasion in Hezekiah's fourteenth year in 2 Kings 18:13, which would appear to be our firmest synchronism, should probably be disregarded. Since the "extension" of Hezekiah's life by fifteen years was assumed by the editors to have occurred in conjunction with Sennacherib's invasion and he ruled for twenty-nine years, the compilers logically assumed that Sennacherib's invasion occurred in his fourteenth year.

Sargon and Hezekiah

If the chronology proposed above for Hezekiah (727–699) is correct,[9] then Assyrian forces under Sargon campaigned in southern Syria-Palestine on three occasions during his reign (720–719, 716–715, 712–711). Sargon's campaign in 720–719, which we have noted formed the background for the final organization of the Assyrian province of Samerina, had the purpose of subduing widespread rebellion in the western area of the empire that had broken out simultaneously with Merodach-baladan's uprising in Babylonia, supported by Elam (*ABC* 73–74). Assyrian opponents ranged throughout the area: Hamath, Simirra, Damascus, and Arpad to the north of Judah, and Gaza to the west. Whether Judah and Hezekiah became involved in any way in the rebellious western affairs cannot be determined. The only hint in presently known Assyrian texts that might suggest that Judah was involved is the single statement in an undated Sargonic inscription, which refers to Sargon as "the subduer of the country Judah which is far away" (*COS* 2:298). Such a reference, however, may denote nothing more than that the state of Judah submitted to Sargon and continued as a satellite of Assyria. Sargon, for example, also described himself as having "subdued seven kings of the land of Ia', a region of the land of Iadnana (Cyprus)" (*COS* 2:300), who actually surrendered voluntarily (*ARAB* II §70). A biblical text already noted that has been related to a possible movement of Sargon against Jerusalem in 720–719 is Isaiah 10:27d–32, but this is very doubtful.[10]

Some evidence does suggest that Judah and Hezekiah fought as a client state on the side of the Assyrians in 720–719, when Sargon moved into Egypt, and were consequently rewarded by Assyria.[11] The general background for this

9. For a different but widely followed chronology in evaluating Hezekiah's reign, see Nadav Na'aman, "Hezekiah and the Kings of Assyria," *TA* 21 (1994) 235–54; repr. in *AIIN*, 98–117. Hayim Tadmor and Mordechai Cogan, "Hezekiah's Fourteenth Year: The King's Illness and the Babylonian Embassy," *ErIsr* 16 (1982) 198–201 (Hebrew with English summary), discuss the problems associated with this date and conclude that it probably originally introduced the account of Hezekiah's illness and recovery.

10. See the references above in n. 4 and K. L. Younger Jr., "Sargon's Campaign Against Jerusalem— A Further Note," *Bib* 77 (1996) 108–10.

11. For a defense of this thesis see P. K. Hooker, "The Kingdom of Hezekiah: Judah in the Geopolitical Context of the Late Eighth Century B.C.E." (PhD diss., Emory University, 1993). Judah's continuing pro-Assyrian stance is suggested by Assyrian documents. One letter of uncertain date (ND 2608) perhaps mentions Judeans who may have been fighting with Assyrians in Urartu (see H. W. F. Saggs,

view is as follows. When he was in Philistia, in 733, Tiglath-pileser set up an Assyrian trading center in the region of Gaza or turned the city of Gaza into a trading center (the reading of the text is somewhat uncertain; see *ITP* 141, 189; *COS* 2:288). Earlier the Assyrians had established such a trading center (*bit kari*) in Phoenicia (see *ITP* 104). These centers would have functioned both to control and to encourage trade, to the benefit of Assyria. During his 720–719 campaign, Sargon (in the Calah Prism; see *COS* 2:296) says he "opened the sealed *karu* of Egypt [the Assyrian emporium in Gaza?], and mingled together the people of Assyria and Egypt. I made them trade [with each other]." Sargon's actions in this regard took place after he had defeated a hostile force in Egypt. At this point in history, Assyria seems to have begun a policy of cooperation and mutual alignment with the Delta Egyptians that would last until the collapse of the Assyrian Empire when, in the end, Egypt remained Assyria's only strong ally. A common enemy for the two was the Ethiopians of Upper Egypt, the Twenty-fifth Dynasty, a dominant force up and down the Nile since about 750.

In the 2 Kings summation of Hezekiah's reign, note is taken of the fact that "he attacked the Philistines as far as Gaza and its territory, from watchtower to fortified city" (18:8). This would certainly have been territory in an arena under Assyrian influence. Tiglath-pileser earlier referred to appointing a supervisory tribe in the vicinity of Egypt (*ITP* 143, 169; *COS* 2:288, 289), and Sargon seems to have assigned the sheikh of Laban some role in the northern Sinai. Sargon probably also assigned Hezekiah administrative control over territory in this region as well. First Chronicles 4:39–43 reports on the settlement of the Simeonites, in the area of Gerar (following the Greek reading), which was near Gaza, during the reign of Hezekiah. These Simeonites took over territory formerly held by Ham (Egypt) and defeated the Meunites. This settlement, carried out with the permission of the Assyrians, was probably the origin of the tribe of Simeon "within the inheritance of the tribe of Judah" (Josh. 19:1).

The movement of Judeans into the Gaza region and the territory near the Brook of Egypt (at this time, Wadi Besor)[12] is probably reflected in the tribal boundaries and city lists for Judah in Joshua 15:1–12, 21–62. These lists envision the Mediterranean Sea as Judah's western boundary and include the Philistine cities of Ekron, Ashdod, and Gaza. Sargon may have granted Judah and Hezekiah oversight of this area. No other time in Judean history would seem to correspond to this particular geographical configuration reflected in the tribal lists. Shortly after Sargon's campaign in 720–719, Judah was probably nominally in control of the entire Philistine region, minus Ashkelon, from the Nahal Soreq at Jabneel (Yebna) to south of Gaza.

The Nimrud Letters, 1952: Cuneiform Texts from Nimrud V [London: British School of Archaeology in Iraq, 2001] 128). Some have claimed that the remains of two queens, consorts to Tiglath-pileser and Sargon, excavated at the site of ancient Calah, were Judeans; see Stephanie Dalley, "Recent Evidence from Assyrian Sources for Judaean History from Uzziah to Manasseh," *JSOT* 28 (2004) 387–401; but cf. K. L. Younger Jr., "Yahweh at Ashkelon and Calah? Yahwistic Names in Neo-Assyrian," *VT* 52 (2002) 207–18.

12. On the Brook of Egypt in Assyrian texts and its early association with Wadi Besor, which drains the Beer-sheba basin emptying into the Mediterranean Sea just south of Gaza, see Nadav Na'aman, "The Brook of Egypt and Assyrian Policy on the Border of Egypt," *TA* 6 (1979) 68–90; repr. in *AIIN* 238–64; and P. K. Hooker, "The Location of the Brook of Egypt," in M. P. Graham et al., eds., *History and Interpretation: Essays in Honour of John H. Hayes* (JSOTSup 173; Sheffield: Sheffield Academic Press, 1993) 203–14.

Isaiah 19 also can be interpreted as reflecting conditions associated with Sargon's battle at Raphia (see *COS* 2:296), where "he made havoc of the land of Egypt."[13] This prophetical oracle accurately describes internal Egyptian conditions at the time.[14] Verses 16–17 describe the Egyptians like women frightened at the mention of the land of Judah. This parallels Sargon's description of his victory over Egypt and the Arabians; "at the mention of my name their hearts palpitated, and their arms collapsed" (*COS* 2:296). In his advocacy of a major role for Judah in the region, presented as prediction, Isaiah spoke of a three-nation coalition:

> On that day there will be a highway from Egypt to Assyria, and the Assyrian will come into Egypt, and the Egyptian into Assyria, and the Egyptians will serve the Assyrians.

> On that day Israel will be the third with Egypt and Assyria, a blessing in the midst of the earth [see Gen. 12:3], whom Yahweh of hosts has blessed, saying, "Blessed be Egypt my people, and Assyria the work of my hands, and Israel my heritage." (Isa. 19:23–24)

In 716 Sargon again campaigned near the Egyptian border. A gift of twelve big horses, probably of Kushite origin, was received from "Shilkanni king of Egypt," perhaps Osorkon IV, the last ruler of the Delta-based Twenty-second Dynasty (*ANET* 286). Deportees were settled in the region of the city of the Brook of Egypt, perhaps south of Wadi Besor, as part of an Assyrian military outpost and placed under the supervision of the sheikh of the city of Laban. It was following this campaign, which was probably more commercial than military, that Arabs from several desert tribes were resettled in Samaria (*COS* 2:293). This settlement of Arabs in Samaria should be understood as connected with trade from the Arabian Desert passing through the region.

The glory of Hezekiah's kingdom, however, was soon to fade. Judah's name appears in a Sargonic inscription describing Assyria's suppression of a revolt spearheaded by the Philistine city of Ashdod in 713–711 in which Judah was implicated (see *AJ* 46, 57; *ANET* 286–87).[15] "Together with the rulers of Philistia, Judah, Edom, Moab, and those who live on islands and bring tribute and *tamartu* gifts to my lord Ashur—they sent countless evil lies and unseemly speeches with their bribes to Pir'u, king of Egypt—a potentate, incapable to save them—to set him at enmity with me and asked him to be an ally" (*ANET* 287, modified).

Sargon's inscriptions indicate that developments in Ashdod associated with the uprising and the suppression of the rebellion occurred in stages and over a lengthy period of time (see the texts in *COS* 2:294, 296–97, 300). In the first stage, the Ashdod king Azuri was deposed for failure to pay tribute and was replaced by a brother Ahimiti. In the second phase, Ahimiti was overthrown by his own people and Yamani (or Yadna in one text) placed on the throne. This

---

13. See the Sargonic text in C. J. Gadd, "Inscribed Prisms of Sargon II of Nimrud," *Iraq* 16 (1954) 198–201.

14. See Alviero Niccacci, "Isaiah XVIII-XX from an Egyptological Perspective," *VT* 48 (1998) 214–38.

15. See Andreas Fuchs, *Die Annalen des Jahres 711 v. Chr.* (SAAS 7; Helsinki: Neo-Assyrian Text Corpus Project, 1998), hereafter abbreviated *AJ*; G. L. Mattingly, "An Archaeological Analysis of Sargon's 712 Campaign Against Ashdod," *Near East Archaeology Society Bulletin* 17 (1981) 47–64; and Younger, "Recent Study," 313–15.

was followed by a time when Yamani along with other states sought to organize a major rebellion and to elicit aid from Egypt. The final phase of the struggle involved Sargon leading his own private forces rather than the main Assyrian army against Ashdod. Yamani fled to Egypt, where he took refuge with the Ethiopian king (Shabako), who moved permanently into the Delta region about this time.[16] Sargon reports that Yamani was later sent as a prisoner to Assyria, and a recently published Sargonic inscription notes that the Ethiopian ruler who extradited Yamani was Pharaoh Shebitku (see COS 2:299–300).

Punitive action was probably taken against Judah because of its participation in the revolt. The so-called Azekah Inscription (see COS 2:304–5), previously assigned to either the reign of Tiglath-pileser or Sennacherib, probably belongs to the reign of Sargon.[17] In this inscription, which lacks the name of the Assyrian ruler, the destruction of the city of Azekah ruled by Hezekiah (whose name is partially restored) is reported.

> [Ashur, my lord, support]ed me {Sargon} and to the land of Ju[dah I marched. In] the course of my campaign, the tribute of the k[ings . . .] the district [of Hezek]iah of Judah . . . the city of Azekah, his stronghold . . . located on a mountain peak, like countless pointed i[ron] daggers . . . I conquered, I carried off its spoil . . . a royal [city] of the Philistines, which He[zek]iah had taken and fortified for himself. (COS 2:304)

This destruction of Azekah and a Philistine city held by Hezekiah probably occurred in conjunction with the Ashdod expedition by Sargon.[18] The "royal city of the Philistines which Hezekiah had taken and fortified for himself" was probably Ekron, taken over in Hezekiah's western expansion.

This revolt led by Ashdod and its Judean consequences are the topic of Isaiah 20–22. According to the prophetic narrative in Isaiah 20, the prophet went about Jerusalem naked and barefoot for three years to demonstrate his opposition to the revolt and promising disaster for the Egyptians and Ethiopians. Isaiah began his prophetic demonstration apparently in the year when the Assyrian commander-in-chief (*turtanu*) led an army against Ashdod. This was probably in conjunction with the first stage of the Ashdod revolt when Azuri was replaced on the throne by his brother, since the final defeat of the city and its disposition were carried out by Sargon personally, who reports on his expedition as follows:

16. See D. B. Redford, "Sais and the Kushite Invasions of the Eighth Century," *JARCE* 22 (1985) 5–15; and A. J. Spalinger, "The Year 712 B.C. and Its Implications for Egyptian History," *JARCE* 10 (1973) 95–101.

17. See the discussion in Eckart Frahm, *Einleitung in die Sanherib-Inschriften* (AfO 26; Vienna: Ferdinand Berger & Söhne, 1997) 229–32; hereafter abbreviated *ESI*.

18. See Hooker, "Kingdom of Hezekiah," 32–38; and Gershon Galil, "A New Look at the 'Azekah Inscription,'" *RB* 102 (1995) 321–29. For development of this theory and the assignment of the tribute noted in 2 Kgs. 18:14–16 to the Ashdod campaign, see Jeremy Goldberg, "Two Assyrian Campaigns against Hezekiah and Later Eighth Century Biblical Chronology," *Bib* 80 (1999) 360–90; so already A. K. Jenkins, "Hezekiah's Fourteenth Year: A New Interpretation of 2 Kings xviii 13–xix 37," *VT* 26 (1976) 284–98. For Isaiah's actions during this period, see Shmuel Vargon, "The Prophecy of Isaiah in the Light of the Revolt of Ashdod Against Sargon II and Its Suppression," in Joshua Schwartz et al., eds., *Jerusalem and Eretz Israel: Arie Kindler Volume* (Tel Aviv: Eretz Israel Museum, 2000) 10*–29*. For other possible dates for the Azekah assault, see Younger, "Recent Study," 313–18.

67. *Siloam Inscription.* This inscription was carved into the wall of the Siloam Tunnel, probably at the point where diggers met after excavating from opposite directions. Discovered in 1880, the inscription was chiseled from the wall and is now in the Istanbul Museum. (*Istanbul Museum*) (See Text 11 for a translation)

> In the ebullience of my heart, I did not gather the masses of my troops, nor did I organize my camp. With my warriors—who never leave my side in (hostile or) friend[ly terri]tory—I marched to Ashdod. . . . I besieged (and) conquered Ashdod, Gimtu (Gath), and Ashdod-Yam. I counted as booty his [Yamani's] gods, his wife, his sons, his daughters, the property, the possessions (and) treasurers of his palace, together with the inhabitants of his land. I reorganized those cities. I settled there the peoples of the lands, the conquest of my hands, from [the area] of the east. [I placed my eunuchs as governors over them.] I counted them with the people of Assyria and they bore my yoke. (*COS* 2:296–97)

Isaiah's actions at that time, demonstrations in public rather than direct confrontation with the king and royal family as during the Syro-Ephraimite conflict, may indicate that the king was inaccessible. One proposed theory to explain this argues that the outbreak of rebellion occurred in Hezekiah's time of illness and was thus led by his subordinates Shebna and Eliakim. The "fourteenth year" noted in 2 Kings 18:13 may have originally been part of the introduction to the account of his sickness (see 2 Kgs. 20). Hezekiah's fourteenth year would have begun in the fall of 714. Isaiah's symbolic act of nude display is said to have lasted three years (Isa. 20:3). If begun in 714, then Isaiah's activity lasted until sometime after the fall festival of 712. This correlates well with the time of Sargon's capture of Ashdod in 712–711.

Isaiah 22 describes an encounter in which the Judean leaders fled from battle, were captured, and executed (vv. 1b–4). (Reference to Elam and Kir in v. 6 could refer to special forces that had been absorbed into Sargon's chariotry.) Condemnation of Shebna and Eliakim (vv. 15–25) and the charge of overly hasty action (vv. 8b–11) suggest that a future revolt plotted and planned by Hezekiah (v. 11) was precipitously carried out by the king's subordinates but without the approval of the king and the prophet, and thus Yahweh.[19] A signif-

19. Reference to creating "a reservoir between the two walls" (Isa. 22:11) and to Shebna's carving out a "tomb" (v. 16) may indicate that what was planned as "Hezekiah's tunnel" was carved during this period.

TEXT 11. The Siloam Inscription

[The matter of the] boring through. And this was the manner of the boring through. While [the workers were wielding] the pick, each one toward his co-worker, and while there was still three cubits to be bored through, [there could be heard] the sound of each worker calling to his co-worker, for there was a fissure in the rock to the right and [to the left]. And on the day of the boring through, the workers struck, each to meet his co-worker, pick against pick. And then the waters from the spring [Gihon] flowed to the pool for twelve hundred cubits. And a hundred cubits was the height in the rock above the head of the workers. (See COS 2:145–46, and Photograph 67.)

icant consequence of this rash rebellion was that "he [Sargon] has taken away the covering of Judah" (v. 8a). This could refer to the Assyrians having taken control of the western approach to Jerusalem, but more likely it refers to Judah having now lost its special status in the eyes of the Assyrian monarch and being treated as a potentially rebellious state. In addition to the loss of territory that Judah had secured in the west following Sargon's 720–719 campaign, the revolt apparently resulted in a settlement of Assyrian troops in Jerusalem.[20]

The attempt of Merodach-baladan (Marduk-apla-iddina), king of Babylon, to gain support and foment rebellion in the west probably influenced the Ashdod revolt. Merodach-baladan, leader of the Bit-Yakin Chaldean tribe in southern Babylonia, had appeared before Tiglath-pileser at Sapiya in 731–730, offered tribute, and kissed the Assyrian's feet (see *ITP* 165–66). Upon the death of Shalmaneser V, while Sargon struggled to secure the throne, however, Merodach-baladan had seized the throne in Babylon and thus shattered the combined Assyrian rule over both Babylonia and Assyria (*ABC* 73). A state of belligerence existed between the two kingdoms for years. According to the Babylonian Chronicles, in his tenth year Merodach-baladan "attacked and ravaged" but the cuneiform text is too broken to determine the objective (*ABC* 75). Probably Merodach-baladan attacked Assyria from the south in conjunction with the Ashdod-led revolt in the west. Second Kings 20:12–19 reports on the appearance of Babylonian ambassadors in Jerusalem. Whether these were sent to seal or encourage Judah's participation in a western and Babylonian combined movement against Sargon, or later during the reign of Sennacherib when Merodach-baladan again occupied the throne of Babylon, cannot be determined with certainty. The biblical material is in a highly legendary narrative, and this creates problems. A date in the reign of Sargon seems more likely.

Following the suppression of the Ashdod-led revolt in the west, Sargon enjoyed four major successes. (1) He attacked Merodach-baladan and drove him from Babylon, then assumed kingship in the city (*ABC* 75). (2) Seven Cypriote

---

20. Josephus twice refers to a site in northwest Jerusalem as "the camp of the Assyrians" (*War* 5.303, 504), which probably does not refer to a camp established by Sennacherib (so David Ussishkin, "The 'Camp of the Assyrians' in Jerusalem," *IEJ* 29 [1979] 137–42) but to the establishment of an Assyrian outpost. Sennacherib never really occupied any area of Jerusalem and had the city blockaded for only a short time. On Assyrian outposts for military control of an area, see Nadav Na'aman, "An Assyrian Residence at Ramat Rahel?" *TA* 28 (2001) 260–80; repr. in *AIIN* 279–97.

kings capitulated and sent submission gifts to Sargon in Babylon (*ARAB* II §70). (3) The Assyrian governor in Cilicia fought Mita of Muski (the golden-touch Midas of Phrygia in Greek legend), who submitted and made tribute payment (*ARAB* II §71). (4) The Ethiopian ruler in Egypt sought at least temporary rapport with Assyria and shipped the exiled Ashdodite king Yamani as a prisoner to Sargon (*COS* 2:299–300). Sargon's dominance in the Near East seemed at its height. He wrote one of his governors in Anatolia: "You, from this side [the east], and the Muskean [Midas], from that side [the west], can squeeze them, so that soon you will tie your rope with them" (ND 2759).[21]

Throughout the remainder of the reign of Sargon, from 711, no further Assyrian campaigns were conducted in southern Syria-Palestine. The temporary peaceful conditions that prevailed between the Assyrians and Egyptians, partially initiated by Sargon in 720 and furthered by continuing internal struggle for power within Egypt itself, brought political stability to Syria-Palestine for several years. The activities of the Assyrians in the region of Judah, however, had probably impressed several lessons upon rulers such as Hezekiah. Among these must have been the recognition that unsuccessful revolts were costly enterprises, that unplanned, spur-of-the-moment rebellions were almost doomed from the beginning, and that help from Egypt could be counted upon only if that country possessed a stronger and better-organized administration than had been the case with the Twenty-third and Twenty-fourth Dynasties.

Hezekiah's Revolt and Sennacherib's Invasion

In 715–714 Sargon had taken action to eliminate once and for all the Urartian threat. He defeated the Urartian king Rusa I (ca. 733–714), decimated the land, and reported his campaign in his famous "letter to (the god) Ashur" (*ARAB* II §§139–78). Unfortunately for him, this diminution of Urartian power opened the Assyrian Empire to the movement of tribal groups into its territory. In 705–704, shortly after dedicating a new capital, Sargon moved against one of these groups and in a subsequent battle lost his life. The Eponym Chronicle notes that the battle was with Qurdi the Kulummaean and that "the king was killed; the camp of the king of Assyria [was captured]." The corpse of the Assyrian ruler was never recovered.

The death of Sargon became the occasion for widespread revolt throughout the empire. His death temporarily ended the vassal relationship between the Assyrian overlord and the subject kingdoms and freed the latter from the threat of divine punishment from their own deities for breaking the treaty. In Jerusalem the prophet Isaiah had long proclaimed that Assyria was only a temporary instrument in the hand of Yahweh that would be broken and destroyed when its task was completed and the divinely appointed, opportune moment arrived (see, for example, Isa. 10:5–27c; 14:24–27).

Sennacherib (704–681) succeeded Sargon to the Assyrian throne. His first campaign was directed against Merodach-baladan, who had reentered Babylon and reclaimed the throne. The Chaldean ruler was quickly driven from

---

21. J. N. Postgate, "Assyrian Texts and Fragments: 5. Sargon's Letter Referring to Midas," *Iraq* 35 (1973) 21–24.

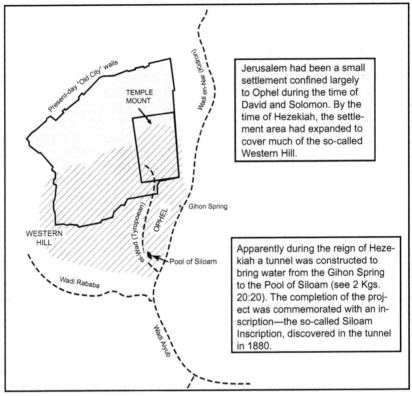

Jerusalem had been a small settlement confined largely to Ophel during the time of David and Solomon. By the time of Hezekiah, the settlement area had expanded to cover much of the so-called Western Hill.

Apparently during the reign of Hezekiah a tunnel was constructed to bring water from the Gihon Spring to the Pool of Siloam (see 2 Kgs. 20:20). The completion of the project was commemorated with an inscription—the so-called Siloam Inscription, discovered in the tunnel in 1880.

MAP 31. Jerusalem at the Time of Hezekiah

southern Babylonia (*COS* 2:300–302). Instead of claiming the throne for himself, however, Sennacherib appointed another to the post: "I installed Bel-ibni, son of a building inspector, a native-born Babylonian, who was raised in my palace like a young puppy" (*COS* 2:302). Only in 701, in his third campaign, did Sennacherib set his sights on the rebellious kingdoms in the west.[22]

Hezekiah's Preparations for Revolt. There are numerous indications both in the biblical traditions and in the archaeological evidence that prior to the death of Sargon Hezekiah had begun to mobilize his state and prepare for revolt. Many of his preparations and programs, planned even earlier on, may have been carried out in the years between Sargon's last western campaign to the region in 712–711 and his death in 705.

Several biblical texts note the strengthening and reorganization of the Judean military: Hezekiah "made weapons and shields in abundance" (2 Chr. 32:5); "he

22. For a recent study of the campaign to the west, see W. R. Gallagher, *Sennacherib's Campaign to Judah: New Studies* (SHCANE 18; Leiden: Brill, 1999). On the problems associated with the sources, the campaign, and reconstructing the course of events, see L. L. Grabbe, ed., *"Like a Bird in a Cage": The Invasion of Sennacherib in 701 BCE* (JSOTSup 363; ESHM 4; Sheffield: Sheffield Academic Press, 2003); and the essays by J. K. Hoffmeier, K. L. Younger Jr., and J. J. M. Roberts in A. G. Vaughn and A. E. Killebrew, eds., *Jerusalem in Bible and Archaeology: The First Temple Period* (SBLSymS 18; Leiden: Brill, 2003) 219–90.

set combat commanders over the people" (32:6); he had "storehouses also for the yield of grain, wine, and oil; and stalls for all kinds of cattle, and sheepfolds," and "provided cities for himself" (32:28–29); he "built up all the wall [in Jerusalem] that was broken down, and raised towers upon it, and outside it he built another wall; and he strengthened the Millo in the city of David" (32:5); "he made the pool and the conduit and brought water into the city" (2 Kgs. 20:20; see 2 Chr. 32:30; Isa. 22:11; Sir. 48:17); and "he planned with his officers and his mighty men to stop the water of the springs that were outside the city" (2 Chr. 32:3). All of this activity, some of which may have been carried out before and some after the actual outbreak of rebellion, suggests a concerted effort to arm the nation, to prepare for war, and to plan for a siege of the capital city. (See Map 31.)

Archaeological evidence and nonbiblical texts support the picture of elaborate military planning and fortification by Hezekiah. Sennacherib's account of his campaign to Syria-Palestine, reported fully in three slightly different versions (see Text 12), mentions taking forty-six strong and walled cities in Judah (*COS* 2:302–3). The so-called Siloam or Hezekiah Tunnel in Jerusalem with its inscription describing the means of construction (*COS* 2:145–46) can with reasonable certainty be ascribed to Hezekiah's planned preparations for the anticipated siege of Jerusalem, although probably executed in conjunction with the Ashdod affair (714–711).[23] This tunnel, almost a third of a mile long, carried the water from the spring Gihon under the Old City (Ophel) to the western side of the mount. Hezekiah probably expanded the city especially westward by enclosing part of the western hill within the city's fortification (note the second wall mentioned in 2 Chr. 32:5), so that the main water reservoir was within the defensive perimeters of the city. On the basis of archaeological evidence, it is clear that the population of Jerusalem during Hezekiah's reign increased significantly, perhaps swelled by refugees from the north. For the first time in Judean history, Jerusalem became a major metropolitan center.[24]

Special types of seal impressions on large storage jars have been unearthed at numerous Judean sites.[25] The hundreds of examples discovered, almost all

23. For a different view see J. R. Rogerson and P. R. Davies, "Was the Siloam Tunnel Built by Hezekiah?" *BA* 59 (1996) 138–49; and the support of the traditional view by R. S. Hendel, "The Date of the Siloam Inscription: A Rejoinder to Rogerson and Davies," *BA* 59 (1996) 233–37. See also David Ussishkin, "The Water Systems of Jerusalem during Hezekiah's Reign," in Manfred Weippert and Stefen Timm, eds., *Festgabe für H. Donner zum 16 Februar 1995* (Ägypten und Alter Testament 30; Wiesbaden: Harrassowitz, 1995) 289–303; Dan Gill, "The Geology of the City of David and Its Ancient Subterranean Waterworks," in D. T. Ariel and Alon de Groot, eds., *Excavations at the City of David 1978–1985*, vol. 4: *Various Reports* (Qedem 35; Jerusalem: Institute of Archaeology, Hebrew University, 1996) 1–28; Stephen Rosenberg, "The Siloam Tunnel Revisited," *TA* 25 (1998) 116–30; and Avraham Faust, "A Note on Hezekiah's Tunnel and the Siloam Inscription," *JSOT* 90 (2000) 3–11.

24. See Magen Broshi, "The Expansion of Jerusalem in the Reigns of Hezekiah and Manasseh," *IEJ* 24 (1974) 21–26; Yigal Shiloh, "Judah and Jerusalem in the Eighth-Sixth Centuries B.C.E.," in Seymour Gitin and W. G. Dever, eds., *Recent Excavations in Israel: Studies in Iron Age Archaeology* (AASOR 49; Winona Lake, IN: Eisenbrauns, 1989) 97–105; Vaughn, *Theology, History*, 59–71; Hershel Shanks, "Everything You Ever Knew About Jerusalem Is Wrong (Well, Almost)," *BAR* 25/6 (1999) 20–29; and Ronny Reich and Eli Shukrun, "The Urban Development of Jerusalem in the Late Eighth Century B.C.E.," in Vaughn and Killebrew, eds., *Jerusalem*, 209–18.

25. See David Ussishkin, "The Destruction of Lachish by Sennacherib and the Dating of the Royal Judean Storage Jars," *TA* 4 (1977) 28–57; Nadav Na'aman, "Hezekiah's Fortified Cities and the *LMLK* Stamps," *BASOR* 261 (1986) 5–21; repr. in *AIIN* 153–78; Hans Mommsen et al., "The Provenience of the *lmlk* Jars," *IEJ* 34 (1984) 89–113; and N. S. Fox, *In the Service of the King: Officialdom in Ancient Israel and Judah* (HUCM 23; Cincinnati: Hebrew Union College Press, 2000) 216–35. See the chart of find spots in Vaughn, *Theology, History*, 166.

at Judean sites, are of three types. Two of these show a four-winged scarab or beetlelike emblem, with one type slightly more stylized than the other. The iconography appears clearly dependent upon Egyptian influence. The third type shows a double-winged sun disk perhaps related to Hittite and Assyrian symbolism. All the impressions were made from a limited number of no more than two dozens seals. Along with the impression of the winged emblem appears the Hebrew inscription *lmlk*, "of, to, or belonging to, the king." In addition, one of four place names occurs: Hebrón, Socoh, Ziph, or *mmsht* (unidentified). The jars on which these impressions appear are generally large, four-handled storage jars. This artifactual evidence has been interpreted as follows. The use of these impressions was introduced under Hezekiah and is evidence for the administrative system used during his reign. The jars were part of a system of tax collection in kind or a royal storage program. The material collected in these containers was sent to four district centers for storage, redistribution, and administrative/military usage. These centers were Socoh for the Shephelah region, Ziph for the Negeb, Hebron for the southern hill country, and *mmsht* for Jerusalem and the northern Judean hill country. In addition, many of these containers were impressed with seals containing the names of officials. If this interpretation of the archaeological evidence is correct, it demonstrates that Hezekiah established or utilized a highly organized administrative system oriented to the effective distribution and storage of goods for national usage.

Finds of *lmlk* stamps indicate that Hezekiah recaptured territory in the Shephelah to the west, which he had lost as a consequence of Judah's participation in the Ashdod revolt. His control seems to have extended from Gezer in the north to Beer-sheba in the south, including Ekron and Gath. Finds of *lmlk* seals at Mizpah, Tell el-Ful, and el-Jib indicate control of territory north of Jerusalem to just south of Bethel. Within this arena a number of fortresses existed, some like Arad no more than half an acre in size. Military and political bureaucracy must have expanded under Hezekiah's highly centralized administration. Among seventy-three official seal impressions discovered at Lachish the names of eighteen different governmental personnel appear.[26]

In addition to Hezekiah's efforts to strengthen Judah's military preparedness and ability to withstand invasion and siege, he also carried out religious reforms related to his nationalistic ambitions. At what time Hezekiah instituted these reforms is uncertain; 2 Chronicles 29:3 claims that he began reforms in the first month of his first year, but this seems highly unlikely. Dating events early or earlier than they occurred in a reign was a means of propaganda and appears rather frequently in Neo-Assyrian inscriptions.[27] The account found in 2 Kings 18:4–6 supplies no date for and provides only a rather generalized

26. See Gabriel Barkay and A. G. Vaughn, "*Lmlk* and Official Seal Impressions from Tel Lachish," *TA* 23 (1996) 61–74; idem, "New Readings of Hezekian Official Seal Impressions," *BASOR* 304 (1996) 29–54; and Vaughn, *Theology, History,* 110–35. On the increase in literacy during the period, see W. M. Schniedewind, *How the Bible Became a Book: The Textualization of Ancient Israel* (Cambridge: Cambridge University Press, 2004).

27. Mordechai Cogan, "The Chronicler's Use of Chronology as Illuminated by Neo-Assyrian Royal Inscriptions," in J. H. Tigay, ed., *Empirical Models for Biblical Criticism* (Philadelphia: University of Pennsylvania Press, 1985) 197–209.

account of Hezekiah's cultic reform.[28] Second Chronicles 29–31 gives the reform pride of place in what appears to be an idealized version emphasizing those elements and cultic groups (the Levites) with which the Chronicler was most in sympathy.

Second Kings 18:4 reports that Hezekiah "removed the high places [local sanctuaries], broke the pillars, and cut down the Asherah. He broke in pieces the bronze serpent that Moses had made, for until those days the people of Israel had burned incense to it; it was called Nehushtan." This verse suggests that Hezekiah took actions to close Yahwistic places of worship outside Jerusalem and to remove some practices and artifacts from the Jerusalem temple.[29] The bronze serpent had played some role in previous Yahwistic practices. Numbers 21:6–9 with its reference to Moses' elevation of the bronze serpent in the wilderness seems to be a story justifying the use of such an image in Yahwism.

Placed on the lips of an Assyrian ambassador,[30] 2 Kings 18:22 makes the following reference to the cultic reforms of Hezekiah: "But if you say to me, 'We rely on Yahweh our God,' is it not he [Yahweh] whose high places [sanctuaries] and altars Hezekiah has removed, saying to Judah and to Jerusalem, 'You shall worship before this altar in Jerusalem'?" This description of Hezekiah's religious innovations clearly suggests a deliberate effort on the part of the Judean king to centralize worship in Jerusalem. Centralization of the cult would have been a drastic move, opposed by some, but intended to make the population more dependent upon Jerusalem and thus upon Hezekiah and the capital city.

---

28. Some scholars argue that Hezekiah carried out no reform or centralization of religion; see, e.g., Nadav Na'aman, "The Debated Historicity of Hezekiah's Reform in the Light of Historical and Archaeological Research," *ZAW* 107 (1995) 179–95; repr. in *AIHH* 274–90. For a defense of the reform, see Jacob Milgrom, "Does H Advocate the Centralization of Worship?" *JSOT* 88 (2000) 59–76, esp. 68–72; and Israel Finkelstein and N. A. Silberman, "Temple and Dynasty: Hezekiah, the Remaking of Judah and the Rise of the Pan-Israelite Ideology," *JSOT* 30 (2006) 259–85. Older discussions are thoroughly reviewed in H. H. Rowley, "Hezekiah's Reform and Rebellion," *BJRL* 44 (1962) 395–431; repr. in his *Men of God: Studies in Old Testament History and Prophecy* (London: Nelson, 1963) 98–132. Recent discussions of the rationale for a religious reform are described in K. A. Swanson, "A Reassessment of Hezekiah's Reform in Light of Jar Handles and Iconographic Evidence," *CBQ* 64 (2002) 460–69. The archaeological evidence for destroyed sanctuaries is surveyed by L. S. Fried, "The High Places (*Bāmôt*) and the Reforms of Hezekiah and Josiah: An Archaeological Investigation," *JAOS* 122 (2002) 437–65, who arrives at a negative conclusion about the reforms. See also Ze'ev Herzog, "The Date of the Temple at Arad: Reassessment of the Stratigraphy and the Implications for the History of Religion in Judah," in Amihai Mazar, eds., *Studies in the Archaeology of the Iron Age in Israel and Jordan* (JSOTSup 331; Sheffield: Sheffield Academic Press, 2001), 156–78; and David Ussishkin, "The Level V 'Sanctuary' and 'High Place' at Lachish," in C. G. den Hertog et al., eds., *Saxa Loquentur: Studien zur Archäologie Palästinas/Israels Festschrift für Volkman Fritz* (AOAT 392; Münster: Ugarit Verlag, 2003) 205–11.

29. A small temple and altar discovered in a citadel at Arad in southern Judah that fell into disuse or was covered over and the secular secondary reuse of an altar at the site of ancient Beer-sheba have been associated with Hezekiah's closure of outlying sanctuaries. Unfortunately, the stratigraphy at the sites does not allow for definite chronological dating. See Yohanan Aharoni, "The Israelite Sanctuary at Arad," in D. N. Freedman and J. C. Greenfield, eds., *New Directions in Biblical Archaeology* (Garden City, NY: Doubleday, 1971) 28–44; idem, "The Horned Altar of Beer-sheba," *BA* 37 (1974) 2–6; David Ussishkin, "The Date of the Judaean Shrine at Arad," *IEJ* 38 (1988) 142–57; Yigael Yadin, "Beer-sheba: The High Place Destroyed by King Josiah," *BASOR* 222 (1976) 5–17; A. F. Rainey, "Hezekiah's Reform and the Altars at Beer-sheba and Arad," in M. D. Coogan et al., eds., *Scripture and Other Artifacts: Essays on the Bible and Archaeology in Honor of Philip J. King* (Louisville: Westminster John Knox, 1994) 333–54; and Fried, "High Places."

30. On the genre and authenticity of this speech, see Chaim Cohen, "Neo-Assyrian Elements in the First Speech of the Biblical Rab-Šāqê," *IOS* 9 (1979) 32–48; Ehud Ben-Zvi, "Who Wrote the Speech of Rabshakeh and When?" *JBL* 109 (1990) 79–90; and Peter Machinist, "The Rab šāqēh at the Wall of Jerusalem: Israelite Identity in the Face of the Assyrian 'Other,'" *Hebrew Studies* 41 (2000) 151–68.

By making the other cities religiously dependent upon the capital city, Hezekiah must have been seeking to tie their political and religious allegiance more firmly to himself, to the Davidic family that had almost been toppled at the time of Ahaz, and to the state causes that he espoused. At the time of Ahaz, centrifugal forces against Jerusalem almost disintegrated Judah, and these may have been lodged in outlying sanctuaries (see Amos 5:4–5). In addition, the religion of the state could be more adequately supervised and the capital city benefit from the economy associated with official religion.

Second Chronicles 30:1 states that Hezekiah also sent letters throughout Ephraim and Manasseh inviting the population in these old Israelite territories, now under Assyrian provincial administration, to worship in Jerusalem. This move, idealistically reported in 2 Chronicles 30:2–27, if historical, would have been an effort on Hezekiah's part to enlist in his cause the support of northern Yahwistic followers and at the same time an expression of his desire to restore the old kingdom under Davidic rule, an ideal no doubt fostered in many Yahwistic circles, given expression even by the prophet Isaiah himself (see Isa. 9:1–7), and now more theoretically possible since no native ruler reigned in the north. (A son of Hezekiah and future king, born ca. 710, was given the name "Manasseh," a name with northern tribal associations.) Thus Hezekiah's religious and cultic innovations would have been part of his efforts to revive nationalistic inclinations and to rally the people to a nationalistic cause that would ultimately mean a clash with the Assyrians. The account of the reform makes no reference to any book or collection of laws that may have provided the basis for Hezekiah's actions, though an early form of Deuteronomy may have served as inspiration.[31]

The final component in Hezekiah's plans for revolt and independence from Assyria was the coordination of his efforts with those of other rulers and the extension of his authority into the territory of the noncooperating Philistine states. In Syria-Palestine rebellion was supported by Luli king of Sidon; Sidqia, who had usurped the throne of Ashkelon; and the city of Ekron, which deposed its noncooperative king Padi and turned him over to Hezekiah. The Philistine city of Gaza, ruled by King Sillibel, remained loyal to Assyria. In addition, Hezekiah may have seized and fortified the city of Gath. Judah at the time was undoubtedly the strongest power in southern Syria-Palestine.

In the east, Merodach-baladan, who had earlier sent envoys to Hezekiah (see 2 Kgs. 20:12–15), led a simultaneous revolt in southern Babylonia (see *COS* 2:300–302 for an account of Sennacherib's attack on Merodach-baladan).[32] Major Anatolian provinces—Que (Kue), Til Garimmu, Tabal, and Hilakku—rebelled as well, but we have no evidence that their action was overtly coordinated with the revolts in Syria-Palestine and southern Mesopotamia.

Egypt was a strong supporter, if not one of the instigators of the revolt. The Twenty-fifth Dynasty from Upper Egypt, having established a base of control in Lower Egypt and the Delta, was now in a position to act with concerted strength. How early the Twenty-fifth Dynasty became involved in the plans for

---

31. See H. L. Ginsberg, *The Israelian Heritage of Judaism* (New York: Jewish Theological Seminary, 1982).

32. On Merodach-baladan see J. A. Brinkman, "Merodach-Baladan II," in R. D. Biggs and J. A. Brinkman, eds., *Studies Presented to A. Leo Oppenheim* (Chicago: Oriental Institute, 1964) 6–53.

rebellion cannot be determined. The return of Yamani to Sargon at the Assyrian capital by Pharaoh Shebitku seems to have taken place in 706, when the Eponym Chronicle notes explicitly that "the king [Sargon] stayed in the land." Between this gesture of friendship and the western campaign of Sennacherib, the Twenty-fifth Dynasty adopted a strong anti-Assyrian posture.

Sennacherib's Invasion. On the basis of the Kings account (2 Kgs. 18:13–19:37 paralleled in Isa. 36–37)[33] and Sennacherib's inscriptions (*COS* 2:302–3), the general course of Hezekiah's encounter with the Assyrians and the campaign of Sennacherib can be reconstructed with some certainty but not in detail (for the Assyrian account see Text 12; for Herodotus's account of the Egyptian version, see above, pp. 402–3).[34] As we have noted, rebellion broke out in numerous regions following Sargon's death—in Anatolia, Babylonia, and Syria-Palestine. After Sennacherib had suppressed rebels led by Merodach-baladan in southern Mesopotamia (*ABC* 77), he turned his attention in his third campaign, in 701, to the revolt in Syria-Palestine. The Assyrian monarch marched down the Phoenician coast into Philistia before he encountered any major opposition. Luli of Sidon had fled overseas, and the cities under his influence submitted—Tyre, Akzib, Acco, and others. A new vassal king, Ethbaal, was installed on the throne in Sidon. Embassies of other kingdoms reaffirmed their loyalty. These included Arvad, Byblos, Ashdod, Ammon, Moab, and Edom. Garrisons of these vassal kingdoms were apparently required to accompany Sennacherib on his march southward.

Without mention of having captured the city of Ashkelon, Sennacherib claims to have taken prisoner and deported its king, Sidqia, and his family ("the gods of his father's house, himself, his wife, his sons, his daughters, his brothers, the seed of his father's house"). He replaced him on the throne with Sharruludari, the son of Rukibtu, the former ruler of the city. One suspects that Sidqia, who had been supported by the anti-Assyrian element of the population, was overthrown by his own subjects and turned over to Sennacherib once the cause had been assessed as hopeless.

---

33. The biblical materials on Sennacherib's invasion are very complex, as noted above in the discussion of sources for the period. Part of the difficulty here may have been created by the following factors. After the death of Hezekiah and during the reign of Amon or early in Josiah's rule, a version of the books of Kings was probably produced that extended through 2 Kgs. 18:12 (on this dating, see I. W. Provan, *Hezekiah and the Books of Kings: A Contribution to the Debate about the Composition of the Deuteronomistic History* [BZAW 172; Berlin, de Gruyter: 1988]; and Baruch Halpern and D. S. Vanderhooft, "The Editions of Kings in the 7th-6th Centuries B.C.E.," *HUCA* 62 [1991] 179–244). When the history was subsequently expanded and extended, for this period the authors possessed only an account of Hezekiah's payment of tribute to an Assyrian king (2 Kgs. 18:14–16; see Goldberg, "Two Assyrian Campaigns") and legends about the deliverance of Jerusalem that had developed around the figure of Isaiah. For a different approach to the traditions, see Nadav Na'aman, "New Light on Hezekiah's Prophetic Story (2 Kings 19:9b-35)," *Bib* 81 (2000) 393–402; repr. in *AIIN* 179–92.

34. No texts in Isa. 1–33 or in the book of Micah are concerned with or reflect Sennacherib's invasion. Isaiah 1:4–9 and Mic. 1:10–16 are most frequently related to this crisis (see the commentaries). The former is devoid of military imagery (see Ehud Ben-Zvi, "Isaiah 1, 4–9, Isaiah, and the Events of 701 Judah," *SJOT* 5/1 [1991] 95–111) and reflects the impact of the earthquake under Uzziah (see Jacob Milgrom, "Did Isaiah Prophesy during the Reign of Uzziah?" *VT* 14 [1964] 164–82). On the significance of this earthquake, see S. A. Austin et al., "Amos's Earthquake: An Extraordinary Seismic Event of 750 B.C.," *International Geology Review* 42 (2000) 657–71. For the date of Micah's oracles, see C. S. Shaw, *The Speeches of Micah: A Rhetorical-Historical Analysis* (JSOTSup 145; Sheffield: Sheffield Academic Press, 1993). The exact course of Sennacherib's third campaign cannot be reconstructed due to the literary qualitites of the inscription; see K. L. Younger Jr., "Assyrian Involvement in the Southern Levant at the End of the Eighth Century B.C.E.," in Vaughn and Killebrew, eds., *Jerusalem*, 235–63.

Sennacherib then set out to reduce all the cities that had been under the influence of Sidqia—Beth-dagon, Joppa, Banai-Barqa, Azor—as well as those under the control of Hezekiah—Ekron, Eltekeh, Timnah, Lachish, Azekah, and others. Sennacherib claims eventually to have conquered forty-six strong walled cities that had been under Hezekiah's control.

Obviously Sennacherib intended eventually to force Jerusalem into submission. While fighting against other Philistine and Judean strongholds, he sent forces and ambassadors to the Judean capital to propose that Hezekiah and the city capitulate. At Jerusalem a blockade line was constructed around the city so that the Assyrian troops could control people entering and leaving the town. The Assyrian king could later speak, in a typical Assyrian cliché, of shutting up Hezekiah as "a prisoner in Jerusalem, his royal residence, like a bird in a cage" (COS 2:303). According to the Kings account, the Rabshakeh, the official Assyrian spokesman representing Sennacherib and probably utilizing Assyrian military intelligence reports, offered reasons that the Judean king and the city should surrender (2 Kgs. 18:19–25; 19:9b–13). The text has the Assyrian diplomat develop a case based on five arguments. (1) Words and baseless confidence are no substitute for strategy and power. (2) Egypt, "that broken reed of a staff," cannot be leaned upon for support. (3) Hezekiah's Yahwism was ambivalent, since he had taken steps to suppress Yahwistic practices outside Jerusalem and thus could be guilty of sacrilege. (4) Jerusalem could not supply two thousand horsemen even if Assyria supplied the horses. (5) The Assyrian invasion of Judah had the sanction and word of Yahweh behind it. In this argument, there is probably a reference to the fact that the Assyrians had carried into exile the Yahwistic cult materials from Samaria (see the fourth item in Text 10) and thus could consult Yahweh and receive his word, or a reference to the earlier treaty with Sargon in which, using ritual and oaths, Hezekiah had participated in becoming a subject. Such treaties included curses and sanctions in the name of the subject's deity, so that the judgment of Yahweh was self-invoked upon Hezekiah should he not remain loyal to his Assyrian overlord. In addressing the city, the Rabshakeh proposed that if Hezekiah was not willing to capitulate, then the population of the town should consider giving up the cause and turning over their king (2 Kgs. 18:28–35), as had probably the people of Ashkelon.

With negotiations under way, and Isaiah offering support for the revolt and encouragement to Hezekiah while denouncing the Assyrians and predicting that Jerusalem would not fall (2 Kgs. 19:6–7, 20–34), an army from Egypt appeared on the scene. Sennacherib notes that the rebels had appealed to the kings of Egypt (apparently the native rulers in the Delta) and to the king of Ethiopia (the ruling pharaoh of the Twenty-fifth Dynasty). At least one Egyptian force was dispatched, probably by the Ethiopian pharaoh, Shebitku, under the command of Tirhakah (2 Kgs. 19:9). Both Egyptians and Ethiopians were apparently involved in the battle. The Egyptian force clashed with the Assyrians near Eltekeh in the coastal plain. Although Sennacherib claimed a great victory, the battle may have been far less than an overwhelming success and his victory less glorious than he claimed.[35] He is rather vague about spoils taken

---

35. The decimation of the Assyrian army, mass burials unearthed at Lachish, and the illness of Hezekiah have long been associated with an outbreak of bubonic plague. For a recent discussion see Margaret Barker, "Hezekiah's Boil," *JSOT* 95 (2001) 31–42.

TEXT 12. Sennacherib's 701 Campaign to the West

In my third campaign I marched against Hatti. Luli, king of Sidon—the terror-inspiring glamor of my lordship overwhelmed him—and he fled far into the midst of the sea [to Cyprus]. The awe-inspiring splendor of the "Weapon" of Ashur, my lord, overwhelmed his strong cities such as Great Sidon, Lower Sidon, Bit-zitti, Sariptu, Mahalliba, Ushu [i.e., the mainland settlement of Tyre], Akzib, and Akko, all his fortress cities, walled and with feed and water for his garrisons, and they bowed in submission at my feet. I installed Ethba'al upon the throne to be their king and imposed upon him tribute due to me as his overlord to be paid annually without interruption.

All the kings of Amurru—Minuhimmu of Samsimuruna, Tuba'lu of Sidon, Abdili'ti of Arvad, Urumilki of Byblos, Mitinti of Ashdod, Puduilui of Beth-Ammon, Chemash-nadbi of Moab, and Ayiarammu of Edom—they brought expensive gifts and—fourfold—their heavy *tamartu*-presents to me and kissed my feet. Sidqia, however, king of Ashkelon, who did not bow to my yoke, I deported and sent to Assyria, his family gods, himself, and his wife, his children, his brothers, all the male descendants of his family. I set Sharruludari, son of Rukibtu, their former king, over the inhabitants of Ashkelon and imposed upon him the payment of tribute and of *katru*-presents due to me as overlord—and he now pulls the straps of my yoke!

In the continuation of my campaign I besieged Beth-Dagon, Joppa, Bene-barak, Azuru, cities belonging to Sidqia which had not bowed to my feet quickly enough; I conquered them and carried their spoils away. The officials, the nobles, and the common people of Ekron—who had put into fetters Padi, under oath and obligation sworn by the god Ashur, and had handed him over to Hezekiah the Judean, and he [Hezekiah] held him in prison, unlawfully, as if he [Padi] be an enemy—had become afraid and had called for help upon the kings of Egypt and the bowmen, the chariot corps and the cavalry of the king of Ethiopia, an army beyond counting—and they actually had come to their assistance. In the plain of Eltekeh, their battle lines were drawn up against me and they sharpened their weapons. Upon a trust-inspiring oracle given by Ashur, my lord, I fought with them and inflicted a defeat upon them. In the mêlée of the battle, I personally captured alive the Egyptian charioteers with their princes and also the charioteers of the king of Ethiopia. I besieged Eltekeh and Timnah, conquered (them) and carried their spoils away. I assaulted Ekron and killed the officials and patricians who had committed the crime and hung their bodies on poles surrounding the city. The common citizens who were guilty of minor crimes, I considered prisoners of war. The rest of them, those who were not accused of crimes and misbehavior, I released. I made Padi, their king, come from Jerusalem and set him as their lord on the throne, imposing upon him the tribute due to me as overlord.

As for Hezekiah, the Judean, he did not submit to my yoke. I laid siege to 46 of his strong fortified cities, and countless small villages in their vicinity, and conquered them by means of well-stamped earth ramps, and battering rams brought thus near to the walls combined with the attack by foot soldiers, using mines, breaches, as well as sapper work. I brought out of them 200,150 people, young and old, male and female, horses, mules, donkeys, camels, big and small cattle beyond counting, and considered them booty. Himself I shut up as a prisoner in Jerusalem, his royal residence, like a bird in a cage. I erected fortresses against him in order to molest those who were leaving his city's gate. His towns which I had plundered, I took away from his country and gave them over to Mitinti, king of Ashdod, Padi, king of Ekron, and Sillibel, king of Gaza. Thus I reduced his country. To the earlier tax, their [the Philistines] annual payment, I added tribute and gifts and imposed there upon them. Hezekiah himself, whom the terror-inspiring splendor of my lordship had overwhelmed and the irregular and his elite troops that he had brought into Jerusalem, as auxiliary forces in order to strengthen it, he sent to me later, to Nineveh, my lordly city. (Oriental Institute Prism; see *ANET* 287–88; cf. *COS* 2:300–301)

(In addition to the) 30 talents of gold, 800 talents of silver, (there were) gems (precious stones), antimony, jewels(?), great *sandu*-stones (carnelian?), ivory beds, house chairs of ivory, elephant's hides, ivory (elephant's tusks, teeth), maple, boxwood, colored (woolen) garments, garments of linen, violet and purple wool, vessels of copper, iron, bronze and lead, iron, chariots, shields, lances, armor, girdle daggers of iron, bows and arrows, spears, countless implements of war, together with his daughters, his palace women, his male and female musicians (which) he had (them) bring after me to Nineveh, my royal city. To pay tribute and to render servitude, he dispatched his messenger(s).

From the booty of those lands which I plundered, 10,000 bows, 10,000 shields I took therefrom and added them to my royal equipment. The rest, the heavy spoil of enemy (captives), I divided like sheep among my whole camp (army) as well as my governors and the inhabitants of my large cities. (Rassam Cylinder, *ARAB* II §284)

and reports only that he personally captured alive Egyptian charioteers and princes and also the charioteers of the king of Ethiopia. Perhaps it was at this time or even before the battle that Hezekiah decided to capitulate, offer his confession, and make assurance of future loyalty. Padi, the king of Ekron, was released by Hezekiah and restored to his throne. With Hezekiah's capitulation, the Assyrian monarch imposed an indemnity on him.

The capture of the Judean city of Lachish, the most important town in the Shephelah, although unmentioned in his texts, was depicted on a wall relief in Sennacherib's palace at Nineveh (see Photograph 68).[36] The king is shown seated, reviewing the captives leaving and the booty carried from the city.[37]

36. See David Ussishkin, *The Conquest of Lachish by Sennacherib* (Tel Aviv: Tel Aviv University Press, 1982); and J. M. Russell, *Sennacherib's Palace without Rival at Nineveh* (Chicago: University of Chicago Press, 1991). Cushites figure prominently in Sennacherib's depiction of Lachish; see R. D. Barnett et al., *Sculptures from the South-West Palace of Sennacherib at Nineveh* (2 vols.; London: British Museum, 1998) 2:322–52. On the more recent excavations at Lachish, see David Ussishkin, *The Renewed Archaeological Excavations at Lachish 1973–1994* (5 vols.; Tel Aviv: Institute of Archaeology of Tel Aviv University, 2004).

37. Pictured among the spoils are some large incense burners. These have been taken as indicating the presence of a temple in the city. The burning of incense, however, was not prohibited in the law of centralization in Deut. 12 and continued to be offered away from temple precincts; see Milgrom, *JSOT* 88 (2000) 59–76.

68. *Sennacherib at Lachish.* This scene, which adorned the Assyrian royal palace, shows the Assyrian king seated on his throne, receiving the booty from his conquest of Lachish; citizens of Lachish kneel in homage to him. The cuneiform inscription reads: "Sennacherib, king of the world, king of Assyria, sat upon a *nimedu-*throne and passed in review the booty from Lachish." (*The British Museum*)

Destruction levels at numerous sites in the Shephelah indicate the widespread havoc wrought by the Assyrians. In the vicinity of Jerusalem, the sites of Ramat Rahel to the south and Tel el-Ful to the north show destruction levels. Occupation in the Shephelah was reduced drastically.

Results and Aftermath of the Invasion. Before leaving Syria-Palestine, Sennacherib consolidated matters so as to preserve Assyrian interests in the area. The rulers in the rebellious kingdoms were replaced with loyal vassals. Ethbaal had been placed on the throne in Sidon, the usurper Sidqia was deported to Assyria and the son of a former ruler installed as a vassal, Padi was returned to Ekron, and Hezekiah was left on the Judean throne after agreeing that he had "done wrong" and was willing to bear whatever the king imposed on him (see 2 Kgs. 18:14). That is, none of the kingdoms was transformed into an Assyrian province as one might have expected. This was consistent with earlier Assyrian policy in which the seaport kingdoms and Judah along with Moab, Ammon, and Edom had been left as semi-independent kingdoms with kings from the ruling families or local populations. As we have seen, Assyria was always hesitant to take over directly the Phoenician and Philistine seaport kingdoms and probably saw Judah and the Transjordanian states as buffer kingdoms best left semi-independent. Hezekiah may have been left on the throne not only because he offered apologies, swore allegiance, and paid imposed fines but also because there may have been no ready suitable candidate from his immediate family to take over the throne. His successor and son Manasseh, whose name, given some few years earlier (ca. 710), may reflect Hezekiah's territorial aspirations to take over the north, would have been a very young lad at the time.

Portions of Judean territory were removed from Hezekiah and given or returned to the Philistine rulers of Ashdod, Ekron, Gaza, and perhaps Ashkelon. Some Philistine cities subsequently underwent drastic economic recovery. At Tel Miqne (Ekron) remains of a vast olive-oil production complex have been excavated, indicating the consolidation of this industry in the town but drawing upon olive production from throughout the region.[38] Citizens

38. See Seymour Gitin, "Ekron of the Philistines—Part 2: Olive Oil Suppliers to the World," *BAR* 16/2 (1990) 32–42; David Eitam, "The Olive Oil Industry at Tel Miqne-Ekron during the Late Iron Age," and Seymour Gitin, "Tel Miqne-Ekron in the 7th Century B.C.: City Plan Development and the Oil Industry," in D. Eitam and M. Heltzer, eds., *Olive Oil in Antiquity* (History of the Ancient Near East 7; Padova: Sargon, 1996) 167–96, 219–43.

were exiled; Sennacherib claims to have taken 200,150 persons as booty (*COS* 2:303), but this figure seems exceptionally large if it is understood as referring to persons actually deported. Sennacherib's inscriptions do note the dispersement of captives but do not stipulate their number (see above, Text 12). The redistribution of territory and the possible assignment of portions of Hezekiah's territory to various Philistine rulers restored political equilibrium in the area, so that no ruler had a balance of power in his favor. Hezekiah paid thirty talents of gold, eight hundred talents of silver, and many valuables as indemnity. This was sent to Nineveh, along "with daughters, his palace women, and his male and female singers" (*COS* 2:303).[39]

Jerusalem's escape from Assyrian devastation was recalled in Hebrew tradition as a fulfillment of Isaiah's prophecy and was retold, like the Egyptian version of its battle with Sennacherib, in legendary form as a time of miraculous deliverance wrought by divine intervention.

Hezekiah's reign had had its moments of glory and hope but also its tragedies and calamities. The nation had temporarily enjoyed the favor of the Assyrian court especially in the period 720–712, and shared in the trade and commerce of the region. Judah's territory had extended from the Jordan to the Mediterranean, and it had shared in the life of the southern extremities of the Assyrian Empire. Two revolts, one almost incidental and the other major, however, had led to an enormous reduction of Judah's territory and influence. Once again, the Davidic kingdom became a backwater client state.

The invasion of Sennacherib was the final blow in what had been fifty years of almost constant turmoil and warfare in Judah. The earlier civil war between the anti-Assyrian Pekah and the pro-Assyrian Samaria and Jerusalem had been accompanied and followed by encroachment on Samarian and Jerusalemite territories by members of the anti-Assyrian coalition. This was then followed by successive waves of Assyrian invaders leaving death and destruction in their wake. Loss of land holdings, disruption in the clan and social structures, movements of refugees, and the general impoverishment of the population must have produced social trauma on a grand scale.

Manasseh

The son of Hezekiah, Manasseh (698–644), became king at the age of twelve and enjoyed the longest reign—fifty-five years—of any monarch in the history of Israel and Judah. If we assume the essential accuracy of the regnal periods recorded for the Judean kings of this time, Hezekiah would have died at the age of about fifty-four, only a few years after resubmitting to Assyrian vassalage. That Hezekiah was already forty-two years old when his successor was born seems most unusual. Sennacherib mentions that Hezekiah's daughters were sent to live at Nineveh but makes no mention of sons. Whether Manasseh was the oldest or only (or the only surviving) son or even grandson of Hezekiah (see 2 Kgs. 20:18), or whether Assyrian pressure was applied to bypass

---

39. The biblical list of tribute in 2 Kgs. 18:14b is somewhat smaller. For the possibility that this may have been indemnity paid in 712–711, see Goldberg, *Bib* 80 (1999) 360–90.

older potential heirs because of previous or possible involvement in the recent rebellion, or whether he was chosen because he was considered to be a "safe" heir by the pro-Assyrian party in Judah cannot be determined. At any rate, his case is unusual.

The youthful Manasseh inherited a reduced and war-torn Judean state.[40] Evidence from Assyrian inscriptions, archaeological data, and some indications in the biblical traditions provide a partial picture of the conditions (see above, Text 12). (1) Sennacherib reports that he had conquered forty-six cities controlled by Hezekiah as well as countless small villages. Even if one allows for some Assyrian exaggeration and assumes that some of these cities were Philistine towns that Hezekiah had occupied temporarily, the devastation in western and southwestern Judah must have been enormous.[41] (2) Sennacherib claims that 200,150 people in Hezekiah's kingdom were counted as Assyrian booty. This figure appears to be an exaggeration even if one assumes that the reference is to the total head count of the cities and villages that Sennacherib captured or even the population of the region rather than to the actual deportees. No claim is made that all of these people were taken into exile or deported, but the population drain on the state must have been great. (3) Portions of Judean territory were removed from Hezekiah's control and turned over to the several Philistine kings. This must not only have disrupted the population in these areas, creating numerous refugees, but also have reduced state resources and income. Assyrian texts refer to Manasseh as "king of the city of Judah," implying he ruled over a city-state kingdom. (4) The continuing payment of tribute was a great economic burden for the impoverished state.

Little is known about the course of historical events in Judah during the more than half century that Manasseh ruled. The editors of the biblical traditions in Kings were content primarily to theologize about his reign.[42] Second Kings 21:1–18 provides only the bare minimum of facts—age at accession, length of reign, mother's name (v. 1)—and then begins to tick off in staccato fashion all his apostate ways (vv. 2–9), following this with a theologizing tirade—which begins with a condemnatory *because*—blaming the fall of Jerusalem and the end of Judah on his reign (vv. 10–15). One last swipe is taken in the description of his shedding innocent blood (v. 16) before he is laid to rest with the typical formulaic statements for concluding the account of a king's

---

40. See Israel Finkelstein, "The Archaeology of the Days of Manasseh," in M. D. Coogan et al., eds., *Scripture and Other Artifacts: Essays on the Bible and Archaeology in Honor of Philip J. King* (Louisville: Westminster John Knox, 1994) 169–87; A. F. Rainey, "Manasseh, King of Judah, in the Whirlpool of the Seventh Century B.C.E.," in Rainey, ed., *"kinattūtu ša dārâti": Raphael Kutscher Memorial Volume* (Tel Aviv Occasional Publications 1; Tel Aviv: Tel Aviv University Press, 1993) 147–64; Ehud Ben-Zvi, "Prelude to a Reconstruction of the Historical Manassic Judah," *BN* 81 (1996) 31–44; and Avraham Faust and Ehud Weiss, "Judah, Philistia, and the Mediterranean World: Reconstructing the Economic System of the Seventh Century B.C.E.," *BASOR* 338 (2005) 71–92.

41. See Blakely and Hardin, "Southwestern Judah," who argue that some of the destruction levels in southwestern and southern Judah, normally assigned to Sennacherib's campaign, were more likely the consequence of Tiglath-pileser's 734–733 activity in the area.

42. See Ehud Ben-Zvi, "The Account of the Reign of Manasseh in II Reg 21:1–18 and the Redactional History of the Book of Kings," *ZAW* 103 (1991) 355–74; W. M. Schniedewind, "The Source Citations of Manasseh: King Manasseh in History and Homily," *VT* 41 (1991) 450–61; P. S. F. van Keulen, *Manasseh through the Eyes of the Deuteronomists* (OtSt 38; Leiden: Brill, 1996); and Baruch Halpern, "Why Manasseh Was Blamed for the Babylonian Exile: The Revolution of a Biblical Tradition," *VT* 48 (1998) 473–514.

reign (vv. 17–18). Since the compilers of the material laid on him the blame for the ultimate fall of Jerusalem, they could say nothing good about his reign.

The Chronicler's account differs somewhat. Beginning with a restatement of the material in Kings (2 Chr. 33:1–9), the Chronicler reports that Manasseh was taken by the Assyrians to Babylon, where he was released after praying to Yahweh for forgiveness. He subsequently became a religious reformer (vv. 9–10, 15–17). In addition, the Chronicler notes that the king carried out certain building and military projects (v. 16). Since the Chronicler has Manasseh repent, Judah's fall could not be blamed on him. The Chronicler seems to have found it unbelievable that a Judean king could be blessed with the longest reign in the state's history without being or becoming a crusading Yahwist.

During the reign of Manasseh, Judah played no consequential role in international affairs. Although Manasseh's reign overlapped those of three Assyrian kings, his name makes an appearance in their inscriptions only in lists. Such scarcity of nonbiblical data about him parallels the paucity of biblically supplied information. This lack of data means that to understand Manasseh's reign at all we must look at the larger history of the period and note where Manasseh is mentioned in nonbiblical texts and where Judean life impinged on that of the larger Assyrian world.

Pax Assyriaca

Three factors about Assyrian history during this period are noteworthy and form the backdrop for understanding Judean history. (1) During Manasseh's reign, Assyrian power was at its apogee. Compared with the eighth century, the first three-quarters of the seventh century under the Pax Assyriaca were rather tranquil times in the Middle East. This does not mean that Assyria enjoyed an era completely free from troubles. It certainly did not. In the northwest, Anatolian regions were rebellious; in the east and southeast, Babylon, Elam, and the Arabs were constant troublemakers; and in the west and southwest, the Phoenician and Philistine states and the Ethiopian rulers of Egypt had to be dealt with. (2) During the seventh century, Assyria increasingly sought to control maritime commerce along the eastern Mediterranean seaboard. In many ways, this intensified Assyrian interest in and domination of the area. (3) Assyria was particularly involved with the rulers of Egypt throughout this period, although the relationship between the two kingdoms varied from hostility during the time of the Twenty-fifth Dynasty when Egypt was controlled by Ethiopian rulers, to friendship and mutual support after the Assyrian-backed native Egyptian Twenty-sixth Dynasty came to dominance.

The early years of Manasseh's rule apparently witnessed no renewed campaign of the Assyrian king Sennacherib into the Syro-Palestinian area. Sennacherib was involved for years with rebellions in Anatolia, Elam, and Babylon. Only in 696 was Sennacherib able to move against rebellious Anatolian provinces. Further campaigns in this area occurred after 689. Troubles with Babylonia finally culminated in Sennacherib's vicious destruction of the city of Babylon in 689 (see *COS* 2:305). A single fragmentary inscription from his reign speaks of an Assyrian campaign against certain Arab rulers, but neither their location nor the nature of the trouble is clear. Sennacherib's rule came to an end

69. *Esarhaddon's Victory Stela.* Victory Stela from Sam'al (Zinçirli) in present-day Turkey, commemorating Esarhaddon's victory over Egypt. Basalt, 3.22 by 1.35 m. (*Vorderasiatische Museum, Berlin*)

when, according to the Babylonian Chronicles (*ABC* 81), he was killed by one of his sons in a rebellion (see 2 Kgs. 19:36–37). The short-lived fraternal six-week civil war in Assyria, which followed Sennacherib's murder, was speedily squelched by the crown prince Esarhaddon, apparently without any major repercussions throughout the empire.

Esarhaddon (680–669) moved quickly to display his authority and Assyrian might in the west.[43] The Ethiopian leaders in Egypt must actually have been, or were suspected of, stirring up trouble in Syria-Palestine. In 679, shortly after solidifying his rule, Esarhaddon plundered the city of Arsa on the Egyptian border, deporting its ruler Ashuli, who, along with his advisers, was displayed like a caged animal in Nineveh, the Assyrian capital (*ANET* 290). This expedition would have had two purposes. First, it reaffirmed Assyrian control over the eastern Mediterranean seaboard as far as the Brook of Egypt, which the Assyrians had claimed since Tiglath-pileser III had set up a victory stela there in 733. Second, it was a warning to the leaders of the Ethiopian dynasty to keep hands off Syria-Palestine and to confine itself to its borders. Egypt at the time was under the control of the aggressive Ethiopian king Tirhakah (ca. 690–664), who had participated, but apparently not as pharaoh, in the battle of Eltekeh

43. Esarhaddon's inscriptions have been edited in Riekele Borger, *Die Inschriften Asarhaddons, Königs von Assyrien* (AfO 9; Graz: Weidner, 1956); hereafter abbreviated as *IAKA*. On Esarhaddon's career see Erle Leichty, "Esarhaddon, King of Assyria," *CANE* 2:949–58.

70. *Tirhakah.* The last ruler of the Cushite Twenty-fifth Dynasty, Tirhakah reigned from about 690 to 664. This was a Negroid dynasty that held sway over all of Egypt and even threatened the Assyrian Empire in Asia. (*Carlos Museum, Emory University*)

in 701 (2 Kgs. 19:9). Tirhakah was already intervening in Syro-Palestinian matters during the last years of Sennacherib.

Esarhaddon's show of force on the Egyptian border was followed by other actions, which asserted Assyrian dominance in the eastern Mediterranean. Assyrian suzerainty over Cyprus was reestablished or reaffirmed (*ANET* 291). Campaigns were conducted against the Phoenician cities of Sidon and Tyre (*ANET* 290–91). Abdimilkutte king of Sidon, along with his ally Sanduarri king of Kundi, was captured, decapitated, and his head paraded in triumph in Nineveh (*ABC* 83). His family, possessions, and many of his subjects were deported. In the vicinity of Sidon, Kar-Esarhaddon ("fort of Esarhaddon") was constructed as a commercial and administrative center, with an Assyrian commissioner appointed to oversee the region. Esarhaddon reports that he "called together all the kings of the country Hatti and from the seacoast and made them build a town on a new location, calling its name Kar-Esarhaddon" (*ANET* 291). Among these "kings of the country Hatti" would have been Manasseh, king of Judah.

The destruction of Sidon was followed by an attempt to consolidate affairs with Tyre. A treaty between Baal king of Tyre and Esarhaddon was concluded (*ANET* 533–34; *NATLO* 24–27). The treaty restricted Tyrian freedom somewhat, requiring that all Assyrian correspondence to the court be read in the presence of an Assyrian commissioner and giving Assyria possession of any Tyrian ships wrecked along the eastern Mediterranean seaboard. At the same time, the treaty granted Baal control of the trade along the coast as far south as Philistia.

TEXT 13. Excerpts from Esarhaddon's Vassal Treaty

(This is) the treaty of Esarhaddon, king of the world, king of Assyria, son of Sennacherib, likewise king of the world, king of Assyria, with Ramataya, city-ruler of Urakazabanu, with his sons, grandsons, with all the people of Urakazabanu, (all the men under his command) young and old, from sunrise (east) to sunset (west), all those over whom Esarhaddon, king of Assyria, acts as king and lord; with you, your sons, your grandsons, all those who will live in the future after this treaty. . . .

(This is) the treaty which Esarhaddon, king of Assyria, has established with you before the great gods of heaven and earth, on behalf of the crown prince designate Ashurbanipal, the son of your lord Esarhaddon, king of Assyria, who has designated and appointed him for succession. When Esarhaddon, king of Assyria, departs from the living, you will seat the crown prince designate Ashurbanipal upon the royal throne, he will exercise the kingship and overlordship of Assyria over you. (If) you do not serve him in the open country and in the city, do not fight and even die on his behalf, do not always speak the full truth to him, do not always advise him well in full loyalty, do not smooth his way in every respect; if you remove him, and seat in his stead one of his brothers, younger or older, on the throne of Assyria, if you change or let anyone change the decree of Esarhaddon, king of Assyria, if you will not be subject to this crown prince designate Ashurbanipal, son of Esarhaddon, king of Assyria, your lord, so that he cannot exercise kingship and lordship over you—

If you do not always offer complete truth to the crown prince designate Ashurbanipal whom Esarhaddon, king of Assyria, has presented to you, as well as to the brothers by the mother of the crown prince designate Ashurbanipal, concerning whom Esarhaddon, king of Assyria, has established this treaty with you; if you do not treat them with proper loyalty, speak to them with a true heart, and serve them in the open country and in the city. . . .

If any (of you) hears some wrong, evil, unseemly plan which is improper or detrimental to the crown prince designate Ashurbanipal, son of your lord Esarhaddon, king of Assyria, whether they be spoken by his enemy or his ally, by his brothers, by his sons, by his daughters, his father's brothers, his cousins, or any other member of his father's lineage, or by your own brothers, sons, or daughters, or by a prophet, an ecstatic, a dream-interpreter, or by any human being whatsoever, and conceals it, does not come and report it to the crown prince designate Ashurbanipal, son of Esarhaddon, king of Assyria. . . .

If anyone instigates you to a revolt or rebellion against the crown prince designate Ashurbanipal, son of your lord Esarhaddon, king of Assyria, concerning whom he has established (this) treaty with you, in order to kill, harm and destroy him, and you, upon hearing such a thing from anybody, do not seize the instigators of the revolt, do not bring them before the crown prince designate Ashurbanipal, (and) if you, being able to seize and kill them, do not seize and kill them, do not eradicate their name and descendants from the country, or, being unable to seize and kill them, you do not inform the crown prince designate Ashurbanipal, do not stand by him and seize and kill the instigators of the revolt. . . .

If you do not love the crown prince designate Ashurbanipal, son of your lord Esarhaddon, king of Assyria, as you do your own lives . . .

(if) you do not say and do not give orders to your sons, grandsons, to your offspring, to your descendants, who will live in the future after this treaty, saying: "Keep this treaty, do not sin against this treaty with you, lest you lose your lives, deliver your land to destruction, and your people to be deported. . . ."

May Ashur, king of the gods, who determines the fates, decree for you an evil, unpropitious fate, and not grant you fatherhood, old age. . . .

May Anu, king of the gods, rain upon all your houses disease, exhaustion, *di'u-* disease, sleeplessness, worries, ill health.

May Sin, the luminary of heaven and earth, clothe you in leprosy and (thus) not permit you to enter the presence of god and king; roam the open country as a wild ass or gazelle! . . .

May all the gods who are named in this treaty tablet reduce your soil in size to be as narrow as a brick, turn your soil into iron, so that no one may cut a *furrow* in it.

Just as rain does not fall from a copper sky, so may there come neither rain nor dew upon your fields and meadows, but let it rain burning coals in your land instead of dew. . . .

Just as this ewe is cut open and the flesh of its young placed in its mouth, so may he (Shamash?) make you eat in your hunger the flesh of your brothers, your sons, and your daughters.

Just as (these) yearlings and spring lambs, male and female, are cut open and their entrails are rolled around their feet, so may the entrails of your sons and daughters be rolled around your feet. (*ANET* 534–41)

Esarhaddon also compelled twenty-two kings of Hatti, the seashore, and the islands to "transport under terrible difficulties, to Nineveh, . . . as building material for my palace: big logs, long beams and thin boards from cedar and pine trees, products of the Sirara and Lebanon mountains, which had grown for a long time into tall and strong timber, also from their quarries in the mountains, statues of protective deities" (*ANET* 291). Among these kings forced to provide this corvée labor, Esarhaddon lists Manasseh of Judah.

Assyrian-Egyptian Rapprochement

Esarhaddon's campaigns in Syria-Palestine and his reordering of the life of the Phoenician cities were related to Assyria's attempt to gain complete control over the important sea commerce in the eastern Mediterranean. A clash with the other Mediterranean power in the area, namely, the Ethiopians in control of Egypt, became inevitable. Indeed, two considerations suggest that Ethiopian influence was a factor behind the Phoenician uprisings and that the pharaoh had encouraged and supported Sidon and Tyre. First, two fragmentary Assyrian texts probably from the early years of Esarhaddon refer to Egypt in association with Syro-Palestinian cities and suggest that a conspiracy was afoot. One text associates a "man of Egypt" with Sidon and another connects Tirhakah with Tyre and Ashkelon, and mentions twenty-two unnamed kings, perhaps the western vassals of Assyria (Nahr el-Kelb Stela; see *IAKA* §67). Second, in 673 Esarhaddon invaded Egypt probably to stem Ethiopian influence at its source. Since the campaign was a failure, it goes unmentioned in Assyrian texts. The Babylonian Chronicles, however, report that "on the fifth day of the month Adar the army of Assyria was defeated in Egypt" (*ABC* 84). Prayers of Esarhaddon to the sun-god Shamash that can be related to this campaign have the king inquiring about whether he would encounter the Egyptians at Ashkelon.[44] This suggests that the Ethiopian pharaoh was operative in southern Syria-Palestine and that Esarhaddon's invasion was a response to hostile actions initiated by Tirhakah. At any rate, Esarhaddon's invasion of Egypt represented a radical change in policy for the Assyrians, who had previously been content with confining Egypt within its borders rather than invading the country itself. The Assyrians, however, seem never to have wanted to annex Egypt into their empire.

In his tenth year (671) Esarhaddon again moved into Egypt. This time he was successful against Tirhakah. After fierce fighting, Memphis was taken. Tirhakah escaped to the south, but his wife, harem, brothers, and heir apparent were captured (*ABC* 85). The Assyrian king's goal was achieved temporarily: "All Ethiopians I deported from Egypt—leaving not even one to do homage" (*ANET* 293). By appointing various rulers throughout the land Esarhaddon sought to establish administrative order in Lower Egypt, which at the time was still a patchwork of competing principalities (*ANET* 292). Many of these appointees were already ruling over various political entities. One of those affirmed in office was Neco I, ruler in Sais. Esarhaddon's actions not only sought to establish some form of Assyrian authority in the country but also to affirm in office many native Egyptians whose vested interests would produce greater support for Assyria than for the non-Egyptian Tirhakah. On his return home, Esarhaddon attacked Baal of Tyre, who had not offered the Assyrians aid on the Egyptian campaign but "had relied on Tirhakah." Tyre was then provincialized and placed under direct Assyrian authority (*IAKA* 86, 110). Two years later Esarhaddon set out again for Egypt to confront Tirhakah, who had moved back into the Delta region, but he fell sick on the way and died (*ABC* 86).

The new Assyrian king, Ashurbanipal (668–627), was immediately confronted with problems in Egypt, where Tirhakah had reestablished himself in Memphis and "turned against the kings and regents whom" Esarhaddon "had appointed in Egypt."[45] Ashurbanipal dispatched his military commander to quell the revolt. The vassal kings in the west were mustered to the cause, required to provide troops as well as ships for transportation, and made to accompany the invading army by land and by sea (*ANET* 294). Among these

---

44. For an English translation see Ivan Starr, *Queries to the Sun God: Divination and Politics in Sargonid Assyria* (SAA 4; Helsinki: Helsinki University Press, 1990) texts numbered 81–90, pp. 94–106.

45. The inscriptions of Ashurbanipal have been edited by Maximilian Streck, *Assurbanipal und die letzten assyrischen Könige bis zum Untergang Ninivehs* (3 vols.; Vorderasiatisches Bibliothek 7; Leipzig: Hinrichs, 1916); hereafter abbreviated *Streck*.

TEXT 14. Parallels between Esarhaddon's
Vassal Treaty and Deuteronomy

§24. If you do not love the crown prince designate Ashurbanipal, son of your lord Esarhaddon, king of Assyria, as you do your own lives. . . .

6:5—You shall love Yahweh your God with all your heart, and with all your soul, and with all your might.

§25. If you do not say and do not give orders to your sons, grandsons, to your offspring, to your descendants, who will live in the future after this treaty. . . .

6:7—Recite them to your children and talk about them when you are at home and when you are away, when you lie down and when you rise.

§37. May Ashur, the king of the gods, who determines the fates, decree for you an evil, unpropitious fate and not grant you fatherhood, old age. . . .

28:20—Yahweh will send upon you disaster, panic, and frustration in everything you attempt to do, until you are destroyed and perish quickly, on account of the evil of your deeds. . . .

§39. May Sin, the luminary of heaven and earth, clothe you in leprosy, and (thus) not permit you to enter the presence of god and king; roam the open country as a wild ass or gazelle!

28:27—Yahweh will afflict you with the boils of Egypt, with ulcers, scurvy, and itch, of which you cannot be healed.

§40. May Shamash, the light of heaven and earth, not give you a fair and equitable judgment, may he take away your eyesight; walk about in darkness!

28:28–29—Yahweh will afflict you with madness, blindness, and confusion of mind; you shall grope around at noon as blind people grope in darkness . . . .

§41. May Ninurta, leader of the gods, fell you with his fierce arrow, and fill the plain with your corpses, give your flesh to eagles and vultures to feed upon.

28:26—Your corpses shall be food for every bird of the air and animal of the earth, and there shall be no one to frighten them away.

§42. May Venus, the brightest among the stars, let your wives lie in the embrace of your enemies before your very eyes, may your sons not have authority over your house, may a foreign enemy divide your possessions.

28:30–32—You shall become engaged to a woman, but another man shall lie with her. You shall build a house, but not live in it. You shall plant a vineyard, but not enjoy its fruit. . . . Your sons and daughters shall be given to another people, while you look on; you will strain your eyes looking for them all day but be powerless to do anything.

§47. May Adad, the canal inspector of heaven and earth, put an end [to vegetation] in your land, may he *avoid* your meadows and hit your land with a severe destructive downpour, may locusts, which diminish the (produce) of the land, [devour] your crops, let there be no sound of the grinding stone or the oven in your houses, let barley rations to be ground disappear for you, so that they grind your bones, (the bones of) your sons and daughters instead of barley rations. . . . Mother shall [bar the door to] her daughter, may you eat in hunger the flesh of your children, may, through want and famine, one man eat the other's flesh, clothe himself in the other's skin; let dogs and pigs eat your flesh, and may your spirit have no one to take care of and pour libations to him.

28:47–54—Because you did not serve Yahweh your God joyfully and with gladness of heart. . . . therefore you shall you shall serve your enemies whom Yahweh will send against you, in hunger thirst, in nakedness, and lack of everything. . . . You will eat the fruit of your womb, the flesh of your own sons and daughters whom Yahweh your God has given you. Even the most refined and gentle men among you will begrudge food to his own brother, to the wife whom he embraces, and to the last of his remaining children.

§48. May Ishtar, the lady of battle, break your bow in a heavy battle, tie your arms, and have you crouch at the feet of your enemy.

28:25—Yahweh will cause you to be defeated before your enemies; you shall go out against them one way and flee before them seven ways.

§49. May Nergal, the warrior among the gods, extinguish your life with his merciless dagger, may he plant carnage and pestilence among you.

28:21—Yahweh will make the pestilence cling to you until it has consumed you off the land that you are entering to possess.

§52. May Gula, the great physician, put illness and weariness [into your *hearts*], an unhealing sore in your body, so that you bathe in [your own blood] as if in water.

28:35—Yahweh will strike you on the knees and on the legs with grievous boils of which you cannot be healed, from the sole of your foot to the crown of your head.

§§63–64. May all the gods who are named in this treaty tablet reduce your soil in size to be as narrow as a brick, turn your soil into iron, so that no one may cut a *furrow* in it. Just as rain does not fall from a copper sky, so may there come neither rain nor dew upon your fields and meadows, but let it rain burning coals in your land, instead of dew.

28:23–24—The sky over your head shall be bronze, and the earth under you iron. Yahweh will change the rain of your land into powder, and only dust shall come down upon you from the sky until you are destroyed.

§96. If you abandon Esarhaddon, king of Assyria, or the crown prince designate Ashurbanipal, and disperse right and left, may swords consume the one who goes to the right, and may swords consume the one too who goes to the left.

(ANET 534–41)

5:32—You must therefore be careful to do as Yahweh your God has commanded you; you shall not turn to the right or to the left.

vassals would have been Manasseh king of Judah.[46] Ashurbanipal notes that Neco I and others whom his "father had appointed in Egypt and who had left their offices in the face of the uprising of Tirhakah and had scattered into the open country" were reinstalled. For some reason, many of these appointees subsequently sided temporarily with Tirhakah, but the Assyrians discovered their plotting (*ANET* 294). Although many of these appointees were punished for breaking faith with Assyria, Neco was given special treatment. Ashurbanipal reports the following about the status assigned him:

> From all of them, I had only mercy upon Necho and granted him life. I made (a treaty) with him (protected by) oaths which greatly surpassed (those of the former treaty). I clad him in a garment with multicolored trimmings, placed a golden chain on him (as the) insigne of his kingship, put golden rings on his hands; I wrote my name (phonetically) upon an iron dagger (to be worn in) the girdle, the mounting of which was golden, and gave it to him. I presented him (furthermore) with chariots, horses and mules as means of transportation (befitting) his position as ruler. I sent with him (and) for his assistance, officers of mine as governors. I returned to him Sais as residence (the place) where my own father had appointed him king. Nabushezibanni [Psammetichus I], his son, I appointed for Athribis (thus) treating him with more friendliness and favor than my own father did. (*ANET* 295)

This continued the alliance between the Assyrians and native Egyptians in the Delta that had originally been inaugurated by Sargon. This alliance eventually produced shared rule between Egypt and Assyria in Syria-Palestine and greatly influenced the course of Judean history throughout the seventh century.

Because of the importance of this Egyptian-Assyrian coalition for Judean history, three more factors about Egyptian history in the early decades of the Twenty-sixth (Saite) Dynasty should be noted.

1. Tirhakah's nephew, Tantamani (664–656), assumed leadership in Upper Egypt and invaded the Delta (665/664). The Delta cities, however, all remained loyal to Assyria. Tantamani besieged the Assyrian forces in Memphis. Loyally supporting his Assyrian overlord, Neco I died in battle opposing Tantamani (Herodotus 2.152). Neco's son, Psammetichus I, fled Egypt, taking refuge in

---

46. Deuteronomy 28:68 probably alludes to this event: "Yahweh will bring you back in ships to Egypt, by a route that I promised you would never see again; and there you shall offer yourselves for sale to your enemies as male and female slaves, but there will be no buyer." See D. G. Schley, "'Yahweh Will Cause You to Return to Egypt in Ships' (Deuteronomy XXVIII 68)," *VT* 35 (1985) 369–72. This suggests that the covenant envelope of Deuteronomy dates from the seventh century.

Syria. From there, he accompanied the Assyrian troops on their return to Egypt. Ashurbanipal marched into the Delta, forced the retreat of Tantamani, retook Memphis, and looted and destroyed Thebes, which was a stronghold for the Ethiopian ruler. (Nahum 3:8–10 recalls the impact made by the conquest of Thebes [called "No-amon" in Hebrew].) With the fall of Thebes, Ethiopian authority in the Delta was shattered. Ashurbanipal and the Assyrians could assume the role of liberators in Lower Egypt. Psammetichus I succeeded his father Neco I and enjoyed the good graces of Ashurbanipal. Ethiopian dominance in Egypt was broken, and Egyptian meddling at Assyrian expense in Syria-Palestine was ended.[47]

2. Gradually, Psammetichus I moved to extend his control over the other Egyptian rulers and eventually to unite the country under his rule. He laid claim to the kingship of all Egypt. This does not seem to have represented any break in Assyrian-Egyptian relations. The only reference in Assyrian texts indicating any hostility toward Psammetichus I speaks of the breaking of his agreement reached with Ashurbanipal (*ARAB* II §785). The agreement between the two had apparently called for the continued rule of various kinglets in the Delta whom Psammetichus I moved to dominate. In order to support his efforts toward unification, Psammetichus I utilized external mercenaries. Sometime after 664, Gyges the king of Lydia dispatched troops to Egypt to aid Psammetichus's cause. In one of his inscriptions (*Streck* 20–23; *NATLO* XVIII–XIX), Ashurbanipal refers to this sending of troops to aid Psammetichus, "who had thrown off my yoke." This statement occurs only in the Rassam Cylinder, a late version of Ashurbanipal's annals. Earlier versions of this account about Gyges' relationship to Assyria do not refer to any activity of Psammetichus that could be regarded as anti-Assyrian. The charge seems to have been an indirect accusation leveled against Gyges for propaganda purposes.[48] Gyges' dispatches along with freebooting Greek pirates may be the Hellenic (Ionian and Carian) mercenaries, "the bronze men from the sea," whom Psammetichus I used in suppressing native rivals (Herodotus 2.152). Judeans may also have served in his mercenary forces. The *Letter of Aristeas* (paragraph 13) speaks of Jews who had been sent to Egypt to help Psammetichus in his campaign against the king of the Ethiopians, apparently having been dispatched or carried there by Ashurbanipal in 664. One component of these Jewish troops may have been those later settled as a border guard at Elephantine in Upper Egypt, probably after Psammetichus I's war with Libya in 655–654.

3. With the unification movement by Psammetichus I under way or successful, after a brief period of civil war and a short interlude when rule was shared by a council of twelve leaders (Herodotus 2.147–150; Diodorus 1.66.1–7), Assyrian forces seem to have been withdrawn from Egypt. There is no evidence that they were forced out or that hostile attitudes developed between Assyria and Egypt. Assyrian actions all along suggest that they were never really interested in occupying Egypt or in turning it into an Assyrian province.

---

47. On Psammetichus see A. J. Spalinger, "Psammetichus, King of Egypt," *JARCE* 13 (1976) 13–47; 15 (1978) 49–57.

48. See Mordechai Cogan and Hayim Tadmor, "Gyges and Ashurbanipal: A Study in Literary Transmission," *Or* 46 (1977) 65–85; and A. J. Spalinger, "The Date of the Death of Gyges and Its Historical Implications," *JAOS* 98 (1978) 400–409.

Their primary concern was to establish Assyrian dominance over the commerce of the eastern Mediterranean seaboard. The Twenty-sixth Dynasty apparently acceded to Assyrian hegemony in this area, and Ashurbanipal was willing to allow Psammetichus to govern his own country under terms similar to those established in his earlier treaty with Neco I.

Manasseh and Assyria

Unfortunately the biblical traditions tell us nothing about the participation and reaction of Manasseh and Judah to contemporary events of the day. (Assyria is not even referred to in 2 Kings after the time of Hezekiah.) The situation suggests that Manasseh, like Ahaz before him, was a loyal Assyrian subject.[49] The political realities of the time left him with little choice. During Manasseh's reign, Assyria probably controlled the economic, religious, and political life of Judah with a strong hand. During the eighth century, in the reigns of Ahaz and Hezekiah, Assyria had not intervened in Judah's internal life or regulated its affairs in any extreme fashion. Matters were probably completely different in the seventh century.

A number of factors contributed to these different modes of relationship between Judah and Assyria. All of them help to explain why Judah was far more strongly influenced and dominated by Assyria after the time of Hezekiah's revolt than before.

1. Ahaz had voluntarily submitted to Assyrian hegemony, turning Judah into an Assyrian satellite, and until the death of Sargon II in 705, Hezekiah appears not to have personally challenged the Assyrians seriously. Judean participation in the Ashdod event (714–711) was probably an adventure of Hezekiah's subordinates, undertaken during the king's illness. On the other hand, Manasseh had come to the throne following a major rebellion by Judah, which now would have been placed under more stringent controls.

2. Ahaz's submission to Assyria had come at a time when Assyrian strength under Tiglath-pileser was seriously challenged but not greatly threatened. Manasseh, however, came to the throne in the context of widespread and serious anti-Assyrian rebellion in Syria-Palestine, Anatolia, and Babylonia. Sennacherib in 696 had just begun to take action against the Anatolian vassaldoms and provinces where revolt had ignited after 705, action that later proved to be less than completely successful. Thus it was not a time for the Assyrians to establish conditions in Syria-Palestine that might allow revolt, much less encourage it.

3. The accessions of both Ahaz and Hezekiah had occurred under Assyrian kings who were secure in their rule. Sennacherib's control of parts of his empire was still in question at the time of Manasseh's accession. Where the Assyrians had the opportunity to exercise firm control, as in Judah, they would certainly have done so.

4. Following Hezekiah's defeat, Judah would have been treated as a vassal state rather than a mere satellite, as was the situation earlier. Vassal states were

---

49. See Roy Gane, "The Role of Assyria in the Ancient Near East during the Reign of Manasseh," *AUSS* 35 (1997) 21–32; and Lynn Tatum, "Jerusalem in Conflict: The Evidence for the Seventh-Century B.C.E. Religious Struggle over Jerusalem," in Vaughn and Killebrew, eds., *Jerusalem*, 291–306.

more firmly controlled than satellite states, and it is quite clear from the inscriptions of both Esarhaddon and Ashurbanipal that Manasseh was treated as a vassal.

5. Manasseh may have been handpicked by the Assyrians to succeed Hezekiah. Earlier we noted the issue of Manasseh's age at his accession. Older siblings or relatives may have been bypassed to place the youngster on the throne. This meant, of course, that Assyria, not Judah, was calling the shots. Manasseh's youth would mean that others were running the government initially. This had to be the members of the Judean pro-Assyrian faction aided by Assyrian officials. Although there is no reference to the appointment of an Assyrian high commissioner in Judah after Hezekiah's revolt, the practice of doing so elsewhere might suggest that this was the case here.

6. During the early seventh century, Assyria was deeply involved in conflict with the Ethiopian leadership of Egypt. Imperial Assyrian troops and outposts dotted the terrain of southern Syria-Palestine. Thus during the early seventh century, at such sites as Tell Jemmeh, numerous Assyrian troops bivouacked within a short distance of the Judean capital. In the eighth century this had not been done to the same degree.

7. In the seventh century Esarhaddon exercised great caution about the accession of his son Ashurbanipal to the throne. Esarhaddon himself had secured the throne after his father's assassination but only after a fraternal struggle against his older brothers (*ANET* 289–90). In order to prevent a situation from developing in his reign that could have produced his own assassination or the usurpation of the throne at his death, Esarhaddon made all his subjects submit to a special treaty and loyalty oath (in 672) pledging their fidelity and the suppression of any rebellious sentiments (*ANET* 534–41; see Text 13). This suggests an Assyrian supervision of subject states unparalleled in the eighth century as well as the requirement that vassal states hold firm lines against any seditious activity.

8. In his vassal treaty with subject states, Esarhaddon made his subject rulers swear to fear the god Ashur and to revere and respect Ashur as they did their own god (*ANET* 538 §§34–35).

All of these factors point to a powerful Assyrian influence in and over Judah from the days of Hezekiah's capitulation.[50] This influence can be seen in a number of ways. (1) The negative assessment of Manasseh by the compilers of Kings suggests that he was probably a loyalist to the Assyrians throughout his reign. Submission to Assyria must have been judged by Manasseh to be the only policy in Judah's best interests. (2) The association of non-Yahwistic worship with Manasseh's reign probably indicates that during his rule many Judeans were attracted to Assyrian religion with its worship of the male god Ashur, Ishtar the queen of heaven, and astral deities ("the host of heaven"). (3) Conflict between strict and syncretistic Yahwists and between those advocating anti-Assyrian and pro-Assyrian policies must have existed throughout the final years of Hezekiah's rule and all of Manasseh's reign. Second Kings 21:16 depicts Manasseh as carrying out suppressive policies. The king probably had

50. For the Assyrian impact on the material culture of Palestine, see Ephraim Stern, *Archaeology of the Land of the Bible*, vol. 2: *The Assyrian, Babylonian, and Persian Periods, 732–332 B.C.E.* (ABRL; New York: Doubleday, 2001) 14–41.

no other choice with Assyrian troops in the neighborhood, Assyrian collaborators and informants in his midst, and Assyrian officials, if not an Assyrian commissioner, at his court. Merchants and other classes as well as governmental officials would have ensured that Assyrian interests were well protected in Judah (see Text 9).

In spite of the biblical negativism toward Manasseh, one must conclude that the Manasseh-Assyria relationship produced some benefits for Judah. The years of his reign were apparently a peaceful time in Judah. Participation in the general economy of the empire must have brought a measure of prosperity to the country. In the course of his rule, portions of Judean territory granted to the Philistines seem to have been returned. His grandson Amon was an offspring of Jedidah daughter of Adaiah of Bozkath, a site in the Shephelah. Archaeological evidence suggests that population increased in the Judean highlands and new settlements were established in fringe areas in the south, perhaps associated with Arabian trade.[51]

An Assyrian document listing receipt of annual tribute from Palestinian states probably dates from the time of Manasseh. It notes the following payments: "Two minas of gold from the inhabitants of Bit-Ammon; one mina of gold from the inhabitant of Moab; ten minas of silver from the inhabitants of Judah; . . . of silver from the inhabitants of Edom" (*ANET* 301). Judah's payment was far less than that of either Ammon or Moab and might imply friendly concession toward the kingdom by Assyria.

The biblical charges of apostasy against Manasseh are numerous (2 Kgs. 21:3–7): (1) rebuilt the "high places" that his father Hezekiah had destroyed; that is, he reversed Hezekiah's policy of religious centralization; (2) erected altars for Baal and the host of heaven in the temple courtyard, which probably indicates the practice of syncretistic religion based on older indigenous forms of religion as well as Assyrian astral worship; (3) "made his son pass through fire," perhaps an allusion to child sacrifice (see 2 Kgs. 16:3);[52] (4) "practiced soothsaying and augury, and dealt with mediums and with wizards," perhaps reference to ancestor veneration and consultation of the dead (see Isa. 8:19–20);[53] and (5) placed a carved image of Asherah in the temple, perhaps indicating some form of veneration of a female consort to Yahweh.[54] Inscriptions discovered at Kuntillet Ajrud (in the southern Negeb) and at Khirbet el-Qom (west of the city of Hebron) refer to "Yahweh and his asherah" (*COS* 2:171–73, 179). Many scholars have assumed this to be an indication that Yahweh was worshiped along with a female counterpart, since Asherah appears in

---

51. See Israel Finkelstein, "Horvat Qitmit and the Southern Trade in the Late Iron II," *ZDPV* 108 (1992) 156–70; idem, "Archaeology of the Days."

52. See Jer. 7:31; 19:5; 32:35; Ezek. 16:20–21; 20:25–26; also G. C. Heider, *The Cult of Molek: A Reassessment* (JSOTSup 43; Sheffield: JSOT, 1985); John Day, *Molech: A God of Human Sacrifice in the Old Testament* (Cambridge: Cambridge University Press, 1989); and Francesca Stavrakopoulou, *King Manasseh and Child Sacrifice* (BZAW 338; Berlin: de Gruyter, 2004).

53. See T. J. Lewis, *Cults of the Dead in Ancient Israel and Ugarit* (HSM 39; Atlanta: Scholars Press, 1989); and Elizabeth Block-Smith, "The Cult of the Dead in Judah: Interpreting the Material Remains," *JBL* 111 (1992) 213–24.

54. See Tilde Binger, *Asherah: Goddesses in Ugarit, Israel and the Old Testament* (JSOTSup 232; Sheffield: Sheffield Academic Press, 1997); and J. M. Hadley, *The Cult of Asherah in Ancient Israel and Judah: Evidence for a Hebrew Goddess* (University of Cambridge Oriental Publications 57; Cambridge: Cambridge University Press, 2000).

Ugaritic texts as a consort to the male god El and there are frequent references in the Hebrew Bible to an Asherah or Asherahs that the NRSV generally translates as "sacred pole(s)" or "pillars" (see Exod. 23:24; 34:13; Deut. 12:3; 1 Kgs. 14:15, 23, etc.). Others have concluded that the asherah was merely some cultic object, perhaps a remnant of the veneration of sacred trees or groves. Associated with the issue of worship of a divine female consort to Yahweh is the presence of scores of clay figurines discovered from this period throughout Judah but especially in the Jerusalem area.[55] Although comprising a variety of forms, the most common is that of a nude upper torso of a female holding her breasts with her hands. Far fewer in number are those of a male rider on a horse. At least the former may have been connected in some way with religion and the veneration of a female deity.

For three reasons, uncertainty exists about how seriously to take the charges leveled against Manasseh. First, the writers of 2 Kings wished to depict him as so religiously villainous that the fall of Jerusalem could be blamed on him (see 21:10–15). Second, the writers, influenced by the laws of Deuteronomy, accused Manasseh of breaking many of the religious prohibitions found in that book (see Deut. 4:19; 7:5; 16:3, 21; 18:9–11; 21:6; etc.). Third, many of the practices referred to may have been remnants of earlier folk religion and not necessarily inspired by Manasseh.[56]

During Manasseh's reign, the Sargonic kings were obsessed with loyalty to themselves and their designated successors. Sennacherib had designated the younger Esarhaddon as his successor and swore the people of Assyria to respect his choice (see *IAKA* 40; *NATLO* XXVIII, 18). After his father's assassination, when Esarhaddon's rule was challenged by his brothers, he appears to have resolved to put everyone under oath to respect his designation of his son Ashurbanipal as future king of Assyria and his son Shamash-shum-ukin as future king of Babylon. Vassal states and the Assyrian population were sworn to fidelity under the threat of severe curses (see Text 13). After Esarhaddon died and was succeeded by Ashurbanipal, the latter's grandmother, Queen Zakutu, required the entire population to swear a loyalty oath and treaty: "with [Ashurbanipal's] brothers, with the royal seed, with the magnates and the governors, the bearded and the eunuchs, the royal entourage, with the exempts and all who enter the palace, with Assyrians high and low" (*NATLO* 62–64). The influence of such loyalty oaths with their stipulations, conditions, and threats probably formed the paradigm for the covenant form of the book of Deuteronomy produced during the reign of Manasseh.

Manasseh in Babylon?

Scholars have labored long and hard to authenticate the tradition about Manasseh found in 2 Chronicles 33:10–13, which reports that "the commanders of the army of the king of Assyria . . . took Manasseh captive in manacles, bound

---

55. See Raz Kletter, *The Judaean Pillar Figurines and the Archaeology of the Asherah* (Oxford: Tempus Raparatum, 1996); Stern, *Archaeology*, 2:205–11; and Ryan Byrne, "Lie Back and Think of Judah: The Reproductive Politics of Pillar Figurines," *NEA* 67 (2004) 137–51.

56. See Jacob Milgrom, "The Nature and Extent of Idolatry in Eighth-Seventh Century Judah," *HUCA* 69 (1998) 1–13.

him with fetters, and brought him to Babylon." Attempts have been made to associate this episode with some known event in the king's career: the rebellion of Sidon in 677/676 during the reign of Esarhaddon, the treaty-swearing conclave held in 672, when many Egyptian rulers sided with Tirhakah (*ANET* 294); the rebellion of Baal king of Tyre in 668/667 against Ashurbanipal (*ANET* 295–96); the period of major Assyrian trouble with the Arabs in the 640s (*ANET* 297–98); the rebellion in Babylon of Ashurbanipal's brother Shamash-shum-ukin in 652–648; or the troubles with Elam in 654–646. None of these efforts has been successful, and 2 Kings suggests that no major changes took place during Manasseh's reign; he was probably not, nor did he become, a Yahwistic reformer (2 Chr. 33:12–13, 15–16; but note 33:22, which implies the continued existence of Manasseh's unacceptable altars and images into the region of Amon). The Chronicler's account may be based on an inherited tradition that told of Manasseh's conversion and even contained his presumed prayer of repentance (see the later "Prayer of Manasseh" in the Apocrypha). Such a tradition reflects what may have been a common Near Eastern folklore motif of the bad king who changes his course of action after some intervening significant event (see the books of Esther and Daniel and the Nabonidus text from Qumran).[57]

Amon

Manasseh was succeeded on the throne by his twenty-two-year-old son Amon (643–642), whose name has been associated frequently with the Egyptian sun-god Amun and who, according to our chronology, would have been born about the time that Ashurbanipal and his western vassals defeated the Egyptians (664/663). Amon was assassinated after a two-year reign (2 Kgs. 21:19–26; 2 Chr. 33:21–25). The biblical text provides the historian with little information about his reign. He is said to have followed the syncretistic religious policies of his father. Amon was killed by his "servants," that is, royal officials. After his death, "the people of the land" intervened and executed those who had conspired against Amon. They then placed his eight-year-old son Josiah on the throne.

Nothing is known about the details of this court conspiracy or about the plans of the people of the land.[58] Were these events inspired by groups who sought change in the cultic and religious life of Judah? Or was it an effort to stifle anti-Assyrian sentiments and preserve the status quo? Or was there some attempted palace coup by other and older sons of Manasseh, who would have been forty-five years old when Amon was born? Or were the assassins inspired by a nationalistic surge that thought the time had come to be done with submission? The historian must simply admit that the course and cause of the events remain a mystery.

---

57. For a defense of the historicity of Manasseh's Babylonian episode and his construction work and reforming activities see Rainey, "Manasseh," who concludes that Josiah simply continued the reforming activity already begun by Manasseh.

58. See Abraham Malamat, "The Historical Background of the Assassination of Amon, King of Judah," *IEJ* 3 (1953) 26–29; repr. in his *History of Biblical Israel: Major Problems and Minor Issues* (CHANE 7; Leiden: Brill, 2001) 277–81.

General Bibliography

The general history of Palestine during this period is discussed in Moshe Elat, "The Political Status of the Kingdom of Judah Within the Assyrian Empire in the 7th Century B.C.E.," in Yohanan Aharoni, ed., *Investigations at Lachish: The Sanctuary and the Residency (Lachish V)* (Tel Aviv: Gateway Publishers, 1975) 61–70; C. D. Evans, "Judah's Foreign Policy from Hezekiah to Josiah," in C. D. Evans et al., eds., *Scripture in Context: Essays on the Comparative Method* (Pittsburgh: Pickwick, 1980) 157–78; and Richard Nelson, "*Realpolitik* in Judah (687–609 B.C.E.)," in W. W. Hallo et al., eds., *Scripture in Context II: More Essays on the Comparative Method* (Winona Lake, IN: Eisenbrauns, 1983) 177–89.

The impact of Assyrian exchange of populations on Judean history is explored by Nadav Na'aman and Ran Zadok, "Sargon II's Deportations to Israel and Philistia (716–708 B.C.)," *JCS* 40 (1988) 36–46; Nadav Na'aman, "Population Changes in Palestine Following Assyrian Deportations," *TA* 20 (1993) 104–24; repr. in *AIIN*, 200–219; and Stephen Stohlmann, "The Judaean Exile after 701 B.C.E.," in Hallo et al., eds., *Scripture in Context II*, 147–75.

The general archaeology of this era is surveyed in Gabriel Barkay, "The Iron Age II-III," in Amnon Ben-Tor, ed., *The Archaeology of Ancient Israel in the Biblical Period* (New Haven: Yale University Press, 1992) 302–73; and Ephraim Stern, *Archaeology of the Land of the Bible*, vol. 2: *The Assyrian, Babylonian, and Persian Periods, 732–332 B.C.E.* (ABRL; New York: Doubleday, 2001) 130–215. On excavations in Jerusalem see Nahman Avigad, *Discovering Jerusalem* (Nashville: Nelson, 1983); Hillel Geva, ed., *Ancient Jerusalem Revealed: Expanded Edition 2000* (Jerusalem: Israel Exploration Society, 2000); idem, "Western Jerusalem at the End of the First Temple Period in Light of the Excavations in the Jewish Quarter," in A. G. Vaughn and A. E. Killebrew, eds., *Jerusalem in Bible and Archaeology: The First Temple Period* (SBLSymS 18; Leiden: Brill, 2003) 183–208 (with bibliography).

14. The Last Years of the Davidic Kingdom

The story of the final years of the Davidic state of Judah forms one subplot in a large drama that involved most of the kingdoms in the Middle East. The major actors in this drama were the three great Near Eastern powers of the day, Assyria, Babylon, and Egypt. Minor but important roles were played by the Cimmerians, the Medes, and the Scythians, and a host of other characters with their bit parts.

Chronologically, this drama covers the final four decades of the seventh (640–600 B.C.E.) and the first decade and a half of the sixth century (600–586). Near the beginning of this period, Judah experienced a brief time of religious reform under King Josiah (641–610). The Davidic state, however, was swiftly sucked into the maelstrom of international affairs from which it was never able to extricate itself. Of its last five Davidic kings, two met their deaths in direct connection with international struggles and the other three died in foreign exile.

Sources for the Period

In comparison with other epochs in Israelite and Judean history, the written source material for this period is reasonably abundant. This includes both biblical and nonbiblical texts. The biblical texts, still our primary source of information about the specifics of Judean history, include the accounts in 2 Kings and 2 Chronicles as well as several prophetical books.

The Accounts in 2 Kings and 2 Chronicles

At the end of this period, that is, with the fall of Jerusalem and with the Judean kings Jehoiachin and Zedekiah in exile, the account of Israelite and Judean history in 2 Kings draws to a close. As the compilers of 1–2 Kings moved in their narration to the reign of Josiah and the exile, they moved nearer to the period of their own day or of the recent past.

Josiah is depicted in 2 Kings 22:1–23:30 as one of the most righteous rulers that either of the two kingdoms ever produced, and earlier events tend to be both depicted and interpreted in the light of events described during his reign. This has influenced the narratives and the content of Joshua–2 Kings in various ways. (1) Many of the preceding reigns—for example, that of Manasseh (2 Kgs. 21)—are depicted as more apostate and unproductive than was probably the case. By deprecating Manasseh, the editors sought to demonstrate the radically different character of Josiah's reign. This endeavor reflects a fairly common Near Eastern pattern in which predecessors are deprecated in order to demonstrate the greatness of the "good," current, or ideal ruler. (2) The reign of Josiah, or portions of it, are depicted as embodying the ideals and programs of the editors. That is, certain factors and impulses in Josiah's reign that became the religious commitments of the editorial compilers were portrayed as the dominant characteristics of his reign. (3) The account of the division of the kingdom of Solomon has been made to focus on the apostate sanctuary at Bethel and anticipates the time when Josiah would destroy it (compare 1 Kgs. 13:1–10 with 2 Kgs. 23:15–18). (4) Each of the kings of both kingdoms has been evaluated with the purification of the cult and the centralization of worship in Jerusalem, considered the hallmarks of Josiah's reign, as the criteria.

The above considerations point, first, to the enormous impact that the compilers' view of Josiah had on the final editing of the books of Kings. Josiah is given such high marks by the compilers of 2 Kings, and his death at Megiddo seems so completely out of step with the theological principle that otherwise pervades much of Joshua–2 Kings (or Deuteronomy–2 Kings)[1]—namely, that a leader's or king's faithfulness to Yahweh would be rewarded by Yahweh's protection and support—that many scholars think an original edition of this material must have been compiled during Josiah's reign, before his untimely death and that later, after the fall of Judah, the account was expanded to cover the reigns of Jehoahaz II, Jehoiakim, Jehoiachin, and Zedekiah.[2] Second, the portrait of Josiah in 2 Kings goes out of its way to depict him as the ideal ruler who embodied and exemplified the religious commitments of the editors; therefore, it must be used with caution by the historian.

The Chronicler's account of Josiah's reform (2 Chr. 34–35) contains some radical deviations from the Kings account. This is partly due to its treatment of the reigns of the preceding kings Hezekiah and Manasseh. Hezekiah is already shown as not only carrying out a cleansing of the Jerusalem temple (29:3–19) and the restoration of worship there (29:20–36) since Ahaz had closed down the temple (28:24–25), but also as celebrating a special Passover (chap. 30), destroying illicit places of worship throughout Judah, Benjamin, Ephraim, and Manasseh (31:1), and reorganizing the priests and Levites (31:11–21). After his repentance (33:10–13), Manasseh is said to have purged the temple, its environs, and the city of Jerusalem of their illicit religious paraphernalia and practices (33:15–17). Thus much of what 2 Kings attributes to Josiah was already carried out earlier according to 2 Chronicles. In addition, the specifics of Josiah's reform, reported in 2 Chronicles, differ from the 2 Kings account and will be noted below.

---

1. This constitutes what is called the Deuteronomistic History. For an examination of the issues related to the theories about this work, see Thomas Römer and Albert de Pury, "Deuteronomistic Historiography (DH): History of Research and Debated Issues," in de Pury et al., eds., *Israel Constructs Its History: Deuteronomistic Historiography in Recent Research* (JSOTSup 306; Sheffield: Sheffield Academic Press, 2000) 24–141; and Thomas Römer, *The So-Called Deuteronomistic History: Sociological, Historical and Literary Introduction* (London: T. & T. Clark, 2006).

2. See F. M. Cross, "The Themes of the Books of Kings and the Structure of the Deuteronomistic History," in *Canaanite Myth and Hebrew Epic* (Cambridge: Harvard University Press, 1973) 274–89; and R. D. Nelson, *The Double Redaction of the Deuteronomistic History* (JSOTSup 18; Sheffield: JSOT Press, 1981).

The Prophetical Books

In addition to the prophetical book of Nahum, which gloats over the (actual or anticipated) fall of the Assyrian capital at Nineveh, the prophetical books of Jeremiah, Ezekiel, Zephaniah, and Habakkuk relate to this period. The prophetical activity of both Jeremiah and Ezekiel spanned the last years of Judah and Jerusalem. The book of Jeremiah, especially, provides important information on this period. Particularly useful are the prose sections of the book, which, interestingly enough, are cast in the same literary style as Deuteronomy and Joshua–2 Kings. Jeremiah's career is said to have begun in the thirteenth year of Josiah (629–628; Jer. 1:1–2). The specific dates scattered throughout the book, however, pick up with his famous temple sermon (Jer. 7; 26) at the beginning of Jehoiakim's reign (608). Although some of the oracles in the early chapters of the book apparently derive from the reign of Josiah, they do not refer to Judean events very explicitly and make no overt reference to Josiah's famous religious reform.

The career of the prophet Ezekiel spanned the last years of the Davidic state. His call is dated to the fifth year of the exile of King Jehoiachin or 593. The dating of oracles throughout the book makes possible a correlation between the prophet's words and international events.[3]

The Babylonian Chronicles

Assyrian texts no longer shed any direct light on Judean history after the middle of the seventh century. No contemporary records from Egypt referring to Judah exist either. A major source of considerable usefulness for reconstructing the history of the period, however, in addition to the biblical materials, are the so-called Babylonian Chronicles (see Text 15).[4] These chronicles do not represent a single document but rather a particular genre of literature. The chronicles, which we have already discussed and utilized, present selective summaries of events during royal reigns, based apparently upon year-by-year records kept in Babylon. Only portions related to this period survive, but these include coverage of the years 626–623 and 616–594. That is, they cover major portions of the reigns of the Babylonian kings Nabopolassar (625–605) and Nebuchadrezzar (604–562). These texts provide the historian with incomparable data concerning the last days of Assyria and the struggles of Assyria, Babylonia, and Egypt. They also make possible the determination of the exact date of Nebuchadrezzar's first capture of Jerusalem.

---

3. See K. S. Reedy and D. B. Redford, "The Dates in Ezekiel in Relation to Biblical, Babylonian and Egyptian Sources," *JAOS* 90 (1970) 462–85. For the entire Babylonian period see R. A. Parker and W. H. Dubberstein, *Babylonian Chronology: 626 BC–AD 75* (Providence: Brown University Press, 1956).

4. Portions of the chronicles have been published in D. J. Wiseman, *Chronicles of Chaldaean Kings (626–556 B.C.) in the British Museum* (London: British Museum, 1961), abbreviated hereafter as *CCK*; and in a more comprehensive form in A. K. Grayson, *Assyrian and Babylonian Chronicles* (Texts from Cuneiform Sources 5; Locust Valley, NY: Augustin, 1975; repr. Winona Lake, IN: Eisenbrauns, 2000), abbreviated *ABC*. See also J.-J. Glassner, *Mesopotamian Chronicles* (SBLWAW 9; Atlanta: Society of Biblical Literature, 2004).

Hebrew Ostraca

Two significant collections of inscriptions on Hebrew ostraca come from this period, the Lachish and Arad Ostraca. These ostraca are broken pieces of pottery vessels used for record keeping and correspondence. Inscriptions were written on the shards in ink. Twenty-one were discovered in the 1932–38 excavations at Lachish, of which about a dozen are letters (see *COS* 3:78–81).[5] These represent correspondence of military officials sent to or copies of letters sent from Lachish during the final years of the Davidic kingdom. Nearby two hundred ostraca were discovered at the military fortress at Arad in the Judean Negeb during excavations in 1952–67 (see *COS* 3:81–85).[6] Written in four different languages (Hebrew, Aramaic, Arabic, and Greek), they span an enormously long time period, although several of the Hebrew texts clearly belong to the last years of Judean independence. Many of these texts are extremely fragmentary and only a few can be clearly understood.[7]

Chronological Problems

In short, we have more useful information for reconstructing the last half century or so of Judah's history than we have had for most of the preceding periods. That still does not mean that we can reconstruct the whole story or that any reconstruction will be free of problems. For example, we possess little material about Josiah's reign except for the extensive accounts in 2 Kings and 2 Chronicles of his religious reform. The information at hand is thus still selective and sometimes contradictory.

This tantalizing situation—rather full and detailed information that almost fits nicely but not quite—is perhaps illustrated best by the chronological data. Both the account in 2 Kings and the book of Jeremiah provide synchronisms between the reigns of the Judean kings and the Babylonian king Nebuchadrezzar. In addition, the Babylonian Chronicles allow for absolute dates for the first twelve years of Nebuchadrezzar's reign. Two difficulties, however, still create problems for any calculation of absolute dates for the Judean kings of this period. (1) There are apparent, even though minor, discrepancies in the biblical dates given for the first and second captures of Jerusalem. Second Kings 24:10–12; 25:8; and Jeremiah 52:12 place Judah's two defeats in Nebuchadrezzar's eighth and nineteenth years. On the other hand, Jeremiah 52:28–30 reports two deportations (which one would assume should have corresponded in time or followed the two defeats), but these are placed in Nebuchadrezzar's seventh and eighteenth years. (2) Uncertainty exists as to whether Judean dates were calculated on the basis of a spring-to-spring (Nisan to Nisan) annual cal-

5. N. H. Tur-Sinai, ed., *Lachish I: The Lachish Letters* (London: Oxford University Press, 1938). See also J. A. Emerton, "Were the Lachish Letters Sent to or from Lachish?" *PEQ* 133 (2001) 11–14.

6. Yohanan Aharoni (with the assistance of A. F. Rainey), *The Arad Inscriptions* (Jerusalem: Israel Exploration Society, 1981).

7. A selection and discussion of the fullest texts can be found in Dennis Pardee, *Handbook of Ancient Hebrew Letters: A Study Edition* (SBLSBS 15; Chico, CA: Scholars Press, 1982); abbreviated *HAHL*; and J. M. Lindenberger, *Ancient Aramaic and Hebrew Letters* (2d ed.; SBLWAW 14; Atlanta: Scholars Press, 2003).

TEXT 15. Selections from the Babylonian Chronicles

In the month of Iyyar [626 B.C.E.] the Assyrian army had come down into Babylonia. On the 12th of the month of Tisri the Assyrian troops when they came against Babylon, on that same day the Babylonians, when they had gone out from Babylon, did battle against the Assyrian army and heavily defeated the Assyrian army, captured their spoil. For one year there was no king in the land. On the twenty-sixth day of the month of Marcheswan, Nabopolassar sat upon the throne in Babylon. (This was) the "beginning of reign" of Nabopolassar. In the month of Adar the gods of the land of Susa which the Assyrians had carried off and settled in Erech those gods Nabopolassar let return to the city of Susa. . . .

(In) the tenth year [616 B.C.E.], in the month of Iyyar, Nabopolassar called out the Babylonian army and marched up the bank of the river Euphrates. . . . In the month of Tisri the Egyptian army and the Assyrian army marched after the king of Akkad as far as the town of Qablinu but did not overtake the king of Akkad and then went back. In the month of Adar the Assyrian army and the Babylonian army attacked each other in the town of Badanu which is in the territory of the city of Arraphu and the Assyrian army broke off contact from the Babylonian army which defeated them heavily and threw them (back) to the river Zab. Their chariots and horses were captured and they took much spoil from them. Many of his (prisoners) they made to cross the river Tigris with them and (so) they brought them into Babylon. . . .

In the twenty-first year [605 B.C.E.] the king of Akkad stayed in his own land, Nebuchadrezzar his eldest son, the crown-prince, mustered (the Babylonian army) and took command of his troops; he marched to Carchemish which is on the bank of the Euphrates, and crossed the river (to go) against the Egyptian army which lay in Carchemish, . . . fought with each other and the Egyptian army withdrew before him. He accomplished their defeat and to non-existence [beat?] them. As for the rest of the Egyptian army which had escaped from the defeat (so quickly that) no weapon had reached them, in the district of Hamath the Babylonian troops overtook and defeated them so that not a single man [escaped] to his own country. At that time Nebuchadrezzar conquered the whole area of the Ḫatti-country. For twenty-one years Nabopolassar had been king of Babylon. On the 8th of the month of Ab he died (lit. "the fates"); in the month of Elul Nebuchadrezzar returned to Babylon and on the first day of the month of Elul he sat on the royal throne in Babylon.

In the "accession year" [605/604 B.C.E.] Nebuchadrezzar went back again to the Ḫatti-land and until the month of Sebat marched unopposed through the Ḫatti-land; in the month of Sebat he took the heavy tribute of the Ḫatti-territory to Babylon. In the month of Nisan he took the hands of Bel and the son of Bel and celebrated the *akitu* (New Year) festival.

In the first year [604/603 B.C.E.] of Nebuchadrezzar in the month of Sivan he mustered his army and went to the Ḫatti-territory, he marched about unopposed in the Ḫatti-territory until the month of Kislev. All the kings of the Ḫatti-land came before him and he received their heavy tribute. He marched to the city of Askelon and captured it in the month of Kislev. He captured its king and plundered it and carried off [spoil from it. . . .] He turned the city into a mound and heaps of ruins and then in the month of Sebat he marched back to Babylon. . . .

In the fourth year [601/600 B.C.E.] the king of Akkad (Nebuchadrezzar) mustered his army and marched to the Ḫatti-land. In the Ḫatti-land they marched unopposed. In the month of Kislev he took the lead of his army and marched to Egypt. The king of Egypt heard (it) and mustered his army. In open battle they smote the breast (of) each other and inflicted great havoc on each other. The king of Akkad and his troops turned back and returned to Babylon.

In the fifth year [600/599 B.C.E.] the king of Akkad (stayed) in his own land and gathered together his chariots and horses in great numbers.

In the sixth year [599/598 B.C.E.] in the month of Kislev the king of Akkad mustered his army and marched to the Ḫatti-land. From the Ḫatti-land he sent out his companies, and scouring the desert they took much plunder from the Arabs, their possessions, animals, and gods. In the month of Adar the king returned to his own land.

In the seventh year [598/597 B.C.E.], the month of Kislev, the king of Akkad mustered his troops, marched to the Ḫatti-land, and encamped against (i.e. besieged) the city of Judah and on the second day of the month of Adar he seized the city and captured the king. He appointed there a king of his own choice (lit. heart), received its heavy tribute and sent (them) to Babylon. (*CCK* 51, 55–57, 67–69, 71–73)

endar, as were the regnal years for the king in Babylonian documents, or from the traditional Judean fall-to-fall (Tishri to Tishri) annual calendar.

The Collapse of Assyria and
the Rise of Babylonia

After a rule of thirty-eight years, the Assyrian king Ashurbanipal (668–627) apparently abdicated the throne in 630 or else elevated his son Ashur-etil-ilani to the kingship of Assyria as coruler.[8] Either Ashurbanipal's fear of a disputed succession, which eventuated anyway at his death (in 627), or his developing physical and administrative ineffectiveness may have been reason for his action. He bequeathed to his successor an empire with many internal and external troubles but an empire far from being impotent. Since the annals of Ashurbanipal do not extend beyond 639, the last years of his rule are largely

---

8. The chronology of the final years of the Assyrian Empire and its last kings is very uncertain. See Nadav Na'aman, "Chronology and History in the Late Assyrian Empire (631–619 B.C.)," *ZA* 81 (1991) 243–67; repr. in *AIIN* 305–28; and Stefan Zawadski, "A Contribution to the Chronology of the Last Days of the Assyrian Empire," *ZA* 85 (1995) 67–73.

unknown.[9] The king's activities in the 640s, however, suggest that he confronted diverse difficulties during this period but did so with a remarkable amount of success. The revolt of his brother Shamash-shum-ukin, the king of Babylon, was suppressed in a vicious four-year war (652/651–648) that saw the destruction of the city of Babylon and the death of Shamash-shum-ukin. Troubles with Elam lasted almost a decade (654–646) and terminated with the destruction of the Elamite capital at Susa in 646. Some Elamites who had been deported as a consequence of these wars were apparently resettled in Samaria following the fall of Susa (see Ezra 4:9–10). A series of campaigns, ending in about 642, were fought against the Arabs who had supported Babylon's earlier revolt. In 644 Ashurbanipal campaigned against Tyre and Usu (the mainland city) on the Mediterranean coast. Sarduri III (ca. 640–610) of Urartu acknowledged Assyrian sovereignty in his territory, and Ashurbanipal received tribute from Kurash (Cyrus I) of Parsumash (Persia). All of this activity suggests that the Assyrian Empire was still vigorous in Ashurbanipal's last years and that the terminal difficulties, involving fraternal claimants to the throne and civil war, set in after his death.

With the demise of Ashurbanipal in 627, an Assyrian military commander, Sin-shum-lishir, was proclaimed king in Babylon. His forces were defeated, however, and Sin-shar-ishkun, the brother of Ashur-etil-ilani, Ashurbanipal's son and successor on the Assyrian throne, proclaimed himself king. Thus began a four-year period of civil strife (627–623), which, when combined with external pressures upon the empire, proved to be overwhelming. Before we examine more closely the final years of the Assyrian kingdom, we need to look briefly at some other historical developments that impinged directly on the Assyrian Empire itself and thus affected, however remotely, Judean life and history.

Cimmerians, Scythians, and Medes

Three groups of seminomadic peoples became major factors in the life of the Fertile Crescent beginning in the late eighth and early seventh centuries. The Cimmerians, barbarian nomadic groups from the north, entered Urartu late in the eighth century and defeated the Urartians, who were ruled at the time by Argishti II (ca. 714–680).[10] Sargon II fought the Cimmerians in the province of Tabal in 705 and died in battle against them. They eventually moved west, taking the city of Gordium in 696/695. They later invaded the kingdom of Lydia, where King Gyges, who had recently made contact with and received support from Ashurbanipal, defeated them in battle (ca. 663). A few years later, a second wave of Cimmerians attacked Lydia (ca. 657). In about 644 King Gyges of Lydia died in battle against the Cimmerians, led by Lygdamis, and the capital city of Sardis was taken. Lygdamis and his followers then threatened the northwestern frontier of Assyria, but a temporary alliance was established between the

9. Ashurbanipal is best known for his collection of ancient literary materials of all types, discovered in 1852 in the ruins of Nineveh by Hormuzd Rassam. See Olaf Pedersen, *Archives and Libraries in the Ancient Near East, 1500–300* (Bethesda, MD: CDL, 1998).

10. See Tadeusz Sulimirski, "The Cimmerian Problem," *Bulletin of the Institute of Archaeology* 2 (1959) 45–64; and E. M. Yamauchi, *Foes from the Northern Frontier: Invading Hordes from the Russian Steppes* (Grand Rapids: Baker, 1982).

Cimmerian leader and Ashurbanipal. After the death of Lygdamis in about 640, his son and successor, Sandakshatru, continued the challenge to Assyria in the northwest. Sardis was again overrun by groups of the Cimmerians (the Trereans and Lycians) in about 637. Shortly thereafter the threat and disturbances of the Cimmerian tribes were brought to a halt by another barbarian group.

This second nomadic group is generally referred to as the Scythians, although various tribes are included in this designation.[11] The Scythians were Indo-Europeans from the Crimean region who had moved into western Asia Minor just after the turn of the eighth century. During the days of Esarhaddon, they had invaded Urartian territory. The Assyrian king entered an alliance with them at that time and married one of his daughters to a Scythian prince. Eventually the Scythian groups occupied an extensive but undefined area along an east-west axis reaching from Asia Minor to the Iranian plateau, from about the Halys River to northwestern Media, but not including Assyrian territory proper. The Scythians apparently also conducted wide-ranging raiding expeditions. Herodotus (1.104) speaks about the Scythians controlling all Asia, but he is probably noting only what might be called Upper Asia (see 1.95, 130; 4.1). In the 630s the Scythians under Madyes defeated the Cimmerians, driving them out of Asia Minor. Following this victory, the Scythians spread eastward, where they encountered the Medes, and southward, into the eastern Mediterranean seaboard. The fourth-century C.E. Christian historian Eusebius declares that the Scythians, as early as 633 B.C.E., had reached as far as Palestine.

The Medes, a third group, centered in northwestern Iran, also consisted of a number of separate but associated tribes.[12] Mentioned frequently in Assyrian texts, in the reign of Esarhaddon they had begun to unite, eventually becoming under King Phraortes (ca. 647–624) a formidable enemy of Assyria. Early in the reign of Phraortes' son and successor Cyaxares (ca. 623–584), the Medes fought the Scythians under Madyes and were defeated but quickly recovered and played a significant role in the downfall of Assyria, as we shall see.

Egypt and Syria-Palestine

The establishment of the Twenty-sixth (Saite) Dynasty in Egypt resulted in a period of cooperative rapprochement between Assyria and Egypt.[13] The treaty alliance between Assyria and the first rulers of the dynasty, Neco I and Psammetichus I, continued until the end of Assyrian rule. As Ashurbanipal became more and more involved with pressures in the north and east, Egypt became more dominant in Syria-Palestine. The expansion of Egyptian influence in the eastern Mediterranean seaboard probably occurred gradually at the start, begin-

---

11. See A. R. Millard, "The Scythian Problem," in John Ruffle et al., eds., *Orbis Aegyptiaorum Speculum—Glimpses of Ancient Egypt* (Warminster: Aris & Phillips, 1979) 119–22; and R. P. Vaggione, "Over All Asia? The Extent of the Scythian Domination in Herodotus," *JBL* 92 (1973) 523–30.

12. See S. C. Brown, "Media and Secondary State Formation in the Neo-Assyrian Zagros," *JCS* 38 (1986) 107–19; and T. C. Young Jr., "The Early History of the Medes and Persians and the Achaemenid Empire to the Death of Cambyses," *CAH* 4:1–52.

13. On the history and presence of Egypt in Palestine during this period, see M. F. Gyler, *Pharaonic Politics and Administrations, 663 to 323 B.C.* (Chapel Hill: University of North Carolina Press, 1959); and Ephraim Stern, "Egyptians in Palestine in the 7th Century BCE," in *Archaeology of the Land of the Bible,* vol. 2: *The Assyrian, Babylonian, and Persian Periods, 732–332 BCE* (ABRL; New York: Doubleday, 2001) 228–35.

ning in the 640s after Psammetichus I was secure at home, and then expanded significantly in the last years of the Assyrian Empire. Nothing in Near Eastern texts would suggest that during this period Egypt saw itself as a competitor to Assyria; everything points to a cooperative attitude between the two powers.

A number of factors indicate Egyptian dominance in Syria-Palestine throughout most of the second half of the seventh century. (1) Herodotus (2.157) reports that Psammetichus I took the city of Ashdod after a siege of twenty-nine years. (Possibly Herodotus mistook the twenty-ninth year of the king's reign for the length of the siege, which would mean that the capture of Ashdod occurred about 635.) The subjugation of Ashdod, which at the time may have been moving to assert its independence from Assyria, illustrates that Egypt was willing to fight the local kingdoms in order to assert its presence in the area. Also according to Herodotus, when the Scythians moved down the eastern Mediterranean coast, they encountered the Egyptians in Palestine. Specifically, Herodotus reports that when "they [the Scythians] were in the part of Syria called Palestine, Psammetichus king of Egypt met them and persuaded them with gifts and prayers to come no farther" (1.105). Other classical sources report military engagements between the Egyptians and the Scythians that undoubtedly refer to this same episode. This Egyptian encounter with the Scythians probably took place in Palestine in the late 630s or, more probably, the 620s. It would have been then that the Scythians plundered the temple of the "heavenly Aphrodite" at Ashkelon (Herodotus 1.105; see Zeph. 1:18). The Scythians seem to have withdrawn from the region soon thereafter, since no further encounter with the Egyptians is reported. Thus by the 620s Egypt was clearly operating as the dominant military power in Palestine. (2) Egyptian campaigns in support of Assyria, reported in the Babylonian Chronicles and the Bible and to be discussed in more detail below, took Egyptian troops across the Euphrates River, which suggests sufficient Egyptian control in Syria-Palestine to operate freely throughout the region. It is apparent from these two sources that the Egyptians possessed major military outposts at Riblah, Carchemish, Haran, and probably Megiddo. Such military entrenchment implies military dominance in the area. (3) Three inscriptional sources indicate that Syro-Palestinian powers were allied to Egypt at this time through treaty arrangements. In an inscription of his fifty-second year (612), Psammetichus I describes the Phoenician region in a manner that clearly indicates the subordination of the Phoenician cities: "Their chiefs were subjects of the (Egyptian) palace, with a royal courtier placed over them; and their taxes were assessed for the (pharaoh's) residence, as though it were in the land of Egypt" (*ARE* 4:493–94). The so-called Wadi Brisa Inscription set up by the Babylonian king Nebuchadrezzar describes the Lebanon area prior to his taking the territory as a region "over which a foreign enemy [no doubt Egypt] was ruling and robbing it of its riches" (*ANET* 307). In about 604/603 Adon the Philistine king of (probably) Ekron wrote to the Egyptian court requesting aid from the pharaoh (*COS* 3:132–34).[14] The form and content of his letter, discovered in Egypt, clearly indicate that Adon was a vassal with a treaty agreement with Egypt (see Text

---

14. Bezalel Porten, "The Identity of King Adon," *BA* 44 (1981) 36–52, contains a study and translation of the text.

16). Finally, (4) statuary and other artifacts from the early Saite rulers have been found as far north as the traditional site of Arvad. This suggests Egyptian presence all along the coast.

Two general conclusions relative to Judean history may be drawn from the above evidence and will be discussed in detail later. First, the Egyptians were in control of the Via Maris, the main highway running north-south through the eastern Mediterranean seaboard by the late 630s and early 620s. This would probably have remained the case until the Egyptians were driven out of Syria-Palestine by the Babylonians after 609. In short, the main route through Palestine was in Egyptian hands during most, if not all, of the reign of Josiah (641–610). Second, Judah enjoyed no political independence during this period. The Assyrian control over Judah, which had been exercised for about a century, would have given way gradually to Egyptian dominance. Perhaps for a time Judah was subservient to both Assyria and Egypt, as is indicated in Jeremiah 2.[15] At any rate, Judah, probably early in the reign of Josiah, became subordinate to Egypt and was part of "all that belonged to the king of Egypt from the Wadi of Egypt to the River Euphrates" (2 Kgs. 24:7).

The Rise of Babylon

For generations, Babylon, the old and widely recognized cultural and religious center of the region, in southern Mesopotamia, had been a trouble spot for Assyria.[16] Sennacherib destroyed the city of Babylon in 689 (see *COS* 2:305), and Esarhaddon subsequently ordered it rebuilt and repopulated (see *COS* 2:306). Continued struggles led to Babylon's further destruction in 648. By the time of Ashurbanipal's rule, Chaldean tribes controlled most of the region south of Babylon and constantly endangered and on occasion seized control of the city.[17] With the death of Ashurbanipal in 627, the Babylonians moved to assert their independence and became entangled in the struggle for the Assyrian throne. This new Babylonian revolt can be seen essentially as the renewal of the struggles that had led to the city's destruction in 648.

As indicated above, with the demise of Ashurbanipal an Assyrian general named Sin-shum-lishir was proclaimed king of Babylon and ruled the southern province for about a year before his own death. Then Sin-shar-ishkun, the brother of Ashur-etil-ilani (630–623), whom Ashurbanipal had designated as his own successor on the Assyrian throne, proclaimed himself and was recognized as king in Babylon for a short time (probably in late 627 or early 626). Babylonia's future and that of the ancient Near East, however, lay with Nabopolassar, the king of the Marshland and founder of the Neo-Babylonian dynasty, who had himself proclaimed king of Babylonia in 626 (for his "autobiography" see *COS* 2:307). Thus three rulers and three armies vied for author-

---

15. Jacob Milgrom, "The Date of Jeremiah, Chapter 2," *JNES* 14 (1955) 65–69.

16. J. A. Brinkman, *Prelude to Empire: Babylonian Society and Politics, 747–626 B.C.* (Occasional Publications of the Babylonian Fund 7; Philadelphia: University Museum, 1984), provides a thorough discussion of the issues and history.

17. On the Chaldeans see Edward Lipiński, *The Aramaeans: Their Ancient History, Culture, Religion* (OLA 100; Leuven: Peeters, 2000) 416–22.

ity over the area.[18] Apparently Sin-shar-ishkun and Nabopolassar temporarily allied their efforts, with the former claiming the throne of Assyria and conceding Nabopolassar's claim to the throne of Babylonia. Nabopolassar emerged victorious. After defeating an Assyrian army sent to subdue him, he gained control of the city of Babylon and the whole southern region in November 626 (*ABC* 88). Seeking to gain support in the east, he returned to the Elamites the gods of Susa taken by the Assyrians in 646 and held in the city of Uruk.

Sin-shar-ishkun gained the throne of Assyria in 623, Ashur-etil-ilani apparently having fallen in battle. Sin-shar-ishkun's agreement with Nabopolassar over shared rule soon lapsed, and the two began their struggle with each other for dominance in Mesopotamia. Involvement of other powers in the Assyro-Babylonian civil war began to complicate matters further. The province of Der on the Elamite border rebelled (*ABC* 89), for example, and Median attacks on Assyrian territory intensified. Phraortes, the leader of the Medes, was killed in battle, however, whereupon Cyaxares, Phraortes' son and successor, was immediately confronted and defeated by the Scythians under Madyes. Whether the Scythians at this time were supporting the Assyrians or merely acting on their own remains unknown, although the long history of reasonably friendly relations between the two suggests the former.

The continuing loyalty to the Assyrian Empire of many of its vassal states and cities is rather surprising at a time when civil struggle was so rampant. Nothing comparable to the widespread revolts early in Sennacherib's reign is evident. Even some cities in the province of Babylonia itself remained loyal to the Assyrian Sin-shar-ishkun until his death and the fall of Nineveh the capital in 612. The existence of groups such as the Scythians and the Medes on the peripheries of the empire may have encouraged the continued alliance of vassal states and cities.

The Last Days of Assyria

When the extant Babylonian Chronicles resume, after a gap from 623 to early 616, they show Nabopolassar firmly in control of the region of Babylonia. After advancing up the Euphrates, however, the Babylonian king was forced to withdraw before a combined Assyrian and Egyptian force (*ABC* 91; see Text 15). In the year following (615), Nabopolassar attacked Ashur, the old Assyrian capital, but was forced to flee the field and take refuge in the city of Tikrit. After a ten-day siege the Assyrian army withdrew and Nabopolassar escaped (*ABC* 91).

For a time thereafter the Medes were the major threat to Assyria. The Scythians appear to have been neutral or even pro-Assyrian at this point. In 614 the Medes attacked several metropolitan districts in Assyria and succeeded in taking Ashur. Nabopolassar and his troops arrived at Ashur only after the city had fallen, but he and the Median Cyaxares sealed their anti-Assyrian opposition with a treaty alliance (*ABC* 93). In 612 Cyaxares and Nabopolassar captured the

---

18. On these wars see P.-A. Beaulieu, "The Fourth Year of Hostilities in the Land," *Baghdader Mitteilungen* 28 (1997) 367–94; and Stefan Zawadski, *The Fall of Assyria and Median-Babylonian Relations in Light of the Nabupolassar Chronicle* (Poznan: Adam Mickiewicz University, 1988).

Assyrian capital at Nineveh, an event celebrated with eloquent boasting in the biblical book of Nahum. The Assyrian monarch, Sin-shar-ishkun, apparently died in the flames of the city's destruction, and the remnants of the Assyrian army were forced to move westward where they could make contact with their Egyptian allies. In Haran, one hundred miles to the west, Ashur-uballit II (611–609), presumably a junior member of the royal family, became the last Assyrian ruler.

During the next two years, Nabopolassar sought to extend his control to include as much of Assyria as possible, especially the Middle Euphrates region. This gave the Egyptians and the Assyrians time to recoup somewhat on the Upper Euphrates (*ABC* 94–95). Neco II had become the new pharaoh in Egypt in late March 610.[19]

Sometime after Iyyar (April–May) of 610, the Babylonians and the Umman-manda (apparently the Medes) took Haran, forcing the Assyrians and the Egyptians to abandon the area temporarily and to withdraw to the west bank of the Euphrates (*ABC* 95). (The term "Umman-manda," used in the Babylonian Chronicles, was an archaic expression revived by Babylonian scribes and employed primarily in reference to the Medes. In the description of the fall of Nineveh, Cyaxares is called king of the Umman-manda [*ABC* 94]. At a late stage in the Assyrian struggles, Scythians and other groups may have been included in the designation.) In 609 Ashur-uballit and the Egyptian army counterattacked the Babylonians in Haran. Although they experienced some initial success evidenced in their victory over the Babylonian garrison, the broken Babylonian Chronicle suggests that the Assyro-Egyptian coalition encountered failure in the long run (*ABC* 96). The name of Ashur-uballit appears no more in the chronicles; the Assyrian Empire was at an end. With this second battle of Haran, the issue shifted to a Babylonian-Egyptian struggle over the control of Syria-Palestine and for dominance along the eastern Mediterranean seaboard.

Judah and International Affairs

Two external factors must be emphasized in order to understand Judean history during the years of Assyria's collapse: (1) Judah was probably under Egyptian control during these years; and (2), like many of the other Near Eastern states at that time, Judah was affected by barbarian movements from the north.

Egypt under the Twenty-sixth Dynasty and Assyria under Ashurbanipal were probably cooperative allies. As Assyria became more and more preoccupied against Babylon, the Elamites, and others in the 640s, Egypt moved into Syria-Palestine in partnership with Assyria. After the death of Ashurbanipal and the outbreak of fraternal struggle for the throne exacerbated by Nabopolassar's rebellion in southern Mesopotamia, Assyria was too preoccupied to control southern Syria-Palestine directly. This task fell to Egypt. (One broken text in the Babylonian Chronicles may be interpreted to suggest that either Ashur-etil-ilani or Sin-shar-ishkun conducted a campaign west of the

19. See M. Smith, "Did Psammetichus I Die Abroad?" *OLP* 22 (1991) 101–9.

CHART 19. The Last Days of the Davidic Kingdom

Judah	Assyria	Egypt	Babylonia
Manasseh (698–644)			
	Ashurbanipal (688–627)	Neco I (665–664) Psammetichus I (664–610)	
Amon (643–642) Josiah (641–610)	*Cooperative alliance between Assyria and Egypt* Ashur-etil-ilani (626–623)		Shamash-shumukin *defeated* *652/651–648* Sin-shum-lishir (627–626) Nabopolassar (625–605)
	Sin-shar-ishkun (622–612) *Fall of Ashur (614) Fall of Nineveh (612)*		
Jehoahaz II (three months) Jehoiakim (608–598)	Ashur-uballit (611–609)	Neco II (610–595)	Victory at Carchemish (605) Nebuchadrezzar (604–562)
Jehoiachin (three months) *Surrender of Jerusalem (March 15/16, 597)*			
Zedekiah (596–586) *Capture of Jerusalem (586)*		Psammetichus II (595–589) Apries (Hophra) (589–570)	

Euphrates as late as 623 [*ABC* 89–90]. Otherwise Assyria was certainly not operative in force in the eastern Mediterranean seaboard after 627.)

Judah as an Egyptian Vassal

Several factors suggest that Judah was under Egyptian dominance and probably an Egyptian vassal throughout Josiah's reign.

1. References in Jeremiah 2 speak of Judah's submission to both Assyria and Egypt (see vv. 16–18 and 36–37). The country is depicted going to Egypt to

drink the waters of the Nile and to Assyria to drink the waters of the Euphrates (2:18). The condition depicted in these verses does not seem to be one in which a choice between Egypt and Assyria is demanded but rather a requirement of serving two masters. A date for this situation is suggested by the date of Jeremiah's call, namely, some time in 629–628, the thirteenth year of Josiah's reign (1:2; 25:3).[20] The condition presupposed by Jeremiah 2 was one in which rule over Judah, and probably other nations in the region, was a hegemony shared between the Egyptian and Mesopotamian superpowers.

2. A Judah subservient to Egypt is suggested by the Egyptian campaigns and tactics described in the Babylonian Chronicles. The chronicle for 616, after a gap of seven years, reports that the Egyptian army with its Assyrian ally pursued Nabopolassar on the Middle Euphrates hundreds of miles from home (*ABC* 91; see Text 15). At least again in 610 and subsequently afterward, the Egyptian army was deep in Syrian territory. How early and how frequently such campaigns occurred cannot be determined. Two things, however, are clear. The 616 campaign, conducted so far from home, was certainly not Egypt's first foray in the area. Such an expedition and deployment of forces indicate a period of ever-increasing involvement in northern Syria prior to 616. In addition, the Egyptian army must have established control and been reasonably certain of its dominance in an area prior to extending its supply lines to such an extent and thus exposing itself to possible attack from the rear. Egypt therefore must have been rather confident of its relationship to Syro-Palestinian states such as Judah; that is, Judah must have been under Egypt's authority.

3. In their efforts to aid the Assyrians and to halt the Babylonian movement into Syria, the Egyptians appear to have been in complete control of the main highways of the eastern Mediterranean seaboard. The most important southern segment of this international roadway was the Via Maris, which passed along the western edge of traditional Judean territory and moved through the Jezreel Valley near Megiddo. This route joined other roads in Syria of which the most important north-south route passed through Riblah, Hamath, and Aleppo. The Egyptian presence in Carchemish and Haran, even farther to the north, indicates control of the entire trade routes along the eastern Mediterranean seaboard and thus direct control over the region where the route passed through Palestine.

4. The employment of Judean troops in the Egyptian military and the presence of Greek mercenaries, apparently in the service of Egyptian pharaohs, in Palestine suggest Egyptian dominance in the area. The evidence of Judean forces in the Egyptian army at the time is threefold. (a) We have already noted the presence of Jewish troops in Egypt in military colonies such as Elephantine. (b) Josephus provides a quote from the fourth-century Chaldean historian Berosus about Nebuchadrezzar's defeat of the Egyptians at Carchemish in 605, which indicates that Judean soldiers were fighting with Egypt in northern Syria. The young Babylonian crown prince had to depart Syria speedily upon receiving word of the death of his father. Berosus reports that "the prisoners—

---

20. Many scholars now date Jeremiah's career to post-Josianic times. See J. P. Hyatt, "The Beginning of Jeremiah's Prophecy," *ZAW* 78 (1966) 204–14; and W. L. Holladay, "A Coherent Chronology of Jeremiah's Early Career," in P.-M. Bogaert, ed., *La livre de Jérémie: Le prophète et son milieu, les oracles et leur transmission* (BETL 54; Leuven: Leuven University Press, 1981) 58–73.

Jews, Phoenicians, Syrians, and those of Egyptian nationality—were consigned to some of his [Nebuchadrezzar's] friends, with orders to conduct them to Babylonia, along with the heavy troops and the rest of the spoils; while he himself, with a small escort, pushed across the desert to Babylon" (*Contra Apion* 1.136–37). Although this text indicates that Judean soldiers were fighting under Egyptian auspices far from their homeland in 605, and thus a few years after Josiah's reign, the same situation probably prevailed earlier as well. (c) Greek mercenaries comprised a major part of the Egyptian army under Psammetichus I and his successors. Evidence of the presence of Greeks, probably in the service of the Egyptian pharaoh, appears in Palestine during the last part of the seventh century. Several letters, unearthed from the site of ancient Arad in southern Judah, refer to Greeks (called Kittim) passing by the settlement and being furnished with supplies by Judean forces (see Text 18). This situation would indicate that Judean forces were aligned with or subservient to Egypt in whose service such Hellenic mercenaries functioned. Excavations at Mesad Hashavyahu and other sites on the Palestinian coast south of Joppa have revealed evidence of Greek settlements from the period, probably also a contingent of Psammetichus I's forces.[21] In addition, an inscription found at the site indicates the presence of a Semitic, probably Judean, force under a commander there (see Text 17). This evidence suggests a situation in which contingents of Greek and Judean forces were employed by the Egyptians and stationed on the Mediterranean coast.

5. The final evidence suggesting that Judah under Josiah was subject to Egypt is found in the narratives of Kings. Second Kings 24:7 reports in connection with Nebuchadrezzar's taking of Judah that "the king of Babylon had taken all that belonged to the king of Egypt from the Wadi of Egypt to the River Euphrates." This implies Egypt's previous control over the entire eastern Mediterranean seaboard including Judah. Also to be taken into account is that when Josiah was killed at Megiddo, the Egyptian pharaoh assumed the authority to appoint the next king over Judah. Specifically, Jehoahaz II, who ascended the throne while Neco II was in northern Syria, was deposed by the pharaoh, Judah was forced to pay a penalty for its rash initiative, and a ruler selected by Egypt was later placed in power (2 Kgs. 23:28–35). All of this takes for granted that Judah was subservient to Egypt, even during Josiah's reign, and that no ruler could hold the Judean throne without Egyptian approval.

Judah and the Barbarian Movements

Like most of the states in the Near East, Judah was affected during the seventh century by barbarian movements from the north. This is most clearly evident in the book of Jeremiah. This prophet viewed affairs to the north as a seething caldron with evil boiling over its sides (1:13–15). In his call vision, Jeremiah claimed to hear Yahweh "calling all the tribes of the kingdoms of the north . . . ; and they shall come and all of them shall set their thrones at the entrance of the gates of Jerusalem, against all its surrounding walls, and against all the cities

---

21. See Alexander Fantalkin, "Meẓad Ḥashavyahu: Its Material Culture and Historical Background," *TA* 28 (2001) 3–165.

of Judah" (1:15). The enemy from the north whose coming the prophet proclaims in Jer. 4:5–6:30 must certainly be connected with the movements of the
Scythian and associated groups.

Although the tribal groups did not overrun Judah as Jeremiah predicted,
they did penetrate into the Palestinian area. The Egyptians battled and bribed
them in Palestine itself but apparently effected their departure. That Egypt was
a cooperative ally of Assyria and that the Scythians were certainly not anti-
Assyrian may have helped moderate their encounter. The most likely date, as
we noted earlier, for the Scythian penetration to the border of Egypt was the
early 620s, the period of Jeremiah's early preaching.

The Reign of Josiah

Following the assassination of Amon, "the people of the land" placed Josiah the
son of Amon, then an eight-year-old youngster, on the throne in Jerusalem.
Josiah ruled for thirty-one years (641–610). Unfortunately neither 2 Kings nor
2 Chronicles provides extensive details about his reign or about international
affairs generally. Both focus almost exclusively on his religious reforms. For reasons indicated above, however, it is evident that Josiah's reign witnessed Judah's
transition from an Assyrian vassal to a position of subservience to Egypt.

Egyptian policy in Syria-Palestine was far more politically laissez-faire in
nature than had been Assyrian policy and was primarily commercial in operation. Egypt did not seem to have had any plans or desire to annex or subjugate
completely Syro-Palestinian states, for example, and thus developed no imposed
provincial governmental system. This means that Egypt was probably little
concerned with internal Syro-Palestinian affairs, such as religious practices and
developments. Accordingly, while Judah under Josiah did not experience a
period of complete freedom unhampered by foreign domination, internal
affairs were certainly more under Judean control with Egyptian than with
Assyrian overlordship. As direct Assyrian control in Judah began to loosen,
and was replaced with an Egyptian program more benevolent in character and
less oppressive in nature, Josiah was able to reform the Jerusalem and Judean
cult. Before discussing the nature of this reform, we must examine the literary
traditions about Josiah's reformation.

Literary and Chronological Matters

The account of Josiah's reign in 2 Kings notes the following episodes:

In Josiah's eighteenth year (624), "the book of the law" was discovered in
the temple while repair work was being conducted (22:3–8).
The book was read to the king; Huldah the prophetess was consulted about
the work; and she responded with an oracle emphasizing its importance
and predicting that judgment would fall upon the land but that Josiah
would be gathered to his grave "in peace" (22:9–20).
The king assembled the elders of Judah and Jerusalem, and after reading
aloud "the book of the covenant," the king covenanted to obey its words
(23:1–3).

A purging of the Judean cult commenced, beginning with the Jerusalem temple and extending from Geba to Beer-sheba, that is, throughout Judah (23:4–14).

The high place and altar at the northern shrine of Bethel was destroyed as well as other shrines in the province of Samerina; human bones were burned on the altars (23:15–20).

The king followed the stipulations of the recently discovered book of the covenant and held the Passover as a pilgrim festival in Jerusalem (23:21–23).

Josiah was killed by Pharaoh Neco II at Megiddo (23:29–30).

On the other hand, 2 Chronicles presents the following course of events for Josiah's reign:

In his eighth year (634–633), Josiah began to seek the God of David his father (34:3a).

In his twelfth year (630–629), Josiah began to purge the cult throughout Judah and Jerusalem, burning bones on the altars and extended the purge into the tribal territories of Manasseh, Ephraim, Simeon, and Naphtali (34:3b–7).

In his eighteenth year (624–623), "the book of the law of Yahweh given through Moses" was discovered in the temple (34:8–18).

The book was read to the king; Huldah the prophetess was consulted about the work; and she responded with an oracle emphasizing its importance (34:19–28).

The king assembled the elders of Judah and Jerusalem, and after reading the book, he covenanted to obey the words of the book and involved the people of Jerusalem and Benjamin and Israel in the observance of its stipulations (34:29–33).

The king followed the stipulations of the law regarding Passover and also appointed priests (35:1–19).

Josiah while disguised was killed in battle at Megiddo (35:20–27).

The primary differences in these narratives concern (1) the relationship of the reform to the law book, (2) whether Josiah's reform was conducted in clearly defined stages in Josiah's eighth, twelfth, and eighteenth years, and (3) the geographical extent of the reform.

The Book of the Law

Numerous issues arise over the nature and extent of Josiah's reform, its relationship to a discovered law book if there was a reform, and the origin of the account or accounts of the reform.[22]

---

22. For general surveys see Norbert Lohfink, "The Cult Reform of Josiah of Judah: 2 Kings 22–23 as a Source for the History of Religion," in P. D. Miller et al., eds., *Ancient Israelite Religion: Essays in Honor of Frank Moore Cross* (Philadelphia: Fortress, 1987) 459–76; idem, "Recent Discussion on 2 Kings 22–23: The State of the Questions," in D. L. Christensen, ed., *A Song of Power and the Power of Song: Essays on the Book of Deuteronomy* (SBTS 3; Winona Lake, IN: Eisenbrauns, 1993) 36–61; and W. B. Barrick, *The King and the Cemeteries: Toward a New Understanding of Josiah's Reform* (VTSup 88; Leiden: Brill, 2002).

1. A plot involving the finding of a book that authorized and resulted in significant cultural and social changes was a rather common feature in ancient Near Eastern literature.[23] The parallels between this topos and the account of the finding of the book in the temple raise the possibility that a common folklore plot was employed to produce a narrative explanation and rationale for changes in the Jerusalem cult.

2. Differences between the accounts of the reform raise additional questions. Was the finding of the book the catalyst for the reform, as in 2 Kings, or was the book found in the course of carrying out a reform, as in 2 Chronicles? Differences exist even in the 2 Kings narratives. In the account of the finding, the book is called "the book of the law" (2 Kgs. 22:8, 11) or just "the book" (v. 16), whereas in the account of the ceremony obligating the king and people to carry out its stipulations, the book is called "the book (or words) of the covenant" (2 Kgs. 23:2, 3, 21).

3. The 2 Kings account has obviously been told so that elements in the narrative are portrayed as fulfillment of a prophecy supposedly given three hundred years earlier. Second Kings 23:15–18 refers back to a prediction found in 1 Kings 13:1–2:

> While Jeroboam was standing by the altar to offer incense, a man of God came out of Judah, by the word of Yahweh to Bethel and proclaimed against the altar by the word of Yahweh, and said, "O altar, altar, thus says Yahweh, 'A son shall be born to the house of David, Josiah by name; and he shall sacrifice on you the priests of the high places who offer incense on you, and human bones shall be burned on you.'"

This prophecy-fulfillment scheme raise serious questions about the historicity of both sets of events involved, especially the idea of a late-tenth-century prophet mentioning by name a late-seventh-century monarch.

4. The anti-Bethel bias of the compilers/authors that runs throughout the books of Kings reaches its climax in the narrative of Josiah's reign. The 2 Chronicles account of the reform, however, does not even mention Bethel. Bethel was seen by the compilers of Kings as a rival sanctuary to Jerusalem. The actual rivalry between the sanctuaries probably continued into and reached its peak in the exilic and later periods.[24] The description of Josiah's actions at Bethel (2 Kgs. 23:4, 15–20) was a way of declaring the sanctuary there defiled and desecrated irrevocably.

5. The narrative of the reform was produced by persons sympathetic to the teachings of the book of Deuteronomy and thus the account has been made to reflect the positions advocated in that book. Second Kings 23:9 even notes that priests from outlying sanctuaries did not come to Jerusalem to officiate in temple worship, a right granted them by Deuteronomy 18:6–8. While the majority of scholars over the past two hundred years have concluded that some form of

---

23. Thomas Römer, "Transformations in Deuteronomistic and Biblical Historiography: On 'Book-Finding' and Other Literary Strategies," *ZAW* 109 (1997) 1–11; and Katherine Stott, "Finding the Lost Book of the Law: Re-reading the Story of 'The Book of the Law' (Deuteronomy–2 Kings) in Light of Classical Literature," *JSOT* 30 (2005) 153–69.

24. See Joseph Blenkinsopp, "Bethel in the Neo-Babylonian Period," in Oded Lipschits and Joseph Blenkinsopp, eds., *Judah and the Judeans in the Neo-Babylonian Period* (Winona Lake, IN: Eisenbrauns, 2003) 93–107.

71. *Arad sanctuary.* Plan of the Arad sanctuary and photograph of the "holy of holies." The arrow in the plan indicates the direction from which the photograph was taken.

the book of Deuteronomy was the law code that formed the basis of Josiah's reform, this view cannot be conclusively demonstrated.[25]

Josiah's Reform

According to the report of 2 Kings 22:3–23:3, the book of the law, found during preparations for temple repair, was turned over to Shaphan the secretary by Hilkiah the high priest, who reported finding the book in the temple. Shaphan then read the book to King Josiah, who reacted strongly to its contents and sent a deputation to make inquiry "concerning the words of this book that has been found" (2 Kgs. 22:13). The officials carried the book to Huldah the prophetess, who "resided in Jerusalem in the Second Quarter," or "New City," perhaps the refugee suburb of Jerusalem, and who was the wife of Shallum the "keeper of the wardrobe" (22:14). Huldah is presented pronouncing a verdict from Yahweh (22:15–20). The king then assembled the people, presented the contents of the book to them, and "made a covenant before Yahweh . . . to perform the words of this covenant that were written in this book. All the people joined in the covenant" (23:3).

25. Thomas Römer, "The Book of Deuteronomy," in S. L. McKenzie and M. P. Graham, eds., *The History of Israel's Traditions: The Heritage of Martin Noth* (JSOTSup 182; Sheffield: Sheffield Academic Press 1994) 178–212, offers a survey of opinions on the book.

72. *Horned altar from Beer-sheba.* Unearthed in the excavations at Beer-sheba and reconstructed, the stones of the altar had been dismantled and reused in another construction. (*Courtesy of Ze'ev Herzog*)

The main focus and surely the initial stage of Josiah's reform had to do with the temple in Jerusalem and with cult places in the immediate vicinity. The editors of the material noted a number of actions taken to purify worship. (We must remember, however, that the editors wanted to glorify Josiah's actions and thus may have exaggerated the non-Yahwistic features associated with earlier monarchs as well as the "purges" of Josiah.) The "idolatrous" priests whom the kings of Judah had appointed to officiate in non-Yahwistic worship were deposed (2 Kgs. 23:5). Some features of this worship were presumably related in some way to Assyrian cultic practices. The cultic artifacts associated with such worship were removed (23:4a). The Asherah was taken from the temple, burned, its ashes beaten to dust, and the dust thrown on the paupers' graves (23:6). Quarters that had been constructed in the temple area for male "holy ones" where the women "wove hangings" (or "wove cubicles") for the Asherah were demolished (23:7). Horses that former kings had dedicated to the sun and placed at the entrance to the temple were removed and "the chariots of the sun" were burned (23:11). Altars constructed on the roof and in the two courts of the temple were pulled down and thrown into the Kidron (23:12). Topheth, an installation in the Valley of Hinnom for sacrificing or dedicating children as Molech offerings, is said to have been defiled (23:10). Also said to have been defiled were the high places (altar shrines) on the mountain east of Jerusalem ("Mount of Olives") dedicated to Ashtoreth, Chemosh, and Milcom that Solomon had erected. Their pillars were broken, the Asherahs were cut down, and the sites strewn with human bones, rendering them unclean (23:13–14). That such places had survived over centuries since the time of Solomon, however, seems doubtful.

A stage of the reform involved an attempt to extend the purge throughout the land—"from Geba to Beer-sheba," that is, throughout Judah proper (23:8). What was involved in Josiah's purge of the cult at large in Judah is not entirely clear. Second Kings 23:5 notes that the king deposed the idolatrous priests in Judah who had earlier functioned under royal patronage. Action must have been taken against some Yahwistic establishments as well, since 23:8–9 notes that "he brought all the priests out of the cities of Judah, and defiled the high places where the priests had burned incense, from Geba to Beer-sheba. . . .

However, the priests of the high places did not come up to the altar of Yahweh in Jerusalem, but they ate unleavened bread among their brethren." These verses suggest that some attempt was made to put the local Yahwistic priests and their sanctuaries out of business by defiling the Yahwistic high places, but that the attempt was not very successful. Apparently the reference in 23:8b to the destruction of "the high places of the gates that were at the entrance of the gate of Joshua the governor of the city, which were on the left at the gate of the city," refers to the destruction of some particular gate shrine.

Second Kings 23:21–23 stipulates that Josiah enforced the observance of the Passover "as it is written in this book of the covenant." That is, he required that particular Passover to be held in Jerusalem (see Deut. 16:1–8). Second Kings 23:23 notes, however, only that such a Passover was held in his eighteenth year, the year when the law book was found. If 23:9 refers to this same celebration, it suggests that even the rural Yahwistic priests did not participate in this centralized Passover observance. Josiah is said also to have banned wizards, mediums, and the like (23:24). This again could have been based on Deuteronomic material but would have been a prohibition very difficult to enforce.

Was there a stage in Josiah's religious reform, namely, a movement beyond Jerusalem and the boundaries of Judah ("from Geba to Beer-sheba"; 2 Kgs. 23:8)? Both 2 Kings (23:15–20) and 2 Chronicles (34:6–7) suggest there was. It is highly doubtful, however, that Josiah extended Judean borders or purged religious cult places outside Judean territory. Except for the case of Bethel, the assertions in 2 Kings and 2 Chronicles that Josiah carried his reformation into old Israelite territory are highly general, sweeping statements, which supply no specific details and appear to be later editorializing notations. That in the later Persian provincial system, which generally followed the situation inherited from the Babylonians, Bethel was part of the province of Judah could suggest that Josiah expanded his kingdom a few miles northward from Geba to include the region around Bethel that was later left under Judean authority by the Babylonians.[26]

The question of Josiah's political ambitions has been a recurring theme in historical studies. For years many scholars argued that Josiah's goal was to reconstitute the earlier kingdom of David and unite the old Israel and the new Judah around the temple and city of Jerusalem.[27] Unfortunately the biblical texts provide no concrete description of internal political affairs under Josiah or about the extent and nature of his kingdom. Sennacherib's invasion had greatly diminished Judean territory, and while there is archaeological evidence of some recovery and rebuilding under Manasseh and Josiah, this is primarily limited to

26. See G. S. Ogden, "The Northern Extent of Josiah's Reform," *ABR* 26 (1978) 26–34. David Ussishkin, "The Date of the Judean Shrine at Arad," *IEJ* 38 (1988) 142–57, argues that Josiah did not even destroy the temple at the administrative center at Arad in the Negeb.

27. See Cross, *Canaanite Myth*, 283; and for an attempt to demonstrate "that biblical literature— including the Deuteronomistic History; the book of Deuteronomy; and the prophetic books of Jeremiah, Zephaniah, Nahum, Habakkuk, Isaiah, Amos, Hosea, and Micah—indeed points to the historical reality of Josiah's reform as a program that was designed to unify Israel and Judah around the Jerusalem Temple under Davidic rule," see M. A. Sweeney, *King Josiah of Judah: The Lost Messiah of Israel* (Oxford: Oxford University Press, 2001), quotation from p. 19. For an idealized account of Josiah's religion and politics, see Israel Finkelstein and N. A. Silberman, *The Bible Unearthed: Archaeology's New Vision of Ancient Israel and the Origin of Its Sacred Texts* (New York: Free Press, 2001) 275–95; but note pp. 347–53 in the same work on the extent of Josiah's kingdom.

73. *Pharaoh Neco II.* This bronze statue represents Pharaoh Neco II kneeling in worship. Second king of the Twenty-sixth Saite Dynasty, Neco executed King Josiah of Judah at Megiddo in 610 B.C.E. Five years later, in 605, Neco was himself defeated at Carchemish and forced to abandon Egyptian imperial interests in Syria-Palestine. (*University of Pennsylvania Museum*)

the Judean Desert and the Negeb. The argument that Josiah had Kittim (Greeks/Cypriots) as mercenary troops under his control and gained a foothold on the Mediterranean, based on the Mesad Hashavyahu finds, can no longer be accepted. Josiah's goal of creating a new Davidic kingdom uniting north and south thus has no basis in either the biblical text or archaeological data.

The Death of Josiah

A late demotic papyrus reports that the corpse of Pharaoh Psammetichus was being imbalmed at Daphnae outside Egypt at the time of a lunar eclipse near sunset. Such an eclipse occurred on 22 March 610. This places the death of the pharaoh shortly after the beginning of his fifty-fifth year on 23 January 610. After his accession to the throne, the new Egyptian pharaoh, Neco II (610–595), probably continued the Egyptian campaign planned by Psammetichus or already under way and marched north to aid the Assyrians and to confront the westward-advancing Babylonians. Probably during the pharaoh's march to the north Josiah was killed by Neco II at Megiddo.[28] Since the Egyptians were at Haran by Marheshvan (October–November; see *ABC* 95), Josiah's death must have occurred sometime between April and October of 610, perhaps in the late

28. See Smith, *OLP* 22 (1991) 101–9; and P. K. Hooker and J. H. Hayes, "The Year of Josiah's Death: 609 or 610 BCE?" in J. A. Dearman and M. P. Graham, eds., *The Land that I Will Show You: Essays on the History and Archaeology of the Ancient Near East in Honour of J. Maxwell Miller* (JSOTSup 343; Sheffield: Sheffield Academic Press, 2001) 96–103.

summer. The Kings account is very vague about the circumstances of Josiah's death: "Pharaoh Neco king of Egypt went up to the king of Assyria to the river Euphrates. King Josiah went to meet him; but when Pharaoh Neco met him at Megiddo, he killed him" (2 Kgs. 23:29). What happened at Megiddo remains a mystery. The Chronicler (2 Chr. 35:20–23) turns the meeting of the two monarchs into a military confrontation, the pharaoh into a Yahwistic preacher, and Josiah into a "second Ahab" who though disguised was accidentally killed in battle (see 2 Chr. 18:28–34). Any proposed scenario about why and how Josiah was killed at Megiddo must be based on pure speculation.[29] Was it the result of some misunderstanding between the new pharaoh and the Judean king on their first meeting? Was there some tension when the new pharaoh sought to impose a new treaty or some new restrictions on his Judean vassal? Were some extenuating circumstances, some accidents of history, to blame? Did Josiah assume that something was to be gained by opposing Egypt and siding with Babylonia? The historian simply cannot know. Both 2 Chronicles and 2 Kings agree on one thing: the Judean king was returned to the capital city and given a proper burial in Jerusalem (2 Kgs. 23:30; 2 Chr. 35:24).

Jehoahaz II

With Josiah's death, "the people of the land" placed his son Jehoahaz on the throne (2 Kgs. 23:30–31), bypassing the latter's elder brother in the succession (23:36). The Judean "people of the land" were again dominating Jerusalem politics. Jehoahaz's mother was from Libnah, one of the major Judean cities, and this may have influenced their specific choice. The reign of Jehoahaz, who was also known in the Bible as Shallum (Jer. 22:11; 1 Chr. 3:15), lasted only three months. As it turned out, it was the Egyptian pharaoh, not "the people of the land," who had the last say. From Marheshvan (October–November) 610 until Adar (February–March) 609, the Egyptian-Assyrian forces fought the Babylonians at Haran but were defeated and forced to withdraw west of the Euphrates (*ABC* 95). In the meantime, Neco had had Jehoahaz brought to the Egyptian camp at Riblah in northern Syria and confined, ending his rule. The Judean ruler was removed from office after a reign of only three months (2 Kgs. 23:33). If the Egyptian ruler had killed Josiah on his way to the Euphrates sometime in Tishri (September–October), then Jehoahaz II would had served as king during the final two months of 610 and the first month of 609. The Egyptian-Assyrian forces were engaged with the Babylonians again in the Haran area until Elul (August–September) 609 and then withdrew (*ABC* 96). On his return in defeat to Egypt, Neco brought along the deposed Jehoahaz and then settled matters in his vassal state of Judah. A modest fine of one hundred talents of silver and a talent of gold was imposed on Judah, and Jehoahaz was taken into exile in

29. Much has been written about the circumstances of Josiah's death. See S. B. Frost, "The Death of Josiah: A Conspiracy of Silence," *JBL* 87 (1968) 369–82; H. G. M. Williamson, "The Death of Josiah and the Continuing Development of the Deuteronomistic History," *VT* 32 (1982) 242–47; Zipora Talshir, "The Three Deaths of Josiah and the Strata of Biblical Historiography (2 Kings xxiii 29–30; 2 Chronicles xxxv 20–5; 1 Esdras i 23–31)," *VT* 46 (1996) 213–36; and Steve Delamarter, "The Death of Josiah in Scripture and Tradition: Wrestling with the Problem of Evil?" *VT* 54 (2004) 29–60.

Egypt, where he eventually died (2 Kgs. 23:33–34). In Jerusalem the prophet Jeremiah advised his countrymen not to lament the dead Josiah but to lament the exiled Shallum (Jehoahaz):

> Do not weep for him who is dead,
>   nor bemoan him;
> weep rather for him who goes away,
>   for he shall return no more
>   to see his native land.
>   (Jer. 22:10; see Ezek. 19:1–4)

Jehoiakim

Neco took Eliakim, the older brother of Jehoahaz, and enthroned him as the new Judean king with the throne name Jehoiakim (2 Kgs. 23:34). Egypt for the moment was still supreme in Syria-Palestine, "from the Brook of Egypt to the River Euphrates" (24:7). Jehoiakim, along with Judean society at large, was clearly pro-Egyptian. To raise the special tribute placed on Judah, Jehoiakim did not raid the royal or temple treasury but instead extracted the silver and gold from the people of the land in a special taxation (23:35). Since he was enthroned after Nisan 609, Jehoiakim's first regnal year did not begin until Nisan 608 (see n. 30). For four years he remained a loyal Egyptian vassal.

In 606 the Egyptian army had temporarily overcome the Babylonian garrison at Kimuhu near Carchemish (*ABC* 98), but the Egyptian-Babylonian struggle was already tilting in favor of Babylon. A year later, in 605, the great encounter for dominance in the eastern Mediterranean seaboard between Babylonia and Egypt occurred at the old Neo-Hittite city of Carchemish (see Jer. 46:1–12). Nebuchadrezzar, the Babylonian crown prince, led his forces to an overwhelming victory. After futilely attempting to halt the Babylonians at Carchemish, the Egyptian army retreated, only to be defeated again in the region of Hamath. The remnants of the Egyptian army were decimated while fleeing Syria for their homeland (*ABC* 99). As we noted earlier, Judean troops formed part of the Egyptian military fighting to halt Nebuchadrezzar's advance westward (*Contra Apion* 1.136–37). From this time on, Nebuchadrezzar regarded himself as master of Syria-Palestine and could portray himself as a liberator freeing the region from Egyptian domination (see *ANET* 307).

Jehoiakim was Neco's man on the Judean throne, and he and most of the Judean population, even after Carchemish, probably hoped that the Egyptian pharaoh could secure the region against Babylonian dominance and resist any attempt on Nebuchadrezzar's part to push farther into the region than northern Syria. The prophet Jeremiah saw matters differently.

King Jehoiakim and the Prophet Jeremiah

Jeremiah must be seen not only as a prophet with his own particular perspectives on Judean life and international affairs but also as the spokesperson for a minority political position concerning the most appropriate foreign policy for the state. He represented those who felt that submission to Babylonia was the

TEXT 16. King Adon's Appeal to Pharoah

To Lord of Kings Pharaoh, your servant Adon King of [Ekron. The welfare of my lord, Lord of Kings Pharaoh may the gods of] Heaven and Earth and Beelshmayin, [the great] god [seek exceedingly at all times, and may they lengthen the days of] Pharaoh like the days of (the) high heavens. That [I have written to Lord of Kings is to inform him that the forces] of the King of Babylon have come (and) reach[ed] Aphek. . . [. . .] they have seized . . . for Lord of Kings Pharaoh knows that [your] servant [. . .] to send a force to rescue [me]. Do not abandon [me, for your servant did not violate the treaty of the Lord of Kings] and your servant preserved his good relations. And as for this commander [. . .] a governor in the land. And as for the letter of Sindur . . . (Bezalel Porten, "The Identity of King Adon," *BA* 44 [1981] 36)

most advantageous policy Judah could take. In criticizing royal practices and state policies, Jeremiah was more than an isolated voice crying in the wilderness. Some members of his immediate family and his personal supporters could have been important and powerful figures in the political and cultic life of Judah.

The names of several members of Jeremiah's immediate family were also the names of leading Judean officials at the time. (It is impossible, however, to know for certain whether an identical name refers to the same or to a different individual.) Jeremiah's father was named Hilkiah, the same name as the high priest at the time of the Josianic reform (Jer. 1:1; 2 Kgs. 22:4, 8). His uncle, Shallum, had the same name as the husband of the prophetess Huldah (Jer. 32:7; 2 Kgs. 22:14). Maaseiah, the son of Shallum (and Jeremiah's first cousin?), was a priestly official, the keeper of the threshold (Jer. 35:4). Zephaniah, another son of Shallum, was second to the high priest in the temple hierarchy (Jer. 21:1; 37:3; 52:24).

In addition, Jeremiah was supported by several high-ranking government officials, many from the family of Shaphan, who possessed strong connections with the reform movement of Josiah. Ahikam, son of Shaphan and court official under Josiah, aided Jeremiah when he was arrested for treason (Jer. 26:24; 2 Kgs. 22:11, 14). Another son of Shaphan, Elasah, carried Jeremiah's correspondence to the exiles in Babylon (Jer. 29:3). Jeremiah's scroll was given a reading in the house of Gemariah, another son of Shaphan (Jer. 36:10–12). Elnathan son of Achbor, a prince in Jehoiakim's court, whose father was involved in Josiah's reform (2 Kgs. 22:12, 14), was at least sympathetic to Jeremiah's preaching (Jer. 36:12, 25).

Jeremiah and Jehoiakim seldom seem to have held similar opinions about either Judean life or international affairs. Already "in the beginning of the reign of Jehoiakim" (between his accession and the beginning of his first regnal year?), Jeremiah had delivered his famous temple sermon (Jer. 7; 26) warning that, unless repentance and strict adherence to the law were forthcoming, the Jerusalem temple would become like the temple of Shiloh (26:6). Just as Shiloh had once housed the ark and functioned as an important sanctuary but now was an insignificant place, so would Jerusalem soon be. The implication

TEXT 17. The Mesad Hashavyahu Letter

May the official, my lord, hear the plea of his servant. Your servant is working at the harvest. Your servant was in Ḥaṣar-Asam. Your servant did his reaping, finished, and stored (the grain) a few days ago before stopping. When your servant had finished his reaping and had stored it a few days ago, Hoshayahu ben Shabay came and took your servant's garment. When I had finished my reaping, at that time, a few days ago, he took your servant's garment. All my companions will testify for me, all who were reaping with me in the heat of the sun—they will testify for me that this is true. I am guiltless of an infraction. (So) please return my garment. If the official does (= you do) not consider it an obligation to return your servant's garment, then have pity upon him and return your servant's garment (from that motive). You must not remain silent when your servant is without his garment. (*HAHL* 20–21; partially restored)

of Jeremiah's sermon, given in Jeremiah 7 in a form strongly reminiscent of Deuteronomic perspectives and terminology, suggests that Jehoiakim was no strict Yahwist cut from the same cloth as his father. Jeremiah 7:31–32 and chap. 19 imply instead that the king had returned to the old-time religion of pre-Josianic days.

Jeremiah was not alone in his evaluation of the situation. The prophet Uriah ben Shemaiah from Kiriath-jearim proclaimed a similar message. Both men angered governmental officials, who must have regarded their words as blasphemy and "un-Judean." In light of the people's reactions, Uriah fled to Egypt but was extradited by an Egyptian government friendly to Judah, returned to Jerusalem, executed on order of the king, and his body thrown into the pauper's graveyard (Jer. 26:20–23). Jeremiah was saved from an identical fate when prophetic precedent was appealed to—the case of the prophet Micah who had preached a similar message provoking, so it is said, King Hezekiah to heed his word and call on Yahweh for help, and Yahweh had changed his verdict (26:16–19). The text notes also, perhaps the more important factor in his escape from execution, namely, that Jeremiah was supported by Ahikam, the son of Shaphan the state secretary (26:24; 2 Kgs. 22:3, 8).

The tensions between Jehoiakim and Jeremiah did not subside with the passage of time. In the fourth year of Jehoiakim (605), the year of the battle of Carchemish, Jeremiah proclaimed that Yahweh would send for all the tribes of the north and for Nebuchadrezzar and would bring them against the land of Judah and utterly destroy it (Jer. 25). He predicted that "this whole land shall become a ruin and a waste, and these nations shall serve the king of Babylon seventy years" (25:11). "Seventy years" was a common figure used in Near Eastern literature to speak of the period of a city's devastation or ruin (see Isa. 23:17, *COS* 2:306, and below, p. 505). Yahweh's scourge at the hands of the Babylonians was to reach other nations as well, including Egypt (Jer. 25:15–26; 46:1–12). Clearly, Jeremiah saw Nebuchadrezzar as Yahweh's new man, as Yahweh's servant, to master the nations for the coming years (25:9).

Jeremiah was barred from entering the temple, possibly as a consequence of his earlier sermon delivered there. To make his oracles public, he engaged Baruch, a scribe, to write his words on a scroll and read them in the temple (Jer. 36). The occasion for the reading was a public fast proclaimed in the fifth year of Jehoiakim (604–603), probably at the time of Nebuchadrezzar's attack on the Philistine city of Ashkelon (*ABC* 100). After the reading, the scroll was taken and privately read to the king, who defiantly burned it and ordered that Jeremiah and Baruch be arrested.[30] The two, having been earlier warned, had taken precautions and were already in hiding. A new scroll was produced containing Jeremiah's message but expanded to include a warning that Nebuchadrezzar would destroy Judah and specifying that Jehoiakim would meet a particularly terrible fate—death without burial.

Sometime in his reign, perhaps before the Babylonians completely took over Syria-Palestine, Jehoiakim began the construction of a new royal palace apparently with the use of conscripted labor. A recently published seal, probably from the late seventh century, contains the inscription: "Belonging to Palayahu, who is over the compulsory labor." Whether the practice of using conscripted laborers on royal land and royal projects had continued throughout Judean history from the time of David and Solomon or was a renewed practice of Jehoiakim's reign cannot be determined. At any rate, Jeremiah denounced Jehoiakim in a scathing oracle:

> Woe to him who builds his house by unrighteousness,
>   and his upper rooms by injustice;
> who makes his neighbors work for nothing,
>   and does not give them their wages;
> who says, "I will build myself a spacious house
>   with large upper rooms,"
> and who cuts out windows for it,
>   paneling it with cedar,
>   and painting it with vermilion.
> Are you are a king
>   because you compete in cedar?
> Did not your father [Josiah] eat and drink
>   and do justice and righteousness?
> Then it was well with him.
> He judged the cause of the poor and needy;
>   then it was well.
> Is not this to know me, says Yahweh.
> But your eyes and heart
>   are only on your dishonest gain,
>   for shedding innocent blood,
>   and for practicing oppression and violence.
>   (Jer. 22:13–17)

---

30. This episode occurred in the ninth month (see Jer. 36:9, 22) when a fire was burning in the winter quarters of the palace. These factors indicate that by this time Judah was operating on a Nisan-to-Nisan calendar when the year began in the spring (March–April) rather than the traditional Judean pattern of a Tishri-to-Tishri calendar when the year began in the fall (September–October). If the change of the calendar was part of Josiah's reform, this could indicate his and the reform's reliance upon priestly or holiness material since only this stream of biblical tradition demanded a year beginning in the spring (see Exod. 12:1–3).

In his denunciations of Jehoiakim, Jeremiah seems clearly to have called for the assassination of the king and his family. In 36:30 the prophet announces an oracle of doom: "Therefore thus says Yahweh concerning King Jehoiakim of Judah: He shall have none to sit upon the throne of David, and his dead body shall be cast out to the heat by day and the frost by night." Jeremiah 22:18–19 is even more explicit: "Therefore thus says Yahweh concerning King Jehoiakim son of Josiah: 'They shall not lament for him, saying, . . . "Alas, lord!" or "Alas, his majesty!" With the burial of a donkey he shall be buried—dragged off and thrown out beyond the gates of Jerusalem.'" Both of these announcements of judgment were proclaimed as rhetorical calls for assassination, but apparently there were no takers.

Judah as a Babylonian Vassal

In 604–603, following his victory at Carchemish, Nebuchadrezzar in his first regnal year marched unopposed into Syria-Palestine, received the tribute of kings in the region, and conquered the defiant Philistine city of Ashkelon (*ABC* 100).[31] This was perhaps the occasion for the national fast noted in Jeremiah 36:9 and for the lamenting oracle of Habakkuk on the growing power of the Chaldeans (Hab. 1–2). For the following two years, 603–602, the Babylonian texts are fragmentary, but Nebuchadrezzar seems to have continued to operate in Syria-Palestine and to secure his control there, anxious to curb Egyptian influence in the area and to confine Egypt to its homeland.[32] Probably following the Babylonian capture of Ashkelon in 604–603 (see above, Text 15), Jehoiakim gave up his tenacious determination not to submit to the Babylonians and became Nebuchadrezzar's vassal. Apparently neither he nor the majority of his officials ever surrendered their confidence in Egypt, however, and remained loyal to Babylonia only long enough to pay annual tribute on three occasions (2 Kgs. 24:1), probably in 603, 602, and 601.

If Jehoiakim transferred his allegiance from Neco II to Nebuchadrezzar sometime in 604–603, then it would have been about 600 that he decided to withhold tribute and challenge Nebuchadrezzar. From the Babylonian Chronicles it becomes obvious why Jehoiakim chose to pursue this action, which otherwise appears irrational. The chronicles report the following:

> Year 4 [601–600]: The king of Akkad [Nebuchadrezzar] sent out his army and marched into Hatti land [Syria-Palestine]. [They marched] unopposed through Hatti land. In the month of Kislimu [November–December] he took the lead of his army and marched toward Egypt. The king of Egypt [Neco]

---

31. On the career of Nebuchadrezzar see D. J. Wiseman, *Nebuchadrezzar and Babylon* (Schweich Lecutres 1983; Oxford: Oxford University Press for the British Academy, 1985). A synopsis of his campaigns is provided in Israel Eph'al, "Nebuchadnezzar the Warrior: Remarks on His Military Achievement," *IEJ* 53 (2003) 178–91. See also L. E. Stager, "The Fury of Babylon: Ashkelon and the Archaeology of Destruction," *BAR* 22/1 (1996) 56–69, 76–77.

32. Nebuchadrezzar may not have campaigned in Syria-Palestine in his second regnal year; see Nadav Na'aman, "Nebuchadnezzar's Campaign in the Year 603 BCE," *BN* 62 (1992) 41–44; repr. in *AIIN* 399–402. For general Egyptian-Babylonian relations, see A. J. Spalinger, "Egypt and Babylonia: A Survey (c. 620 B.C.–550 B.C.)," *Studien zur altägyptischen Kultur* 5 (1977) 228–44; and Oded Lipschits, "Nebuchadrezzar's Policy in 'Hattu-Land' and the Fate of the Kingdom of Judah," *UF* 30 (1998) 467–87.

heard (of it) and sent out his army; they clashed in an open battle and inflicted heavy losses on each other. The king of Akkad and his army turned back and [returned] to Babylon. (*ANET* 564; cf. *ABC* 101)

This frank Babylonian report demonstrates that Nebuchadrezzar attempted to invade Egypt late in 601 but was either defeated or fought to a draw. This Egyptian-Babylonian battle also appears to be noted in Herodotus, who reports that "with his land army, he [Neco] met and defeated the Syrians [= Babylonians?] at Magdolus [= Migdol in Egypt?], taking the great Syrian city of Cadytis [= Gaza?] after the battle" (2.159). Jeremiah 47:1 also refers to the Egyptian capture of Gaza. Probably in late 601/early 600, Nebuchdrezzar invaded Egypt, was severely defeated and repelled from Egypt, and Neco carried the conflict into Palestine, where he captured the city of Gaza. According to the Babylonian records, Nebuchadrezzar spent the year following his defeat in Babylon refurbishing his chariot forces (*ANET* 564; *ABC* 101; see above, Text 15). For the first time since 604, no Babylonian campaign was conducted in the direction of Syria-Palestine. Perhaps Jehoiakim, encouraged by the pharaoh's showing and by the absence of the main Babylonian army, took the occasion to withhold tribute and thus to rebel.

Following their victory in 600 over the Babylonians, Neco and the Egyptians, while still attempting to foment rebellion in Syria-Palestine, were either unable or unwilling to reassert themselves further in land battles with Nebuchadrezzar. Neco turned his attention more to the sea. Perhaps recognizing that the Babylonians had control of the land area of the eastern Mediterranean seaboard, Neco sought a greater share of naval commerce. A canal joining the Mediterranean and the Red Sea was begun, and large seagoing triremes were introduced into the Egyptian fleet. Thus, although an Egyptian victory triggered Jehoiakim's revolt, the Egyptians proved not to be a major support in the long run partly because of their naval preoccupation.

In the sixth year of his reign (599–598), Nebuchadnezzar moved back into Syria-Palestine, but the period was spent primarily in raids against Arab tribes in the desert (*ANET* 564; *ABC* 101; see above, Text 15). The main Babylonian forces took no direct action against the rebel Jehoiakim. Second Kings 24:2 notes that "Yahweh sent against him bands of the Chaldeans, bands of the Arameans, bands of the Moabites, and bands of the Ammonites." Apparently Nebuchadnezzar contented himself for the moment with allowing the Jerusalem situation to be handled by auxiliary forces and the Babylonian (Chaldean) garrisons stationed in the region. Probably at this time Jeremiah had his famous encounter with the Rechabites (Jer. 35). The group had moved into Jerusalem "for fear of the army of the Chaldeans and the army of the Syrians" (35:11). Jeremiah used the Rechabites as an object lesson for the people: according to the prophet, they manifested a fidelity to their commitments that was in stark contrast to the unfaithfulness of Judah and Jerusalem.

In the following year, Nebuchadrezzar marched out with his main army. The Babylonian Chronicles report his suppression of the Judean revolt in the following terms:

Year 7 [598–597 B.C.E.], month Kislimu [18 Dec. 598–15 Jan. 597]: The king of Akkad [Nebuchadrezzar] moved his army into Hatti land, laid siege to the city of Judah [Jerusalem], and on the second day of the month Addaru he captured the city and seized its king. He appointed in it a king of his liking, took heavy booty from it and sent it to Babylon. (See *ANET* 564; *ABC* 102)

The second of Adar in Nebuchadrezzar's seventh year would correspond to either the 15th or the 16th of March 597. The uncertainty over the day is due to the fact that the Babylonians reckoned the day from dusk to dusk.

Jehoiachin

The king whom Nebuchadrezzar captured when Jerusalem surrendered was Jehoiachin (also called Jeconiah and Coniah), the eighteen-year-old son and successor of Jehoiakim. The biblical texts assign three months (2 Kgs. 24:8) or three months and ten days to his reign (2 Chr. 36:9). This means that he would have become king sometime early in December 598 before Nebuchadrezzar personally arrived on the scene in Jerusalem. There are diverse traditions about what happened to Jehoiakim, the previous king and instigator of the rebellion. Second Kings 24:6 reports that he slept with his fathers, thus implying that he died a natural death. Second Chronicles 36:6 says that Nebuchadrezzar bound him in fetters to take him to Babylon. The Lucianic recension of the Greek for both 2 Kings 24:6 and 2 Chronicles 36:8 reports that he was buried in the Garden of Uzzah, outside the wall of Jerusalem (see 2 Kgs. 21:18, 26). Finally, Josephus has Jehoiakim killed by Nebuchadrezzar after Jerusalem fell (*Ant.* 10.96). Second Kings 24:6 is probably the more reliable. Jehoiakim must have died in office, still anticipating the arrival of the Egyptians, but "the king of Egypt did not come again out of his land" (2 Kgs. 24:7).

After a reign of three months, upon the arrival of Nebuchadrezzar on the scene, "King Jehoiachin of Judah gave himself up to the king of Babylon, himself, his mother, his servants, and his officers, and his palace officials" (2 Kgs. 24:12). These and other leading citizens along with the temple and royal treasures were carried away by Nebuchadrezzar to Babylon. According to 2 Kings 24:12b, the exile of Jehoiachin occurred in the eighth year of Nebuchadrezzar, although Jerusalem was captured in his seventh year. Jeremiah 52:28b states that 3,023 Judeans were deported in Nebuchadrezzar's seventh year. One would presume that after the city was captured, the Babylonian king returned to Babylonia to observe the *akitu* festival before the beginning of the next regnal year. Exiles were probably carried back with him. According to 2 Chronicles 36:10 Nebuchadrezzar "in the spring of the year . . . sent and brought Jehoiachin to Babylon . . . ," thus after the new year and in Nebuchadrezzar's eighth year.

Zedekiah

The "king of his liking" whom Nebuchadrezzar placed on the Judean throne was Mattaniah, an uncle of Jehoiachin, who bore the throne name Zedekiah (2 Kgs. 24:17). Zedekiah was subjected to a treaty and made to swear an oath of fidelity to the Babylonian ruler in the name of Yahweh (2 Chr. 36:13; Ezek.

17:12–20), "that he would surely keep the country for him and attempt no uprising nor show friendliness to the Egyptians" (so Josephus, *Ant.* 10.102).[33] He ascended the throne after the major spring festival had passed; thus his first regnal year began in Nisan 596. His rule lasted for eleven years (596–586).

The capture of Jerusalem and the exile of Jehoiachin left the people stunned and polarized. There were those—perhaps a majority—who could not believe that this had really happened, that Jerusalem, Yahweh's city, had been taken. Yahweh had stepped in before, at the last moment, and saved the city during Hezekiah's reign. Moreover, the Zion theology proclaimed the inviolability of the city (Pss. 46; 48; 76). Surely the capture had been only an historical accident. In short, there were hopes, encouraged by prophetic announcements, that the whole bad dream would be reversed in the immediate future and Jehoiachin and the exiles would return.

Feelings were partially polarized around the figures of Jehoiachin and Zedekiah. Dates in the biblical text are frequently given with references to Jehoaichin's exile (Ezek. 1:2; 8:1; 20:1, 24:1, etc.; see 2 Kgs. 25:27) suggesting that many still considered him the real king and looked forward to his release and reinstatement. Zedekiah had been put on the throne by a foreign monarch, not installed by his own people. On the other hand, Jehoiachin was considered totally unacceptable by Jeremiah (Jer. 22:24–30; referred to here as Coniah). Jeremiah and Judah were also divided over what course of action to take, whether to continue hoping in Egypt or to submit completely to the Babylonians. In all of this, Zedekiah seems to have lacked full control over his own people and to have vacillated in his actions or to have been forced into positions he would rather not have taken. In addition, many of the seasoned Judean diplomats and officials were in exile, no longer present to offer advice.

Judah under Babylonian Hegemony

Little is known about international events during Zedekiah's reign. The account in 2 Kings moves directly from his accession to the outbreak of rebellion in his ninth year (2 Kgs. 24:18–25:1). The Babylonian Chronicles are fragmentary for this period. Fortunately some information has been supplied in the books of Jeremiah and Ezekiel. Jeremiah 27–29, for example, which belongs primarily to the beginning of the reign of Zedekiah (27:1; 28:1), provides some information about international affairs. (The reference to "the fifth month of the fourth year" in 28:1 probably is a calculation associated with a seven-year or sabbatical cycle [see Deut. 15] rather than the chronology of the reign of Zedekiah.[34])

In 597, after Nebuchadrezzar had quickly returned to Babylon, as was his custom after completing a campaign, a six-nation regional conclave was held in Jerusalem. Representatives from Edom, Moab, Ammon, Tyre, and Sidon gathered in the Judean capital to discuss possible plans and to coordinate strategy (Jer. 27:3). The absence of any representatives from Philistia suggests that

33. See Matitiahu Tsevat, "The Neo-Assyrian and Neo-Babylonian Vassal Oaths and the Prophet Ezekiel," *JBL* 78 (1959) 199–204.

34. See Nahum Sarna, "The Abortive Insurrection in Zedekiah's Days (Jer. 27–29)," *ErIsr* 14 (1978) 89–96; repr. in his *Studies in Biblical Interpretation* (Philadelphia: Jewish Publication Society, 2000) 281–94.

74. *Discovery of an Arad ostracon.* Members of the excavating team at Tell Arad gather around to see and photograph a newly discovered ostracon—in this case a bowl inscribed with the letters *qdsh* (meaning "holy"). Yohanan Aharoni, director of the excavations, stands at the center of the photograph.

this area had been placed under strong Babylonian control, since it was located close to Egypt, Nebuchadrezzar's primary enemy. Apparently the Transjordanian and Phoenician ambassadors discussed with Zedekiah the prospects of a united revolt to take place two years later in conjunction with a simultaneous rebellion being planned by states in the east that were subject to Babylon. Whether Zedekiah initiated the meeting and what his stance was on the planned rebellion remain unknown.

Jeremiah vigorously opposed the conclave and picketed the meeting wearing thongs and yoke bars (Jer. 27:2). He denounced all plans for rebellion and called upon all the nations and especially Zedekiah to remain loyal to Babylon, threatening them with divine judgment if they did not serve Nebuchadrezzar. Apparently the anti-Babylonian sentiment had the support of many religious leaders, especially some of the prophets (27:9, 16). In his letter to the exiles, which Zedekiah allowed him to send to Babylon with royal emissaries, Jeremiah referred to the prophetical activity in Babylon that was apparently aware of the movement underfoot (29:8–9, 20–23). Jeremiah also responded to the attempt to have him arrested and the charge that he was a madman (29:24–28). In his letter Jeremiah advised the exiles not to place any hopes in a speedy return but to settle down in their new locale and cause no trouble (29:4–7).

The nationalistic prophet Hananiah spoke out in Jerusalem promising that the yoke of the king of Babylon would be broken in two years and that King Jehoiachin and the exiles would soon return home (Jer. 28:1–4).[35] He seems to

---

35. See Henri Mottu, "Jeremiah vs. Hananiah: Ideology and Truth in Old Testament Prophecy," in N. K. Gottwald, ed., *The Bible and Liberation* (2d ed.; Maryknoll, NY: Orbis, 1983) 313–28.

TEXT 18. Lachish and Arad Letters

Lachish Letters

1. Your servant Hoshayahu (hereby) reports to my lord Ya'ush. May YHWH give you good news. . . . And now, please explain to your servant the meaning of the letter which my lord sent to your servant yesterday evening. For your servant has been sick at heart ever since you sent (that letter) to your servant. In it my lord said: "Don't you know how to read a letter?" As (Y)HWH lives, no one has ever tried to read *me* a letter! Moreover, whenever any letter comes to me and I have read it, I can repeat it down to the smallest detail. Now your servant has received the following information: General Konyahu son of Elnatan has moved south in order to enter Egypt. He has sent (messengers) to take Hodavyahu son of Ahiyahu and his men from here. (Herewith) I am also sending to my lord the letter (which was in the custody) of Tobyahu, servant of the king, which was sent to Shallum son of Yada from the prophet and which begins "Beware." (*HAHL* 84–85; partially restored)

2. May YHWH give you good news at this time. And now, your servant has done everything my lord sent (word to do). I have written down everything you sent me (word to do). As regards what my lord said about Beth-HRPD, there is no one there. As for Semakyahu, Shemayahu has seized him and taken him up to the city. Your servant cannot send the witness there today. For if he comes around during the morning tour he will know that we are watching the Lachish (fire-)signals according to the code which my lord gave us, for we cannot see Azeqah. (*HAHL* 91; partially restored)

3. To my lord Yaush. May YHWH make this time a good one for you. Who is your servant (but) a dog that my lord should have sent (him) the king's letter and those of the officials asking (me) to read them? The [officials'] statements are not good—they are of a kind to slacken your courage and to weaken that of the men . . . my lord. Won't you write to them as follows: "Why are you acting thus." . . . As YHWH your God lives, ever since your servant read the letters he has not had a moment's peace. (*HAHL* 100; partially restored)

Arad Letters

1. To Elyashib. And now, give to the Kittim three *bat*-measures of wine and write down the date. From what is left of the first meal have one *homer*-measure(?) of meal loaded to make bread for them. Give (them) the wine from the craters. (*HAHL* 31)

2. To Elyashib. And now, give to the Kittim two *bat*-measures of wine for the four days, three hundred loaves of bread, and a full *homer*-measure of wine. Send (them) out tomorrow; don't wait. If there is any vinegar left, give (it) to them (also). (*HAHL* 33)

3. To Nahum. [And] now, go to the house of Elyashib son of Eshyahu and get from there one (*bat*-measure?) of oil and send (it) to Ziph right away. (*HAHL* 51)

4. To my lord Elyashib. May YHWH concern himself with your well-being. And now, give Shermaryahu a *letek*-measure(?) (of meal?) and to the Qerosite give a *homer*-measure(?) (of meal?). As regards the matter concerning which you gave me orders: everything is fine now: he is staying in the temple of YHWH. (*HAHL* 55)

5. To Elyashib . . . . king . . . . army . . . . servant . . . , from Arad fifty and from Qinah. . . . and send them to Ramat-negeb under Malkiyahu son of Qerabur. He is to hand them over to Elisha son of Yirmeyahu at Ramat-negeb lest anything happen to the city. This is an order from the king—a life and death matter for you. I have sent you this message to warn you now: These men (must be) with Elisha lest (the) Edom(ites) go there. (*HAHL* 59–60; partially restored)

6. Your son Gemaryahu, as well as Nehemyahu, hereby send greetings to (you) Malkiyahu. I bless you to YHWH. And now, your servant has applied himself to what you ordered. I (hereby) write to my lord everything that the man wanted. Eshyahu has come from you but he has not given them any men. You know the reports from Edom. I sent them to [my] lord before evening. Eshyahu is staying in my house. He tried to obtain the report but I would not give (it to him). The king of Judah should know that we are unable to send the. . . . This is the evil which the Edom(ites) have done. (*HAHL* 64; partially restored)

have placed his faith in the planned forthcoming rebellion, proclaimed it as Yahweh's will, and condemned Jeremiah for lack of faith. According to Hananiah, the yoke of Babylon would be broken "from the neck of all the nations" (28:11). To symbolize his prophecy, Hananiah had removed the yoke bars from Jeremiah and broken them (28:10). Jeremiah subsequently replaced these with iron yokes to symbolize that Nebuchadrezzar's rule was a rule of iron (28:12–14). Jeremiah prophesied Hananiah's death, and apparently someone in Zedekiah's administration or in the pro-Babylonian segment of the society saw to it that the prophecy was fulfilled, since "in that same year, in the seventh month, the prophet Hananiah died" (28:15–17).

In Nebuchadrezzar's ninth and tenth years (596–595, 595–594), trouble did break out in the east. Although the Babylonian Chronicles are fragmentary at this point, they refer to a movement from the east by the king of Elam against Nebuchadrezzar in the king's ninth year. Elam may have been influential earlier in the call of the planning meeting held in Jerusalem to plot revolt in the west (see Jer. 49:34–38). The Elamite advance was met by a Babylonian response and the Elamites fled. For most of his tenth year Nebuchadrezzar remained in Babylonia, where he had to put down a local rebellion that broke out in December 595 and involved elements in his own army. Later in the year he marched to the west and collected tribute (*ABC* 102). So far as is known, none of the nations that sent representatives to the Jerusalem conference rebelled during Babylonia's troubles in 596–594.

In Zedekiah's fourth year (594–593), we hear of a trip of the Judean king or a royal emissary to Babylon (Jer. 51:59). Such a trip undoubtedly had a political purpose: to offer to Nebuchadrezzar assurances of Judean loyalty in light of the recent uprisings. On this occasion Jeremiah is said to have sent a letter (51:60) containing an oracle proclaiming the ultimate downfall of Babylon (51:1–58), with orders that the document be read and then thrown into the Euphrates (51:61–64). Such an oracle makes sense as Jeremiah's response to the demoralized Judean exiles who had set their hopes on the success of the recently suppressed insurrection. All along, it seems, Jeremiah had viewed the exiles in a positive light, comparing them to good figs and those left in Jerusalem and the pro-Egyptians who had fled to Egypt to bad figs (Jer. 24).

In Egypt, meanwhile, Psammetichus II (595–589) had succeeded Neco II. Two events in this pharaoh's reign had enormous impact on Judean politics and tipped the scales toward a second revolt against Babylonia. (1) The pharaoh carried out a successful campaign against Nubia (Ethiopia). The Egyptian army marched south, apparently encountered no overwhelming opposition, and returned home victorious in 592 (Herodotus 2.161; *AEL* 3:84–86). The pharaoh sought to make the most of this victory to counter Egyptian lack of success against Babylonia. (2) In 591, shortly after the return from Nubia, Psammetichus II went on a victory tour of Palestine. This journey is reported in the so-called Rylands IX papyrus. The following extract from the papyrus text describes the visit:

> In the fourth regnal year of Pharaoh Psamtek Neferibre they sent to the great temples of Upper and Lower Egypt, saying, "Pharaoh (Life, Prosperity, Health) is going to the Land of Palestine. Let the priests come with the bouquets of the gods of Egypt to take them to the Land of Palestine." And they sent to Teudjoy saying: "Let a priest come with the bouquet of Amun, in order to go to the Land of Palestine with Pharaoh." And the priests agreed and said to Pediese, the son of Essamtowy, "you are the one who, it is agreed, ought to go to the Land of Palestine with Pharaoh. There is no one here in the town who is able to go to the Land of Palestine except you. Behold, you must do it, you, a scribe of the House of Life; there is nothing they can ask you and you not be able to answer it, for you are a priest of Amun. It is only the priests of the great gods of Egypt that are going to the Land of Palestine with Pharaoh." And they persuaded Pediese to go to the Land of Palestine with Pharaoh and he made his preparations. So Pediese, son of Essamtowy, went to the Land of Palestine, and no one was with him save his servant and an hour-priest of Isis named Osirmose.[36]

---

36. F. L. Griffith, *Catalogue of the Demotic Papyri in the John Rylands Library* (3 vols.; Manchester: Manchester University Press, 1909) 2:64–65; see Julie Galambush, "The Northern Voyage of Psammetichus II and Its Implications for Ezekiel 44.7–9," in L. L. Grabbe and A. O. Bellis, eds., *The Priests in the Prophets: The Portrayal of Priests, Prophets and Other Religious Specialists in the Latter Prophets* (JSOTSup 408; London: T. & T. Clark, 2004) 65–78.

Two factors about this text are noteworthy and must be taken into consideration in its interpretation. First, the text presents the expedition to Palestine as if it was fundamentally a religious, festive occasion. Second, the focus in the narrative is on Pediese the priest and his fate and not on the larger historical issues. In the story's continuation, the account reports how Pediese returned to Egypt to find that he had been cheated out of his priestly income and was forced to appeal unsuccessfully to the pharaoh.

The visit of Psammetichus II to Palestine must, however, be seen as more than a triumphant religious procession. After all, Babylonian troops were stationed in the area and the states of Syria-Palestine were committed to Nebuchadrezzar by treaty. Such a visit by a long-standing anti-Babylonian power could not help but carry political and military implications. Psammetichus's visit must have been seen as Egypt's reassertion, even if somewhat ceremonial, of its claims over Syria-Palestine.

The Judean Rebellion and the Fall of Jerusalem

Sometime very late in the 590s or early in the 580s, Judah rebelled against Babylon, a move presumably symbolized by Zedekiah's failure to render annual tribute (2 Kgs. 24:20b) and by "sending ambassadors to Egypt in order that they might give him horses and a large army" (Ezek. 17:15). The account in 2 Kings offers no explanation for the rebellion, nor does it provide any clues about why the Judean political hierarchy thought it had a chance to succeed. In fact, this account moves quickly to the final days of the two-year Babylonian siege of Jerusalem.

Two factors must be seen as contributing causes to Zedekiah's revolt. (1) Nebuchadrezzar had apparently not put in an appearance in Syria-Palestine since 594. The Babylonian Chronicles report that in his eleventh year (594–593) Nebuchadrezzar mustered his army and marched to Hatti (*ABC* 102), but they provide no details about this western campaign. As we have noted, even prior to this date, Nebuchadrezzar was fairly consistently occupied in the east. (2) Psammetichus II's triumph in Nubia must have stirred the hopes of Judean circles who still believed that Egypt could offer military salvation. Undoubtedly a large portion of the Judean leadership held this view. Likewise, the visit of Psammetichus II to Palestine and his "triumphant tour" in the area must have fed the fires of revolt. It is not out of the question that Psammetichus may have visited Jerusalem, conferred with Zedekiah, and entered into a treaty with him. (Ezekiel 8 has been interpreted in terms of such a visit, and the reference in v. 17 to putting "the branch to the nose" has been associated with the garlands of the Egyptian gods.) Ezekiel 17:15 clearly refers to Zedekiah's negotiations with Egypt over supplying him with horses and troops. It cannot be determined when this negotiation took place. If the date in 8:1 (September 592) is applicable to the whole section of chapters 8–19, then negotiations with Psammetichus II could certainly be alluded to in 17:15.

It may have been these Egyptian negotiations, therefore, which led to the breaking of Zedekiah's treaty with Babylonia (Ezek. 17:13–21). At any rate, Zedekiah was clearly relying on Egyptian aid in his endeavors. Among the ostraca (inscribed potsherds) discovered at the site of ancient Lachish was a letter mentioning the visit to Egypt of Coniah son of Elnathan, a general in the Judean army (*ANET* 322, ostracon III; see Text 18), possibly to conduct negotiations for assistance.

No evidence exists to suggest that Judah's uprising was coordinated with any country other than Egypt. Neither does there appear to have been any broad move of insurrection against Babylonia in Syria-Palestine at the time or a united anti-Babylonian front in Judah. Of the other states in the region, only Ammon (see Ezek. 21:18–23) and Tyre, which was subsequently placed under a thirteen-year siege by Nebuchadrezzar (Ezek. 26–28; 29:17–20; Josephus, *Ant.* 10.228), rebelled. Likewise, elements of the population, including Jeremiah and his followers and associates, strongly opposed rebellion. One of the Lachish ostraca can be interpreted to suggest that there was dissension and tension even in the military over the best attitude to take toward Babylonia (*ANET* 322, ostracon VI; see Text 18).

Many episodes in the book of Jeremiah concern events associated with the days of Jerusalem's siege and illustrate the diverse sentiments in the city. As Nebuchadrezzar's army approached the city, for example, Zedekiah is reported to have sent a delegation of nobles to Jeremiah to "inquire of Yahweh" (Jer. 21). Jeremiah responded very negatively, announcing that Yahweh would fight on the side of the Babylonians and recommending that the citizens surrender to the Chaldeans. Jeremiah 19:1–20:6 may belong to this same context. In Jeremiah 19 Jeremiah proclaimed in a symbolical act, and publicly, the same message that had been transmitted privately to Zedekiah's delegation. Thereupon Pashhur, the priest who had been a member of the delegation, beat Jeremiah and had him put in stocks in the Upper Benjamin Gate of the temple. When released the next day, Jeremiah reaffirmed his position that Judah would fall to the Babylonians and added that Pashhur and his family would die in exile.

While the siege of the city was under way, Apries (Hophra, 589–570), the new Egyptian pharaoh, sent an Egyptian army into Palestine, causing the Babylonians to lift the siege temporarily (Jer. 37:1–10). It is impossible to know how seriously Apries took his commitment to Judah. Classical sources note that he fought against Tyre and Sidon and defeated the armies of Cyprus and Phoenicia (Herodotus 2.161; Diodorus 1.68.1). This would suggest that Apries was more concerned with naval exploits and Mediterranean trade than with aiding landlocked Judah.

Apparently while the Egyptian army was on the scene and the Babylonian army temporarily withdrawn, Zedekiah sent yet another delegation to Jeremiah requesting that he pray for the people. Again the prophet responded negatively and offered his evaluation of Egyptian assistance: "Pharaoh's army, which set out to help you, is going to return to its own land, to Egypt. And the Chaldeans shall return and fight against this city; they shall take it and burn it with fire" (Jer. 37:7–8; see Ezek. 17:17).

Also while the Babylonian army was temporarily withdrawn, Jeremiah sought to leave the city for business reasons (perhaps to buy a plot of land in Anathoth; see Jer. 32). He was arrested again, charged with deserting to the Babylonians, beaten, and imprisoned (37:11–15). While imprisoned in the house of Jonathan the secretary, he was summoned to Zedekiah for a private meeting. To the king he reaffirmed his negative assessment of the situation and appealed for release from prison. Zedekiah removed him to the court of the guard with orders that he be given a daily ration of bread as long as there was food in the city (37:16–21).

Apparently no major encounter occurred between the Egyptians and the Babylonians. The former may simply have withdrawn from Palestine. The siege of Jerusalem was again taken up in earnest, and the situation in the town became desperate. Among the Judean cities, only Jerusalem, Lachish, and Azekah remained in Judean hands (34:7).

Jeremiah apparently continued his preaching throughout the Babylonian campaign against Judah (Jer. 38). A delegation went to Zedekiah urging the king to put the prophet to death, "because he is discouraging the soldiers who are left in this city, and all the people, by speaking such words to them. For this man is not seeking the welfare of this people, but their harm" (38:4). The king turned the prophet over to the accusers, and Jeremiah this time was put into the cistern of Malchiah, the king's son, which was in the court of the guard. An Ethiopian in the royal service, Ebed-melech, appealed to the king for permission to draw Jeremiah out of the mire of the cistern. Following his rescue, Jeremiah remained in the court of the guard. Again the texts report a meeting between Zedekiah and Jeremiah. The prophet tried to talk Zedekiah into surrendering, and the king admitted that he was afraid to capitulate to the Babylonians lest they hand him over to the Judeans who had deserted to Nebuchadrezzar for fear they would abuse him. (As we shall see in the next chapter, this probably refers to pro-Babylonian Judeans who had set up headquarters in Mizpah.) After Jeremiah described for the king the consequences to his family of their capture, Zedekiah begged the prophet not to divulge the contents of their secret conversation, and Jeremiah agreed.

Two oracles in Jeremiah 34 relate to Zedekiah. In the first, Jeremiah predicts the fall of Jerusalem, but promises Zedekiah that he will die in peace (not be executed) after seeing the Babylonian king eye to eye and speaking with him face to face (34:1–5). In 34:8–22 he condemns the king and his officials for granting liberty to their slaves (so they would not have to feed them?) when the city was besieged but then reenslaving them as soon as the Babylonians moved away at the approach of the Egyptians.

As Jerusalem's situation became increasingly desperate and the city appeared doomed, Jeremiah seems to have shifted his preaching to pronouncements about the future. Of the city's impending ruin, he had no uncertainty, but he attempted to give hope for the more distant future. While still a prisoner in the court of the guard, for example, he reported on his earlier purchase of land in Anathoth (Jer. 32). The point he made was that, although Jerusalem would surely fall, things would someday surely return to normal: "Houses and fields and vineyards shall again be bought in this land" (32:15). The same point is made in Jeremiah 33. The houses that had been dismantled for stones to strengthen the city defenses would be rebuilt.

After a two-year siege, which began on the tenth of Tebet of Zedekiah's ninth year (about January 587; 2 Kgs. 25:1; Jer. 39:1), the people who were defending Jerusalem ran out of food. The city wall was breached on the ninth of Tammuz in Zedekiah's eleventh year (mid-July 586; 2 Kgs. 25:3; Jer. 39:2). Zedekiah with a military escort fled by night in the direction of Transjordan.

The Babylonians gave chase and overtook them near Jericho. Zedekiah was captured and carried before Nebuchadrezzar, who was encamped at Riblah. There sentence was passed, no doubt in terms of the treaty to which Zedekiah's and Yahweh's names had been earlier affixed: Zedekiah's sons were slaughtered before his eyes, he was blinded, bound in fetters, and taken to Babylon (2 Kgs. 25:3–7; Jer. 52:5–11; 39:1–7).

General Bibliography

H. W. F. Saggs, *The Greatness That Was Babylon* (2d ed.; London: Sidgwick & Jackson, 1988), provides an excellent treatment of Babylonian history, culture, and religion. B. T. Arnold, "Babylonians," in A. J. Hoerth et al., eds., *Peoples of the Old Testament World* (Grand Rapids: Baker, 1994) 43–75, competently covers the essentials, as does Arnold's *Who Were the Babylonians?* (SBLABS 10; Atlanta: Society of Biblical Literature, 2004).

Several significant articles on the period are found in Abraham Malamat, Part Four, "Twilight of Judah and the Destruction of the First Temple," in *History of Biblical Israel: Major Problems and Minor Issues* (CHANE 7; Leiden: Brill, 2001) 277–337. Oded Lipschits, "Nebuchadrezzar's Policy in 'Ḫattu-Land' and the Fate of the Kingdom of Judah," *UF* 30 (1998) 467–87, surveys Babylonian-Judean relations to the fall of Jerusalem.

The issues of the extent and nature of Josiah's kingdom are discussed by Nadav Na'aman, "The Kingdom of Judah under Josiah," *TA* 18 (1991) 3–71; repr. in *AIIN* 329–98. The archaeology of the period is surveyed in Ephriam Stern, *Archaeology of the Land of the Bible*, vol. 2: *The Assyrian, Babylonian, and Persian Periods, 732–332 BCE* (ABRL; New York: Doubleday, 2001) 303–50; and Raz Kletter, "Pots and Politics: Material Remains of Late Iron Age Judah in Relation to Its Political Borders," *BASOR* 314 (1999) 19–54. The articles in L. L. Grabbe, ed., *Good Kings and Bad Kings* (JSOTSup 393; ESHM 5; London: T. & T. Clark International, 2005), discuss many of the issues noted in this chapter.

Erik Eynikel, *The Reform of King Josiah and the Composition of the Deuteronomistic History* (Otst 33; Leiden: Brill, 1996); W. B. Barrick, *The King and the Cemeteries: Toward a New Understanding of Josiah's Reform* (VTSup 88; Leiden: Brill, 2002); and Antti Laato, *Josiah and David Redivivus: The Historical Josiah and the Messianic Expectations of Exilic and Postexilic Times* (ConBOT 33; Stockholm: Almqvist & Wiksell, 1992), survey issues and theories related to Josiah's reform, the nature of the biblical accounts, and the influence of the reform on the so-called Deuteronomistic History. Josiah is treated along with other kings in R. H. Lowery, *The Reforming Kings: Cults and Society in First Temple Judah* (JSOTSup 120; Sheffield: JSOT Press, 1991).

15. The Period of Babylonian Domination

Babylonian troops, under the direction of Nebuzaradan the captain of the royal bodyguard, ravaged Jerusalem in August 586 B.C.E., a few weeks after the city's capture (2 Kgs. 25:8; Jer. 52:12).[1] The temple, the royal palace, and the homes of citizens were burned. The city walls, already breached, were pulled down (2 Kgs. 25:9–10; Jer. 52:13–14). The remaining vessels and treasures from the temple, as well as reusable bronze, were carted away (2 Kgs. 25:13–17; Jer. 52:17–23). The conquering army, no doubt, had already plundered the city in the interval between its capture and its burning. The top priests, some surviving royal officials and commanders, and provincial leaders were rounded up, escorted to Riblah, and there executed in the presence of Nebuchadrezzar (2 Kgs. 25:18–21; Jer. 52:24–27). Many persons were led away into exile (2 Kgs. 25:11–12). Indeed, "the pleasant land" was in ruins (Zech. 7:14). Nebuchadrezzar had taken out his vengeance on the disloyal house of David.

Sources for the Period

The biblical sources for the time of Babylonian domination over and control of Judean life (586–539) are very meager. Second Kings 25:8–29, 2 Chronicles 36:17:23, and Jeremiah 52:12–34 provide accounts of Jerusalem's destruction and the subsequent exile of Judeans but with significant variations. Second Kings 25:13–17 reports on the looting of the temple and the removal of all the religious equipment, giving the impression that the bronze, silver, and golden items were carried away for their metal (see 2 Kgs. 24:13; Jer. 52:17–23). Second Chronicles 36:18 notes that all the sacred utensils and other temple treasures were carried intact by Nebuchadrezzar to Babylon. The Kings and Jeremiah narratives designate the number of Judean exiles (see below) and comment on the people left in the land of Judah. From the Chronicles account the reader would assume that all surviving Judeans were carried away into Babylonian captivity, leaving an "empty land" to rest and "keep sabbath" (2 Chr. 36:20–21). The Babylonian disposition of the conquered land is described briefly in 2 Kings 25:22–26 but not mentioned in either Jeremiah 52 or 2 Chronicles 36.

Biographical narratives about Jeremiah (Jer. 37–44) describe the activities of the prophet during the latter part of his career and provide our fullest accounts

---

1. Scholars differ over whether the date was 587 or 586; see Ormands Edwards, "The Year of Jerusalem's Destruction. 2. Addaru 597 B.C. Reinterpreted," *ZAW* 104 (1992) 101–6; and Michael Avioz, "When Was the First Temple Destroyed According to the Bible?" *Bib* 84 (2003) 562–65.

of life in Judah under Babylonian rule. Jeremiah 39:1–43:7 provides stories about the prophet set in the period immediately following the fall of Jerusalem.

The prophet Ezekiel was carried into Babylonian exile after Nebuchadrezzar's first capture of Jerusalem in March 597. The inauguration of his prophetic career is dated to the fifth day of the fourth month of the fifth year of the exile of King Jehoiachin, or about July 593. Many of his subsequent oracles shed light on conditions experienced by Judeans settled in Babylonia.

The book of Lamentations (and perhaps Pss. 74 and 79) gives expression to the impact of the destruction of Jerusalem and the temple. Although written in poetic and metaphorical terminology, these poems doubtlessly express sentiments felt during the time.

Unfortunately very few nonbiblical texts provide any information on Judean life under the Babylonians. The known Babylonian Chronicles break off after the eleventh year of Nebuchadrezzar (594–593) and do not resume for some decades. Thus we do not have a Babylonian description of the second capture of Jerusalem and its consequences. A few references in Babylonian lists and business texts offer an occasioned glimpse at the life of Judeans in exile.

Judah after the Fall of Jerusalem

The suppression of Judah's rebellion and the destruction of the city of Jerusalem were no doubt severe cultural and theological shocks for Judean society. The fall of the city and the exile of many of its citizens marked a watershed in Judean history and have left fissure marks radiating throughout the Hebrew Scriptures. The "day of judgment" heralded in prophetic pronouncements had not just dawned—it had burst on Judah with immense ferocity.

General Destruction in the Land

The immediate results of the Babylonian conquest of Judah are clear. Much of the country, especially in the west, south, and east and in the immediate environs of Jerusalem, was destroyed by the foreign invaders. Archaeological excavations at many Judean sites show evidence of destruction that scholars have related to Nebuchadrezzar's campaigns. Evidence for destruction extends from Tell ed-Duweir (Lachish) in the west, to Arad and environs in the south, to En-gedi and Jericho in the east. This is not to suggest, however, that every Judean city was left in ruins. Primarily those cities that served as fortress towns and where anti-Babylonian sentiment was high would have been the most likely targets for the Babylonians. One area, however, is the exception to the rule. Cities north of Jerusalem, in the traditional territory of Benjamin, suffered little or no destruction.[2]

At the southern site of Arad, excavations have revealed a destroyed military fortress that included remains of a Yahwistic sanctuary whose usage seems to

---

2. See Oded Lipschits, "The History of the Benjamin Region under Babylonian Rule," *TA* 26 (1949) 155–90. On the difficulties in identifying destruction levels caused by the Babylonians, see Joseph Blenkinsopp, "The Bible, Archaeology and Politics or the Empty Land Revisited," *JSOT* 27 (2002) 169–87; and Ephraim Stern, "The Babylonian Gap: The Archaeological Reality," *JSOT* 28 (2004) 273–77.

have been discontinued decades earlier, in the late eighth century.[3] To associate this discontinuation with the reform of either Hezekiah or Josiah is tempting.[4] A second category of finds consists of over two hundred Hebrew and Aramaic ostraca, or inscribed potsherds, many in letter form and dating from the last years of Judah (see Text 18). Most of the letters are addressed to a certain Eliashib, presumably the commander of the military garrison. The letters contain references to Kittim, Hellenic mercenaries apparently in the service of the Egyptian pharaoh and stationed in the Palestinian area. In addition, the letters refer to the Jerusalem temple and to Edomites in the area of Arad.

At the site of Tell ed-Duweir, generally identified with ancient Lachish, between twenty and thirty inscribed ostraca were found in stratum II belonging to the last years of Judah (see Text 18). Apparently to be dated before Nebuchadrezzar's final invasion, some refer to the preparations for battle, the use of fire signals, the employment of some code for communicating between towns, the sending of a delegation to Egypt, concern for the harvest, differences of opinion among the population over strategy and the forthcoming conflict, and the presence of prophets.

The destruction of most Judean cities meant a disruption in the governmental apparatus as well as in the industry and economics of the country. Because soldiers profited from the spoils of war, plundering was the conqueror's privilege and the conquered's fate. Thus one must assume that much of the people's possessions became Babylonian spoils of war. Many cities, like Jerusalem, that had once been thriving centers were left as depleted, subsistence-level villages if occupied at all. The primary economy of the country was probably reduced to a purely agricultural base.

A significant percentage of the manpower and leadership was killed off. There is no way to estimate the number of casualties who died at the hands of Babylonian troops, but it certainly would have been a sizable portion of the population, even though the Babylonians had no reputation for needless destruction and excessive killing. Nebuchadrezzar had taken a lenient attitude toward the country in 597, but no ancient ruler was very hospitable to a rebellious subject on the second military visit.

Judean Exiles

The biblical materials contain two parallel accounts of the Judean revolt, the fall of Jerusalem, and the deportation of Judeans: 2 Kings 24:18–25:21 and Jeremiah 52:1–30. These texts are identical, with one major exception. Jeremiah 52:28–30, which provides figures and dates for the two exiles, disrupts the parallel with the account in Kings and contradicts the dates and figures in both 2 Kings 24:8–16 and 25:8–27 concerning the number of Judeans taken into exile. In addition, Jeremiah 52:30 speaks of a third deportation. The following illustrates the differences between the accounts:

---

3. See Ze'ev Herzog, "The Fortress Mound at Tel Arad: An Interim Report," *TA* 29 (2002) 3–109.

4. See Ze'ev Herzog, "The Date of the Temple at Arad: Reassessment of the Stratigraphy and the Implications for the History of Religion in Judah," in Amihai Mazar, ed., *Studies in the Archaeology of the Iron Age in Israel and Jordan* (JSOTSup 331; Sheffield: Sheffield Academic Press, 2001) 156–78; and L. S. Fried, "The High Places (*Bāmôt*) and the Reforms of Hezekiah and Josiah: An Archaeological Investigation," *JAOS* 122 (2002) 1–29.

	2 KINGS	JEREMIAH
First Deportation	All Jerusalem, 10,000 captives (24:14) 7,000 brought to Babylon, plus 1,000 craftsmen and smiths (24:16) Eighth year of Nebuchadrezzar (24:12)	3,023 Judeans (52:28) Seventh year of Nebuchadrezzar (52:28)
Second Deportation	The rest of the people left in the city and the deserters together with the rest of the multitude (25:11) Nineteenth year of Nebuchadrezzar (25:8)	832 from Jerusalem (52:29) Eighteenth year of Nebuchadrezzar (52:29)
Third Deportation		745 Judeans in the twenty-third year of Nebuchadrezzar (52:30), making a total of 4,600

Various attempts have been made to harmonize or explain these figures, but none is completely satisfying. One approach is to assume that both accounts are talking about the same events in the statements on the first two deportations. The difference in the dates given would be due to the use of different systems of calendar reckoning in the two texts, one calculated from a spring and the other from an autumn new year. The difference in the head count would be due to a gradual stylization in the presentation: from Jeremiah's rather concrete count, to the round figures in Kings, to the assumption in 2 Chronicles 36:17–21 that the entire population was deported. A second approach assumes that the figures in Jeremiah for the first two deportations refer to deportations that occurred in 599–598 and 587–586 before the actual captures of Jerusalem. The first group would have been Judeans captured in Nebuchadrezzar's seventh year when he was fighting the Arabs but at a time when Jerusalem was already in revolt (*ANET* 564; Jer. 49:28–33). The second group would have been Jerusalemites captured in the early stages of the two-year siege of Jerusalem during the second revolt, perhaps those seized before the Babylonian siege was temporarily lifted when an Egyptian army appeared on the scene (Jer. 37:5). This approach assumes that Jeremiah 52:28–30 represents a special source originally unconnected with the rest of Jeremiah 52, which seems otherwise to be based on 2 Kings 24:18–25:30. The account in Kings would then be a report of the main deportations after the city surrendered.

Under either circumstance, we must assume that sizable groups of Judeans were taken by Nebuchadrezzar into Babylonian exile. Whether the figures given refer only to a male headcount cannot be known. Such deportations frayed the total fabric of society, siphoning off many of the upper and artisan classes. At the same time, such deportations would have led to some redistribution of Judean property and wealth and thus benefited portions of the lower classes. Those left behind could occupy the land of those taken into exile (see Ezek. 11:15), and debtors may have been left suddenly without creditors to whom they were indebted.

Verification of Prophetic Proclamation

Judah, which had been ruled for over four centuries by Davidic kings, except for one short interlude, now saw another Davidic monarch led away into exile. The temple and sacred city lay in ruins. A particular theological reading of Judean history—namely, the prophetic and the Deuteronomic—could now point to the end of the kingdom and the destruction of the temple as historical verification of its theology. The classical prophets and Deuteronomy had argued that the people's fortune and fate were determined by their fidelity or infidelity to God, and the former had proclaimed the fall of the state as a result of the people's immorality and apostasy. This understanding of history provided the means by which the people could now interpret their tragic conditions and understand their fate as a punishment from God rather than as an indication of Yahweh's weakness. Thus they could remain faithful to their God even in the midst of calamity and even look forward to the future with some hope and expectation. God had destroyed their nation and their temple because of their religious infidelity, but this did not mean that Yahweh had deserted his people. This perspective became a dominant lens for viewing the traditions of the past and a dominant concern in the editing of these traditions. That this was not the only way in which to understand the historical conditions and the fall of Jerusalem is indicated by the statement of those who felt that it was Josiah's suppression of religious pluralism that had been the source of their trouble: "We will do everything that we have vowed, making offerings to the queen of heaven and pour out libations to her, just as we and our ancestors, our kings and our officials, used to do in the towns of Judah and in the streets of Jerusalem. We used to have plenty of food, and prospered, and saw no misfortune" (Jer. 44:17). For many, the city's destruction probably led to a loss of faith in Yahwism or to a continuation and even intensification of syncretistic practices.

The Rule of Gedaliah

It is easy to paint a very dreary and dismal view of Judean life and to overemphasize the drastic and debilitating consequences of the fall of Jerusalem and the triumph of Babylonian forces. Various aspects of life were certainly greatly modified, but Babylonian policy was not overly oppressive. Judeans were not systematically tortured or annihilated. Unlike the Assyrians, over a century earlier, however, the Babylonians did not move into Judah, restore the capital city, and partially repopulate it with foreigners. Instead, only minimal actions seem to have been taken to make the region a viable political and economic entity. Since earlier Assyrian military installations established in the area now came under Babylonian hegemony, Nebuchadrezzar did not need to establish new major military centers or to settle the area with soldiers or foreigners. Instead, a local administration was drawn from the local population.

One should think of the calamity that befell Judah in terms of crisis and change rather than in terms of total collapse. Earlier exiles under Sargon (in 720–719 and following) and Sennacherib (in 701) had probably resulted in greater depopulation than the deportations of 597 and 586. As we shall see below, life and activity, but at a greatly reduced level, continued in the land.[5]

The exact details of the political status of Judah immediately following the destruction of Jerusalem are unclear and disputed. We are told that Nebuchadrezzar "appointed over them" Gedaliah the son of Ahikam, the son of Shaphan (2 Kgs. 25:22 and Jer. 40:7; many translations supply the title "governor" in these and other passages about Gedaliah but without textual warrant). To what office he was appointed we are not told, but three lines of evidence suggest that he may have replaced Zedekiah on the throne as king. (1) The failure to mention any title whatever in the text could suggest that the final editors of the Kings material did not wish to reveal his real title. The reason was probably that it would have required the admission that a non-Davidic person was appointed as king. (See 2 Kgs. 25:27–30, which reports the later release of Jehoiachin from prison, but this text does not hold open any real expectation of a future for the Davidic family. The report acknowledges that the exiled king has died and makes no reference to any offspring.[6]) (2) Two texts in Jeremiah 40–41 speak of "the king" in describing conditions after the fall of Jerusalem, and these can be interpreted as references to Gedaliah. In the first, mention is made of "the king's daughters" at Mizpah (41:10). The king's daughters could have been either the actual daughters of Gedaliah or the women at his court (perhaps women of Zedekiah's court whom Gedaliah had inherited as part of his new appointment?). One could presume that had these been daughters of King Zedekiah they would have been carried into exile or executed with his other offspring (2 Kgs. 25:7; "sons" could be read "children"). The second text (Jer. 41:1) describes Ishmael as "one of the chief officers of the king," that is, as an officer of Gedaliah under whose authority he had earlier placed himself (40:8). Here "the king" appears to be Gedaliah. (3) One of the Judean military commanders who joined Gedaliah at Mizpah was Jaazaniah son of the Maacathite (2 Kgs. 25:23; see Jer. 40:8). (It is uncertain what "Maacathite" denotes: one from the Judean clan of Maacah [1 Chr. 2:48], from the Galilean region of Abel-beth-maacah [2 Sam. 20:14], or the Aramaean kingdom of Maacah [Josh. 13:11, 13]?). Among the artifacts discovered at Tell en-Nasbeh (= Mizpah) was an onyx seal recovered from a tomb. An inscription on the seal reads *ly'znyhw 'bd hmlk*, "belonging to Jaazaniah servant of the king." Was "the king" Zedekiah or Gedaliah? One cannot be certain. If Gedaliah was made king, it would suggest that the Babylonians were not only following the old Assyrian policy of not incorporating the southern Palestinian states into their provincial system but also allowing them limited independence as vassal states. Gedaliah would thus have been viewed as the successor to Zedekiah but simply not from the old ruling family. Since Gedaliah was not of the family of David, his appointment as king could have been deliberately suppressed by the compilers of the biblical text, thus explaining the absence of any reference to his exact office. The support given to Gedaliah by Jeremiah and the general population in Judah

5. See H. M. Barstad, "On the History and Archaeology of Judah during the Exilic Period: A Reminder," *OLP* 19 (1988) 25–36; R. P. Carroll, "The Myth of the Empty Land," *Semeia* 59 (1992) 79–93; and Ephraim Stern, "The Babylonian Gap," *BAR* 26/6 (2000) 45–51, 76.

6. A survey of approaches to the concluding verses of 2 Kings is provided in D. F. Murray, "Of All the Years the Hopes—or Fears? Jehoiachin in Babylon (2 Kings 25:27–30)," *JBL* 120 (2001) 245–65.

would suggest that large segments of the population were willing to go along with a non-Davidic monarch, just as had been the case during the crisis of kingship at the time of Ahaz when the Davidic ruler was almost deposed and replaced by a son of Tabeel.

Gedaliah came from a prominent family. His grandfather, Shaphan, served as royal "secretary" and thus was a high governmental official under Josiah (2 Kgs. 22:8). Shaphan's son Gemariah and his grandson Micaiah were prominent leaders at the time of Jehoiakim (Jer. 36:11–13). Another son, Elasah, was one of Zedekiah's envoys to Babylon (29:3). Gedaliah's father, Ahikam, had supported the prophet Jeremiah when the latter was placed on trial for his inflammatory denunciation of Jerusalem's citizens and their confidence in the temple and the city's inviolability (26:24). A seal impression unearthed at Tell ed-Duweir reads, "Belonging to Gedaliah, who is over the household." If this refers to the biblical Gedaliah, then it could suggest that even before the siege of Jerusalem he had held a prominent position in the Judean administration. The choice of Gedaliah was no doubt based on his pro-Babylonian sentiments. Many in Judah, like the prophet Jeremiah, had favored submission and surrender to Babylonia rather than war (see 38:19), and Nebuchadrezzar now placed this group, the earlier minority opposition party, in charge of Judean affairs.

Mizpah of Benjamin (Josh. 18:26), located about eight miles northwest of Jerusalem, was the seat for Gedaliah's administration. Mizpah had been an important cultic center in premonarchical days, had special connections with Samuel (Judg. 20:1–3; 21:18; 1 Sam. 7; 10:17) and Saul (1 Sam. 10:17–25), and its renown as a prominent place of worship continued into Maccabean times (1 Macc. 3:46). Several factors indicate that Mizpah was already functioning as an administrative center even before the fall of Jerusalem. First of all, there was no major Babylonian destruction of sites in the Benjaminite area. Mizpah, Tell el-Ful, Gibeon, and Bethel survived on into the sixth century. Mizpah itself seems to have undergone some rebuilding and expansion at the time.[7] Second, Babylonian-type artifacts and portions of a cuneiform inscription have been found at the site.[8] This indicates a Babylonian settlement. Third, King Zedekiah expressed fear that if he surrendered to the Babylonians he might be handed over to the pro-Babylonian Judeans who had deserted to the Chaldeans (Jer. 38:19). This suggests that there may have been some administrative structure of Judeans sympathetic and cooperative with the Babylonian authority in the region rather than simply renegade deserters. Fourth, Jeremiah's desire to leave Jerusalem to go to the land of Benjamin, apparently to complete a land transference from his cousin (Jer. 37:1–16; see 32:6–75), indicates that conditions approaching normalcy prevailed in the Benjaminite region. Finally, immediately following the burning of Jerusalem Jeremiah was turned over to the custody of Gedaliah, who was already established in Mizpah, which suggests a preexisting political structure. Mizpah remained the political capital of Judah

---

7. See J. R. Zorn, "Mizpah—Newly Discovered Stratum Reveals Judah's Other Capital," *BAR* 23/5 (1997) 29–38, 66; idem, "Tell en-Nasbeh and the Problem of the Material Culture of the Sixth Century," in Oded Lipschits and Joseph Blenkinsopp, eds., *Judah and the Judeans in the Neo-Babylonian Period* (Winona Lake, IN: Eisenbrauns, 2003) 413–47.

8. J. R. Zorn, "Mesopotamian-style Ceramic 'Bathtub' Coffins from Tel en-Nasbeh," *TA* 20 (1993) 216–24.

for over a century, from the days of Gedaliah until Nehemiah's refortification of Jerusalem. In support of his cause, Gedaliah seems to have been supported by a contingent of Babylonian (Chaldean) troops or at least advisers (see 2 Kgs. 25:24–25 and Jer. 40:10; 41:3).

Nebuzaradan, the captain of the Babylonian bodyguard, quickly took steps to normalize life in Judah. The poor in the land, "who owned nothing," were provided with vineyards and fields (Jer. 39:10; 2 Kgs. 25:12), that is, there was some redistribution of property to the benefit of previously landless classes. Pro-Babylonians like Jeremiah were given preferential treatment (see Jer. 39:11–14 and 40:1–5, although the details differ). Judeans were encouraged by Gedaliah to resume ordinary agricultural pursuits and live peacefully under Babylonian hegemony. Jews from neighboring areas—Moab, Ammon, Edom, and elsewhere—who had fled the country returned and submitted themselves to Gedaliah's authority (Jer. 40:10–12).

Although little is said about the status of the general population, we should assume that the Babylonians exploited the region to their advantage. Reference to the fact that "the poorest elements of the population . . . were left . . . to be vine-dressers and field hands" (Jer. 52:16 NJPSV; see also 39:10; 2 Kgs. 25:12) indicates not only a redistribution of property among "the remnant in Judah" (Jer. 40:11) but also Nebuchadrezzar's need to supply his homeland with products like wine, grain, and olive oil.[9]

An Attempt at Davidic Restoration

Peaceful conditions, counseled by Gedaliah, did not immediately materialize. Some Judean field commanders and their troops had survived the recent struggles. Second Kings 25:22–24 and Jeremiah 40:7–13 imply their submission to Gedaliah and their continuation as a military force under his command. Ishmael, one of these commanders, was or claimed to be a member of the Davidic family, though perhaps not from the immediate ruling line (2 Kgs. 25:25; Jer. 41:1). He apparently belonged to the Davidic family strand that went back to Elishama, a son of David (see 2 Sam. 5:16; 1 Chr. 3:8; 14:7). Ishmael submitted, at least temporarily, to the authority of Gedaliah (Jer. 40:8–10) and was placed in a position of power (note that Jer. 41:1 refers to Ishmael as "one of the chief officers of the king" [Gedaliah]). At the instigation of Baalis, the Ammonite king,[10] Ishmael and a contingent of his troops assassinated Gedaliah, his entire entourage, and the Babylonian military contingent at Mizpah (2 Kgs. 25:25–26; Jer. 40:13–41:3). The biblical text offers no rationale for these murders, but one must assume they were the act of nationalistic patriots who wished to reestablish an independent Judean state under a Davidic ruler with the support of a foreign monarch, the Ammonite king. After further killings, Ishmael and his force were opposed by other Judean officers, especially Johanan the son of Kareah (Jer. 41:11–14). The Judean population was in no mood to support the ambitions of a would-be Davidic messiah. Without the sympathy and support

9. See J. N. Graham, "'Vinedressers and Ploughmen': 2 Kings 25:12 and Jeremiah 52:16," *BA* 47 (1984) 55–58.

10. A seal of this king was recently discovered; see R. Deutsch, "Seal of Ba'alis Surfaces—Ammonite King Plotted Murder of Judahite Governor," *BAR* 25/2 (1999) 46–49, 66.

of the general population, which seems to have placed its hope in the non-Davidic Gedaliah (see 42:7–11), Ishmael's plans faltered and he took refuge in Ammon (41:4–16). Fearful of Babylonian retaliation, some of the military leaders and general population fled to Egypt, carrying along the protesting prophet Jeremiah (41:17–43:7).

Direct evidence about the status of affairs in Judah following Gedaliah's assassination is almost nonexistent. Jeremiah 52:30 reports a third Babylonian deportation of Judeans—745 persons were exiled in the twenty-third year of Nebuchadrezzar (581). What precipitated this deportation is not discussed by Jeremiah. Many scholars, perhaps correctly, associate it with the Gedaliah affair, although 2 Kings 25:25 and Jeremiah 41:1 seem to imply that Gedaliah had been killed only two months after the fall of Jerusalem. This seems hardly sufficient time for all the activities attributed to Gedaliah and does not fit with his recommendation to the general population that they go about normal agricultural pursuits (Jer. 40:10–12). The Jewish historian Josephus reports that Nebuchadrezzar was again in Syria-Palestine in 582–581:

> The Deity revealed to the prophet [Jeremiah] that the king of Babylonia was about to march against the Egyptians, and He bade the prophet foretell to the people that Egypt would be taken and that the Babylonian king would kill some of them and would take the rest captive and carry them to Babylon. And so it happened; for in the fifth year after the sacking of Jerusalem, which was the twenty-third year of the reign of Nebuchadnezzar, Nebuchadnezzar marched against Coele-Syria and, after occupying it, made war both on the Moabites and the Ammanites. Then, after making these nations subject to him, he invaded Egypt in order to subdue it, and, having killed the king who was then reigning and appointed another, he again took captive the Jews who were in the country and carried them to Babylon. (*Ant.* 10.180–82)

Some suspect that Josephus based his account on his desire to have Jeremiah's prophecies of Babylon's capture of Egypt fulfilled literally (see Jer. 27:1–7; 44:30; 46:13–24; 48:1–49:6). Certainly, Nebuchadrezzar did not invade Egypt and kill and replace the Egyptian pharaoh in 581, since Apries (Hophra), who had become pharaoh in 589, continued to reign until 570, If Josephus does preserve the recollection of trouble in Syria-Palestine in 582–581 involving Moab and Ammon, however, then this may have been the setting for Ishmael's attempted coup or at least the background for Jeremiah's report that 745 Judeans were taken captive to Babylon in Nebuchadrezzar's twenty-third year. Egyptian influence may have been asserted in Syria-Palestine in support of anti-Babylonian uprisings. At any rate, Egypt seems to have been receptive to the Judeans fleeing Palestine for fear of Babylonian reprisal. At the time Tyre on the coast was under Babylonian siege, a siege that lasted thirteen years (586–573; *Ant.* 10.228; *Contra Apion* 1.156) and whose immediate lack of success may have stimulated hopes that Babylonia would prove not to be invincible. Also, efforts at revolt in Syria-Palestine in the mid-580s would have occurred while Nebuchadrezzar was preoccupied with matters in Asia Minor.

If Gedaliah was appointed king over Judah, his assassination may have brought this experiment in non-Davidic monarchy to an end. After his death, Judah continued as a Babylonian province, but we have no firsthand information on Judean politics for the period immediately following Gedaliah's murder. If Judah was given provincial status, it would have had its own governor, perhaps a native Judean, appointed by the Babylonians. One would assume that normal life as a Babylonian province continued.

Continuation of Cultic Life

The general perception gained from the books of 2 Kings and Ezra, the latter describing conditions in the later Jerusalem community, is that all cultic activity ceased in Judah following the destruction of the temple in Jerusalem.[11] This perception has, however, probably been retrojected onto a situation that was actually quite different, although the exact details escape us.

In reporting the Gedaliah-Ishmael episode, the book of Jeremiah notes that "eighty men arrived [at Mizpah] from Shechem and Shiloh and Samaria, with their beards shaved and their clothes torn, and their bodies gashed, bringing grain offerings and incense to present at the temple of Yahweh" (Jer. 41:5). This text suggests two things: (1) cultic worship continued in Judah during the Babylonian period, and (2) Mizpah seems to have been the site of such worship.[12] That no sacrificial animals are mentioned may be coincidental, since these were often purchased at the site of worship (see Deut. 14:25–26). As the new administrative center, Mizpah would have been the logical place for worship. The old sanctuary center for northern Israel at Bethel was only three miles from Mizpah, and it may have retained its role; thus it could have been Bethel (Tel Beitin) that served as the province's religious center.

Some form of cultic activity may have continued also at the site of the temple in Jerusalem. The cultic laments in the book of Lamentations seem to presuppose some type of worship at the site of the destroyed sanctuary and city. This may not have involved sacrificial activity but may have consisted of lamenting comparable to modern activity at the Jerusalem Wailing Wall. That one of the first activities of the returning exiles was to rebuild the altar in Jerusalem (Ezra 3:1–3) indicates that no such functioning altar was in existence (see Lam. 2:7).

The continuation of cultic activity would of course have required priests. We hear nothing in the books of 2 Kings and Jeremiah about the condition of the priesthood after the destruction of Jerusalem except the notice that Seraiah the chief priest, Zephaniah the second priest, and the three keepers of the threshold were put to death by Nebuchadrezzar at Riblah (2 Kgs. 25:18–21; Jer. 52:24–27). At any rate, however, 2 Kings 25:18–21 suggests that the Jerusalem priestly hierarchy was decimated as a consequence of Babylonian action. Once the capital of the region shifted away from Jerusalem, the priesthood at the sanctuary at Mizpah or that region, probably Aaronite, may have risen to greater prominence in Judah and even replaced in leadership the Zadokite line established under David and Solomon.

---

11. D. R. Jones, "The Cessation of Sacrifice after the Destruction of the Temple in 586 B.C.," *JTS* 14 (1963) 12–31.

12. See Joseph Blenkinsopp, "The Judaean Priesthood during the Neo-Babylonian and Achaemenid Periods: A Hypothetical Reconstruction," *CBQ* 60 (1998) 25–43; idem, "Bethel in the Neo-Babylonian Period," in Lipschits and Blenkinsopp, eds., *Judah and the Judeans*, 93–107.

The Era of Babylonian Dominance

At the end of the seventh century, four major powers existed in the Near East—Babylonia, Egypt, Media, and Lydia. Babylonia, in spite of being the strongest of the four powers, was never able to dominate Near Eastern affairs as had the Assyrians earlier or as the Persians would later. The Medes, who had aided Babylonia in its conquests of Assyria, controlled the highlands north and east of the Mesopotamian plain. Most of the Fertile Crescent was in Babylonian hands, but the Medes largely controlled the eastern trade routes, forcing the Babylonians to turn their economic interests more to the west.

The Medes also expanded westward. Cyaxares had overrun the Urartian kingdom and extended his rule into Asia Minor. The growth of Median power led some Jews to suppose that the Medes might topple Babylonia (Jer. 51:11). Nebuchadrezzar, however, remained on good terms with Media. Median expansion into Asia Minor eventually resulted in a clash with Lydia. About 585 the Babylonians served as mediators in Lydian-Median territorial disputes. A Babylonian officer and future king, Nabonidus, mediated a treaty of peace, which established the river Halys as the boundary between the two kingdoms' spheres of influence (see Herodotus 1.72).

In the eastern Mediterranean, Babylonia and Egypt vied for control of the area and its maritime commerce. The Babylonians seem never to have been as successful as the Assyrians in dominating this area. The Phoenician city of Tyre, for example, held out for thirteen years against Nebuchadrezzar's siege.[13] What role Egypt may have played in the Babylonian-Phoenician struggle remains uncertain. Herodotus reports that the Egyptian pharaoh Apries (Hophra) sent an army against Sidon and fought a naval battle with the Tyrians (11.161). That Egypt fought against the Phoenician states while Tyre was under siege by Nebuchadrezzar, and thus in support of the Babylonians, seems highly unlikely. Perhaps Herodotus has confused his information. The Egyptian pharaoh may have aided the Phoenicians against the Babylonians as he had earlier offered some assistance to Judah. If Egypt attacked Phoenicia, it must have been before Tyre was placed under Babylonian siege.

We have noted earlier in this chapter that Babylonia had to deal with additional troubles in Syria-Palestine in the late 580s (see above, p. 486). These too may have been partially precipitated by Egypt. According to Ezekiel 29:17–20, an oracle dated to April 571, Nebuchadrezzar received the spoils of Egypt as wages for his unprofitable siege of Tyre that ended with less than overwhelming success for the Babylonians. The Ezekiel text would suggest an invasion of Egypt. (In *Ant.* 10.182 Josephus reports that Nebuchadrezzar in his twenty-third year did invade Egypt and replace the reigning pharaoh with another ruler.) Only fragmentary cuneiform evidence and late legendary stories can be mustered, however, to support Josephus's and Ezekiel's claim of a Babylonian invasion of Egypt. The following cuneiform text, greatly restored, points to a military engagement between the two powers but does not unequivocally imply an invasion: "In the 37th year, Nebuchadnezzar, king of Babylon

13. H. J. Katzenstein, *A History of Tyre from the Beginning of the Second Millennium B.C.E. until the Fall of the Neo-Babylonian Empire in 539 B.C.E.* (2d ed.; Beer Sheva: Ben Gurion University of the Negev Press, 1997).

marched against Egypt to deliver a battle. Amasis, of Egypt, called up his army . . . from the town Putu-Iaman . . . distant regions which are situated on islands amidst the sea . . . many . . . carrying weapons, horses and chariots . . . he called up to assist him" (see *ANET* 308). Unfortunately such a fragment is more tantalizing than informative. The thirty-seventh year of Nebuchadrezzar (568–567) would have been shortly after Amasis (570–526) had replaced Apries as pharaoh following a period of Egyptian civil war (Herodotus 2.161–69). Whether Nebuchadrezzar took advantage of the civil strife to invade Egypt or even to attempt to remove Apries from the throne remains unknown.

Amasis brought Egypt to a period of great prosperity (Herodotus 2.177). His predecessor had relied greatly on Greek mercenaries, earning him the epithet "Philhellene," and during his reign Greek merchants were widespread in Egypt. The city of Naucratis in the western Delta had become an international trading center where the Greeks had special prerogatives. Amasis took more direct control of matters both internally and externally than had Apries. Greek mercenaries and traders were brought under more disciplined control. Legal practices were reformed. Treaties were made with Croesus king of Lydia and Polycrates king of Samos in Asia Minor, and friendly relations were established with the Greek colony of Cyrene. The island of Cyprus, which had formerly been under Assyrian control, came under the dominance of Amasis and was subjected to tribute (Herodotus 1.77; 2.177–82). Egyptian expansion and prosperity must have been partially at the expense of Babylonia.

The Babylonian kingdom, in spite of its inability to emulate the Assyrians, thrived reasonably well throughout the reign of Nebuchadrezzar. By the time of his death, a constellation of factors heralded the deep troubles about to beset the kingdom. These included excessive economic inflation in Babylon precipitated in part by extravagant royal building projects; Median, Lydian, and Egyptian pressures on trade routes leading into Mesopotamia; and a lack of effective leadership among the royal family.

A quick succession of rulers followed Nebuchadrezzar. His son Amel-marduk (561–560), the Evil-merodach of 2 Kings 25:27 and Jeremiah 52:31 who released Jehoiachin from prison, reigned for only two years before being killed in a revolution. A son-in-law of Nebuchadrezzar, Neriglissar (the Nergal-sharezer of Jer. 39:3), succeeded to the throne.[14] His reign (559–556) witnessed a Babylonian campaign into southeastern Asia Minor against King Appuashu of Pirindu, who had invaded Syria (*ABC* 103–4). Following Neriglissar's mysterious death upon returning to Babylon, his young son Labashi-marduk, "a minor who had not yet learned how to behave" (*ANET* 309), assumed the throne but ruled only for a short time before being replaced in a rebellion led by officers of the kingdom.

The new ruler, Nabonidus (555–539), a Babylonian military commander from Haran in northern Syria, was the son of a nobleman and the high priestess of the moon-god Sin in his native city.[15] Although Nabonidus's reign would

---

14. R. H. Sack, *Neriglissar—King of Babylon* (AOAT 236; Neukirchen-Vluyn: Neukirchener Verlag, 1994).

15. See P.-A. Beaulieu, *The Reign of Nabonidus King of Babylon 556–539* (Yale Near Eastern Researches 10; New Haven: Yale University Press, 1989); R. H. Sack, "Nebuchadnezzar and Nabonidus in Folklore and History," *Mesopotamia* 17 (1982) 67–131; and André Lemaire, "Nabonidus in Arabia and Judah in the Neo-Babylonian Period," in Lipschits and Blenkinsopp, eds. *Judah and the Judeans* 285–98.

mark the end of the Babylonian kingdom and he himself would be remembered in popular tradition as the mad monarch par excellence, he seems to have made some gallant efforts to stabilize the tottering kingdom.

First of all, Nabonidus sought to reform Babylonian religion and to use the worship of the moon-god Sin as a unifying force in the empire. His emphasis on the worship of Sin was, of course, not to the exclusion of the other religious cults. The moon-god, unlike Marduk, a Babylonian sun-deity, was worshiped by many peoples in the empire, including Arabs and Aramaeans. The king took as his pious duty the restoration of the Sin sanctuary (Ehulhul) in Haran, where his high priestess mother survived to the age of 104 (see *ANET* 560–62).[16] The sanctuary had been destroyed in 610 and was subsequently held by the Medes until military pressure from Cyrus I forced their withdrawal from the area. In addition, Nabonidus constructed a special Sin sanctuary at Ur and installed his daughter as high priestess. His support and encouragement of the worship of Sin alienated elements of the religious establishment in Babylon headed by the Marduk priesthood (for texts reflecting his building activity and his religious devotion see *COS* 2:310–14).

Most of Nabonidus's military activity and economic interests were centered in the west. In his early years as king, he was active in eastern Asia Minor and Syria, in Hume in Cilicia and Hamath in Syria. After a short stay and period of sickness in the Anti-Lebanon region, Nabonidus turned his attention to the Arabian Desert (*ANET* 305). He stayed there for over a decade without returning to the capital city, where his son Bel-shar-usur (the Belshazzar of Dan. 5:22; 7:1; 8:1) served as regent. Nabonidus notes the following reasons for leaving the capital city and for his stay in Arabia:

> But the citizens of Babylon, Borsippa, Nippur, Ur, Uruk (and) Larsa, the administrators (and) the inhabitants of the urban centers of Babylonia acted evil, careless and even sinned against his [Sin's] great divine power, having not (yet) experienced the awfulness of the wrath of the Divine Crescent, the king of all gods; they disregarded his . . . rites and there was much irreligious and disloyal talk. They devoured one another like dogs, caused disease and hunger to appear among them. He (Sin) decimated the inhabitants of the country, but he made me leave my city Babylon on the road to Tema, Dadanu, Padakku, Hibra, Jadihu even as far as Jatribu [later Muslim Medina]. For ten years I was moving around among these (cities) and did not enter my own city Babylon. (*ANET* 562)

The activity and stay of Nabonidus in the eastern Mediterranean seaboard and in Arabia were probably necessitated by economic and trade considerations. He must have been attempting to establish and exercise control over the overland trade routes in the region. There is a strong possibility that Jewish soldiers and families accompanied him to Arabia, because practically all the oases he claims to have visited were later strong centers of Jewish settlement. As we shall see in the next chapter, by the time Nabonidus returned to Babylon his former ally King Cyrus II of Anshan had risen to a position of dominance

16. See C. J. Gadd, "The Harran Inscription of Nabonidus," *AnSt* 8 (1958) 35–92.

throughout Mesopotomia and was merely waiting for the proper occasion to seize the Babylonian capital.

The Diaspora

Nebuchadrezzar's deportations of Judeans to Babylonia and the flight of many others to Egypt greatly increased the number of Judeans and Israelites living outside the Palestinian area. The fate of most of these deportees is unknown, although later Jewish communities in many areas throughout the Middle East may have originated from these exiled groups. The families of some of these deportees eventually returned to Palestine and were a strong influence on Jewish life in the area during the Persian period. Although we shall consider the return of these exiles in the next chapter, a discussion of the exiled groups is appropriate at this point, since the dispersion of groups from Palestine reached a climax in the Babylonian period.

The Diaspora did not have its beginnings in the days following the destruction of Jerusalem. The Assyrians had exiled peoples from Galilee and Transjordan in 733–732 (2 Kgs. 15:29; *ANET* 283). After Samaria fell in 720–719, according to his inscriptions Sargon II deported 27,290 persons from the land of Samaria (*ANET* 284–85) and resettled them in Assyrian provinces in Upper Mesopotamia and Media (2 Kgs. 17:18; 18:11; 1 Chr. 5:26). After Sennacherib's successful campaign in Judah in 701, he claimed to have counted 200,150 persons driven from Hezekiah's towns as booty (*ANET* 288). Certainly some of these must have been exiled and settled elsewhere (see above, Text 10). One of Sennacherib's palace reliefs in Nineveh depicts the deportation of Judeans from Lachish. Nebuchadrezzar's deportations of 597, 586, and 582 (Jer. 52:29) only increased the number of Israelites and Judeans living in the east; it did not inaugurate the Diaspora.

The Judeans who fled to Egypt after the assassination of Gedaliah were not the first from Palestine to go to Egypt. Several texts refer to earlier Jewish communities there. Isaiah 11:11 mentions Judeans dwelling in various regions along the Nile. Jeremiah 44:1 introduces the words of Jeremiah addressed to his countrymen living in Egypt at Migdol, Tahpanhes (Daphnae), and Memphis and in the land of Pathros (Upper Egypt; see Jer. 46:14). This presupposes widespread Jewish settlements in Egypt. The Elephantine archives, which we will describe below, note that this community was founded before Cambyses' capture of Egypt in 525 (*ANET* 492; see below, Text 20). The *Letter of Aristeas* (paragraph 13) states that Jews were sent to Egypt as mercenary soldiers during the reign of Pharaoh Psammetichus (probably Psammetichus I rather than II). Similarly, Judean troops had been taken to Egypt during the reign of Manasseh (*ANET* 294). (Note the reference to being taken to Egypt in ships in Deut. 28:68.) In both of these cases, Jewish troops may have subsequently been stationed in Egypt as military garrisons. In addition to Mesopotamia and Egypt, Judean refugees and emigrants were found also in those small nations surrounding Judah (see Jer. 40:11–12; 41:15).

What can we know about Jewish life in the Diaspora? Of the two main centers of the dispersed—Mesopotamia and Egypt—the former was by far the most significant in terms of both its contribution to the later development of Jewish faith and its role in Jewish life in the Persian period. Before we discuss what can be known about Diaspora life, a word about the extent and nature of the available primary source material on the issue is in order.

The Biblical Source Material

Very little biblical material directly describes life in the Diaspora. Neither of the two main historical sources—Genesis–2 Kings and 1–2 Chronicles—covers the period following the fall of Jerusalem or overtly concerns itself with life and culture outside Palestine. Our primary biblical sources are the books of the prophets Jeremiah and Ezekiel and Isaiah 40–55.

Jeremiah was a witness to both captures of the city of Jerusalem (in 597 and 586), and he participated in the life of the Judean community during the rule of Gedaliah. After the latter's assassination, Jeremiah was carried to Egypt, and some of his book relates to this period (Jer. 43–44). The prophet had earlier carried on correspondence with the exiles deported to Babylonia in 597, and he appears to have been informed about conditions there (see Jer. 28–29; 50–51). Thus the book of Jeremiah supplies some valuable but very limited information about both the Babylonian and the Egyptian diasporas.

The ministry of the prophet Ezekiel seems to have been carried out completely in the Babylonian exile. His career spanned the period from 593 (Ezek. 1:2) to at least 571 (29:17). The sermons and narratives in the book of Ezekiel thus provide many insights into the life of the exiles in Babylonia.

Much of Isaiah 40–55 is now dated by many scholars to the closing years of the Babylonian exile. The anonymous prophet, frequently referred to as Second or Deutero-Isaiah, who produced this material proclaimed the rise of the Persians under Cyrus as ground for renewal and hope for the exiles. The historical conditions reflected in the book shed light on the circumstances of the Babylonian Jewish exilic communities at the transition point between the Babylonian and Persian periods.

Nonbiblical Sources

Nonbiblical texts from both Babylonia and Egypt cast some, although not extensive, light on the life and status of Jews living in the Diaspora. Among the Babylonian materials are royal cuneiform tablets that refer to Jehoiachin in exile (see *ANET* 308). In addition, Jewish names appear in tablets discovered at the site of Nippur in 1893, which reveal the commercial and land-leasing activity of the Murashu firm. These tablets, although dating from the second half of the fifth century (455 to 403) and thus from the Persian period, provide evidence of the involvement of Jews in the economic life of the communities where they were settled.[17]

---

17. M. D. Coogan, *West Semitic Personal Names in the Murašû Documents* (HSM 7; Missoula, MT: Scholars Press, 1976); and Ran Zadok, *The Jews in Babylonia During the Chaldean and Achaemenian Periods According to the Babylonian Sources* (Studies in the History of the Jewish People and the Land of Israel, Monograph Series 3; Haifa: Haifa University Press, 1979).

Numerous documents in Aramaic from Egypt provide information related to the Egyptian diaspora. The most significant of these are the so-called Elephantine papyri.[18] Discovered in Egypt at Elephantine Island opposite Aswan, these legal and epistolary documents were found in three major caches near the turn of the twentieth century. The papyri came from a Jewish military settlement and present us with many facets of the legal and religious conditions existing in the colony. Although dating from the Persian period (495 to 399), they can be used to reconstruct the life of Jews in Egypt during the Babylonian period, since it is probable that this community was already in existence during the preceding Assyrian period and changed little over the years.

The Exiles in Babylonia

The Babylonian treatment of exiled Judeans probably varied. Many captives who had leadership roles in the revolt were sent into exile in chains and were presumably imprisoned or confined. This was the case with both Judean kings—Jehoiachin (2 Kgs. 25:27) and Zedekiah (2 Kgs. 25:7)—and other members of the royal family. Those, however, who were deported in order to weaken the rebellious nation, to siphon off the superpatriots, or to provide service for the conquerors were treated differently.

The Babylonian texts that refer to Jehoiachin as king of Judah mention foodstuffs provided him and his five sons as pensionary payments (*ANET* 308). Such payments were made to numerous persons of diverse national backgrounds (even Greeks!), status, and professions. They do not in themselves reflect any preferential position but do suggest the humane treatment given Jehoiachin and Judean nobles. Seal impressions discovered at several Judean sites inscribed "Belonging to Eliakim steward of Yaukin (Jehoiachin)" could suggest that even after being exiled Jehoiachin was allowed to retain possession of some Judean crown property that was administered by Eliakim. Jehoiachin, in the thirty-seventh year of his exile (561–560), was released from prison by the Babylonian king Evil-merodach (Amel-marduk) and given, in the terms of the text, "a seat above the seats of the kings who were with him in Babylon" (2 Kgs. 25:27–30), although what this status involved goes unexplained. The royal family seems to have remained intact; the cuneiform texts that mention Jehoiachin also refer to his sons.

The exiles were not forced to live in inhuman conditions. There seems to have been no opposition to them or limitation of their privileges because of their origin or religion. They were treated like the exiles from any other nation. Something of the nature of exilic conditions can be seen in Jeremiah's recommendations to the Judeans carried away in 597: "Build houses and live in them; plant gardens and eat their produce. Take wives and have sons and daughters; take wives for your sons, and give your daughters in marriage, that they may bear sons and daughters; multiply there, and do not decrease. But seek the welfare

---

18. See Bezalel Porten, *Archives from Elephantine: The Life of an Ancient Jewish Military Colony* (Los Angeles: University of California Press, 1968). The texts are available in Bezalel Porten and Ada Yardeni, *Textbook of Aramaic Documents from Ancient Egypt* (4 vols.; Jerusalem: Hebrew University Press, 1986–99); hereafter abbreviated *TAD*. The most important of these are translated in *COS* 3:116–31, 141–98.

of the city where I have sent you into exile, and pray to Yahweh on its behalf, for in its welfare you will find your welfare" (Jer. 29:5–7; see also 2 Kgs. 18:31–32, where the Assyrian Rabshakeh describes the conditions of exilic life).

Exiles were settled by both Assyrians and Babylonians not only in ruined cities that needed rebuilding and in areas that needed agricultural development but also in administrative centers. The appearance of the term "tel" in various place names where Judean exiles lived (Tel-Melah, Tel-Harsha, Tel-Abib) could suggest that Judeans were sometimes settled on abandoned or destroyed sites, since "tel" may mean "mound" (often a city ruin). The prophet Ezekiel lived in Tel-Abib on the river Chebar (Ezek. 1:3; 3:15). Thus the Jews received land to till and sites to rebuild and settle, and as tenants to the king would have provided labor, paid taxes, and served in the military. The appearance of Jewish names in about 8 percent of the prosaic business texts of the Murashu firm illustrates that Judean exiles became involved in various commercial activities. Biblical texts indicate that they could own property (Jer. 29:5), even slaves (Ezra 2:65), and many became quite wealthy (Ezra 1:6; 2:68–69). Administrative positions were open to them, as they were to the exiles of other nations.

The exiles remained relatively free and certainly should not be understood as imprisoned slaves.[19] They would have been under no overt governmental pressure to assimilate and lose their identities. Like many other exiled groups, the Jews preserved some communal cohesion and national identity and may have formed their own ethnic corporations in various towns. References to "the elders of Judah/Israel" (Ezek. 8:1; 14:1; 20:1, 3) and "the elders among the exiles" (Jer. 29:1) indicate a state of limited internal autonomy in which they were able to live and govern themselves according to traditional customs and to preserve their family structures. The presence of Davidic family members probably contributed to the sense of identity and perhaps to some optimism about the future. Years were reckoned by reference to Jehoiachin's reign (Ezek. 1:2; 33:21; 40:1). While the practices of ritual purity, Sabbath observance, and circumcision tended to isolate Jews from the local culture, they also contributed to the people's sense of distinctiveness and communal cohesion. Deported Philistines and Phoenicians also lived in colonies named after the cities from which they had been exiled.[20]

Deportees could continue to practice their national religion in the land of their exile, although there was also the tendency to combine this with some form of worship of the gods of the lands in which they dwelt (see Ezek. 14:3; 20:29). The foreigners who were settled in Samaria, for example, continued the worship of their gods while also serving the god of Israel (see 2 Kgs. 17:24–33). Many Judeans taken to Babylonia probably continued their ancestral religion and traditional worship. For some this meant the continuation of syncretistic

19. Even slaves in Babylonia lived reasonably well and enjoyed numerous privileges; see M. A. Dandamaev, *Slavery in Mesopotamia from Nabopolassar to Alexander the Great* (DeKalb: Northern Illinois University Press, 1984); idem, "Free Hired Labor in Babylonia during the Sixth through Fourth Centuries BC," in M. A. Powell, ed., *Labor in the Ancient Near East* (AOS 68; New Haven: Yale University Press, 1987) 271–79.

20. Israel Eph'al, "The Western Minorities in Babylonia in the 6th-5th Centuries B.C. : Maintenance and Cohesion," *Or* 47 (1978) 74–90.

worship and the service of many gods (see Ezek. 14; 20:31; Deut. 4:27–28; 28:36, 64). Many of the exiles, strongly Yahwistic, continued to advocate the worship of only one God.

Little is known about the practice of Yahwism in exile. The Jews at Elephantine in Egypt possessed their own temple where sacrifice was offered, but whether similar conditions prevailed in Babylonia is uncertain. Some take Ezekiel 11:16 to refer to a "temporary sanctuary." According to Ezra 8:15–20, temple personnel were congregated at the "place" Casiphia. Since Hebrew *maqom* (= place) can denote a temple precinct, this text has been understood as specifying a temple. Such argumentation, however, is founded as much on conjecture as on evidence. Jews in Mesopotamia probably worshiped in a nonsacrificial cult characterized by prayer, praise, and the reading and exposition of traditional texts. Sermons, such as those found in Ezekiel and the prose passages of Jeremiah, were perhaps also commonplace. This type of worship could function anywhere, requiring only a meeting place (Greek synagōgē). Exilic worship no doubt possessed many characteristics analogous to later synagogue services.

Jewish life in an alien culture naturally led to some cultural assimilation even among the most conservative. The use of the Aramaic language and the square Aramaic script became widespread, although they did not totally replace Hebrew and the older script. The presence of Babylonian names among the exiles illustrates some accommodation to the host culture, although many Jews continued to give their children Hebrew names, and the fact that a Jewish person bore a theophoric name referring to a god other than Yahweh does not in itself denote conversion. Babylonian names for the months replaced the old Canaanite-Hebrew names used in Palestine. Political and economic pressures were no doubt influential in the level of assimilation among persons of prominence. Undoubtedly many Judeans, like most of the Israelites exiled by the Assyrians, assimilated the culture so thoroughly as to lose their Jewish identity.

Prophets as radically different as Ezekiel and Second Isaiah (the author of Isa. 40–55) wrote and preached during the period of Babylonian domination. Ezekiel, with his priestly orientation, especially condemned his contemporaries for their abominations and impurities, their adherence to idolatry, and their syncretistic worship of other gods in addition to Yahweh. Ezekiel held out hope to the exiles that they would return to the land and purge it of its detestable things and abominations (see Ezek. 11:14–25). Like Jeremiah in his earlier preaching, Ezekiel saw the exiles as the hope for the people—they were the "very good figs, like first-ripe figs," and those left in Judah were the "very bad figs, so bad that they could not be eaten" (Jer. 24:2; but cf. Jer. 42:7–22). Like Ezekiel, Jeremiah or his followers and editors spoke of the transformed persons that would live in the renewed land (see Ezek. 11:19–20; Jer. 31:31–34; 32:36–41) when Israel and Judah would exist together again as one. Ezekiel or his circle of associates proceeded to draw up a blueprint for the idyllic life in a transformed Palestine (Ezek. 40–48). Second Isaiah, about whom more will be said in the next chapter, gave expression to an elevated monotheism that declared all gods besides Yahweh to be merely impotent idols and other religions to be mere delusions: "Thus says Yahweh, the King of Israel, and his Redeemer, Yahweh of hosts: 'I am the first and I am the last; besides me there is no god'" (Isa. 44:6).

The Egyptian Diaspora

The Egyptian diaspora was less significant for the immediate future of Judaism, and the status and life of the Judeans there are even less known than the Mesopotamian diaspora. The only direct, firsthand information, except for the material in the book of Jeremiah (Jer. 43–44; 46), comes from the legal documents and letters of the Elephantine archives (see *ANET* 491–92, 548–49; *COS* 3:116–31, 141–98; and *TAD*). These texts, even though from the later Persian period, reveal a number of interesting features about life in the Egyptian diaspora. (1) The Elephantine community was a small military colony that included women and children. Since it was a military outpost protecting the southern border and Nile commerce, the soldiers received payments as well as land grants from their overlords. Jewish settlements at Migdol, Tahpanhes, and Memphis were probably military garrisons similar to Elephantine (see Jer. 46:14). (2) There was intermarriage with Egyptians and assimilation in both directions. There is evidence of Egyptians becoming members of the Jewish community, and no doubt the reverse conditions also obtained. (3) Some Jewish persons rose to high position in local administrative matters, and some accumulated significant wealth. (4) The community retained contact with the religious authorities in both Jerusalem and Samaria. (5) The colony possessed limited internal autonomy. Contracts and legal documents suggest that there was a great similarity between the practices of the Jewish community and Egyptian culture. At Elephantine, for example, a woman apparently possessed the right to divorce her husband. This may, however, reflect some otherwise unknown ancient Israelite practice rather than a modification of Jewish legal procedures in an alien culture. (6) The community was at least aware of many traditional Jewish practices, including observance of the Sabbath and such festivals as Passover and Unleavened Bread. (7) They possessed a temple that bore structural similarity to the one in Jerusalem, and in which the ancestral god Yahweh (Yahu) was worshiped and sacrifices were offered. The existence of such a temple in Egypt would not necessarily have been understood as an infringement of the provision in the Deuteronomic law specifying only one place of sacrifice to Yahweh, since the biblical law speaks of conditions pertaining "in the land," that is, within Canaan (see Deut. 12:1, 10). Isaiah 19:19 speaks in a positive tone of the day when "there will be an altar to Yahweh in the midst of the land of Egypt, and a pillar to Yahweh at its border," and thus the prophet seems earlier to have endorsed a sacrificial cult outside Palestine. (8) Indications suggest that the Jews at Elephantine were syncretistic in their worship. Oaths and blessings and other evidence refer to a variety of Syro-Palestinian deities venerated in the Elephantine and surrounding Aramaic community: Anat, Sati, Bethel, Harambethel, Ashambethel, and so on. (For reference to some of these deities elsewhere in Palestine in the Assyrian period, see *ANET* 534.)

Biblical texts in general take a decidedly negative attitude toward the members of the Egyptian diaspora. This is especially the case with the prophet Jeremiah: "Lo, I swear by my great name, says Yahweh, that my name shall no longer be pronounced on the lips of any of the people of Judah in all the land of Egypt, saying, 'As Yahweh God lives.' I am going to watch over them for harm and not for good; all the people of Judah who are in the land of Egypt shall perish by the sword and by famine, until not one is left. And those who escape the sword shall return from the land of Egypt to the land of Judah, few in number" (Jer. 44:26–28).

General Bibliography

T. C. Mitchell, "The Babylonian Exile and the Restoration of the Jews in Palestine (586–c. 500 B.C.)," *CAH* 3/2:410–60, provides a general survey of this period. H. M. Barstad, *The Myth of the Empty Land: A Study in the History and Archaeology of Judah During the "Exilic" Period* (Symbolae Osloenses Fasciculus Suppletionis 28; Oslo: Scandinavian University Press, 1996); Oded Lipschits, *The Fall and Rise of Jerusalem: Jerusalem under Babylonian Rule* (Winona Lake, IN: Eisenbrauns, 2005); and Jill Middlemas, *The Troubles of Templeless Judah* (Oxford: Oxford University Press, 2005), stress the role and continuity of life in Judah during the Babylonian epoch.

Various problems associated with this period are discussed in L. L. Grabbe, ed., *Leading Captivity Captive: 'The Exile' as History and Ideology* (JSOTSup 278; Sheffield: Sheffield Academic Press, 1998); Oded Lipschits and Joseph Blenkinsopp, eds., *Judah and the Judeans in the Neo-Babylonian Period* (Winona Lake, IN: Eisenbrauns, 2003); and Bob Becking and M. C. A. Korpel, eds., *The Crisis of Israelite Religion: Transformation of Religious Tradition in Exilic and Post-exilic Times* (OtSt 42; Leiden: Brill, 1999). A sociological approach to the exile is offered by D. L. Smith, *The Religion of the Landless: The Social Context of the Babylonian Exile* (Bloomington, IN: Meyer-Stone, 1989). P. R. Ackroyd, *Exile and Restoration: A Study of Hebrew Thought of the Sixth Century B.C.* (OTL; Philadelphia: Westminster, 1968), and R. W. Klein, *Israel in Exile* (OBT; Philadelphia: Fortress, 1979), provide discussions of theological and literary developments. A special focus on the origin of biblical materials characterizes Rainer Albertz, *Israel in Exile: The History and Literature of the Sixth Century B.C.E.* (SBLStBL 3; Atlanta: Society of Biblical Literature, 2003). D. S. Vanderhooft, *The Neo-Babylonian Empire and Babylon in the Latter Prophets* (HSM 59; Atlanta: Scholars Press, 1999), traces the influence of Babylonia in the prophets.

16. The Era of the Persian Empire

The middle decades of the sixth century (559–539 B.C.E.) witnessed the rise of a new ruling power in the Near East. The Persians, an Indo-European people whose origins and center of power lay in the territory north and east of the Fertile Crescent, quickly established the most comprehensive Near Eastern empire that had existed until that time.

The architect for the new empire was Cyrus II. His meteoric career and far-flung conquests took advantage of the weaknesses of the Babylonian, Lydian, Median, and Egyptian kingdoms and appealed to those who favored internationalism over the more limited ethnic kingdoms that had temporarily replaced the Assyrian Empire. Cyrus's son Cambyses added Egypt to the Persian holdings. Darius I, the third of the Persian rulers, further expanded the imperial holdings and implemented organizational structure for the huge Persian Empire.

For over two centuries, from the Persian capture of Babylon in 539 until the fall of Tyre to Alexander the Great in 332, Palestine and the Jewish community in Judah were under Persian hegemony. The most significant events in Jewish history during this period, at least from the perspective of the final editors of the Hebrew Bible, were the return of exiles from Babylonia, the reconstruction of the Jerusalem temple, the refortification of the city of Jerusalem, and the attempts to reform Judean life by two returning Jewish leaders from the Diaspora—Ezra and Nehemiah. Unfortunately, as we shall see, the biblical materials, our primary explicit sources for Jewish history in the land of Palestine during this period, by focusing on the restoration efforts of exilic returnees, practically ignore the ongoing life and history of the Judean community that remained in the land and never experienced the exile. Thus any reconstruction of the history of Palestinian Judaism for this period is at the mercy of the narrow documentation that has survived.

Sources for the Period

The primary Jewish sources for the period are the historical books of Ezra and Nehemiah, the prophetical books of Haggai and Zechariah (Zech. 1–8), the apocryphal book of 1 Esdras, and Josephus's *Antiquities* (book 11). (Although given a Persian setting, the book of Esther is a romantic novel and supplies no precise historical information on the period.) Ezra 1–6 purports to narrate the history from the return to Jerusalem until the rededication of the temple.[1] A number of "documents" are included in this section. Ezra 1 reports that Cyrus granted permission for exiled Judeans to return and rebuild the temple (Ezra 1:1–4; cf. 6:1–5) and that he restored the temple vessels taken into exile by Nebuchadrezzar, sending these home under the care of Sheshbazzar "the prince of Judah" (1:5–11). After supplying a list of the returnees (Ezra 2; see Neh. 7:6–73), the story of the returning exiles focuses on the work of reconstructing the temple led by Jeshua (Joshua) and Zerubbabel (Ezra 3:1–4:5; see 5:13–16), on opposition to the work of the returnees (4:6–24), and on the eventual reconstruction and rededication of the sanctuary (5:1–6:22). The remainder of Ezra–Nehemiah is taken up with the stories about Ezra (Ezra 7–10; Neh. 7:73b–10:39) and Nehemiah (Neh. 1:1–7:73a; 11–13). First Esdras offers a summary in Greek of the book of Ezra and Neh. 7:38–8:12 along with 2 Chronicles 35–36. The prophets Haggai and Zechariah were active at the time of the reconstruction of the temple (Ezra 5:1–2), and oracles in their books are dated to the reign of the Persian king Darius I (522–486). Other prophetical material probably originates from this period—Joel, Malachi, Jonah, Isaiah 56–66—while Deutero-Isaiah (chaps. 40–55) reflects the period of Persia's rise to dominance. The Jewish historian Josephus discusses the Persian period in book 11 of his *Antiquities* and offers some information not found in the biblical texts.[2]

Some inscribed nonbiblical Hebrew and Aramaic materials from this period also exist. The most important include the Elephantine documents, which contain correspondence addressed from and to the Jewish military colony settled at Aswan in Egypt (see *TAD* and *COS* 3:116–32, 141–98), papyri and other materials from a cave in the Wadi ed-Daliyeh southeast of Samaria carried there when Alexander the Great razed the city about 331,[3] and scores of seals and seal impressions (see *COS* 2:203–4)[4] and coins,[5] some of which provide the names of leaders of the Jewish community.

1. For a discussion of the issues related to these chapters and their use in historical reconstruction see H. G. M. Williamson, "The Composition of Ezra i–vi," *JTS* 34 (1983) 1–30; repr. in *SPPHH* 244–70; Baruch Halpern, "A Historiographic Commentary on Ezra 1–6: A Chronological Narrative and Dual Chronology in Israelite Historiography," in W. H. Propp et al., eds., *The Hebrew Bible and Its Interpreters* (Winona Lake, IN: Eisenbrauns, 1990) 81–142; Bezalel Porten, "Theme and Structure of Ezra 1–6: From Literature to History," *Transeu* 23 (2002) 27–44; and L. S. Fried, "The Land Lay Desolate: Conquest and Restoration in the Ancient Near East," in Oded Lipschits and Joseph Blenkinsopp, eds., *Judah and the Judeans in the Neo-Babylonian Period* (Winona Lake, IN: Eisenbrauns, 2003) 21–54. A survey of issues related to the history of the period can be found in H. G. M. Williamson, "Exile and After: Historical Study," in D. N. Baker and B. T. Arnold, eds., *The Face of Old Testament Studies: A Survey of Contemporary Approaches* (Grand Rapids: Baker, 1999) 236–65; idem, "Early Post-Exilic Judaean History," in *SPPHH* 3–24; D. V. Edelman, *The Origins of the 'Second' Temple: Persian Imperial Policy and the Rebuilding of Jerusalem* (London: Equinox, 2005) 151–208.

2. See C. G. Tuland, "Josephus, *Antiquities*, Book XI: Correction or Confirmation of Biblical Post-Exilic Records?" *AUSS* 4 (1966) 176–92; and H. G. M. Williamson, "The Historical Value of Josephus' *Jewish Antiquities* XI. 297–301," *JTS* 28 (1977) 49–66; repr. in *SPPHH* 74–89.

3. P. W. Lapp and N. L. Lapp, *Discoveries in the Wâdī ed-Dâliyeh* (AASOR 41; Cambridge: American Schools of Oriental Research, 1974); M. J. W. Leith, *Wadi Daliyeh I: The Wadi Daliyeh Seal Impressions* (DJD 24; Oxford: Clarendon, 1997); and D. M. Gropp, *Wadi Daliyeh II: The Samaria Papyri from Wadi Daliyeh* (DJD 28; Oxford: Clarendon, 2001).

4. Nahman Avigad and Benjamin Sass, *Corpus of West Semitic Stamp Seals* (Jerusalem: Israel Academy of Sciences and Humanities, 1997).

5. See Yaakov Meshorer, *Ancient Jewish Coinage, I. Persian Period through Hasmoneans* (Dix Hills, NY: Amphora Books, 1982); J. W. Betlyon, "The Provincial Government of Persian Period Judea and the Yehud Coins," *JBL* 105 (1986) 633–42; and Leo Mildenberg, "On the Money Circulation in Palestine from Artaxerxes II till Ptolemy I: Preliminary Studies of Local Coinage in the Fifth Persian Satrapy, Part 5," *Transeu* 7 (1994) 63–71.

A number of cuneiform texts provide information on the rise and rule of the Persians. Most important among these are the so-called Nabonidus Chronicles (*ABC* 104–11), which describes the rise of Cyrus, his capture of Babylon, and the events immediately following; the Cyrus Cylinder (*COS* 2:314–16; *ANET* 315–16), produced early in the Persian king's rule, which presents him as a liberator of oppressed people; and the multilingual Behistun Inscription, inscribed on a mountain face at Naqsh-i Rustam near Persepolis, which describes the rise and early years of Darius I.[6]

Since the Greeks and Persians were engaged in conflict throughout the period of Persian rule, several Greek writers provide reference to Greco-Persian relations, often providing snippets of information not attested elsewhere, but few that bear directly on Judean history.[7]

The Rise of Cyrus and the Persians

Since the biblical sources supply only a few vignettes of Jewish life for this period, the story is best carried by the narrative of the larger Persian history. The ancient world was familiar with several legends about the origins and early career of Cyrus (Herodotus 1.95). The account based on the motif of the threatened and/or abandoned child who grows up to be a great leader (see *ANET* 119; Exod. 2; Matt. 2) fascinated Herodotus (1.107–30) but probably provides little of historical value. Cyrus, apparently the son of King Cambyses I of the minor kingdom of Anshan, and Mandane, the daughter of the Median king Astyages (ca. 585–550), began his career as ruler in his father's rather insignificant province in southwestern Persia. Cyrus was able to expand his power at the expense of his Median overlord and grandfather Astyages and probably with the blessings of the Babylonian king Nabonidus, who was suspicious of Median power. A fragmentary portion of the Nabonidus Chronicle reports that Cyrus acquired Astyages' kingdom in 550 as a consequence of the desertion of the Median forces:

> King Ishtumegu [Astyages] called up his troops and marched against Cyrus, king of Anshan, in order to meet him in battle. The army of Ishtumegu revolted against him and in fetters they delivered him to Cyrus. Cyrus marched against the country Agamtanu [Ecbatana]; the royal residence he seized; silver, gold, other valuables of the country Agamtanu he took as booty and brought them to Anshan. (partially restored; see *ANET* 305; *ABC* 106)

Thus Cyrus took control over the Median empire. Instead of moving against Babylonia, as might have been expected, Cyrus turned his attention westward. According to Herodotus (1.73–90), he carried on negotiations with the Greek

---

6. The original inscription was written in Elamite, Akkadian, and Old Persian but was circulated throughout the empire in other languages as well; see E. N. von Voigtländer, *The Bisitun Inscription of Darius the Great: Babylonian Version* (Corpus Inscriptionum Iranicarum: Part I: Inscriptions of Ancient Iran, vol. 2: The Babylonian Versions of the Achaemenian Inscriptions, Texts 1; London: Humphries, 1978); and J. C. Greenfield and Bezalel Porten, *The Bisitun Inscription of Darius the Great: Aramaic Version* (Corpus Inscriptionum Iranicarum: Part I: Inscriptions of Ancient Iran, vol. 5: The Aramaic Versions of the Achaemenian Inscriptions, Texts 1; London: Humphries, 1982). The Old Persian version is translated in R. G. Kent, *Old Persian: Grammar, Text, Lexicon* (2d ed.; AOS 33; New Haven: American Oriental Society, 1953), hereafter abbreviated *OP*.

7. See Robert Drews, *The Greek Accounts of Eastern History* (Cambridge: Harvard University Press, 1973).

CHART 20. The Persian Empire

Persian Rulers	*Events in Palestine*
Cyrus II (559–530)	
Became king of Anshan (559)	Judah as a Babylonian province or
Conquered Astyages of Media (550)	subject kingdom
Defeated Croesus of Lydia (546)	
Captured Babylon (539)	Shesh-bazzar as head of Judean province
Edict allowing Jews to return and	First return of Jews from Babylonia
rebuild the temple (538)	(538?)
	Work begun on Jerusalem temple
	restoration(?)
Cambyses (530–522)	
	Zerubbabel as governor
	Palestine fully under Persian control
Conquest of Egypt (525)	Work begun on Jerusalem temple
Political turmoil after the death of	restoration(?)
Cambyses (522–520)	
Darius I (522–486)	
Codification of Egyptian laws under	Prophets Haggai and Zechariah active
Persian supervision	in Jerusalem (520)
Ionian cities, aided by Athens, revolt	Jerusalem temple rebuilt (520–515)
against Persians	
Persian expedition against Athens	
defeated at the battle of Marathon	
(490)	
Egypt rebelled against Persia just	
before Darius's death (486)	
Xerxes I (486–465)	
Egyptian revolt suppressed (483)	
Persians invaded Greece; Persian fleet	
defeated at Battle of Salamis (480)	
Persian army defeated by Greeks at the	
Battle of Plataea; Persian fleet	
destroyed at the battle of Mount	
Mykale; Persia lost control of	
Macedon, Thrace, and Cyrenaica	
(478)	
Delian League formed by Athens to	
liberate Greek cities from Persians	
(478)	

Persian Rulers	*Events in Palestine*
Artaxerxes I Longimanus (465–424)	
Egyptians, under Inaros and aided by Athens, again rebel against Persians (465–455)	
	Ezra's mission to Jerusalem (458?)
Rebellion of satrap Megabyzus (449/448)	
Peace of Callias between Persia and Athens (449)	Nehemiah sent to Jerusalem to refortify the city (445)
Peloponnesian War in Greece (431–404)	
Darius II Nothus (424/423–405/404)	
Greek cities in Asia Minor reclaimed by Persia (404)	Elephantine Jews appealed to Jerusalem and Samaria for help in rebuilding their temple (407)
Artaxerxes II Memnon (405/404–359/358)	
Egypt regained its freedom from Persia (after 401)	Egyptians moved into southern Palestine for a time (about 399)
	Ezra's mission (398?)
Revolt of several satraps (366–360)	Egyptians moved back into southern Palestine for a short time (360)
Philip II came to power in Macedon (359)	
Artaxerxes III Ochus (359/358–338/337)	Revolt of Phoenicians led by Tennes (ca. 350)
Persians regain control of Egypt (342)	
Arses (338/337–336)	
Darius III Comodamus (336–330)	
Philip assassinated (336)	
Alexander invaded the Persian Empire (334)	
Darius defeated at Issus (333)	
Capture of Tyre (332)	
Death of Darius (330)	

city-states in Ionia and in 547 attacked Croesus, the legendary king of Lydia who had initially attacked Cyrus to get revenge for the latter's actions against Astyages, a brother-in-law of Croesus (so Herodotus 1.73). Following up an inconclusive victory, Cyrus unconventionally attacked Croesus, after the latter had dismissed his provincial levies, prior to the onset of winter. After fourteen days, Cyrus had taken Sardis, the capital city (see *ANET* 306). In addition to Lydia and Lycia, the Greek states in Asia Minor were subdued and added to Cyrus's holdings in Armenia, Cappadocia, and Cilicia that he had taken on his march to fight Croesus. It was probably during Cyrus's campaign into western Asia Minor that Cyprus voluntarily submitted to Persian control (Herodotus 3.19). Thus two of the major powers of the time—Media and Lydia—fell to the Persians.

Before moving against the third major power, Babylonia, Cyrus extended his control to the east, securing the entire Iranian plateau and the territory extending to northwest India. In Babylonia itself, discontent with Nabonidus and pro-Cyrus support seems to have accelerated. Probably three classes especially hoped for a Persian triumph. (1) The Marduk priesthood was strongly opposed to Nabonidus's predilection for the moon-god Sin, even through he had continued to worship and support the other Babylonian deities.[8] The absence of the king from Babylon during his stay in the Arabian oasis in Tema had curbed religious celebrations. In strongly anti-Nabonidus tones, the Nabonidus Chronicle monotonously demurs: "The king stayed in Tema; the crown prince [Belshazzar], the officials and his army were in Akkad [Babylonia]. The king did not come to Babylon for the ceremonies of the month Nisan, . . . Nebo did not come to Babylon, . . . Bel did not go out of Esagila in procession, the festival of the New Year [*akitu*] was omitted" (partially restored; see *ANET* 306; *ABC* 106). (2) Babylonian merchants who had seen their markets disrupted and trade routes disappear probably yearned for the renewal of an empire where far-flung trade routes and ever-increasing markets created demands and stimulated supplies. (3) Foreigners now living in Babylon must have felt that chances for a return to their homelands were better under anyone other than the presently ruling establishment.

Nabonidus was an old man, perhaps past seventy, when he returned from Arabia, probably in October 543, to prepare the capital city for the inevitable invasion of the Persians. He hastily sought to fortify the city of Babylon and the outlying regions for the onslaught of Cyrus and participated in the spring New Year (*akitu*) Festival, which his absence had suspended for a decade. But the city and the region—torn by internal dissensions, cut off from external trade and military aid, defended primarily by mercenary seminomads, and plagued by famine and inflation—were no match for Persian forces now joined by defectors from the Babylonian military hierarchy. In early October 539 the Babylonian army was defeated at Opis, and the ancient city of Akkad was destroyed and its population slaughtered by Cyrus. The pro-Persian Nabonidus Chronicle reports the capture of Babylon itself in the following terms:

8. On the impact of Nabonidus's theology on his activities, see P.-A. Beaulieu, "King Nabonidus and the Neo-Babylonian Empire," in *CANE* 2:969–79. See also Amélie Kuhrt, "Nabonidus and the Priesthood of Babylon," in Mary Beard and John North, eds., *Pagan Priests: Religion and Power in the Ancient World* (London: Lutterworth, 1990) 119–55.

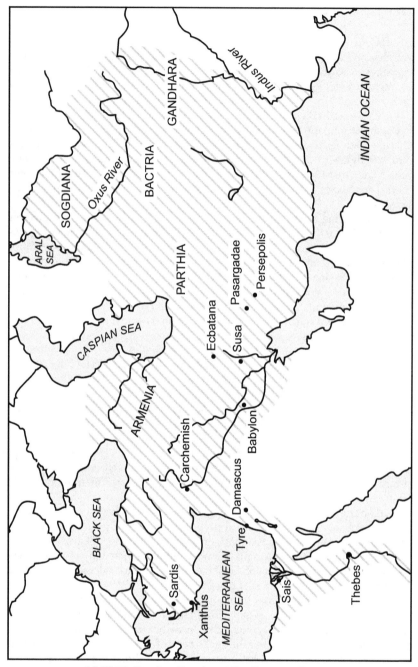

MAP 32. Persian Empire at Its Greatest Extent

On the sixteenth day [of the month Tishri = 12 October 539] Gobryas (Ugbaru), governor of the Guti, and the army of Cyrus entered Babylon without a battle. Afterwards, after Nabonidus retreated, he was captured in Babylon. Until the end of the month, the shield-bearing troops of the Guti surrounded the gates of [the temple] Esagila. But there was no interruption of rites in Esagila or the other temples and no date for a performance was missed. On the third day of the month Marchesvan [= 29 October 539] Cyrus entered Babylon. . . . There was peace in the city while Cyrus spoke his greeting to all of Babylon. (*ABC* 109–10)

With the fall of the capital city, Babylonia—the third major Near Eastern power of the sixth century—fell to Persian control. The territory ruled by Nabonidus—Babylonia proper, Arabia, Transjordan, and the eastern Mediterranean seaboard—was all added, theoretically at least, to the Persian Empire.

Cyrus as Liberator and Propagandist

It is not accidental that history has remembered Cyrus as a great liberator of captured peoples. (See Text 19.) It is an image that he and his officials sought to foster and that the historical conditions of the time facilitated. In this endeavor he was building upon and exploiting an age-old royal tradition. The portrait of the good ruler as "the gatherer of the dispersed" and "the restorer of the gods and their sanctuaries" was a common feature of Near Eastern royal ideology.[9] Already in the eighteenth century Hammurabi could boast that he was the one "who gathers together the scattered people" (*COS* 2:336; *ANET* 164). Such motifs were especially stressed by the Assyrian rulers Esarhaddon and Ashurbanipal. For example, after Sennacherib had destroyed Babylon and its Esagila temple in 689, Esarhaddon depicted himself as the great restorer of people and temple. The following quotations from texts concerning Esarhaddon's rebuilding of Babylon illustrate the point:

Seventy years as the period of its [Esagila's] desolation he [Marduk] wrote (down in the Book of Fate). But the merciful Marduk—his anger lasted but a moment—turned (the book) upside down and ordered its (the city's) restoration in the eleventh [a reversed 70 in cuneiform script] year. (*ARAB* II §650; *COS* 2:306)

As for the enslaved Babylonians, who had been the feudatories, the clients, of the gods Anu and Enlil, their freedom I established anew. The "capitalists," who had been brought into slavery, who had been apportioned to the yoke and fetter, I gathered together and accounted them for Babylonians.

Their plundered possessions I restored. The naked I clothed and turned their feet into the road to Babylon. To (re)settle the city, to rebuild the temple, to set out plantations, to dig irrigation-ditches I encouraged them. Their clientship which had lapsed, which had slipped out of (their) hands, I restored. The tablet (charter) of their freedom I wrote anew. Toward the four winds of heaven I opened up their ways so that, establishing their tongue (language) in every land, they might carry out their plans. (*ARAB* II §659E)

---

9. Geo Widengren, "Yahweh's Gathering of the Dispersed," in W. B. Barrick and J. R. Spencer, eds., *In the Shelter of Elyon: Essays on Ancient Palestinian Life and Literature in Honour of G. W. Ahlström* (JSOTSup 31; Sheffield: JSOT Press, 1984) 227–45.

The building inscriptions of Ashurbanipal abound with similar claims about how he "renewed the sanctuaries of all the metropolises and revived in them the ancient cults and restored their regular offerings which had ceased" (*ARAB* II §956). Similarly, Nabonidus repaid the god Sin for raising him to the throne by restoring his city and cult:

> I carefully executed the command of his (Sin's) great godhead, I was not care-less nor negligent but set in motion people from Babylon and Upper Syria, from the border of Egypt on the Upper Sea to the Lower Sea, all those whom Sin, the king of the gods, had entrusted to me, (thus) I built anew the Ehul-hul, the temple of Sin, and completed this work. I (then) led in procession Sin, Ningal, Nusku and Sadarnunna, from Shuanna (in Babylon), my royal city, and brought (them) in joy and happiness (into the temple), installing them on a permanent dais. I made abundant offerings before them and lavished gifts (on them). (*ANET* 563)

With a grand flair for propagandistic impact, Cyrus too played the role of liberator, accepting and acknowledging the patronage of the gods worshiped by those capitulating to and supporting him. The so-called Cyrus Cylinder (*COS* 2:314–16), reflective of and modeled on earlier inscriptions of Esarhad-don and Ashurbanipal, for example, ascribed his success in Babylon to Mar-duk, who "scanned and looked through all the countries, searching for a righteous ruler willing to lead him in the annual procession. Then he pro-nounced the name of Cyrus, king of Anshan, declared him to be the ruler of all the world" (*ANET* 315; see Text 19).

Against this background, the hope of the Judean exiles to return home and Second Isaiah's preaching and expectations become more understandable. This prophet sought, in poetry of great lyrical expression and in enormously per-suasive rhetoric, to convince his fellow exiles that the activity of Cyrus and the international developments of the time were under the control of Yahweh and that all of this forebode a good future for the exiles. The prophet hailed Cyrus as savior and redeemer, as the chosen of Yahweh: "I [Yahweh] stirred up one from the north, and he has come, from the rising of the sun he was summoned by name. He shall trample on rulers as on mortar, as the potter treads clay" (Isa. 41:25). In order to emphasize Cyrus as Yahweh's "chosen," he even bestowed upon Cyrus the title borne by Davidic kings: "Thus says Yahweh to his messiah, to Cyrus, whose right hand I have grasped to subdue nations before him and strip kings of their robes, to open doors before him and the gates shall not be closed" (45:1). The prophet has Yahweh address Cyrus per-sonally (see 45:1–7) and proclaim the fall of Babylon (Isa. 46–47). The hope for the future is already placed in the mouth of Yahweh and the hands of Cyrus: "'He is my shepherd, and he shall carry out all my purpose'; and who says of Jerusalem, 'It shall be rebuilt,' and of the temple, 'Your foundation shall be laid'" (44:28). The words of the prophet must be seen therefore as intended not only for his exilic audience but also for the Persians to demonstrate that it was Yahweh who had chosen Cyrus and that his people expected reciprocation (45:13).[10] "Predictions" about what would happen in the future were a means of advocating what should happen in the future. Josephus reports that Cyrus

---

10. See Morton Smith, "II Isaiah and the Persians," *JAOS* 83 (1963) 415–21.

TEXT 19. An Inscription of Cyrus

Upon their complaints the lord of the gods {Marduk} became terribly angry
and [he departed from] their region, (also) the (other) gods living among
them left their mansions, wroth that he {Nabonidus} had brought (them) into
Babylon. . . . (But) Marduk [who does care for] . . . on account of (the fact that)
the sanctuaries of all their settlements were in ruins and the inhabitants of
Sumer and Akkad had become like (living) dead, turned back (his countenance) [his] an[ger] [abated] and he had mercy (upon them). He scanned and
looked (through) all the countries, searching for a righteous ruler willing to
lead him (i.e. Marduk) (in the annual procession). (Then) he pronounced the
name of Cyrus . . . , king of Anshan, declared him (lit.: pronounced [his]
name) to be(come) the ruler of all the world. He made the Guti country and
all the Manda-hordes bow in submission to his (i.e. Cyrus') feet. And he
(Cyrus) did always endeavour to treat according to justice the black-headed
whom he (Marduk) has made him conquer. Marduk, the great lord, a protector of his people/worshipers, beheld with pleasure his (i.e. Cyrus') good
deeds and his upright mind (lit.: heart) (and therefore) ordered him to march
against his city Babylon. . . . He made him set out on the road to Babylon
going at his side like a real friend. His widespread troops—their number, like
that of the water of a river, could not be established—strolled along, their
weapons packed away. Without any battle, he made him enter his town
Babylon . . . , sparing Babylon . . . any calamity. He delivered into his (i.e.
Cyrus') hands Nabonidus, the king who did not worship him (i.e. Marduk).
All the inhabitants of Babylon as well as of the entire country of Sumer and
Akkad, princes and governors (included), bowed to him (Cyrus) and kissed
his feet, jubilant that he (had received) the kingship, and with shining faces.
Happily they greeted him as a master through whose help they had come
(again) to life from death (and) had all been spared damage and disaster, and
they worshiped his (very) name. . . .

When I entered Babylon . . . as a friend and (when) I established the seat of
the government in the palace of the ruler under jubilation and rejoicing, Marduk, the great lord, [induced] the magnanimous inhabitants of Babylon . . . [to
love me], and I was daily endeavouring to worship him. My numerous troops
walked around in Babylon . . . in peace, I did not allow anybody to terrorize
(any place) of the [country of Sumer] and Akkad. I strove for peace in Babylon . . . and in all his (other) sacred cities. As to the inhabitants of Babylon . . . ,
[who] against the will of the gods [had/were . . . , I abolished] the corvée (lit.:
yoke) which was against their (social) standing. I brought relief to their dilap-
idated housing, putting (thus) an end to their (main) complaints. Marduk, the
great lord, was well pleased with my deeds and sent friendly blessings to
myself, Cyrus, the king who worships him, to Cambyses, my son, the offspring of [my] loins, as well as to all my troops, and we all [praised] his great
[godhead] joyously, standing before him in peace.

All the kings of the entire world from the Upper to the Lower Sea, those
who are seated in throne rooms, (those who) live in other [types of buildings

as well as] all the kings of the West land living in tents, brought their heavy tributes and kissed my feet in Babylon. . . . (As to the region) from . . . as far as Ashur and Susa, Agade, Eshnunna, the towns Zamban, Me-Turnu, Der as well as the region of the Gutians, I returned to (these) sacred cities on the other side of the Tigris, the sanctuaries of which have been ruins for a long time, the images which (used) to live therein and established for them permanent sanctuaries. I (also) gathered all their (former) inhabitants and returned (to them) their habitations. Furthermore, I resettled upon the command of Marduk, the great lord, all the gods of Sumer and Akkad whom Nabonidus has brought into Babylon . . . to the anger of the lord of the gods, unharmed, in their (former) chapels, the places which make them happy. (*ANET* 315–16)

took his lenient attitude toward the Judean exiles after reading Isaiah's prophecy about Cyrus, written 210 years before the Persian took Babylon (*Ant.* 11.1–9). This, of course, assumes too much; Josephus did not know about a Second Isaiah. However, it is not beyond the range of possibility to assume that Cyrus and the Persians knew the Jewish sentiments reflected in Isaiah 40–48, if not the material itself.

Cyrus's treatment of groups that had been deported and settled throughout the Assyrian and Babylonian empires probably varied from case to case. The Cyrus Cylinder, obviously seeking to gain as much propagandistic mileage as possible, probably presents a reasonably accurate picture of Cyrus's policy toward people and cults at least in the Babylonian area.[11] (See Text 19.)

Although Cyrus and his successors earned a reputation for tolerance and benevolence, we should note that Persian kings could be as severe in their treatment of subject peoples as others, depending upon the needs of the situation. For example, later kings often took harsh actions against their subjects, even against cultic centers: Darius I had the temple at Didyma in Asia Minor destroyed (Herodotus 6.20), Xerxes destroyed Babylon in reprisal for a revolt (Herodotus 1.183), the residents of Barca in Lydia were resettled in Bactria by Darius I (Herodotus 4.204), the Paeonians were moved from Thrace to Phrygia (Herodotus 5.13–16), citizens of Miletus were resettled on the Persian Gulf (Herodotus 6.20), and late in Persian history Sidonians were exiled to Babylon and Susa (*ABC* 114).

Persian Policy toward the Judean Exiles

The book of Ezra contains two ordinances dated to the "first year" of Cyrus, presumably the year following his capture of Babylon (539), that speak of a return of the Jews from exile and of the restoration of the temple. One is written in Aramaic and is described as the official record of Cyrus's edict preserved in the official archives at Ecbatana in Persia (Ezra 6:1–5). This document has Cyrus stipulate that the temple should be rebuilt according to certain dimensions and specifications, that royal funds along with voluntary contributions

11. See Amélie Kuhrt, "The Cyrus Cylinder and Achaemenid Imperial Policy," *JSOT* 25 (1983) 83–97.

should be used for the project, and that the vessels taken from the old temple to Babylon should be restored (cf. 5:13–15). The other ordinance, written in Hebrew, is described as a proclamation distributed in writing throughout the kingdom (1:2–4). This text notes that Cyrus was charged by Yahweh the God of heaven to reconstruct the temple in Jerusalem. Further, it notes that permission was granted to any Yahweh worshipers wishing to return to work on the rebuilding to do so; Jews not returning might contribute toward the expense of those who did return as well as to the cost of temple restoration.

The differences in these ordinances are significant. Ezra 6:3–5 concentrates on the rebuilding of the temple at royal expense but makes no reference to returning exiles. Ezra 1:2–4 focuses on the issue of returning exiles and contains no particulars about temple reconstruction. If both texts are authentic and from the first year of Cyrus's reign, as they purport, then these could be seen as two types of Persian administrative documents with different functions. The Hebrew text in Ezra 1 would be a form of the message that was proclaimed by official heralds in various Jewish communities and subsequently posted in written form. The Aramaic text in Ezra 6 would represent the form of an official memorandum stored in the royal archives. Such memoranda would have been based on royal decrees and were written down on clay tablets for filing or on papyrus sheets, which were glued together to form archival scrolls.

If these texts refer to two different decrees but have in common their interest in the restoration of the temple, then the text in Ezra 6:3–5 may be seen as Cyrus's decree ordering temple reconstruction and the return of the sacred vessels. (Note that in this text the reference to "the first year of Cyrus" appears to be part of the document.) The decree in 1:2–4 would then be a subsequent decree granting the right of Jews to return and aid in restoration but making no reference to the vessels or temple specifications, since these were covered in the earlier decree. (Note that in 1:1–5 the dating of the decree is part of the editorial frame rather than a part of the document.) Even if these decrees came from two different occasions in the reign of Cyrus or served two different functions, there is not sufficient reason to doubt that such decrees were issued, although their present wording and specific content may have been shaped by the biblical editors.[12]

Such a decree or decrees concerning the reconstruction of the temple and the return of the exiles should not be taken as an expression of Persian favoritism toward the Jews. In the first place, such action was typical of Cyrus when such a policy was judged in the best interests of the Persian cause. Second, his affirmation that it was Yahweh who had given him all the kingdoms of the earth was comparable to similar affirmations made about Marduk. Third, such actions could be viewed as reciprocation for the pro-Persian sentiments held by many Judean exiles, such as Second Isaiah. Fourth, by providing support for the Jerusalem temple, Cyrus was assuming the role of successor to Jerusalemite royalty, since the temple had been a "royal shrine" under the

---

12. On the authenticity of the decrees see E. J. Bickerman, "The Edict of Cyrus in Ezra 1," *JBL* 65 (1946) 249–75; repr. in his *Studies in Jewish and Christian History* (3 vols.; AGJU 9; Leiden: Brill, 1976–85) 1:72–108. For arguments against authenticity see L. L. Grabbe, "Reconstructing History from the Book of Ezra," in P. R. Davies, ed., *Second Temple Studies, 1: Persian Period* (JSOTSup 117; Sheffield: JSOT Press, 1991) 98–106.

special care of the king. Fifth, the political realities on the southwestern borders of his empire could have made expedient such a friendly and supportive gesture. Although "all the kings of the West land living in tents" had submitted to Cyrus shortly after his capture of Babylon, bringing tribute and kissing his feet (*ANET* 316; *COS* 2:315), others may not have submitted so readily, if at all. Egypt was still ruled by the aged Pharaoh Amasis (570–526), a former ally of Croesus. The inevitable attack against Egypt could only be aided, not hindered, by a Judean community favorably disposed to the Persians.

Two final matters should be noted about these decrees. (1) They did not require or allow for the gathering of the dispersed Jews throughout the Persian Empire. Thus no return en masse was envisioned. (2) The decrees are primarily concerned with the reconstruction of the temple, not the return of exiles per se.

The Political Situation in Judah

Unfortunately all the Jewish historical sources for the Persian period focus almost exclusively on the exilic returnees and their efforts to affect life in the province of Judah. Practically all of these sources assume that the territory of Judah existed during the Babylonian period as something of an occupational vacuum awaiting repopulation from those taken into exile and that all the major impulses of the time came from the returnees. As we noted in the last chapter, however, one should assume that a vigorous life continued in the area, although with a reduced population. The important aristocratic family of Shaphan had moved into leadership following the destruction of Jerusalem. After Gedaliah's assassination, we should assume that Nebuchadrezzar appointed a successor and political life continued. Presumably Mizpah continued as the capital for the region.

In the early chapters of Ezra, there appears the figure of Sheshbazzar, described as "the prince of Judah" (1:8) and said to have been appointed as governor by Cyrus (5:14).[13] Although it must remain in the arena of speculation, we could surmise that Sheshbazzar, who bore a Babylonian name, was the incumbent ruler of the Judean province at the time of Cyrus's triumph. As such, the title "prince of Judah" either would be equivalent to the term "king," as perhaps in the book of Ezekiel (Ezek. 45:7–8), or would be the Hebrew equivalent of a Babylonian title. After assuming authority in the area, Cyrus continued Sheshbazzar in office but with the title "governor" (Ezra 5:14).

The province or district of Judah, if we may judge from the evidence of the books of Ezra and Nehemiah, was composed of the territory extending from just north of Bethel to south of Beth-zur and from the Jordan River to just west of Emmaus and Azekah. This would give an area of about twenty-five miles north to south and thirty or so miles east to west, or an area of about eight hundred square miles. This would probably have corresponded to the boundaries recognized by Nebuchadrezzar following the fall of Jerusalem.

---

13. See Sara Japhet, "Sheshbazzar and Zerubbabel: Against the Background of the Historical and Religious Tendencies of Ezra-Nehemiah," *ZAW* 94 (1982) 66–98; and Nadav Na'aman, "Royal Vassals or Governors? On the Status of Shesbazzar and Zerubbabel in the Persian Empire," *Hen* 22 (2000) 35–94; repr. in *AIIN*, 403–14.

The Extent of the Return

Surprisingly, the biblical materials contain practically no information on the return of exiles from Babylon during the early years of Persian rule. (This contrasts noticeably with the accounts of returns at the time of Ezra [Ezra 7–8] and Nehemiah [Neh. 2:1–10].) Mention is made of the fact that temple vessels were turned over to Sheshbazzar to be returned (Ezra 1:7–11; 5:14–15). The transport of these cultic artifacts is noted also in Second Isaiah:

> Depart, depart, go out from there!
>> Touch no unclean thing;
> go out from the midst of it [Babylon], purify yourselves,
>> you who carry the vessels of Yahweh.
> For you shall not go out in haste,
>> and you shall not go in flight;
> for Yahweh will go before you,
>> and the God of Israel will be your rear guard.
>> (Isa. 52:11–12)

Otherwise, we are told only that "the heads of the families of Judah and Benjamin, and the priests and the Levites—everyone whose spirit God had stirred—got ready to go up and rebuild the house of Yahweh in Jerusalem" (Ezra 1:5).

Two lists of returnees, almost identical, appear in Ezra 2 and Nehemiah 7. The appearance of the list in Ezra 2 immediately following the comments about Sheshbazzar would imply that the list should be associated with the return of about fifty thousand persons (see Ezra 2:64–67) under Sheshbazzar. The officials associated with the list, however, are not Sheshbazzar but Zerubbabel, Jeshua, Nehemiah, and others who belong to later periods (Ezra 2:2; Neh. 7:7). Thus if the document is a genuine list of returnees, it probably comes from a time later than Sheshbazzar. Doubts can be raised, however, about whether it is even an authentic tabulation of returnees at all. The list contains no indication of date nor any references to Cyrus. It may be some census count, a tax document, or a population count (see Ezra 5:4–10) from a later period that has been incorporated into the text and treated as a list of returnees.

In all probability, the initial return from Babylon was a rather limited matter. Several factors indicate this. (1) The permission to return was related to reconstruction work on the Temple and not a full-fledged grant of exilic repatriation. Thus only those "whose spirit God had stirred to go up to rebuild the temple of Yahweh" (Ezra 1:5) would have left Babylon. (2) The Persians apparently did not move into southern Syria-Palestine in force until Cambyses, the successor of Cyrus, invaded Egypt in 526/525. Thus conditions prior to this time were not conducive to mass movement of exiled Judeans to the area. (3) The books of Haggai and Zechariah, concerned with the period around 520, do not indicate any large conglomerate of returnees anxious to complete temple construction. (4) The rather favorable status of the exiles in Babylonia vis-à-vis conditions in Palestine may have made it more desirable for Jews to remain in Babylon, "being unwilling to leave their possessions" (Josephus, *Ant.* 11.8).

Perhaps we should think of only an initial return of small numbers that may, however, have swelled with the movement of Persian forces into Palestine

during the reign of Cambyses (530–522). The outbreak of troubles which especially plagued the city of Babylon at the time of Cambyses' death and the subsequent turmoil in the early years of Darius I (522–486) may have encouraged
migration back to Canaan.

The Reconstruction of the Jerusalem Temple

A temple to Yahweh in Jerusalem built with Cyrus's patronage never became a
reality during his reign. The rebuilt temple was not dedicated until the reign of
Darius I (Ezra 6:15). This, of course, does not call into question either the
authenticity of Cyrus's decree concerning the temple or his utilization of the
orders for propaganda purposes. The issuing of the decree and the assumption
of the role of "restorer of the old order" were apparently as consequential as the
execution of the role itself. Esarhaddon's inscriptions, for example, speak of
him as the one who rebuilt Esagila and Babylon, protected their arrangements,
and returned the gods deported to Ashur. Yet it was twelve years later and long
after his death, during the reign of his successor Ashurbanipal, when his decree
was brought to fruition.

Various interpretations and differing accounts of the "restoration" of
authentic Jewish existence after the calamitous judgment of Yahweh in the fall
of Jerusalem are found in Jewish tradition. Underlying these are the assumptions that the exile marked a radical break in authentic existence, that proper
restoration was the work of those who had actually experienced being in exile,
and that the renewed community must in some sense be new and uncontaminated and yet stand in continuity with conditions that had existed prior to the
exile. Diverse narratives and traditions thus exist about when, under whom,
and how this restoration was effected. This can be seen in the various ways in
which temple restoration and renewal of worship in Jerusalem are described.
In one form it was Ezra who was the real restorer. This can be seen in the biblical traditions about Ezra as well as in the apocryphal book of 2 Esdras.
Another form is found in 2 Maccabees 1:18–2:15, where it is Nehemiah who is
the restorer of temple and altar. First Esdras, Josephus who follows 1 Esdras,
and some of the biblical texts in Ezra, Haggai, and Zechariah assign Zerubbabel a unique role as restorer. (One can say that for the author of the book of
Daniel [see Dan. 9], true restoration of people and temple was to be realized
finally in the second century B.C.E.)

In Ezra 1–6 there appear to be three different presentations of the temple
restoration.[14] One line of tradition, in Ezra 1 + 5:6–17, sees Sheshbazzar as the
initiator of work on temple rebuilding at the time of Cyrus that continues unin-
terrupted into the time of Darius I. A second line of tradition, in Ezra 3 +
6:19–22, sees Zerubbabel and Jeshua (Joshua) as the restorers. A final form, in
5:1–5 + 6:1–18 and in Haggai and Zechariah, assigns the restoration work to

---

14. On the issue of temple reconstruction see Sara Japhet, "'History' and 'Literature' in the Persian
Period: The Restoration of the Temple," in Mordechai Cogan and Israel Eph'al, eds., *Ah Assyria . . . !
Studies in Assyrian History and Ancient Near Eastern Historiography Presented to H. Tadmor* (ScrHier 33;
Jerusalem: Magnes, 1991) 74–88; and J. M. Trotter, "Was the Second Jerusalem Temple a Primarily Per-
sian Project?" *SJOT* 15 (2001) 276–94.

Zerubbabel and Joshua, but they carry out the work in conjunction with the prophetical activity of Haggai and Zechariah.

A plausible interpretation of the restoration of the Jerusalem temple, one that we follow here, sees reconstruction as having begun under Sheshbazzar and then reaching a new phase under the leadership of Zerubbabel and Joshua at the time of Darius's accession to the throne. Our approach to the matter, however, assumes that Sheshbazzar was not necessarily an exile, or if so, he had already been appointed as head of the Judean community prior to the rise of Cyrus and the Persians. Sheshbazzar would have been given custody of whatever temple vessels had survived to return them to Jerusalem. (The figures for the temple vessels in Ezra 1:9–11, however, appear to be greatly exaggerated.) He also began, in his position as Persian-appointed governor of the province, to carry out the decree of Cyrus to begin reconstructing the temple (Ezra 5:16), but he did not bring the task to completion. We are not told what happened to him. Perhaps he functioned as governor until his death and was succeeded in his post by Zerubbabel.

Under Zerubbabel, reconstruction entered a new phase but a phase reflective of and with a new impetus given by conditions under the successors of Cyrus, to which we now turn.

Cambyses

Cyrus died fighting in the east in 530. Before his final battle he had designated his son Cambyses as heir apparent and had Cambyses accompany him on much of the march eastward, probably to familiarize the subjects with the king's successor (Herodotus 1.208). After his father's death, Cambyses, who was remembered in tradition as a harsh ruler, "being naturally bad" (so Josephus, *Ant.* 11.26), subdued the eastern region of the empire and then invaded Egypt in 525. He assembled his invasion force at the Palestinian coastal town of Acco (Strabo, *Geography* 16.2.25). Arabic tribes aided the Persian forces in their march through the Sinai desert, supplying them with water (Herodotus 2.7–9) as they had the Assyrians in an earlier era. Speaking of these Arabs, Herodotus claims they "never submitted to the Persian yoke, but were on friendly terms, and gave Cambyses a free passage into Egypt; for, without the consent of the Arabians, the Persians could not have penetrated into Egypt" (Herodotus 3.88). Cyprus, along with the Phoenicians, supplied ships for the Persian expedition.

The aged and resourceful Egyptian pharaoh Amasis died, after a reign of forty-four years, while the Persian force was moving toward Egypt. The new pharaoh, Psammetichus III, was defeated after a hard-fought battle in the Delta and withdrew to Memphis, where he was quickly overcome. Persian conquest was apparently aided by the defection of Udjahorresnet, the commander of the Egyptian fleet.

Cambyses remained in Egypt for three years. Udjahorresnet, who was also a leading priest, prepared a royal titulature for the Persian monarch, who was duly crowned as the legitimate pharaoh of Upper and Lower Egypt. Cambyses apparently wanted to be seen as the legitimate successor of the old Saitic Dynasty whose last king Apries had been replaced by Amasis. The latter's name was removed from many Egyptian monuments. A legend that Cambyses was the son of a daughter of Apries circulated in various forms (see Herodotus 3.1–3) and may have been part of Persian propaganda. During his stay in Egypt, where he was later remembered, perhaps falsely, as an intolerant madman, Cambyses carried out several expeditions, with only limited success: a campaign against Ethiopia apparently achieved some objectives, a force sent into the desert to the oasis of Amun disappeared in a sandstorm, and an expedition to Carthage failed when the Phoenicians refused to fight against their kinsmen. (Much of the material provided by Herodotus [3.1–38] on Cambyses' invasion and stay in Egypt is colored by the Egyptian disdain for the monarch.[15])

Something of Cambyses' interest in local life and religion in Egypt and probably a more realistic and unbiased view of the king can be seen in the autobiographical inscription of the much rewarded Udjahorresnet (see *AEL* 3:36–41). According to this text, Cambyses, "the Great Ruler of Egypt and Great Chief of all foreign lands," not only visited the temple of the goddess Neith (mother of the sun-god Re) in Sais and provided offerings but also ordered that the temple be purged of all foreigners and purified for its proper ritual, and that all the priestly personnel be returned to the sanctuary. The reconsecration of the temple, which had been the cult sanctuary and dynastic center for the Saite Dynasty, and the restoration of normalcy after the turmoil of invasion were supervised by Udjahorresnet, who requested in his inscription that his pious deeds be remembered by the gods:

> I am a man who is good in his town. I rescued its inhabitants from the very great turmoil when it happened in the whole land, the like of which had not happened in this land. I defended the weak against the strong. I rescued the timid man when misfortune came to him. I did for them every beneficence when it was time to act for them. . . .
>
> One honored by Neith is he who shall say: "O great gods who are in Sais! Remember all the benefactions done by the chief physician, Udjahorresne. And may you do for him all benefactions! May you make his good name endure in this land forever!" (*AEL* 3:39–40)

(Later, Udjahorresnet was with Darius in Elam and was sent back to Egypt by the Persian king to restore the establishment called the House of Life, where medicine, theology, temple administration, and ritual were studied and practiced.)

Cambyses was far less tolerant and benevolent with regard to other temples in Egypt. Surprised at the extent of temple and priestly revenues, he curtailed the income and powers of many sanctuaries.

When Cambyses was in Syria (at Ecbatana according to Herodotus; in Damascus according to Josephus, *Ant.* 11.30) on his return home, he learned that his brother, Bardiya (Smerdis in Greek), had usurped the throne (Herodotus 3.62). Cambyses, however, never made it home to suppress the revolt. He died in Syria of uncertain causes: Herodotus speaks of an accidental stabbing while mounting his steed (3.64).

Although Cambyses passed through Palestine on his journeys to and from Egypt and his forces congregated at Acco for the invasion, no contemporary

---

15. See T. S. Brown, "Herodotus' Portrait of Cambyses," *Historia* 31 (1982) 387–403.

document refers to any contacts between him and the Jewish community. (1 Esd. 2:16–25 and Josephus in *Ant.* 11.20–30 do, however, associate the content of Ezra 4:7–24 with Cambyses rather than Darius.) One thing is clear: by the time of Cambyses, Palestine and the eastern Mediterranean seaboard were securely in Persian hands.

Darius I

The rebellion in Persia was probably led by Cambyses' true brother and thus the son of Cyrus rather than by a pretender as later claimed by Darius. Even among the Persians, according to Herodotus, Cambyses was considered a tyrant, "severe and arrogant" (3.89), and the widespread extent of the support for Bardiya prior to or even upon the death of Cambyses suggests that he had a large following. Darius admitted that "all the people became rebellious from Cambyses, (and) went over to him [Bardiya], both Persia and Media and the other provinces" (*OP* 120 §11). In the self-serving Behistun Inscription, Darius gives the following account of how matters occurred:

> A son of Cyrus, Cambyses by name, of our family—he was king here. Of that Cambyses there was a brother, Smerdis [Bardiya] by name, having the same mother and the same father as Cambyses. Afterwards, Cambyses slew that Smerdis. When Cambyses slew Smerdis, it did not become known to the people that Smerdis had been slain. Afterwards, Cambyses went to Egypt. When Cambyses had gone off to Egypt, after that the people became evil. After that the Lie waxed great in the country, both in Persia and in Media and in other provinces. . . . Afterwards, there was one man, a Magian, Gaumata by name; he rose up. . . . He lied to the people thus: "I am Smerdis, the son of Cyrus, brother of Cambyses." After that, all the people became rebellious. (*OP* 119–20, §§10–11)

This version of events, reported in the massive Behistun Inscription recorded in three languages—Elamite, Akkadian, and Old Persian—was widely circulated and apparently believed in the ancient world (see Herodotus's version in 3.61–69). Fragments of a version of the Behistun Inscription in Aramaic were found at Elephantine. In all probability, Darius, supported by an inner circle of seven prominent families, took over the throne from Bardiya, who had either sought to take advantage of the absence and dislike for his brother Cambyses to seize power or assumed power upon Cambyses' death. Cambyses himself had no children, although he had married two of his sisters. Darius, although from the same general ancestral line as Cyrus, was not from the immediate ruling branch; he was a usurper. In the Behistun Inscription he does not mention Cyrus among his ancestors but traces his genealogy back to Achaemenes (thus the terms "Achaemenid" and "Achaemenian").

Three factors about the early years of Darius (522–486) are significant for the subsequent course of events in Judah.[16]

Widespread Revolts at the Beginning of His Reign. At the beginning of his reign, Darius was confronted with numerous political and military obstacles. These

---

16. For succinct depictions of Darius and his reign, see L. L. Grabbe, "Another Look at the Gestalt of 'Darius the Mede,'" *CBQ* 50 (1988) 198–213; and Heleen Sancisi-Weerdenburg, "Darius I and the Persian Empire," *CANE* 2:1035–50.

involved suppressing the popular support given Bardiya and the subsequent major revolts that followed Darius's assumption of power. Although Bardiya reigned for only a short time—Herodotus says seven months (3.67); the Behistun Inscription gives three months (*OP* 120 §§11–13)—his support was widespread. Darius assumed power without popular support, and opposition to his rule broke out in various regions. He notes that rebellions occurred in the provinces of Persia, Elam, Media, Assyria, Egypt, Parthia, Margiana, Sattagydia, and Scythia (*OP* 123 §21). Some of the strongest opposition was in Babylon, which had quickly recognized Bardiya as king. After his death, Nebuchadrezzar III, the son of Nabonidus whom Darius called Nidintu-Bel, was acclaimed king in Babylon and other cities. After defeating the Babylonian army, Darius entered Babylon and executed Nidintu-Bel and the city's leading citizens. A second revolt in Babylon broke out in August 521, led by Nebuchadrezzar IV, and was finally suppressed in November. Herodotus reports that this second capture involved harsh treatment of the population: "When Darius had made himself master of the Babylonians, first of all he demolished the walls and bore away all the gates; for when Cyrus had taken Babylon before, he did neither of these things; and, secondly, Darius impaled about three thousand of the principal citizens, and allowed the rest of the Babylonians to inhabit the city" (Herodotus 3.159). The extent of troubles throughout the empire can be seen in Darius's claim that he fought nineteen battles and took nine kings captive in a single year (*OP* 131 §52). That Babylon was ravaged by turmoil for months may have been an encouragement to Jewish exiles to leave the region and return to Palestine.

Administrative Reforms. The struggles of Darius to secure his throne in 522–519 were followed by his efforts to provide the empire with an effective administrative system. According to Herodotus, Darius was remembered above all for his organizational skills: "The Persians say Darius was a trader, Cambyses a master, and Cyrus a father. The first, because he made profit of everything; the second, because he was severe and arrogant; the latter, because he was mild, and always aimed at the good of his people" (3.89). This assessment is given in the context of a discussion of Darius's organization of the empire into provinces, or satrapies, each with its assigned tribute. Darius intensified the efforts to give organizational structure to the empire, but the exact details and geography are somewhat uncertain. The Behistun Inscription claims twenty-two regions plus Persia as Darius's domain (*OP* 119 §6). Herodotus claims that twenty satrapies existed (3.90–97) which may reflect the condition of his own time, that is, the middle of the fifth century. Later texts suggest a different number. (See Map 32.)

When Darius began the reorganization into provinces, or satrapies, cannot be determined, but indications point to a period early in his reign immediately following the turmoil that accompanied his rise to power. Each satrapy was subdivided into smaller provinces. According to Herodotus (3.91), Palestine fell into the fifth satrapy, called Abir-Nari ("Beyond the River" or "Trans-Euphrates," as viewed from Mesopotamia), an administrative division already known in Assyrian times.[17] This satrapy was composed of "Phoenicia, Syria

17. See A. F. Rainey, "The Satrapy 'Beyond the River,'" *AJBA* 1 (1969) 51–78; and M. W. Stolper, "The Governor of Babylon and Across-the-River in 486 BC," *JNES* 48 (1989) 283–305.

75. *Achaemenid tombs.* Three Achaemenid tombs carved in the face of cliffs at Naqsh-i Rustam near Persepolis. The one on the right is that of Darius I. The other two, moving to the left, probably belong to Artaxerxes I and Darius II. A fourth tomb, probably that of Xerxes, is not shown in the photograph.

called Palestine, and Cyprus," and extended "from the city of Posidium, . . . down to Egypt, except a district belonging to the Arabians, which was exempt from taxation." The fifth satrapy thus included the eastern Mediterranean seaboard and Cyprus, with which the seaboard was closely associated. The territory comprising the fifth satrapy plus Babylonia had been part of the territory Cyrus inherited from Nabonidus, and the two areas formed one Persian administrative unit for a time. When Babylonia and Abir-Nari were separated still remains a disputed point. Gobryas, father-in-law of Darius, for example, served as satrap over Babylon and Abir-Nari under Cambyses, yet a text like Ezra 5:3 suggests that the two were separate early in the reign of Darius, although some evidence suggests that a certain Ushtani was satrap over Babylonia and Abir-Nari under Darius. If Darius created the separate satrap of Abir-Nari, then the rebellions of the usurper Nebuchadrezzar III (522) and Nebuchadrezzar IV (521) may have led to this separation that was intended to facilitate better control over the Babylonian area. It may, however, have been later, at the time of troubles under Xerxes, that the two satrapies were created.

Darius seems to have taken a personal interest in specific matters of rather limited administrative concern throughout the empire, a factor reflected in his concern with the Jerusalem cult. We have already noted his interest in local Egyptian matters in his commission of Udjahorresnet's revival of the House of Life at Sais. Additional actions are also indicative. Darius ordered his satrap Ariandes to collect wise men from the military, scribes, and priests of Egypt to collect and write down the laws of Egypt in effect at the death of Amasis. The commission worked for sixteen years, and the results were made available in both the Egyptian (demotic) and Aramaic languages, but no such collection has survived and its contents remain uncertain.[18] Such codification of earlier laws and regulations existing prior to Cambyses' restriction of temple privileges supposedly endeared Darius to the Egyptian priesthood. The later Demotic Chronicle preserves the fact that Darius reversed some of the policies of his predecessor. Various temples were restored and a major sanctuary to Amun-Re was constructed at el-Kharga. As we shall see in the next section, Darius may have taken similar interests in the Jerusalem cult.

Darius in Egypt. As part of his campaigns from the Indus to the Nile, Darius visited Egypt during the fourth year of his reign (518–517). It was probably at this time that a flotilla of ships passed through the canal joining the Nile and the Red Sea, marking the completion of a project partially realized earlier by Neco II. Stelae with inscriptions in Elamite, Akkadian, Old Persian, and Egypt-ian hieroglyphs commemorating the occasion were set up.

On his trip to Egypt, Darius, like Cambyses, would have passed through Palestine, and the conditions there could have come under his immediate perusal.

The Completion of Temple Reconstruction

The early years of Darius's reign form the historical background for the com-pletion of reconstruction work on the Jerusalem temple. Restoration work, begun by Sheshbazzar, apparently entered a new phase under the leadership of Zerubbabel and Jeshua (Joshua). Their role in the rebuilding is emphasized in the account of Ezra 3 + 6:19–22 and, in conjunction with the prophets Hag-gai and Zechariah, in Ezra 5:1–5 + 6:1–18 and in the book of Haggai and Zechariah 1–8 (see Sir. 49:11–12).

Who were Zerubbabel and Jeshua? In Ezra–Nehemiah Zerubbabel is referred to only by name (Ezra 2:2; 4:2–3; Neh. 12:47) or with reference to his father, Shealtiel (Ezra 3:2, 8; 5:2; Neh. 12:1). Ezra–Nehemiah never assigns him a title, unless he is the person called "ruler" or "governor" in Ezra 2:63; 6:7. Haggai clearly refers to Zerubbabel as governor (Hag. 1:1, 14; 2:2, 21) and presents him as a "messianic" figure (Hag. 2:2–9, 20–23). Zechariah likewise stresses Zerubbabel's important role, calling him one of the "anointeds" (Zech. 4), and seems to apply to him the political-messianic title "Branch" (Zech. 6:12–13). The Chronicler (in 1 Chr. 3:17–24) unequivocally makes Zerubbabel a member of the Davidic family, although listing him as a son of Pedaiah, not of Shealtiel. If Zerubbabel had been a member of the Davidic family line, it seems almost unbelievable that neither Ezra, Nehemiah, Haggai, nor Zechariah noted this. In all probability, therefore, Zerubbabel was a non-Davidic Jewish leader whom the Chronicler has made into a member of the Judean royal family in order to emphasize what he considered to be essential—the continuity of the leadership in preexilic and postexilic times.

Whether and when Zerubbabel returned from exile are unknown data. Ezra–Nehemiah clearly depicts him as a returnee from exile (see Ezra 2:1–2;

---

18. See D. B. Redford, "The So-Called 'Codification' of Egyptian Laws under Darius I," in J. W. Watts, ed., *Persia and Torah: The Theory of the Imperial Authorization of the Pentateuch* (SBLSymS 17; Atlanta: Society of Biblical Literature, 2001) 135–59.

Neh. 7:6–7), but this material presents only the returnees, "the children of the exile," as carrying out significant work in the community during the Persian period. Since he was an important figure, he had to be presented as a returnee. In spite of the questionable nature of much of the traditions, there seems to be no reason to doubt that Zerubbabel served for a time as governor of Judah, perhaps having succeeded Sheshbazzar already in the days before Darius (see Ezra 3:7; 4:3–5). It is far more uncertain that he was a returnee from exile.

Associated with Zerubbabel in work on the temple was the priest Joshua (Jeshua), son of Jozadak. As with Zerubbabel, Ezra–Nehemiah does not assign Joshua any title but refers to him either by name alone (Ezra 2:2, 36; 4:3, Neh. 12:1, 7, 10) or with reference to his father (Ezra 3:2, 8; 5:2; 10:18; Neh. 12:26). He is called "the high priest" in both Haggai (Hag. 1:1, 12, 14; 2:2, 4) and Zechariah (Zech. 3:1, 8; 6:11). In 1 Chronicles 6:1–15 the Chronicler provides a "genealogy" of the high priests from Aaron to Jozadak (Jehozadak). This list notes twelve high priests from Aaron to the building of the temple and then seems to have supplied eleven high priests from the building of the temple until Jehozadak (Jozadak), who "went into exile." Joshua would thus be the twelfth high priest following the construction of the First Temple. Such a listing is schematic in the extreme, being calculated on two successions, one before and one after the building of the temple, of twelve high priests, with forty-year reigns each. Jehozadak (Jozadak) appears nowhere in the biblical traditions except in the texts we have noted and is associated with the "official" line of Jerusalem priests only by the Chronicler. Second Kings 25:18–21 reports that Seraiah the chief priest at the time of the Babylonian capture of Jerusalem, and father of Jehozadak according to 1 Chronicles 6:14, was put to death by Nebuchadrezzar, but no reference is made to Jehozadak or the family of Seraiah as having been carried into captivity.

Two possibilities exist for understanding Joshua's predecessor and origins. (1) Joshua's father could have been a son of Seraiah, been carried into captivity, died there, and been "succeeded" by Joshua. Thus Joshua would have been a priest descended from the family of Zadok, the ruling priestly family in Jerusalem. This, of course, is the assumption behind 1 Chronicles 6:14–15 and fits the view of those biblical compilers who claimed or believed that all the significant persons involved in the restoration returned from exile. At the same time, this would satisfy the Chronicler's desire to have continuity between the preexilic and postexilic priesthood. (2) One could assume that Joshua's ancestor had functioned as the chief priest in the cult that continued in Judah after the destruction of the temple, most likely, at or near the provincial capital at Mizpah. If one assumes this view, then Jehozadak (Jozadak) may not have been a son of the high priest ruling at the time of Jerusalem's destruction. He would have risen to prominence as chief priest in the province after the city's destruction. His son Joshua then would simply have been his successor in the land of Judah.[19]

A major problem that has baffled biblical interpreters for years has been the issue of when the Aaronite priestly line came to dominance. There is no evidence,

19. For a different construction see F. M. Cross, "A Reconstruction of the Judean Restoration," *JBL* 94 (1975) 4–18; in an expanded form in his *From Epic to Canon: History and Literature in Ancient Israel* (Baltimore: Johns Hopkins University Press, 1998) 151–72. See also L. L. Grabbe, "Josephus and the Reconstruction of the Judean Restoration," *JBL* 106 (1987) 231–46.

76. *Persian dignitaries.* Persian dignitaries depicted on the northern stairway to the Apadana (great audience hall) at Persepolis.

other than genealogical references in the Chronicler, that Zadok and his successors in the Jerusalem temple were Aaronite, yet the final editing of the biblical materials gives the Aaronites dominance and subsumes other groups under them. Jehozadak and Joshua may have been representatives of the Aaronite priestly line, which had connections with Bethel, Mizpah, and other northern sanctuary centers (see above, p. 108). The period following the fall of Jerusalem may have been the time when the Aaronites, represented by Jehozadak and Joshua, came to prominence.[20] Of course, one must realize that it is finally impossible to be certain about the origins of the priestly line represented by Joshua.

The concerted Jewish effort that finally rebuilt the temple is best understood in light of the developments on the international scene from the time of Cambyses' death until the early years of Darius and the expectations these stirred in the Judean community. The widespread turmoil, dissension, and revolts in the Persian Empire ignited prophetic fervor among the Jewish community and incited renewed efforts on temple reconstruction. The prophets Haggai and Zechariah, active during the early years of Darius's reign, proclaimed a radical, impending action of God that would transform the status of the community and the world (see Hag. 2:6–7, 21–22). Zerubbabel was cast by these prophets in the role of the new ruler-to-be of the Jewish community (see Hag. 2:23; Zech. 4:6–10; 6:9–14). How personally involved Zerubbabel became in this zealous enthusiasm cannot be determined.

20. See Joseph Blenkinsopp, "The Judaean Priesthood during the Neo-Babylonian and Achaemenid Periods: A Hypothetical Reconstruction," *CBQ* 60 (1998) 25–43.

Evidence within the biblical traditions, especially in the books of Ezra and Zechariah, suggests conflicts and tensions between groups in Judah during the time of Zerubbabel and the temple reconstruction. The nature of these tensions is more hinted at than discussed. In addition, the material in Ezra related to this period (Ezra 1–6) reached its final form after the other traditions in Ezra–Nehemiah; further, its presentation has been colored by the descriptions of the Judean opponents of this later period. The editor of the material in Ezra 1–6 has attempted to reinterpret all opposition as being from outside the local community (see 4:1), even reading material descriptive of a later period back into this era (4:7–23). The hostility between the community in Jerusalem and the surrounding peoples dates primarily from the time of Ezra and Nehemiah and nearer to the editor's time than to the period of temple reconstruction.

Some apparently opposed any reconstruction of the Jerusalem temple. This is hinted at in Isaiah 66:1–3, which may come from this period. Neither the rationale for this position nor any indication of the extent of this opposition is noted. A primary tension of the time seems to have centered around conflicts between "the people of the land" (those who had not gone into exile) and "the sons of the exile" (those returning from exile). Nonreturning Yahweh worshipers, who no doubt included some persons from the province of Samaria, sought to participate in the rebuilding of the temple but were rebuffed by the returnees: "You shall have no part with us in building a house to our God; but we alone will build to Yahweh, the God of Israel, as King Cyrus the king of Persia has commanded us" (Ezra 4:3). This exclusivism of the returnees and rejection of the offer of help were probably partially based on economic conflict over the rights to property that had been taken over by those not exiled (see Jer. 39:10; 2 Kgs. 25:12; Ezek. 11:15). The people of the land opposed the returnees (see already Ezra 3:3) and are said to have "bribed officials to frustrate their plan, throughout the reign of King Cyrus of Persia, and until the reign of King Darius of Persia" (Ezra 4:4–5). Legal measures to defend the land rights and privileges they held under the Babylonians may not have been the only means used to frustrate the dominance of the returnees, since Zechariah 8:10 reports that there was no safety in the town since the laying of the temple's foundation.

Most of the returnees were strongly Yahwistic and seem to have operated on the basis of the nationalistic and exclusivistic theology of Deuteronomy, thus advocating a strict adherence to Deuteronomic law on behalf of the worshipers. This meant that one considered impure by the stricter Yahwists would have been admissible to the Jerusalem cult only after they had "separated themselves from the pollutions of the nations of the land to worship Yahweh, the God of Israel" (Ezra 6:21). The visions of the prophet Zechariah show even the high priest Joshua as originally falling short of this strict Yahwism: "The angel said to those who were standing before him [Joshua], 'Take off his filthy clothes.' And to him he said, 'See, I have removed your guilt away from you, and I will clothe you with festal apparel'" (Zech. 3:4). This opposition could have been based on the fact that Joshua was not a "son of the exile" and a returnee. On the other hand, priestly theology with its radical but universalizing monotheism was less concerned with election and nationalism than was Deuteronomic theology. The high priest Joshua, like many of his later successors, seems to have been less exclusive and ritually demanding than stricter Yahwists wished.

Before he was acceptable to function as high priest, to have legal charge of the Jerusalem temple and its courts, and to be a mediator of revelation, Joshua was required to agree to walk in Yahweh's ways, that is, agree to follow the law as interpreted by the strict Yahwists (Zech. 3:6–10). For the strict Yahwists, he was at best only "a brand plucked from the fire" (3:2). The work on the temple could not proceed harmoniously until a compromise between the strict Yahwists, led by Zerubbabel, and the less strict Yahwists, represented by Joshua, had produced a "peaceful understanding" and cooperation (6:13).

Whether these tensions within the Judean community, the messianic fervor associated with temple restoration, or some other reason explains Zerubbabel's removal from office remains uncertain. He simply disappears from history. The references to him in Zechariah 4 are dated to February 519, probably just prior to the time when Darius marched through Palestine on his way to Egypt. According to Ezra 5:3–6:15, however, when the authority to rebuild the temple was questioned by Tattenai, the governor of the province "Beyond the River" to which Judah belonged, search was made for a copy of Cyrus's permission and a memorandum was found. Darius gave his approval and order for work to continue. This cooperative spirit of the Persians does not suggest that the Jewish messianic enthusiasm of the time was interpreted as rebellion. However, no reference is made in the correspondence with the Persian court to Zerubbabel's presence, of his later work on the temple, or of his presence at the temple dedication (in 515; Ezra 6:15). Was Zerubbabel exterminated by the Persians? Removed from office and exiled? Or did he simply die? An enigmatic passage in Zechariah, sometimes related to Zerubbabel, could suggest that he may have been killed, perhaps by a pro-Davidic faction as a result of an internal dispute: "I will pour out a spirit of compassion and supplication on the house of David and the inhabitants of Jerusalem, so that, when they look on the one whom they have pierced, they shall mourn for him, as one mourns for an only child, and weep bitterly over him, as one weeps over a firstborn" (Zech. 12:10). Any theory about what happened to Zerubbabel is, of course, purely speculative.[21] At any rate, it was Joshua, the high priest, who ended up wearing a crown as the only "anointed" (= messiah) in the community (6:9–14).

Judah as a Persian Province after Darius I

Under the organizational scheme of Darius I, the tiny province of Judah took its place in the massive Persian Empire and for decades practically disappears from view (see Map 32). Darius not only secured the territory held by Cyrus and Cambyses but also extended the Persian frontier, so that he ruled over the largest empire the world had seen. It stretched from the Indus Valley in southeast Asia to the Danube River in the Balkans, from the steppes of southern Russia to Libya in North Africa. As the "king" in the kingdom, the Persian monarch claimed absolute control and ruled under the "shadow" of the god Ahura Mazda. It was the king, not the Persians, whom Ahura Mazda had made to rule (see *ANET* 316–17).

---

21. See Leroy Waterman, "The Camouflaged Purge of Three Messianic Conspirators," *JNES* 13 (1954) 73–78.

Under Darius the families of his original supporters filled most major posts, both at the court and in the military, as well as governorships of the satrapies. "The king's ears," special intelligence inspectors, and cooperative local officials served to keep the monarch informed on matters throughout the kingdom. Although Indo-Europeans (as Xerxes I says, "Aryan of Aryan descent," *ANET* 316), the Persians utilized Aramaic as the official language, thus providing some linguistic unity for the empire. An international bureaucracy and army, capable courier service, royal coinage, extensive trade, and limited local freedom created a generally widespread sense of security and cooperation among the various national groups, but as in the case of most alien overlordships did not totally win over the hearts and loyalty of the king's subjects or extinguish the embers of a dormant hostility. Especially later when their positions tended to become hereditary and private armies developed, the satraps posed more of a threat to the peace of the empire than national uprisings. The size of the empire, however, meant that Persia's external enemies were too widely separated to cooperate effectively.

As a small province, Judah, or Yehud as it is designated on seals and coins, was part of the administrative satrapy Abir-Nari ("Beyond the River"), which lay west and south of the Euphrates River and was made up of Syria, Phoenicia, Palestine, and Cyprus. Judah occupied the plateau lying between the Dead Sea and the coastal piedmont (the Judean Shephelah). As a distinct political unit, Judah probably continued to be ruled by an appointed governor.[22] The biblical text provides no names of the holders of this office between Zerubbabel and Nehemiah. From archaeological remains such as seals, bullae (stamped clay sealings), and stamped jar handles, the names of other governors are known. It is uncertain, however, whether these governors preceded or followed Nehemiah. The recovered names of the governors Elnathan, Yehoezer, and Ahzai are Jewish, which suggests that the Persians appointed rulers from among the local populace.[23] Except when Persian affairs were directly involved, self-government was apparently enjoyed by the province. The collection of taxes for the royal coffers was a primary responsibility of the governor (Neh. 5:15). The evidence from the time of Nehemiah (Neh. 3) suggests that the province of Judah was composed of five (or six) districts, each divided into two subdistricts, and each with its ruler or rulers: Jerusalem (3:9–12), Beth-haccherem (3:14), Mizpah (3:15), Beth-zur (3:16), and Keilah (3:17–18).[24] (See Map 34.)

22. A long-held theory argues that Judah was included in the province of Samaria until the time of Nehemiah when it became a separate province; see S. E. McEvenue, "The Political Structure in Judah from Cyrus to Nehemiah," *CBQ* 43 (1981) 353–64. J. P. Weinberg (*The Citizen-Temple Community* [JSOTSup 151; Sheffield: Sheffield Academic Press, 1992]) has argued that the returning exiles gradually developed into a strictly religiously based temple community that was self-regulating but under the political control of Samaria. For a refutation of this theory, see H. Williamson, "Judah and the Jews," in Maria Brosius and Amélie Kuhrt, eds., *Studies in Persian History: Essays in Memory of David M. Lewis* (Achaemenid History 11; Leiden: Nederlands Instituut voor het Nabije Oosten, 1998) 145–63; repr. in *SPPHH* 25–45.

23. See Nahman Avigad, *Bullae and Seals from a Post-Exilic Judaean Archive* (Qedem 4; Jerusalem: Hebrew University Press, 1976); and H. G. M. Williamson, "The Governors of Judah under the Persians," *TynBul* 39 (1988) 59–82; repr. in *SPPHH* 46–63.

24. The exact boundaries of the province cannot be determined; on the issue and various mappings see C. E. Carter, *The Emergence of Yehud in the Persian Period: A Social and Demographic Study* (JSOTSup 294; Sheffield: Sheffield Academic Press, 1999) 75–113. Carter estimates the population of the province at about 11,000 in late sixth/early fifth century and about 17,000 in the late fifth/early fourth century. Such figures seem a bit low. For a discussion of the occupied sites, see Edelman, *Origins*, 281–331.

Persia and the West from Darius I to Artaxerxes III

After highlighting the return from exile and the reconstruction of the Jerusalem temple, the biblical traditions move to focus on the activity of Ezra and Nehemiah. Unfortunately, numerous problems plague any reconstruction of their work. It is impossible to know with any certainty, for example, to what particular historical period or periods the careers of the men belong. Josephus assigns them consecutive careers during the reign of Xerxes I (486–465). First Esdras describes the work of Ezra without mention of Nehemiah. The present books of Ezra–Nehemiah present them as having overlapping careers and assign both to the reign of an Artaxerxes, but do not specify which Artaxerxes of the three Persian kings who bore this name.

Both Ezra and Nehemiah, like the Egyptian official Udjahorresnet whom we mentioned earlier, conducted their reforming and restoration work with the permission and under a commission from the Persian authorities (see Ezra 7:11–26; Neh. 2:1–8).[25] Their activity, therefore, was not only condoned but also encouraged by the ruling government and thus must have been viewed as in the best interests of the Persians. This means that their activities must be understood not just in terms of the religious conditions and needs of the Jewish community in Palestine but in terms of the political interests of the Persians in Syria-Palestine. In this section we shall outline the main events in Persian history during the fifth and fourth centuries, especially noting those periods of tension in the western part of the empire, tension that may have made special intervention into Judean life by the Persians both timely and opportune.

Of prime significance during the later reign of Darius I (522–486) was the beginning of Greco-Persian hostilities. In 512 Darius extended his empire westward into Europe, crossing the Bosporus, conquering Thrace, and pursuing the Scythians to the mouth of the Danube (Herodotus 4.83–144). East and west, Asia and Europe, now became embroiled in a struggle that would last for generations. After a period of increasing tensions, Greek (Ionian) cities in Asia Minor as well as Cyprus rebelled against the Persians in 499, being encouraged and supported in their endeavor by Athens. Utilizing their naval strength to good advantage, the rebels threatened the peace of the empire for half a decade. After suppressing the uprising, Darius set out to retaliate against the Athenians. He invaded Greece but was humiliated especially at the battle of Marathon (490). The Persian ruler hoped to wage further war against Athens, but during the course of making preparations he was confronted with a rebellion in Egypt early in 486. Darius's death later in the year left the subjugation of Egypt and the invasion of Greece to his successor, Xerxes I (486–465), Darius's son by Atossa, a daughter of Cyrus. The Egyptian revolt was suppressed three years later, but only after heavy fighting. The fact that Xerxes appointed his own brother as satrap in Egypt might suggest that the previous satrap was implicated in the uprising.

Before Xerxes could move against Greece, revolt erupted again in Babylon but was severely repressed. By 481 Xerxes ceased calling himself "king of Baby-

---

25. See Joseph Blenkinsopp, "The Mission of Udjahorresnet and Those of Ezra and Nehemiah," *JBL* 106 (1987) 409–21; and David Janzen, "The 'Mission' of Ezra and the Persian-Period Temple Community," *JBL* 119 (2000) 619–43.

lon," a change that suggests governmental restructuring in the area. It was perhaps following this revolt that Babylonia was made into an independent satrapy and separated from Abir-Nari.

Xerxes' great expedition against Greece, begun in 481, proved to be a Persian fiasco. In battles at Artemisium, Thermopylae, and Salamis, the Greeks routed the Persians from most of Europe. The Greek allies took the fight into Asia Minor and Cyprus. At Plataea, Mykale, and Eurymedon, the Greeks won significant victories. Xerxes gave up the struggle with the Greeks and was subsequently murdered by his vizier, Artabanus. Xerxes' youngest son, Artaxerxes I (465–424), had to fight his way to dominance at the Persian court. The Egyptian Inaros, a son of Psammetichus III, took the occasion of the struggle over the throne to organize a revolt. Athens not only encouraged the uprising but also dispatched naval forces to aid the effort. The main Egyptian rebels and an Athenian fleet were defeated and Egypt was brought back under Persian control in 455 after a lengthy war led on the Persian side by Arsames the satrap of Egypt and Megabyzus the satrap of Abir-Nari. Following the Egyptian uprising, in what has been called the Peace of Callias (449), which was adhered to for some time, Persia and Athens agreed that Athens would not intervene in affairs in Egypt and Cyprus and that the Persian king would keep hands off the Greek cities along the southern and western coasts of Asia Minor.

In 448 Megabyzus, the satrap of "Beyond the River," and his two sons rebelled against Artaxerxes. After two victories over forces sent to subdue him, Megabyzus was reconciled to the Persian king and peace was restored to the area.

Additional fraternal strife erupted at the death of Artaxerxes. Three of his sons assumed the throne within a year. The "year of the four emperors" saw Xerxes II, Sogdianos, and finally Darius II (424/423–405/404) each rule after slaying his predecessor. Darius II's reign also witnessed troubles in the west. Revolts broke out in Anatolia and Syria. Arsames was recalled from Egypt to assist in suppressing the opposition. In his absence, widespread discontent occurred in Egypt, and the Yahwistic temple in the Jewish military colony at Elephantine was destroyed (see Text 20).

Under Artaxerxes II (405/404–359/358), Persian control in the west collapsed further. The Egyptians, led by Pharaoh Amyrteus (404–399), gained their independence when Artaxerxes was forced to fight his brother Cyrus to retain the throne. For sixty years (404–343) and during the rule of three dynasties (Twenty-eighth to Thirtieth), Egypt retained its independence and even launched a counteroffensive against Persia that involved the invasion of Syria-Palestine. Persia considered Egypt to be nothing more than a rebellious province and expended enormous effort in an attempt to return the renegade to the fold.

In alliances, first with Sparta, then with King Evagoras, ruler of the Cypriot kingdom of Salamis, and then with Athens, Egyptian rulers sought friends wherever they could find a Mediterranean opponent of the Persians. Archaeological and inscriptional evidence indicates that pharaohs Nepherites I (399–393) and Achoris (393–380) extended their influence along the coastal plain of Palestine and into Phoenician territory. For a time the Egyptians, with the aid of Evagoras, held Tyre and Sidon. Two major efforts by the Persians, including the amassing of a fleet and thousands of Greek mercenaries at Acco, pushed the Egyptians out

TEXT 20. Correspondence on Rebuilding the Elephantine Temple

To our lord Bagoas, governor of Judah, your servants Yedoniah and his colleagues, the priests who are in the fortress of Elephantine. May the God of Heaven seek after the welfare of our lord exceedingly at all times and give you favor before King Darius and the nobles a thousand times more than now. May you be happy and healthy at all times. Now, your servant Yedoniah and his colleagues depose as follows: In the month of Tammuz in the 14th year of King Darius [410 B.C.E.], when Arsames departed and went to the king, the priests of the god Khnub, who is in the fortress of Elephantine, conspired with Vidaranag, who was commander-in-chief here, to wipe out the temple of the god Yaho from the fortress of Elephantine. So that wretch Vidaranag sent to his son Nefayan, who was in command of the garrison of the fortress of Syene, this order, "The temple of the god Yaho in the fortress of Yeb is to be destroyed." Nefayan thereupon led the Egyptians with the other troops. Coming with their weapons to the fortress of Elephantine, they entered that temple and razed it to the ground. The stone pillars that were there they smashed. Five "great" gateways built with hewn blocks of stone which were in that temple they demolished, but their doors *are standing*, and the hinges of those doors are of bronze; and *their* roof of cedarwood, all of it, with the . . . and whatever else was there, everything they burnt with fire. As for the basins of gold and silver and other articles that were in that temple, they carried all of them off and made them their own.—Now, our forefathers built this temple in the fortress of Elephantine back in the days of the kingdom of Egypt, and when Cambyses came to Egypt he found it built. They knocked down all the temples of the gods of Egypt, but no one did any damage to this temple. But when this happened, we and our wives and our children wore sackcloth, and fasted, and prayed to Yaho the Lord of Heaven, who has let us see our desire upon that Vidaranag. The dogs took the fetter out of his feet, and any property he had gained was lost; and any men who have sought to do evil to this temple have all been killed and we have seen our desire upon them.—We have also sent a letter before now, when this evil was done to us, <to> our lord and to the high priest Johanan and his colleagues the priests in Jerusalem and to Ostanes the brother of Anani and the nobles of the Jews. Never a letter have they sent to us. Also, from the month of Tammuz, year 14 of King Darius, to this day, we have been wearing sackcloth and fasting, making our wives as widows, not anointing ourselves with oil or drinking wine. Also, from then to now, in the year 17 of King Darius, no meal-offering, in[cen]se, nor burnt offering have been offered in this temple. Now your servants Yedoniah, and his colleagues, and the Jews, the citizens of Elephantine, all say thus: If it please our lord, take thought of this temple to rebuild it, since they do not let us rebuild it. Look to your well-wishers and friends here in Egypt. Let a letter be sent from you to them concerning the temple of the god Yaho to build it in the fortress of Elephantine as it was built before; and the meal-offering, incense, and burnt offering will be offered in your name, and we shall pray for you at all times, we, and our wives, and our children, and the Jews who are here, all of them, if you do thus, so that that temple is rebuilt. And you shall have a merit before Yaho the God of Heaven more than a man who offers to him burnt offering and sacrifices worth a thousand talents of silver and (because of) gold. Because of this we have written to inform you. We have also set the whole matter forth in a letter in our name to Delaiah and Shelemiah, the sons of Sanballat the governor of Samaria. Also, Arsames knew nothing of all that was done to us. On the 20th of Marheshwan, year 17 of King Darius [407 B.C.E.].

Memorandum of what Bagoas and Delaiah said to me: Let this be an instruction to you in Egypt to say before Arsames about the house of offering of the God of Heaven which had been in existence in the fortress of Elephantine since ancient times, before Cambyses, and was destroyed by that wretch Vidaranag in the year 14 of King Darius: to rebuild it on its site as it was before, and the meal-offering and incense to be made on that altar as it used to be.

Your servants Yedoniah the son of Ge[mariah] by name 1, Ma'uzi the son of Nathan by name [1], Shemaiah the son of Haggai by name 1, Hosea the son of Yatom by name 1, Hosea the son of Nathun by name 1, 5 men in all, Syenians who [ho]ld proper[ty] in the fortress of Elephantine, say as follows: If your lordship is [favo]rable, and the temple of ou[r] God Yaho [is rebuilt] in the fortress of Elephantine as it was for[merly buil]t, and n[o] *sheep,* ox, or goat are offered there as burnt offering, but (only) incense, meal-offering, [and drink-offering], and (*if*) your lordship giv[es] orders [to that effect, then] we shall pay into your lordship's house the s[um of . . . and] a thous[and] *ardabs* of barley. (*ANET* 492)

of Palestine-Phoenicia temporarily but failed to resubjugate Egypt proper. The "revolt of the satraps" in the 360s raised havoc in many parts of the empire. In 360 Pharaoh Tachos pushed north toward Syria, but dissension in Egypt led to the abortion of his campaign and Tachos's surrender to the Persians.

When the octogenarian monarch Artaxerxes II died, he was succeeded by his ambitious and ruthless son Ochos (Artaxerxes III; 359/358–338/337). Under his administration, some of the old glory of the empire was restored. After subduing the revolting satraps, he set out to reconquer Egypt (Diodorus 16.40–52.8). The initial effort, after a year's fighting (351–350), was abandoned. Ochos's failure triggered widespread revolt along the eastern Mediterranean seaboard. Phoenicia and Cyprus, encouraged and aided by Pharaoh Nectanebo II (359–341), were the prime movers in the area. Sidon, under King Tennes, took an important role but was eventually subdued by the Persians when its leaders betrayed the city. The city was destroyed and its surviving inhabitants deported (see *ABC* 114). Another assault was made on Egypt, led by the Persian king's associate Bagoas and Mentor of Rhodes, the latter having been earlier in the employ of the Egyptian pharaoh. In 342 Egypt was reconquered and in spite of occasional disturbances remained under Persian control until it was "liberated" by Alexander the Great in 332.

The Activity of Ezra and Nehemiah

This larger world of the Persian Empire receives little consideration in the biblical traditions, and we are left to wonder about the course of life in the Palestinian Jewish community during the time. Only two snippets of biblical tradition, except for the materials about Ezra and Nehemiah, have been preserved relating to this period. These, in Ezra 4:6–23, have been preserved out of chronological order, as if they belonged to the period between Cyrus and Darius I. They have been employed to illustrate the theme of "opposition to restoration," the topic of Ezra 4. The first, in 4:6, merely notes that an accusatory letter was written against the inhabitants of Judah and Jerusalem. If the Ahasuerus of the biblical text was King Xerxes I, then this letter written in the beginning of his reign (his accession year, 486/485) would date to the time of the Egyptian revolt (486–483) suppressed by Xerxes. The sending of such a letter of accusation might indicate that Judah was suspected or implicated in the anti-Persian activity in the region, but this is only speculation, since nothing is given of the letter's content. The second tradition, in 4:7–23, reports that officials of the province Abir-Nari wrote to Artaxerxes I (465–424) warning against the rebuilding of the city of Jerusalem undertaken by Jewish returnees. The king ordered that work on the reconstruction cease. Again it is impossible to determine the actual historical context of this interchange. If the monarch was Artaxerxes I, then the attempted rebuilding of the city could have been related in some fashion to the Egyptian revolt led by Inaros (465–455).

Unlike the fragmentary items in Ezra 4:6–23, the biblical traditions about Ezra and Nehemiah are rather extensive. The present form of these traditions, in Ezra 7–10 and the book of Nehemiah, is apparently based on originally independent collections. The Ezra traditions are found in Ezra 7–10 and Nehemiah 7:73b–10:39. Some of these are composed in a first-person account, the so-called memoirs of Ezra (Ezra 7:12–9:15). The first-person "memoirs of Nehemiah" are found in Nehemiah 1:1–7:73a; 11–13. (Serious questions, however, can be raised about whether all the material in Neh. 7:5b–73a and 9:1–13:3 belonged to the Nehemiah source used by the editor.) These memoirs, especially those of Nehemiah, are similar in form to the autobiographical inscription of the Egyptian official Udjahorresnet, who, like Nehemiah, operated as a Persian appointee. The Ezra and Nehemiah traditions have been edited to make their activity contemporaneous, and, in describing the work of one, the editor makes occasional reference to the other (see Neh. 8:9; 12:26, 36). The lack of any real interaction between the two and the indication of the traditions' original independence, however, suggest that their careers were unrelated.

The Chronological Problem

As we noted earlier, the historical contexts within which Ezra and Nehemiah worked remain uncertain. Ezra 7:7–8 and Nehemiah 2:1 associate both men with an Artaxerxes, Ezra with the seventh year of the king's reign and Nehemiah with the twentieth. If both worked under Artaxerxes I, then Ezra would have returned to Jerusalem in 458 and Nehemiah in 445; if under Artaxerxes II, then the years would have been 398 and 384. Artaxerxes III (359/358–338/337) might be a candidate for Ezra's mission, but Nehemiah 5:14, which refers to the thirty-second year of Artaxerxes, rules out this latter Persian as the monarch under whom Nehemiah functioned, since his reign was too short.

Any conclusions about the relationship of the work of the two men and the historical contexts to which they belonged must remain highly uncertain and partially rely on intuition and speculation.[26] If both were historical figures, we assume that Nehemiah preceded Ezra and that the former worked under Artaxerxes I and the latter under Artaxerxes II.[27] Placing Nehemiah before Ezra, and thus discounting the present biblical order, is based on several considerations. (1) Chronological precision, as we noted in discussing Ezra 4:6–23, is not characteristic of the editing of the material in Ezra–Nehemiah, where thematic interests are more evident. (2) Ezra is considered by the final biblical editor to be the real restorer of Jewish life after the exile, and this could have led to giving him priority over Nehemiah. In the traditions about Ezra, he is presented as the true successor to the preexilic high priests (Ezra 7:1–5), his activity is seen as the true continuation of activity following temple restoration (the subject of Ezra 1–6), and the return under Ezra is depicted as a second exodus under this postexilic "Moses" (Ezra 7). (3) Ezra's work in Jerusalem seems to presuppose a reconstructed and repopulated city, conditions not restored until the work of Nehemiah. (4) The high priest at the time of Nehemiah was Eliashib (Neh. 3:1, 20; 13:4), whereas at the time of Ezra the high priest was Jehohanan the son (or grandson) of Eliashib (Ezra 10:6). One of the Elephantine letters, written to Bagoas the governor of Judah in 407 requesting permission to rebuild the temple of Yahweh previously burned at the direction of Egyptian priests, refers to a recently written letter addressed "to the high priest Johanan and his colleagues the priests in Jerusalem" (*ANET* 492; *COS* 3:128). If this Johanan can be identified with the Jehohanan of Ezra's day, then this would place Ezra near the end of the fifth or the beginning of the fourth century.

The names and order of the high priests in the Persian period are, however, a complex issue. Nehemiah 12:10–11 supplies the following order: Jeshua, Joiakim, Eliashib, Joiada, Jonathan, and Jaddua, while 12:22 supplies an alternative list of the same group or else a list extending the line to the time of "Darius the Persian" (Darius III?): Eliashib, Joiada, Johanan, and Jaddua. From Josephus it is possible to reconstruct the following order: Jeshua, Joiakim, Eliashib, Johanan, Joiakim, Eliashib, Joiada, Johanan, and Jaddua (*Ant.* 11.121, 147, 158, 297, 302). The association of Eliashib with Nehemiah and Jehohanan (= Johanan) with Ezra would, at any rate, suggest the priority of Nehemiah.

The correlation of Nehemiah with the twentieth year of Artaxerxes I and Ezra with the seventh year of Artaxerxes II makes it possible to relate their

---

26. See J. C. VanderKam, "Ezra-Nehemiah or Ezra and Nehemiah," in Eugene Ulrich et al., eds., *Priests, Prophets and Scribes: Essays on the Formation and Heritage of Second Temple Judaism in Honour of Joseph Blenkinsopp* (JSOTSup 149; Sheffield: Sheffield Academic Press, 1992) 55–75; J. R. Shaver, "Ezra and Nehemiah: On the Theological Significance of Making Them Contemporaries," ibid., 87–99; R. J. Saley, "The Date of Nehemiah Reconsidered," in G. A. Tuttle, ed., *Biblical and Near Eastern Studies: Essays in Honor of William Sanford LaSor* (Grand Rapids: Eerdmans, 1978) 151–65; and Aaron Demsky, "Who Came First, Ezra or Nehemiah? The Synchronistic Approach," *HUCA* 65 (1994) 1–19.

27. The classical defense of this position was made by H. H. Rowley, "The Chronological Order of Ezra and Nehemiah," in D. S. Lowinger and J. Somogyi, eds., *Ignace Goldziher Memorial Volume*, I (Budapest: Globus, 1948) 117–49; repr. in his *The Servant of the Lord and Other Essays on the Old Testament* (Oxford: Blackwell, 1965) 135–68.

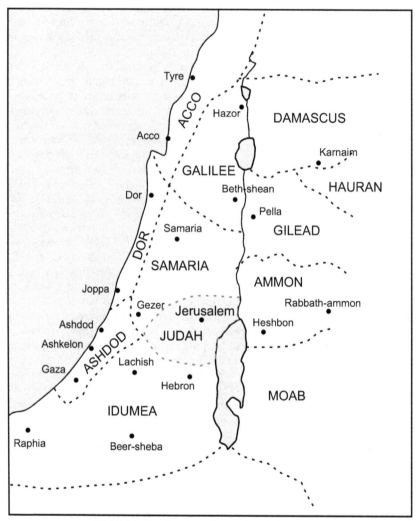

**MAP 33. Persian Province of Judah among
Other Provinces "Beyond the River"**

activity in Palestine with times when having Jewish support in the area could
have been especially advantageous to the Persians. The year of Nehemiah's
return, 445, was a time just following a long Egyptian revolt as well as the
revolt of the satrap over the province Beyond the River. It was thus a time for
reestablishing firm Persian support in the region. The year of Ezra's return, 398,
was at a time when Egypt not only had asserted its independence from Persia
but also had begun to move into the coastal region of Syria-Palestine.[28]

28. K. G. Hoglund, *Achaemenid Imperial Administration in Syria-Palestine and the Missions of Ezra and
Nehemiah* (SBLDS 125; Atlanta: Scholars Press, 1992), has argued that after the Egyptian revolts Persian authorities took special effort to induce loyalty in the region, and has associated the increase of
military fortresses throughout the area with this effort.

The Work of Nehemiah

Thus Nehemiah, if we are correct in our dating, rose to the office of cupbearer to King Artaxerxes I (Neh. 2:1), a position, according to his memoir, that gave him opportunity for personal contact with the king.[29] The occasion of Nehemiah's interest in returning to Jerusalem is said to have been the arrival at Susa of persons coming from Judah (1:1–2). Perhaps this group consisted of an embassy hoping to make an appeal directly to the royal court regarding the rebuilding of Jerusalem, thereby bypassing the uncooperative administrators of the satrapy Beyond the River (see Ezra 4:7–23). Nehemiah was informed that "the wall of Jerusalem is broken down, and its gates are destroyed by fire" (Neh. 1:3). He requested and was granted permission by Artaxerxes to return to Jerusalem and rebuild the temple fortress and the city walls (2:1–8). He left for Jerusalem, probably in 445, in the company of "Persian troops and cavalry" and with the authority of letters that vouchsafed passage to Judah and, once there, use of timber from the royal estates (2:7–9). His reconstruction of the temple fortress may have been for internal control of the population and for housing the Persian military forces. Although no mention is made of it in connection with the initial arrangements of Artaxerxes, he had apparently been appointed governor of the district (5:14). Further, he may have returned to Judah not just to refortify Jerusalem but also to establish the restored city as a new capital for the province, replacing Mizpah.

After a nocturnal, secret survey of the conditions of the city's fortifications, Nehemiah rallied support for reconstruction (Neh. 2:11–20). Various segments in the society including the priesthood, landed gentry, and district rulers worked on different sections of the wall (Neh. 3). Opposition to the refortification came from the leaders of neighboring provinces: Sanballat the Horonite in Samaria, Tobiah the Ammonite, Geshem the Arabian, and the citizens of Ashdod (2:10, 19; 4:7). Since these groups were on generally good terms with the local Judeans (6:17–19; 13:4–5, 23, 28), these opponents must have seen correctly that the refortification and Nehemiah's leadership were a threat to their authority and influence in the area. Sanballat, Tobiah, and Geshem had all established local dynastic rulership in the area. Work was carried out with special military precautions, utilization of the Persian forces, speed, and long hours of work (Neh. 4), although the biblical text says nothing about any enemy force being employed to frustrate reconstruction. Nehemiah's opponents sought to entice him away from Jerusalem to do him harm and threatened to file an accusation charging him with fomenting a rebellion and pretensions to kingship (6:1–9). In addition, local prophecies were circulated that sought to discourage him. Some of the prophets opposed to his work were apparently Judeans (see 6:10–14, especially 6:14). Other occasional hints of the unwillingness of some Judeans to aid the restoration are noted (3:5; 4:10). Nonetheless, the city wall was restored in fifty-two days, according to 6:15 (Josephus in *Ant.* 11.179 says the work required two years and four months). Such work, which necessarily would have involved arousing support, organizing

---

29. On the difficulties of using autobiographical material for reconstructing history, see D. J. A. Clines, "The Nehemiah Memoir: The Perils of Autobiography," in *What Does Eve Do to Help? and Other Readerly Questions to the Old Testament* (JSOTSup 94; Sheffield: Sheffield Academic Press, 1990) 124–64. See also J. L. Wright, *Rebuilding Identity: The Nehemiah-Memoir and Its Earliest Readers* (BZAW 348; Berlin: de Gruyter, 2004).

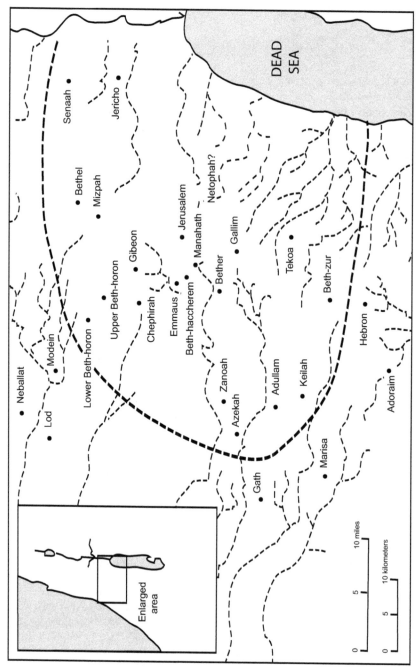

MAP 34. Persian Province of Judah

(see also Map 33)

labor, and securing necessary stone and timber, could certainly not have been carried out immediately after Nehemiah's arrival in Jerusalem but must have required some period for planning and preparation.[30]

Two economic moves were made by Nehemiah to alleviate the exploitation of the poorer classes by the landed gentry and provincial officers. Both activities would have aided in creating support for him among the peasantry and rural populations. Some of the poorer Judean classes complained of poverty, others protested that conditions demanded the mortgaging of their property, while some argued that they were forced to sell members of their families into slavery. Such complaints were made against the exploitation by their Judean brothers (Neh. 5:1–5). Plotting his moves to secure the greatest public support for himself and his cause and to produce the greatest pressure on the oppressors and aristocracy, Nehemiah confronted the nobles and officials in a public assembly (5:6–13). Noting that he and his party had redeemed Judeans sold into foreign slavery, he pointed out that the local men of wealth, on the other hand, had engaged in the slave traffic by selling Judeans. Admitting that he, his family, and his servants had lent Judeans money at interest contrary to the law (see Deut. 23:19–20), Nehemiah swore that this interest would not be collected and challenged his countrymen to return property taken at interest and to cease the practice. The leaders submitted and agreed to the abolition of interest and the return of property seized for nonpayment of debts.

A second economic measure was Nehemiah's remission of taxes that previous governors had imposed for the support of themselves and their staff; the taxes consisted of food, wine, and forty shekels of silver (Neh. 5:14–15). He was apparently able to do so since he was a man of means. There was evidently no subsequent reduction of the standard of living at the governor's palace, since Nehemiah brags that "there were at my table a hundred and fifty people, Jews and officials, besides those who came to us from the nations around us [foreign visitors]. Now that which was prepared for one day was one ox and six choice sheep; also fowls were prepared for me, and every ten days skins of wine in abundance" (5:17–18).

Nehemiah 11:1–2 reports that Jerusalem was repopulated by moving one-tenth of the people into the city. Nehemiah is not explicitly referred to in the description of this action (but see 7:4–5), and much of the material in Nehemiah 11–12 does not appear to have been part of his memoirs. Thus it is impossible to say anything certain about Nehemiah's role in the resettlement. The period just following the restoration of the city's fortification, however, would seem to have been a natural time for such a repopulation of the city, which may have coincided with making the city the province's capital. Nehemiah 3:7 implies that at the time of Jerusalem's refortification Mizpah still held a special status in the province.

After twelve years, from 445 to 433 (but compare Neh. 13:6 with 5:14), Nehemiah returned to the Persian court for a time. No reason is given for this trip, but he may have had to defend himself against charges brought by his opponents in the neighboring provinces (see 2:19; 6:5–9). After his return to

---

30. See H. G. M. Williamson, "Nehemiah's Walls Revisited," *PEQ* 116 (1984) 81–88; repr. in *SPPHH* 64–73.

77. *Human-headed bull.* Human-headed bull guarded the "Gate of All Nations" near the main entrance to Persepolis.

Jerusalem, Nehemiah initiated action geared to produce several religious reforms. The first move was the expulsion of Tobiah the Ammonite (see Deut. 23:3–6) from a special chamber in the temple where he had been installed by the high priest Eliashib (Neh. 13:4–9). Apparently Tobiah was a Yahwist. His reason for having a special chamber in the temple is uncertain, although he was an influential person in Judean circles, especially among the Judean nobles or landed gentry. The role of Eliashib in granting Tobiah such a prerogative demonstrates that the high priest and the priesthood were far more open to religious relationships with foreigners and their participation in the cult than such strong Yahwists as Nehemiah and his followers. Thus Nehemiah must be viewed as a strong lay representative of a strict Yahwism that sought to bring the priesthood and religious establishment into conformity with a conservative position, a position based primarily on the laws of the book of Deuteronomy. His further actions confirm this.

The Levites had been deprived of their income and status in the temple and thus forced to make their livelihoods completely from agricultural pursuits. Nehemiah gathered and reinstated these strong Yahwists in the temple, outlined their duties vis-à-vis the priests, put some in places of leadership, and ensured that the tithe of grain, wine, and oil, or a portion thereof, went for their upkeep (Neh. 13:10–13, 30). Probably as a concession to the priests for this diminution of their power, he made arrangements for "the wood offering, at appointed times, and for the first fruits" (13:31). He found that there was also great laxity in Sabbath observance. Rural Judeans were working and, along with Tyrians, were running markets in Jerusalem on the Sabbath. Nehemiah remonstrated with the nobles, ordered the city gates closed and guarded during the Sabbath, and gave the Levites power to supervise and enforce observance of the day as a holy occasion (13:15–22).

The move to prevent mixed marriages, oriented apparently toward producing a purified Judean community and the loss of property, power, and influence to outsiders, was probably the most radical of Nehemiah's actions (Neh. 13:23–28). Judean men had married women from Ashdod, Ammon, and Moab, and children of such marriages were giving up speaking the language of Judah. Nehemiah sought to force the Judean community to desist from such practice by taking an oath in the name of God not to give their daughters or marry their sons or themselves to aliens. One of the high priest's grandsons was apparently banished for having married the daughter of Sanballat the Horonite, leader of the community in Samaria. The highly authoritative, even tyrannical, nature of Nehemiah's activities has been frequently noted: "I contended with them and cursed them and beat some of them and pulled out their hair. . . . Thus I cleansed them from everything foreign" (13:25, 30).[31] Such behavior, as well as the capacity to issue and enforce edicts and regulations, was authorized by his role as governor, which made him an agent and extension of the Persian imperial power.

Ezra's Attempted Reform

According to the biblical sources (Ezra 7–10; Neh. 7:73b–10:39), much in autobiographical form, Ezra returned to Jerusalem with a special commission from the Persian king in the seventh year of Artaxerxes (Ezra 7:7). He is described as "the priest, the scribe of the law of the God of heaven" (7:12). His genealogy in 7:1–5 makes him a descendant of the preexilic high priestly family, but he is never designated high priest.

The royal decree designating Ezra as a special commissioner and outlining his work (Ezra 7:11–26) is said to have contained a number of stipulations.[32] (1) Permission was granted for any of the people of Israel, their priests, or Levites to return with Ezra. (According to the list in 8:1–14, about five thousand returned with him.) (2) Ezra was commissioned to investigate conditions in Judah and Jerusalem in the light of the law of God in his hand. (3) Silver and gold contributed by the king and his counselors were to be carried to Jerusalem, along with the gifts and freewill offerings made by the members of the Diaspora as well as special vessels prepared for the temple. (4) Treasurers in the satrapy Beyond the River were ordered to cooperate with Ezra and provide, within limits, all necessary assistance and funds, as well as exemption from taxation for all religious personnel associated with the temple. (5) Ezra was granted authority to appoint magistrates and judges to administer and teach the law of God and to execute punishments for failure to obey the law of God (and the law of the Persian monarch!). The present form of the king's decree first speaks about Ezra (7:12–20), then the treasurers of the provinces (7:21–24), and then, once again, of Ezra (7:25–26), which seems unusual.

31. There are also many parallels between Nehemiah's actions and those of "tyrants" in certain contemporary Greek city-states; see E. M. Yamauchi, "Two Reformers Compared: Solon of Athens and Nehemiah of Jerusalem," in Gary Rendsburg et al., eds., *The Bible World: Essays in Honor of C. H. Gordon* (New York: Ktav, 1980) 269–92. See also L. S. Fried, "The Political Struggle of Fifth Century Judah," *Transeu* 24 (2002) 9–21.

32. See L. S. Fried, "'You Shall Appoint Judges': Ezra's Mission and the Rescript of Artaxerxes," in Watts, ed., *Persia and Torah*, 63–89.

78. *Provisions for the palace.* Reliefs on the stairway entrance to Darius's palace at Persepolis depict servants bringing provisions into the royal palace.

Ezra and his followers reportedly returned to Jerusalem in festive procession without military escort as a mighty pilgrimage to the Holy Land. In his hand was "the law of God." The identity of this book of law supposedly possessed by Ezra has been a much-debated issue.[33] Attempts to define its contents have ranged from the suggestion that it was a special, but no longer extant, code developed under Persian supervision to the hypothesis that it was the Pentateuch in basically its present form. About this law we are told (1) that it was in Ezra's hand (although nothing is said about the law being already known in Jerusalem), (2) that the people requested Ezra to read as if they were unfamiliar with the law (Neh. 8:1), (3) that the people reacted unexpectedly or perhaps ceremoniously and wept after hearing the law (8:9–10), (4) that the Levites had to aid the people in understanding the law (8:7–8), and (5) that the Feast of Tabernacles that was celebrated on the basis of Ezra's law was so innovative that "from the days of Jeshua [Joshua] the son of Nun [at the time of the conquest] to that day the people of Israel had not done so" (8:17). The stress on the innovative aspect of the law, however, may be partly a literary device used by the editor to heighten the significance of the law's promulgation (see 2 Kgs. 23:21–23). The contents of Ezra's law, perhaps recently codified, can no longer be determined with any exactitude. Some of its content may have been subsequently incorporated into the Pentateuch.

33. For a survey see Cornelius Houtman, "Ezra and the Law: Observations on the Supposed Relation between Ezra and the Pentateuch," *OtSt* 21 (1981) 91–115.

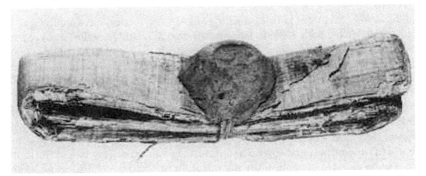

79. *Elephantine papyrus.* This and other documents from the Jewish colony at Elephantine in Egypt were published in three groups, one in 1906, another in 1911, and a third in 1953. Consisting mostly of letters and legal documents, these Persian period writings shed light on religious and legal conditions in a Jewish colony in the Diaspora (see Text 20). (*Brooklyn Museum, gift of Charles Wilbour*)

Ezra presented the law code to the people in a public reading (Neh. 8:1–12), led them to observe the Festival of Tabernacles according to the code's stipulations (8:13–18), and secured a covenant of the people to obey the law (9:38).

The concern of the Persian monarchs with the traditional law of subject peoples has already been noted in the case of Darius I and Egypt. The Persians could concern themselves with various elements in the local cults: one of the Elephantine letters, dated to 419, refers to the fact that Darius II had written to Arsames the satrap in Egypt about the regulations for the observance of the Jewish Feast of Unleavened Bread in the Elephantine community (*ANET* 491; *COS* 3:106–8).

On the assumption that the Persian administration often approved and authorized local customs and laws, scholars have argued that the Torah (Pentateuch) brought to Jerusalem was produced through the influence or at the bequest of Persian imperial authority.[34] Such a theory would help to explain the diverse components that go to make up the books of Genesis through Deuteronomy: various elements in the culture with their diverse traditions were compelled to agree to a document that embodied multiple viewpoints and thus represented a compromise.[35] At the same time, if the Pentateuch was authorized as the law for Yahwists throughout the territory of the satrapy of Beyond the River, this would explain why it became the sacred writings of the Jews in the province of Samaria as well as the province of Judah. There is, however, no direct evidence for such compilation, codification, and authorization of the Pentateuch as an imperially approved law book and, in many ways, the Pentateuch is much more than a collection of laws.

Ezra, we are told, learned that intermarriage with foreign women was widespread in the community, "thus the holy seed has mixed itself with the peoples

---

34. For exposition, discussion, and critique of this theory, see the articles in Watts, ed., *Persia and Torah*.

35. On the Pentateuch as a "compromise" document, see already Morton Smith, *Palestinian Parties and Politics That Shaped the Old Testament* (1971; 2d ed.; London: SCM, 1987).

of the lands, and in this faithlessness the officials and leaders have led the way" (Ezra 9:2). He led the people to take an oath that they would make "a covenant with our God to send away all these wives and their children" (10:3). Here Ezra, probably attempting to implement the edicts of Nehemiah, moved beyond the action ascribed to his predecessor, who sought only to stop intermarriage with foreigners but did not seek to force the dissolution of such existing marriages. An assembly was called to deal with the matter and to implement the policy of divorcing foreign women, but it was shortened by a heavy December rain and winter cold (10:9–15). According to 10:7, this assembly consisted of only those who had returned from exile. This would indicate that some features of community organization that had developed in the exile were retained by the returnees. Confiscation of property (by the temple?) and exclusion from the congregation are noted as penalties for failure to appear at the assembly (10:8). A commission was appointed to examine the matter and investigate the extent of the intermarriage. After three months the committee produced a list of offenders, which included some priests and Levites (10:16–43).

Unfortunately nothing is noted about the final outcome of Ezra's work and his effort to force the divorce of foreign women and thus purify the "holy seed." After providing a list of offenders, the final chapter of Ezra concludes abruptly and enigmatically: "All of these took foreign wives and there are still wives of theirs and they have had sons" (10:44; so the Hebrew text). All appearances suggest that Ezra's work was aborted and never carried to completion. Had he been successful, this would surely have been reported. One could speculate that such a policy would have aroused opposition from the officials in neighboring provinces and from the local constituency and that he was either forced to retire or was removed from the scene.

Far more problems surround any attempt to determine the role and activity of an historical Ezra than is the case with either Sheshbazzar, Zerubbabel, or Nehemiah.[36] Elements in the narrative are incredible: the gold and silver returned to the temple according to 8:24–30 would have weighed about thirty tons. Since Ezra was not govenor, the lack of any reference to Persian officials in the Ezra materials leaves his activities floating in a vacuum. (Neh. 8:9 appears to be an editorial addition to include Nehemiah; the verb "said" is singular.) The description of Ezra's commission in Ezra 7:25–26, which included the appointment of judges throughout the satrapy Beyond the River, seems extravagant.[37]

Later Developments in the Period

We know practically nothing about the history of the Jewish community between Ezra–Nehemiah and the conquest of Alexander the Great. What effect the Persian-Egyptian wars, the revolt of the satraps, the Phoenician rebellion

---

36. See L. L. Grabbe, "What Was Ezra's Mission?" in T. C. Eskenazi and K. H. Richards, eds., *Second Temple Studies, 2: Temple and Community in the Persian Period* (JSOTSup 175; Sheffield: Sheffield Academic Press, 1994) 286–99.

37. Fried, "You Shall Appoint Judges," has argued that this was Ezra's fundamental commission, namely, to function as a Persian agent to appoint Persian judges throughout the region.

initiated by Tennes, and the Persian reconquest of Egypt may have had on the Jerusalem community remains unknown. Josephus reports one incident which, in spite of problems of interpretation, probably relates to the reign of Artaxerxes III (*Ant.* 11.297–301). According to this account, the Jewish high priest Johanan slew his brother Jeshua in the temple. Jeshua had sought to acquire the high priesthood with the help of his friend, the Persian general Bagoas. As a consequence of the murder and the Jewish protest against his entry of the temple, according to Josephus, Bagoas "made the Jews suffer seven years" by imposing a special tribute tax on every sacrifice made in the temple (*Ant.* 11.297, 301). This general Bagoas appears to be the same Bagoas who, according to Diodorus Siculus, was Artaxerxes III's closest associate (16.47.2).[38] He was a major leader in the Persian conquest of Egypt and a kingmaker at the royal court. Diodorus describes him as "master of the kingdom, and Artaxerxes did nothing without his advice. And after Artaxerxes' death he designated in every case the successor to the throne and enjoyed all the functions of kingship save the title" (16.50.8). Diodorus also reports that, after the Persian troops plundered the Egyptian shrines in 342 carrying off the inscribed records from the ancient temples, Bagoas returned these to the Egyptian priests "on the payment of huge sums by way of ransom" (16.51.2). Eventually he murdered Artaxerxes and then, disappointed with his own selection as successor, Arses (338/337–336), Bagoas had him and most of the royal line put to death as well (Diodorus 17.5.3–6), before he himself was poisoned.

Unfortunately this little vignette provided by Diodorus casts no major light on the course and shape of Jewish history. Attempts to relate this event to the larger Persian history, such as the fourth-century Egyptian invasion of Syria-Palestine or the rebellion of Tennes,[39] have failed. Nonetheless, three factors are noteworthy. (1) The friendship of Jeshua of the Jerusalem high priestly family with a member of the upper echelon of Persian administration suggests that the Jewish community was not without standing in the Persian Empire and that Jewish affairs were not completely isolated from the larger world. (2) Bagoas's intervention in the life of the Jerusalem temple illustrates the exercise of tight Persian control and supervision over many facets of life throughout the empire. (3) The struggle between Johanan and Jeshua illustrates the internal conflicts that could tear at Judean life, especially over such an important post as high priest and particularly when exacerbated by the intervention of outside powers.

General Bibliography

J. M. Cook, *The Persian Empire* (New York: Schocken, 1983); Joseph Wiesehöfer, *Ancient Persia from 550 BC to 650 AD* (London: Tauris, 1996); and Maria Brosins, *The Persians: An Introduction* (London: Routledge, 2005), provide succinct and informative surveys of Persian history. The most recent and comprehensive history of the

---

38. Since more than one Bagoas and Jewish high priest named Johanan are known, one cannot be certain of the persons involved. See L. L. Grabbe, "Who Was the Bagoses of Josephus (*Ant.* 11.7.1. §§297–301)?" *Transeu* 5 (1991) 49–55, and the articles cited in n. 2 above.
39. See the speculative article by D. Barag, "The Effect of the Tennes Rebellion on Palestine," *BASOR* 183 (1966) 6–12.

period is Pierre Briant, *From Cyrus to Alexander: A History of the Persian Empire* (Winona Lake, IN: Eisenbrauns, 2002).

Four relatively recent works survey particular aspects of the history and culture of the Persian province of Yehud: J. L. Berquist, *Judaism in Persia's Shadow: A Social and Historical Approach* (Minneapolis: Fortress, 1995), focuses on the impact of Persian power on Judaism in a colonial state; K. G. Hoglund, *Achaemenid Imperial Administration in Syria-Palestine and the Missions of Ezra and Nehemiah* (SBLDS 125; Atlanta: Scholars Press, 1992), interprets the roles of Ezra and Nehemiah in light of the struggles between Persia and Egypt and the latter's allies, the Greeks; C. E. Carter, *The Emergence of Yehud in the Persian Period: A Social and Demographic Study* (JSOTSup 294; Sheffield: Sheffield Academic Press, 1999), pays particular attention to archaeological and survey data to reconstruct the extent, population, and culture of the Persian province; and L. S. Fried, *The Priest and the Great King: Temple-Palace Relations in the Persian Empire* (Biblical and Judaic Studies from the University of California, San Diego; Winona Lake, IN: Eisenbrauns, 2004), examines the relationship of Judean leadership to Persian administration. A more comprehensive history is L. L. Grabbe, *History of the Jews and Judeans in the Second Temple Period*, vol. 1: *Yehud: A History of the Persian Province of Judah* (London: T. & T. Clark International, 2004). D. V. Edelman, *The Origins of the 'Second' Temple: Persian Imperial Policy and the Rebuilding of Jerusalem* (London: Equinox, 2005) argues that the temple was reconstructed at the time of Nehemiah in the reign of Artaxerxes (465–433 B.C.E.).

Many of the problems associated with the history of this period are discussed in P. R. Davies, ed., *Second Temple Studies, 1: Persian Period* (JSOTSup 117; Sheffield: Sheffield Academic Press, 1991); T. C. Eskenazi and K. H. Richards, eds., *Second Temple Studies, 2: Temple and Community in the Persian Period* (JSOTSup 175; Sheffield: Sheffield Academic Press, 1994); and Josette Elayi and Jean Sapin, *Beyond the River: New Perspectives on Transeuphratene* (JSOTSup 250; Sheffield: Sheffield Academic Press, 1998). Problems and issues associated with the reconstruction of the temple are discussed in P. R. Bedford, *Temple Restoration in Early Achaemenid Judah* (JSJS 65; Leiden: Brill, 2001). Problems of priestly rule and succession are treated in James VanderKam, *From Joshua to Caiaphas: High Priests after the Exile* (Minneapolis: Fortress, 2004).

W. D. Davies and Louis Finkelstein, eds., *The Cambridge History of Judaism*, vol. 1: *Introduction; The Persian Period* (Cambridge: Cambridge University Press, 1984), contains a number of valuable essays, as do Bob Becking and M. C. A. Korpel, eds., *The Crisis of Israelite Religion: Transformation of Religious Tradition in Exilic and Post-Exilic Times* (OtSt 42; Leiden: Brill, 1999); Rainer Albertz and Bob Becking, eds., *Yahwism after the Exile—Perspectives on Israelite Religion in the Persian Period* (Assen: Van Gorcum, 2003); H. G. M. Williamson, *Studies in Persian Period History and Historiography* (FAT 38; Tübingen: Mohr Siebeck, 2004); and Oded Lipschits and Manfred Oeming, eds., *Judah and the Judeans in the Persian Period* (Winona Lake, IN: Eisenbrauns, 2006).

The archaeology of the period is discussed in Ephraim Stern, *Material Culture of the Land of the Bible in the Persian Period, 538–332 B.C.* (Warminster: Aris & Phillips, 1982); and idem, *Archaeology of the Land of the Bible*, vol. 2: *The Assyrian, Babylonian, and Persian Periods, 732–332 B.C.E.* (ABRL; New York: Doubleday, 2001) 351–582.

Scripture Index

Name Index

CPSIA information can be obtained
at www.ICGtesting.com
Printed in the USA
LVHW011729240721
693442LV00008B/91

9 780664 223588